BORIS KARLOFF

MORE THAN A MONSTER

THE AUTHORISED BIOGRAPHY

Stephen Jacobs

"A shoemaker should stick to his last, and a monster should stick to his monstrosities."
Boris Karloff

TOMAHAWK
Press

First published in 2011 by

Tomahawk Press

PO Box 1236

Sheffield S11 7XU

England

www.tomahawkpress.com

ISBN 13: 978-0-9557670-4-3

Proofread by Kenneth Bishton - kenbishton@talktalk.net

Edited by Bruce Sachs

Designed by Steve Kirkham – Tree Frog Communication 01245 445377

Printed in the EU by Gutenberg Press Limited

For Tania & Amelia

CONTENTS

FOREWORD
by Sara Karloff

I can't imagine there could be anything at all to add about my father, Boris Karloff, except "Thank you, Stephen Jacobs," once you have read this remarkably well written and superbly researched and documented biography.

Mr. Jacobs has literally spent years meticulously making certain that every possible person has been interviewed, every document and file has been read and re-read for dates, names and details, every possible heretofore unseen photograph, both personal and professional, has been reproduced for the reader's enjoyment, every question asked and answer verified. No stone has been left unturned.

Mr. Jacobs has certainly succeeded in opening many of the doors in my father's life which, until this book, had remained closed even to his family. As my father would have said: "Full marks, Stephen Jacobs, on a job jolly well done!"

Thank you Stephen for sharing my father so brilliantly with his family and his fans.

Sara Karloff
Rancho Mirage, California
May, 2010

ACKNOWLEDGEMENTS

My interest in Boris Karloff began in the 1970s when my older brother, Paul, told me of a film he had seen in school that day. He described the opening scene, played out in a cemetery, where the branches of a tree appeared to form an arrow pointing towards a statue of Death. He then explained the story of the scientist obsessed with the creation of life, and of the monster he made. The picture, Paul said, was called *Frankenstein*.

I hoped I, too, would get to see *Frankenstein* in school and was excited when told one day that my classmates and I were to assemble in the hall to watch a film. However, I was to be disappointed. Where Paul had had the opportunity to see James Whale's 1931 horror picture, we were presented with *The Angry Silence* (1960) starring Richard Attenborough. It was a very good film—but it was not *Frankenstein*. I was, however, fortunate to discover a copy of Richard J. Anobile's book of the Karloff movie in my local library. It contained the complete dialogue of the movie, accompanied by stills, but this only served to further pique my interest.

Living in England in those pre-home video days, it was difficult for the majority to view movies at their own convenience. Unless you had the funds to invest in a movie projector and a cine version of the desired film, you would have to wait, sometimes for years, for it to be shown on television or, if you were very lucky, gain a cinema re-release. I, however, was unlucky and *Frankenstein* remained conspicuously absent from the television schedules. The BBC, however, would eventually rectify this situation.

In the mid-1970s the broadcaster began showing seasons of late Saturday night horror movie double-bills, usually consisting of a classic Universal picture followed by a more modern Hammer horror. It was during one of these seasons that I finally got to see not only *Frankenstein* but also many other Karloff classics, including *Bride of Frankenstein, The Mummy* and *The Body Snatcher*. It had been worth the wait. *Frankenstein* did not disappoint.

I had now seen the movie, but knew little of the cast and crew who had made this picture. My main task was to find out more about the man who had played the iconic Monster. I recall being thrilled to discover that the actor—Boris Karloff—was, despite his name, an Englishman born less that 15 miles from my own birthplace. A paltry connection, perhaps, but, to a 12-year-old, a connection nevertheless.

Finding out more about Karloff's life, however, proved rather difficult. Books solely on the subject seemed few and far between. There was Peter Underwood's *Horror Man*—the first of the biographies on the star—and Denis Gifford's *Karloff: The Man, The Monster, The Movies*. I was also fortunate to discover Gregory William Mank's excellent *It's Alive: The Classic Cinema Saga of Frankenstein* and Cynthia Lindsay's *Dear Boris*. Still, I was determined to find out more about Boris Karloff and began my own research. When this data began to contradict the known facts about the horror star, I contacted his daughter, Sara Karloff, to inform her of my findings. She immediately proved receptive, and throughout the writing of this book Sara's help and encouragement never wavered.

Despite Sara's involvement, I never imagined this biography would ever be an authorised work. Such a thought had never occurred to me, especially as this honour had already been bestowed upon Nollen's 1999 biography *Boris Karloff: A Gentleman's Life*. It was only when my publisher, Bruce Sachs of Tomahawk Press, suggested I ask Sara if she would give my own book her seal of approval that I felt I could approach her with the request. I was, and still am, thrilled that she consented.

While researching this book I have been privileged to talk to and correspond with many of Boris Karloff's friends and colleagues. For their kindness in sharing their memories with me I would like to thank: Merritt Blake, Claire Bloom, Tom Bosley, Tony Britton, Marcie Christensen, Pat Christensen, Sybil Clutton, Bernard Coleman, Elisabeth Crowley, David Del Valle, Mark Eden, John Elliott, Peter Foy, Richard Gordon, Michael Gough. John S. Hayward, Robert Hardy, Jack Hill, Rosamund James, Gloria Jean, Norman Jewison, Jean Kent, Stanley Long, Francis Matthews, Marianne Means, Dick Miller, Leslie Nielsen, Ian Ogilvy, Nehemiah Persoff, Angela Plant, Mark Pratt, Richard Randall, Jeremy Read, Steve Reid, Olwen Simmon, Arianne Ulmer Cipes, Peter Underwood, Dan Walden, Eli Wallach, Bill Warren and Robert Wise.

For their kind assistance in gathering information, checking facts and responding to numerous queries (and with my sincere apologies for any omissions), I would also like to thank: Sheryl Abrams, Bettina Adragna, Bill Alford, Len Barnett, Gillian Butler and Sujan Nandanwar (The School of Oriental and African Studies, London), Keith Call (Wheaton College), Rebecca C. Cape and David K. Frasier (The Lilly Library, Indiana University), May P. Chan (Regina Public Library), Karine Chirico (National Archives of Canada), James Chliboyko, Mary Joan Cornett (Red Deer Branch Alberta Genealogical Society), Vena Dacent (Conway Van Gelder), Graham Dalling and Kate Godfrey (Local History Unit, Enfield Libraries), Mary Ellen Daugherty, Steven Davenport (San Francisco Maritime NHP Library), Michael Dawe and Mitra Shakibanejad (Red Deer and District Archives), Julie Day (GKT Registry, Guy's Campus), Mark DeCew, Hugh Dempsey, Kim Doyle, Elizabeth Duckworth (Kamloops Museum & Archives), Sabina Ebbols (Archives Assistant, Kings College London), Jackie Edwards, Ken Favrholdt, Kerry Gammill, Elaine Gibb (BC Archives, Royal BC Museum Corporation), Maggie Gibbons and Julia Lamb (Mind), J.L. Green (British Board of Film Classification), Jill Grey, Norm Gillespie (Brigham Young University), James Hansen, Susan Hikida (University of Southern California), Sarah Hobbs (Manchester Archives and Local Studies, Manchester Central Library), Mrs V. Howe and the staff of the British Library Newspaper Library, Tim Hunt (Guildford Crematorium), Mrs. Sunita John (Principal, Auckland House School, Shimla), Dwight Kemper, James Kern (Vallejo Naval and Historical Museum), Dr. Robert J. Kiss, Elaine M. Kozakavich (Frances Morrison Library, Saskatoon), Kristine Krueger (Margaret Herrick Library, Academy of Motion Picture Arts and Sciences), Dorian Leveque (Oriental and India Office Collections, British Library), Richard Longhurst, Janet Lorenz (National Film Information Service, The Academy of Motion Picture Arts and Sciences), Jo Macleod (The Spotlight), Gregory William Mank, Richard Manning, Janet Moat (British Film Institute), Olivia Moore (Public Affairs, British Consulate General, Chicago), Wendy Moore, Dwight A. Macpherson, J. Jeffrey O'Brien (City Archivist, City of Saskatoon Archives), J.R. Piggott (Keeper of the Archives, Dulwich College), Nic Price, Gordon Reid, Anthony Richards (Imperial War Museum), Lucy Robinson (Chatto & Linnit), Alan Rode, Jack Ruttan, Tricia Roush (San Francisco Performing Arts Library and Museum), John Salmon (St. Mary Magdalene's Church, Enfield), Lisa Jo Sagolla, Gordon B. Shriver, Ray Stothers, Alex Tassell (Heritage Collections, State Library of Tasmania), Robert Taylor, Rory Tennant (BC Hydro Information Centre), Mark Timbrook (Ward County Historical Society), Genevieve Troka (California State Archives), Sarah

Vidler (English Heritage), Peter Walmsley (Brown & Simcocks), Nicole Watier (Canadian Genealogy Centre, Library and Archives Canada), Lisa Wehrmann (History & Genealogy Department, Los Angeles Public Library), Jennifer White (Flinders University), Peter Williamson (Peachey & Co LLP), Caroline Yates and Jane Zambra.

My biggest thanks, however, must be reserved for a select few. To Sara Karloff, for her continual encouragement and assistance over the years it has taken me to write her father's biography; to my publisher Bruce Sachs, for having the faith, and patience, to invest in a neophyte writer; to Kenneth Bishton, for his proof reading skills, and Steve Kirkham who designed the book. To the Screen Actors Guild historian Valerie Yaros, who not only provided information but also kindly read and corrected my writings on the organisation; and to Canadian historian Greg Nesteroff, whose award-winning 2006 article *Boris Karloff in British Columbia* first made public the existence of the horror star's first wife, Grace Harding. Greg kindly shared with me his own research on Karloff's first theatrical troupe, the Jeanne Russell Players, and we embarked on a lengthy course of correspondence, sharing new discoveries and discussing our own Karloff related theories. He also kindly read and corrected my chapters on Karloff's time in Canada. The resultant friendships with Greg and others I have corresponded with during this project have proven to be some of the unexpected highlights of writing this book.

I would also like to thank my family and friends who, for years, have suffered my eternal Karloff mumblings with amazing forbearance – especially my brother Paul, who encouraged me to continue with a full-blown biography, and then presented me with his own laptop to put the idea into practice. Finally, and most importantly, to my wife Tania and my daughter Amelia who have borne my absences with good grace when they really deserved my full attention. It is to them I dedicate this, my first book.

Stephen Jacobs
Woodside, Surrey
May, 2010

INTRODUCTION

"I didn't set out to chill anyone. I was just an actor willing to try anything. I had no special interest in terror subjects. My private tastes are still very catholic."[1]

Boris Karloff (1965)

On the evening of Wednesday, 20 November 1957, Boris Karloff arrived at NBC's television studio in Burbank to watch his friend, the television host Ralph Edwards, record another episode of his popular show *This Is Your Life*. The evening was supposed to have been a relaxing one. Following the show Karloff and his wife, Evelyn, were due to join the Edwards for a post-show dinner. However, instead, Karloff found himself announced as that evening's subject.

Although he amiably sat through the evening's proceedings, greeting each guest and listening to their recollections, it later emerged he had, in fact, loathed the whole experience. It had been an unwelcome intrusion into his private life. His past and his family were his own business – not a tale to be told on national television.

For Boris Karloff was a private, even secretive, individual. Always amiable with press and public alike, there were, however, certain areas of his personal life he would forever remain guarded about. Not the closest of friends, not even his wives, were given full access to the actor's past. Instead he would fashion a new biography – a version journalists and biographers have adhered to ever since.

The 'deceptions' had begun before he ever set foot in Hollywood. His fortuitous stage name conjured up the image of an exotic immigrant from the land of the Czars, and many newspapers repeated his claims that he was an Englishman of Russian extraction. As he became better known brief details of his English background emerged and, in the wake of *Frankenstein*'s success in 1931, were included in Universal Studio's biography of its newest horror star. Yet even these, often incorrect, 'facts' were repeated for decades afterwards.

Karloff's Canadian period, like much of his early life, poses a problem for any biographer. The often-reported details of his time in the western provinces are largely gleaned from Karloff himself and, as we shall see, the veracity of his claims is often brought into question when one compares his recollections with the existing evidence. This holds as true for his childhood years as it does for his later time in Canada. However, Karloff's occasional appearance in official records and newspaper reports of the time means it is not impossible to trace his journey across Canada. His movements between these appearances is, however, harder to ascertain and so, for these instances we must rely upon, or at least report, the recollections of Karloff himself.

The continuing efforts of archives across the world to digitise their collections have given researchers far easier access to these collections. Papers relating to Karloff's time in Canada – prior to his successful infiltration of Hollywood – no longer require the biographer or historian to make a personal visit to search through a repository's collections, a time-intensive and often expensive prospect. The digitisation process has proved a boon to researchers across the world and can turn up some interesting, and sometimes surprising, results.

A decade after arriving in Canada, Boris Karloff found himself in Hollywood. It was then an industry blighted by racial prejudice – an industry in which white actors were often required to 'black up' to play African characters. Then, in 1930, the Motion Picture Production Code (also known as the Hays code) banned inter-racial relationships in the movies. 'Miscegenation (sex relationships between the white and black races) is forbidden,' the Code advised. Such regulations offered just more reasons for Karloff to keep his Anglo-Indian heritage hidden.

Karloff, though, was not alone in his caution. Many actors hid, or disguised, their origins. While some merely chose – or were ordered – to anglicise their names, others were forced to go to greater lengths. Actress Merle Oberon – the daughter of a British father and a Ceylonese mother – was given a new background, and adopted the mantle of a Tasmanian. To keep her Asian mother close, Oberon was forced to employ a deception and retain the woman as her personal maid.

Karloff took a simpler tack, blaming his mahogany-coloured skin on, simply, 'too many hours in the sun'. However, his skin tone was not the result of excessive sunbathing but merely the result of genetics – of the union of two people from different continents: Europe and Asia. This early saga in the actor's story is a tale of love, loss and disappointment, a story of rejection and of abandonment, and began in Warwickshire, England, almost a century before Boris Karloff's birth.

Chapter 1

ORIGINS
(1796-1887)

"He always said his mother was Russian. Later I met the
British Consul in San Francisco. He said Boris's mother was
the most beautiful Indian woman he had ever seen."[1]
Dorothy Karloff (née Stine)

Boris Karloff's paternal grandfather, Edward John Pratt, was born in a country at war. On 1 February 1793, eleven days after King Louis XVI was guillotined in Paris, France declared war on England and drew the country into a conflict that would last, with a single 13-month hiatus, for 22 years.

Three years later, on 10 February 1796, Edward John Pratt was born to Edward and Mary Pratt in Warwick, England. By 1809, however, the boy had left his hometown and made his way (presumably not alone) to India, a country then under the rule of the East India Company.

In April 1812 Edward joined the Bombay Marines in Bengal and that October received his commission as a Midshipman and began a life at sea, initially employed 'in the Cruizers at Bengal.'[2] Six years later, on 20 July 1818, Edward – now Lieutenant Pratt – married Miss Margaret Sheals at the Anglican St. Thomas' Cathedral in Bombay. Less than nine months later, on 6 April 1819, the union was blessed with the birth of their first child, Margaret Caroline.

Edward, it would appear, spent most of his married life at sea and it is likely that, as a result, his wife took residence with her friend, the widowed Mrs. Charlotte Bellasis (née Cameron) and her two daughters. Late in 1824, however, tragedy struck. Margaret had fallen pregnant earlier in the year and on 5 November, while

St. Thomas' Cathedral in Bombay.

her husband was at sea, she gave birth to a baby boy. Sadly, Margaret died the same day leaving her two children motherless and Edward a widower. She was 32 years old.

Edward arrived back in Bombay aboard the *S.S. Fulk* on 23 December and learned the tragic news. It is unknown what became of the child as no further reference to him has been found. However, the Pratt family tradition of naming the first child Edward suggests this child also died in infancy. Whatever the case it is certain that this child was *not* Boris Karloff's father – for the next child born to Edward Pratt would also be named Edward, and it is this child who became the horror star's father.

Sometime between his arrival in Bombay in December 1824 and October 1826 Edward married for a second time. It seems likely his new wife, Charlotte, was in fact the widow Charlotte Bellasis, the friend of his deceased wife.[i] The union produced two children. The first, a boy – named Edward John after his father – was born on 15 October 1826 in Bombay. The following September his sister, Charlotte Catherine, was born.

By July 1829 Edward and family (including his two step-daughters) had returned to England where they took a house in Hampstead. Later than year, on Christmas Day, Charlotte and her four children arrived back in Bombay on the ship *Charles Kerr*. Lt. Pratt, however, had decided to remain in England where he received a yearly pension until the final payment dated 31 December 1834. He then disappears from the records and his fate is unknown. It seems doubtful, however, that he ever saw his wife or children again and was probably unaware that his daughter, Charlotte, later died and was buried in Bombay. She was ten years old.

In February 1842 the young Edward, now aged 15, became an 'Uncovenanted Civil Servant' when he joined the Indian Civil Service as a clerk at the General Post Office in Bombay. He would remain there for 12 years. Uncovenanted Civil Servants such as Edward held the lowest ranks of the service. These posts, which were made almost entirely from those born in India (whatever their origins), were poorly paid and provided no pension.

During his time there Edward met Juliana Campbell,[ii] the Indian born daughter of the 'Head Clerk with the office of the Auditor and Account of Military Stores,' Archibald Campbell and his wife, Margaret. On 10 April 1849 Edward, then 22, married the 17-year-old Juliana in Bombay.

The new bride soon fell (or possibly already was) pregnant for on 12 January 1850 she gave birth to a daughter, Emma Caroline. Within months Juliana was pregnant again, this time resulting, on 14 December, with the birth of a son, Edward. The joy, however, was short lived for the child died the following day. Hard on the heels of one tragedy came another. On 2 February 1851, less than two months after the death of her son, Juliana, too, died. She was 19 years old.

Edward did not remain a widower, however. Within a few years he had found himself a new companion and, on 6 February 1853 he married Charlotte Campbell, the sister of his dead wife. She must have been pregnant at the time for the couple's first child, James Douglas, was born three months later, on 9 May 1853.

The following year Edward left the Post Office and became an 'Uncovenanted Assistant Secretary to Government in the General and Ecclesiastical Departments' in Bombay. His

i Lt. Pratt's grandson, also named Edward, searched for the records of his father's mysterious marriage when he was Legal Remembrancer to the Governor of Bombay. "I can find no record of the second marriage of John Pratt with the widow Mrs. Bellasis," he wrote, "but the ecclesiastical records of these years have been destroyed."
ii The birth, marriage and death records all state the spelling *Juliana* and not *Julianna* as is often cited.

Boris Karloff's parents – Edward and Eliza Pratt.

home life was also changing. In the latter half of the year Charlotte fell pregnant for the second time and on 27 March 1855, two months after James was baptised in St. Thomas', his sister was born. She was named Eliza Julia. Within months, however, baby Eliza began to fade and on 19 August she died. It was a year of loss for Edward for that same year his mother passed away. She was laid to rest in the Back Bay cemetery beside her friend, her husband's first wife, Margaret Pratt (née Sheals).

Four years later, on 6 February 1859, Edward Pratt's life was again touched by tragedy when his wife Charlotte, then only 32 years old, died as a result of a snakebite. She was buried in Back Bay cemetery[iii] the following day.

Edward was now a widower for the second time. His work life, too, began to deteriorate and the following year he received the first of a series of suspensions that would punctuate the rest of his career. The causes appear to have been the same. There was, as Edward's son Frederick later wrote, "the controversy about salt taxation with Sir Charles Pritchard who was the head of the Salt Department. I know no details except that our father held that the tax was harsh & oppressive and disobeyed or refused to carry out orders for its levy. He was in fact 'Protector of the poor' – *Gharib Parwer*."[3]

In December 1857 Edward was made 'Honorary Secretary' of the 'David Sassoon Industrial and Reformatory Institution', a home for orphaned, delinquent and destitute

iii Back Bay cemetery was closed in the late 1890s and now no longer exists.

boys in Bombay. It was here he became acquainted with one James Millard who, in 1858, became the institution's superintendent.

Millard had arrived in India in 1826 after having enlisted for unlimited army service. In 1845 the 38-year-old military man married Eliza Julia Edwards.[iv] She was 15 years old. Their first child, James, was born the following year. A second child, Eliza Sara (Boris Karloff's mother), was born on 25 June 1848.

Edward Pratt's association with Millard later brought him into contact with Eliza and on 27 October 1864 Edward, then 38 years of age, married for the third and final time. The bride was, at 16, less than half the groom's age and it seems likely that her marriage, like her mother's before her, had been one of convenience.

The following April, Edward left work at the beginning of what would become an extended period of sick leave. He and Eliza, now several months pregnant, travelled to Paris where, on 29 August 1865, Eliza gave birth to their first son, Edward Millard Pratt.

Edward did not go back to work until the following May. Within months of his return Eliza had fallen pregnant again and the couple's second son, George Marlow, was born on 13 April 1867. Before the end of the year Eliza was pregnant again and the couple's third son, Charles Rary, was born on 30 August 1868.

Edward's life as a civil servant was, by now, one of disillusionment and on 1 December 1869 he left on another period of sick leave. Three days later a fourth son, Frederick Greville, was born in Bombay. Edward's absence extended for over a year during which time he again travelled to England as his son, John, later recorded. "In his later years his official career was one of continual strife with the Bombay Government," John wrote. "He corresponded with John Stuart Mill who promised to bring his grievances to the notice of Parliament. In 1870 he went to England to brief Mill. He took my mother and me with him, and though I was then only 5 years of age I remember the excitement caused by the news of the declaration of war between France and Germany, which reached us in the train crossing the Isthmus of Suez. The war so engrossed the attention of Parliament that Mill thought it useless to take up the case. My father returned to India a disappointed man…"[4]

Early in 1871 Eliza fell pregnant for a fifth time resulting, on 3 November, with the birth of another son, David Cameron.[v] The couple's only daughter, Julia Honoria, was the next to be born, entering the world on 5 November 1874. Julia was followed, on 13 January 1876, by the couple's sixth son, John Thomas Pratt. He would be the last of Edward and Eliza's children to be born in India.

Edward remained in the service until his forced retirement. "In the end," wrote John Pratt, "the Bombay Government got the better of him and compelled him to retire on a reduced pension in 1878."[5] It was an ignominious end to his Government career and left Edward Pratt an embittered man. In 1879, with nothing left to keep him in India, Edward bade his homeland farewell and, accompanied by his wife and children, sailed for England.

The 1881 census, taken on 5 April, shows Edward, Eliza and family (Edward Jr., George, Charles, Frederick, David, Julia, and John) living at 23 Landcroft Road in Camberwell, South London. It was here, on 11 October the following year, a seventh son was born. He was named, appropriately, Richard Septimus.[vi] By 1887, the year of Queen Victoria's

iv Eliza's younger sister Ann would later gain fame as Anna Leonowens, the Governess of the children of the King of Siam. Her story was later told in the musical *The King and I*.
v David Cameron was not, as has previously been claimed, Edward's son by a previous marriage.
vi Septimus – the Latin for 'seventh.'

Golden Jubilee, the family had moved to 15 Forest Hill Road, less than a mile from their previous address.

That year the Queen had initially been reluctant to celebrate her Jubilee but, encouraged by the Prince of Wales, finally relented. Jubilee paraphernalia was produced and Victoria ventured from Osborne House on the Isle of Wight to meet her subjects. It was a rare foray into the crowds, having become a virtual recluse since the death of her husband, Prince Albert, 26 years before.

For Eliza Pratt, now 39 years old, the festivities probably held little interest. Having fallen pregnant earlier in the year she was, by November, readying herself for the birth of the latest, and last, of her children.

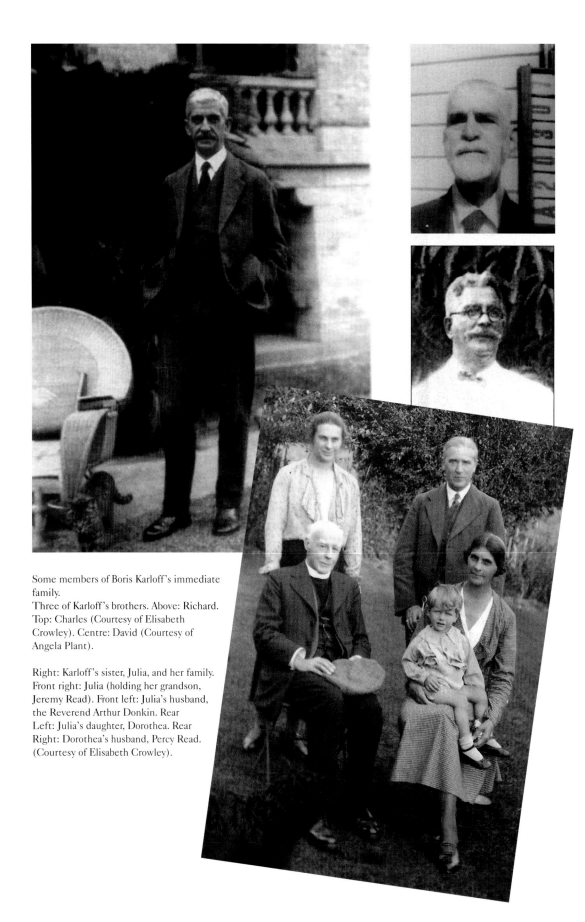

Some members of Boris Karloff's immediate family.
Three of Karloff's brothers. Above: Richard. Top: Charles (Courtesy of Elisabeth Crowley). Centre: David (Courtesy of Angela Plant).

Right: Karloff's sister, Julia, and her family. Front right: Julia (holding her grandson, Jeremy Read). Front left: Julia's husband, the Reverend Arthur Donkin. Rear Left: Julia's daughter, Dorothea. Rear Right: Dorothea's husband, Percy Read. (Courtesy of Elisabeth Crowley).

Chapter 2

The Early Years

(1887-1909)

"Actually I am assured that I was a quiet infant, and a gentle boy. No whippings by cruel step-parents scarred my childhood. No sadistic governesses read me horror stories by flickering candlelight. My childhood as William Henry Pratt in the serene London suburb of Enfield was extraordinarily tame."[1]

Boris Karloff (1962)

For Queen Victoria 1887 had been a good year. "Never, never can I forget this brilliant year," she wrote in her journal, "so full of marvellous kindness, loyalty & devotion of so many millions, which I really could hardly have expected."[2] For Eliza Pratt the ongoing year held the burden of pregnancy and, ultimately, the pain of childbirth she had endured eight times before. On Wednesday, 23 November – a fine day in London, with a light north-easterly wind – the child, another boy, was born in the family home at 15 Forest Hill Road, Camberwell. His parents, Edward (then 61 years of age) and Eliza (39), named him William Henry. "As I was the youngest, mother rather spoiled me,"[3] he later recalled. But being the baby of the family had its drawbacks. "My brothers were always keeping me in my place," he said, "or what they considered was my place."[4]

Edward Millard, 22 at the time of Billy's birth and the oldest of the brothers, had been educated at Dulwich College (1880-1884) and University College London before joining the Indian Civil Service, having been appointed following his exam in 1884. He arrived in Bombay on 21 December 1886. George had also been educated at Dulwich College (1881-1886). Then, on 7 October 1886, he registered at Guy's Hospital Medical School. He was not alone in his medical aspirations. The following October, Charles – who had also been educated at Dulwich College (1881-1887) – followed his brother by also registering at Guy's. Frederick, meanwhile, was still studying at Dulwich College (1881-1888). He then attended Hertford College, Oxford, before entering the Indian Civil Service. He arrived in Bombay on 24 November 1890. At the time of Billy's birth the rest of his siblings, David (aged 16), Julia (13), John (11) and Richard (5), were all still at school.

Despite the birth of another baby Edward and Eliza's marriage had reached the end of the road. It was never a happy union and had been a trying ordeal for Eliza. "I know that my mother was married at a very early age to someone who must have been not far short of a devil," Richard later wrote. "I know she was a bundle of nerves for years before she died – poor soul."[5] George also later described his mother's lingering illness saying that, at times, she suffered from a "suicidal mania".[6] In 1897

Boris Karloff's birthplace (left) in Forest Hill Road (Author's photograph).

Kate Martin, one of the Pratt's domestic servants, also revealed, "Mrs. Pratt had suffered mentally for several years and razors were never left about the house."[7]

Within 18 months of Billy's birth, and after more than 20 years of marriage and nine children, Eliza had had enough. The services of the London solicitors Field Roscoe and Co., of 36 Lincoln's Inn, were engaged to handle the legalities and on 8 May 1889 Eliza Pratt filed for a judicial separation. Unlike a divorce, judicial separation (usually petitioned on the grounds of cruelty, adultery or desertion) meant the couple would remain married, so neither party was free to re-marry. Any property or earnings belonging to the wife were protected and the husband was no longer liable for any debts incurred by his wife. He could also be ordered to pay maintenance costs. Eliza's petition fully laid out her reasons for the suit:

> The Petition of Eliza Sara Pratt now residing at No. 15 Forest Hill Road, Forest Hill in the County of Surrey, the lawful wife of Edward Pratt of the same place, retired Indian Civil Servant. –
>
> Showeth:
>
> 1.   That for several years before this suit the said Edward Pratt treated your Petitioner and her children with great unkindness and cruelty.
> 2.   That in the year 1880 at Boulogne in the Republic of France he dragged her up the stairs and pushed her down and pulled her hair.
> 3.   That in the Summer of 1881 at Southampton in the County of Hants – he pushed her against the wall and swung her round and tore the sleeve of her dress.
> 4.   That in the year 1884 and afterwards he refused to occupy the same bedroom with her.
> 5.   That in the Summer of 1885 at No. 15 Forest Hill Road aforesaid he pushed her about, knocked her against the table and threw a jug full of water over her.
> 6.   That in March 1887 at No. 15 Forest Hill Road he threatened to crush her head and said that she deserved to be kicked out of doors.
> 7.   That he frequently insulted, abused and threatened her and kept her without servants and without clothing and without money and insisted on offensive and uncleanly arrangements in the household.

8. That when teaching his children their lessons he spat upon their exercises and dragged the girl about by her hair.
9. That he frequently threatened and frequently beat his children with great cruelty and called them vile names.
10. That on the 15th March 1889 at 15 Forest Hill Road he swore at your Petitioner and beat the daughter Julia and caused your Petitioner to have an attack of hysteria.
11. That on the 1st April 1889 at 15 Forest Hill Road he swore at your Petitioner and called her vile names.
12. That on the 22nd April 1889 he left your petitioner without means of support.
13. That by reason of his ill treatment and misconduct as aforesaid your Petitioner's health was greatly impaired.
14. That it is unsafe for your Petitioner to continue to cohabit with the said Edward Pratt.

Your Petitioner therefore prays:
That your Lordship will be pleased to decree to her
1. A judicial separation.
2. The custody of such of the children as are under the age of 16 years.
3. Such further and other relief as the case may require. –

Eliza Sara Pratt[8]

The separation was granted on 13 Dec 1889 and with it Edward Pratt left his fatherly responsibilities behind. For years afterwards Eliza relied on her solicitors to issue numerous petitions for costs, which Edward appears to have generally ignored. More drastic action was called for and, on 9 July 1894, the court ordered "that the Respondent Edward Pratt be restrained from receiving by himself or through his bankers or agents the moneys payable to him in respect of the pension of £175 per annum payable to him by HM's Secretary of State for India."[9] Even so, according to Edward's son Richard, all efforts by Eliza Pratt proved fruitless and her husband "steadily refused to pay her afterwards one penny of alimony!"[10]

Edward's final 'fatherly' act occurred when, one day, he abducted Richard from the house in Forest Hill Road. "I don't suppose he had a special feeling for me," Richard later said, "and I expect he would have kidnapped Boris instead if Boris had been old enough."[11] Edward took his son to Dover and absconded with the child across the English Channel. In a letter to Karloff's last wife, Evelyn, Richard described what happened next: "I was rescued in Calais by an uncle, whose name I can't remember,[i] snatching me from the Calais apartment when my father was out, blurring his track by driving by road to Dunkirk and crossing back to England by what must have been an exceedingly dirty cattle boat. It has stuck in my memory because I caught ringworm on the cattleboat and in due course was taken weeping to a barber to have my head shaved and the ringworm attended to!!"[12]

---

i Richard had only one uncle, his mother's brother, James Millard (b. 1846). It has been suggested that Richard's saviour was his older brother, Edward, although it seems strange that Richard would not remember his own sibling. Another possible contender is Richard's half-brother, James Douglas Pratt (b. 1853).

Following the legal separation some sacrifices were made. George had continued to study at Guy's and was doing well, having been awarded the *Open Scholarship in Arts*. During his three years there George had attended a total of 196 lectures in subjects which included anatomy, physiology, surgery, chemistry and midwifery. His efforts at dissection were particularly successful. In January 1890, however, his prospects of a career in medicine ended when he decided to leave the college, probably as a result of the financial difficulties following his parents' separation. A note was entered against George's name on the *Pupils Returns – Guy's*: "Jan/90. Absent for family reasons – may return at end of 1890."[13]

The young Billy Pratt.

Charles, who was studying 'Preliminary Science' at the medical school, had attended 53 lectures but had yet to take an exam. Before he could do so he, too, decided to leave. A note written against Charles' entries simply states: "Jan/90. Left the profession. Gone to India."[14] Whether it was ever Charles' intention to leave the country is unknown, but the census taken in April of the following year reveals he was still living at home.

'Home' by then was at 175 Friern Road, some four streets from their old address. The move from Forest Hill Road was necessitated by the straitened circumstances the family were now in. The new abode was, as Richard later recalled, "a much smaller, cheaper house."[15] The burden of responsibility seems to have fallen upon the shoulders of Edward, the oldest of Billy's brothers. His actions gained his brother Richard's admiration "because," Richard later wrote, "out of his no doubt meagre salary as a junior in the I.C.S. he must have borne the brunt of the expenses of Friern Road together with most of the cost of my own education…"[16]

The 1891 census, taken on 5 April, shows Eliza, then aged 43 and still listed as married, as 'living on own means'. George (23) was now teaching elocution and pursuing an acting career, while Charles (21), Julia (16), John (14) and Richard (8) were all 'scholars'. Of the children only three-year-old Billy remained permanently at home with his mother and Harriet Eaves, the 25-year-old servant.

Within a few years[ii] Eliza and the family moved further afield, this time to 'Chase View' on the north side of Chase Green Avenue in Enfield, Middlesex. "From that time on, I began to see less and less of my brothers," Karloff later said. "They seemed always to be abroad, either in India or China."[17] The family was to move twice more, both times to houses close by. First they relocated to 'The Willows' (later No. 21) in Slades Hill (or East Barnet Road as it was also known). Then, by 1899 they were residing at 'Norgrove', 38 Uplands Park Road.[iii]

Billy's early years, however, were not easy as childhood friend Mrs. Noel Horsey (née Hearns) recalled. "He was very shy and no wonder," she said. "He was, I think, a very lonely little boy. We had a large house, full of young people – he liked that. He loved our house because he was always welcome. His brothers were never at home, his mother was so ill – and his father was a very severe man. He found something with us, and we enjoyed having him. Billy was an awfully good-natured boy. He had to be, to put up with all of us as well as his treatment at home... He was put down a lot. In fact, he was downright squashed. His mother was frail and he was very much on his own – then one or another of his brothers would return home from somewhere or other and bully him. He was a generous boy – he never seemed to hold it against them, just sort of got on with it."[18] Another of Billy's friends, Mrs. Horsey's cousin Winifred Cumming (later Lady Cocke), observed, "Billy had a pretty stiff time. His was a strange, uncommunicative family..."[19]

To make matters worse, young Billy was afflicted by a stammer and a lisp that were to stay with him his entire life. It would prove an encumbrance during his acting years. As Evelyn Karloff later explained, "He frequently had to rephrase dialogue to encompass them."[20] In addition to the speech disorders, Billy was bowlegged. "We used to tease him about it," said Lady Cocke.[21] It was a condition that would cause him great pain in his later years. Evelyn Karloff recalled, "That's one of the reasons the arthritis became so agonising later on..."[22] It was not in Billy's nature to gripe, however. "We loved him," said Lady Cocke. "Admired him for being such a good sport. He never showed any sign of rejection – he just made a joke about the family, never moaned about his rotten childhood."[23]

Following Billy's transformation into the world famous horror star, Boris Karloff, the tales of his childhood took on an aspect more in keeping with his screen persona. Following a 1933 interview with the star, one reporter wrote:

> He was a serious child. As soon as he could read (his mother taught him long before he entered school)[iv] he spent hours each day poring over imaginative stories of goblins, ghosts and other weird creatures. On the first Christmas which he remembers, he received a small box of paints. Immediately he retired from the family group, hieing himself to the attic where he painted his face in a series of atrocities as horrible as his juvenile mind could make them. This was his first escapade into the art of make-up and he continued tampering with it all his life. Just off the main attic of the house was the room in which trunks and luggage were stored. It was always kept locked, but young Karloff finally found the key. Upon his first exploration of the room, he was delighted that it was even darker than the attic. Knowing that his brothers thought of the room as "haunted", he invented numerous contrivances that would make strange sounds and shrieks at intervals. After frightening his older brothers almost out of their wits by his strange noises, he would walk calmly into the trunk room and close the door! Once inside, he proceeded to "haunt" the room in an even louder and more gruesome manner until he had the rest of the boys afraid to climb the attic stairs. This accomplished a two-fold purpose: respect and solitude.[24]

Karloff told the journalist other rather suspect tales of his youth. Being the last of nine children, he said, had removed any element of novelty from the occasion of his birth. His father could, Karloff claimed, recall nothing of his final son's birth save the 'beastly, shrieking weather'.[25] In fact, Karloff had been born on a clear day.

---

iv Eliza Pratt's signature has the same angular quality inherited by her son and suggests that she did have a hand in his early education.

As the boy grew, his father, it was also alleged, thought his son a 'strange one' although his mother delighted in her youngest's individuality. "William," she boasted, "was more like *her* people... more Russian than British... truly a *Karloff*!"[26] By the age of seven, Billy's foibles – reading, exploring attics and cellars, and making "weird, crazy noises that didn't seem to mean anything (except to him)"[27] – resulted in his father sarcastically referring to the boy as 'Karloff' in mock deference to his wife's forebears. This, however, is all pure fiction. No Russian ancestry can be found in Karloff's maternal family, let alone any ancestor bearing the surname 'Karloff'. More conclusive, however, is the fact that by the time Billy was seven his father had long since departed the family home. Living in a household with a poorly mother Billy's upbringing was in the hands of his siblings.

Recreation provided some escape from his brothers' rebukes. Billy and his friends would play games such as *Mumbledy Peg*, *Crawlers*, *Bangers* and *Up Jenkins, Down Jenkins* as Mrs. Horsey recalled. "We had great games – he loved games, and he was terribly good at them... We played a lot of charades," she said. "Our mother and father had brought clothes from India and we dressed up... Billy particularly enjoyed charades and was definitely good at them."[28] Lady Cocke recounted one particular game. "We did a beautiful Bluebeard," she said. "We cut holes in an old sheet to stick our heads through and put red paint under the holes for where our heads were chopped off by Bluebeard. I'll bet you'd like me to say Billy played Bluebeard, wouldn't you? Well – he didn't. But you can say so."[29]

Sometimes events would take Billy and his friends further afield. "Billy took me to the opening of the two-penny tube," Lady Cocke recalled. "It was the first tube – went from Shepherd's Bush to the Bank... that's the Bank of England, you know."[30] Other excursions were not quite so formal. "We would cycle over and play hockey in the brickfields in front of Wormwood Scrubs Prison," said Lady Cocke. "Believe me, mixed hockey is the most dangerous game ever invented... Billy was very keen!"[31]

Billy's favourite pastime, however, was the theatre. "Billy adored the theatre," said Mrs. Horsey. "We saved every penny to buy seats way up in the gods... We saw Lewis Waller play Monsieur Beaucaire."[32] For Billy this trip to the Lyric Theatre in London's Shaftesbury Avenue was the source of great amusement, as Lady Cocke recalled. "I was dressed in white satin," she said, "and wore a hat with a nest of robins on it that kept falling into my eyes. Billy couldn't see the play for laughing!"[33]

Billy's enthusiasm for acting had already taken him onstage. The family's proximity to nearby St. Mary Magdalene's church had made attendance almost compulsory and, although not enamoured by the prospect, Billy soon discovered that the vicar, George Passand Turner,[v] arranged occasional stage plays, which were presented in the church hall. This increased the boy's interest and, as he later told the journalist Walter Ramsey, he would find time each day to visit the church and wander around in silence. He also enjoyed listening to the music master as he practised upon the church organ. Yet the boy's interest masked an ulterior motive – he wanted a part in the next church play.

For two nights each Christmas a parish play, or pantomime, was produced at the church for the parishioners' children. "Then the Band of Hope[vi] put on an entertainment, and I was always in those things," Karloff later explained, "giving everything in me, acting lustily and loudly."[34]

---

v Rather than being the 'old rector' Walter Ramsey described, Rev. Turner would have been only 46 in December 1896.
vi The Band of Hope, established in 1845, was a temperance organisation for working-class children.

Left: The stage of St. Mary Magdalene's church hall where the young Billy Pratt first took the stage (Courtesy of John Salmon).

At Christmas 1896, at the age of nine,[vii] Billy made his acting debut appearing in one of the plays – a version of *Cinderella*. "Instead of playing the handsome prince, I donned black tights and a skullcap and rallied the forces of evil as the Demon King," he recalled.[35] Billy later claimed the vicar was compelled to advise him to tone down his portrayal. "You mustn't make *Evil* so strong, my boy," Turner had said. "*Evil* is always weak when it encounters *Right!*"[36] But the vicar was ignored as the young actor continued to perform with gusto, even adding horns to his costume for further performances. The role had ignited the passion. "From then on," he proclaimed, "I resolved to be an actor."[37]

The family had already produced one actor in George. "[He] had been on the stage under the name George Marlowe when I was about eight years old," Karloff revealed. "He was the one I knew best when the others were abroad. He played with Fanny Ward at the old Strand Theatre in *The Royal Divorce*. Giving up this stage life, he went into the city as a partner in a Swedish firm of paper merchants. Still, the theatre interested him deeply. He coached clubs and assisted at the Enfield Amateur Dramatic Society. Each year he put on a show at the Enfield Cricket Club."[38]

Karloff's statement is, however, characteristically inaccurate. There never had been a production of *A Royal Divorce* (the play's correct title) at the Strand Theatre. The play, a drama about Napoleon and the Empress Josephine, was produced at the Olympic Theatre in 1891, then at the Princess Theatre the following year but neither featured Fanny Ward or George Marlowe. However, George had appeared in the play on tour with W. Kelly's company during which Ronald Bayne had played Napoleon with Edith Cole as Josephine. In early December 1894 the troupe played at Her Majesty's Theatre in Aberdeen and a week later were in Dundee where *The Era* described George's portrayal of the Marquis de Beaumont as "vigorous".[39] When the company took the stage in Darlington on 31 December George was considered "very satisfactory"[40] in his role.

The only recorded appearance by George Marlowe in London is a single matinee performance of Arthur Fry's comedy *A Rescued Honour* at the Avenue Theatre on 4 June 1896. George played a character named Tommy Tabor. But within a few years George had retired from the stage and become a salesman – not a partner – for the paper merchants Eberstein & Co.[viii]

---

vii In an interview with Colin Edwards circa 1963, Karloff stated he was 'about ten' when he appeared in the play. In 1960 he claimed the play was staged when he was eleven.

viii Eberstein & Co. has previously been incorrectly referred to as Elverstein & Co.

Although his theatrical career had not been too successful, George was to prove an influence on Billy. Mrs. Horsey recalled, "He worshipped his brother George, who was the only one who was good to him. George was an actor. I expect possibly that's why Billy always wanted to be one."[41] Of this brotherly influence Karloff said, "His dramatic experience was really no encouragement for me. Despite the fact that George was an extraordinarily handsome man, he never went very far on the stage, which was the reason he gave it up for a city job. But I tried to emulate him."George, however, was not a perfect role model. In September 1897 Billy's favourite brother fell foul of the law in an episode that made the national newspapers. On the afternoon of Sunday, 5 September George Marlow Pratt shot and killed his neighbour, Frederick Grant Lockyer. A 'very distressed'[43] George was later arrested and taken into custody. The following day he was taken before the Enfield magistrates and formally charged with causing Lockyer's death.

The jury was told how George and Lockyer had arranged to go cycling on that fatal Sunday but the inclement weather had prevented it. Instead, George visited Lockyer who, he found, was sitting in the drawing room smoking a pipe and reading the newspaper. George took his neighbour's match and carried it across the room, pushing back the curtain to check the weather. Then, George explained, he put his hand in his jacket pocket to take out his tobacco pouch. As he was fumbling for the pouch he heard a loud report. The gun, which he had purchased to send to his brother Charles in Brazil, had gone off. George threw off his coat then noticed Lockyer was not moving. Then he saw the blood coming from his friend's mouth. He ran to the kitchen and sent for a doctor. Despite Lockyer's maid hinting at impropriety between George and Mrs. Lockyer the jury accepted the evidence that the shooting had been an accident. George, it was reported, "wept bitterly"[44] as the listening public applauded the verdict.

At ten years old it seems likely that Billy would have been aware of his brother's arrest and the subsequent hearing. Still, regardless of George's troubles, his influence on Billy remained. The acting bug had bitten and Billy took to the stage in future productions at the church hall, such as *Mike the Gypsy*, "acting lustily and loudly"[45] until the brothers intervened. "My older brothers saw which way the wind was blowing after I'd played in, oh, two or three of these things as a small boy," he said. "Well, they put their foot down and stopped it. But the seed had been planted... I was determined somehow or another that I was going to go on the stage."[46]

For his brothers, however, this remained an unwelcome decision. "There was always one or another of them home on leave," Karloff later recalled. "He saw me at my various stages of boyhood and adolescence. Each one would try to reform me during his six months on leave. There was always the general comment that I was going to the dogs and someone would have to do something about it. This brotherly benevolence became a trifle annoying. In time I got used to it and recognized that their intentions were sound. But I feel that I owe much to that interest. All men of substance and standing, they impressed me with a sense of rightness and the need for doing the right thing."[47]

Regardless of Billy's wishes for an acting career the plan remained that he would follow his brothers into the Civil Service. "Two were in the Indian Civil Service [Edward and Frederick]," he explained, "two were in the Chancellor's Service in China [John and Richard] and I was supposed to go to the Chancellor's Service in China with them... I didn't want to."[48]

Curiously, when speaking of his childhood, Karloff made scant mention of his mother. "Both my parents died during my childhood," he later said. "I was reared by one amiable stepsister [Emma, who was actually Billy's half-sister] and seven stern older brothers, who knew exactly what I was to be – a government servant in the family tradition."[49]

Despite such claims Eliza was, in fact, alive throughout Billy's childhood. The 1901 census records Eliza (aged 52), her sons George (33),[ix] Richard (18) and Billy (13), Eliza's nephew, Havelock J. Millard (20), and the family servants, the cook Rosetta E. Brightman (18) and, presumably, her sister – the housemaid Eliza J. Brightman (16) – as being in residence at 38 Uplands Park Road on 31 March of that year.

According to Billy, his education began at a small military prep school comprising only 40 pupils. It had been George's idea to send him there with the intention that his sibling would graduate and pass straight into the army. However, the classrooms were dark and draughty and the pupils were presided over by an aged and eccentric master named 'Starky'. The pedagogue had a pointed head and bad teeth through which he would draw in breath in a hissing manner whenever he spoke. "Had the worthy but detestably ugly master known that years later he would prove the inspiration for one of the most grotesque make-ups ever imagined for the Hollywood screen," Walter Ramsey later wrote, "he would no doubt have seized the occasion to 'wallop' Karloff mightily!"[50] Coincidentally, perhaps, the 1901 census lists one 'Sefton Starkey' as the 38-year-old headmaster of the Ridgeway School in Enfield, an educational establishment run from Starkey's home on a local road known as The Ridgeway.

Karloff claimed he did not like the prep school and wanted to leave. His brother George had died, he said, and he received no opposition. As Karloff later told Ramsey, his mother had "seldom refused *her* boy anything."[51] Instead he enrolled at Merchant Taylors' School in Charterhouse Square, London. This, he said, happened when he was "about 15".[52] Upon closer examination, however, these claims appear merely spurious. In fact, Billy's formal education began at Enfield Grammar School then, from September 1899, he attended Merchant Taylors'. His brother Richard had also been a pupil there, having attended between January 1896 and 1899. When Billy joined the school he was two months short of his twelfth birthday, not "about 15" as he had claimed. Perhaps more convincing, George was still alive at the time.

In 1901 Billy's father, Edward, died. He is last recorded as living at 9 Stockwell Park Road in Lambeth, South London. On 28 October 1901 he made his will at St. Thomas' Home, part of St. Thomas' Hospital in Lambeth. Edward appointed his son, Edward Millard Pratt, and the honourable Mr. Justice Chandavarter of the High Court, Bombay, as his executors and requested £100 from his estate be used "for drawing attention to the grievances of poor India and to her claims for just treatment as a dependency of this great Kingdom."[53] He also left £200 asking "that the money be regarded as a nucleus of a fund to be augmented hereafter from every possible source and that the annual income therefrom may be used for assisting the several Ethical Societies in promoting their ends & aims."[54] The rest of his estate, which had a net value of £5,067 5s 7d, "may be used in the grant of old age pensions to one or more cultivators of land in the Bombay Presidency."[55] He left no provision for his family from his sizeable estate. Edward Pratt died two days later, on 30 October 1901, aged 75.

---

ix It would appear that, following his brush with the law, George returned to live with his mother and siblings. George's profession is listed as 'Paper Agent'.

In Karloff's later recollections he repeatedly made clear he had had no relationship with his father. "I'd lost my father when I was an infant," he said on one occasion.[56] Other times he would be more specific, explaining his father had died when he was still a baby. Although this was untrue – Karloff was 13 when Edward passed away – it is indicative of Edward's absence from his son's life.

In September 1903 Billy's schooling continued at Uppingham, a boarding school in Rutland in the East Midlands. Founded in 1584 the school remained small for 270 years, having only two staff and some 30 to 60 students. The school grew under the headmastership of Edward Thring (1853-87) who commissioned new buildings, including a gymnasium (the first in an English school) and a chapel. The number of students increased to some 330 pupils.

Initially Billy's attendance at Uppingham was on a daily basis but in 1904 he began to board full-time, lodging at 'Fircroft', one of the school's 12 houses, presided over by the housemaster, Robert N. Douglas. Douglas had, that year, succeeded Billy's original housemaster, the Reverend T.E. Raven. In later years Karloff recalled that Rev. Raven was known to the boys as The Old Bird. The two housemistresses also acquired nicknames. They were unflatteringly referred to as Big Bum Ada and Pee Drawers Elsie.

Early in the New Year Billy lost his favourite brother when George died. He had never married and was still earning a living as a salesman for the paper firm when, in January 1904, he fell ill with double lobar pneumonia. He was taken to the Manchester Private Hospital but his future looked bleak. Richard and his mother made the journey from London to see him. Sadly, George passed away at the hospital on 23 January. He was 36 years old.

Back at Uppingham Billy found a friend in fellow pupil Frank Geoffrey Taylor.[x] Commonly known as Geoff, Taylor hailed from Birmingham. The two were often late for morning class. The walk downhill would quicken to a sprint in an attempt to reach class on time. They would invariably fail and find, as Karloff later recalled, "the door being closed in our faces."[57] Such concerns could be dismissed later by a trip to Uppingham High Street where the two would treat themselves to, as Taylor later recounted, "fruit salads with the cream and the bananas…"[58]

Although presented with the opportunity to learn Billy preferred the challenge of the playing fields to the mental exertions of the schoolroom. "I was the enthusiastic rabbit, you know, at cricket and rugger," he said.[59] While cricket was to remain his favourite sport Billy expanded his sporting repertoire. In the third term of 1903 (i.e. September to December) Billy played forward for the second side of the 8th Rugby Football game. They won 11 games. In 1905 he joined Taylor on the Fircroft hockey team and in the summer of that year played cricket against Meadurst and F.A.E Ashwell's XI. In 1906, in the annual schools comprehensive sports competition, Fircroft was placed fifth. Within the 32 places in Fircroft Billy came a respectable third, one place behind Taylor. Billy even tried his hand at weightlifting, coming seventeenth.

Although the shortcomings of his academic career did not cause Billy any undue worry the mastery of one subject did cause some remorse. "One thing I regret is that I did not satisfy my love of music," he later said. "I sang in the choir and did two years of piano

x It has been claimed that Karloff's friend was J.G. Taylor. However, there was no J.G. Taylor listed in 'Fircroft' during Karloff's stay.

practice under pressure. If I had decided to work a little more at music, I should have had a great opportunity. The music master [P.J.P. David] was a brilliant man. If any boy had any music in his soul, he would have brought it out…. Yes, I made a great mistake then, apart from no particular aptitude for music, in not taking advantage of that man's knowledge and patience."[60]

Throughout his schooldays Billy's enthusiasm for the stage remained undiminished. In the autumn of 1905 he took part in the Fircroft show and at Christmas that year won a prize for 'Music and Choir'. He won another prize, on 6 July 1906, at the school's annual Speech Day for his performance in German. Yet despite his success on Uppingham's stage and playing fields his enthusiasm never extended to the classroom, as he was later to admit. "I was a lazy little devil at school because I knew exactly what I wanted to do, go on the stage. I was not going to pass any examinations if I could possibly help it. I wanted to be an actor."[61] Geoff Taylor concurred, later admitting, "I'm afraid the young Bill Pratt was not a very distinguished scholar at Uppingham."[62]

With his heart defiantly set on an acting career Billy's brothers took action, as he later explained:

> My brother's experience was held up to me by the elders of my family as the horrible example of what happens when you try to get on the stage. Forming a tribunal they pronounced:
>
> 1. That I could not possibly succeed because I did not have George's looks or his talents.
> 2. That it would be complete folly for me to try it.
> 3. Finally they would not countenance it!
>
> They urged me to see that the dignity and stability of a consular career was vastly to be preferred to the insecurity and uncertainty of the stage. They were right.[63]

After the spring term of 1906 Billy's time at Uppingham came to an end. The years of schooling he had spent were, he said, merely routine. "He learned to smoke with the usual digestive difficulties – saw his first French postal cards – got drunk to see what it was like, and didn't like it," Walter Ramsay later reported. "All during this time, however, his flair for drama was given an even greater incentive."[64]

Although his academic career had been unimpressive, his brothers' expectations for a consular service career remained. "After I left school I went to a crammer in London," Karloff recalled. "I was supposed to be reading for the exams, instead of which I haunted the galleries of all the theatres of that time. I used to haunt His Majesty's Theatre, with Tree and Lyn Harding and Constance Collier, that wonderful trio that held forth there. I saw Tree in *Richard II* and *Antony and Cleopatra* and *The Tempest*."[65]

The time at King's College, in which he specialised in Chinese customs and languages, proved fruitless. "The first-term reports amply reflected the fact that I had attended more plays than classes," he said. "I was, in fact, fast becoming a disgrace to the family name."[66]

On 15 December 1906, three weeks after his nineteenth birthday, Billy suffered another major loss when his mother, Eliza, died. The cause was later recorded as 'cerebral apoplexy'.[67] She had been living with her stepdaughter, Emma, at 12 Uplands Park Road, having made her will there on 24 November 1905. "She [Emma] was about my mother's age and her great friend," Richard later wrote. "On retirement she lived with mother in Enfield and outlived her by a good many years."[68]

Following the death of her stepmother Emma took possession of 38 Uplands Park Road and moved in. Billy later recounted how his half-sister was constantly displeased with his mischievous antics. He was, he later confessed, "a miserable little brat… I was the black sheep of the family and rarely out of hot water for more than five minutes!"[69] Years later one Enfield resident, Harry Ford, regaled his grandson, Graham Dalling, with the tale of the day he had gotten into a fistfight with Billy Pratt. "My grandfather as a young man was a very good amateur boxer," Dalling said, "and it is likely that the future film star's good looks may have suffered in the encounter."[70]

Billy's more outrageous exploits would result in threats by Emma to cut the boy from her will. She would always relent, however, though she would warn Billy to mend his ways lest she die suddenly and leave him penniless. "Dear old Emma!" he later said. "In the end she left me £100 a year, and jolly useful it was too! It kept a roof over my head when I shouldn't have had one otherwise."[71]

Perhaps Billy found some solace with his love, Alice Roe. Alice, who was five years Billy's senior, lived with her parents, William and Mary (both elementary school teachers), brother Albert, and sister Edith at 59 Birkbeck Road, less than 1½ miles from Billy's house in Uplands Park Road. Mrs. Sybil Clutton (née Aughton), who later knew both sisters, explained: "They went to St. Mary Magdalene's Church where he [Billy] joined the drama group. Both of them [Alice and Edith] were in the choir and probably they were in drama as well. That would be before my time, of course, but this is how she [Alice] started falling in love with him, I think, when they were in drama together."[72]

Billy once encountered Edith on her way to school. Edith had a penchant for chocolate cream buns and Billy persuaded her to play truant from school for an afternoon on the promise that, if she would, Billy would reward her with as many buns as she could eat. The offer was too good to resist and Billy was true to his word. "A very lasting memory for that girl," Karloff's first biographer Peter Underwood wrote, "is of having tea with Billy and eating many, many chocolate cream-buns!"[73]

Billy would often visit Alice at her home. "I was shown Billy's favourite garden seat under the mountain ash in that quiet, secluded garden in Enfield," wrote Underwood. "Here the youthful Billy would sit on a summer's evening and once, sitting on this very seat with Alice on one side of him and Edith on the other, their mother, Mrs. Roe, of whom Billy was very fond, took a delightful photograph which the sisters still possess…"[74]

Billy once presented Alice with his tie pin, probably as a token of his love. It was adorned by six black Indian pearls. Upon Alice's mother's suggestion the pin was made into a dress ring. "This was done and a very charming ring it made," wrote Underwood in 1971. "I had the opportunity of admiring it, for the lady concerned [Alice] still proudly possessed the ring a few years ago."[75] The romance blossomed. "She told me they were informally engaged,"[76] Underwood later revealed.

On his twentieth birthday – 23 November 1907 – Billy accompanied Alice to His Majesty's Theatre in London's Haymarket to see Henry Ainley and Lily Brayton appearing in Shakespeare's *As You Like It*. At the theatre Billy bought a presentation copy of the play, inscribed it *23.11.07 from W.H.P.* and presented it to his beloved. When she got home Alice realised she had left the gift behind. Billy immediately returned to the theatre to retrieve it. It became one of Alice's most treasured possessions.

An opportunity to escape the harassment of his home life came when Billy turned 21. His half-sister Emma and his brother Frederick had, on 16 July 1907, arranged an indenture in which Billy would, on turning 21, receive £150 from his mother's estate. When Billy collected the money at the office of the family solicitor in Lincoln's Inn he had already determined to leave the country, despite his commitment to Alice. "The family had been informed that I intended to leave home," Karloff later said. "I felt I had to get away and work things out on my own."[77] He limited his choice to two destinations but, unable to decide, trusted to

Karloff's first love - Alice Roe (ca. 1935) (Courtesy of Sybil Clutton).

chance. "I remember tossing a shilling to decide whether I'd go to Australia or Canada."[78]

The "unfortunate losers"[79] were the Canadians. "Just about that time the Canadian Government was sending out an appeal for immigrants," he explained. "I had no idea what Canada was like. It was all a fantastic and frightfully exciting adventure."[80] A second-class passage was arranged. "With part of the legacy I bought my steamer ticket for Montreal."[81] Billy gave his occupation as 'farmer' and was issued with ticket number 27525.

His travel arrangements complete Billy left home, bound for Liverpool, on the first leg of his journey. His departure was surprisingly easy, as he later recalled. "Fortunately, there were no brothers at home at the actual time of my departure," he said. "I don't remember that any obstacles were placed in my way or that I had to overcome any great difficulties."[82]

But Billy had not intended to go alone. He had asked Alice to accompany him in his new life abroad – but it was not to be. "Her mother didn't want her to go so that was the end of it," Mrs. Clutton revealed. "I don't know if the father had any objections. Father was never, ever, very much mentioned to me. He died – actually I think he fell down the stairs – and that was the end of him, really. He wasn't teetotal, put it that way."[83] Alice later revealed that she and Billy had argued, probably about her decision to stay. Later, on the evening before he was due to sail, Billy came to see Alice and asked for a single dark-red rose from a bunch he had bought her. She presented him with a flower and he left.

Billy Pratt in 1907 (Courtesy of Sybil Clutton).

The *Empress of Britain*.

Alone at Liverpool Billy boarded his ship, the *S.S. Empress of Britain*, and sailed for Canada. He was finally free from his nagging brothers and they, equally, were free of him. "I imagine," he said, "that, when I got on the ship, brotherly sighs of relief could be heard in various far-flung British outposts. There was no weeping and no distress. I was on my way. To what, I didn't exactly know."[84]

Chapter 3

FIRST STEPS

(1909-1912)

"I was educated at Uppingham and Merchant Taylors' and they tried, Heaven help them, to teach me Latin and history and all sorts of things – but nobody ever showed me how to use a pick and shovel. And at that time my existence depended on being able to use a pick and shovel."[1]
Boris Karloff (1953)

On Friday, 7 May 1909 the *Empress of Britain* left Liverpool bound for Montreal. Aboard ship that same day Billy had a marriage application prepared in apparent expectation of another's arrival on board. The paperwork, however, was never completed as only Billy's name was entered on the document. In the space reserved for the signatures it simply states 'No records of marriage at sea'. Alice Roe later told Peter Underwood the reason why. "[They] planned to be married aboard ship on the way to Canada," Underwood revealed, "but they had a disagreement and she got cold feet at the last moment and did not turn up… At all events Alice never saw him again."[2] Ten days later, on Monday 17 May, the ship docked in Montreal and Billy began his new life in Canada – alone.

At the London offices of the Canada Company Billy had arranged for employment as a farmer. He was told that when he reached the company's Toronto office he would be given his assignment. "There were some plans to go on to a farm in Ontario to learn farming," he said, "then to buy some virgin land and develop it by myself."[3] The Toronto office directed him to a farm in Caledonia, near Hamilton, Ontario run by an Irishman, Mr. Terrance O'Reilly. Billy was unconvinced that this stint would prepare him for a farmer's life. "How six weeks with an Irish farmer, son of a retired country gentleman, who had come over to Canada on a windjammer, could fit me for a life on the soil, I don't know," he said. "Still, that was the idea."[4] He hitched a ride with a horse and buggy for the journey to the farm but on arrival found things had not gone to plan. "I arrived all smiles and blushes – but the fellow had never heard of me, wasn't expecting anybody, didn't want anybody. Farmer O'Reilly and I just looked at each other – I had only pennies left, no way to get back to Toronto. Thank God it was spring and work on the farm was beginning. O'Reilly finally said, 'All right, you can stay.' I stayed three months[i] at ten dollars a month – and what a rough ride! O'Reilly would get me out of bed with a pitchfork at four in the morning to catch the horses in the fields and bring them in. I'd never known a horse personally before and knew nothing about them... I soon learned."[5]

Terrance O'Reilly and the farm near Caledonia figured frequently in Billy's recollections of his early days. The 1911 Canadian census, however, contains only one Irish-born Ontario farmer that comes close to Billy's description.[ii] The record shows a 33-year-old Terrance O'Reilly living with his parents, John and Mary and their adopted daughter, Mary, in the township of Oneida, in Haldimand County eight miles south of the town of Caledonia.

After leaving the farm Billy's story begins to differ, sometimes radically, in the telling. In a 1932 interview with John Moffat, Karloff revealed that after leaving the farm he went home. "When the crop was in and his pay was in his pocket," Moffat wrote, "he obeyed a momentary flash of nostalgia and sailed for home and England. It was an uncomfortable trip home. He felt like a quitter... He stayed in England for a week, received some money from his father's estate and took another boat back to Canada."[6] It is a curious statement and one that is echoed, albeit with variations, in Karloff's biography issued by Universal in the wake of his success in *Frankenstein* (1931). This document, issued by the studio's publicity director John LeRoy Johnston on 9 January 1932 claimed, "Toward the end of 1909 Karloff's father died in England and Boris went home for a few weeks and then returned to Canada, proceeding to Banff, Alberta, where he remained several months and spent most of his money. Realising that he could not earn much of a salary in Banff, Karloff made his way to Vancouver, British Columbia, arriving in the Western metropolis with exactly $5.00."[7]

However, no evidence to support this story has been found. The claim that Billy returned to England due to his father's death is clearly untrue, as Edward Pratt had passed away in October 1901, over seven years *before* Billy left for Canada. Moffat's story about Billy receiving money from his father's estate is also suspect, as the will had left no provision for his family.

In another, more likely, version of the tale Billy later related how, after leaving O'Reilly's farm, he made his way westward by train and disembarked at Lake Louise. He liked the place so much, he said, he stayed for three months. When his money began to run low he left and continued his journey west. "The rugged beauty and impressive grandeur of the Rockies will always remain a deep memory," he later said. "Banff appealed to me, but it was no use as a place to find a job. So I went on to Vancouver."[8] He arrived in the city with five dollars in his pocket. Within days he was down to 15 cents.

His search for employment proved fruitless. All he found was disappointment. "There wasn't a hope of stage work," he explained. "There was little doing in the theatre at that time and, in any case, managers were not interested in gangling youths with no experience. The dire necessity of eating was soon apparent."[9] Billy took what work he could. "Men

---

i Karloff is inconsistent about the amount of time he spent on O'Reilly's farm. In a 1936 interview with Jonah Maurice Ruddy he said, "From Ontario, where I lasted six months, I went on to Banff." In another interview, from 1953, Karloff said, "They took me on for about ten weeks." Ten years later he told Colin Edwards he had stayed on the farm for "about two months".

ii There is another Terrance O'Reilly on the 1911 Canadian census. However this 60-year-old Irish born farmer lived in Augusta, some 250 miles from Hamilton.

were wanted to dig a race track[iii] and a fair ground," he said, "and the pay was one and threepence an hour.[iv] I reported for work without having had any breakfast as I didn't have the money to buy it. The first day was a long, dreary 10 hours of pick and shovel. My hands were blistered at the end of that day. By the end of the week they were merely calloused. For three days I lived on threepence a day because the arrangement, made by an astute foreman, was that we were to be paid on Saturday. The steak I bought that Saturday night was the finest meal I have ever tasted."[10]

According to Karloff his time in the city[v] was punctuated by a series of chance encounters. The first, he claimed, happened shortly after arriving in Vancouver. "I was wondering what to do next," he said, "when a man stopped me in the street and asked if my name was Pratt. I said it was – "Boris Karloff" didn't exist then. The man was a school friend of my brother Jack's at Dulwich, and he recognised the likeness. He gave me a note to the Works Superintendent of the British Columbia Railway, and I got a job at 28 cents an hour with a pick and shovel laying tracks. I wasn't much good at laying tracks."[11] Although Billy neglected to give the name of this person it was probably the family friend Henry Hayman Claudet who, like four of Billy's brothers, had attended Dulwich College.

Over the years Hayman Claudet would occasionally meet up with the Pratt brothers, as Karloff later reminisced in a 1951 letter to his brother John. "I keep thinking of our famous reunion with Hayman Claudet in the winter of 1943," Karloff wrote, "and the many laughs we had together at the most unseemly hours."[12]

After Claudet died in 1955 Karloff wrote to his friend's widow. This private correspondence clearly indicates Claudet was instrumental in obtaining his first job in Vancouver. Karloff wrote:

> I can never forget what a good friend he was to me, and how kind you both were to me in my early days in Vancouver. I was so completely at a loss to what to do and Hayman gave me exactly this right advice and not content with that he implemented it by getting me my first job and keeping an eye on me and helping me in so many ways… I always think that true immortality lies in the love and the memories that are left behind in the hearts of those who knew you. Hayman's immortality is safe.[13]

Another chance encounter with a family friend allowed Billy to put aside the pick and shovel, albeit temporarily. "Walking on the street one day, Hugh Arthur,[vi] a friend of a brother of mine in China, spotted me," he said. "There was a boom in land at the time. He suggested that I should become a real estate salesman."[14]

Billy took Hugh's advice and gained employment as a broker with Ward, Burmester and von Graevenitz. The company dealt in real estate, insurance and loans and were sales agents for the British Columbia Homes Trust Ltd. They worked out of two offices with

---

iii The racetrack and fairground Karloff referred to are probably those built for the first Pacific National Exhibition (then known as the Industrial Exhibition) which opened in Vancouver's Hastings Park on 16 August 1910.

iv In Karloff's original interview he gave all currencies in English monies. This was later converted to dollars when printed overseas.

v The 1910 Vancouver City Directory reveals Billy had found accommodation at Hornby Mansions, a building at 530 Hornby Street, which still stretches from West Hastings Street southwards to Pacific Street.

vi Hugh Arthur was born on 27 May 1876. Like most of Billy's brothers he, too, had attended Dulwich College. During the Great War Arthur was awarded the Military Cross but sadly, on 29 May 1918, he was killed by a shell.

a Head Office in Pender Street West and a branch office at 443 Lonsdale Avenue.

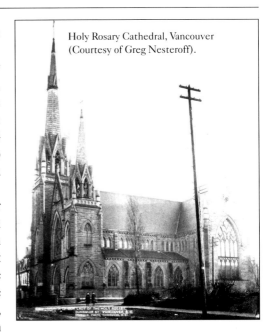

Holy Rosary Cathedral, Vancouver (Courtesy of Greg Nesteroff).

It was during his time with the company that Billy met Jessie Grace Harding. Grace, as she was known, was, like Billy, born in England. As a child she had emigrated with her parents to New Zealand. Around 1904 they moved again, this time relocating to Canada. They settled in British Columbia two years later.

Grace had been born on 16 December 1885 at 'Hill View', Birdhurst Rise in Croydon, Surrey – a mere seven miles from Billy's Camberwell birthplace. Perhaps it was this common thread that first drew the two together. It is not known how the couple met or for how long they were courting but, on 23 February 1910, 22-year-old William Henry Pratt wed 23-year-old Grace Harding in the Holy Rosary Cathedral at 646 Richards Street in Vancouver.[vii] The ceremony was performed by Father Ambrose Madden and was witnessed by Billy's boss, Charles Mansel Burmester, and Grace's mother, Mary.

Along with a new wife came new responsibilities. Unfortunately, the broker job was not as productive as Billy had wished. "Little better than a glorified office boy, I made some money and gave Hugh £2 occasionally towards buying a lot for me," he recalled.[viii] "This did not work so successfully and, when there were no immediate returns, I shovelled coal and did some more ditch-digging. It was less of a hardship this time. Youth soon gets used to work, no matter how rigorous it may be."[15]

While in the metropolis Billy received an interesting business proposition. "Probably one of the greatest things that happened for me was in Vancouver when I was 22 years old," he later said. "Someone offered me a half interest in a goldmine for £100. I had the money. I asked the advice of a banker friend. He said, 'No'. That mine was subsequently sold for £3,000,000. But imagine what would have happened to me. It would have ruined me."[16] Again, Karloff never mentioned the source of this offer but it seems likely it was his friend, the mining engineer, Hayman Claudet.

However, fortune did occasionally smile on Billy. "Late in December, 1910, I called at the Hotel Vancouver for some reason," he explained. "A man passed through the lobby. His face seemed distinctly familiar to me. Upon inquiry, I found he was my brother John on his way from China to London. Sportingly he loaned me £20, enough to keep me going for a while in my planned attempts to get on the stage."[17]

So far Billy's work experience had extended mainly to manual labour. Despite this, and regardless of his newly married status, his theatrical ambitions remained undiminished. "For months, I had made overtures to three Vancouver stock companies," he said. "There didn't

---

vii Curiously, the wedding certificate gives Billy's religious denomination as Catholic. Born an Anglican it is not known when, if ever, he converted to Catholicism. His brother Charles had converted in 1898. His sister Julia also converted.
viii According to the *Quesnel Cariboo Observer* of 18 June 1910, Billy intended to apply for permission to purchase a plot of land a few miles south west of Big Lake in the Central Cariboo region of British Columbia.

seem a chance, not even a faint hope, of becoming an assistant to the assistant stage manager."[18] Then one day, while looking through an old copy of *The Billboard*, Billy noticed an advertisement for a theatrical agent in Seattle. "His name was [Walter] Kelly. I went to see him[ix] and shamelessly told him I'd been in all the plays I'd ever seen, that I was forced to retire to Canada temporarily for my health and was now hale and ready for a comeback."[19]

While despondent at his lack of success Billy saw an advertisement in a newspaper. A stock company, the Jeanne Russell Players,[x] were looking for a character actor. "I applied for the job,"[xi] he later said, "using the name Boris Karloff."[20] He explained, "The 'Karloff' comes from my mother's family – there were some Russian ancestors, and the 'Boris' I took out of the air or a book or something. After all, you can't be Billy Pratt on the stage."[21]

Karloff's siblings, however, thought this explanation lacked credibility. "I think Boris's explanation of Karloff was a flight of his imagination," his brother Richard wrote

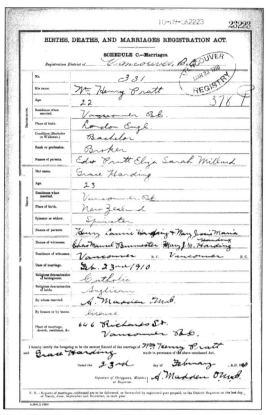

Karloff's 1910 marriage certificate.

in 1971. "I remember agreeing with my brother Jack some time (he had met Boris and had corresponded with him) that B. chose a Russian name because it sounded somehow romantic at that time, so I think any family connection is OUT."[22]

The origin of Billy's stage name has caused much speculation. In her book *Dear Boris* Cynthia Lindsay states she did discover a man named Lazarus Kholoff who was living in Bombay at the same time as Karloff's parents. It may be possible that Billy's parents had spoken of the man. More likely though, as Canadian historian Greg Nesteroff has indicated, is the notion that the actor took his surname from the villainous character Count Karloff in Harold MacGrath's 1904 novel, *The Man on the Box*.[xii] MacGrath's book was serialised in the U.S. press and a stage version did appear in Canada in 1909. It is, therefore, entirely possible that Karloff had seen the play and been influenced by it. It is known he did attend the theatre in Vancouver. It was there he first saw the actor C. Aubrey Smith, then appearing

---

ix In his interview with Ruddy, Karloff said he only wrote to Kelly.

x Karloff sometimes referred to this troupe as the Ray Brandon Players.

xi In 1962 Karloff told a different story claiming it was "On the train [to Kamloops] I concocted my stage name."

xii It has also been suggested Billy derived his stage name from one of two possible literary sources. *Tarzan* author Edgar Rice Burrough's novelette *The Rider* includes a character named Prince Boris of Karlova, while Harold MacGrath's novel, and subsequent play, *The Drums of Jeopardy* features a mad Russian scientist by the name of Boris Karlov. However, Karloff's stage reviews date back to at least February 1912 predating both these supposed influences. Burroughs did not start work on his story until October 1915 while MacGrath's work first appeared in *The Saturday Evening Post* in January 1920.

in *A Woman's Way*, many years before the two men became friends in Hollywood. Of course, we can never be certain of the origins of Billy's stage name. Only the actor knew the truth and even his own account would often change in the telling. Perhaps it is appropriate the name that sent shivers around the world should remain shrouded in mystery. Whatever its origins it was a fortunate choice.

Two months after the trip to Seattle, Billy was working for the British Columbia Electric Co. on a survey party at Lillooet Lake. "We were surveying a couple of lakes 40 miles out of Vancouver, and 30 miles up into the bush," he said, "also for the BC Electric"[23] when he received word from Walter Kelly. "A letter from him arrived… telling me that I had been engaged to join the company at Kamloops at the princely salary of £6 a week."[24] Karloff left without hesitation. "I left my axe in the air, practically, and hot-footed it down to Kamloops and joined this little company," he said, "and that was the beginning of my so-called theatrical career in western Canada"[25]

It is likely that Karloff 'hot-footed' alone, leaving his wife in Vancouver. Extant hotel records that list Karloff as a guest during his days with the Jeanne Russell Stock Company show no sign of Grace. Whether Karloff was aware of it at the time or not, his departure from Vancouver to join the Jeanne Russell Players would also signal the end of his marriage.

Jeanne Russell Alford was born in Salt Lake City in 1875. Her Scottish mother, Margaret, had been married before but her husband, Captain John Ripley, had been lost at sea. Margaret took her only surviving child,[xiii] her daughter Helene, and emigrated to America, settling in Salt Lake City in 1871. There she met and married an Englishman, John Alford. The union produced five children: John (b. 2 July 1873), Jeanne, Frances (who died aged 8), William (who died aged 6) and Robert.

Jeanne had a natural aptitude for the stage. While still a girl she wrote a successful one-act playlet entitled *Traps*. Jeanne began touring, often accompanied by actor/playwright Willard Mack and in August 1906 she married 30-year-old fellow thespian Ray Fowler Brandon in a typically theatrical manner – on the stage of the Tacoma Theatre.

The Jeanne Russell Stock Company had been in existence since around 1908 and regularly played at Edmonton's Dominion Theatre, which was managed by Ray's brother, Lee Brandon. Others in the company for the 1911/12 season included Irving Cook, Donald Gray, Frank Burton, G.C. Garretts and Miss Pinky Mullally. Jeanne's much-married half-sister, Helene Ripley, was also a member of the troupe acting under the stage name Margot Beaton.

In 1889 Helene had married Colonel George Angus Bethune, a mining engineer who had earned his military title as commander of San Francisco's crack regiment. The couple spent the next few years in Tacoma, Washington before settling in San Francisco. The marriage, however, was not a success and they divorced in May 1892.

Within a decade, Bethune had struck it rich from his mining endeavours. This prompted his ex-wife, in April 1902, to commence suit against him – even though she had since remarried, this time to one George W. Walthew. As the Californian divorce laws did not prevent her from receiving alimony, despite remarrying, Helene now wanted her share and demanded $21,600 in arrears. Unfortunately, it is not reported if she was successful in her endeavour, although her subsequent acting career suggests she was not. In 1898 Helene's second husband died in San Francisco. Six years later she married again, this time to one George Noble.

---

xiii Margaret Ripley's son, Robert, died in infancy.

When Karloff joined the Jeanne Russell Players their repertoire included such pieces as *The Galley Slave, Friends, Paid in Full, The Flag of Truce, The Heart of Kentucky,* and *The Young Mrs. Winthrop.* Yet, although the critics and public alike thought well of the troupe, by 1911 this feeling did not extend to the acting community. The company, Karloff recalled, "had such a bad reputation that nobody would join it. That's why he sent for me."[26] So, with no professional acting experience, Karloff arrived one afternoon in the city of Kamloops, "feeling no slight trepidation at the prospect of my first professional stage work. I hadn't the foggiest idea of how to take stage direction. Rehearsal routine and make-up were both completely foreign to me."[27]

Although he joined the troupe in Kamloops Karloff did not tread the boards there. "They were rehearsing new plays for the new season," he later wrote, "and all I had to do for the few days I was there before we moved on to the next town was to watch the rehearsals. And thank God that WAS all as I was a green amateur and I didn't know right from left so far as the stage was concerned."[28]

Yet Karloff had very nearly not joined the troupe at all. Upon entering the theatre he had sat in a rear seat and watched the actors at rehearsal. The company's manager was sitting in the orchestra pit giving orders to the players on the stage. But as soon as he heard the manager's voice, and the manner in which he spoke to the actors, Karloff knew he could not work for this man. He rose from his seat and left the theatre without even seeing the man's face.

Karloff walked around the block but soon realized he was broke with no means to return to Vancouver. He had no choice; he simply had to take the job. He returned to the theatre and politely introduced himself to the manager of the troupe – a thick-necked, bristly-haired man whose penchant for chewing tobacco had left him with a perpetual stain in the corner of his mouth. The man's name, Karloff said, was Ludie and Karloff immediately sensed they both disliked each other. Soon it became apparent that his instincts were

Jeanne Russell (Courtesy of the Glenbow Archives).

correct. Ludie took every opportunity to upbraid the neophyte actor, usually making comments about his appearance and, more often than not, his face. Karloff's feelings for the man soon intensified, as he later related:

> The hatred between this man Ludie and myself is one of the most amazing experiences of my life. Strangely enough, it was unfounded. That is, we did not have the usual reasons for hating each other… a quarrel over a woman… a drunken fist brawl. It was something far stronger than this. If you can believe that a great love can have its inception in some 'other life'… then the same thing might have been the reason for the intense hatred between us. I don't suppose I shall ever forget that first feeling of revolt that I had when I saw his back from the last seat in the theatre. That feeling of unbelievable irritation! It grew with the months. For a whole year we travelled and played and lived together… hating! He was unbelievably cruel… and while none of us likes to believe that the puppy dog tail-pulling cruelty of childhood extends into manhood – this man had that sort of cruelty. He vented it upon human beings. Once, in a bar, I saw him hold a steaming cup of coffee up to the lips of a poor, helpless old beggar… and just as the old fellow had managed to reach the cup, Ludie dashed it in his face![29]

This loathsome character Ludie presents something of a problem. Although he features prominently and later, rather shockingly, in an early Boris Karloff interview not a single trace of the man can be found in any extant documents or reviews concerning the Jeanne Russell Players. Assuming the man was not a figment of Karloff's imagination it may be that, perhaps, the corpulent, tobacco-stained manager was, in fact, a disguised reference to the company's manager and leading man, Ray F. Brandon.

It is known that Brandon could be unscrupulous, as Canadian historian Greg Nesteroff explained. "Ray Brandon had a bad reputation with actors," he said, "He was kind of a hothead, frequently quarrelling with theatre managers, and on at least two occasions with his cast (which led to his arrest in 1925 on a charge of criminal libel)."[30] If Ludie was, in fact, Brandon the later, and uncharacteristically violent, episode Karloff would later describe still lay in the future. For now the actor was merely learning the ropes of the business.

If his recollections about this period are accurate then it was in the city of Nelson, possibly on the occasion of his 24th birthday – 23 November 1911 – that Karloff made his professional debut playing Hofmann, the 60-year-old banker in Ferenc Molnar's 1907 play *The Devil*.[xiv]

Although he had bluffed his way into the troupe his performance betrayed his lack of experience. "I had finally become an actor, but I mumbled, bumbled, missed cues, rammed into furniture and sent the director's blood pressure soaring," he admitted. "When the curtain went up, I was getting 30 dollars a week. When it descended, I was

xiv In a 1953 interview for the *Radio Times* Karloff claimed he had made his stage debut in Nelson. There is some doubt about the veracity of his statement, however, for the Players had already been performing Molnar's play that season, while Karloff was a member of the troupe. In October they had presented *The Devil* in Salmon Arm (the company's first stop after Kamloops), and later in Vernon. It is entirely possible, therefore, that Boris Karloff made his professional debut on one of these nights.

down to 15 dollars."[31] These wages, Karloff later mentioned were, "just enough to exist on – if they paid you. As often as not, they didn't."[32]

Karloff had ample opportunity to learn his new craft, however. The troupe travelled through western Canada playing in towns and cities such as Grand Forks, Rossland, Nelson, Cranbrook and Fernie, even occasionally taking in towns in the northern United States.

Occasionally, when funds would allow, they would take accommodation in the towns' hotels but, more commonly, would stay in rooming houses where they were forced to live as best they could. "Karloff was a profound student on this subject," Samuel Grafton later wrote. "A stock-company actor had to learn to fry an egg on the bottom of an electric iron, propped up on his hotel room floor between the bedpost and the Gideon Bible. (No butter was used, because that would have made the egg slide off, and one had to keep jiggling the iron.) Canned soup, always mulligatawny, because it had meat in it, was cooked in a dresser drawer over a canned-heat fire. New suits were selected from uncalled-for garments at cleaning establishments at a standard price of $5. Since the cast pressed their own clothes, a man's electric iron, which also served as his egg cooker, was his most precious possession, thoughtfully bought and fiercely guarded. 'If you were going to be in a small town for any length of time and needed a boarding house,' says Karloff, 'you enquired around as to where the local schoolteachers stayed and asked for lodging there. You could be sure the place would be very cheap and very clean'."[33]

On Monday, 19 February 1912 Jeanne Russell and her company opened at the Majestic Theatre in Lethbridge with *The American Girl*. The play told the story of a young Southern girl who falls in love with an English artist. After they are secretly married the artist is called back to England by the illness of his brother. While he is away a former suitor of his wife obtains the mortgage for their farm and evicts the girl and her mother. They go to the city but when the husband returns he cannot find them. After years of searching he concludes they must be dead and returns, in grief, to England. 12 years later, however, the man and wife meet by accident in London.

A review appeared in the *Lethbridge Daily Herald* the following day. "Not for many nights has the theatre claimed so large an audience," the newspaper wrote, "and this testified to the popularity of the Jeanne Russell company... The players certainly deserved the compliment, and were far from disappointing to those who had come to greet them. There was a mixture of fun and pathos, neither of which was allowed to run loose, and the outcome was a night of solid entertainment."[34] The piece also contains an early reference to the future horror movie star. Already he was making a mark as the heavy. "Boris Karloff," the paper reported, "was a capable villain."[35]

The following night the troupe presented *The Man from Home*. This four-act satirical comedy, by Booth Tarkington and Harry Leon Wilson, was set at the Hotel Regina Margherita in Sorrento, Italy and told the story of Daniel Voorhees Pike [Ray F. Brandon], a lawyer from Kokomo, Indiana. He arrives in Sorrento to meet his ward, Ethel Granger-Simpson [Jeanne Russell] but finds her engaged to the worthless Almeric St. Aubyn, the son of the treacherous Earl of Hawcastle. Pike exposes the pair, frees Ethel's brother, Horace, from an equally unsavoury alliance and, in doing so, wins the hand of Ethel. Pike, Ethel, and Horace agree to return to Kokomo.

Karloff took the role of the Russian Grand Duke Vasili Vasilivitch, described in the play as, "a portly man of forty-five, but rather soldierly than fat. His hair, pompadour, is reddish blond, beginning to turn gray, like his mustache and large full beard, the latter somewhat 'Henry IV' and slightly forked at bottom. His dress produces the effect rather of carelessness than of extreme fashion. He wears a travelling-suit of grey, neat enough but not freshly pressed, the trousers showing no crease, the coat cut in 'walking-coat style,' with big, slanting pockets, in which he carries his gloves, handkerchief, matches, and a silver cigarette-case full of Russian cigarettes. On his head is a tan-colored automobile cap with buttoned flaps."[36]

Fort Macleod, Alberta (ca. 1911) (Courtesy of the Glenbow Archives).

On Wednesday, the company performed *Emanuella*, a comedy written especially for Jeanne Russell by her half-sister, Helene Ripley.[xv] "Another capacity audience attended the Majestic Theatre last evening to witness the very mirth-provoking farce in three acts, *Emanuella*, by the Jeanne Russell Company," wrote the reviewer for the *Lethbridge Daily Herald*. "The reception given the play by the large audience was a tribute to the excellence of the performance from a popular standpoint."[37] The following night the troupe gave a performance of Molnar's *The Devil* and on Friday they completed their stay in town with *The Half Breed*.

Leaving Lethbridge the troupe made their way to Fort Macleod, Alberta some 30 miles away, where they were booked to play for a single night. On Saturday, 24 February the troupe presented *Emanuella* in the town hall. The subsequent edition of the weekly newspaper recorded that the play, "was very spiritedly put on and the laughter provoked by the situations did approach the 'screaming' stage on several occasions. Miss Russell is always good and she is supported by a capable company. It was a first-rate evening's entertainment."[38]

Following their performance the troupe packed up the costumes and props and headed north on the Canadian Pacific Railway, possibly stopping along the way for short periods as they made towards Calgary and, this time, a longer engagement. On the evening of Monday, 4 March the company took to the stage of the Lyric Theatre on 8th Avenue in *The Man from Home*, which ran for three nights. *Emanuella* was the next presentation, which ran from Thursday through to Saturday.

On Monday the company produced J.M. Barrie's *The Little Minister*. The play concerned the 21-year-old minister, Gavin Dishart, who takes charge of the little Scottish parish of Thrums where the rise in the price of web weave has caused dissention between the local weavers and the King's troops. Lady Barbara Rintoul (known as Lady Babbie), the daughter of Lord Rintoul, dresses as a gypsy to warn of the troop's approach. Dishart falls in love with her and, to avoid trouble with the soldiers, claims the gypsy as his wife. He then discovers, due to Scottish custom, he has unwittingly married her. "J.M. Barrie's quaint comedy of Scotch life, *The Little Minister*, was produced at the Lyric Theatre last night to a well-filled house," wrote the *Calgary Daily Herald*. "Miss Jeanne Russell is an ideal Lady Babbie, and it would be difficult to find a more worthy successor to Maude Adams in this role than Miss Russell proved herself to be last night. She was given able support by Ray F. Brandon whose masterful interpretation of the little minister, Gavin Dishart, proved him

xv Helene co-wrote *Emanuella* with her second husband, George Walthew. The play was copyrighted in 1895 and re-registered on 25 June 1907.

to be an actor of sterling abilities. The cast was excellent throughout and *The Little Minister* should play to capacity houses tonight and tomorrow night."[39]

Karloff played the violent drunkard Rob Dow in the play and a photograph exists showing the actor in his stage costume. On his knees, and with his hands on his chest, Karloff posed in a scene from the play. Upon his head he wears the traditional Scottish beret, the tam.

On Thursday the bill changed again and the company staged *The American Girl*. The following day the *Calgary Daily Herald* wrote, "*The American Girl*, an intensely interesting comedy drama of life on two continents, was given at both performances at the Lyric yesterday and found instant favor with both audiences. It is easily the best production that has been staged by the Jeanne Russell company since the beginning of their stock

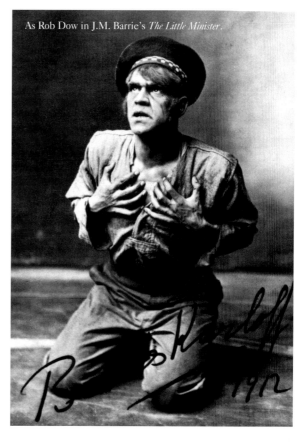

As Rob Dow in J.M. Barrie's *The Little Minister*.

engagement at the Lyric. Miss Russell has a strong emotional role, which she handles with ease and finish… Ray Brandon was a laugh forty ways as the tramp theatrical manager who afterwards became a regular Charles Frohman, with theatres in New York and London. The balance of the long cast gave excellent support."[40]

The following week the company presented three plays instead of the usual two. Monday (St. Patrick's Day) began with a revival of the Irish comedy *Cousin Kate* for two nights, including a Tuesday matinee.

Hubert Henry Davies's 1903 play told the story of Kate Curtis, a young novelist who falls in with a young Irishman, Heath Desmond. When she discovers her relative, Amy Spencer, has split from her betrothed Kate attempts to reconcile the pair, unaware that Amy's fiancé is, in fact, her beloved Desmond.

"The play was enthusiastically received," the *Calgary Daily Herald* reported, "and several individual hits were scored. Miss Jeanne Russell, in the name part, originated by Ethel Barrymore, appeared to great advantage. Miss Russell has had quite a run with comedy roles lately, and in each successive part she seems to excell [*sic*]. Her *Cousin Kate* is an artistic masterpiece."[41]

Cousin Kate was followed by *Moths*, a dramatisation of Ouida's novel of 1880. The play told the story of Vere Herbert [Jeanne Russell] who is persuaded to marry the Prince Zuroff. The Prince, however, is a violent man who beats and berates his new wife. Vere, though, has two admirers, the Marquis de Corréze (whom she loves) and Lord Jura. At the end of the play Jura kills, and is killed by, the Prince leaving Vere free to marry the

Marquis. "The theme deals with the smart set of Russia and is typically Ouidaesque," wrote the *Morning Albertan*. "The story is too well known to need a review. Miss Russell has the personality described by the author, and her work was artistic. Ray Brandon was a capable Duke of Coureze [*sic*], and Irving Cook a manly and lovable Lord Jura."[42]

The week's run concluded, on Friday and Saturday, with Harry D. Cottrell's play *The Half Breed*, "a sensational play of the modern west."[43] The play, revealed the *Morning Albertan*, "presents the stage Indian in a new light, namely a true light, showing the inborn hate that the redskin bears the pale face. The play calls for a long cast and all the members of the company will appear in congenial roles. This play will mark the last appearance of the Jeanne Russell company at the Lyric for some time."[44]

Leaving Calgary the troupe made their way eastward into Saskatchewan. By April 1912 they had arrived in the province's capital city Regina where they were booked to play the 800-seat Regina Theatre on 12th Avenue and Hamilton Street.

On Monday, 1 April they took to the stage in *The American Girl*. The play and its performance, however, did not meet with the approval of the newspaper's theatrical reviewer who later commented that, "the insipid melodrama... with its idiotic plot and amateurish lines without doubt prejudiced many of the audience against the company, but the error of including such rubbish in the repertoire was undoubtedly righted to a large extent by the rather clever bill of last evening."[45] This second production, *The Man from Home*, was, the reviewer noted, "so distinct an improvement on that of the night before... that one should never have known without glancing at the programme that it was the same company which was playing it... The title part is taken by Ray F. Brandon, and is fairly well handled... Miss Jeanne Russell is also good in the part of the girl... The role is not a brilliant one, but Miss Russell does as well as possible with it... It would be impossible to say how truly Boris Karloff presented the character of a philanthropic Russian grand duke [Vasili Vasilivitch] – the species being up to the present unknown. He appeared quite convincing, however, and the character was pleasing if not familiar."[46]

Although the reviewer praised the production in general, one aspect of the evening's entertainment proved irksome. "One thing with which the company might well dispense is the so-called vaudeville between acts," he wrote. "It spoils the theme of the play, and further, is distasteful to those who are yet forced to sit and listen. More than that, it cheapens the quality of the company as a whole. This, however, in no way refers to the singing of G.D. Gray, who could not be classed as a "vaudeville singer." He is well known in this city as the finest baritone who ever made Regina his temporary home. He also has the good taste to choose songs universally known and liked. *Thora* and *Three for Jack* were those he chose for last evening. Mr. Gray was a one-time resident of this city, and his excellent voice is still remembered by many."[47] After an extended stay the company concluded their tenure on 11th April with a performance of *A Texas Ranger*.

In mid-April the company arrived in the city of Saskatoon heralded, on 13 April, by an announcement in the *Daily Phoenix*. "Canada's representative stock organisation, the Jeanne Russell company, will be the attraction at the Empire theatre [for] three nights starting Thursday, April 18th," the newspaper wrote. "The opening play will be Booth Tarkington's and Harry Leon Wilson's clever satirical comedy, *The Man from Home*. This play, founded upon the prevailing tendency of American heiresses to marry titled foreigners, has enjoyed a popularity both in the United States and England that has never been surpassed."[48]

Days later a tragic story was filling the newspapers. On Monday, 15 April the 'unsinkable' *R.M.S. Titanic* struck an iceberg on its maiden voyage from Southampton to New York and sank in the cold Atlantic with the loss of 1,523 lives.

That Thursday the Jeanne Russell Players took to the stage in Saskatoon. According to the *Daily Star*, the performance of *The Man from Home* attracted "a fairly large audience, and the show was one of an enjoyable character. The opening act was not so well done as it might have been, but as the play progressed the work of the company improved. Mr. Ray F. Brandon has many admirers in Saskatoon, and in the role of a hardheaded, although romantic, Yankee he was seen to great advantage. Miss Jean [*sic*] Russell possesses considerable talent and her interpretation of the role of the young lady, who was determined to marry a title no matter what it might cost her in the way of money, she was spirited and attractive. Mr. Boris Karloff, as the Russian grand duke, proved himself a capable artiste..."[49]

The *Daily Phoenix* wrote:

> Ray F. Brandon's friends were glad to see him again last night though he was hardly to be recognised in his Indiana slicker and accent. He was "the man from home" who had journeyed to Sorrento to save his ward from marrying a title at a cost of hundreds of thousands of dollars in stage money. A real monkey-wrench and a more or less saleable motor car had a part among the stage settings, the car furnishing a splendid hiding place for the escaped Russian insurgent… Miss Russell was the American girl who would be a countess even though the title was costing as much as a whole street in Sorrento was worth... Mr. Karloff gave a good portrayal of the Russian nobleman and Mr. Cook was quite admirable as the smartly dressed American. Between acts were vaudeville stunts. Among the best of them were two songs **Italian Love** and **Which would you rather, a grand baby or a baby grand** sung by a young lady act in Venetian red costume.[50]

The following night the company staged Barrie's comedy *The Little Minister* and on Saturday, 20 April presented a matinee and evening performance of Molnar's *The Devil*.

On Monday the *Daily Phoenix* headlines ran: "INVESTIGATION INTO *TITANIC* DISASTER ADJOURNED TO MEET IN WASHINGTON." Inside, the paper announced a performance of *A Texas Ranger*, to be staged that night by the Jeanne Russell Players. The review appeared the following day. "A full house got round to the Empire last night to see the Texas Ranger range and to watch how cowboys make love and war with the accents on the war," the newspaper wrote. "Ray F. Brandon was the hero of this play of the plains, who graduated from ranching to being a mine owner. Miss Jeanne Russell played leads for the ladies. Her role got her into a mock marriage from which she gets rescued in the last act at which point also the villain dies a melodramatic death… *American Girl* will be the play presented tonight by Mr. Brandon and his company."[51]

On Wednesday, the Players presented *The Squaw Man* and followed this, the following evening, with *Jesse James*. We cannot know how these plays fared in Saskatoon as, unfortunately, none of the local newspapers ran reviews for these one-night productions.

The next evening the company staged *Emanuella*. "It is not often that an absolutely new play is seen in Saskatoon," wrote the *Daily Phoenix*, "but Miss Jeanne Russell will appear tonight at the Empire in the title role of *Emanuella*, a three-act farce written especially for her by Helene Riplay [*sic*], whose stage name is Margot Beaton. Miss Russell determined to make it part of her repertoire in order to test its power with critics and public. The verdict of both has been so encouraging that she has determined to make it her only vehicle next season, opening for a run in Chicago, before touring the United States and Canada... The weak point in the play is the name. It seems to indicate a religious subject. In spite of Shakespeare, there is everything in a name. Can you suggest a good name for this farce? A prize of $10 will be given for the best name suggested. Study the situations carefully tonight and present your suggestion at the box office before five o'clock tomorrow evening, at the end of the third act of *The Halfbreed* which is Saturday's bill."[52] It would appear the offer of a $10 prize did the trick, for *Emanuella* was latter presented by the troupe – albeit in a condensed version – under the title *A Star By Mistake*.

It is unclear whether the company remained in the city or did a brief stint elsewhere but according to the *Daily Phoenix* they began a three-night run of *The Moonshiner's Daughter* on 9 May. It is a curious claim as this play was not a part of their regular repertoire. Still, the play, the newspaper explained, was "a gripping story of life among the makers of moonshine whiskey."[53]

Life in a stock company was an exhausting existence. They had been on tour for a year. "How we worked!" Karloff said. "We rehearsed all day and every day, and we played in the evenings in any sort of barn or shack wherever we happened to be."[54] But by June the company found themselves in the centre of the Canadian plains stranded back in Regina.

Karloff later made a curious confession about his time with the troupe, one that involved the mysterious Ludie, which may possibly have occurred around this time. He claimed:

> By roundabout means, I got wind of the fact that Ludie was planning to jump the show... leave us stranded. And the worst part of it was that he owed most of us a lot of back pay and was planning to leave us helpless. I figured that if I let him know that I was on to his little game that I might delay his departure at least until he paid off the troupe.
>
> So I went to his little room in a cheap hotel. He was lying on an unmade bed... a bottle of liquor on the nightstand beside him. I didn't want to fight. I greeted him as amicably as possible, removed my hat and placed it with my cane across the end of the bed. Then I sat down to talk.
>
> I started out by talking of other subjects. But Ludie knew why I was there and it infuriated him that I would be the one to learn his secret. Suddenly, before I had even broached the subject and without warning, he jumped to his feet. Like a fat snake, he jumped from the bed with my cane in hand and before I could grasp the situation he crashed it down on my hand and face.
>
> Something happened inside me! As the blood from the gash on my head poured into my eyes, blinding me with fury and my own blood... something terrible came over me. Suddenly I knew the feeling that must come over a murderer just before he commits his crime. I went insane... and for the moment I was as much the beast as he.
>
> I don't know how I got the stick away from him, but when the first vestige of sanity returned, I was conscious of my arm – rising and falling... rising and

falling, cutting deep welts into his prostrate form with my cane. Like a crazy subtitle in a movie, it flashed across my mind: *"I am beating this man to death!"* Yet I couldn't stop. Rising and falling… rising and falling… that cane went on.[55]

Whether this ever happened is, of course, impossible to know. However, the truth remains that when the company arrived in Regina they were in trouble. "Everyone in the company, including myself of course, was absolutely flat broke," Karloff said. "The situation was rotten and the prospects dismal. Maybe the finger of Fate was pointing at me. The day after the manager announced our complete lack of funds and inability to proceed, there was a terrific storm in Regina…"[56]

At 5 p.m. on a hot Sunday, 30 June 1912 a 500-mph tornado tore through Regina's downtown. 28 people died, 2,500 were rendered homeless and $4 million of property was damaged. The tornado had ripped through the city in three minutes. "However," Karloff mused, "it was a case of an ill wind blowing no good all right – because we all got jobs clearing up the debris…"[57]

It has been claimed that, following the devastation, the Jeanne Russell Players announced it would stage a benefit performance of the comedy *The Real Thing* and donate half the receipts to the city. The performance, we are told,

MR. RAY F. BRANDON
LEADING MAN AND PRODUCER WITH THE JEANNE RUSSELL COMPANY AT THE ORPHEUM THEATRE—FOUR NIGHTS, STARTING WEDNESDAY 4TH.

The aftermath of the 1912 Regina tornado (Courtesy of the Glenbow Archives).
Ray F. Brandon (Courtesy of Greg Nesteroff).

never occurred and the Players disbanded. In fact, the play *was* performed on 4 July but it was *not* by the Jeanne Russell Players. Regina's daily newspaper *The Leader* announced:

> Regina Benefit Tonight – Miss Crosman and the members of her company have made a tour through the tornado devastated district of our city and painfully realized what the disaster means to the grief-stricken victims. She and the members of her company are so impressed with what they saw that they wish to do something to show their sympathy. They have announced, therefore, that the performance of **The Real Thing** tonight will be in the nature of a benefit for those who have suffered through Sunday's disaster.[58]

When the debris was cleared, and with no prospect of any further stage work, Karloff searched for other jobs. He discovered the Dominion Express Company, a haulage concern owned by Canadian Pacific, required men. "Being fairly husky, I got temporary employment," he said.[59]

After the company broke up Jeanne Russell and Ray Brandon continued to work on the stage. After some time in stock in Calgary they entered into vaudeville. By May 1913 Jeanne had returned to Salt Lake City where she and her husband took to the stage in her playlet, *Traps*. The following year the couple were touring in a successful production of *A Star By Mistake*, which the newspapers described as a "riot".[60]

The young Boris Karloff.

Sadly, Jeanne Russell died at the age of 44 on Wednesday, 9 June 1920 at her mother's home in Salt Lake City. She had, the newspapers reported, been suffering for a year from a nervous breakdown. Her husband was not present when she died as he was on an important business trip to Phoenix, Arizona. Jeanne's cause of death was officially recorded as 'tabes dorsalis,' a slowly progressive degeneration of the spinal cord caused by an untreated syphilis infection.

Following the death of his wife, Ray Brandon continued in showbusiness. He married again, to one Jean Spawr, and although the marriage produced two children – a boy and a girl who were named after their parents – it too ended in tragedy when, in 1928, Brandon's second wife drowned. Then, on 7 August 1933 Ray F. Brandon, now working as an 'advance man' [61] for an animal show,[xvi] died when his car left the road in Bend, Oregon. He was found near the wreckage 45 feet down an embankment near the highway. The police were at a loss to explain the accident, as they could find no evidence of a collision. He was 57 years old.

Karloff, of course, fared better. While employed by the Dominion Express Company the actor received a stroke of good luck. "The company sent me to the railway station to collect some crates of goods," he explained. "As I crossed the tracks to the warehouse, someone threw an old copy of *The Billboard*, a theatrical journal, from a train window. Casually I picked it up and glanced at it. I saw an announcement that the Harry St. Clair Players, a repertory company, at Prince Albert, wanted a young leading man. I dashed off a letter of application post haste and, to my surprise, I received a reply a few days later asking me to join them in Prince Albert."[62]

---

xvi An advance man oversaw the necessary preparations (licences, sponsorship, publicity, etc.) ahead of the show's arrival.

PINNEY THEATRE

TWO NIGHTS

MONDAY AND TUESDAY, NOV. 12 & 13

THE NEW YORK PRODUCING CO. OFFERS

"THE VIRGINIAN"

CAST OF CHARACTERS

Honey Wiggins......................................Edwin Holt
Trampas ....Lloyd Redfield
Mrs. Taylor......................................Nellie Holland
Mollie Woods.......................................Marie Wells
THE VIRGINIAN.....................................Boris Karloff
Steve ....Herbert R. Connor
Spanish Ed.......................................Elmer Nordseth
Shorty...C. R. Hanna
Nebrasky ....Lloyd Brummett
Judge Henry.....................................David B. Kennedy
Uncle Hewie......................................T. J. Fadden
Simpson..C. E. Robert
Taylor ....Dan Hailey
Dollar Bill......................................Fred Steinmetz
Mrs. Hewie.......................................Olive Whitney

SYNOPSIS

Act I—Office of "Here's How" Hotel.
Act II—Judge Henry's Ranch.
Act III—Horse Thief Pass.
Act IV—Street in Medicine Bow.

Executive Staff for the New York Producing Co.

W. B. Bennett..Manager
J. A. Redfield..................................Business Manager
Lloyd Brummett.....................................Electrician
E. Nordseth.................................Master of Properties
D. Hailey.......................................Stage Manager

COMING ATTRACTIONS

"THE FLAME," Friday and Saturday, November 16-17
IKE & ABY, Monday, November 19

Flyer for the touring production of *The Virginian*, starring Boris Karloff, 1917 (Courtesy of the Red Deer and District Archives)

Chapter 4

FROM CANADA TO CALIFORNIA
(1912-1919)

"Frequently we would skip the entire second or third act simply because we were tired and wanted to go home. Beside, it served the audience right. They had no business being there in the first place, wasting their time on such terrible theatre!"[1]

Boris Karloff (1960)

With the promise of another acting job Karloff made his way to the Harry St. Clair Players. "St. Clair was absolutely honest," Karloff said. "If there was no money in the office, the ghost didn't walk, but when business was good he paid us what he owed us. In some towns we stayed a week, in others we settled down for a run. I was a quick study and the quickest study got the longest part. So I played leads in *Paid in Full*, *Charley's Aunt*, *East Lynne*, *Way Down East*, *Bought and Paid For*, *Baby Mine*, *What Happened to Jones*, *Why Smith Left Home* and many other melodramas. We all took turns at being stage manager, and we never had a dress or prop rehearsal."[2]

Being constantly on the road, however, took its toll on Karloff's marriage. It has become apparent that, during his time with the Jeanne Russell Players, Karloff's relationship with fellow thespian Margot Beaton had assumed a more intimate nature. It is not known how Karloff's wife, Grace, became aware of her husband's indiscretions but she petitioned for divorce citing 'Helene Russell' – another of Margot's many aliases – as co-respondent.

On 8 January 1913 the document was placed before the Honourable Mr. Justice Murphy in the Supreme Court of British Columbia. Neither Grace nor Karloff were in attendance when the decision was reached:

> This Court doth order and decree that the marriage of the Petitioner Grace Harding Pratt to the Respondent William Henry Pratt be and the same is hereby absolutely dissolved. And it is further ordered and adjudged that the

> Respondent William Henry Pratt do pay to the Petitioner her costs of this
> action as between Solicitor and client forthwith after the taxation thereof.[3]

The District Registrar, A.B. Pollinger, entered the verdict into the records two days later. It must have been an unwelcome financial burden on an already meagre existence. However, Grace's second marriage, to a realtor named Cecil Angus Hadfield, conducted a mere ten days after the verdict, suggests at least the possibility that Karloff and Grace had mutually agreed to end their marriage. Whatever the case, with his marriage now dissolved, Karloff was free to pursue a career on the stage.

Grace joined her new husband in Calgary and there they raised a son, Philip Leon. Sadly, Cecil died of typhoid fever in 1918, aged only 38. Grace never remarried and died on 1 August 1962, aged 76. Philip died in New York on 17 July 1980. He was 66 years old.

Karloff had joined St. Clair's company in the city of Prince Albert, Saskatchewan. Unfortunately, the city's newspaper archives for these years were destroyed in a fire and so there are no theatrical reviews for the time Karloff played there. According to the entertainment newspaper the *New York Clipper*, the Harry St. Clair Stock Company stayed in the city from at least the 21 October to the end of December 1912.

From 30 December, they started a series of six-day stints in towns and cities across central Canada, travelling on Sundays when there were no shows. They began in Brandon, Manitoba, a city some 400 miles south east of Prince Albert. Then it was 80 miles along the train line east to Portage la Prairie. The following Monday the troupe was in Virden, 125 miles to the west before moving on to Moosomin, Saskatchewan. A week later, on 27 February 1913, the Harry St. Clair Players opened in Broadview, some 45 miles away. By April they were back in Brandon where the *New York Clipper* listed them as playing an 'indefinite' engagement until that September. Despite the paper's claim, however, (and assuming St. Clair was not also running a second company) the troupe did, in fact, leave the city during this period, for on Monday 23 June they opened in Wainwright, Alberta for a week-long residency, appearing in such plays as *Moths, Facing the Music, Paid in Full, Young Mrs. Winthrop, Lena Rivers, Mabel Heath*, and *A Terrible Tangle*.

"I remember we had been guaranteed $300 for a week in Wainwright, Alta," Karloff later said. "We looked forward to that for days; it was a lot of money for the company to make in one week. The night before we got there the theatre burned down. So we got to work on the old skating rink. We rigged up curtains, and set up board seats and we played our scheduled week, a new play each night, to packed houses with audiences coming from miles around. They wanted a good show and didn't care if the fixings weren't up to scratch. And we did our best."[4] Upon investigation, however, it appears Karloff's story of the fire had been appropriated from elsewhere.

On the morning of Sunday, 26 May 1912, while Karloff was still with the Jeanne Russell Players, a fire broke out in Wainwright's business section. Within hours the fire had spread, consuming shops, poolrooms, the Union Bank and the Auditorium. The damage was estimated at $100,000.

The Eckhardt Stock Company had been due to play the Auditorium but the fire put an end to that. Instead, the troupe's engagement was postponed while the skating rink was converted into an opera house. Eckhardt's players finally opened at the Rink Opera House on 10 June with *Paid in Full*.

Initially Karloff stayed with Harry St. Clair's troupe for a year, performing in its gamut of plays. "At the end of the engagement I had $800 simply because St. Clair held back a certain amount each week and paid it at the conclusion of the season," Karloff later explained.[5] Then, taking his savings, he decided to go to Chicago to take a crack at the big time. On Monday, 12 October 1913 Boris Karloff left Saskatchewan and passed through the border control in Portal, North Dakota. According to the border-crossing list, however, he was not alone.

Fellow St. Clair Players Chester [Charles] Jackson and his wife Constance had, like Karloff, also recently left the city of Weyburn, Saskatchewan on their journey to America. According to the documentation completed at the border, however, there was a fourth member of the party – a woman named 'Margot Karloff'.

While it seems safe to assume that this Mrs. Karloff was the actor's paramour Margot Beaton, her claim to be the legal spouse of the actor has proven, so far, unverifiable. For, while both Margot and Karloff are shown on the document as being 'married', neither British Columbia, Saskatchewan, Manitoba or Alberta (those provinces most heavily travelled by their touring companies) have any record of a marriage between the two, by any of their known names – although, of course, the two could have married during one of the travelling troupe's excursions into America.

According to the list, the last time Karloff and Margot had returned from the U.S. had been in January 1912 when they left Whitefish, Montana on their way back to Canada. This would have been while they were still members of Jeanne Russell's Stock Company.

At the border Karloff, then a month shy of his 26th birthday, had his details entered on the list. He was, the official recorded, six feet in height with a dark complexion, brown hair and brown eyes. His place of birth, however, was entered as *Odessa, Russia*. Clearly, Karloff was not being entirely honest with the border officials. He was not the only one. Margot's height, we are told, was five feet three inches. She had brown hair and blue eyes. Her place of birth is recorded as Bombay, India – a fact consistent with data from the 1880 U.S. census taken when Margot was 13 years old. When she crossed the U.S. border 33 years later, however, Margot claimed she was 31 years old. 'Mrs. Karloff' had knocked 15 years off her age.

The border paperwork of October 1913 also reveals that Karloff had $30 to his name and had purchased tickets for Margot and himself to travel to Kenmare, North Dakota some 30 miles away. The Jacksons, too, were bound for Kenmare though details of the group's later wanderings remain obscure. They probably took employment with other theatrical troupes.

On 21 October, nine days after he had passed through the border, Karloff's first – and only – theatrical piece was registered. According to the Library of Congress 1913 *Catalogue of Copyright Entries* covering dramatic compositions, the piece had been written in Hardisty, Alberta.

The manuscript languished in the library, ignored and forgotten, until 1981 when Dr. Patrick O'Neill of Newfoundland's Mount Saint Vincent University unearthed it while searching for unpublished Canadian plays. It was copied and microfilmed, along with some 800 other plays, and deposited in the University's drama collection from where it was retrieved, almost 30 years later, by Canadian historian Greg Nesteroff. The piece, *With a Grain of Salt* (by Helene Ripley and Boris Karloff), contains only two roles: a married couple called the Beverlys – roles obviously intended for its authors.

In the playlet Mrs. Beverly threatens to kill herself to teach her husband a lesson for keeping late nights. "And everybody will know that your cruel inhuman treatment drove me to suicide," she says.[6] She drinks 'poison' but is angered when her husband's only concern seems to be how he will now find another woman. "She'll be wondering all the time if my wife really did commit suicide or not," he says.[7] As his alarmed wife looks on Mr. Beverly contemplates what he should do with her body. He then phones his paramour, Maybelle. He tells her of his wife's 'death' and arranges to meet her at the train station, once he has interred his wife's body in the cellar.

After he leaves the room Mrs. Beverly rises from the sofa and phones Maybelle, but the person on the other end of the line denies the existence of any such person on that number. Mrs. Beverly hangs up the phone and puts on her husband's hat and coat just as he re-enters the room. He claims he can see his wife's ghost, which enrages her even more. He then reveals where he had been earlier. "What a pity she can never know that I spent the entire evening with an insurance agent."[8] His wife then asks, "But Maybelle?" "I left her in the coal cellar," he tells her, "which is wet."[9] The curtain is then directed to descend quickly. It is unknown whether the playlet was ever publicly performed but, with its macabre undertones, it already presented a persona in keeping with the Boris Karloff the world would later come to know.

Karloff eventually made his way to Chicago arriving, he later claimed, on 13 October 1914 – exactly a year after he had crossed the U.S. border. His search for work, however, proved fruitless. "There was a frightful slump in the theatrical business at the time and I just couldn't get an engagement," he explained.[10] The discouraged actor eventually found employment at the Brinkman Theatre in Bemidji, Minnesota. "This was very dull," he recalled, "and I was very happy to rejoin Harry St. Clair."[11]

St. Clair held no qualms about re-employing actors who had previously left his company. In fact, as his various newspaper adverts show, he actively encouraged it. One such advert had appeared in the *New York Clipper* in November 1911:

> WANTED QUICK
> For the Harry St. Clair Stock Co.
> LEADING MAN
> Salary moderate. I pay all. Old friends write.
> Address MGR. HARRY ST. CLAIR
> Macklin, Sask.[12]

Another from April 1913 read:

> A No. 1 Leading and Character Man
> Other good people write. Make Summer salary low, as it is sure. Booze fighters
> and disorganisers need not apply. Must be good dressers on and off. Address
> HARRY ST. CLAIR, Sherman Theatre, Brandon, Manitoba, Indefinite.[13]

After returning to St. Clair it was business as usual. "We used to play towns at the end of a branch line…" Karloff explained. "If business was good we got paid. If not, St. Clair would hand us a statement and let it go at that."[14]

In 1915 the Players arrived in the city of Minot, North Dakota. It would be, as Karloff recalled, the start of "years of bitter oblivion".[15] The troupe performed at the Jacobson Opera House on the northeast corner of Central Avenue. Situated above a large hardware store, the Opera House, which could seat almost one thousand people, had opened in 1903 with an adaptation of Alexandre Dumas' *The Count of Monte Cristo*. "We were up in about 18 plays and we played those in the first three weeks," Karloff said. "So with no money to move on, we had to stay there and start expanding the repertoire. We did two new plays a week for 53 weeks. Three rehearsals and you were on! It was rugged, but good training, and it stood me in good stead. I was forced to become a fast study – or starve to death. I think we were really a very good company actually. Of course, frequently we would leave out an entire act and no one noticed, so maybe the audiences were just not paying attention. I'll say one thing for them, though: the audiences of the sticks were in no way unintelligent. When at the end of a run we'd ask for repeat requests, they invariably chose the best plays."[16]

J. Warren Bacon, the manager's son (and chief errand boy), recalled Karloff's time in Minot. "He could play any part convincingly," Bacon said. "In spite of the fact that he played mostly villainous roles, they [the people of Minot] loved Boris. And to give you an idea, George Magnusson used to keep the drugstore fountain open at night so [he] could go there and have a coke every evening… [It was] right across the street."[17]

By July 1916 the troupe had reached Hutchinson, Kansas where they were engaged to play the Home Theatre. For a week the troupe trod the boards there, presenting such pieces as *Facing the Music*, *The Builder of Bridges* and *A Cheerful Liar*. They opened on Monday, 24 July with *The Spendthrift*. The star of the piece was Margot Beaton.

By that October the pair were topping the Players' bill. Following a week at Newk's Theatre in Burlington, Kansas, the theatre's manager, J.J. Newcomb, reported, "Played the Harry St. Clair Co. Fair week, Oct. 2, to very good business at 35c top, receipts doubling every night. I want to say to brother managers that this is the best rep show I have had in 15 years. All very nice people. Boris Karloff and Miss Margot Beaton are the two greatest leading people I ever saw at any price and I've seen a few of the big ones. Harry St. Clair is a prince to do

Karloff on stage, 1914.

business with. The support of the leading people is very good. You will make no mistake in throwing out any feature pictures and letting them have your time."[18]

Within months of sharing top billing in Burlington, Karloff and Beaton had parted company. Margot later married fellow actor Maurice Atherton Francillon and together the pair continued to tread the boards. By October 1923 they had joined the John Winninger Players and six years later Margot could be found as a member of the Metropolitan Players back in the actress's adopted hometown of Salt Lake City where she appears to have stayed. Maurice seems to have given up the actor's life and around 1937 he took a job as the secretary of the State Employees Union, Local 99. He died on 4 December 1952, aged 71. Margot's fate, however, is unknown.

By early 1917, with $60 in his pocket, Karloff had left the Harry St. Clair Players for the last time. "Realising that success would come only by playing the large cities, once more I went to Chicago," he said. "And once more I failed."[19] He secured accommodation – a furnished room with a stove – at four dollars a week and continued his search for employment.

For Karloff, Chicago was always a daunting place. "It was terrifying," he said. "Alone, no help, no one to turn to, no food, and rent to be paid. I never got over my fear of the place. Years later I played there in *Arsenic and Old Lace*, staying in total luxury at the Ambassador, and still later in *Peter Pan*, for which we broke every record including *South Pacific*, but I couldn't get over my feeling. Chicago has always given me the willies – the knife is really at your throat there."[20]

Karloff's movements after Chicago are sketchy and the actor's own recollections about the period have proven characteristically unreliable. He later claimed, "Billie Bennett's *The Virginian* company was going on tour. They took me with them, and we toured through Minnesota, Iowa, Kansas, Colorado and Nevada, finally arriving in Los Angeles in December of 1917… *The Virginian* tour did not last long. The San Pedro stock company had a series of engagements in Southern California for about six weeks. Through them I enjoyed my first wanderings in this part of the world. Then another repertory company went on a tour through the San Joaquin Valley and ended at San Francisco."[21]

The first hard evidence of Karloff's movements during this period, however, can be found in early 1917 when the actor is listed as one of the Patti McKinley Players. On 3 February the *New York Clipper* announced the troupe's extended stay in Zanesville, Ohio:

> The Patti McKinley Players, under the management of Dave Heilman, who opened a temporary engagement at the Orpheum Theatre, have decided to remain the rest of the season. The company includes besides Miss McKinley, Pauline LeRoy, Hazel Wylde, Olive Whitney, Walter King, Earl Suffraine, Ronald Rosebraugh, Boris Karloff, Fred Cantway, Walt. Williams, Robert Fleming, carpenter and Chas. Montgomery, scenic artist.[22]

On Monday, 12 March 1917 the troupe opened at the Sun Theatre in Portsmouth, Ohio where they would stay for six weeks. Presenting two plays a week the troupe performed such plays as the comedy *Johnny Get Your Gun*, *The Lure* (a play about the white slave trade), the war play *The Girl I Left Behind Me*, and *The Vampire*.[i]

---

i *The Vampire* was an adaptation of a play entitled *A Fool There Was*. It was made into a film in 1915, starring Theda Bara.

Karloff can next be found with Lona Fendell's Stock Company, a touring theatrical troupe that, in January 1916, was reported to be in possession of "a carload of special scenery and electrical effects".[23] By that time they had been touring through the state of Wisconsin for the last three seasons playing, it would appear, inside a large tent the troupe carted from town to town. "Miss Fendell has won her way into the hearts of the theatre-going public," one newspaper noted. "All her plays are high-class and refined, and the vaudeville between the acts is made up of the best vaudeville material. The gowns and costuming displayed by this company is beyond comparison and up-to-the-minute."[24]

At the end of April 1917 Fendell's company began a three-night run in the town of Grand Rapids, Wisconsin.[ii] Tickets cost 10c and 20c. "They are here and they are good," asserted the *Daily Leader*. "Come early."[25]

At 8:00 p.m. on Monday, 30 April the Players took the stage at the town's Palace Theatre. Although the name of that evening's entertainment has gone unrecorded the following night the troupe presented *Rebecca of Sunnybrook Farm*. As was the norm for Fendell's company, a new play was presented each night and on 2 May they ended their brief engagement in town with *The Whole Dam Family*.

Two weeks later they were back in Grand Rapids for another three-night stint at the Palace Theatre opening, on 14 May, with *Don't Lie to Your Wife*. *The Spendthrift* was the following evening's entertainment, and on 16 May they ended their engagement with *The Divorce*. Although there are no reviews or cast lists for their time in Grand Rapids it seems likely that Karloff was with Fendell's company at this point. It is certain he was a member of the troupe a month later when the troupe passed through Chicago. Before they left that city, however, Karloff was required to register for the draft.

The Great War had now been raging in Europe for almost three years. After initially pursuing a policy of non-intervention the United States declared war on Germany on 6 April 1917. The following month Congress approved conscription and on 5 June the first draft was held for all men between the ages of 21 and 31. Karloff, although a non-national and therefore not subject to induction into the American forces, was still required to register – which he did in Chicago on 1 June as, presumably, he would not be in the city on draft day. It was not, according to Karloff, the actor's first brush with the military. The first occasion, he later claimed, was in Chicago almost three years earlier. "I arrived there October 13, 1914," he said, "and found that no one was the least bit interested in my experience. The British army had rejected me because of a heart murmur, my money was disappearing rapidly and I decided that I had better get back to the sticks where I was appreciated."[26] It is a claim that was often repeated but has so far proved unverifiable.

Karloff's claim suggests he had attempted to enlist with the British Army, presumably in Chicago, not long after Britain had declared war on Germany in August 1914. A tantalising letter survives from the actor's brother John to his half-sister Emma which may refer to this event. "That yarn about Billy and the Consul at Chicago and its advertisement was interesting and characteristic – and also, if viewed from an entirely detached point of view, amusing," John wrote. "Billy, of course, is hopeless, but I trust, now that America is in the war, a way may be found for making things warm for him. A shell in the trenches would do him a power of good!"[27] Although written in December 1917 John's phrase "now that America is in the war" suggests Billy's visit to the Consul was *prior* to U.S. involvement

---

ii In 1920 the town's name was changed to Wisconsin Rapids to avoid confusion with Grand Rapids, Michigan.

Karloff's WWI draft papers.

and may, therefore, relate to Karloff's alleged earlier attempt to enlist. It is impossible to know for sure. Unfortunately, Emma's original letter describing the incident has not survived and neither the Chicago consulate nor British Army archives have any record of an attempt by William Henry Pratt to enlist. Nevertheless, on 1 June 1917 he presented himself to the U.S. draft board.

The registrar entered Karloff's data on a draft board registration card and recorded the actor as being a tall Caucasian of medium build with brown eyes and black hair. He was an actor then residing at 307 Deliarse Boulevard (36 W. Randolph Street), Chicago, Illinois and was 'en route' with the Leona [sic] Fendell Stock Company. He had no disabilities and had experienced no military service. Although ineligible for enlistment Karloff's draft card makes it clear that the actor claimed exemption from the draft due to a 'varicocele and dilated valve'.[28] Karloff signed the card using his full real name *William Henry Pratt* and the registrar noted at the end of the form *"The professional name used as actor is Boris Karloff."*[29]

Once again an official document pertaining to the actor makes an interesting claim. Like the 1913 border-crossing list, the draft registration card also records the actor's status as 'married'. On first appearances one would assume that this too referred to Margot Beaton. By now, however, Karloff had a new partner – the actress Olive de Wilton.

Olive was born Edith Doreen de Wilton on 25 March 1898 in Ropley, Hampshire to Sussex Gerald de Wilton of the First Class Army Reserve (later of the Royal Scots Greys) and his wife Edith Juliet (née Holloway). In 1903, following Sussex's retirement, the family emigrated to Canada and settled in the Hill End district just south of Red Deer, Alberta, where Edith attended class in a one-room log schoolhouse. Six years later they moved to a homestead near Hardisty – the same town where Karloff and Margot Beaton would pen their playlet *With a Grain of Salt*.

On 3 April 1915 Edith, then 17 years old, married an immigrant Englishman, Herbert Warren Cluff. However, the marriage was a very brief and unhappy one. A wedding photograph – or, more accurately, half a wedding photograph – exists which attests to the incompatibility of the union. For, sometime following the wedding, Edith had torn the picture in two to remove the image of her rejected husband. She left Hardisty and embarked upon a theatrical career that would last for the rest of her life. Edith initially took the stage name Olive Whitney and within two years was acting alongside Boris Karloff as a member of the Patti McKinley Players.

There has been some debate about Olive's relationship with Karloff and it has been assumed that the two were legally wed. Olive had even told her friend, the theatrical producer Brian Doherty, that this was so. Doherty later passed this information on to Karloff's friend and biographer, Cynthia Lindsay. "Doherty says Olive de Wilton spoke of Boris with no animosity but with considerable affection and a strong memory of near starvation," Lindsay added. "She was dark and sallow, dressed strangely, wore no makeup, and was, according to an actor who knew her, 'almost a Charles Addams character'."[30] However, an extant 1948 letter from Olive to theatrical director Robert Anderson finally solves the mystery about her relationship with Boris Karloff. "I was not legally his wife," she confessed, "as I was unable to get my first divorce but he would never tell you that…"[31]

Seven weeks after Karloff registered for the draft Lona Fendell and her stock company were playing in Virginia, Minnesota when trouble struck and the troupe was forced to fold.

One Willia Gogin of Red Granite, Wisconsin, apparently unable to gain recompense for monies owed to her by Fendell, issued a writ of attachment and an auction was conducted on 30 August. Fendell's "large tent, three handpainted scenes, seats and an automobile"[32] were sold, effectively closing the company. It seems unlikely, however, that Karloff and Olive were still with Fendell when the writ was served for on Thursday, 23 August they took the stage at the Orpheum Theatre in Aberdeen, South Dakota as members of The New York Producing Company in a touring production of Owen Wister's western drama *The Virginian*.

Once again the facts do not tally with Karloff's tales. According to the star, he had toured in the play during this period with Billie Bennett's company. He also claimed he had, on that tour, played the villain, Trampas. However, an extant flyer reveals Karloff had, in fact, played the title role, the hero of the piece – and rather capably as one reviewer noted. "Boris Karloff, as the Virginian," wrote the *Idaho Statesman*, "portrays the spirit of the west as Wister knew it when he was living at Medicine Bow, and Marie Wells as Mollie Woods, the eastern schoolma'am, gives strength to the play."[33] The play toured South

Top: Olive de Wilton (ca. 1915) (Courtesy of the Red Deer and District Archives). Bottom: Her torn wedding photo (Courtesy of the Red Deer and District Archives).

Dakota, Wisconsin, North Dakota, Idaho, Utah, and Nevada where they opened at the Rialto Theatre on 2 December 1917.

When the run ended Karloff and Olive left the company and found employment with the Robert Lawrence Stock Company. This time, however, it would appear Olive abstained from stagework. At the end of July 1918 the troupe was booked into the Airdome Theatre on the corner of York Street and Sonoma Boulevard in Vallejo, California where they would put on two shows a week. The company consisted of its owner and leading man, Robert Lawrence, Orville Sperzlet, Florence Elsen, Albert Van Antwerp, Hazel Van Haltern, Evelyn Hambly,[iii] A.J. (Buck) Thiele and Karloff. The non-acting members of the company were the carpenter William McCarthy and the musical director Oliver Alberti. The company were still playing the Airdome 11 weeks later and expected to stay in Vallejo indefinitely.

Although Olive appears not to have been a member of the troupe at the time she was certainly living with Karloff in the city, for the couple had rented accommodation at 614b Capitol Street. The stay in Vallejo had also been sufficiently lengthy to warrant an entry in the 1918 city directory where they were listed as 'Karloff, Boris (Olive W.)[iv] actor Airdome Theatre'. Life had been one stock company after another until, said Karloff, "an influenza epidemic ruined theatrical business in the west."[34]

On 11 March 1918 Private Albert Gitchell reported to the camp hospital at Fort Riley in Kansas complaining of a fever, sore throat and a headache. By noon over one hundred soldiers had reported with the same symptoms. By the end of the week that number had risen to five hundred. Before the year was out the virus had killed 675,000 people in America and another estimated 20 million worldwide.

Stranded in Vallejo with the theatres closed and no hope of an acting job, Karloff was forced to revert to his trusted standby – manual labour. "Being addicted to roughly three meals a day I went to work for the Sperry Flour Mills," he explained, "waiting for the flu scare to be over so the theatres could re-open."[35]

For two months he earned a living "piling sacks of flour and loading lorries",[36] but when the epidemic subsided Karloff renewed his search for stagework. "My top salary on the stage up to now had never been more than £10 a week," he said. "Somehow, I managed to keep intact a tiny capital of £12, enabling me to have a little security and to venture afield in search of engagements."[37] He found stage work with his friend Alfred Aldridge.[v]

Aldridge had arranged a vaudeville act in San Jose based on 'the Mooney Case'. In San Francisco on 22 July 1916 ten people were killed and 40 injured when a bomb exploded during a Preparedness Day parade. Two labour leaders, Thomas Mooney and Warren Billings, were among those arrested and charged with the crime. Billings received a life sentence while Mooney was condemned to death. However, many – including the presiding judge – later came to feel the trial had been unfair and had contained questionable 'evidence'. In 1918 the President, Woodrow Wilson, intervened and the Governor of California commuted Mooney's sentence to life imprisonment.[vi]

Karloff made his way to San Jose to join his friend. The journey, by lumber schooner, was not a pleasant experience. "There was no place for anything on deck except this great

---

iii This is probably the same Hambly who had been with the Harry St. Clair Stock Company in 1912.

iv *Olive W.* is most likely an abbreviation of *Olive Whitney*.

v Aldridge's surname is often misspelt. Even adverts of the day often announced him as Alfred Aldrich

vi In 1939 Billings was released and Mooney was pardoned.

load of lumber," Karloff recalled. "No place to sit, or lie; below decks was so filthy you couldn't go there and the sea was too rough anyway."[38]

At 7 p.m. on Tuesday, 31 December 1918 the curtain rose on the *1919 International Vaudeville Road Show* at the Victory Theatre in San Jose. "Nine big acts and featuring Alfred Aldrich [*sic*] & Co., in *Bolsheviki*, The Pros and Cons of the Mooney Case," the *Evening News* announced. "Admission, All Seats, 25c. The Greatest New Year Show in San Jose."[39]

The entertainment included singers, dancers, a juggler, a strong man, a couple of blackface entertainers and Alfred Aldridge's company. "A playlet entitled *Bolsheviki*... is given by the Alfred Aldrich [*sic*] company of three people – a girl and two men," revealed the *San Jose Mercury Herald*. "The men give a dialogue of harangue about politics, police and graft, while the girl chews gum, telephones and jumps into the dialogue whenever the spirit of devilry moves her.

Karloff's friend, Alfred Aldridge (Courtesy of the Red Deer and District Archives).

The playlet will interest people who keep up with the San Francisco law courts."[40]

Unfortunately there is no advert or review for the playlet that gives the names of the trio in Aldridge's company. Yet, if the two actors in *Bolsheviki were* Karloff and Aldridge, it seems likely that Olive played the 'girl'.

Karloff's vaudevillian career in San Jose was short-lived, lasting only those two nights. "Its existence was brief indeed," he later confirmed, "and, when Aldridge tried to get a booking in Los Angeles, he had no success. Yet he sent for me to join him there. Wondering what it was all about, I joined him."[41]

It is unknown whether Olive accompanied Karloff to Los Angeles. Her parents had returned to England in 1915 and by early 1919 Olive had followed them. Her split from Karloff, she later revealed, had been acrimonious and initiated by the malicious machinations of others, possibly Alfred Aldridge himself. In 1948 she wrote to theatre director Robert Henderson suggesting Karloff as a possible source of financial backing for a play. The letter gives a tantalising, though obscure, insight into the relationship. "Honestly, Robert," she wrote, "I do not know how I stand with him [Karloff] after all these years. He was terribly hurt with me and a lot of mischief was made at one time by a so-called mutual friend which resulted in our breaking up and was at the time rather tragic for both of us... Anyhow, if you do see him, please somehow let him know that I am really quite a decent member of society and not just a heartless rotter as he was made to believe."[42] Unfortunately the letter contains no further details about Olive's relationship with Karloff and one can only speculate as to the circumstances behind the break-up. "We were very happy for three years until the trouble came," she added.[43]

Olive continued her theatrical career and founded the Northern Repertory Theatre with her then husband Richard Meadows-White. In 1929 Olive gave birth to a daughter, Rosalind Edith Charlotte, but her marriage to Richard had declined and the couple soon parted. Olive later returned to Canada where she remained for most of her life. She continued to act, in addition to her work for the Montreal Repertory Company and the National Film Board. In 1964, now in her mid-sixties, Olive moved to Lacombe, Alberta where she died four years later.

Olive, like Grace and Margot before her, never spoke publicly about her time with Boris Karloff. She did, however, ingratiate herself with at least one member of the actor's family although the exact circumstances are not known. In 1948 Olive drafted a letter to Karloff informing him she would soon be visiting New York and would like to see him, "if you would care to see me after all these years."[44] "One other thing," she added, "is your brother Charles still alive? I have completely lost touch with him since the start of the war, and often wonder how he made out in the Channel Islands. Charles and I were very good friends, and if he is still alive I very much want to see him again before I leave England, probably for several years."[45] It is not known if the letter was ever sent.

Arriving in Los Angeles, Boris Karloff took lodgings in a boarding house at the top of Angel's Flight in Bunker Hill and, supported by Aldridge, continued his search for employment. "He must have had some belief in me," Karloff said, "for he loaned me sufficient money for food and lodging until I made the rounds of the only possible outlet, the film studios. I appeared before the camera for the first time in a crowd scene being directed by Frank Borzage at Universal City."[46] The name of that movie is, however, still a mystery.

Some have claimed Karloff's first film appearance had occurred years earlier in *The Dumb Girl of Portici* (1916), a drama starring the famous ballerina, Anna Pavlova. The picture was partly shot in Chicago in July 1915 but Karloff always denied involvement. He had, however, made appearances in two 15-episode serials. In late July 1918 Pearl White returned from holiday to begin shooting her new serial *The Lightning Raider*. The cliffhanger, which was released that November, featured Boris Karloff in his first screen role. His second serial, *The Masked Rider*, starred Jack Chapman and was released in May 1919. Long presumed lost, 21 reels of film were discovered in 2003. The remaining footage – although edited of its opening credits and missing the first reel of episode one (which had deteriorated beyond repair) – was almost complete and ran to three and a half hours. The reels revealed Karloff had appeared as a Mexican roughneck in a bar scene in chapter two – *In the Hands of Pancho*.[vii]

Boris Karloff was now an actor in Hollywood. It would take him another 13 years to be a star.

---

vii Pancho was played by Bavarian born actor Paul Panzer who was later seen as one of the graveside mourners at the beginning of *Frankenstein* (1931).

Chapter 5

EARLY FILMS

(1919-1931)

"Things were a little more slapdash in the silent days. The actors didn't have lines to learn; you just had an outline of the script. And they shot for much longer, sometimes, in the making of a film. Those were the very extravagant days."[1]
Boris Karloff

Karloff's initial entry into pictures was brief, lasting only a single day. He was paid five dollars. "Certainly no one there [at Universal City] thought anything at all about me," he explained. "Similarly, I didn't think very much of my prospects in pictures. This was well proved, for that was the only day's work I managed to obtain. In despair I gave up calling at the studio casting offices and went to San Francisco, to the Bob Lawrence Company at the Majestic Theatre for a three month season."[2]

James Edwards, a member of the company who shared a dressing room with Karloff at the Majestic recalled, "Boris was a very capable character actor… and he was tremendously popular with children. And it was a common sight to see Boris striding down Mission Street, smiling happily and always followed by an admiring group of six or eight small fry… I can still see Boris sitting in the dressing room, hour after hour, working with grease paint, nose putty, crepe hair and wigs trying to perfect the art of changing his appearance."[3]

In May 1919 Karloff appeared at the Fulton Theatre at Franklin and 15th Streets in Oakland with Nana Bryant and the 'Famous Fulton Players' in *Eyes of Youth*, the story of a young woman who has three possible futures revealed to her by a mystic. Although the theatre usually presented plays on a 'one-week run' basis, *Eyes of Youth*, which opened on Monday, 5 May, proved so successful the management extended the play's run for another week.

While Karloff was treading the boards, Alfred Aldridge remained in Los Angeles and looked for work on his behalf. "Reports from him were hopeful," Karloff said. "Returning to Los Angeles,[i] he introduced me to Al MacQuarrie, an agent."[4] MacQuarrie was also a part-time actor who had appeared in small roles in a number of films produced by 'Douglas Fairbanks Pictures'. Production had now begun on Fairbanks' latest film *His Majesty, the American*, the first film to be produced by the newly formed United Artists and, through MacQuarrie, Karloff got work on the picture. "For a week I chased Fairbanks all over the back lot," Karloff recalled. "It was heaven. I was in films, I was making five dollars a day, and I worked for a solid week. I'm not at all sure that that wasn't more money than I earned in all my ten years in the theatre in any one week. I thought I had made my fortune!"[5]

Having earned $30, less a small percentage for MacQuarrie's services, Karloff decided to try his luck in pictures. "The film magnates of those days did not wax enthusiastic about my particular type," he said. "But, while I was in the vicinity, I thought I might as well expose myself to any opening. I made the rounds of all the agencies. Late one afternoon I was entering the office of Mabel Condon. She saw me and enthused at once about my type. Thanks to her good offices, I obtained small bits and little parts in independent film productions."[6] His work resulted in a rise in pay to seven and a half dollars a day. "A great promotion," he said. "Well, if not great, it was a 50 percent jump."[7]

Later that year Karloff rose from the ranks of extras to become a bit-part player and made his first major screen appearance. "William Desmond and Blanche Sweet were the stars in the Jesse Hampton picture in which I played," he said. "I can't remember the name of it."[8] The picture, *The Prince and Betty*, was adapted from P.G. Wodehouse's novel and starred, not Blanche Sweet as Karloff believed, but Mary Thurman. Then came what Karloff called "quite a decent role"[9] in *The Deadlier Sex*, starring Blanche Sweet. Like his previous picture it was directed by Robert Thornby and produced by Jesse Hampton.

Filmed in the town of Truckee, nestled in the Sierra Nevada Mountains, the picture gave Karloff his first screen credit as Jules Borney, a villainous French-Canadian trapper who, during the course of the picture, attempts to knife the hero and rape the heroine.

In his next picture, *The Courage of Marge O'Doone*, filmed in March 1920, Karloff played another disreputable character, Tavish, who abducts the heroine (Billie Bennett) and her daughter (Pauline Starke). "Working in several pictures," he said, "encouraged me to forget the stage for a while and remain working as long as I could in Hollywood. The typing system was used even in those days. Casting directors regarded me as a French-Canadian type and I worked in a number of pictures in that category."[10]

A 15-part serial followed for Kosmik Films, and was in production by early May. Karloff played two roles in *The Hope Diamond Mystery*, the purportedly true story concerning the theft of a sacred diamond and its resulting curse. In the early episodes (set in 16th century India) he played the Priest of Kama-Sita, and Dakar, the Hindu servant of an American jewel collector, James Marcon, in the latter, contemporary half.

Next came an uncredited role as an Indian in Maurice Tourneur's film adaptation of James Fenimore Cooper's *The Last of the Mohicans*. It was the first picture for 'Associated Producers', the new company formed by Tourneur, Allan Dwan, Thomas H. Ince, Marshall Neilan, J. Parker Read Jr. and Mack Sennett.

Production of the Robert A. Dillon script began in spring 1920 with Tourneur as director. An accident on set, however, soon resulted in his replacement. "We hadn't been on that picture more than two weeks," recalled Clarence Brown, "when Tourneur fell

i On the 1920 census Karloff is listed as a 'lodger' at a residence in Hope Street, Los Angeles.

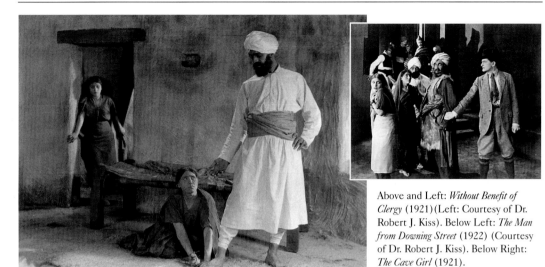

Above and Left: *Without Benefit of Clergy* (1921)(Left: Courtesy of Dr. Robert J. Kiss). Below Left: *The Man from Downing Street* (1922) (Courtesy of Dr. Robert J. Kiss). Below Right: *The Cave Girl* (1921).

off a parallel and was in bed for two months. I made the whole picture after that."[11] The exteriors were shot in California at Big Bear Lake, Yosemite Valley, Lake Arrowhead and Malibu.

By the time production had begun on Tourneur's picture Karloff was lodging at 327 South Hope Street in Los Angeles. Karloff and Olive had parted at least a year earlier and in July 1920 he married for the second time. His new wife was 24-year-old musician Montana Laurena Williams, the New Mexico-born daughter of William R. and Annie Williams (née Keeler). It seems to have been a whirlwind romance for only six months before the wedding Williams was lodging in El Paso, Texas, while her future husband was residing in Los Angeles.

In 1921 the Karloff home moved to 210 South Flower Street, a short distance from the old Hope Street address. That year he also appeared in three pictures. In *Without Benefit of Clergy* (based on a short story by Rudyard Kipling) he played an Asian, Ahmed Khan. Shooting began at Robert Brunton's studio in early March and was completed two months later.

In *The Cave Girl*, Karloff returned to the villainous French-Canadian type he would repeatedly play. "I know it's fashionable to complain about being typed," he once said, "but that's nonsense. All actors are typed. If you're a young man you play juveniles, and as you get older, if you're lucky, you turn into a character man. And if you become known for a certain type of role, a certain type of part, a certain line of country, I think you are a very lucky actor."[12]

His final picture of the year was *Cheated Hearts* in which he played yet another villain, this time an Arab named Nei Hamid. Also featured were Karloff's actor/agent friend Al MacQuarrie and his brother, Murdock.

During 1922 Karloff moved home again (approximately three miles) to 1225 McCadden Place. He also featured in *The Man from Downing Street* playing Dell Monckton, the head of a gang of jewel thieves and his *alter ego*, the Indian Maharajah Jehan of Dharwar. Production ended in February. Karloff also appeared as the Nabob of Menang, the ruler of a South Sea island, in *The Infidel*, his second picture with director James Young.

In *The Woman Conquers*, Karloff played Raoul Maris, another in his increasing repertoire of villainous French-Canadian characters. Then, following the picture's completion in mid-May, Karloff was afforded a change of character in Richard Walter Tully's *Omar the Tentmaker* when he played the sympathetic role of Imam Mowaffak, the heroine's father. "[It] featured me prominently,"[13] he recalled.

A role, as Hugo, in another South Sea island drama, *The Altar Stairs*,[ii] followed before there came a change in fortunes. "Prospects were encouraging," Karloff recalled, "when there came a ghastly slump in production. I carried on as long as I could until my small capital was exhausted."[14]

He then appeared in only two 1923 releases. In *The Gentleman from America* he was an unbilled character who is shot by the hero, Dennis O'Shane (played by western star Hoot Gibson). In Universal's adventure picture, *The Prisoner* (based on George Barr McCutcheon's novel, *Castle Craneycrow*), Karloff played Prince Kapolski.

Legend has it that during this time – possibly while working on the Hoot Gibson picture at Universal City[iii] – Karloff was introduced by long-term character actor William Taylor to Lon Chaney. It was the first of many encounters with the star, as Karloff recalled:

> I used to go to the Legion Stadium for the fights, and since I often lacked sufficient funds to go inside, I would stand outside and watch the more fortunate people enter. Chaney never missed a boxing bout and he always spoke to me pleasantly as he passed…
>
> One day after work, as I walked through the studio gates and set off home, I heard a big car honking behind me. I thought the driver wanted me out of the way. I had only 15 cents in my pocket, but I had plenty of pride and I resented the honking. I slowed down and walked calmly ahead…
>
> The car slowed down too and a voice said: "Don't you recognise old friends, Boris?"
>
> I looked inside the car and saw Lon Chaney smiling at me. He invited me to ride with him and for more than an hour he talked to me of the picture industry and asked me about my ambitions…

ii *The Altar Stairs* was directed by Lambert Hillyer. Karloff would work with him again on *The Invisible Ray* (1936).
iii It is often claimed that Karloff met Chaney at Universal in 1926, while Karloff was appearing in the Hoot Gibson western *The Man in the Saddle*. Chaney's last picture at Universal, however, was *The Phantom of the Opera*, which premiered on 6 September 1925. On 6 January 1926 Chaney signed a contract with MGM and all his remaining pictures were made for that studio. It is possible that Chaney was filming *The Hunchback of Notre Dame* at the time of his meeting with Karloff. The picture was in production at Universal between 16 December 1922 and 3 June 1923.

Top and Left: *Omar The Tentmaker* (1922) (Left – Courtesy of Dr. Robert J. Kiss). Above: *The White Panther* (1924) (Courtesy of Dr. Robert J. Kiss).

That talk with Lon gave me the courage to keep trying in later years when the going was far from easy. One of the things Lon said was: "If you're going to act – you're going to act. Even if you have to starve, never give up. It's the only way."

Yes, there will only be one Lon Chaney because he understood so well the souls of afflicted people. On that fateful afternoon he told me how he had suffered because his mother and father were deaf mutes. None of us can do what Chaney did, because none of us feels it just as he did. He said too, "The secret of success in Hollywood lies in being different from anyone else. Find something no one else can or will do – and they'll begin to take notice of you. Hollywood is full of competent actors. What the screen needs is individuality!"[15]

In January 1924 *The White Panther*, starring Australian athlete Rex 'Snowy' Baker and Boomerang the Wonder Horse, opened at Loew's in New York. "*The White Panther* is a picture of horsemanship and sword play laid in a locale of Oriental exotic beauty," one newspaper explained, "with a background of stern mountains inhabited by cruel, vengeful natives."[16] Karloff's role, as a 'native', would prove to be his last movie appearance for a while – for, by now, the work had dried up.

Karloff was then living at 1404 North Catalina, but with no income things looked bleak. "I was faced with a decision," he said. "I was known to casting directors as a $150-a-week available actor – too available. In order to eat, I could have gone back to the extra ranks and probably would have gotten work. But I felt if I did that, it would 'put paid' to everything, because once you play parts and then go back to being an extra – you're dead."[17] At times he even considered giving up acting altogether, as he later explained:

I would just get out of debt, then – no work – away went my savings, and I would go from one casting office to another, listening to opinions that I was "too much one type". I not only got discouraged but rather disgusted. I made up my mind I would rather be a successful truck driver than a starving actor who had his feelings hurt every time he asked for work. At first the truck driver idea was just an expression; then I thought, "Well, why not?" And off I went to find some one to teach me how to drive a car. A friend taught me the levers and pedals on a truck on Sunday and took me to his boss on Monday. I got a job driving a cement truck. When I was told to back up to the warehouse I was baffled. On a pretence that I had to get some tobacco I asked another driver to back my truck up to the warehouse. He did and my ignorance was not discovered.

I had a deathly fear of breaking the truck, and the warehouse, too. The first few days I lived in terror, but finally I managed to keep on the right side of streetcars and turn corners without running over the sidewalk. My job was a bit different from acting. Each sack of cement weighed 200 pounds. I had to pick these sacks off the floor, put them on my shoulder, carry them a half block to the truck, fill the truck with sacks, drive to the other end of town, then unload the sacks and pile them a considerable distance from where I was parked.[18]

For this, Karloff recalled, "I received £1 a day. It wasn't really so bad except that I was a little older, and for the first few days, I ached in every muscle."[19]

During the 18 months he worked at the yard Karloff re-acquainted himself with his niece, Dorothea Donkin (the daughter of his sister, Julia), who was working in California as Governess to the children of the Bishop of Los Angeles. As the actor had little money, Dorothea fed him with occasional meals. She later spoke of this time with her uncle's first biographer, Peter Underwood. "She visited him in America – long before *Frankenstein* – and found him living with a young actress in appalling poverty," Underwood explained. "She took them out for a meal and they told her it was the first real meal they had enjoyed in a long, long time. 'Uncle Billy really deserved better.' She tried to help with a little money but 'he had always been a proud man and could be stubborn'. Dorothea told me her uncle, for whom she had great affection, made a habit of dumping his girlfriends and his wives and offspring and somehow seeming to erase them from his memory."[20]

Dorothea was probably the only family contact Karloff had during these lean years. "I never wrote home in those days," he admitted. "I had nothing to tell them except I was broke."[21] He did, however, write at least once to his old flame, Alice Roe, sending her photographs of himself in cowboy costume.

Helen Vivian Soule a.k.a. 'Polly' Karloff (Courtesy of Greg Nesteroff).

Some time during this period Karloff met a 23-year-old dancer named Helen Vivian Soule.[iv] Born in Maine to Greenwood Everett and Etta Melvina Soule (née Rich), Helen was employed by the Fanchon and Marco troupe. Known professionally as 'Pauline', Karloff, reportedly, called her Polly. His marriage to Montana Williams had ended in divorce sometime earlier[v] and so he was free to wed again. The civil ceremony was performed on Sunday, 3 February 1924 by J. Walter Hanby, Justice of the Peace and was witnessed by one Harry S. Sheket.

Karloff was now living at 951 Venego Avenue. Yet, within a year, he had moved home again, this time to 1549 Western Avenue. The work at the yard continued but the yard foreman, an Englishman named Charlie Curtis, was sympathetic to Karloff's situation and allowed him the occasional day off to act in pictures. "We carried on this way for over a year," Karloff explained.[22]

He then made two pictures for Sunset Pictures. In the first, the western *The Hellion*, he played an outlaw. Then, in early May, Karloff began work on the boxing picture *Dynamite Dan* in which he played a character named Tony Garcia. Both pictures were written and directed by Bruce Mitchell. Karloff also played a bit part in the 15-chapter western serial *Riders of the Plains* (now lost) for the Arrow Film Corporation. Then, in September, he played a character named Diego in Eastern Productions' *The Prairie Wife*.

---

iv The marriage record lists Soule's occupation as 'actress on stage'.

v Although the divorce must have occurred some time between July 1920 and February 1924 no record has yet come to light.

Parisian Nights (1925)

Karloff next obtained an unbilled bit part in *Never the Twain Shall Meet*, an adaptation of Pete B. Kyne's novel made by William Randolph Hearst's Cosmopolitan Pictures. This story of a South Sea Island princess who comes to America was filmed in Tahiti and San Francisco.

In order to take the role, however, Karloff asked Curtis for a week's leave of absence. "Curtis, who was a nice fellow, gave it to me," he said, "and I left for San Francisco on location. What a windfall! We got five dollars a day for meals, stayed at the Palace in $25-a-day rooms. I was rich! Then I returned to report back to my job on the truck. My leave of absence was for one week and we were gone three so they replaced me. I was pitchforked back into films."[23]

The picture had completed shooting by mid-January 1925 but Karloff was soon employed in more film work. "People were very kind," Karloff said, "as I think they always have been to me. Through Robert Florey, who later became a director at Universal, I got a job in an Elaine Hammerstein film at the old F.B.O. Studios."[24] The 'job' was the role of a Parisian Apache (a member of the criminal underworld) in the picture *Parisian Nights*.

Then came the role of the first mate, Pietro Castillano, alongside Evelyn Brent and Robert Ellis in the rum smuggling picture *Forbidden Cargo*, which was shot in Balboa, California. It was another villainous part that, in one scene, required Karloff to prepare to pour molten lead into the hero's eyes. "Robert Ellis… is a sound hero," wrote *Kinematograph Weekly*, "and Boris Karloff a typical teeth-gritting villain."[25]

Next he appeared in the small part of a scissors grinder in First National's *The Greater Glory*,[vi] which began shooting in early June 1925. This was followed by the role of a robber in the Hoot Gibson western *The Man in the Saddle* for Universal.[vii]

In *Lady Robinhood* Karloff again appeared with Brent and Ellis and once more featured as the villain, this time playing Cabraza, a Spanish version of the Sheriff of Nottingham. "I'm going to horse-whip Boris Karloff this morning," Brent told a reporter

---

vi *The Greater Glory* was originally announced as *The Viennese Medley*.
vii *The Man in the Saddle* was shot in June/July 1925.

during filming that July, "which, you might say, is a fairly good handful to a young woman as a morning's work."[26]

In her later years Evelyn Brent recalled Karloff's early days in pictures. "Boris," she said, "was just one of a pool of actors who would hear of a film being shot, then go and stand in front of the studio and the director would come out and say 'Okay, you' and grab one. I saw Boris picked that way twice. He worked, I think, in about three films with me."[27] A role in another 15-episode serial (now presumed lost) followed when Karloff appeared in Universal's *Perils of the Wild*. Then, in September 1925, it was off to Portland, Oregon to play a railroad bandit, Blackie Blanchette, in Lewis H. Moomaw's *Flames*.

In the New Year work began on the contemporary crime drama *Her Honor The Governor*, starring Pauline Frederick. In it Karloff played yet another criminal. "Snipe Collins, a weak creature, half crazed with drugs, is well played by Boris Karloff," wrote the *Los Angeles Times*. "Many such a wretch has been dragged into Police Headquarters. His shaken, jerky figure, the twitching mouth, the vicious anger which vents itself on a helpless man who has tormented him for years, is, next to Miss Frederick's, the most authentic piece of work in the picture."[28] *Variety* agreed. "Boris Karloff does a very good drug addict heavy," it said.[29]

In the melodrama *The Golden Web* Karloff played another disreputable character, this time a blackmailer, Dave Sinclair, who is murdered. Then came the role of The Mesmerist in *The Bells*. Based upon Emile Erckmann and Alexandre Chatrain's 1869 play *Le Juif Polonais* [*The Polish Jew*] the picture told the story of Mathias [Lionel Barrymore], an unconvicted murderer who is haunted by his conscience. The story had been filmed several times before but this adaptation, directed by James Young, gave Karloff the opportunity to work with Barrymore. "A great man," Karloff said of his co-star, "a much better actor than his brother, John."[30] Barrymore also aided Karloff in the design of his make-up. "Lionel was a stimulating man – a marvellous, a great man," Karloff explained. "Because my make-up for this part was a conventional Svengali-like job, Lionel sat down and on an envelope sketched an idea for James Young and the make-up person. What he sketched was Caligari."[31] In Paramount's *Old Ironsides*, a picture based upon Oliver Wendell Holmes' 1830 poem of the same name, Karloff appeared as a Saracen. Although it was only a small role in a big picture he was afforded a close-up in which he mouthed the subtitle "Touch not the white woman. She belongs to the Caliph!"

Another sea-faring picture followed. In Paramount's swashbuckler *The Eagle of the Sea* Karloff played one of a band of "half-naked cut-throats".[32] He also appeared in his first, and only, slapstick comedy – the three-reel Hal Roach production *The Nickel Hopper*. The picture, which starred comedienne Mabel Normand in one of her final films, was co-written by Stan Laurel and featured Oliver Hardy (as a dance band drummer) and James Finlayson. Karloff played a lecher who tries to entice Normand with a ten-dollar bill. When she gives the money to a blind beggar he attempts to retrieve it but is chased away by a policeman.

Another role as a French-Canadian villain followed when Karloff played Gaspard in the dog picture *Flaming Fury*. He then made an uncredited appearance in Metro-Goldwyn-Mayer's Spanish romance *Valencia*, which was shot in October 1926. Karloff followed this in November with the role of Owaza, a native in Robertson-Cole Pictures' *Tarzan and the Golden Lion*. James Pierce, who played Tarzan in the picture, later said, "Because of poor direction, terrible story treatment and putrid acting, the opus was a stinkeroo. I emerged

Left: *Soft Cushions* (1927). Right: With Louis Wolheim and William Boyd in *Two Arabian Knights* (1927)

with nothing to show for my strenuous effort except being typecast as Tarzan. I was out of a job."[33]

That December Paramount's comedy *Let it Rain* went into production. Douglas MacLean starred as 'Let-It-Rain' Riley, a marine sergeant who falls in love with a telephone operator, and together they foil a plan to steal a mail train. On 24 January 1927 the cast, which included Karloff as a crook known as X, left Los Angeles for the Mexican border to shoot the picture's climax – a chase involving a runaway mail train. The company made their temporary headquaters at Jacumba, where they remained for ten days before returning to Los Angeles.

A small role as a French anarchist named Pavel followed in the comedy *The Princess from Hoboken*. Blanche Mahaffey starred as Sheila O'Toole, an Irish restaurant belle who assumes the role of a Russian princess and falls in love with a nobleman. Karloff then appeared in two low-budget westerns. In *The Meddlin' Stranger* he played Al Meggs, the hired killer of a crooked banker, and Ramon, a Mexican border smuggler, in *The Phantom Buster*.

Yet more villainy followed. In March Karloff took a small role as the ship's purser in the Howard Hughes production *Two Arabian Knights*. Then, in June, it was announced the actor had joined the cast of Paramount's Arabian Nights comedy-adventure *Soft Cushions*, starring Douglas MacLean and Sue Carol (later Mrs. Alan Ladd). Karloff played the Chief Conspirator. He then played Fleming – another villainous character – in First National's *The Love Mart* starring Billie Dove, Gilbert Roland and Noah Beery.

On 6 October 1927 *The Jazz Singer*, starring Al Jolson, was released. Although it contained only a small portion of dialogue and five songs it ushered in a new era of the motion picture – the talkies. While the advent of sound marked the beginning of the end for silent pictures some, most notably Charlie Chaplin, held out against the inevitable. "A good talking picture," Chaplin believed, "is inferior to a good stage play, while a good silent picture is superior to a good stage play."[34] The transition would, as Karloff later commented, prove the end to many an acting career. "The sad thing was that when sound came in, so many established film actors just did not make the grade," he said. "Sometimes it was their fault, sometimes it wasn't, but I am sure that a great many of them were rather sacrificed to the crudity of the early sound equipment. But, of course, when sound came along, you had to have some training behind you in speech. It was then that the stage actor came into his own."[35]

Although Karloff's stage training placed him in an enviable position he was, as he later confessed, "rather cynical about film acting, certainly silent film acting. In silent films anybody could be made to act, could get by, because it could all be done for you. It could be done by the cameraman, by the cutter, by the director. The great requisites for silent films were large eyes, good physique, lots of hair, and that was it!"[36]

As Hollywood scrambled to be a part of the talkie revolution Karloff returned to his first love. "The stage still enthralled me," he said. "A brilliant English actor and producer, Reginald Pole, gave me a good part in *The Idiot*. He must have had astounding faith in my acting ability, as I had not read a line for almost seven years."[37] To take the role as the murderer, Parfyon Rogozhin, Karloff travelled to the Belmont Theatre, on First and Vermont Avenue, from his apartment at 6040 Eleanor Avenue, his home since the previous year.

The play opened on Wednesday, 25 January 1928. Marquis Busby's review appeared in the *Los Angeles Times* the following day. "Reginald Pole gives a remarkable performance as Myshkin, the frail Russian prince," he wrote. "Pole has a marvellously sensitive face, on which expressions are mirrored with perfect fidelity. There are times in *The Idiot* when he appears almost in an eerie fashion as the true Redeemer... Boris Karloff as Rogozhin, the man of the earth-bound, passionate love, is a perfect type in keeping with the Russian locale. His performance was a bit uneven yesterday, but this can be easily remedied. Olga Zacsek... is a picturesque, interesting Nastasya and the possessor of a splendid voice. Miss Zacsek, although displaying emotional power, is a bit inclined toward overacting."[38]

Only two days later it was announced that, as Karloff must fulfil his motion-picture contract with Universal,[viii] the play would be forced to close with a final matinee on Saturday, 28 January. "The production has received the undivided support of the intelligentsia," reported the *Los Angeles Times*, "and an effort is being made to arrange additional performances after Karloff's contract is filled."[39] Three months later the actor returned to the stage with Olga Zacsek and William Stack in *Monna Vanna*, a drama concerning the surrender of the Italian city of Pisa in 1509.

The play opened on 23 April at the Trinity Auditorium at 9th and Grand in Los Angeles. "The presentation, which featured Olga Zacsek, was effective to the tiniest detail," wrote *The Los Angeles Times*. "The cast was an excellent one, and the costumes and settings harmonised in a highly effective manner, the whole blending into colourful tableaux... Olga Zacsek, in the role of the heroine, Monna Vanna, completely captured last night's audience, not only with her histrionic ability but with her charm and exceedingly lovely appearance. Boris Karloff gave a splendid characterisation in the difficult role of Guido Collona, commander of the Pisan garrison, and William Stack shared honours with his interpretation of the Florentine general, Prinzivalle."[40]

The success of the play resulted in a short extended run until 2 May. Then, at 8:30 p.m. the following evening, the Guild presented the world premiere of *For the Soul of Rafael* at the same venue, with ticket prices at $1.60 and $1.90 and with matinees on Wednesday and Saturday.

Adapted from Marsh Ellis Ryan's novel the play, set in the Mission days of California, told the story of Raquel Estevan [Zacsek] who, while at a convent in Mexico, had fallen in love with an American traveller. After arriving in California, however, she is told the

---

viii Karloff's contract was probably to appear as the villain in the ten-episode western serial *The Vanishing Rider*, starring William Desmond and Ethlyne Claire. The serial is now presumed lost.

American is dead and so is influenced by her guardian to marry his wayward son. She then learns that her lover is, in fact, alive and living at San Juan Capistrano. "How she remains true to both," wrote the *Los Angeles Times*, "forms a fascinating tale in the midst of intrigue."[41]

Following the play's closure Karloff, Olga Zacsek and others of the Drama Guild joined the newly formed Sydney Sprague Repertoire Company. Sprague, in association with Warren Millais, had leased the Egan Theatre for a year in order to present new plays, all to be directed by Millais, with the cast taking a share of the receipts. The theatre, which had been closed for several weeks, opened on Wednesday, 23 May with the world stage premiere of Lajos Biro's war drama *Hotel Imperial*, presented by the Sprague Repertoire Company.

The play centred upon a hostelry, the 'Hotel Imperial' of the title. Located in a war-torn border town, the hotel is occupied by the Russians whose officer, General Juskievica, assumes charge of the hotel's chambermaid, Anna Zedlak. Anna, however, is in love with a Hungarian officer. The 20-strong cast was headed by Karloff as the General, Olga Zacsek as Anna, and William Stack as her Hungarian love.

The day after the play's opening Edwin Schallert of the *Los Angeles Times* wrote, "While it could hardly be said that the production was adequate to the demands of the play, the third act attained a very fair level dramatically. This is the episode in which following the shooting of the spy the Hungarian officer is cross-examined by the general, and the girl is forced to resume her servant's garb at the behest of that worthy. Pitch and tempo, which were subnormal earlier in the play, improved considerably in this act. Boris Karloff as the general was rather effective in the scene of the denunciation, as was Olga Zacsek…"[42]

By the second week interest in the play had increased. "The staging of the production," wrote the *Los Angeles Times*, "the… unusual professional strength of the combined cast and the outstanding performances of Boris Karloff and Olga Zacsek particularly have occasioned a widespread buzz of curiosity and comment that is said to be bringing in growing audiences each evening."[43] The play closed in the last week of June.

Karloff trod the boards of the Egan Theatre again when he joined Sarah Padden and the rest of the cast of the play *Window Panes*. Olga Printzlau's play, a "dramatic story of the colourful peasant life,"[44] had opened on 6 July. On 5 August, six weeks into the run, Karloff took over the role of the tyrannical and avaricious husband, Artem Tiapkin.

Also in the cast was Peter Richmond, a 22-year-old actor who would later become better known as John Carradine. "We both started on the stage here in Los Angeles at the same time and, strangely enough, in the same play," he later explained. "It was called *Window Panes* and the year was 1928. Boris played a black-bearded villain, they had him a bit typecast even then."[45] It was, as many would later discover, the antithesis of Karloff's true character. "Boris was a very gentle man," Carradine later said.[46]

After the play's run ended on Saturday, 8 September Karloff returned to pictures. In Universal's western *Burning the Wind* Karloff appeared, once more, in a Hoot Gibson picture, this time as kidnapper Pug Doran. He then featured in the ten-episode adventure serial *Vultures of the Sea*, for producer Nat Levine. Karloff was back in the Canadian North West, though, for his role as a heavy, Maurice Kent, in *The Little Wild Girl*.

Another Nat Levine serial followed – the ten-episode mystery *The Fatal Warning* in which Karloff played a bank clerk. He then played a conspirator named Boris in *The Devil's Chaplain*. In *Two Sisters* Karloff played Cecil, yet another criminal, before taking a bit part in the melodrama *Anne Against the World*.

In early 1929 Karloff met Dorothy Stine. Although it is often stated that the two met at a dinner party, in 1935 Stine told a reporter, "I was a librarian. One day Karloff walked in, and during the course of his browsing around, I happened to recommend a number of books that I thought he might possibly like. My suggestions led to the discovery that we shared a number of tastes. And from that discussion of books came our courtship, our marriage and all that you can see."[47]

Two Sisters (1929)

Born in Charlotte, Michigan in 1900, Stine was working for the Los Angeles Library Central Supply System and lived with her mother. Karloff's marriage to Helen Soule had ended in divorce when, according to Hollywood gossip columnist Sidney Skolsky, Soule had "packed up to go to Panama. She had a job there in a café, dancing. A divorce followed."[48] Although no record has emerged it is certain the couple divorced prior to 20 November 1928. For this was the date a court order was issued detailing the sums of settlement that Karloff, now living at 1835 North Wilcox Avenue, should pay to his ex-wife. However, due no doubt to his constant lack of funds, Karloff reneged on the order. As a result, on 5 December 1928, another order was made requiring him to "then and there show cause why he should not be found guilty of contempt of court for failing to pay Plaintiff the sums set forth in this court's order of November 20, 1928."[49] This was followed by a further order six months later, on 10 June 1929, regarding attorney's fees and alimony. This time Karloff was ordered to pay his ex-wife, Helen V. Pratt, $100 cash and an additional $240 at $50 a month. The order also required Karloff to pay Helen $15 a week for 54 weeks plus payment of all community bills. Only upon compliance with this order would the charge of contempt of court be dropped.

It is unlikely that Dorothy was aware of her husband's legal troubles. She later confessed she had known nothing of her husband's previous marriages. "I found out only inadvertently that I was the fourth," she explained.[50] She never discussed it with him. "None of my business," she said.[51]

Karloff's next picture, *The Phantom of the North*, was also his last silent. Cast as a killer, Jules Gregg, he returned to the villainous French-Canadian trapper type he had begun playing nine years earlier. In his first talkie, *Behind That Curtain*, he played an unnamed Soudanese Servant. The picture was also notable for an early, albeit brief, screen appearance of Earl Derr Biggers' oriental detective, Charlie Chan. Karloff's third Nat Levine serial, *The King of the Kongo*, followed in which he played Macklin, the leader of a gang of ivory thieves.

Then came an uncredited appearance as Abdoul in the murder mystery *The Unholy Night*, which reunited him with Lionel Barrymore. The picture, which was shot in March 1929 under the title *The Green Ghost*, boasted an all-British cast.[ix] "The reason," explained Barrymore, "is partly that the British actor has, invariably, a perfect speaking voice, and hence is ideal for talking dramas."[52] As Karloff recalled Barrymore, who directed the picture, was as helpful as ever. "In those days it often took several hours to light a set and Lionel would use this time to help me and other players to improve our scenes," he said. "He would interrupt us with a word here, a bit of business there. When I played my

---

ix In fact, both cast members Dorothy Sebastian and Polly Moran were American.

big scene – finding the body of my dead wife – I realised that Lionel had analysed the scene inside out and had given me hints that enhanced my own interpretation. When I finished he exclaimed: 'By God, you cunning old devil you, I knew you could do it! That performance was as different as chalk from cheese.'"[53]

Karloff then returned to the stage to play Kregg in Chester de Vonde and Kilbourn Gordon's play *Kongo* at the Capitol Theatre in San Francisco. Then, returning to pictures, he appeared, unbilled, in United Artists *The Bad One*, starring Dolores Del Rio.

In January 1930 Karloff and another 62 players and technicians travelled to Mazatlan on the Gulf of Mexico to make *The Sea Bat* for MGM. Karloff would play a sailor (credited as a Corsican). Director Wesley Ruggles was in charge of what was reported to be the "largest company ever to leave California for another American country".[54] When, on 24 February, the company returned to the U.S. at Nogales, Arizona, Boris Karloff and fellow cast members Gibson Gowland and Fred T. Walker were denied admittance by United States immigration officials, "pending the clearing of their quota status".[55] Although the problem was finally

With Gibson Gowland in *The Sea Bat* (1930).

resolved there were concerns at the time that the detention of the three men would hold up the completion of the picture.

Karloff next featured as Baxter in *The Utah Kid*, his only western talkie, before working on another serial, the 12-part *King of the Wild*, which was filmed in Yuma, Arizona and the Bronson Caverns in Los Angeles Griffith Park.[x] The actor appeared as a villainous African sheikh named Mustapha.

An unbilled appearance as a murder victim in the First National drama *Mothers Cry* followed. The picture featured Helen Chandler and David Manners who were both subsequently signed by Universal and would soon appear alongside Bela Lugosi in *Dracula* (1931).

Away from the studios Karloff's relationship with Dorothy Stine blossomed and the couple were married on Saturday, 12 April 1930 at the Hollywood Presbyterian Church. As Stine recalled, the wedding day was chaotic. "I can't really remember much about the wedding," she said, "except it was total confusion. Somebody got lost or drunk or something, there wasn't any money for a honeymoon, so we drove Boris's old wreck of a car back to his shack – and I do mean shack – in Laurel Canyon. We lived there for two years. I continued working, he was doing bits. There was very little money and it was Prohibition, but we always loved to entertain, so we made beer in the bathtub. Nobody could ever wait for it to ripen, or whatever you call it, so we'd all gather around and drink the green beer through straws right from the tub – wonder it didn't kill us – but we were young and strong – and we had an awfully good time."[56]

Twice a week Karloff would drive into Hollywood in his old car to visit a theatrical agent in the hope of securing employment. "One day I called and he was out," he later said. "I was told he'd be back in an hour. So I decided to hang about. I couldn't go into the

---

x *King of the Wild* was re-edited into a feature-length version that was released in Argentina under the title *Bimi* – the name of a half-man, half-beast creature played in the serial by Victor McLaglen's brother, Arthur.

Maskers' [*sic* Masquers] Club because I hadn't paid my club dues.[xi] I would have liked a cup of coffee, but didn't have the cash. So I walked into the Actors' Equity, to see if there were any letters. Of course there weren't any letters, but as I turned away from the desk, the girl said, "By the way, are you working?" I said no. She told me that a play called *The Criminal Code*, which had run in New York, was being rehearsed, and they needed players for the small parts."[57]

Karloff rushed to the Belasco Theatre and landed the role of Ned Galloway. "It was a small part," he said, "but a showy one. The character was a trusty in prison. He was the killer; he had only four scenes in the play, but they were key scenes."[58] One 'key' scene, a murder committed by the

Karloff in an unidentified role
(Courtesy of Reimund Schultheis).

trusty, was particularly effective. "The highspot," Karloff explained, "was a prison scene in which I had to come on and kill a 'stool-pigeon'. It was a gripping scene, and you could have heard a pin drop in the theatre. Yet it required no acting. The stool-pigeon was on first. He had his back to the audience. Then I came on. As I walked across the stage I was staring at the stool-pigeon. The audience couldn't see my face fully. Then I turned and had my back to them as well. There was a moment of deathly silence, then the stool-pigeon turned. Before he could do a thing I had plunged a knife into him. He flopped to the floor. The audience still couldn't see my face. But they were imagining the most terrifying expressions on it – far more spine-chilling expressions than I could possibly have achieved. I had simply provided the frame; they had filled in the picture."[59]

The play opened on 12 May 1930. "*The Criminal Code* came to the Belasco Theatre last evening, and found a notable first-night audience eager to experience its sober actuality," wrote Edwin Schallert of the *Los Angeles Times*. "The enthusiasm and response that the initial presentation here met was engrossing to behold. There were nearly a dozen curtain calls after the final scene... The cast, in its major principals, is the New York one, and Byron as the District Attorney, who later becomes the warden of the prison, justifies the

---

xi 'The Masquers' had its clubhouse at 6735 Yucca Street in Hollywood. Karloff had applied for membership of the Hollywood social men's club on 7 March 1926 while living at 1012 Larrabee Street in Sherman. He was recommended for membership by Guy Coburn and seconded by Australian born actor, Fred Esmelton.

high reports of his work... I thought the work of Boris Karloff as the avenger excellent... *The Criminal Code* is a striking and splendidly done play."[60]

Karloff had hoped his performance would prove the turning point of his career. "I remember thinking, here, by golly, I go," he said. "I'll show these chaps! I always left my dressing room door open after opening night, expecting all the producers and agents in town to come pouring in, but not a soul came near me. I got some nice notices, but I didn't get any work, which was discouraging, because in those days that was the show window. I thought, well, I've shown them, but nobody's paid any attention."[61] However, Karloff was unaware that the head of Columbia Pictures, Harry Cohn, had seen the play and arranged to purchase its rights. He assigned the project to director Howard Hawks.

During the picture's casting Arthur Byron, who had played Warden Brady on stage, was replaced. "Vic Fleming had been working with Walter Huston," Hawks said, "and I'd met him – and thought he'd be great for it. He was one of the greatest actors we've ever had."[62] Karloff, however, was more fortunate. "[As] I had been seen in the play," he said, "I had the opportunity to do the part and that is the thing that sort of turned the tide for me."[63]

Karloff's casting was a happy choice, as Hawks recalled. "Boris was one of the few grateful actors in the business," he said. "Actors are funny people – suddenly, they make it, and the Lord tells them they did it all on their own. They start telling me which is the better side of their face photographically, and I know I'm in trouble. I've got a story to tell, got no time for that sort of thing. Boris was a different breed of actor. He was self-effacing, he never talked about himself, he was completely charming, and he always knew his lines. With [*The*] *Criminal Code* I gave him a face. Boris had played the part on stage and knew what he was doing, but he had no form. I've always said that if an actor had a face you couldn't caricature, he'd never be a star. Look at Gable, Bogart, Cooper – even Carole Lombard – easy caricatures. Boris had that kind of face..."[64]

When Hawks came to shoot Galloway's big scene – the murder of the stool-pigeon – the director turned to Karloff for advice. "[Hawks] asked me how that scene had been played on stage," Karloff explained. "I told him and persuaded him to film it in exactly the same way. He wanted to take one or two close-ups of me as well, but I talked him out of the idea. I knew that a single shot showing my face would have spoilt the effect. Imagination alone provide those thrills. Imagination is the quality most needed in screen thrillers..."[65]

In late 1930 Karloff appeared in *Sous Les Verrous* for Hal Roach Studios, the French language version of Laurel and Hardy's first full-length picture *Pardon Us*. At the time MGM was distributing Roach's pictures and therefore allowed him the use of various studio facilities. Roach intended to shoot a two-reeler Laurel and Hardy comedy utilising the prison set from MGM's recent picture *The Big House* but the studio added the proviso that, in return, Laurel and Hardy should make a picture for them. Roach refused and instead had his own prison set built. To help recoup the increase in costs he expanded the planned two-reeler to feature length.

As well as the English version, the picture was also filmed in French, German, Italian and Spanish. As neither Laurel nor Hardy could speak these additional languages they were required, with the aid of a voice coach, to write their lines phonetically on blackboards from which they could read during filming. As the picture is presumed lost Karloff's role in *Sous Les Verrous* has always been subject to speculation, fuelled by the existence of a single still showing him, in prison uniform, with the stars. It is often cited that Karloff was Le Tigre (The Tiger) as played in the English version by Walter Long. However, the foreign language versions were shot from mid-September to 1 December 1930 and it is certain that Long played The Tiger in the three surviving foreign versions. It seems more likely, therefore, that Long also played that role in the French version and Karloff appeared in another, additional, scene.

On 3 January 1931 *The Criminal Code* went on release. *Variety* called the picture, "An excellent interpretation of the play of the same name… Plenty of action all the way, in and out of the prison yard, with the performances of Huston, Phillips Holmes and Boris Karloff always holding it together…"[66] *Bioscope* later commented, "Boris Karloff, as the one chosen to avenge his fellows, is the embodiment of the crafty, stick-at-nothing criminal."[67]

The release of the picture signalled a change in fortunes for Karloff. "[Work] began to pour in," he said, "work of all kinds. Nothing very exciting but at least it was work which was the important thing."[68] In keeping with the new success the Karloffs moved from the 'shack' in Laurel Canyon to a home in Las Palmas Avenue in Hollywood, perched at the top of 92 steps. Soon they would move again, this time down to the San Fernando Valley.

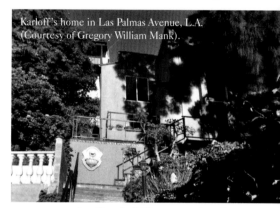

Karloff's home in Las Palmas Avenue, L.A. (Courtesy of Gregory William Mank).

In contrast to his role in *The Criminal Code*, Karloff took the role of a prison warder in the drama *The Last Parade* starring Jack Holt and Constance Cummings. A role as a revolutionary followed in the RKO-Radio Pictures comedy *Cracked Nuts*, starring Bert Wheeler and Robert Woolsey. Woolsey's character, a milk bottle cap seller, arrives in the mythical kingdom of 'El Dorania' where he is made king. Problems arise with the arrival of the revolutionary, Wheeler.

Karloff stayed with RKO for a further two pictures, both starring Richard Dix. In *Donovan's Kid* Karloff played a dope-pusher known as Cokey Joe.[xii] In the second Dix picture, *The Public Defender*,[xiii] he played The Professor, an associate of crime-buster Pike Winslow (a.k.a. The Reckoner). "Richard Dix's comeback is still further assured by his excellent performance as Pike Winslow," wrote *Kinematograph Weekly*. "Good character studies come from Boris Karloff as the ex-forger, and Paul Hurst as the cat burglar."[69]

Karloff then went to Warner Brothers to appear in *Smart Money*, the only picture to co-star Edward G. Robinson and James Cagney. Robinson played Nick Venizelos, a barber who runs an illegal gambling den. Karloff made an uncredited appearance in the picture as Sport Williams, a gambler who is evicted from the den for cheating. Staying with Warners for the comedy romance *I Like Your Nerve*, starring Douglas Fairbanks Jr. and Loretta Young, Karloff had a small role as a butler named Luigi.

Karloff's next film for Warners came about as a result of a misconception. "I was called in for an interview by Michael Curtiz," Karloff explained. "Seeing me, he at once hesitated, and then said, 'Well, I called you over, so I suppose I shall have to use you.' I didn't understand what he meant. He gave me the role of a Russian, however, in *The*

---

xii Karloff signed for the picture in February 1931. Originally entitled *Big Brother* the picture was also known as *Young Donovan's Kid*.

xiii This picture was originally announced as *The Million Dollar Swindle*.

Mad Genius, the John Barrymore picture he was directing for Warners."[70] Years later, when working together on *The Walking Dead*, Curtiz explained their earlier meeting, as Karloff revealed: "'The reason I called you in,' he explained, 'was because I thought you actually were a Russian. Your name is Karloff – it certainly sounds Russian. When you came in you seemed so anxious to get the job that I decided to let you have it.'"[71]

The Mad Genius was produced as a follow-up to Barrymore's previous hit *Svengali* (1931). Adapted from Martin Brown's play *The Idol*, the picture concerned Vladimir Ivan Tsarakoff [Barrymore], a club-footed puppeteer with the unrealisable dream of being a ballet dancer. He takes into care Fedor [Frankie Darro], a boy who has fled his abusive father, and trains him as a dancer. Trouble ensues when the grown Fedor [Donald Cook] falls in love with fellow dancer Nana Karlova [Marian Marsh]. Karloff had the small, uncredited role early in the picture as the boy's brutal father.

Karloff's brief work on the picture paid dividends. "Mervyn LeRoy saw my work in *The Mad Genius*," he explained. "Even though he was impressed, I think it took great courage on his part to give me that fairly important role in *Five Star Final*. George E. Stone, one of my oldest friends, had a lot to do with my getting it. He literally worked for me, talked about me, made sure that the producers would not miss knowing about me."[72]

Five Star Final was based upon the play *Late Night Final* by ex-tabloid journalist Louis Weitzenkorn. It told the story of newspaper editor Joseph Randall [Edward G. Robinson] who, pressured to increase circulation, revives a 20-year-old murder case concerning a woman, Nancy Townsend [Frances Starr] who shot her lover. Karloff played T. Vernon Isopod, an ex-divinity student who had been expelled for sexual misconduct.

In Fox's *The Yellow Ticket*, directed by Raoul Walsh, Karloff appeared for the third time in a Lionel Barrymore picture. Set in Czarist Russia in 1913, the picture also starred Elissa Landi and Laurence Olivier. "I remember Boris Karloff extremely well and I liked him very much," Olivier later said, "[but] I have no memory of his being in the picture."[73] This is not surprising, however, as Karloff's few shots as a drunken orderly were not shared with Olivier.

Karloff's next picture, *Scarface*, reunited him with director Howard Hawks. "[Howard] Hughes had a story about two brothers," Hawks said. "One was a cop and one was a gangster. Same old story you've heard a few hundred times, and he wanted me to do it. I got an idea and asked Ben Hecht, 'Would you do a picture?' Ben said, 'What?' and I said, 'A gangster picture.' He said, 'You don't want to do that,' and I said, 'Well, Ben, this is a little different. This is the Borgia family in Chicago today, and Tony Camonte is Caesar Borgia.' And he said, 'We'll start tomorrow morning.' We took 11 days to write the story and dialogue. And then we showed it to Hughes and he kind of grinned and said, 'This is quite a story. Where's the brother?' I said, 'Well, Howard, you can just use that story all over again.'"[74]

Casting the picture, however, proved problematic as the director recalled: "[Hughes] said, 'What are you going to do about casting it?' I said, 'I don't know, we can't get anybody. All the good actors and actresses are under contract and the studios won't loan them out. I think I'd better go to New York.' He said, 'OK. Let me know.' So I went back and found Paul Muni at the Jewish theatre downtown around 29th Street; Osgood Perkins I saw in a play, doing the lead in a love story; George Raft I saw at a prizefight; Ann Dvorak was a chorus girl down at Metro-Goldwyn, making forty a week, and I got her out of her contract because a vice-president at Metro-Goldwyn liked me; Karen Morley went around with some fellow I knew, and I thought she was attractive. Boris Karloff had just been in *The Criminal Code*. He said, 'I don't care how small it is – I'm going to have a part.' He thought I was good for him. Little Vince Barnett had been hiring out as a waiter – insulting people at the Coconut Grove. So we just collected actors and went into a little dust-covered studio and opened it up. We were an entity unto ourselves and we made a picture."[75]

Throughout the movie Hawks employed a visual motif to signal imminent slayings. "In the papers, in those days," he explained, "they'd print pictures of where murders occurred and they always wrote 'X marks the spot where the corpse was'. So we used X's all through the film.[xiv] When any one connected with the picture thought up some way of using an X, I'd give him a bonus."[76]

Karloff's character, a rival gangster named Gaffney, meets his end gunned down in a bowling alley pre-empted by the ominous 'X' – in this instance, a strike written on his score card. The French director Francois Truffaut later commented, "The most striking scene in the movie is unquestionably Boris Karloff's death. He squats down to throw a ball in a game of ninepins and doesn't get up; a rifle shot prostrates him. The camera follows the ball he's thrown as it knocks down all the pins except one that keeps spinning until it finally falls over, the exact symbol of Karloff himself, the last survivor of a rival gang that's been wiped out by Muni. This isn't literature. It may be dance or poetry. It is certainly cinema."[77]

The picture, which began production in June 1931, was completed that October. However, the film immediately ran into trouble. "There were a few things that had to be done to get by the censors," Hawks explained. "We did a completely different ending for Muni's death. In some states he had to be hanged. And we no longer had Muni, so we had to do it with feet, trapdoor, rope, hangman and music. They didn't like the other ending."[78] Originally Tony 'Scarface' Camonte [Paul Muni] was shot down by the police but, as Hawks recalled, "They said that was a little too heroic."[79] The censorship problems meant that the picture was not premiered until 31 March 1932. It was released just over a week later, on 9 April.

Following *Scarface* Karloff lent his voice to the 12-part serial *The Vanishing Legion*, starring Harry Carey. "It is described as a melodramatic mystery story of the new West," the *New York Times* explained, "with the oil fields of California for a background." An uncredited Karloff played The Voice, a criminal mastermind who commands his followers, The Vanishing Legion, in an attempt to halt the production of oil at Carey's well.

Then, in June 1931, Karloff took the role of another criminal, Terry, in the crime drama *Graft*. The picture would mean his return to Universal City, where the executives were having problems producing their latest horror opus – *Frankenstein*.

---

xiv Even Hawks appeared in the picture as a victim. "I was the man who was spread-eagled on the bed in the form of a cross with just his underwear on in one of those "X marks the spot" dissolves," he said.

Early, unused Monster makeup for *Frankenstein* (1931).

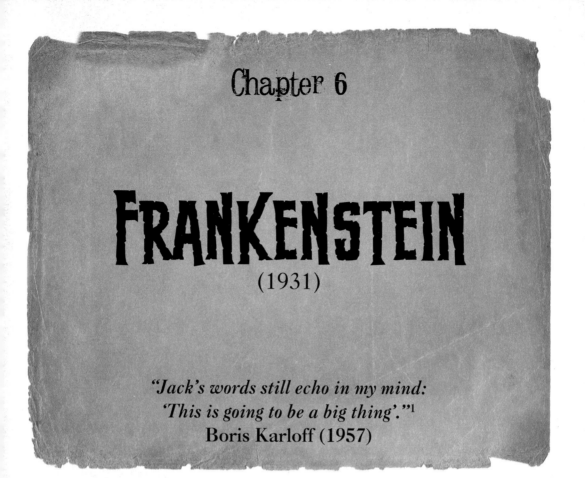

Chapter 6

FRANKENSTEIN

(1931)

*"Jack's words still echo in my mind:
'This is going to be a big thing'."*[1]
Boris Karloff (1957)

In 1914 Bavarian immigrant Carl Laemmle paid $165,000 for 230 acres of land in the foothills of California's San Fernando Valley, five miles north of Hollywood. On 15 March 1915 Universal City opened its gates and over the next 15 years produced a steady stream of pictures, including such classics as *The Hunchback of Notre Dame* (1923) and *The Phantom of the Opera* (1925) – both starring Lon Chaney. By 1931, however, the studio was in trouble. It had lost $2½ million the previous year and, despite the success of *All Quiet on the Western Front* (1930) and *Dracula* (1931), the studio was desperate for another hit to help refill its emptying coffers. In March 1931, 350 employees were laid off and the studio shut down for six weeks. Laemmle's son, Vice President in Charge of Production, Carl Laemmle Junior,[i] decreed a new picture be made to highlight its latest star, *Dracula*'s Bela Lugosi, and ordered a suitable property be found.

Universal scenario editor Richard Schayer met with the 30-year-old Frenchman Robert Florey at the Musso and Frank Grill on Hollywood Boulevard to discuss the *Dracula* follow-up. Florey, a writer/director who had previously worked for Paramount,[ii] had returned from Europe and was looking for work. Various stories were discussed (including Edgar Allan Poe's *The Murders in the Rue Morgue* and H.G. Wells' *The Invisible Man*) but Florey's interest lay with *Frankenstein*.

---

i Carl Laemmle Junior (1908-1979) received the post on 28 April 1929 as a 21st birthday present.
ii While at Paramount, Florey directed the Marx Brothers in their first feature *The Cocoanuts*.

The story of *Frankenstein* was conceived in June 1816 at the Villa Diodati, the rented residence of Lord Byron, situated on the shores of Lake Geneva. 18-year-old Mary Wollstonecraft Godwin and her lover, the poet Percy Bysshe Shelley,[iii] joined Byron and his physician, Dr. John Polidori, and, on the stormy night of 16 June, Byron suggested all present should write a ghost story. Dr. Polidori was the only one to write anything of substance that night – the beginnings of *The Vampyre*. While Shelley and Byron attempted their own tales, Mary had been uninspired and had not put pen to paper.

In the introduction to the 1831 edition of her novel Mary related how a discussion between the poets concerning the possibility of reanimating a corpse proved to be the inspiration for her tale:

> Night waned upon this talk, and even the witching hour had gone by, before we retired to rest. When I placed my head on my pillow I did not sleep, nor could I be said to think. My imagination, unbidden, possessed and guided me, gifting the successive images that arose in my mind with a vividness far beyond the usual bounds of reverie. I saw – with shut eyes, but acute mental vision – I saw the pale student of unhallowed arts kneeling beside the thing he had put together. I saw the hideous phantasm of a man stretched out, and then, on the workings of some powerful engine, show signs of life, and stir with an uneasy, half vital motion. Frightful must it be; for supremely frightful would be the effect of any human endeavour to mock the stupendous mechanism of the Creator of the world.[2]

The next day Mary began to write what would become chapter four of her novel.[iv] *Frankenstein; or, The Modern Prometheus* was completed in May 1817 and was published anonymously in three volumes by Lackington, Hughes, Harding, Mavor and Jones of Finsbury Square, London on 1 January 1818.

The first play version of Shelley's novel, *Presumption: or, the Fate of Frankenstein* by Richard Brinsley Peake, was premiered at the English Opera House on 28 July 1823. Starring James William Wallack as Frankenstein and Thomas Potter Cooke as the Monster, Peake's adaptation had various elements that would be reflected in the 1931 movie, all of which were not to be found in Shelley's original novel: both contained a creation scene, an assistant named Fritz and a mute monster.

The play initially ran for only 37 performances but Cooke, whose portrayal of the Monster was, according to the *London Morning Post*, "tremendously appalling"[3] went on to portray the Monster in another adaptation, *The Monster and the Magician*, in 1826. Mary Shelley, who attended a performance of Peake's play, wrote of the evening to her friend, Leigh Hunt. "The play bill amused me extremely," she wrote, "for in the list of dramatis personæ came, ——— by Mr. T. Cooke: this nameless mode of naming the unameable [*sic*] is rather good.[v] On Friday, Aug 29th Jane, my father, William & I went to the theatre to see it... The story is not well managed – but Cooke played ——— 's part extremely well – his seeking as it were for support – his trying to grasp at the sounds he heard – all

---

iii Mary and Shelley were married on 30 December 1816.
iv This became chapter five in the 1831 edition.
v This device was reversed in the opening credits of the 1931 movie. While the Monster was listed, Karloff's name was replaced by '?'.

indeed he does well imagined & executed. I was much amused, & it appeared to excite a breathless eagerness in the audience."[4]

Various other adaptations followed: *The Man and the Monster! Or, the Fate of Frankenstein* (1826), *Frankenstein; or, The Model Man* (1849) and even burlesque versions of Shelley's novel – *Humgumption; or, Dr. Frankenstein and the Hobgoblin of Hoxton* (1823) and *Frank-in-Steam; or, The Modern Promise to Pay* (1824).

In 1910 Shelley's novel made its first appearance in the relatively new medium of film. The Thomas Edison Company produced the short film *Frankenstein* starring Augustus Phillips as the scientist and Charles Stanton Ogle as the Monster. Five years later the first full length movie version of the story, entitled *Life Without Soul*, appeared with William Cohill as the creator and Percy Darrell Standing as the Monster. In 1920 Italian producer Luciano Albertini starred as Frankenstein in *Il Monstro di Frankenstein* with Umberto Guarracino as the Monster.

In 1924 the Irish born actor/producer Hamilton Deane adapted Bram Stoker's novel *Dracula* for the stage. The play, whose London opening was at the Little Theatre on Valentine's Day 1927,[vi] was a great success and gained the interest of American publisher and producer Horace Liveright. He hired the American playwright and newspaperman John Lloyd Balderston, then living in England, to adapt the play for the American stage. This new version, featuring Bela Lugosi as the Count, opened at the Fulton Theatre, New York, on 5 October 1927. Like its English predecessor it, too, was a big hit.

Back in England, Hamilton Deane wanted a new play to alternate with *Dracula* in his tour of the English counties. *Frankenstein: an Adventure in the Macabre* was written by Peggy Webling, an acquaintance of Deane's, and premiered in Preston in late 1927. The play was revised several times during its tour and finally opened at the Little Theatre in London on 10 February 1930. Shortly after, the *Times* announced the play was to be produced on Broadway. As with Deane's *Dracula* Horace Liveright once again engaged Balderston to revise and adapt the play. Balderston retained Webling's curious decision to swap the forenames of Victor Frankenstein and his friend Henry Clerval[vii] but added a creation scene (missing from both Shelley's novel and Webling's play) and had Frankenstein treat the Monster cruelly, like an animal, viciously beating him with whips and hot irons.

The Broadway production was initially planned for 1931. Problems arose, however, when Liveright had his own ideas for revising the play, ideas that did not sit well with either Balderston or Deane. Unhappily for Liveright the matter was soon resolved. The stock market crash wiped out his finances and, unable to make the royalty payments on *Dracula* or stage the new production of *Frankenstein*, he sold his option on the *Frankenstein* film rights to Webling and Balderston. The playwrights subsequently offered the material to Universal.

Despite Florey's enthusiasm for the material, Schayer remained unconvinced of the novel's adaptability. He did, however, arrange for Florey to meet with Junior and, as Florey recalled, he pitched the idea to a preoccupied Head of Production. "The crimes committed by the Monster were relatively easy to imagine, and during an unusual interview, while Carl Laemmle Jr. surrendered his fingers to a manicurist, his hair to

---

vi The movie version also opened on Valentine's Day (in 1931). It was billed as 'The story of the strangest passion the world has ever known!'

vii This exchange remained in the final movie, with the creator now named Henry Frankenstein and his friend, Victor Moritz.

a barber, his thoughts to his secretaries, and his voice to a dictaphone, I explained the general plan of the film to him. He told me to type up the story right away and send it to the head of the scenario department."[5]

Florey duly wrote a five-page synopsis in which he reduced Frankenstein's creation from the eloquent, literate creature of Shelley's novel (and Webling's play) to a grunting, thuggish monster. The synopsis was submitted and another meeting with Junior was arranged. In a letter to James Whale's biographer James Curtis, Florey described how, at that second meeting, Junior was just as distracted as before. "Junior had listened impatiently – playing with the carnation in his lapel – to my first two lines before talking to some girl for 15 minutes on the phone, then had gone out for half an hour, returning to say, 'Well, go on,' and I was saying, 'The monster...'. He interrupted me with 'What monster? Who is the monster?' before placing a bet on a race... Schayer decided to leave him a copy, adding he would try to catch him early in the morning, or sometime when he was not as busy. In any case, we went along."[6]

Despite Junior's apparent disinterest he gave his approval to Florey's treatment. Laemmle Senior, however, had his reservations. "I knew that most of the studios in town had turned it down," he explained. "I said to Junior, 'I don't believe in horror pictures. It's morbid. None of our officers are for it. People don't want that sort of thing.' Only Junior wanted it. Only Junior stood out for it and he said to me, 'Yes they do, Pop. They do want that sort of thing. Just give me a chance and I'll show you.' Well, he showed me. He showed us all."[7]

Shelley's novel was in the public domain and so, to secure what rights it could, Universal registered the title with the Motion Picture Producers and Distributors of America (MPPDA) and arranged for the purchase of the rights to Webling's play, as adapted by Balderston. The deal was concluded on 8 April 1931 with Universal agreeing to pay $20,000 plus 1% of the world gross. The agreement also included a stipulation that Balderston would provide a screenplay adapted from the play. Within days it was announced that Lugosi would star and, on 16 May, the *Hollywood Filmograph* announced Florey as *Frankenstein*'s director.

Schayer gave Florey the go-ahead to proceed with the full screenplay. The Frenchman refused, however, stating he would not continue until he was presented with a contract guaranteeing that he could write and direct *Frankenstein*.[viii] Universal acquiesced and presented him with a contract which he duly signed, not noticing that, although the contract stated Florey would write and direct a film, it did not state that the film would be *Frankenstein*. Unaware of his oversight, Florey began work on the screenplay.

To assist him, Schayer assigned Garrett Fort, who had previously worked on the *Dracula* screenplay. Florey would work on the plot, Fort would write the dialogue. It was during this partnership that Florey had the idea of inserting a criminal brain into the Monster. The windmill climax was also created when Florey saw the windmill trademark of the Van de Kamp bakery from his apartment window. It was this ending that caused some disagreement between the writers. "I had typed the many cuts of the final chase," Florey explained "ending with the monster cornered on the mill's balcony and seeing the peasants piling their burning torches around the base of the mill and the flames commencing to

---

viii It is possible that Florey's refusal was due to the fact that Balderston was to provide Universal with his own screenplay for *Frankenstein*. The advance publicity for Frankenstein stated "Adapted by John L. Balderston from the play by Peggy Webling".

lick up the sides. Fort came up with the idea that the
Monster should pick up Frankenstein and hurl him
down over the rail at the peasants, killing him instantly.
Thinking of a follow-up in case of success, I was against
the idea, but Dick Schayer, taken as a referee, decided
that 'For the time being, let's end the picture with the
double death of the monster and its creator and a short
sequence in the village church written by Garrett.'"[8]

Florey claimed it was always his intention for Lugosi
to play the role of Frankenstein and not the Monster.
Junior, however, had other plans. The new horror star
of *Dracula* would now play the Monster in *Frankenstein*.
Lugosi learned of Laemmle's wishes and was deeply
unhappy. He would, he felt, be wasted in a role that
could be played by "any half-wit extra".[9] Junior, however,
could not be dissuaded.

French *Frankenstein* poster with credit for
Robert Florey.

The task of transforming Lugosi into the Monster
went to Universal's head make-up artist, Jack P. Pierce. Born in Greece on 5 May 1889, Jack
Piccolo Pierce emigrated to America and in 1914, after a variety of jobs, including a period
as a semi-professional baseball player and a nickelodeon projectionist, joined Universal as
an assistant cameraman. Pierce had dabbled as a make-up artist since 1910 while working
for a number of independent companies, and in 1926 had transformed Jacques Lerner
into an ape for the film *The Monkey Talks*. His first make-up job for Universal followed.
For the adaptation of Victor Hugo's *The Man Who Laughs* (1928) Pierce was called upon to
supply Conrad Veidt with a permanent, leering grin.

Pierce's next assignment was *Dracula*, but it was not long before disharmony grew
between the film's star, Bela Lugosi, and the make-up man. Lugosi refused to let Pierce
experiment with the vampire's make-up and insisted on doing it himself. Things were no
easier when the two reunited for *Frankenstein*. Once again, Lugosi wanted to do his own
make-up. "Lugosi thought his ideas were better than everybody's," Pierce explained.[ix]
Unhappy with Lugosi's make-up, Junior suggested that Pierce should base the Monster's
look on the clay man portrayed by Paul Wegener in the 1920 silent *Der Golem*.

The Florey/Fort draft was completed on 8 June. The screenplay contained 475
scenes and was credited solely to Garrett Fort. Yet even with a complete screenplay, all
was not well. Two days later, while the Laemmles were away in New York, the *Hollywood
Reporter* announced:

"FRANKENSTEIN" HELD UP
Production on Frankenstein has been temporarily halted at Universal with
Robert Florey, director,[x] being passed up until a production okeh can be had
from New York.[10]

---

ix Boris Karloff was later to hear about Lugosi's creation. "I was once told that he insisted on doing his make-up himself,"
Karloff said, "and did this awful, hairy creature, not at all like our Monster."

x The numerous statements in the Press that Robert Florey was to be the director of *Frankenstein* may not have been
entirely accurate. On 15 June Garrett Fort sent a memo to Richard Schayer in which he stated that a director had not
been 'definitely assigned' to the project.

On 18 June the paper re-affirmed its earlier statement and now added that pictures "cancelled on the current programme during Junior's absence from the studio will remain definitely off the schedule."[11]

It was decided, possibly by Schayer, Florey's "only direct contact with the Universal management",[12] that a test of the creation scene should be shot with Lugosi in the role of the Monster. The footage would be filmed on the still-standing sets from *Dracula*.[xi] As Florey recalled, "The *Dracula* set had not been modified or rebuilt but simply dressed as a lab. We shot the test in two days, I believe, three at most. Of course, we used other actors in the test – we could hardly have photographed a couple of thousand feet of the monster alone!"[13]

A cast including Edward Van Sloan and Dwight Frye, both of whom had appeared with Lugosi in the movie version of *Dracula* (and would be retained for *Frankenstein*), and two stock players (to play the parts of Henry and Victor) were assembled. According to Van Sloan the revised Monster make-up was unimpressive. When made up, Lugosi's head "was about four times normal size, with a broad wig on it".[14] The Monster had "polished, claylike skin"[15] and, rather than befitting a movie monster, looked, Van Sloan thought, "more like something out of BABES IN TOYLAND."[16]

The test was filmed on 16 and 17 June during which time Lugosi's increasing dissatisfaction became evident. "As I was working with the other actors," Florey said, "during a time when the Monster had not yet come to life, Lugosi kept exclaiming, 'Enough is enough', that he was not going to be a grunting, babbling idiot for anybody and that any tall extra could be the monster. 'I was a star in my country, and I will not be a scarecrow over here!' he said repeatedly."[17]

Junior returned from New York on Sunday, 21 June having secured "sufficient finances to carry through their programme for 1931-32"[18] and began work again the following day. To view the 20-minute long *Frankenstein* test Florey, Lugosi and the cameraman Paul Ivano joined Junior in the screening room. The screening was a disaster. Instead of instilling fear, the appearance of the Monster's face caused Junior to burst out laughing. When the screening was over an unimpressed Junior rose from his seat and left in silence. Unlike Junior, however, Lugosi was delighted with the footage and exclaimed to the cameraman: "Ivano! My close-up was magnificent."[19] He then thrust a fistful of cigars into Ivano's hand and left. Ivano, a non-smoker, passed the cigars to Florey. Yet, despite Junior's reaction, Florey claimed that Junior was "not displeased"[20] with the footage and that "on the contrary, he often projected it".[21] In later years, however, when asked if he recalled the test reel, Junior replied, "Yes, but it wasn't very good."[22]

Following the disastrous screening, Florey's removal from the picture was assured. Outraged, he checked his contract but was shocked to find that *Frankenstein* was not named as his project. He tried to enlist Lugosi's support but, as the star's companion (and later fourth wife)[xii] Lillian Arch recalled, Lugosi's enthusiasm for the project had waned: "Bela wanted out! He said, 'I'll get a doctor's excuse' because it was a six-hour make-up and all that sort of stuff. Bela, you see, was the actor. And he couldn't see himself moaning and grunting – and that's all the Monster did in the original one. Bela thought, 'You don't need an actor for that part! Anybody can moan and grunt! I need a challenging part – a part where I can act!' He had a stupid agent – this I must add! I think it was a woman. And if

xi The *Dracula* sets were designed by Herman Rosse. He would also be the set designer on *Frankenstein*.
xii Bela Lugosi and Lillian Arch were married from 1933 to 1953.

she had an ounce of brains, she would have said, 'Look Bela. I don't care what you think. You are right now the top in horror. You did Dracula. Now here's the Monster. Don't refuse it.' If only he had a smart agent – but he had a stupid woman."[23]

With no backing from the star, Florey was off the picture. Ironically, Florey was given, as his contracted writing and directing project, one of the stories previously discussed with Schayer at the Musso and Frank Restaurant – Poe's detective story *The Murders in the Rue Morgue*. Its star would be Bela Lugosi.

With news of the test reel doing the rounds of the Universal lot, James Whale paid a visit to Junior's office. Whale had been born in Dudley in the West Midlands of England on 22 July 1889. His student days at the Dudley School of Arts and Crafts ended in August 1914, cut short by the outbreak of the First World War. Whale, a homosexual, reluctantly enlisted in October 1915 and, by the summer of 1916, he became a commissioned 2nd Lieutenant. Taken prisoner by the Germans at Passchendaele, he was sent to a prison camp at Holzminden in Brunswick where he spent the remaining 15 months of the war. For entertainment the POWs would produce plays in the camp's barracks and it was here that Whale's interest in the theatre began. His artistic talents were put to use designing and painting scenery and he would even turn his hand to writing new material for the performers.

After the war Whale rejected a career as a cartoonist and, joining the Birmingham Repertory Company, began his theatrical career in earnest. Over the following years he turned his hand to all aspects of theatre work. He was a stage manager, actor, set and costume designer, and in June 1923 he directed his first London play.

In 1928, Whale directed R.C. Sherriff's First World War drama *Journey's End*. Starring a 21-year-old Laurence Olivier as Captain Stanhope, the play had only two performances, opening on 9 December at the Apollo Theatre, London. The play had a much longer run when it opened at the Savoy Theatre on 21 January 1929. With Colin Clive now in the role of Captain Stanhope the play was a great success and ran for 593 performances.

Whale took the play to America where it played in Chicago, New York and on tour. While there he attracted the attention of Paramount and was engaged as 'Dialogue Director' on the Richard Dix picture *The Love Doctor*. Whale's next project was to direct dialogue sequences for Howard Hughes' new, and previously silent, World War I aviation picture *Hell's Angels*. He then directed his first picture, *Journey's End*, once again starring Colin Clive as Captain Stanhope. The picture opened on both sides of the Atlantic to rave reviews. The *New York Evening Post* wrote, "It bears the stamp of all round perfection, and James Whale has unquestionably placed himself along with the foremost screen directors."[24] Whale's first film for Universal followed – *Waterloo Bridge*, a First World War story of Myra [Mae Clarke], a prostitute, who falls in love with a Canadian soldier, with tragic consequences. With the success of *Journey's End*, and *Waterloo Bridge* still in post-production, Whale was to choose his next picture. He chose *Frankenstein*. "At first I thought it was a gag," he said, "but *Frankenstein*, after all, is a great classic of literature, and I soon became absorbed in its possibilities. I decided I'd try to do something with it to sort of top all thrillers."[25]

Junior was happy with the change of director, believing Whale "could do a better job of it."[26] Despite Whale's later claim that he was "forced more or less against my will"[27] to direct the picture, he gave his reasons for choosing *Frankenstein* in an article printed in the *New York Times*. "I chose *Frankenstein* out of about 30 available stories because it was the strongest meat and gave me a chance to dabble in the macabre," he said. "I thought it would be an amusing thing to try and make what everybody knows to be a physical impossibility into the almost believable for 60 minutes. A director must be pretty bad if he can't get a thrill out of a war, murder [or] robbery. *Frankenstein* was a sensational story and had the chance to become a sensational picture. It offered fine pictorial possibilities, had two grand characterisations and dealt with a subject which might go anywhere, and that is part of the fun of making pictures."[28]

After accepting the project Whale turned his attention to the screenplay. He read Florey's original script and Balderston's adaptation. Whale had decided that the picture "might just as well be as horrible as possible"[29] and recalled Garrett Fort, who could only give two weeks, to make 'minor changes'.[30] For inspiration Whale screened *Der Golem* (1920), Fritz Lang's *Metropolis* (1927), Rex Ingram's *The Magician* (1926) and *The Cabinet of Dr. Caligari* (1920), all of which would furnish him with elements to use in *Frankenstein*.[xiii]

On 11 July the *Hollywood Filmograph* reported, inaccurately, that Whale would begin production on *Frankenstein* "within a fortnight".[31] The screenplay was still not completed to Whale's satisfaction and only three parts had been cast. Dwight Frye would play the hunchback assistant Fritz, and Edward Van Sloan would play Frankenstein's mentor, Dr. Waldman. For the part of Henry Frankenstein's father, the Baron, Whale asked for 72-year-old Frederick Kerr. Whale, who had worked with Kerr previously on *Waterloo Bridge*, said, "Frederick Kerr is an asset to any picture and I wanted him because he is conventionally well-bred enough not to interfere with the personal liberty of any son over 18 years old."[32]

Yet, as the parts were being filled, Lugosi, never happy with his role, asked to be released from the picture. Junior readily agreed and the studio was suddenly without a monster. Whale, however, was unconcerned about the loss. There would be "terrible confusion",[33] Whale felt, if the star of *Dracula* also played Frankenstein's Monster. Whale's companion, film producer David Lewis, explained, "Lugosi was all wrong for the part and Jimmy knew it."[34]

Despite Junior's preference for Leslie Howard in the role of Henry Frankenstein, Whale wanted his *Journey's End* star, Colin Clive. "I chose Colin Clive for *Frankenstein*," the director said, "because he had exactly the right kind of tenacity to go through with anything, together with the kind of romantic quality which makes strong men leave civilisation to shoot big game. There is also a level-headedness about Clive which keeps him in full control of himself even in his craziest moments in the picture."[35]

John Boles was given the thankless role of Victor and for the part of Henry's fiancée, Elizabeth, Whale asked that his star of *Waterloo Bridge* be tested.[xiv] "I asked for Mae Clarke for Elizabeth," he explained, "because of her intelligence, fervour and sincere belief that *Frankenstein* would claim the public's interest."[36] Clarke would join the cast in August, although with some doubts on the merit of her role. "*Waterloo Bridge* was definitely for me but *Frankenstein* was not," she later said. "It was a great thing to be connected with. It's always nice to be in a success, but it didn't really give me any scenes to play. I remember

---

xiii *Der Golem* concerned a man of clay, brought to life by magic. *Metropolis* contained a laboratory complete with elaborate electronic equipment, while *The Magician* had a hunchback assistant who hobbles down tower steps similar to those in *Frankenstein*. In *The Cabinet of Dr. Caligari* Cesare, the somnambulist, enters a woman's bedroom in order to abduct her.
xiv Bette Davis, a new Universal contractee, was also considered for the role of Elizabeth but was rejected. "She's got as much sex appeal as Slim Summerville," Junior said.

thinking, 'Oh well, at least it's Whale and the same people I loved. I'll enjoy myself and it's going to be a prominent film.'"[37]

Only the Monster now remained to be cast. Various actors had been considered including, so he claimed, John Carradine. "I've never played a monster," he later explained. "I was offered one and turned it down – I turned down *Frankenstein*, and Boris took it… They sent me to the make-up department, and the make-up man started mixing up a bowl of plaster, and I, being a sculptor, knew just what he was up to – a life mask! I said, 'Wait a minute – what is this?' He said, 'You play a Monster.' I said, 'Oh! Do I have any dialogue?'

"'No. You just grunt.'

"'This is not for me!' I said, and walked out… I never regretted it…"[38]

The inability to find a suitable actor was now causing Whale some concern, a fact he reflected to David Lewis. "Jimmy was absolutely bewildered," Lewis said, "although I didn't realise they needed a monster as badly as they did until he told me one day."[39] Then, during the filming of his latest assignment *Graft*,[xv] Boris Karloff entered the Universal commissary. "I was having lunch," Karloff explained, "and James Whale sent either the first assistant or maybe it was his secretary over to me, and asked me to join him for a cup of coffee after lunch, which I did. He asked me if I would make a test for him tomorrow. 'What for?' I asked. 'For a damned awful monster!' he said. Of course, I was delighted, because it meant another job if I was able to land it. Actually, that's all it meant to me. At the same time I felt rather hurt, because at the time I had on a very good straight make-up and my best suit – and he wanted to test me for a monster!"[40]

Although the circumstances of Karloff's 'discovery', or variations of it,[xvi] are generally acknowledged as being the most plausible, in the wake of *Frankenstein*'s success others claimed to have had a hand in finding the Monster. David Lewis told how he saw Karloff in the role of Galloway at the Belasco Theatre and was so impressed by the actor that he "never left my mind.[41] I had seen Boris Karloff in *The Criminal Code*, and he was so good, I cannot tell you. His face – the way he moved – everything about him stuck in my mind. He was powerful, and you had to have a powerful monster."[42] Lewis then informed Whale of his find: "Jimmy said, 'Boris – who?' He hadn't even heard of him."[43]

Even Lugosi, in a 1935 interview, claimed the credit for Karloff's discovery. "I made up for the role and had tests taken, which were pronounced O.K," he said. "Then I read the script, and didn't like it. So I asked to be withdrawn from the picture. Carl Laemmle said he'd permit it, if I'd furnish an actor to play the part. I scouted the agencies – and came upon Boris Karloff. I recommended him. He took tests. And that's how he happened to become a famous star of horror pictures – my rival, in fact."[44] It was a story Lugosi rigidly adhered to. In 1953 he said, "After I did *Dracula* at Universal, they wanted me to do the monster in *Frankenstein*. But when I tested the make-up it was heavy and painful. Then I read the script. I didn't have a word of dialogue. I got out of the role by having my doctor say it would be bad for me. I suggested Karloff for the role. You might say I created my own Frankenstein Monster – competition for horror roles."[45]

To prepare for the test Karloff was sent to Jack Pierce who had once again been called upon to create the Monster's make-up. "Jack was nothing short of a genius, besides being a lovely man," Karloff later said. "So, at the end of the day's work on *Graft*, I would stay,

xv *Graft* was in production between 22 June and 21 July 1931.
xvi Karloff told a slightly different story in a later interview. "James Whale, the director," he said, "was lunching at a nearby table. Suddenly he caught my eye and beckoned me over."

and he would stay, and nightly he worked on the make-up until we felt it was ready. People in production were constantly calling and saying, 'Aren't you ready yet?' And we would answer, 'No – we're not ready yet.'"[46]

Pierce's stalling tactic was, Karloff believed, instrumental in getting him the role. "I was just a freelance actor, but he [Pierce] was on the inside of the studio and he knew the importance of the film and of the part. Because of his own position in the studio he was able to forestall the test until he felt we were quite ready to do it. In fact he stalled it off for about three weeks. If I had asked for that I would have been thrown out on my ear, but in his position he was able to do it."[47]

According to Pierce, during the four months in total he worked on the Monster's make-up, he made "hundreds of sketches and models"[48] and a "life-size mould".[49] Ignoring Mary Shelley's brief description of the Monster[xvii] Pierce finally submitted just one sketch, which was approved. In an interview given during the production of *Son of Frankenstein* eight years later, Pierce described how the original make-up was developed:

> I figured that Frankenstein, who was a scientist but no practising surgeon, would take the simplest surgical way. He would cut the top of the skull off straight across like a potlid, hinge it, pop the brain in and then clamp it on tight. That is the reason I decided to make the monster's head square and flat like a shoebox and dig that big scar across his forehead with the metal clamps holding it together.
>
> Those two metal studs sticking out at the sides of the monster's neck… are inlets for electricity – plugs such as we use for lamps or flatirons. Remember, the monster is an electrical gadget. Lightning is his life force… he carries a five-pound steel spine – that you can't see – to represent the rod which conveys the current up to the monster's brain.
>
> Here's another thing. I read that the Egyptians used to bind some criminals hand and foot and bury them alive. When their blood turned to water after death, it flowed into their extremities, stretched their arms to gorilla length and swelled their hands, feet and faces to abnormal proportions. I thought this might make a nice touch for the monster, since he was supposed to be made up from the corpses of executed felons. So I fixed Karloff up that way.
>
> … I made his arms look longer by shortening the sleeves of his coat, stiffened his legs with two pairs of pants over steel struts and… covered Karloff's face with blue-green greasepaint, which photographs grey. I blacken[ed] his fingernails with shoe polish.[50]

Karloff also removed a dental bridge from the right side and sucked in his cheek. The resulting hollow was accentuated by Pierce to give the Monster's face a more cadaverous look. Yet, with the make-up almost complete, Karloff felt that the Monster's eyes were not right. They seemed "too normal and alive and natural for a thing that had only just

---

xvii Shelley wrote: 'His limbs were in proportion, and I had selected his features as beautiful. Beautiful! Great God! His yellow skin scarcely covered the work of muscles and arteries beneath; his hair was of a lustrous black, and flowing; his teeth of a pearly whiteness; but these luxuriances only formed a more horrid contrast with his watery eyes, that seemed almost of the same colour as the dun-white sockets in which they were set, his shrivelled complexion and straight black lips.'

been put together and born"[51] and so mortician's wax was added to his eyelids to make them "heavy, half-seeing".[52]

Whale had also been involved in the Monster's make-up design. He made drawings of Karloff's head and added "sharp, bony ridges where I imagined the skull might have joined."[53] He also added two large, clamped scars to the forehead of the Monster. Although these were removed from the make-up before production began Universal's publicity department had already issued advance stills and advertisements that showed this earlier make-up. To add height to the Monster, Karloff wore a pair of asphalt spreader's boots. "The boots weighed about 16 pounds apiece. All told, the entire outfit weighed about 40 to 45 pounds,"[xviii] Karloff recalled.[54]

Meanwhile, the script still needed work. Schayer hired John Russell, a short story writer, "to do dialogue".[55] Russell, however, proved incompatible with Whale's requirements and lasted only a week. To complete the screenplay Schayer recruited Universal contractee Francis Edwards Faragoh. Faragoh, a Hungarian-born playwright, was in demand following his success with the screenplay for *Little Caesar* (1931), the hit gangster movie starring Edward G. Robinson. Faragoh's *Frankenstein* draft was dated 7 August 1931.

Earlier versions of the script had placed Frankenstein's laboratory in the old windmill, and at the end of the picture the Monster was to seek the mill, the place of its creation. Faragoh moved the location of the laboratory to the abandoned watchtower.[xix] He also gave dialogue to the previously mute Fritz and introduced the premise of the criminal brain being used as a replacement for the dropped normal brain. Faragoh also made Frankenstein and the Monster more sympathetic characters, akin to Shelley's novel and Webling's play, and more to Whale's liking. As Karloff recalled, "I don't think the main screenwriter, Bob Florey, really intended there to be much pathos inside the character. But Whale and I thought that there should be; we didn't want the kind of rampaging monstrosity that Universal seemed to think we should go in for. We had to have some pathos, otherwise our audiences just wouldn't think about the film after they'd left the theatre, and Whale very much wanted them to do that. He wanted to make some impact on them. And so did I."[56]

Colin Clive arrived in New York aboard the *Aquitania* in August 1931 and was met by a Universal emissary who presented him with a copy of the unfinished script and a letter from Whale. "I am sending you herewith a copy of the script for *Frankenstein*," Whale wrote. "It is a grand part and I think will fit you as well as Stanhope. I think the cast will be old Frederick Kerr as your father Baron Frankenstein, John Boles as Victor, Bela Lugosi or Boris Karloff as the Monster,[xx] Dwight Frye as the Dwarf, Van Sloan as Dr. Waldman, and I am making a test of Mae Clarke as Elizabeth. Although it is largely an English cast, I do not want too much English accent about it, so in studying the part please keep this in mind. Of course I do not want an American accent, but it is well to talk to as many Americans as you can to get that looseness, instead of what Americans think of as English tightness, in speech. Do not let this worry you, it is merely a note."[57]

On 21 August the *Hollywood Filmograph* announced John Boles and Mae Clarke had joined the cast of *Frankenstein*. More importantly the Monster was also finally cast. After

xviii Other sources have estimated the boots weighed 11, 13 or 15 pounds each and the total additional weight of the make-up and costume amounted to an extra 48 pounds.
xix Despite the location change, in the finished picture, due to an oversight, the Baron asks why his son goes "messing around an old windmill".
xx Although Pierce's stalling tactic eventually proved beneficial to Karloff, the Universal front office, concerned by the delay, had considered recalling Lugosi for the role.

Whale had approved the make-up, Karloff had the decisive screen test. On seeing the footage Junior happily approved the casting. "Karloff's eyes mirrored the suffering we needed," he said.[58] With a budget of $262,000 and production scheduled at 30 days, filming began on Monday, 24 August 1931.

Whale began by shooting the opening cemetery scene. While Colin Clive and Dwight Frye were collecting cadavers, Boris Karloff's costume and make-up were being finalised. Van Sloan's first scenes – the lecture at Goldstadt Medical College followed by Fritz's bungled attempt to procure a normal brain – were shot next.

On Saturday, 29 August Karloff arrived at Universal for his first day of filming. To ensure he was ready for the 9 a.m. start the actor would arrive at the studio at 4 a.m. He would then report to Dressing Room No. 5 and place himself in Pierce's hands for the lengthy task of transformation. "It took from four to six hours a day to make me up," Karloff said. "I felt like an Egyptian mummy as Jack ladled the layers of make-up on me."[59] In 1932 *Picturegoer* described the daily routine:

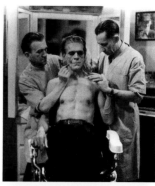

Top: Being made up by Jack Pierce and his assistant. Bottom: Jack Pierce leads Karloff to the set.

> Each time the monster was created, Karloff had to sit in the make-up chair for exactly three and a half hours. First his eyes must be given that heavy, half-dead, insane look – a matter of applying coats and coats of wax to his eyelids to weigh them down.
>
> Then invisible wire clamps over his lips to pull the corners of his mouth out and down. Then the overhanging brow and high, square-shaped crown of the head, supposedly 'grafted' from the head of another man. These, as well as his face and neck, were shaped and built up by means of thin layers of cotton, applied with a special liquid preparation so that it went on smoothly like so many thin layers of flesh. Then the greyish make-up on top of all. Heavy bolts were placed on the side of his neck (where the head had been bolted on to the body in case you did not see the strange operation on the screen) and held there by means of more layers of cotton and adhesive liquids.
>
> Karloff still carries two little scars on his neck, where those bolts were fastened.[60]

Dressing Room No. 5 – or 'The Bugaboudoir' as it became known – was a 20-foot-square cabin. It was here that Lon Chaney had applied his famous make-up for *The Hunchback of Notre Dame* (1923) and *The Phantom of the Opera* (1925). Jack Pierce had applied Conrad Veidt's disfigured grin for *The Man Who Laughs* (1928) in the cabin while, earlier in 1931, it had been the location of Bela Lugosi's transformation into Dracula.

Upon leaving the dressing room on his first day as the Monster, Karloff turned left to reach the soundstage. This set a superstitious precedent and all those actors who used the dressing room in the actor's wake would turn left on leaving the cabin, regardless of the direction they needed to go.

One of the first people to see the Monster in its full regalia, or so he claimed, was Karloff's friend, Groucho Marx. "I was in a back room playing my guitar when the doorbell rang," Groucho later explained. "The maid opened it. I heard her scream. She later fainted. Then I heard these heavy footsteps coming down the hall to my room. The door opened and there stood this monster. It was Karloff in his get-up."[61]

Karloff's first day on set was for the filming of the creation scene.[xxi] As Whale affirmed this was the most important moment in the picture. "I consider the creation of the Monster to be the high spot of the film," he said, "because if the audience did not believe the thing had been really made, they would not be bothered with what it was supposed to do afterward. To build up to this, I showed Frankenstein collecting his material bit by bit. He proves to the audience through his conversation with Professor Waldman that he actually did know something about science, especially the ultra-violet ray, from which he was expecting the miracle to happen. He deliberately tells his plan of action. By this time the audience must at least believe that something is going to happen; it might be a disaster, but at least they will settle down to see the show. Frankenstein puts the spectators in their positions, he gives final orders to Fritz, he turns the levers and sends his diabolic machine soaring upward to the roof, into the storm. He is now is a state of feverish excitement... The lightning flashes. The Monster begins to move. Frankenstein merely has to believe what he sees, which is all we ask the audience to do."[62]

To dress Herman Rosse's laboratory set Universal leased elaborate electrical equipment from Kenneth Strickfaden. Strickfaden had begun creating the apparatus as a hobby, constructing gadgets from any odds and ends he could acquire. "I'd put something together and then sit back and marvel at it," he later explained. "Then I found there was a market. The styling depended upon what kind of junk I had at hand."[63] The equipment was operated by Ray Lindsay and Frank Graves during the creation scene, although Strickfaden remained on hand to make adjustments and replace any burned out equipment.

Universal staff were invited to witness the scene being shot. "Everybody for miles around came to watch when they pulled the switch!" Mae Clarke recalled.[64] The fascination for some, however, was short lived. "The first time they did it, it was fascinating," Clarke said. "But the sixteenth time it was a goddamn bore... Everything went wrong. One at a time, you know. 'Try that again.' Oh, they did it too soon. But the first time it was fascinating to see how that all pulled together."[65]

Although required to do little more than lie swathed in bandages on the operating table the scene caused Karloff some concern. "For a while I lay half-naked and strapped to Doctor Frankenstein's table," he said. "I could see directly above me the special effects men brandishing the white-hot, scissorlike carbons that made the lightning. I hoped that no one up there had butterfingers."[66]

On the tenth day of filming Karloff appeared in full costume for the first time. First seen entering backwards, the Monster turns and a series of progressively closer shots reveal its face in startling close-up. "Part of the reason for the Monster's frightening realism," Karloff explained, "was the look of *pores* in the skin. Jack achieved this by a

---

xxi On the same day as the creation scene was shot Karloff's casting was announced in the press. When Lugosi learned of the casting he telephoned Karloff. "The part's nothing," Lugosi said, "but perhaps it will make you a little money."

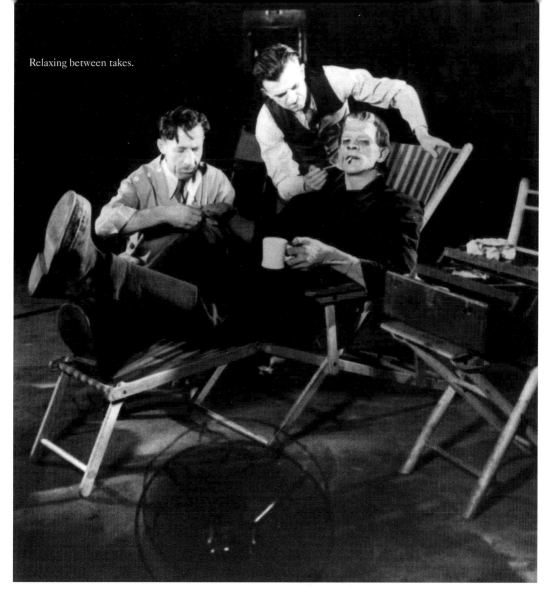

Relaxing between takes.

special technique in which he carefully built up the make-up from layers of cheesecloth. When he was done you couldn't tell where my real face ended and the Monster's began."[67] Pierce remained on set during the shoot to attend to any emergency make-up repair work. "Sometimes it was an eyelid that came loose – another time the wig would slip in a fight, or one of the heavy bolts came loose in a particularly frenzied scene," *Picturegoer* reported.[68]

Mae Clarke recalled that, during the Monster's first scenes, a rapport appeared to develop between Whale and Karloff. "He [Whale] and Boris got on well together after the first couple of scenes were done and they knew they had something," she said. "They were so at ease they would just whisper and agree. I remember all the gestures the monster did were Whale's – I saw him do them. When he first said 'Sit down' Whale mapped it all out. He said 'Now you don't know what sit down means, but you know – because his hands are going that way – that he means back. So you go. What am I doing? Hands. Where do I go? You hit the chair, you go down.'"[69]

Karloff and Whale were also in agreement regarding the nature of the Monster. "Whale and I both saw the character as an innocent one," Karloff said. "Within the heavy restrictions of my make-up I tried to play it that way. This was a pathetic creature who, like us all, had neither wish nor say in his creation, and certainly did not wish upon itself the hideous image which automatically terrified humans whom it tried to befriend. The most heartrending aspect of the creature's life, for us, was his ultimate desertion by his creator. It was as though man, in his blundering, searching attempts to improve himself, was to find himself deserted by his God."[70]

In the summer heat and under the glaring Klieg lights it was not long before Karloff began to suffer the effects. The waxen eyelids would melt and crumble with pieces falling, painfully, into his eyes. The extra weight of the costume was also an added burden in the heat and humidity. "To fill out the monster costume I had to wear a doubly quilted suit beneath it," Karloff explained. "We shot *Frankenstein* in midsummer. After an hour's work I would be sopping wet. I'd have to change into a spare undersuit, often still damp from the previous round. So I felt, most of the time, as if I were wearing a clammy shroud myself. No doubt it added to the realism."[71]

Early in production Karloff took a walk outside the sound stage in an attempt to cool down. In full costume and make-up he unexpectedly encountered a young studio secretary who, on seeing the Monster, promptly fainted. When Laemmle Senior heard of the incident he issued orders that, when walking around the lot, Karloff should keep his face covered. "Because," Laemmle explained, "some of our nice little secretaries are pregnant and they might be frightened if they saw him!"[72] As a result Karloff was led, with his head covered by a blue veil, to and from the soundstage by Jack Pierce. Once there, Karloff was forbidden to leave except to have lunch. Two guards were also placed at the stage door to stop unauthorised people entering (and Karloff leaving).

Film Weekly reported the studio's increase in security. "At the Universal studio Boris Karloff, playing the synthetic Monster 'made' from fresh corpses in *Frankenstein*, is under an oath of secrecy. Once made up, he is not allowed to leave the studio or see visitors until the make-up is removed. His journeys to and from his dressing-room and the soundproofed stages are made with a hood over his head and face, and with gloves covering his hands. His meals are served to him in private."[73] Mae Clarke recalled, "He didn't have lunch with us in the studio commissary because it was easier for him, due to the make-up, to eat alone in his dressing room bungalow."[74]

The lunch break would also present the opportunity for Karloff to gain some temporary relief from the heat by stripping naked. With lunch over he would climb into fresh undergarments, his spare quilted undersuit and Monster costume and, a little refreshed, would be led, his face hidden by the obligatory blue veil, back to the soundstage to continue the day's filming. Another brief respite was offered by the daily ritual of tea breaks every mid-afternoon, which also gave Karloff the chance to smoke a cigarette.

With the day's filming complete, Karloff would return to Dressing Room No. 5 where Pierce would begin the make-up removal process. "Removing the make-up was not much simpler than putting it on, and certainly more painful," *Picturegoer* reported. "It required an hour and a half of prying, pulling and coaxing, plus special oils and acids, "plus a great deal of bad language!" as Karloff added. First the eyelids came off – most painful, to say the least, and enough to inspire any quantity of questionable language. The deep scar on the monster's forehead was then pried into, as a starting point, and from then it was just one pry and push and acid-soaking after another until Boris was himself again."[75]

On 28 September the unit moved to Malibou Lake in the Santa Monica Mountains to shoot the scenes with Little Maria. In the picture the child meets the Monster

The Monster menaces Elizabeth (Mae Clarke).

and, unafraid, leads him in play, throwing flowers onto the water. When the flowers are exhausted, the Monster tosses her into the lake in the misguided belief that she, like the flowers, will float. The child drowns and the Monster runs away, horror-stricken by his actions. Mae Clarke said of the scene, "This was the nearest the Monster came to having a soul, without having one."[76]

In order to be ready for the start of that day's filming Karloff was required to report to Pierce at 3:30 a.m. On the journey to the lake he found an unexpected travelling companion in seven-year-old Marilyn Harris who had been cast to play Little Maria. "Boris Karloff was in his make-up," she recalled, "and nobody wanted to ride with him but he didn't bother me. I had such love for that man. I went over to him and said, 'May I please ride with you?' and he said I could."[77] Instead of being frightened by the monstrous visage, Harris was simply curious. "I remember asking him about the bolts in his neck and he said, 'Oh, those are glued on.'"[78]

Although Harris remained unfazed by the Monster's appearance, Whale was aware that the shooting of the drowning scene could prove difficult for a seven-year-old and was, therefore, suitably sensitive when dealing with the child. "Here was this beautiful direction by Whale," said Mae Clarke. "He told little Marilyn Harris, 'Here is Mr. Karloff in a funny costume who's just being friendly. You look up at him and say, I am Maria.'"[79] Karloff, however, was not enthused by Whale's direction of the scene and disagreed with the method used to toss the girl into the water. "Well, that was the only time I didn't like Jimmy Whale's direction," Karloff later said. "My conception of the scene was that he would look up at the little girl in bewilderment, and, in his mind, she would become a flower – and, to his horror, she would sink. Well, Jimmy made me pick her up and do THAT [motioning violently] over my head which became a brutal and deliberate act... The whole pathos of the scene, to my mind, should have been – and I'm sure that's the way it was written – completely innocent and unaware."[80] The cast and crew, reportedly, took Karloff's side. "He fumbled for his words," Karloff recalled, "as he tried to convey why to us, because in a strange way we were all very hostile about it. Then he said, 'You see, it's all part of the *ritual*.'"[81]

When it came to shooting the scene, other problems arose. With men in rowboats out of camera ready to fish Harris out of the water, Karloff threw the girl into the lake for the first time. However, instead of sinking, Harris was kept afloat by her dress, which had billowed with air. "They wanted to do it again," she recalled, "but it hurt my back when I hit the water, so I didn't want to. They were drying me out and James Whale came over to me and said, 'If you do it again, I'll give you anything you want.' So I went over to Boris Karloff and asked him not to throw me in so hard next time."[82] Karloff was apologetic. "But I have to," he explained. "I have to get you under the water."[83]

On the second take Whale got what he wanted. "The second shot went fine," Harris said. "Boris Karloff threw me in again and I went underwater out of camera range."[84] Having had only a few swimming lessons she was not adept at swimming underwater. "I managed to stay under and swim out of camera," she said, "but that wasn't skill. I did it out of fear."[85] Although Whale was happy with the take, Harris's mother appeared dissatisfied and shouted, "Throw her in again! Farther!"[86] "My mother wanted to be in the movies," Harris explained, "but she wasn't talented enough or good looking enough, so she went to the orphanage and said, 'I want the prettiest, blondest, blue-eyed baby you've got'. In those days, you could do that."[87]

True to his word, Whale asked Harris what reward she wanted for suffering a second soaking. To her mother's amazement, Harris, who was on a strict diet, asked for a dozen hard-boiled eggs. "My mother almost killed me," she said. "You could have had a doll, a bicycle – anything! I think James Whale was so relieved, he sent me two dozen eggs."[88]

The lake scene was completed but the day's filming was far from over. "We were out on the edge of the lake for the scene with the little girl," said Karloff, "and then we went back to the studio in the evening to have some supper, and then... back onto the backlot and worked all night until five in the morning... I had it [the make-up] on for over 25 hours. It was a long pull."[89]

Following supper, Karloff was required back on the soundstage to film Frankenstein's confrontation with his creation. Frankenstein is struck down and the Monster carries him up a hill towards the old windmill. It was this scene that proved, for Karloff, to be the most physically demanding of the entire shoot. Although filmed in long shot where stand-ins or, in Clive's case, a dummy could easily have been used, Whale insisted on no substitutes. Karloff would carry Clive up the hill. The scene was repeated over a dozen times before Whale was content. Karloff's daughter, Sara Jane, recalled: "The most difficult part of the shoot was my father carrying Colin Clive up that hill time and time and time again until they got it right. Ultimately, he ended up having three back surgeries. He really suffered for the rest of his life, physically, because of… the physical difficulties in shooting that film."[90]

Unlike the young Marilyn Harris, Mae Clarke had been terrified by Karloff in costume. For Clarke, the bedroom confrontation between Elizabeth and the Monster posed a particular problem. "Between Karloff's perfect performance and my throwing myself so thoroughly into my role, I feared I would drop dead," Clarke explained. "I asked Boris if he knew any tricks which would help me. 'Remember,' he said, 'when I am coming at you to keep your eye on my up-camera little finger. I'll keep wiggling it. Then you'll know it's only Boris underneath all this make-up.' Fortunately for me, Boris didn't forget to wiggle his finger!"[91]

Filming ended on Saturday, 3 October five days over schedule and almost $30,000 over budget. For Karloff the end of the shoot meant simply another job done, but it had been hard work. From the beginning he had been used to working long hours on the picture, usually required to put in a 15 to 16-hour day, but towards the end of the shoot the

The Monster with Little Maria (Marilyn Harris).

excessive demands became too much and Karloff appealed to the Academy, as Donovan Pedelty reported in *Film Weekly*:

> Now Boris Karloff is playing the synthetic Monster, and the make-up for that weird role takes five hours to put on and two to take off. Boris quite naturally contends that that prodigious task constitutes work; Universal points out that unless Boris makes up during his rest period, there are only five hours a day left in which to make the picture.
>
> So far the studio has won, and the unfortunate 'monster' reports at the studio at 4 a.m. in order to be ready for a 9 o'clock call, and does not get away at night until two hours after all the other players have departed. But Karloff has appealed to the Academy, and that body has flung the Universal lot into mourning by defining character make-up as work.[92]

Some concessions were made following the Academy's ruling but they came too late to make much difference to Karloff. He was permitted to arrive at 5:30 a.m. instead of his usual 4 a.m. start and could finish slightly earlier. Jack Pierce, always sympathetic to Karloff's cause, also managed to reduce the make-up application process to three and a half hours.

When Karloff's work on the picture was over, he informed his agent he was available again. He was reportedly paid $500 for his work and kept the Monster's headpiece and boots. He had also shed 20 pounds caused by the combination of the heat, the costume and the sheer physical demands of the role.

On Thursday, 29 October *Frankenstein* had its first public showing at the Granada Theatre in Santa Barbara. Laemmle Junior, James Whale and companion David Lewis, associate producer E.M. Asher and editorial supervisor Maurice Pivar were all in attendance. Colin Clive was on a train bound for Chicago and Mae Clarke had begun shooting at Columbia and so both were unable to attend. Boris Karloff was not invited. "I was just an unimportant freelance actor," he said, "the animation for the monster costume."[93]

The audience was treated first to the latest William Haines picture, *The New Adventures of Get-Rich-Quick Wallingford*, a comedy following the capers of a con-man [Haines] and his partners [Jimmy Durante and Ernest Torrence]. Then, at 8:15 p.m., *Frankenstein* began. Its effect was instantaneous. "Up came the first shot in the graveyard[xxii] and you could hear the whole audience gasp,"[94] Lewis explained. As the screening continued, the reaction grew. "The film has been imitated so much that today those scenes don't bother people," he said. "But in 1931, this was awfully strong stuff. As it progressed, people got up, walked out, came back in, walked out again. It was an alarming thing."[95] When the film ended there was no applause, only shocked silence. According to *Film Weekly* the manager of the Granada Theatre[xxiii] was, "aroused at 2 a.m. by his house telephone and a man's voice which said, 'I saw *Frankenstein* at your place and can't sleep – and I have no intention that you should either!'"[96]

---

xxii In 1935 the first shots, of the mourners' procession, were removed for inclusion in the flashback in *Bride of Frankenstein*.

xxiii In 1955 James Whale told the story to a writer for *Good Housekeeping* but adapted the story, claiming he was the recipient of the call.

The preview cards were not kind. "Story is about a man destroyed by his own creation. Look out this doesn't happen to Universal," one viewer wrote. "Junior was scared to death," Lewis recalled. "He said, 'Jesus, God, we've got to do something! This thing's a disaster!' He thought no one was going to come to see it."[97]

Changes had to be made. The film was booked to play the entire RKO circuit of 175 screens from 21 November so time was short. Over the Halloween weekend a new ending for the picture was planned. Henry would survive the fall from the burning mill and be re-united with his bride. Mae Clarke was recalled from Columbia but Colin Clive was unavailable. He had already left the country by ship, bound for Europe.

The new scene was shot on Tuesday, 3 November. Frederick Kerr returned as the Baron to toast "a son to the House of Frankenstein". Behind him, through a doorway, could be seen Henry, lying in his sickbed, being nursed by Elizabeth. An unidentified actor[xxiv] took Clive's role in the scene. When interviewed later that month Clive was oblivious to the changes. "I think *Frankenstein* has an intense dramatic quality," he said, "that continues throughout the play and culminated when I, in the title role, am killed by the Monster that I have created. This is a rather unusual ending for a talking picture, as the producers generally prefer that the play end happily with the hero and heroine clasped in each other's arms."[98] When he did learn of the changed ending Clive was disappointed. Whale, however, remained reflective. "The semi-happy ending," Whale explained, "was added to remind the audience that after all it is only a tale that is told, and so could easily be twisted any way by the director."[99]

A prologue was also added, delivered by Edward Van Sloan who appears from behind a stage curtain to address the audience:

> How do you do? Mr. Carl Laemmle feels it would be a little unkind to present this picture without just a word of friendly warning. We are about to unfold the story of Frankenstein, a man of science, who sought to create a man after his own image without reckoning upon God. It is one of the strangest tales ever told. It deals with the two great mysteries of creation – life and death. I think it will thrill you. It may even shock you. It might even horrify you. So, if any of you do not care to subject your nerves to such a strain, now's your chance to… Well, we've warned you!

Laemmle Senior, reportedly, also wanted the entire lake scene cut. Whale resisted. "Without it," David Lewis explained, "the audience was left to imagine what he [the Monster] had done to her [Little Maria] before he had drowned her. The implication with the cut was that he had raped her."[100] According to Whale's friend Jack Latham, the scene had already been trimmed prior to the Santa Barbara preview. Originally, bubbles rose from the water as the girl drowned. "It was pretty awful," Latham recalled, "and he [Whale] made the decision to cut it down before the preview."[101]

On Friday, 13 November *Frankenstein* was reviewed and awarded its MPPDA seal. The picture was passed uncut. The following day the *Motion Picture Herald* ran its review. "*Frankenstein* is a thriller, make no mistake," it wrote. "Women come out trembling, men

---

xxiv It has been suggested Clive's stand-in was Robert Livingston (1904-1988). Livingston appeared as Lt. Young in *Mutiny on The Bounty* (1935) and was considered for the lead in the Greta Garbo film *Camille* (1936). He lost out to Robert Taylor.

The iconic Frankenstein Monster. Inset: With James Whale.

exhausted. I don't know what it might do to children, but I know I wouldn't want my kids to see it. And I won't forgive Junior Laemmle or James Whale for permitting the Monster to drown a little girl before my very eyes. That job should come out before the picture is released. It is too dreadfully brutal, no matter what the story calls for. It carries gruesomeness and cruelty just a little beyond reason or necessity.[102]

Frankenstein opened in Detroit, Milwaukee and Seattle on 21 November,[xxv] taking $25,000 in its first week in Detroit and breaking the house record for the Rialto theatre in Seattle. The picture moved on to Kansas City where it again broke house records. Then Minneapolis (where, according to *Variety*, people were fighting to get in) and Boston (breaking a house record by taking $41,200 in its first seven days).

On Friday, 4 December *Frankenstein* opened in New York. The 1,734 seats at the Mayfair Theatre at Broadway and 47th were quickly sold out and within a week the picture had taken almost $54,000. To meet the demand the theatre put on extra showings, selling advance tickets until 2 a.m. In his article for the *New York Times*, Mordaunt Hall wrote:

> It is naturally a morbid, gruesome affair, but it is something to keep the spectator awake, for during its most spine-chilling periods it exacts attention... Boris Karloff undertakes the Frankenstein creature and his make-up can be said to suit anybody's demands. He does not portray a robot but a monster made out of human bodies, and the reason given here for his murderous onslaughts is that Frankenstein's Man Friday stole an abnormal brain after he had broken the glass bowl containing the normal one. This Frankenstein does not know.
>
> No matter what one might say about the melodramatic ideas here, there is no denying that it is far and away the most effective thing of its kind. Beside it *Dracula* is tame...[103]

A December issue of *Exhibitor's Forum* offered theatre owners suggestions on how to promote the picture. "SELLING SEATS: Advertise this as a thrill shocker," it advised. "Every star is a bet. Use large cut-outs of 'The Monster' in your lobby. Arouse public curiosity by stating: 'To have seen *Frankenstein* is to wear a badge of courage.'"[104]

The film played for three weeks at the Mayfair in New York, taking $122,600, before being pulled by Universal to play in other theatres. The *Hollywood Reporter* observed:

> To date, *Frankenstein* has played about nine spots on which we have received reports. In seven of the nine, it has been HELD OVER. In all of the nine it has BROKEN EVERY HOUSE RECORD. At the New York Mayfair Theatre last Saturday it ran up a day's gross in excess of $13,000, establishing a record. Jules Levy, RKO booking head, writes us: "The picture will roll up the greatest gross of the past ten months."[105]

"Not everyone, however, felt enthusiasm for monsterism," Karloff recalled. "Some parent and civic groups felt *Frankenstein* was too horrifying for children to see and should be limited to 'adults only'. The children thought otherwise. On the very first Halloween after the film's release, a crowd of laughing, pint-sized ghosts and goblins rang my doorbell

---

xxv Some early prints of *Frankenstein* were released with a green tint - "The Color of Fear!"

and invited me to join in their trick-or-treat rounds. As I wasn't appropriately costumed, I had to decline. Over the years thousands of children wrote, expressing compassion for the great, weird creature who was so abused by its sadistic keeper that it could only respond to violence with violence. Those children saw beyond the make-up and really understood."[106]

Colin Clive's work in the picture also prompted people to write. One package the actor received contained a 'corpse-reviver'. The device consisted of wires, pipes, pulleys, miniature motors and an electric battery. The accompanying letter read:

> Dear Mr. Clive, - Having seen your picture *Frankenstein* I want you to look over my own invention, similar to the one you use in your picture. It can't make a living man, but if you put the current through the body of a dead mouse it will restore life.[107]

On the evening of Sunday, 6 December 1931 *Frankenstein* had its west coast premiere in Santa Barbara. Once again, the Laemmles and Whale were in attendance. Colin Clive and Mae Clarke had also received invitations. Both had declined. Clive was in England[xxvi] and Clarke was too tired, having contracts with both Universal and Columbia. Once again, Boris Karloff was not invited.

As with previous showings, the audience reaction was extreme with more reports of people walking out. Yet as the people flocked to see the picture they were unaware that, for many, they were viewing an incomplete film. The always contentious lake scene was cut in Massachusetts, Pennsylvania, New York and many other cities and towns with the scene now ending when the Monster reaches for the girl. Likewise, some censor groups cut the creation scene, editing Colin Clive's line, "In the name of God? Now I know what it feels like to *be* God!" Frankenstein's speech now resulted in a jump-cut with the offending dialogue obscured by a clap of thunder.[xxvii] Scenes of Fritz tormenting the Monster with a burning torch were cut, as was a close up of Dr. Waldman injecting the Monster.[xxviii] The censor's scissors were busiest, however, in Kansas City where the State Board of Censors made 32 deletions, citing 'cruelty' as the reason for the cuts. Responding to a request from Junior, Colonel Jason Joy of the MPPDA viewed *Frankenstein* on 11 December and telephoned the Kansas Board, urging them to moderate the number of cuts. Joy's call proved persuasive. The Board acquiesced and reduced the deletions from the original 32 to 10. Reacting to parental complaints, theatres in Virginia stopped admitting children under the age of 14, unless accompanied by an adult. Newspapers in Rhode Island refused to run advertisements for the picture on the grounds that they were "too excessive" and some towns in Massachusetts banned the film outright.

The picture provoked similar reactions further afield. The film was banned in Italy despite being shown at the Venice Film Festival in August 1932.[xxix] Australia, Sweden and Czechoslovakia also refused to show the picture. In England the censors demanded

---

xxvi On the day of the premiere Colin Clive fell from his horse while attempting to jump a gate and fractured a hip.
xxvii In 1937 the stricter Production Code Administration decreed the cuts be removed from the negative prior to re-issue. They remained missing until the film was restored in 1985.
xxviii There is a continuity error in this scene. The drugged Monster collapses and lies on the ground face-up. The next time he is seen the Monster is lying face-down.
xxix The Venice Film festival, *Mostra Internazionale d'Arte Cinematografica*, ran from 6 to 21 August 1932 and was inaugurated by Benito Mussolini at the Lido in Venice. It was the world's first film festival.

the removal of several scenes. Frankenstein's discovery of Fritz's body, the Monster in Elizabeth's bedroom (with its implication of rape) and the killing of Dr. Waldman were all deleted. The lake scene, however, remained intact.[xxx]

It was not until late December that Karloff finally got to see the film. During production he had not been happy with his portrayal and one night, on viewing the day's rushes, told Van Sloan it would ruin his career. Van Sloan disagreed. "Not so, Boris, not so," he replied. "You're made!"[108]

The opportunity to judge his performance came on a trip with his wife to San Francisco to visit one of her school friends. "To our surprise," Karloff recalled, "we found that *Frankenstein*, which we had not yet seen, was playing across the bay in Oakland. What could be more natural than to invite our friend to a performance? I had, of course, seen rushes of the picture, but never a connected version, and as the film progressed I was amazed at the hold it was taking upon the audience. At the same time I couldn't help wondering how my own performance would weather all the build-up. I was soon to know. Suddenly, out of the eerie darkness and gloom, there swept on the screen, about eight sizes larger than life itself, the chilling, horrendous figure of me as the Monster! And, just as suddenly, there crashed out over the general stillness the stage whisper of my wife's friend. Covering her eyes, gripping my wife by the shoulder, she screamed: 'Dot, how can you live with that creature?'"[109]

Frankenstein opened in Los Angeles on 1 January 1932 where it played for four weeks. Paramount's *Dr. Jekyll and Mr. Hyde*, starring Fredric March, was also due for a January release[xxxi] but was rushed out and opened one week before Whale's picture. Regardless, *Frankenstein* broke the house record for the 2,200 seat Orpheum and within a week had taken $25,000.

The *New York Times* listed the picture as number seven in its "ten best" for 1931 and amongst the top hits of the 1931/32 season. In June 1932 *Variety* revealed the foreign and domestic rentals (i.e. the monies returned to the studio by exhibitors) totalled $1,400,000. In 1943 Universal reported that *Frankenstein* had made a profit of $708,871. As Whale biographer James Curtis later pointed out, the estimated $12 million profit often cited stems from a 1953 settlement with John L. Balderston and the heirs of Peggy Webling over their contracted 1% share of the world gross and probably refers to the entire *Frankenstein* film series.[xxxii]

Despite *Frankenstein*'s success Robert Florey's work on the project received little recognition. At Whale's insistence Florey's name had been removed from the credits and appeared only on French posters. For Boris Karloff, it was a different matter entirely. He had given a star-making performance and with his portrayal, and Jack Pierce's make-up, created one of the most instantly recognisable cultural images of the 20th century. "I think the popularity was due to the compassion people felt for him. He was helpless, alone, confused and terrified – how could one not feel sympathy for such a creature?" Karloff later said.[110] "My dear old Monster, I owe everything to him. He's my best friend."[111]

---

xxx Another curious lapse in continuity occurs in this scene, possibly due to pre-release cutting. When the Monster throws Little Maria into the lake, he is standing. The girl hits the water and suddenly the Monster is now on his knees, his body obscuring a view of the drowning girl.

xxxi *Dr. Jekyll and Mr. Hyde* opened in New York on 31 December 1931.

xxxii *Frankenstein* (1931), *Bride of Frankenstein* (1935), *Son of Frankenstein* (1939), *Ghost of Frankenstein* (1942), *Frankenstein Meets the Wolfman* (1943), *House of Frankenstein* (1944), *House of Dracula* (1945) and *Abbott and Costello Meet Frankenstein* (1948).

1950's re-release poster for *The Mummy* (1932).

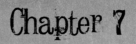

Chapter 7

After Frankenstein

(1931-1933)

"I always hope to play strange, unusual characters... They have always interested me. One day I hope to appear on screen as Shakespeare's Caliban."[1]
Boris Karloff (1933)

In the seven weeks between the completion of his work on *Frankenstein* and the picture's release in November 1931 Karloff remained busy. The role of a bootlegger, Tony Ricca, in *The Guilty Generation*, a gangster film loosely based on Shakespeare's *Romeo and Juliet*, took him to Columbia Pictures. The *Los Angeles Times* found Karloff "acceptably pleasant as the suitor".[2]

Then it was off to United Artists to play a waiter in *Tonight or Never*, a Mervyn LeRoy directed comedy starring Gloria Swanson and Melvyn Douglas. Returning to Columbia in November, Karloff appeared in *Behind the Mask* as Jim Henderson, part of a drug smuggling operation. The film's criminal mastermind, Mr. X, was played by Karloff's *Frankenstein* co-star Edward Van Sloan.

Following the success of *Frankenstein* the studio decided to capitalise on the Monster's success. "...My agent called one morning," Karloff explained, "and said, 'Boris, Universal wants you under contract.' I thought, *Maybe for once I'll know where my breakfast is coming from, after more than 20 years of acting.*"[3] The two year contract stated he would get $750 a week for the first year, with a $250 increase at the end of that period, followed by another $250 increase at the end of 18 months. The document was signed on 2 December 1931.

However, with the new contract came a problem. Universal had nothing suitable for Karloff to star in. A number of properties were considered including a remake of *The Hunchback of Notre Dame*, an adaptation of Robert Louis Stevenson's story *The Suicide Club*, and an unscripted project called *The Wolf Man*, to co-star Bela Lugosi.[i] The rights to

---

i The picture was eventually made in 1935 as *Werewolf of London* with Henry Hull playing Dr. Wilfred Glendon, the role originally intended for Karloff. Warner Oland played Lugosi's role of Dr. Yogami.

Left: Lobby card for *Behind the Mask* (1932).
Right: *The Miracle Man* (1932).

H.G. Wells' *The Invisible Man* had also been purchased in September 1931 as a follow up to *Frankenstein*, but the technicalities of the project meant it could not be completed quickly. So, with no horror pictures to star in, Karloff was given an uncredited cameo appearance in the comedy *The Cohens and Kellys in Hollywood*. He then played an autopsy surgeon in the medical drama *Alias the Doctor*, starring Richard Barthelmess. The *New York Times* commented that Karloff's character in the picture was a man "who seems to be disappointed when an operation is successful. His presence sometimes is obviously symbolic of death or the shadow of death."[4] Karloff did not appear, however, in the British version of the movie. Unhappy at the 'gruesome' nature of his character, the British censor ordered the offending sequences be removed. Unable to recall Karloff for re-shoots, he was replaced by Nigel Du Brulier.

In August, Karloff went to Fox to play a sheikh in the Will Rogers comedy *Business and Pleasure*, travelling in from his new house at 9936 Toluca Lake Avenue in Hollywood. Months later, at 8:30 p.m. on 3 January 1932, Karloff made his first appearance on radio, a medium he would grace for almost four decades. In addition to Karloff, the show, *California Melodies*, featured actor Ken Murray, the Hallelujah Quartet and soloist Vera Van.

He was then loaned to Paramount for his next picture, a remake of the 1919 *The Miracle Man*. Instead of being cast in the logical role of Frog – as played in the original by Lon Chaney – Karloff played a crook named Nikko.

When he returned to Universal in March 1932 *The Invisible Man* was still being mentioned. *Frankenstein* director James Whale had been attached to the project late in 1931 but passed when he was offered *The Road Back*,[ii] the sequel to Universal's 1930 hit picture *All Quiet on the Western Front*. With Whale now seemingly off the picture *The Invisible Man* passed, albeit briefly, into the hands of Robert Florey.[iii] With no timetable for the production of Wells' tale, Karloff was instead put in *Night World*, a drama set around a nightclub. *Film Weekly* commented, "The boyish charm of Lew Ayres imparts some

---

ii *The Road Back* was shelved in November 1932. Whale finally directed the picture in 1937 although, following completion, the picture was taken from his hands. To placate German sensibilities some scenes were cut and new ones, directed by Edward Sloman, were added.
iii As on an early version of *Frankenstein*, Florey collaborated on a screenplay for *The Invisible Man* with Garrett Fort, submitting a script on 9 April 1932. Universal dispensed with Florey's services a week later.

Karloff and Lugosi.

interest to our hero, and Boris Karloff gives a powerful study of a night-club proprietor. The vividly staged nightclub background gives opportunity for some clever dancing,[iv] and there is any amount of noisy gunplay."[5] Receiving third billing behind Lew Ayres and *Frankenstein* co-star, Mae Clarke, Karloff played the club's owner, 'Happy' MacDonald.

Night World (1932).

"NIGHT WORLD" *A Universal Production* ———

Karloff's next film was to be *The Old Dark House*, an adaptation of J.B. Priestley's novel, to be directed by James Whale. It is believed the picture had its origins in the latter half of 1931 when, during a trip to England, Carl Laemmle Sr. met James Whale's old acquaintance – the playwright Benn W. Levy. Having been impressed by Levy's work on the script for *Waterloo Bridge*, Laemmle invited him to Universal to write the screen adaptation of *The Invisible Man*. Levy left for America on the *S.S. Bremen*. He arrived in New York on 25 October 1931 and made his way to Universal City. Unfortunately, Laemmle had neglected to tell anyone at the studio of Levy's appointment. He was therefore loaned to Paramount where he was put to work writing the screenplay for *The Devil and the Deep* (1932). When the script was completed Levy returned to Universal to work on *The Old Dark House* and completed the screenplay in early March 1932.

Priestley's novel *Benighted* was published by William Heinemann Ltd. in 1927. "Written late at night, [*Benighted*] was an attempt, familiar enough now but unusual then in the Twenties, to transmute the thriller into symbolical fiction with some psychological depth," Priestley explained. "I don't think I succeeded in this, though the tale itself was readable and sufficiently engrossing. There was none of this fancy work in America, where my publishers [Harpers], calling it *The Old Dark House*, handled it as a thriller and sold about 20,000 copies."[6]

Despite the novel's popularity Priestley had not been enthused by the prospect of adaptation. "I refused many applications to dramatise it," he said, "believing that the queer inmates of that house would shrivel under the spotlights..."[7] Despite his initial misgivings the author finally agreed to an adaptation and the rights to the book were purchased for $12,500 on 6 January 1932. According to David Lewis, they were bought specifically for James Whale. Whale was an admirer of Paul Leni's 1927 silent picture *The Cat and the Canary* with its mix of comedy and horror, and wanted to direct a picture in a similar vein.

Karloff was to play Morgan, the brutish mute butler of the novel, described by Priestley as both a 'giant troll' and 'a tongueless hulk'. The butler is introduced in the novel, as he would be in the film, when he first opens the door to the sodden travellers. "The door opened an inch or two, and Penderel saw an eye," Priestley wrote. "There was no talking to an eye so he waited. The eye withdrew and then the door was slowly pulled back. A huge lump of a man stood there, blankly staring at him; a shapeless man with a full black beard and matted hair over a low forehead. For a minute Penderel himself was all eyes and no tongue, staring blankly back. Then he recovered himself and rapidly plunged into speech."[8]

---

iv The picture's choreography was by Busby Berkeley.

Left: Herald for *The Old Dark House* (1932). Above: Early, unused makeup for *The Old Dark House* (1932).

In addition to Karloff, who would receive top billing for the first time, Whale collected together a cast of, primarily, English actors,[v] many of whom he had already worked with during his time in the theatre. Colin Clive was initially announced for the lead role of Penderel but was committed to filming *Lily Christine* in England. He was replaced by Melvyn Douglas. Both Douglas and Raymond Massey joined the cast when their picture *Adventure Lady* was postponed. Gloria Stuart took the role of Margaret Waverton, Massey's wife and the object of Morgan's unwanted attentions. Lillian Bond was cast as chorus girl Gladys Du Cane and Whale's old friend, Ernest Thesiger, joined the cast following his role, alongside Basil Rathbone, in Benn Levy's play, *The Devil Passes*, at New York's Selwyn Theatre. Thesiger would play Horace Femm in Whale's picture, a character described by Priestley as "a man so thin, with so little flesh and so much shining bone... he was almost a skeleton."[9] For the role of Horace's sister, Rebecca Femm, Whale cast 62-year-old Eva Moore. Moore was in Los Angeles visiting her daughter, the actress Jill Esmond (then married to Laurence Olivier), when she received the offer of the role.

For the role of insane sibling Saul Femm, Whale requested Brember Wills, an actor Whale had worked with in 1929.[vi] In casting Wills, Whale departed from Priestley's description of the mad pyromaniac. In the book Saul was described as a "much older man than Penderel, but he was also much bigger and heavier and seemed to be unusually powerful."[10] Whale made Saul a small, nervous and seemingly harmless man. Whale's quirkiest piece of casting, however, was reserved for the role of 102-year-old Sir Roderick Femm, the bedridden head of the household.[vii] Billed as John Dudgeon, the identity of the actor remained a mystery for many years. "Jimmy couldn't find a male actor who looked old enough to suit him," revealed David Lewis, "so he finally used an old stage actress he knew called Elspeth Dudgeon. She looked a thousand."[11]

---

v Of the cast Douglas, Stuart and Wills were American. Massey was Canadian.
vi Wills had appeared in two 1929 theatre productions designed by Whale: *The Mock Emperor* and *Mafro, Darling*.
vii In Priestley's novel, Sir Roderick is not the father, but the eldest of the Femm brothers.

Dudgeon's identity was also kept from the cast as Stuart recalled. "He mentioned the fact that there was an old man up in the attic that was going to come down at the end of the picture," she said. "Well, I wasn't terribly impressed because there were always people coming down who were strange. But the last day… when she was finally disrobed, shall we say, and the wig came off and everything, and James said, 'This is Elspeth Dudgeon', everybody went 'Oh, James! What a wonderful idea – what a great joke!' He was very happy with it."[12]

Charles Laughton joined the cast when his picture at Paramount, *The Devil and the Deep*, ran into difficulties. Laughton had been cast as Tallulah Bankhead's jealous husband, the submarine commander Charles Sturm, after being suggested for the role by his friend, Benn Levy. Laughton and his wife, actress Elsa Lanchester, arrived in California in late March and that night dined with old acquaintance[viii] James Whale and his companion, David Lewis. "We met him for supper at the Brown Derby the first night we arrived in Hollywood…" Lanchester recalled. "James said that night, 'You'll like it here, Charles – I'm pouring the money from my hair!'"[13]

When *The Devil and the Deep*'s star, Tallulah Bankhead, fell ill production was postponed. Paramount therefore agreed to loan Laughton to play Sir William Porterhouse in Whale's picture on condition *The Old Dark House* would only be released after *The Devil and the Deep*.

Filming on *The Old Dark House* began in the week of 18 April 1932. For Douglas, Massey and Stuart their first scenes in the picture were an ordeal to shoot. The travellers, lost in a storm, drive through the Welsh countryside in search of shelter before coming upon the home of the peculiar Femm family. "We had wind machines, rain machines, it was cold, it was windy… we were wet," Stuart said. "It was an all night shoot and it was my introduction to James Whale's meticulous direction."[14] Douglas and Massey were not happy. "They complained a lot all evening about the conditions," Stuart recalled. "It being my first location shoot and my second movie, I thought it was wonderful. I thought it was such fun and I really enjoyed it."[15]

Fortunately for the cast, the majority of the film was shot inside the Femm household, a set on a Universal soundstage. "There were no fun and games on that set, like there were on many, many, many sets," Stuart said. "The scene was rehearsed, the cameras were set, the scene was shot. It was a very tight company."[16]

Shooting was broken twice daily by a ritual of tea breaks. "The first morning at 11 o'clock the commissary sent over a lot of trays of tea and, I guess, crumpets," Stuart explained. "I was never asked to observe them, or have them – and the whole English contingent, with the exception of Melvyn Douglas and me, were asked to have tea. So they had elevenses that morning and Melvyn and I sat off by ourselves and the British contingent sat by themselves with James. And then later in the afternoon at 4 o'clock the commissary sent over more tea and they had fourses – and Melvyn and I sat by ourselves and talked… and this went on every single day and we were never, never, never asked to have tea with the rest of the actors."[17]

Whale's relationship to his countrymen was somewhat different. "The English were very respectful of James," Stuart recalled, "and did precisely what he wanted them

---

viii Laughton and Whale had appeared together on stage in the 1928 production of Benn W. Levy's stage adaptation of Hugh Walpole's *A Man with Red Hair*. Whale played Laughton's son, Herrick Crispin, in the production, which opened on 27 February 1928 at the Little Theatre in London and ran for 79 performances.

to."[18] Thesiger, in particular, took benefit from Whale's suggestions. "The two of them loved creating bits of business," said Stuart, "such as the throwing the flowers from the vase into the fireplace... sniffing the gin, the way he held his hands... in a cathedral sort of way... James directed everything – how you dressed, how you walked, how you moved, how you talked, whether you picked the line up fast or let it go for a minute – and Thesiger, being an actor's actor, got it very fast. They were wonderful together."[19]

Although the majority of Thesiger's dialogue was lifted from Priestley's book the Whale/Thesiger collaboration provided the picture with its wittier moments. "He and James seemed to enjoy reading," said Stuart. "I remember several times Thesiger saying 'How does it sound this way?' or 'Would you like it this way?' Or James saying 'I think, Ernest, that you should give a little more emphasis here.'"[20] It was an amiable partnership as Stuart observed. "I would say that the two of them enjoyed each other very, very much during the entire film," she said.[21]

Charles Laughton required a different approach. Plagued by self-doubt he had difficulties with the acting process that would remain with him his entire life. Alfred Hitchcock, who later directed Laughton in *Jamaica Inn* (1939), recalled, "Charles was a very charming man – very nice and also very troubled. He had great, great difficulty in getting into the role. He took everything so seriously – it would somehow get almost exasperating."[22]

Although Laughton had appeared in a few pictures and shorts in England *The Old Dark House* was his first for an American studio. "Charles was very pleased to get the camera experience for the larger parts to come," Elsa Lanchester said. "He knew he had to bridge a large technical gap in one giant stride."[23]

Laughton's character, Sir William, and chorus girl Du Cane make their entrance just under a third of the way into the picture when they come in out of the storm. "Before this scene was shot he was running up and down the sound stage," recalled Gloria Stuart, "and I said to James, 'What's he doing?' He said, 'He's running up and down to get out of breath.' I said, 'James, I can be out of breath without running up and down.' And he just turned and walked away from me. This was Method acting which I had not heard of and was not used to, and his turning and walking away from me was a real rebuff."[24]

Boris Karloff, meanwhile, remained relatively in the background. To Whale's chagrin he had received most of the credit for *Frankenstein*'s success. As a result Whale believed the picture's reception had changed the star, as he told his friend Curtis Harrington. "He said Karloff was very amusing and amused," explained Harrington. "He didn't take himself too seriously. Then when he suddenly became a big star because of *Frankenstein* and became the king of horror films, he began to take himself very seriously."[25] Whale found ways to express his annoyance as Elsa Lanchester witnessed. "There was a thing in which James Whale was rather nasty," she explained. "He was very derogatory about Boris Karloff; he'd say, 'Oh, he was a *truck driver*.' Maybe in the early days, he had to do some hard work, but Boris Karloff was a well-educated, very gentle, nice man."[26]

Despite his attitude towards Karloff, Whale's irritation did not reveal itself on set. "I understand that Boris and James were not great friends at that point," said Stuart. "I didn't know that. I was not aware of it and I don't think that anyone in the cast was aware of it. I think maybe Karloff was aware of it. I think that James gave him his due. I think that James wanted him in every scene that he was written into and larger than life, and giving a great performance. I never had the feeling that there was any difficulty at all between James and any of the cast. I heard later that Karloff and he were not friendly but it was not apparent at all and I was on the set almost every day."[27] Unlike Whale, Stuart had nothing but admiration for her co-star. "Boris was so gentle, so soft spoken, such a gentleman," she said. "Never raised his voice, was as charming and considerate an actor as you could possibly work with. He was the antithesis of this 'Morgan' person."[28]

To prepare for Morgan's drunken pursuit of Mrs. Waverton, Whale required Stuart's character, somewhat incongruously, to change her clothes. Stuart was confused by Whale's choice of attire. "James had me change into a Jean Harlow-style, bias-cut, pale pink velvet gown with spaghetti straps and earrings and pearls, as I recall," Stuart explained. "And I said, 'Why me, James? Nobody else is changing. Why am I changing?' He said, 'Because Boris is going to chase you up and down the corridors, up and down the stairs, and I want you to appear as a white flame.' So, all right, I put on the dress… and Boris chased me up and down the corridors, and I was a white flame. It was strictly a matter of camera and style. There was no legitimate reason for me being in that dress. Lillian Bond didn't have to change, and she came in very wet. But Karloff didn't chase her."[29]

Production ended towards the end of May and following two weeks of editing the picture was ready for exhibition. On 24 June MPPDA representatives Jason Joy, Lamar Trotti and James B.M. Fisher arrived at Universal for a screening of the picture. The following day Joy penned a letter to Laemmle Junior. "Mr. Whale," he wrote, "as well as the members of the cast, are to be congratulated on the excellence of their work. We, ourselves, enjoyed the picture thoroughly and wish you every success with it."[30]

The Old Dark House previewed in early July but the *Hollywood Filmograph* was not impressed, calling it a "somewhat inane picture…"[31] Following the preview Whale re-called Melvyn Douglas and Lillian Bond to appear in an additional scene. Originally the picture ended after Massey and Stuart leave in the morning to fetch an ambulance for the injured Penderel.[ix] Thesiger waves them off then re-enters the house. This ending, however, left elements of the plot unresolved. Would Penderel live and, if so, would his romance with Du Cane blossom? The new final scene, where Penderel awakens and proposes marriage to Du Cane, was possibly written by R.C. Sherriff[x] who later revealed he was consulted for spur of the moment dialogue changes.

After *The Devil and the Deep* was released in August 1932 the way was clear for the release of Whale's picture. *The Old Dark House* opened on Thursday, 20 October and included a pre-title card:

> PRODUCERS NOTE: - Karloff, the mad butler in this production, is the same Karloff who created the part of the mechanical monster in "Frankenstein." We explain this to settle all disputes in advance, even though such disputes are a tribute to his great versatility.

However, the main credits (like some advertisements) curiously misspelt the author's name, crediting the novel to J.B. *Priestly*.

The Old Dark House was booked for a three week run at the Rialto theatre in New York where it opened on 27 October 1932, taking $24,500 in its first week. Mordaunt

---

ix Although Levy's script adhered closely to Priestley's novel Whale changed the ending so that Penderel, who is killed in the novel as a result of his fight with the madman Saul, survives.

x By the time the additional dialogue was written Levy had returned to England.

Hall of the *New York Times* liked the picture. "This current thriller," he wrote, "like *Frankenstein*, had the advantage of being directed by James Whale, who again proves his ability in this direction… [Charles Laughton] gives a splendid portrayal. Raymond Massey makes the most of the role of Waverton. Gloria Stuart is both clever and charming as Mrs. Waverton… Mr. Thesiger is very capable as Horace Femm and Eva Moore is distinctly fearsome as Rebecca Femm. Brember Wills, an English actor, went to Hollywood solely to act Saul Femm and his performance causes one to consider that his long journey was well worthwhile to the picture. Mr. Karloff is, of course, thoroughly in his element as Morgan. He leaves no stone unturned to make this character thoroughly disturbing."[32] Despite good reviews *Variety* reported the picture's takings were down to $13,600 in the second week and dropped to $6,200 for the third. It fared little better elsewhere. At the 3,000-seat RKO Hillstreet in Los Angeles it took a paltry $4,000 in a week.

The picture found a more appreciative audience, however, in England where it broke the house records at the Capitol Theatre in London. "Like most of its type," *Picturegoer* wrote, "this eerie thriller is somewhat vague and incredible and wholly fantastic; but there is this difference – it is exceedingly cleverly acted and characterised and the direction is quite brilliant."[33]

The picture was later re-issued in 1939 with minor cuts. Universal's rights to the picture lapsed in 1957 and within a decade *The Old Dark House* had disappeared and was presumed lost. In 1968, following a concerted effort by James Whale's friend Curtis Harrington, the original negative and a lavender protection print was discovered in Universal's vaults in New York. "They had analysed the first reel and it could not be printed, it was already decaying. So that meant that a new dupe negative had to be made of the first reel. Well, so far so good except for the fact Universal had no interest whatsoever in paying for this restoration of the film."[34] Fortunately, Eastman House offered to pay for the work.

Curtis Harrington was later able to pass on the good news personally to Karloff. "I only met him once," said Harrington. "I didn't

With Elsie the Borden cow.

know him though. I can say that after I rescued *The Old Dark House* one day I was on the Universal lot. I found out that Karloff was playing a guest role on a TV series. So I just went on the set and introduced myself to him and told him that the film had been saved. I think he was pleased."[35]

A two-month break from filming followed Karloff's work on *The Old Dark House*. He spent time tending his garden and menagerie which within a few years would grow to include Buff Orpington chickens, ducks (both named Donald), turkeys, a cow named Elsie, and a Poland China sow named Violet, a joke gift from a banker friend. Violet, presented to the Karloffs when she was very young, had a ravenous appetite and gained a pound and a half a day until she weighed nearly a quarter of a ton. Her eating habits were so rapacious that, in 1936, the Karloffs were later forced to part with their porcine pet.

The Karloffs also kept more traditional pets. They originally owned a single Bedlington terrier (named Silver), at that time one of only three in the United States. "It is a new breed of dog," the *Washington Post* revealed, "evidently obtained by crossing a Simmons with an Ostermoor, or something!"[36] By 1936 they owned four Bedlingtons (three white and one mouse grey – two of which were named Agnus Dei and Silly Bitch), two Scottish terriers and a tortoise named Lightning Bill. Karloff had trained the terriers from pups and when they were stricken with the potentially fatal disease distemper their master nursed them night and day. However, neither medicine nor a special diet helped. Karloff, therefore, decided to concoct his own regimen and added a generous shot of Scotch whisky to their medicine. He eventually used up his last two bottles but the dogs did improve and, as a tribute to the cure, he renamed his pets Whiskey and Soda.

At the weekends Karloff indulged in his sporting passion of cricket. In 1934 he wrote:

> My own cricket history goes back to 1919 in Los Angeles, but the game was struggling along under adverse conditions, lack of suitable grounds being the principal drawback. It was only due to the tenaciousness of such enthusiasts as Ernest Wright of Los Angeles and two great sportsmen who have since passed on, Sam Milbourne and Pat Higgins of the old Overseas Club, that the game staggered on at all.
>
> Then, about 1931, a change came over the spirit of the dream. A promising young cricketer named C. Aubrey Smith, better known as "Round the Corner" Smith, came to Hollywood, and today, thanks to his untiring efforts, the game is on a firm footing for the first time. Aubrey found us playing on rough fields under dangerous conditions. He at once went to see Mr. Moore at UCLA Westwood, who with extraordinary generosity gave us the use of the campus for our Saturday and Sunday games, with the single proviso that we try to get the lads at the school interested in the game. It was a long, uphill pull: a few of them came, looked, sniffed and departed. But little by little the idea took hold, until this year, aided by Peter Kinnell and Eugene Walsh, the latter a brilliant cricketer from South Africa, and also students at the University, Aubrey has been able to keep his word to the school, and any Tuesday or Thursday he may he found enthusiastically coaching 20 or 30 youngsters at the nets.[37]

The club played every Sunday and, for a time, Karloff could be seen driving his Ford with 'Hollywood Cricket Club' emblazoned on the car's spare tyre cover. "We'd have a tremendously long season," Karloff explained. "About five months!"[38] Among the club's membership were some of the star's fellow actors. "Nigel Bruce played with us," he said. "Basil Rathbone played, H.B. Warner played. Not a great many actors played.[xi] That's about it I think. Oh, but there were an awful lot of people there who, when they heard there was cricket, would turn into aged enthusiasts."[39]

Although many of his colleagues were British, Karloff dismissed any charges of nationalism. "I don't know that there really was a British Colony," he later said. "I think that was an American phrase... there's a lot of English actors out there. But I had friends

xi Clive Brook, Ronald Colman, Claude King, Noel Madison and R.C. Sherriff (when in Hollywood) also played, while Vivien Leigh and Merle Oberon were often spectators. Later Cary Grant, Errol Flynn and David Niven also became members of the club.

English, I had friends American. You don't cling together quite as tight as it used to be... or at least I hope not. It would be far too provincial."[40]

Eugene Walsh later recalled Karloff's commitment to the game, which extended beyond the weekly match days. "He spent much of his spare time teaching students at UCLA how to play cricket... He was not a great bat or bowler himself, but he was an excellent coach," Walsh said. "He had a very wide knowledge of the game, and I remember many times we sat up to the early hours of the morning discussing cricket. In my opinion, Boris was one of the greatest ambassadors that England had in California."[41]

In August 1932 Karloff was loaned to MGM to play Sax Rohmer's Chinese villain, Dr. Fu Manchu. Rohmer had introduced the character of the evil scientist in the 1912 short story *The Zayat Kiss* and some of the stories had been filmed before. Harry Agar Lyons had appeared in two serials, 1923's *The Mystery of Fu Manchu* (comprising 15 episodes) and the 18 episode *The Further Mysteries of Fu Manchu*, the following year. Warner Oland had also played the 'Yellow Peril' in three films for Paramount: *The Mysterious Dr. Fu Manchu* in 1929, *The Return of Dr. Fu Manchu* (1930) and *Daughter of the Dragon* the following year. This story was also serialised in 12 parts on American radio in *The Collier Hour* between 9 March and 25 May 1930. Arthur Hughes played Fu Manchu on the show, which was created to promote the magazine *Collier's Weekly*. CBS also produced a series of half-hour radio programmes entitled *Fu Manchu* starring John C. Daly, broadcast between 26 September 1932 and 24 April 1933.

Karloff was to star in an adaptation of the novel *The Mask of Fu Manchu*,[xii] first serialised in 12 parts in *Collier's Weekly* between 7 May and 23 July 1932. Joining Karloff would be Lewis Stone as Fu Manchu's archenemy, Nayland Smith, Lawrence Grant as Sir Lionel Barton, Karen Morley as Sir Lionel's daughter, Sheila, and Charles Starrett as Sheila's fiancé Terence Granville. Myrna Loy was also cast in the last of her many 'oriental' roles as Manchu's daughter, the 'sadistic nymphomaniac',[42] Fah Lo See.

The Mask of Fu Manchu (later published by Doubleday in October 1932) concerned Manchu's search for the tomb of Genghis Khan and the sword and mask that where contained within. Sir Lionel Barton leads a British expedition in an attempt to beat the Chinaman to the tomb for, as Sir Lionel explains, "If Fu Manchu wears that mask across his wicked eyes, puts that scimitar into his bony, cruel hands, all Asia arises!"

It was to be a troubled production. Even prior to shooting there were problems. "It was a shambles," Karloff recalled. "It really was. It was simply ridiculous. I shall never forget, for about a week before we got started, I kept asking for a script. I was met with roars of laughter at the idea that there would be a script."[43]

On Saturday, 6 August Karloff reported to make-up for the first day of filming. During the next few hours the make-up artist, Cecil Holland, went to work, transforming Karloff into the Chinese megalomaniac. Karloff's ears and nose was reshaped, and his eyebrows were painted. Oriental eyepieces were applied and thin shell teeth covered his own. "I could not use any of the many types of false teeth which were such potent parts of disguises in silent days," Karloff said. "Lon Chaney once told me speech had made impossible about 50 of his best make-up devices."[44] To finish the effect long fingernails were applied and a moustache was added. Curiously, although Fu Manchu's long moustache became his trademark, in the novels the Chinaman was clean-shaven.

xii The mask in the film was based on the original illustrations in *Collier's*, designed by the artist and mask-maker, W.T. Benda.

Yet as Karloff sat in the make-up chair for the two and a half-hour application process the problems with the script continued. "On the morning we were to start shooting," Karloff explained, "I went into the make-up shop and worked there for about a couple of hours, getting this extremely bad make-up on... And, as I was in the make-up chair, a gentleman came in and handed me about four sheets of paper, which was one enormous, long speech. That was to be the opening shot in the film and I was seeing it for the first time, then and there. And it was written in the most impeccable English. And I said, 'This is absolute nonsense. I can't learn this in time...' He said, 'Oh, it will be all right.' So I got my make-up on and, on my way from the make-up shop to the stage, I'm intercepted by somebody else who took those pages away from me and gave me some others that were written in pidgin English!... This was happening all through the film."[45]

Above: With Myrna Loy in *The Mask of Fu Manchu* (1932). Below: Karloff, Myrna Loy and director Charles Brabin on the set of *The Mask of Fu Manchu* (1932)

Things did not improve. Within weeks both the director Charles Vidor and screenwriter Courtenay Terret were replaced. Charles Brabin, who had been removed from the equally troubled *Rasputin and the Empress* (1932), was given directorial duties and new writers Irene Kuhn, Edgar Allan Woolf and John Willard were appointed.

Production restarted on 3 September. Yet even with a new team of writers the problems with the script continued. "Some scenes were written in beautiful Oxford English, and others were written in God knows what!"[46] Karloff said. Such was the chaotic nature of the project that within Hollywood the picture was dubbed *The Mess of Fu Manchu*.

Despite the films troubles at least one incident during filming caused some amusement, as Charles Starrett recalled. "Boris was a subtle, good-humoured man," he said, "an actor's actor – a most adaptable man – he could think himself into any part. Never blew a line – except once – in *Mask*. I, the hero, was lying face down strapped down to a table; he as Fu Manchu was about to do me in by injecting a hypodermic needle into the back of my neck – we couldn't get it right – it never looked like the real thing – so the director, I think it was Charles Brabin, suddenly yelled, 'I've got it!' He sent to the commissary for four especially baked potatoes – he tucked one of them into the collar of my shirt and said to Boris, 'Go ahead – jab it in – you can't hurt him – it will only go into the potato.' We started the scene, Boris plunged the needle into (allegedly) my neck – the potato exploded with a great pop, got all over Boris and all over me. The two of us couldn't stop laughing – we went through three more takes, using up the rest of the potatoes with the same results until we were hysterical. Finally,

As Dr. Fu Manchu.

the director said 'You two just go home – you're no use – we'll shoot it in the morning.'"[47] Another interruption occurred when Don Bradman and the Australian Cricket Team, then on a North American tour, visited the production and posed for photographs with Brabin and members of the cast.[xiii] *The Mask of Fu Manchu* wrapped on 21 October with a final cost of $327,627.

Opening on 5 November the picture garnered generally lacklustre reviews. "Everybody is handicapped by the story and situations," wrote *Variety*. "It's strange how bad such troupers as Stone and Jean Hersholt can look when up against such an assignment as this."[48]

---

xiii The Australian cricket team arrived in Vancouver on 16 June 1932 and embarked on a 75-day private tour of Canada and the USA. They arrived in Hollywood in late August and toured the film sets meeting, amongst others, Clark Gable and Jean Harlow on the set of *Red Dust*. The team also played – and beat – the Hollywood Cricket Club's team, which included C. Aubrey Smith, Leslie Howard and wicketkeeper Boris Karloff.

The picture opened at the Capitol in New York on 1 December. "And still the cinema goes busily about its task of terrorising the children," wrote the *New York Times*. "The latest of the bugaboo symposium arrived at the Capitol yesterday under the fairly reticent title of *The Mask of Fu Manchu*. Its properties include Boris Karloff, one well-equipped dungeon, several hundred Chinamen, and the proper machinery for persuading a large cast to divulge the location of the mask and sword of the late Genghis Khan. To accomplish all, Fu must acquire the Khan's sacred paraphernalia… It is Scotland Yard's intention to frustrate Fu if it takes all winter – and at the Capitol the new film does manage to create the unhappy impression that it is taking at least that long."[49]

By 10 December the picture had taken over $40,000 at the Capitol. However by Christmas *The Mask of Fu Manchu* was, according to *Variety*, performing 'just fairly' having taken $7,000 at the 2,000-seat Broadway Theatre. The picture eventually went on to recoup its costs and made a profit of $62,000.

Years later Myrna Loy saw the picture again. "It astonished me how good Karloff and I were," she remarked. "Everyone else just tossed it off as something that didn't matter, while Boris and I brought some feeling and humour to those comic-book characters. Boris was a fine actor, a professional who never condescended to his often unworthy material."[50]

While Karloff worked on pictures for other studios Universal was preparing a suitable vehicle of their own. Writer and journalist Nina Wilcox Putnam was asked to provide a story that could be used as the basis for a screenplay. In early February 1932 she wrote a nine-page treatment entitled *Cagliastro*. Universal's scenario editor, Richard Schayer, joined Putnam to develop the piece and they submitted a story, dated 19 February.

Putnam's story concerned the machinations of a 4,000-year-old Egyptian priest who, staying alive by the injection of nitrates, had spent the ages destroying all women who resembled the ancient love that had betrayed him. In 18th century Paris he was Count Cagliastro, the popular medium and healer. Living as Doctor Astro in contemporary San Francisco he poses as a blind spiritualist and commits robbery and murder using a surveillance system and death ray before he is discovered and destroyed.

To work on the script Universal engaged John L. Balderston. Although Balderston had previously supplied adaptations of *Dracula* and *Frankenstein*, which were used as the basis for the hit pictures, this was to be his first screenplay. Arriving in Hollywood at the end of March he submitted an incomplete script, dated 30 June. A complete draft followed, dated 13 July. Balderston completed five more versions throughout August and September initially using the title *King of the Dead* but by the time he submitted his final screenplay (dated 12 September), the story had been re-titled *Im-Ho-Tep*.

The finished screenplay differed significantly from Putnam's original story. Balderston, a keen amateur historian who had covered the opening of King Tutankhamun's tomb in November 1922[xiv] while working for the *New York World*, changed the story's location from San Francisco to Egypt and drew on elements from his *Dracula* adaptation. He even considered having the Mummy return regularly to his mummy case, much like Dracula's need to return to his coffin, but abandoned the idea.

In late September 1932, while *The Mask of Fu Manchu* was still in production, Karloff returned to Universal for *The Mummy*. Also joining the cast were Karloff's *Frankenstein* co-star Edward Van Sloan as Dr. Muller, Arthur Byron as Sir Joseph Whemple, and David

xiv The burial chamber was finally cleared of its treasures in November 1930, eight years after the discovery of the tomb.

Manners as Sir Joseph's son, Frank. In his later years Manners, then aged 97, recalled working with Karloff. "Very grand," Manners said of the star, "but so withdrawn. But he was always polite. A gentleman."[51]

Although Balderston had initially suggested casting Katherine Hepburn in the role of Helen Grosvenor (the re-incarnation of Princess Anck-es-en-Amon) the part went to the 28-year-old Austro-Hungarian born Broadway actress, Zita Johann.

Johann had been under contract with MGM where she was afforded script approval rights. However, after turning down two scripts, she was dropped by the studio and so returned to the stage. Following a stint at RKO (who loaned her to Warner Brothers for the 1932 Edward G. Robinson picture *Tiger Shark*), Johann signed with Universal to appear in the John Huston scripted *Laughing Boy*. "All I did was just a test with actors for the lead – but they couldn't find a Laughing Boy! Humphrey Bogart wasn't a star then, but I called him up and I said, 'Would you mind very much if I suggested you for *Laughing Boy*?' And he said, 'Oh please do.' But the film was never made. I felt that I owed Universal something – you know, they paid me for *Laughing Boy*, but I didn't make the picture – so they wanted me for *The Mummy*."[52]

To direct the picture Universal assigned noted German cinematographer Karl Freund. Freund had previously shot Universal's *Dracula* (1931) and *Murders in the Rue Morgue* (1932), as well as Fritz Lang's *Metropolis* (1927), but *The Mummy* was his directorial debut, having been promoted on 29 August. The choice, however, was not a happy one for Zita Johann. "Well, the director [Freund] needed somebody he could blame, you know," she explained. "He needed to be able to say 'I can't take it with her', so that, if he was running late with the production he could say 'Well, it's her fault – she's so temperamental', you see. On the first day of shooting *The Mummy*, Freund said that I would have to appear nude from the waist up. Well, he expected me to have a fit… but I said 'Well, that's okay with me, if you can get it past the censors.' So, since that stunt didn't work, he pulled all kinds of little tricks. You know how actors have their own chairs to sit in, but I didn't have one with my name on it, you see. So Sascha, my driver, said 'I will get one for you, Miss Johann, and I will have your name on it in Russian.' I should have let him do that. I regret now that I didn't, but at the time I didn't want to draw attention to myself."[53]

Freund's antagonistic behaviour continued throughout the production. "We worked a lot of long hours," Johann said. "There were no 12-hour days like we were supposed to have, and Freund was riding me very hard. For instance, I didn't have a chair like they usually had on sets – I had to stand for two days upright, all day long, because he didn't want a crease in my skirt. The scene he was concerned with was a long shot, and it would have taken me two minutes to put on the skirt when he was ready for the shot. Instead, I had to stand around. By the last Saturday night of the shooting, I was very exhausted…"[54]

Johann was more fortunate, though, in the choice of co-star. "Karloff was really, truly a great gentleman," said Johann. "He minded his own business and was very seclusive, very good, very kind and very nice! There was in Karloff a hidden sorrow that I sensed and respected – a deep, deep thing. Still, whatever that may have been, there was a true respect between us as actors. He was a marvellous person."[55]

To prepare for his first scenes in the picture Karloff reported to the make-up room at 11 a.m. and put himself, once again, in the capable hands of Jack Pierce. "He was a gentleman," Pierce said, "always on time, and everything an actor should be."[56] Working from a photograph of the mummy of Pharaoh Seti II, it took Pierce eight hours to

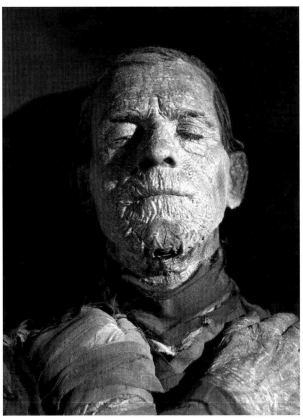

Left: Poster for *The Mummy* (1932). Right: As the embalmed Imhotep.

transform Karloff into the 3,700-year-old mummy – twice as long as the process required for Frankenstein's Monster. Karloff's ears were glued back and the bridge of his nose built up. Then his entire face and hands were covered with thin strips of Egyptian cotton, covered with collodion (a highly flammable syrupy solution of pyroxylin, ether and alcohol) and dried with an electric dryer. At 1 p.m. Karloff's hair was smeared with beauty clay into which Pierce carved cracks as the mixture hardened. An hour later his face and hands were covered with make-up. At 5 p.m. Pierce wrapped Karloff in 150 yards of linen, artificially aged with a treatment of acids and heated in an oven. Then, at 7 p.m., a complete dusting with Fuller's Earth completed the make-up. It was only then, however, that Karloff discovered an oversight in the Mummy's apparel. "You've done a wonderful job," Karloff told Pierce, "but you've forgotten to give me a fly!"[57] Karloff later told his friend, the actor Christopher Lee,[xv] of another problem with the costume. "He told me," Lee recalled, "that when he was all bound up, he barely dared to take a breath lest the bandages break, and if he breathed out too much they'd come loose. Perforce he'd spent hours in this condition because the whole process was too complex to repeat."[58]

Karloff found a unique way to test the effectiveness of his make-up. "When I was working on *The Mummy*," he later recalled, "my make-up was so grotesque and so disgusting that none of my friends recognised me. For an experiment, I sent home for my two Scotties to see if they would know me. The make-up didn't fool them for a second.

xv Christopher Lee also played a Mummy, Kharis, in Hammer's *The Mummy* (1959).

They didn't even seem to notice it. They galloped across to me and jumped up to be petted, the moment they were let into the studio."[59]

James Whale later told his friend Curtis Harrington that Karloff had summoned him to the set. "James said that one day he was sitting in his office and an emissary from the make-up department at Universal came to his office and said 'Mr. Karloff would like to see you in the make-up department'. He said he was ushered with great ceremony into the make-up department, into one of the rooms there, where Karloff was sitting in a chair covered by a sheet. They did a kind of unveiling for Jimmy. He said it was the make-up for *The Mummy*. The way James Whale put it, he said it looked like he had every piece of make-up on his face. He said Karloff looked at him and said 'I think this will be the most marvellous thing ever seen on the silver sheet!'"[60]

As on *Frankenstein* Pierce walked his creation to the set for the day's filming. Ironically, despite the lengthy application process, the make-up was used for only one scene in the picture. While the archaeologists discuss their finds the Mummy can be seen mainly in long shot, standing upright in its sarcophagus. Pierce's make-up can be seen only twice in close-up – once when the Mummy is examined by Dr. Muller and again when the Mummy is revived. Although a still exists where the Mummy can be seen reaching for the Scroll of Thoth, no such shot appears in the picture. Freund refrained from showing the Mummy in motion, except for minimal movements when the Mummy is revived, relying instead on the audience's imagination.

Except for a tea break, which he shared with his wife Dorothy who had visited her husband on the set (and posed for photographs), Karloff was required, most of the time, merely to stay in his sarcophagus. The scene finally wrapped at 2 a.m., having taken seven hours to shoot, and Karloff reported back to Pierce for the painful process of make-up removal.

Using solvents and acids Pierce spent the next two hours removing the make-up he had worked so long to apply. "Physical exhaustion was nothing compared to the nervous exhaustion I suffered," Karloff later said. "I am glad it is over!"[61] The experience, he said, was "the most trying ordeal I have ever endured."[62] Fortunately for Karloff he spent the rest of the movie as the mummy's unwrapped *alter ego*, Ardath Bey. According to Karloff, though, this second make-up still took four hours to apply. His face and hands were 'aged' by the application of more cotton and collodion.[xvi] It was uncomfortable in the extreme," the star later recalled, "as the wrappings were put on wet and as they dried they tightened, and it was very difficult to speak lines with my throat so constricted."[63]

The director's shooting regime also proved trying. Throughout the production Freund would shoot for long periods without breaks. This eventually became too much for Johann and towards the end of production, during the filming of the pool scene where Anck-es-en-Amon's death and burial are revealed to Helen, she collapsed from exhaustion. "Suddenly I just toppled over and was out for an hour – I was dead! I have had two death experiences. If you know the occult, then you know that we do go. Once I went from here and I was up there in the trees – oooh, the lighting was great! So anyway, over I went and I experienced death, that was it. You see, you become so exhausted or so fearful of a situation that you choose to go somewhere else. And

---

xvi Following *The Mummy*'s release Jack Pierce was given an award for his make-up on the picture, which was presented to him by Boris Karloff. Many years later, when Universal's make-up rooms were refurbished, the award was discovered underneath a sink in Pierce's former make-up room.

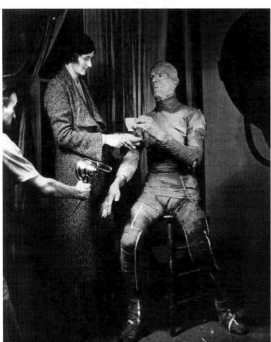

Top: Cleaning up the set on *The Mummy* (1932). Inset:
The director Karl Freund. Left: Dorothy Karloff visits
her husband during production.
Right: With Zita Johann.

I think I had become so fearful that I didn't realise yet what I had ahead of me."[64] Johann came to with a concerned Karloff, in costume and covered by layers of make-up, leaning over her. "He just sat there and was sorry," she said. "It was 10 o'clock at night on Saturday and they couldn't get a doctor. So, they tried to give me whiskey, but I wouldn't take it. And when I finally came round, Ruby [Johann's assistant] told me that the crew had prayed me back. They said they wanted to get Freund for what he had done to me! So Ruby said to them, 'You don't know the half of it.' Because on my menstrual days – the producers always ask you your menstrual days before you sign a contract – and then they make those the light days. Freund made those the heaviest, deliberately, and the longest."[65]

The picture wrapped towards the end of October 1932 on schedule and under budget with a total cost of $196,000. There was no wrap party at the end of the shoot. "Everybody just walked away," said Johann, "and that was it."[66] Johann's troubles with the picture, however, were not over yet. "I was being interviewed by a simply dreadful interviewer," Johann recalled, "and Junior Laemmle called up. He had seen the final print of *The Mummy* and was very exuberant. I listened to him enthuse and then, partially out of boredom due to the interview, I said 'Do me a favour. I had a lousy rotten time at your studio. *Don't pick up my option for another picture.*' Well, he almost died! In a way I'm sorry I did that, because Junior Laemmle was an awfully nice person, a very sensitive man, and we did have a great mutual respect."[67]

Johann's outburst had its repercussions when, prior to release, a number of changes were made. Originally it had been the studio's intention to give Johann top billing

Universal's 1932 pool of talent. Studio owner Carl Laemmle front centre wearing ribbon. Boris Karloff, back row 4th from left. Others in the line-up include John Boles, James Whale, Bela Lugosi, Raymond Massey, Noah Beery Jr., Lew Ayres, Tom Mix, Mickey Rooney and Karl Freund.

alongside Karloff. Laemmle Jr. had planned to team the pair in further pictures and hoped to feature Johann both in a sequel to *Frankenstein* and the studio's proposed adaptation of *The Invisible Man*. When the actress refused to commit to another film, however, she lost both her shared top billing and several scenes in the picture.

Shot but deleted on Laemmle Jr.'s orders was a scene in which Helen, influenced by Ardath Bey, visits the Museum. There she examines a display of Anck-es-en-Amon's personal effects, which includes a circular bronze mirror. Ardath Bey enters and, by discussing the objects with her, awakens a memory of her past life. He tells Helen to visit him the next day and exits, leaving behind a dusty handprint. Another major change occurred during Helen's subsequent visit to the house of Ardath Bey. In the release print Helen views her death and burial in Ancient Egypt in Bey's pool. Also shown is Imhotep's arrested attempt to steal the Scroll of Thoth and his subsequent burial alive. As originally scripted by Balderston and shot by Freund – these revelations were shown in two separate scenes. Only Anck-es-en-Amon's death and burial and Imhotep's arrest were shown in the pool.

During the final scene in the Museum, footage was shot in which Helen views scenes from her other past lives in the bronze mirror. She discovers she was an aristocrat in 18th century France and a 13th century noblewoman. In the 8th century she was a Saxon Princess who kills herself to escape the ravages of the Vikings, and in 1st century Rome a Christian fed to the lions.

Following the images of her later incarnations, scenes of Helen's life in Ancient Egypt are revealed to her. She sees herself embrace Imhotep in the Temple of Isis and witnesses the priest's burial. On orders from Laemmle Jr. however, the museum footage of Helen's past lives was dropped. Only Imhotep's burial was retained and moved to the pool scene. While the deletions serve to tighten the picture, the removal of the mirror scene obscures the meaning of Ardath Bey's line, uttered to Helen in the pool scene: "But the rest you may not know – not until you are about to pass through the great night of terror and triumph." Despite the deletions an oversight ensured that Henry Victor still received screen credit for his portrayal of a Saxon warrior. In addition, publicity materials listed both Victor and Arnold Grey, who had appeared as a knight in the 13th century segment.

For the movies advertising campaign Karloff was billed by his surname only – 'KARLOFF the Uncanny' – an accolade previously only afforded to a select few such as [Greta] Garbo, [Alla] Nazimova and [John] Barrymore. When the picture previewed on 29 November 1932 at the Pantages Theatre on Hollywood Boulevard, it was an event not without incident, as actor Eugene Walsh explained. "As we entered the foyer," he said, "a middle-aged lady came out of the theatre… She seemed very apprehensive and nearly bumped into us. Then suddenly she sank to the floor and Boris helped the attendant to revive her. I don't think the lady had any idea who Boris was, but she was most grateful for the help he had given her."[68]

Following the Hollywood preview the *Los Angeles Times* wrote, "Surely the mantle of the late Lon Chaney will eventually fall upon the actor Karloff, whose portrayal of an unholy thing in this film, aided of course by magnificent make-up, establishes him as not just a good character actor but a finished character star… *The Mummy* beggars description. It is one of the most unusual talkies ever produced."[69]

On 23 December, the day after *The Mummy* was released, *Film Weekly* reported Universal's recurring difficulty to find suitable material for its star:

Wanted: Wicked Men!
Out-of-Work Monster Seeks Worthwhile Crimes

Who were the world's wickedest men? Answers to this question are anxiously sought by young Carl Laemmle who is trying to find a character bad enough for Boris Karloff. Mr. Laemmle has read the Newgate Calendar and the lives of the Roman Emperors without discovering a villain inhuman enough for the ex-Monster of **Frankenstein**. He ruled out Ivan the Terrible as a possible Karloff part because Ivan was too religious, and disqualified Cesare Borgia and Dr. Crippen for similar reasons. H.G. Wells' **The Invisible Man**, recently planned for Universal production, has been postponed because Mr. Laemmle feels that, although the leading character is eerie, he is not really evil in the Karloff sense. The latest suggestion is that Karloff shall play a modernised Bluebeard, whose story has been handed to a Universal scenarist to see if he can repaint the wife killer black enough for admission to Universal's gallery of horrors. A story about a mad electrical genius, entitled **The Wizard**, is also being considered. Meanwhile Karloff has completed his gruesome part of a revivified Egyptian mummy in **The Mummy**, and until Mr. Laemmle finds him a new crime worth committing, he must remain out of work.[70]

On 3 January 1933, while Karloff tended his garden, *Variety* reported that the actor was now listed among Universal's top stars ranking aside Tom Mix, Lew Ayres and Walter Huston.

The Mummy opened at the Mayfair Theatre in New York three days later. *Variety* wrote, "There are more reasons than not why *The Mummy* should show a nice profit. It has an excellent title, some weird sequences and it is the first starring film for Karloff. Primarily, it lends itself to exploitation. Any exhibitor who avails himself of a fraction of such opportunities in this direction should check "Mummy" off in black. Revival of the mummy comes comparatively early in the running time. The transformation of Karloff's Im-Ho-Tep from a clay-like figure in a coffin to a living thing is the highlight. The sequence in the museum with Im-Ho planning to kill Helen Grosvenor, of Egyptian heritage, to revive her ancient state, is too stagey. The mustiness of the tombs excavated is also over-suggestive of the Hollywood set."[71]

The picture took a respectable $21,250 in its first week at the Mayfair, although this was $3,500 *less* than takings from the Lupe Velez comedy *The Half-Naked Truth* the week before. In early January 1933 *Variety* reported on the success of the picture at Keith's, a 2,400-seat theatre in Baltimore: "Femmes are not frequenting particularly, but the kids are rushing the register during this no-school interim, and on this strength may account for $5,000, one of the best marks here in recent weeks."[72]

The film was more enthusiastically received by the British critics. "The film is wildly incredible," wrote *Kinematograph Weekly*, "but the brilliant acting of Boris Karloff, together with some very notable technical work and imaginative direction, invest it with a realism which rivets the attention and excites grim suspense. An unusual offering, one which by reason of its novel theme and amazing star, cannot fail to win full box-office honours. Boris Karloff's make-up is remarkable and the coming to life of the mummy is an amazing piece of transformation. The star's acting is also brilliant and his clever histrionics make the figure a vital force."[73] *The Mummy* premiered at the Capitol in London on 5 February 1933. The picture was a great success and the demand for tickets was such that hundreds of picturegoers had to be turned away.

The end of work on *The Mummy* signalled a period of rest for Karloff that would last for four months. Iris Foster of *Film Weekly* asked the star what his future plans were. "Right now I am going around to make the boys pay up their Rugger Club subscriptions, and then I am going to order my wife a bicycle for a present," he said. "This year, if I can make my escape, I am going to England. I've been away since 1909. I have three hefty brothers who are dying to 'take me in hand' and knock spots off me for not visiting them all these years… I don't want to see London… I would sooner remember it all as I knew it as a kid. I'm going to buy the oldest ramshackle car I can find. And then I'm going to toss a coin into the air. If it falls down 'heads' I'll go to John o'Groats. If it's 'tails' I'll motor to Land's End. I've seen enough bricks and mortar to last me a lifetime. I want to see purple heather on the moors. I want to go to Deal, where I spent my schoolboy holidays. I'm pining for the emerald green fields, poppies in corn, thatched cottages in cobbled streets, cider apples, Devonshire cream, Kentish strawberries."[74]

He did not have to wait long.

Chapter 8

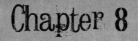

THE TRANSATLANTIC STAR

(1933-1934)

"Mr. Karloff, appropriately, occupies the dressing room formerly used by Lon Chaney. For diversion he does not eat babies; he plays golf and cricket and fancies a pot of tea in the afternoon."[1]
New York Times (28 January 1934)

I n early March 1933 Karloff's desire to return to England was unexpectedly realised. Earlier in the year Lord Lee of Fareham, a Gaumont-British executive, had arranged with Universal for the loan of the star. The deal was convenient for Universal. The early 1930s had not been profitable for the studios. The Depression had caused a decline in cinema attendance and, combined with rising production costs, resulted in financial despair for the studios. In 1932 Universal had lost $1.7 million and would lose another $1 million the following year. However, they fared better than most. Over the same two year period Warners lost $20 million and Fox, Paramount and RKO either went bankrupt or into receivership.

On 7 March 1933 (while unemployment was at its highest with 28% of the country's labour force out of work) the Producers Association announced an eight-week 50% salary cut for most of the studio's employees. However, due to Universal's earlier deal with Lord Lee, Karloff's salary remained unaffected.

On 2 March, two days before Franklin Delano Roosevelt began his first term as President, the studio telephoned the Karloffs residence. "Universal called at 9 a.m. on Thursday," Dorothy Karloff recalled, "to say we were to catch a plane at 4:30 that afternoon. Neither of us had flown before, neither of us had passports, neither of us had any money."[2] A panic rush by the public to withdraw their funds from banks had resulted in their closure so, with no other source of funds available, the Universal payphones were raided and the monies, totalling $12, were presented to Karloff in a paper bag.[i] "Don't worry," Karloff was told, "we'll wire ahead for money."[3]

They caught the plane – a Ford tri-motor – and occupied two of its four bucket seats. "The plane trip was no fun at all," Dorothy later wrote to her mother, "more like a nightmare as we look back at it now – but a nightmare with no sleep attached. Never ever have I sat in harder seats, or been so rushed and pushed about. The plane came down only for 5 to 15 minutes at a time to allow you to stretch and grab a bit of horrible food at some terrible lunch stand miles from anywhere."[4] The landings, which included a five-hour stop in Cleveland, allowed for refuelling but little else. All banks along the route were closed so no further funds could be obtained.

They finally arrived in New York two days later, as Dorothy recalled. "We actually did get to New York at 12 noon on Saturday," she said, "and with a police escort raced to the *S.S. Paris*."[5] Arriving at the dock, the Karloffs found the other passengers had already boarded, the gangplank was up and the ship had sailed. A small boat ferried them to the ship and they climbed aboard with all eyes upon them. "We were certainly two tired and disreputable-looking people," said Dorothy.[6] Stepping on deck the Karloffs were hailed by some familiar faces. Although the Gleasons (James, Lucile and their son, Russell)[ii] had until then been mere casual associates of the Karloffs, the week-long sea voyage would allow ample opportunity to become better acquainted. By coincidence James Gleason had also been employed by Michael Balcon to act in a picture at Gaumont – in his case, the army comedy *Orders Is Orders*.

Aboard the *S.S. Paris* passengers were treated to a life of luxury. The ship boasted Art Nouveau interiors with opulent staterooms, some complete with telephones and even square portholes. The cuisine was first-class with service to match. The ships daily entertainment included a Punch and Judy show at 3 p.m. and feature films two hours later. The Karloffs attended a showing of *Rasputin and the Empress* (1932) starring the Barrymore siblings, Ethel, Lionel and John. Another form of relaxation was

1933 - Boris Karloff approaches England for the first time in 24 years.

offered by the ship's bar but the Karloffs were still without money. "So we signed for everything," said Dorothy, "and arrived in England with a spectacular bar bill."[7]

The ship reached port on 10 March. "It was late on Friday that we arrived at Southampton,"[8] Karloff recalled. They were met by four representatives from Gaumont who ushered them onto a train. The ensemble arrived in London at 10:30 p.m. that evening where they were met by fans and photographers. "It was thrilling to be on English soil once more," Karloff said. "I wanted to see London and to know all about the changes."[9]

i Edward Muhl, who became Universal's Head of Production in 1952, recalled a curious incident: "One odd thing I've never forgotten. Somewhere in the middle thirties, I can't remember exactly when, we wanted him [Karloff] for a picture. He agreed to do it but only if I would come to the set personally and give him a paper sack containing $2,500 in cash and no record go through the front office. I did it, but I've often wondered about it. Does seem odd, doesn't it?"

ii Russell Gleason was best known for having played Müller, one of the four friends in Universal's hit picture *All Quiet on the Western Front* (1930).

The party was then escorted to the Dorchester Hotel in Park Lane. "We were… given a suite of rooms such as you've never seen," said Dorothy. "Champagne sent up and loads of people about. Boris was too excited to go to bed so we were taken to the Kit Kat Club – a very swell night club – then for a drive around the city until about 3 a.m."[10]

That weekend the Karloffs spent time at leisure with walks in Hyde Park. However, they soon decided to leave the Dorchester, which Dorothy complained was costing "about $20 a day".[11] Along with the Gleasons they rented service flats in Duchess Street in Mayfair. The Karloffs abode had a large living room, two bedrooms and a dining room, resplendent with a pipe organ. Included in the rent were the services of a valet, maid, butler and a cook.

Although the accommodation was more to their liking the lack of some home staples prompted Dorothy to write to her mother and request her friends Edith Havenstrite and her husband, soon to visit England, to "bring 200 Lucky Strikes for us… And if they want any decent coffee… bring a can with them – or 5 or 6 cans. The coffee is foul here."[12]

Before beginning work on *The Ghoul* Karloff decided to pay an impromptu visit to his brother, Sir John Pratt, at his office at the Foreign Office in London's Whitehall. Wishing to surprise his brother after so many years away Karloff was shown into Sir John's office unannounced. Although the last time the two brothers had met, and then only briefly, was in December 1910 when Karloff borrowed £20 from his sibling his appearance did not seem to surprise his older brother who looked up from his work and said, "Oh, Billy – how amusing!"[13]

On Monday, 13 March Karloff arrived at Gaumont's Lime Grove Studio at Shepherd's Bush in West London to begin work on *The Ghoul*. Karloff would play Professor Morlant, a dying Egyptologist who believes he can gain everlasting life through 'The Eternal Light', a jewel stolen from an Egyptian tomb. When Morlant is buried without the jewel he returns from the dead to seek revenge. Although credited as an adaptation of the novel by Dr. Frank King and Leonard Hines, it bore little relation to the 1928 tale.

The picture, with a budget of just over £30,000, was directed by American T. Hayes Hunter who, along with his wife, the actress Millicent Evans, had left Hollywood in 1927 to settle in England. In addition to Hunter, Gaumont had hired the services of two German nationals, cinematographer Günther Krampf, who had shot F.W. Murnau's *Nosferatu, eine Symphonie des Grauens* (1922) and art designer Alfred Junge. Junge's sets in particular resulted in production costs rising by a third and Hunter brought the picture in at a little under £40,000.

The Ghoul, like *The Old Dark House*, had a small cast. Among those joining Karloff were Cedric Hardwicke, Anthony Bushell, Dorothy Hyson, Kathleen Harrison and Karloff's co-star from *The Old Dark House*, Ernest Thesiger. For the role of the 'vicar' Nigel Hartley, Cedric Hardwicke suggested Ralph Richardson in what would be Richardson's first speaking part.

Making the picture, however, was not a pleasant experience for Karloff as Dorothy revealed in a letter to her mother. "Boris as usual doesn't like the story – or his part – and they're having an awful time with the make-up," she wrote. "He says the make-up man doesn't know anything about Boris's type of work – is German besides and can't understand a word Boris says. So it's the same agony of starting a new picture even if it's in England."[14] The make-up by Heinrich Heitfeld received further criticism after the picture's release. "Boris Karloff's make-up is clever," wrote *Kinematograph Weekly*, "but why an Egyptologist should be so absurdly grotesque passes all reason, and is detrimental to the drama."[15]

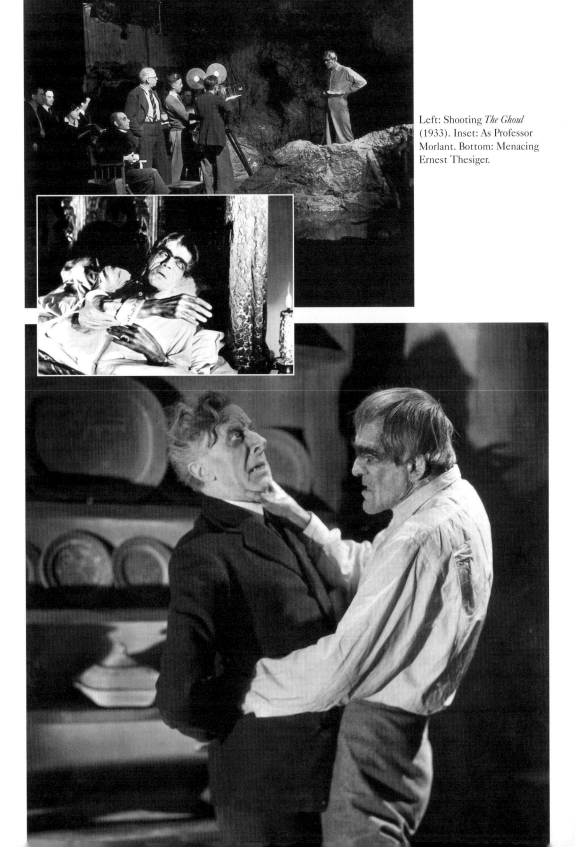

Left: Shooting *The Ghoul* (1933). Inset: As Professor Morlant. Bottom: Menacing Ernest Thesiger.

The Ghoul's assistant stage manager, John Croydon,[iii] was a friend of the make-up man and would often watch Heitfeld at work. "Karloff was always called very early for make-up and was never ready for the set until mid-morning," he said. "In all the time I spent watching the applications of layers of make-up – collodion to draw the facial muscles tight and what I heard described as "fish skin" – he never spoke. Maybe he couldn't! He had only one speech in the opening sequence of the film. Thereafter, he uttered not a word, which was no surprise. His make-up must have caused a form of lock-jaw."[16]

During the days, while Karloff was confined within the studio, Dorothy spent the time "dashing around"[17] in a "very elegant"[18] car, complete with driver, she had been loaned by the studio. Any costs Dorothy incurred during her excursions, however, were covered by her husband who paid all his wife's expenses.

To publicise Karloff's work on *The Ghoul* a press reception was held in Piccadilly.[iv] As members of Karloff's family were invited the event also served as an impromptu family reunion. Of Karloff's surviving siblings three were present that evening. "My two eldest brothers, Ted and Fred, had retired from Indian Civil Service and were living in London," Karloff explained. "Jack had been transferred from China to take charge of Far East affairs in the Foreign Office."[19]

Karloff's brother George had died in 1904 after having contracted pneumonia. On 4 August 1924 his half-sister, Emma, had passed away at 38 Uplands Park Road. She was 74 years old.[v] Sir John wrote of Emma, "She never married but she was a remarkable woman and amassed a small fortune entirely by her own exertions. She was a great musician and for many years she was Headmistress of a school in Delhi."[20] In fact, Emma had been Principal of the Auckland House School in Simla (now Shimla) in the North-West Himalayas, from 18 February 1890 to 16 December 1904.

Emma's estate was valued at the sizeable £12,400 4s 1d. In her will the house in Uplands Park Road was bequeathed to her half-sister Julia with the stipulation that when Julia died the house would pass on to her daughter, Dorothea. The document also made provisions for all of her half-siblings, a sum of 20 pounds a year to her servant Edith Harriett Young, and a likewise amount to Mary Elliot Pratt, "the widow of my brother James Douglas Pratt." In fact, James was also a half-sibling but Emma may not have been aware of the fact.[vi]

Also absent from the reunion, though still living, were Charles, David, Julia and Richard. Charles had worked for the South American Cable Company in Pernambuco, Brazil. In 1898 he converted to Catholicism and married one Alfenia Ward Dowling two years later. Sadly, Charles' wife died in 1903 and he later returned to England. At the time of Emma's death he was unemployed and living with her at Uplands Park Road. He later settled on the Channel island of Guernsey.

David had also worked in South America. As well as working with his brother in Pernambuco, David had lived in Buenos Aires working as an engineer, designing and

iii John Croydon would work with Karloff over 25 years later, when he produced the star's pictures *Grip of the Strangler* and *Corridors of Blood* (both 1958).
iv In 1962 Karloff recalled this event slightly differently. "A little later I got a surprising reaction from my staid and proper British brothers," he said. "Some friends from Hollywood were in London, and before they left for home we gave a sort of joint cocktail party. All went well until a newspaper photographer approached me. 'I understand you've some brothers here,' he said. 'Could we get a photograph or two?'"
v Emma's death notice in *The Times* on 7 August (and again the following day) mistakenly records her age as 75.
vi James and Emma's mothers were the sisters Juliana and Charlotte Campbell.

Four of the Pratt brothers. L to R. Edward, Frederick, Sir John and William.

building the Argentine Railway. He later returned to England and married Bertha Immisch, the daughter of the inventor and electrical engineer Moritz Immisch. The couple lived at 11 Beavual Road, Dulwich and on 29 March 1909 a son, David Charles Pratt, was born. His sister Gwendoline was born two years later. The family later left Dulwich and settled in Leigh-on-Sea, Essex.

Karloff's sister, Julia, lived at the Rectory in Semer, Suffolk with her husband, the Reverend Arthur Donkin. It may be that Julia had met Donkin while he was Curate of St. John's Church in Enfield (1895-97). The couple were married in 1895 and their daughter Dorothea was born later that year. "Boris admired the vicar tremendously," said Evelyn Karloff, "because although Arthur was Church of England, he allowed Julia Honoria to convert to Catholicism and he even entertained the local priest at his church because he said that what she did was quite her own business 'as long as you do your duty to the parish.' Boris considered this to be a very civilised attitude."[21] Sir John, however, thought differently of his brother-in-law. "She [Julia] is not an amiable character," he wrote to his half-sister, Emma, in 1924, "but after all she is one of the family & she has had a hard life of grinding poverty, married to a man who is in every way inefficient."[22]

Richard, like his brother John, worked for the British Consular Service in China and in 1933 was living in Swatow, China. Both brothers had been coached for the entrance examination at the Civil Service Department in King's College, London. Prior to his work for the Consul, Richard had studied in Peking for two years as a student interpreter learning to speak Mandarin. During the process Richard was required to learn to read and write two thousand Mandarin characters.

However, the Pratt's Anglo-Indian heritage proved to be a handicap to both brothers when working in China, for each was subjected to racial bigotry. When John was the acting-consul in Shanghai members of the British community referred to him, behind his back, as the black consul. Likewise, when Richard was serving as consul a leading British subject found it amusing to ask him to perform the Indian rope trick. Such treatment depressed Richard – but it would get worse.

In July 1926 the Commander-in-Chief of the National Revolutionary Forces, Chiang Kai-shek, began a military campaign to rid China of the controlling northern Warlords. The Northern Expedition, as it was known, aimed to unify the country under the forces political party, Kuomintang.

At this time Richard was stationed in Chunking. In January 1927 the situation had become so bad that soldiers cursed him, cried "kill him," or even aimed their rifles at him when he ventured onto the streets. The situation, exacerbated by his isolation from other foreigners, caused him acute mental depression.

In March 1927 the Nationalist Army attacked the city of Nanking and American, British and Japanese ships were sent to aid in the evacuation of foreign residents. In Chungking, on 17 March, Richard Pratt accompanied a naval lieutenant and seven British Marines to retrieve supplies intended for the British canteen, which had been seized by Chinese pickets. Pratt, the lieutenant and the Marines gave chase and retrieved the goods. The mob, however, then rounded on the unarmed men, beating them with spears and pelting them with bricks and stones. The British were forced to abandon the supplies and flee. While the Marines received no serious injuries Richard, it was reported, received a head injury from a thrown brick.

Richard's daughter, Rosamund, later recounted how her father received a more severe wound during his Chinese service. While mediating in the evacuation of foreign residents, Richard received a spear in his back. It left him with a large scar.[vii] Such events did nothing to endear the country to Richard Pratt and in 1928 a confidential report remarked that although he was a fast and efficient worker Richard had developed a discernible dislike for China and its people. Although he longed to retire Richard was obliged to serve another nine years before his wish was fulfilled.

Had Richard been in England at the time of the family reunion it is unlikely he would have attended. He was always very retiring and hated entertaining. His sister Julia recalled that when he came home from college he would stay with her at the rectory in Semer. If guests arrived he would retire to his room. Julia later told her niece, Richard's daughter Rosamund, "He would have lived the life of a hermit if he could."[23] It has been claimed that Richard withdrew and refused to communicate with his family. This, however, is not true as he did write to his brother, Charles. Sir John's remaining papers, too, contain some correspondence with Richard.[viii] The earliest surviving letter from Richard is dated 1929 whilst the other, written in 1947, contains his detailed comments on Sir John's proposed manuscript for his book *The Expansion of Europe into the Far East*.

Karloff approached the reunion with some trepidation. "The meeting again with my brothers was quite different to what I anticipated," he later said. "There is a little

---

vii According to Rosamund, her father's services during the evacuation resulted in the offer of a knighthood, which he refused.

viii "During the blitz on London in 1940 a land mine dropped by parachute from a German plane alighted on the roof of my flat," Sir John wrote in 1946. "It blew the whole block to pieces and destroyed all my worldly possessions including family photographs and other such records."

difference in my suddenly attaining fame, when my mature family had taken years to establish themselves in their respective diplomatic posts. But Jack immediately put me at my ease by saying 'It's simply grand, and we're all delighted to see you come home in triumph!' The 25 years we had been apart made a difference. The strangeness had to wear off. We had to find the common touch. Then there came that lovely sense of well-being, of deep understanding and warm friendship."[24] A curious Sir John asked his brother, "Tell me, Billy, how much do you get paid for this sort of thing you do?"[25] When informed Sir John said, "Billy, save every farthing… this can never last!"[26]

When a photographer wanted to take a picture of the reunited brothers he asked Karloff if he could arrange it. "This was the moment I had been dreading. I felt that they would consider it beneath their dignity, and expected to be told in no uncertain terms that such a thing was impossible. But I hunted them up and put the proposition to them. 'I realise,' I said apologetically, 'that I make my living in rather a queer fashion, and I only bring this to your notice because the man is so insistent. I assure you it is not an idea of my own, but – well, there is a photographer here who wants to take our pictures together.' 'Where is he?' asked Sir John excitedly. 'Bring him in here and let's be photographed in front of the fireplace!' They were as pleased as three boys and, when the photographer had come in from the other room, they began to argue as to where each should stand. Finally, it was decided that we should line up according to age, with my brother John on one end and myself on the other. No sooner was the picture taken than all three brothers began to inquire how soon they could secure prints – and by this time I was in a positive glow of relief. A film actor had been received in the British diplomatic circles and had made good!"[27]

Karloff's recollection of the order of the brothers in the photograph is incorrect as the content of a 1946 letter reveals. His brother, Sir John Pratt, wrote, "The short dumpy one on the left (he looks short but his actual height is 5' 11") is my eldest brother E.M. Pratt, or Mr. Justice Pratt, formerly a Judge of the High Court in Bombay but now over 80 years of age and living on a pension in retirement in England. Next to him is F.G. Pratt, formerly in the Indian Civil Service as Commissioner of Poona, a large city near Bombay; now also retired aged 76. Next comes myself, a mere youngster at 71, and next to me, roaring with laughter, is… Boris Karloff. To his friends in England he is known as William Henry Pratt, or Billy, the youngest of a family of nine…"[28]

To Karloff the acquirement of fame and its resulting benefits seemed unjustified. "I have often thought how absurd and lopsided it is that men like my brothers should spend their lives in the service of their country, and be comparatively unknown," he said, "whereas I, because of a series of lucky accidents, have been granted fame and some fortune. Anything I have achieved in life in no way compares to anything they or the hundreds of men like them have done."[29]

Karloff spent more time with his family on his days away from the studio. One afternoon was spent with Sir John and his family. He also met his sister Julia whose daughter Dorothea had provided him with the occasional meal while a struggling actor in Los Angeles. One Wednesday night was spent dining with six members of his brother David's family. Then, on Monday 27 March, Karloff returned to his old stomping grounds of Enfield. He saw his house in Uplands Park Road, his old Grammar School and visited Enfield's cricket ground where he used to play under the tutelage of his brother George. He also paid his respects at the graves of his mother, brother George and half-sister Emma in Enfield's Lavender Hill cemetery. "Poor Boris," Dorothy wrote to her mother, "except for his two Sundays with his brothers, has seen nothing but the studio and the flat – but he gets a tremendous thrill about hearing about them every night... We never have dinner until 7:30 or 8 – then we go for a walk every night – for it's the only air Boris gets all day long – as the studios here are entirely enclosed – and he likes poking about the streets anyway."[30] Dorothy's statement was, however, an exaggeration. In fact, much of the Karloffs leisure time was spent socialising.

They met with the playwright R.C. Sherriff and Ernest Thesiger. An invitation had also taken them, along with the Gleasons, to a party at Lady Ravensdale's, the daughter of Lord Curzon and, at that time, the sister-in-law of Oswald Mosley, the founder of the British Union of Fascists. Some evenings were spent at the theatre. They saw Mary Ellis in *Double Harness* at the Apollo Theatre in Shaftesbury Avenue and saw his *Ghoul* co-star Anthony Bushell appearing with Ivor Novello in *Fresh Fields* at the Criterion. One night, however, there was a tragedy. Bushell shared a flat with his brother Nicholas, a young lawyer. One evening Nicholas failed to show for a pre-evening dinner with the Gleasons as had been arranged. When Russell Gleason went to the Bushell's flat to investigate he discovered Nicholas's body. The reason for Nicholas's suicide was never ascertained.

On a happier occasion Dorothy arranged a night out with the Gleasons to see the American actress and comedienne Charlotte Greenwood[ix] in the Hammerstein/Hart musical *Three Sisters* at Drury Lane.[x] It was supposed to be a quiet affair. "Somehow people got to know," Karloff recalled. "There was a tremendous crowd gathered round the entrance. As I got out of the cab, many of them shouted in a most friendly fashion: 'Welcome home, Mr. Karloff, welcome home.' They came around, some wanting autographs, some simply to extend friendly greetings. A welcome to me! I was overcome almost to the point of tears. Then a man in the crowd came to the rescue. 'It's all right, Mr. Karloff, we'll wait until after the show. This is a good play. We don't want you to miss any of it. You go to the theatre with your party and we'll be waiting after the performance.' It was terribly touching to have extended to me those lovely sentiments and that great kindness and consideration, which came from the heart. They were waiting for me after the show. I was deeply impressed with their friendly good will, and I realised what a great thing, literally beyond price, is the friendship of the people. Somehow, I felt it could have happened only in London and was fully representative of the heart of its people, of my people."[31]

In early April Dorothy wrote to her mother:

> Boris looks fine – he's so thrilled and happy all the time that he looks heavier and more rested. But I don't think he'll be contented to live in California ever again – not really contented – he'll always want to come back to this, I know... There is still talk of a second picture here. Boris is with the men now, talking about it. He'll be broken-hearted if we don't stay – Universal have given their permission, but Gaumont couldn't start another picture until about the first of May or later – so I don't know.[32]

At the end of the letter Karloff added, "Hello, Mother dear... Don't you believe what Dorothy says about my not being contented in California. She is the one to distrust. She

---

ix Greenwood was also the star of the picture *Orders Is Orders*, which co-starred James Gleason.
x *Three Sisters* premiered at the Theatre Royal, Drury Lane on 9 April 1934. The cast included Stanley Holloway, Adele Dixon and a gaggle of live geese. It closed after 72 performances.

gets positively lyrical about everything, and everyone says 'What a charming wife you have and how she has fallen into everything over here! We never met anyone who enjoyed England so much.' It is lovely – the weather has been marvellous and the excitement of being here again is almost too much. But still I have some pretty deep roots in California."[33]

During the filming of *The Ghoul* Karloff was interviewed at the studio by O. Bristol, a reporter for *Picture Show*. "I live a very quiet, rather uneventful life apart from my work," Karloff told Bristol. "I am very fond of reading, and I do a great deal of gardening in my Hollywood home."[34]

While the interview was being conducted Heinrich Heitfeld adjusted the star's make-up with a pair of scissors. "It takes us five hours every morning before the others get here to finish this make-up," Heitfeld explained.[35] "Yes, five hours, about twelve cups of tea, and quite a lot of bad language," Karloff added. "I've been elected president of the Make-up Artistes Tea Club. We drink it all day."[36] It was wonderful, Karloff told Bristol, to be back in England – although the trip did have a downside. "My hobby is dog breeding, and I'm very keen on Aberdeens," Karloff said. "My favourite dog had five puppies just before I left, and I think that leaving them behind was the only regret I had about setting off for England so suddenly."[37]

When the second picture for Gaumont came to naught the Karloffs readied to leave. One matter, however, had to be resolved, a matter that was causing Dorothy some concern. She had written to her mother Louise several times to obtain a copy of her birth certificate, without which she would be unable to re-enter the United States. "Boris was able to get a re-entry permit while we were in London," she said, "but the record of my birth had been burned in the courthouse in Charlotte, Michigan."[38] Dorothy requested her mother send a copy of the Stine family Bible in place of the lost certificate. Fortunately, Louise located the thought-lost certificate and sent it to her daughter.[xi] "Needless to say I was glad to get it," Dorothy wrote, "for just that morning I had been to the consul's, and he told me I'd have trouble getting in... But now everything is fine."[39]

With the visa problem resolved the Karloffs embarked on a ten-day paid holiday. The whistle-stop tour took in Canterbury and Dover, then up to Warwick, Kenilworth, the Lake District, Windermere and the lowlands of Scotland. "I found great changes... Not so much in London that was a rather peculiar thing," Karloff later said. "I found much more changes in the countryside because I left England in 1909 to go to Canada and, in the interval, there had been the great advent of the motor car, you see. That opened up great arterial highways and all the rest of it. There were lots of new buildings and that sort of thing, of course. In London, with the smoke and the grime, they weather so quickly; it all becomes part of the scene, you know, and you don't notice it so much."[40]

The Karloffs then travelled down to York before journeying on to Karloff's schoolboy stomping ground of Rutland. "I went back up to Uppingham, and it was during the holiday time, so I crept around like a ghost." Fortunately there were no encounters with the pupils. "I would have been terrified... terrified to face those little wretches!" he confessed.[41]

---

xi Dorothy later gave an alternate version of events. "My mother eventually had to have a photostat made of the family Bible and to get two of her friends who knew her when I was born to go before a notary and swear I'd been born. The joke of the whole situation was that Boris – a non-native American – could return at will, but I was left stranded in England unable to get home until eventually all papers arrived. Only then was I issued a passport and allowed to come back – two weeks later!"

With their holiday over the Karloffs headed back for Southampton where they boarded the *Europa* bound for New York. They were back in Hollywood by 19 May.

The Ghoul opened in London on 24 July 1933. *Kinematograph Weekly* thought the picture a "fantastic thriller, a picture devised on lines similar to that of *The Mummy*, but lacking its plausibility in presentation, treatment and dramatic construction... Still, as a vehicle designed solely to exploit the macabre histrionics of Karloff, the picture will no doubt find a ready market with the masses."[42]

The picture was received less favourably after it opened in the United States on 25 November. The *New York Times* complained that, "a newsreel of a Sunday School picnic would have been more thrilling."[43] *The Ghoul* took $18,500 in its first week in the city but during the next five days takings dropped to $8,000 before it was succeeded by the adventure picture *Devil Tiger*. It was a disappointing reception for Gaumont's attempt to enter the American horror picture market.

When Karloff returned to Universal in May he found the question of suitable pictures had not been resolved. As the script for *The Invisible Man* had still not been completed[xii] Karloff put his energies to use elsewhere. At the end of the month (28 May) he attended the annual dance of the Hollywood Cricket Club, held in the Blossom Room of the Hollywood Roosevelt Hotel. "Every year at the start of the cricket season," he later explained, "we used to stage something of the sort to promote interest in the club and raise funds for the season just beginning."[44]

During the evening he was approached by his actor friend Kenneth Thomson, as Karloff recalled:

> As he is not too well known for his prowess as a cricketer, I suspect that he had been lured there in the hope of knocking him over for a small financial contribution to the cause of cricket – to be rewarded, of course, with a fancy card proclaiming him to be a non-playing associate, non-voting, dues-paying member of the Hollywood Cricket Club. Anyhow, as the evening advanced and I was circumnavigating the floor in my customary slow and stately manner, Ken dropped anchor alongside me and muttered in my ear the magic words, "Would you be interested in an autonomous organisation for film actors with an affiliation with Actors' Equity?" Hastily scrambling off my unfortunate partner's foot, I practically yelled, "How... when... where?" At which he hissed, "Next Thursday, 8:00 P.M. my house.... Don't park too close to the house," and practically vanished in a puff of smoke... with his pocketbook intact, I trust."[45]

The idea of a new open-to-all actors' union had been the subject of previous discussions at the Masquers Club in Hollywood. However, after 7 March when the Producers Association announced an eight-week 50% salary cut for most studio employees, it was decided that the time had come for action. Kenneth Thomson and his wife Alden Gay arranged a meeting at their home with fellow actors Berton Churchill, Charles Miller, Grant Mitchell and Ralph Morgan to discuss the practicalities of forming a self-governing union.

The group was well served to instigate the creation of a new organisation. Mitchell had, in 1913, been a founding member of the theatrical union Actors' Equity Association.

---

xii In all, *The Invisible Man* went through a total of six treatments and nine screenplays until the final draft – the tenth – was approved by the MPPDA on 12 June 1933.

In 1919 the union demanded better working conditions for its members but the refusal by producers to recognise Equity resulted in the first-ever strike in the history of the American 'legitimate' theatre.[xiii] During the action Berton Churchill had run Equity's New York headquarters. In 1924 Ralph Morgan briefly served as the union's acting president and, like Churchill and Mitchell, was a long-time Equity Council member. Charles Miller was Equity's current West Coast representative and, in addition, both Mitchell and Morgan held law degrees.

The Thursday after the HCC dance Karloff arrived at the Thomson household for the planned meeting. In 1960 Karloff recalled:

> Well, I went, I listened, and I was conquered. Dear Ralph Morgan was presiding over a crowded meeting of perhaps half a dozen people. Ken Thomson, of course, and his wife Alden, Jim and Lucille [sic] Gleason, Noel Madison, Claude King, and perhaps one or two others whom I dare not mention for fear I get the names wrong after so long a time. Anyhow, from then on it was a regular weekly event with one or two new recruits coming in… a rather thin trickle, but still a trickle. Amongst that trickle were Sir Aubrey Smith, Ivan Simpson, Murray Kinnell, all members of the Cricket Club… Among others who joined the group before the actual formation of the Guild were Leon Ames, Bradley Page, Charles Starrett, Lyle Talbot and Alan Mowbray, whose personal cheque paid for the Guild's legal incorporation.
>
> From time to time various well-known luminaries in the film world came to listen and admire but not to enlist. But in the meantime, Ralph and Ken and the rest, with the invaluable aid and counsel of Larry Beilenson, plugged away. The general idea was to set the skeleton of an organisation for film actors with a constitution and the machinery for making it work, get what recruits we could, but in the meantime sit back and hold the fort and wait for the producers to make the inevitable booboo that would enable us to interest the stars, without whose support we knew the Guild could not hope to function successfully.
>
> Well, the months ticked away and our growth was hardly phenomenal and sometimes, in spite of the coffee and sandwiches so generously supplied by Ken and Alden, our spirits flagged a bit but never our firm belief that the producers would do the job for us by putting the cat among the pigeons and getting everybody into an uproar.[46]

John L. Dales, later the Guild's Executive Secretary, recalled Karloff's contribution during these early days. "Boris was marvellous in these meetings," he said. "He was firm, courageous, at a time when it was actually dangerous…"[47] Such activity, if discovered by the studios, would almost certainly mean the end of an actor's career. Eugene Walsh recalled, "I was present at one of the first meetings… at Boris's Toluca Lake home… Boris personally had everything to lose, but his determination to help other actors was the driving force behind his decision."[48]

---

xiii In February 1901 the White Rats of America, an organisation formed by vaudeville performers, went on strike for the first time over, the *Washington Post* explained, "exaction by the managers of a commission for booking the acts." The strike was successful and the commission was abolished.

On 1 June Karloff had his own run-in with the studio, as *Variety* reported five days later:

MONEY-STAR DUMPING BY UNIVERSAL HITS KARLOFF

Universal is continuing its policy of dumping contract players as soon as they reach the big money class and substituting them with new people at less money. Latest Universal star to go off the list is Boris Karloff. At the studio 18 months, Karloff had been drawing $750 per week, and was scheduled to get $1,250 on his coming option jump. The sum represented a jump of $500 or $250 each for two option periods. Karloff waived the previous option increase, which would have boosted his salary to $1,000, on condition that he would get the full amount on the next option. Universal refused to meet the figure, which came due Thursday, and Karloff walked.[49]

The split from Universal was, however, brief. In July the studio lured Karloff back with a contract that provided a salary of $2,000, included freelance clauses and guaranteed top billing as 'KARLOFF'. The contract, stated the *Los Angeles Times*, "is for two maybe three pictures a year – with Universal, and runs five years. It was negotiated by Harry Gould. First up will be *The Return of Frankenstein*."[50]

On 30 June the Screen Actors Guild's articles of incorporation were filed. Just over a week later, on 8 July, the Guild created its contract. Boris Karloff applied to join eleven days later. On 25 July Kenneth Thomson wrote back to Karloff informing him of the Guild's temporary headquarters at the Hollywood Centre Building at 1655 N. Cherokee.[xiv] Thomson added, "As you know, we will soon have a rather large payment to make to the attorneys, and it will help us considerably if you can find it possible to send us a cheque for the full amount; or if that is not convenient, for the initiation fee and the first quarter's dues... In the meantime, if you know of anyone who might be interested in joining the Guild, please use all your persuasive powers, as we need members at once."[51] Four days later Thomson received Karloff's cheque for the full amount of $25.

It was important to expand membership so, on 3 August, the Guild's membership committee chairman, Arthur Vinton, wrote to Karloff. "With a little diligent effort on your part we can get results," the letter read.[52] It was urged that all committee members phoned, every other day, a list of members who were recruiting. "Should any of your people contact actors or actresses who are important or semi-important," Vinton continued, "I will be very glad to arrange a get-together at Ralph Morgan's home."[53]

Karloff went to work recruiting. Actress Mary Brian, who joined the Guild on 6 November 1933, recalled, "When I was doing *Hard to Handle* [1933] with Jimmy Cagney, he was very enthusiastic and fired up about the cause... I can remember hearing stories of Boris Karloff and Bela Lugosi recruiting fellow actors on the sets of their Universal horror movies. You can imagine the persuasive spectacle of Frankenstein's monster and Dracula in full make-up, bringing you an application and urging, 'Join the Guild now!'"[54]

Around this time a new face was introduced into Karloff's circle of friends. Cynthia Hobart had left her boarding school, prematurely, in mid 1932 due to lack of funds to

---

xiv The building remained the Guild's headquarters from July 1933 to August 1936.

complete her schooling. "I was totally unequipped to make a living at anything," she later wrote, "but I was a good athlete and Warner Brothers was about to shoot Busby Berkeley's famous "By a Waterfall" number for *Footlight Parade*, starring Ruby Keeler, James Cagney, and Dick Powell."[55]

Two of Hobart's friends were Ruby Keeler's sisters, Marjorie and Gertrude. "One day," Hobart recalled, "they said they were going to the Brown Derby to join some boys for lunch and why didn't I come too? The 'boys' turned out to be friends from *All Quiet on the Western Front*. They had become inseparable friends off the *Front* as well as on; in fact, they ran in a pack. I started seeing Russell [Gleason] steadily and through him I met and became close to the Karloffs."[56]

Despite his split from Universal in June Karloff was not out of work for long. He soon signed with RKO to play the religious fanatic Sanders in *The Lost Patrol*, to be directed by John Ford, a "wonderful man... wonderful director", as Karloff later said.[57] The picture, with a budget of $227,703, would be filmed in the searing heat of the Buttercup Valley sand dunes west of Yuma, Arizona. Production on Ford's picture was set to begin at the end of the month.

On 30 August Karloff boarded a train bound for Yuma and reported on location for *The Lost Patrol* shoot at 6:30 a.m. the next morning. Based on Philip MacDonald's novel *Patrol*,[xv] the story concerned a First World War British cavalry unit who, after their officer is shot dead by an Arab, become lost in the Mesopotamian desert. They reach an oasis where Arab snipers pick them off, one by one, until only the Sergeant remains.

To adapt MacDonald's novel for the screen, Ford called upon the talents of screenwriter Dudley Nichols. "I was working at Fox again," said Nichols, "when Ford, who had gone to RKO... called me, in some urgency. He was to start shooting in about ten days – and had no script. What had been done he considered a mess and unshootable. Eager to help, I got leave from Fox and we sat down together with the novel, taking a fresh concept and starting from scratch. I wrote, and Ford would spend part of the time with me. The script was finished in eight days, very long days I must say..."[58]

If the order of the actors listed on Ford's paper *"Patrol" Suggestions for cast* suggests an order of preference then Karloff was not the first choice for the role of Sanders, for Walter Huston's name appears above him on the list. The paper also reveals that Spencer Tracy, Fredric March, Walter Huston and Leslie Howard were considered for the role of the Sergeant played in the picture by Victor McLaglen,[xvi] who only featured on Ford's list under the roll of Corporal Bell. Basil Rathbone and Laurence Olivier were also listed as possibles for Reginald Denny's role of Brown.

The cast and crew were roused by a bugler every day at 4:30 a.m. and breakfast was served an hour later. Shooting began at 6:30 a.m. and would last until 11 a.m. when the intense desert sun would necessitate a halt to production. Shooting would resume at 2:30 p.m. RKO executives, however, deemed the lunch break too lengthy and requested it be reduced to speed up production. Ford refused to cut the break from three and a half hours to 30 minutes. "I'm not going to have a lot of sick people on my hands – sunstroke and everything else," he said.[59] His words soon proved prophetic. Thirty minutes later the executive who made the request was taken to hospital suffering from sunstroke. Ford

---

xv A version of MacDonald's novel had been filmed before. Also entitled *The Lost Patrol* the 1929 picture stared Victor McLaglen's brother, Cyril, in the role of the Sergeant.
xvi Richard Dix was originally cast in the Sergeant's role but was replaced shortly before filming began.

visited him. "God," the director later explained, "he was the sickest man I've ever seen in my life – lying there – pale, with his eyes back in his head… he had to stay there about four days."[60]

The 110-degree heat also took its toll on the equipment. On the first day of shooting the sound equipment generator broke down and Ford was only able to shoot a single scene. The second day's shooting was interrupted by a windstorm and another hit the following day, halting the production at 9:45 a.m. To compensate Ford shot some scenes inside a plaster mosque set. To make up on lost time he also shot on Sundays and on Labor Day, 3 September.

For one scene an artificial oasis was made with palm trees and water. As the sun was setting water was poured into the prepared pool ready for the arrival of the patrol. The water had only been there a few minutes when a great flock of wild doves came flying in. They turned and descended upon the water. As twilight fell the patrol emerged from the desert. "We and the horses had been practically all day without anything to drink," Karloff explained. "When we reached the pool, we broke before the water. The men flung themselves from their saddles and lay on their bellies between the legs of their parched horses to plunge their faces into the pool and drink as greedily as their mounts. That was a wonderful shot – and you can't imagine what bliss that water was after a whole day in the heat."[61]

Shooting lasted for two weeks during which tempers sometimes frayed. On one occasion a drunken Victor McLaglen took to firing a pistol which, as was then the norm, contained live ammunition. A bullet grazed Frank Baker's foot (Baker was cast as an Arab) and, understandably irate, he charged at the inebriated actor. Wallace Ford also resorted to violence, punching a cook who refused to serve a black worker. The picture wrapped on 22 September, two days over its 21-day schedule.

Two days earlier the *Los Angeles Times* announced that Karloff would be "importantly present"[62] in Universal's *Bombay Mail*, starring Edmund Gwenn. The picture, the newspaper reported, "will be of the "Shanghai Express" type, with its

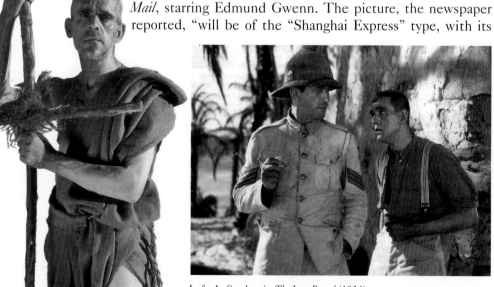

Left: As Sanders in *The Lost Patrol* (1934).
Above: With Victor McLaglen.

locale in India instead of China… The story is an original by L.G. Blochman, and Edwin L. Maria will direct, while Tom Reed will essay his first supervision. He also adapted."[63] However, when the film went into production in early October Karloff was no longer a member of the cast.

On 7 October Karloff joined his co-stars Victor McLaglen and Reginald Denny on NBC radio's *Hollywood on the Air* (a.k.a. *Hollywood on Parade*) to promote *The Lost Patrol* by acting scenes from the picture. On 24 October Karloff appeared on *California Melodies* for a second time where he gave an interview. Others on the bill included Raymond Paige's Orchestra and the violinist Margit Hegedus.

On 27 January 1934 Karloff appeared once again on the radio's *Hollywood on the Air* to promote *The Lost Patrol* and gave an 'interview,' scripted by RKO's publicity department, to the show's host, Jimmy Fidler. The *Washington Post* revealed that the singing of comedienne Maxine Doyle, who also appeared on the show, received "as much applause as any on the programme, not excepting Boris Karloff's reception and Mr. Karloff, the "Frankenstein" of the picture of that name, was the honour guest of the evening."[64]

The Lost Patrol received a "special world premiere"[65] at RKO-Keith's in Washington on Friday, 9 February 1934 and played there for the following week. "Not since *Journey's End* has there been so grim and stark a drama of the heroism of men as this tragic tale of doom that overtook a little band of British cavalry, lost in the Mesopotamian desert," wrote the *Washington Post*.[66] The picture was, the newspaper concluded, "a sterling example of realistic and thrilling drama."[67]

At 7:30 p.m. on 15 February radio station KNX made an experiment that promised to be an "innovation in radio broadcasts that has possibilities of opening up an entirely new field of either entertainment"[68] when they broadcast the entire soundtrack of *The Lost Patrol*. The soundtrack, which included "all the dialogue, sound effects and music will reach listeners via a special line from the motion-picture studio's projection room to the control room of KNX," revealed the *Los Angeles Times*.[69]

The picture opened at the RKO Hillstreet Theatre in Los Angeles the following day. "With Wallace Ford as guest star during the day and the cast of *The Lost Patrol*, headed by Victor McLaglen, Boris Karloff and Reginald Denny appearing in person tonight, the RKO Hillstreet this morning will launch a unique two-premiere programme," announced the *Los Angeles Times*. "One of the most unusual pictures, *The Lost Patrol* is declared to be a stark study of men on the burning sands of the Far East's desert. Screen stars will preside as guests of honour at each performance during the week of the programme, *Hollywood on the Air*, which will be seen for the first time on any stage in conjunction with the showing of *The Lost Patrol*. Tomorrow night *Hollywood on the Air* will present its usual national broadcast, but this time from the stage."[70]

The broadcast from the Hillstreet stage was made at 9 p.m. the following evening. "Jimmy Durante," revealed the *Los Angeles Times*, "is to sing his number 'Inka Dinka Doo', and others appearing on the bill include Rauol [*sic*] Roulien, Jimmy Fidler, Charles Irwin and the members of the cast of *The Lost Patrol*."[71] The cast continued to make personal appearances throughout the run at the RKO Hillstreet and marked the closing of the picture on Thursday, 1 March by attending a "theatre party"[72] for the California Posts of the Canadian Legion.

Throughout the picture's run the reviews continued to be favourable. Still, some did not think much of Karloff's portrayal. "Boris Karloff strikes the most insistent theatric [*sic*] note as Sanders," wrote the *Los Angeles Times*, "he is never quite believable."[73] Mordaunt

Hall of the *New York Times* agreed. "It is, however, with the exception of Boris Karloff, who plays a religious fanatic, an exceptionally well-acted production…"[74] Some, like *Variety*, thought differently. "As a Bible nut, Boris Karloff is on a somewhat different assignment," it wrote. "He gives a fine account of himself."[75]

Both the *New York Times* and the *National Board of Review* voted *The Lost Patrol* as one of the ten best pictures of the year. In addition Max Steiner's score[xvii] was nominated for an Academy Award (he lost to Louis Silvers' score for the musical *One Night of Love*). Steiner would, however, win the following year for his music for another John Ford picture – *The Informer*.

In late September 1933 the 'inevitable booboo' occurred when the contents of the Code of Fair Competition for the Motion Picture Industry were revealed. In June President Roosevelt had introduced the National Industrial Recovery Act (NIRA) in an attempt to boost the nation's failing economy. As part of the incentive the National Recovery Administration established Codes of Fair Competition for industries to abide by. At the Government's request the MPPDA assisted in the creation of a code for the motion picture industry. The result did not, however, meet the approval of the acting community, which objected to several of its provisions. Controversially, the code included an agreement amongst producers not to bid competitively for talent and imposed a $10,000 penalty for doing so. Other contentious elements included the imposition of an annual limit of $100,000 on the earnings of actors, directors and writers and the requirement that agents had to be licensed by the producers, instead of the actors.

"The producers chose the moment when our evening quota of visiting nobility and gentry consisted of Groucho Marx and the late Charlie Butterworth," Karloff recalled. "They, of course, knew what the row was about and we told them what we had been up to. Proudly we dangled our skeleton before them and trotted out the proud roster of our members… all 50 or 60 of them. That did it. They sent telegrams to every important star in the business and they all convened at Frank Morgan's house the following Sunday and the Guild was off to the races at last…"[76]

James Cagney, who was present at the subsequent meeting, had previously discussed working conditions with Karloff. "The need for the Guild was dramatized for me by that very gentle gentleman, Boris Karloff (Boris playing monsters, by the way, was typecasting in reverse)," Cagney later wrote. "Boris came to me one day saying, 'Jim, I'm having a terrible time. Every morning I have to report three and a half hours before work commences in order to put on these fanciful make-ups. By day's end, I'm thoroughly exhausted, and then it's another hour getting the damned stuff off. Sometimes they keep me working through to eleven or twelve o'clock at night. It's terribly, terribly trying.' I said, 'Boris, this is exactly what we're doing at Warner Bros., too.'"[77]

The result of the meeting of Sunday, 1 October was revealed in *Variety* the following day:

STARS IN STAMPEDE QUIT BODY
The Academy of Motion Picture Arts and Sciences is today virtually a defunct organization in so far as its actor membership is concerned.
    Dissatisfied with the fashion in which their interests have been represented at NRA code hearings in Washington and believing that in the course of its hectic four year life the Academy has become a producer-ruled body

xvii Steiner would later incorporate elements of *The Lost Patrol* score into his music for *Casablanca* (1942).

misrepresentative of the acting profession, 23 picture stars met last night at the home of Frank Morgan and resigned by wire from the Academy to form a new actors' organization for the protection of all Hollywood players…

The following telegram was sent to the Academy: 'The undersigned hereby resign from the Academy of Motion Picture Arts and Sciences in all capacities, this resignation to take place at once. We have no feeling of resentment in resigning but feel that an organization for actors only can produce better results for the members of our profession. (Signed) Adolphe Menjou, Fredric March, Robert Montgomery, Chester Morris, George Bancroft, James Cagney, George Raft, Gary Cooper, Ralph Bellamy, Boris Karloff, Warren William, Frank Morgan, Kenneth Thomson.'[78]

At 8:30 p.m. the following evening, 3 October, a meeting was held at Kenneth Thomson's house. The entire board of directors and officers stood down to enable more prominent stars to take up the posts. Eddie Cantor, a long time member of Equity who had taken part in the 1919 strike, was at Lake Arrowhead at the time of the meeting but was elected President *in absentia*. Cantor was also a member of Equity's Council and, importantly, was friends with President Roosevelt. Ann Harding, Fredric March and Adolphe Menjou were elected Vice-Presidents with Groucho Marx as elected Treasurer. Lucile Gleason was voted in as Assistant Treasurer.

On 8 October, five days after that pivotal council, the Guild's first public meeting was held at Hollywood's El Capitan Theatre chaired by the Guild's new president, Eddie Cantor. "By this time, however, everyone, including the big stars… wanted to join the Guild and support it," said Eugene Walsh.[79]

The stars converged to add their support in a call to rewrite the controversial codes. The meeting swelled the membership of the Guild to 529 members. Within weeks that number grew to 4,000. In November Eddie Cantor's friendship with President Roosevelt bore fruit when the two met in Warm Springs, Georgia, to discuss the Guild's concerns resulting in the suspension of the offending articles. "What days," Karloff later wrote, "what fun – what excitement – what glorious results and what leaders: Ralph Morgan, Bob Montgomery, George Murphy, Jim Cagney, Ken Thomson. If one may be permitted to paraphrase Wordsworth – They were the Happy Warriors, that every man in arms would wish to be."[80]

Except for the two radio appearances Karloff had remained unemployed since *The Lost Patrol*. In December he travelled to the fledgling Twentieth Century (later to become 20th Century Fox) to appear as the villainous, rabble-rousing Ledrantz, in *The House of Rothschild*. Set during the Napoleonic Wars the picture told the story of the Jewish banker, Nathan Rothschild [George Arliss], who overcomes anti-Semitism to rise within British society.

It was a controversial choice of material for the studio. On 23 March Adolf Hitler had become Dictator of Germany. Twelve days later, on 1 April, the persecution of German Jews began when Jewish businesses, including doctors, lawyers, and shopkeepers, were boycotted. On 7 April the "Law for the Restoration of the professional Civil Service" was passed which banned Jews from holding Government jobs. Yet despite the climate in Germany the picture's producer, Darryl F. Zanuck, had confidence in his picture. "Even the Jew-haters are going to come and see it," he said.[81]

Arliss, who had won an Academy Award for his portrayal of Benjamin Disraeli in 1929, had originally planned to make *Rothschild* in 1931 while contracted to Warner Brothers. The project was, however, shelved and only revived after Arliss joined Twentieth Century and persuaded the studio to purchase the property. After Maude T. Howell and Sam Mintz prepared a script outline Arliss responded with 14 pages of suggestions. He then wrote to the Zanuck. "I do not wish Howell's and Mintz's hands to be tied in any way to this scenario of mine," Arliss explained, "I only desire that you should take the best there is in it."[82] After completing another draft Howell wrote to Zanuck, "I have followed G.A.'s suggestions as closely as possible. As he wished to emphasize the anti-Jewish feeling, I have made Ledrantz more important."[83]

The final script, by Nunnally Johnson, included a fervent speech by Ledrantz. "I wrote for him a savagely anti-Semitic speech to which, needless to say, Arliss is called upon as Rothschild to reply – and tops him," said Johnson.[84] This speech, however, caused Twentieth Century's co-founder, Joseph Schenck, some concern. "Look, that anti-Semitic speech that Karloff delivers," he told Zanuck, "I'm a little worried about that."[85] Zanuck, though, did not share Schenck's anxiety. "People are not going to complain about its nastiness once they hear what Arliss says in reply," he said. "That's not what I'm worried about," Schenck replied. "What I'm afraid of is that when Karloff finishes saying what he thinks about the Jews, a lot of people are going to get up and cheer."[86] Happily, Schenck's fears proved to be unfounded. Most audiences listened to the speech in silence and cheered and applauded Rothschild's eloquent reply. "Actually, I think we may have leaned over backwards a bit too much," Johnson later said. "Certainly the general effect of the film was so pro-Semitic that a lot of Jews I know reacted the opposite way Joe had done, and were made uncomfortable about it because it was just too sweet, lacked a sense of balance. But what Darryl and I found particularly interesting, and what in the end made the film such a big success, was the fact that we were showing it in that climate at that particular time, and that for once in a way the movies were not shying away but dealing with a real touchy subject right there on the screen."[87]

Joining Arliss and Karloff was a cast that included C. Aubrey Smith (as the Duke of Wellington), Loretta Young and Robert Young. "Most of the actors I knew well; I had either met them on the screen or played with them on the stage," Arliss later wrote. "The only one I had never met was the terrible Boris Karloff – the professional bogeyman. I was therefore considerably surprised to find him one of the most retiring and gentle gentlemen it was ever my lot to meet."[88]

The picture premiered at the Astor in New York on 14 March and was on general release from 7 April. "A fine picture on all counts; in the acting, writing, and directing, and in its financial prospects," wrote *Variety*. "It handles the delicate subject of anti-Semitism with tact and restraint... *House of Rothschild* is one of those occasional 100% smashes which Hollywood achieves."[89] Curiously, aside from the cast list, the review made no mention of Karloff.

Mordaunt Hall of the *New York Times* also liked the picture. "In fact," he wrote, "the picture is engrossing throughout. The dialogue is smart and often witty and the direction and staging are excellent... Not only does Mr. Arliss's work here excel that which he has done in any other picture, but most of the other roles are acted expertly. Boris Karloff, without any facial disguise, appears to advantage as the sinister Baron Ledrantz."[90]

A nationwide poll of exhibitors, conducted by *Film Daily*, placed *The House of Rothschild* second in the year's top ten films. The picture was also nominated, along with another 11 pictures, for the Best Picture Academy Award. It lost to *It Happened One Night*.

On 17 January 1934 Karloff returned to Universal City to attend Carl Laemmle Sr.'s 67th birthday party. Any ill feeling resulting from Karloff's departure the previous June was forgotten as the star took his seat beside the studio's founder. During the event, which was held at noon, Laemmle, surrounded by his studio workers, cut a 67-pound chocolate cake which had been made in the form of Universal's trademark globe with circling aeroplane. As if to announce Karloff's acceptance back into Universal's fold, the same day the *New York Times* announced Karloff would appear in the studio's screen version of Edgar Allan Poe's story *The Black Cat*.

The Black Cat, Karloff's first picture for Universal in over a year, was the brainchild of 29-year-old Austro-Hungarian émigré director, Edgar G. Ulmer. Ulmer had initially worked in the German theatre with Max Reinhardt before starting his film career working on the set design for Paul Wegener's 1920 picture *Der Golem*. He later served as (uncredited) set designer for Fritz Lang on *Die Nibelungen* (1924), *Metropolis* (1927), *Spione* (1928) and *M* (1931). Ulmer moved to America in 1923 and soon signed to Universal. "I got a contract with Laemmle," he recalled, "which was a 'catch-all' contract – assistant art director and production assistant with Willy [William] Wyler and that whole bunch out there."[91]

Fortunately, along with the Universal contract, Ulmer gained a supportive producer. "[A] lot of credit must be given to Junior Laemmle on that picture," Ulmer later said. "Junior was a very dear friend of mine, and a very young man... And when I came to him with the idea of *The Black Cat*... Junior gave me free rein to write a horror picture in the style we had started in Europe with *Caligari*. He was a very strange producer; he didn't have much education, but had great respect for intelligence and for creative spirit."[92]

Ulmer co-wrote the story with Peter Ruric (the screenwriting pseudonym of mystery writer George Sims) using, as a basis for the plot, recent news reports concerning the occultist Aleister Crowley. Crowley had been irate over the publication of *Laughing Torso*, the 1932 autobiography of his author friend Nina Hammett, and chose to prosecute for

Left: As Count Ledrantz in *The House of Rothschild* (1934). Right: With George Arliss.

libel. One passage in particular riled him. "He was supposed to practise Black Magic there," Hammett wrote, "and one day a baby was said to have disappeared mysteriously. There was also a goat there. This all pointed to Black Magic, so people said, and the inhabitants of the village were frightened of him."[93]

Crowley maintained in court that he was a practitioner of white magic and opposed to the darker arts. To aid the defence Hammett's solicitor called into court Betty May Loveday. Loveday claimed that, in 1923, she and her husband Raoul were invited to study 'magick' at Crowley's 'Abbey of Thelema',[xviii] situated in the Sicilian town of Cefalù. During the stay, however, Raoul died of enteritis. His death, Loveday claimed, was due to his participation in a ritual involving a black cat. *The Times* reported Loveday's claim that "after an invocation lasting three hours, the cat was killed. Its blood fell into a bowl and her husband had to drink a cup of that blood."[94]

Crowley lost the case. The judge, Mr. Justice Swift, commented, "I have nothing but this to say about the facts of the case. I have been over 40 years engaged in the administration of the law in one capacity or another. I thought that I knew every conceivable form of wickedness. I thought that everything which was vicious and bad had been produced at some time or another before me. I have learnt in this case that we can always learn something more if we have long enough. I have never heard such dreadful, horrible and abominable stuff as that which has been produced by the man who describes himself as the greatest living poet."[95]

Using elements from the case Ulmer and Ruric fashioned a bizarre tale which, although for commercial reasons was advertised as Edgar Allan Poe's *The Black Cat*, bore no relation to the original 1843 story.

The Black Cat was to be the first teaming of Universal's two horror stars: Boris Karloff and Bela Lugosi. Karloff signed on to play the picture's villain, the Satanist Hjalmar Poelzig, for a fee of $7,500. The character was created from an amalgamation of Crowley and German architect Hans Poelzig, whom Ulmer had met during the production of *Der Golem*. The architect was one of the picture's art directors, responsible for the expressionistic sets of 16th century Prague. Poelzig, like his cinematic namesake, held an interest in the occult sciences. He and his wife, Marlene, also held séances at their home, during which their daughter would serve as the medium.

Lugosi had just completed a stint on the stage. On Tuesday, 12 September 1933 he opened in Earl Carroll's mystery-comedy *Murder at the Vanities* at the New Amsterdam Theatre in New York. He stayed with the show until late November. On 8 December Lugosi began a short tour heading a vaudeville bill in a condensed version of *Dracula* and planned to follow this run with another play. In January 1934 he acquired the rights to S.J. Warshawsky's play *Pagan Fury* with the intention of playing the lead role of a bohemian artist. He planned to open the play in Chicago in the spring. However, when offered the role of Poelzig's nemesis, Dr. Vitus Werdegast in *The Black Cat*, Lugosi accepted and *Pagan Fury* fell by the wayside. Lugosi's fee for the picture was $3,000, less than half the amount Karloff would receive.

Initially, *The Black Cat* had not been intended as a picture. "I wanted to write a novel, really," said Ulmer, "because I did not *believe* the literature during and after the war, on both sides: in Germany *and* in England, it was very much the heroic thing, where enemies were friends like you never saw before. I couldn't believe that. Therefore, I took two men

xviii In reality the 'Abbey' was little more than a dilapidated, five-room, single-story farmhouse that lacked sanitation and electricity.

who knew each other and who fought their private war during the time when capitalism flourished. I thought it was quite a story, stylistically. I had a wonderful cameraman [John J. Mescall], and Junior let me do the sets and everything at the same time."[96]

The interiors of Poelzig's mansion (where "even the phones are dead") reflected Ulmer's expressionistic background. "My father had very definite ideas all the time about the look that he wanted for the film," said Arianne Ulmer Cipes, "and, again, it goes back to his German background. At the time you had an architecture that was called the Bauhaus and my father loved Bauhaus. The set designs of that apartment, that house, is definitely Bauhaus. Plus the fact that he wanted to give it the German expressionistic design and look – the shadow and light. And... he just had a wonderful time with it. It was one of his happiest experiences. I know that he always loved this film."[97]

In *The Black Cat* Poelzig's home is built on the ruins of a fort, overlooking the site of one of the First World War's bloodiest battles. "Tens of thousands of men died here," explains the bus driver [George Davis] in the picture. "The ravine down there was piled twelve deep with dead and wounded men. The little river below was swollen red, a raging torrent of blood. And that high hill yonder where Engineer Poelzig now lives, was the site of Fort Marmorus. He built his home on its very foundations. Marmorus, the greatest graveyard in the world."

This idea sprang from the time Ulmer had worked on *The Golem*. "At that time I met Gustav Meyrinck," Ulmer explained, "the man who wrote *Golem* as a novel. Meyrinck was one of those strange Prague Jews, like Kafka, who was very much tied up in the mystic Talmudic background. We had a lot of discussions, and Meyrinck at that time was contemplating a play based upon Doumont, which was a French fortress the Germans had shelled to pieces during World War I; there were some survivors who didn't come out for years. And the commander was a strange Euripedes figure who went crazy three years later when he was brought back to Paris, because he had walked on that mountain of bodies. I thought it was an important subject, and that feeling was in the air in the twenties."[98]

On 27 February 1934, due to the absence of both Laemmles, the script was approved by production supervisor, E.M. Asher. Filming of the picture, budgeted at $91,125 and with an estimated four-week shoot, began the following day. Lugosi was joined by Jacqueline Wells and David Manners (as newlyweds Joan and Peter Alison).

Although Manners had worked with Lugosi before – in *Dracula* (1931), *The Death Kiss* (1932) and *The Devil's in Love* (1933) – the two actors did not have a close relationship. "I never did get to know him – not really," said Manners. "He was not someone I cared to know."[99] Manners had also previously worked with Karloff on *The Mummy* two years earlier. "He was a friendly, gentle person," Manners recalled, "not at all like the monsters he portrayed. He and I had a kind of friendship – and he always spoke with a lisp."[100]

On Friday, 2 March Karloff reported to Jack Pierce to prepare for his first day on *The Black Cat*. This time the make-up was far simpler to apply than previous Pierce creations. Instead of the accustomed layers of cotton and collodion Karloff's make-up consisted of a distinctive angular hairstyle, white face-paint and black lipstick.

Yet despite his character's inherent wickedness, Karloff found it difficult to take the role seriously. "My biggest job was to keep him in the part, because he laughed at himself," Ulmer explained. "Not the Hungarian, of course: You had to cut away from Lugosi continuously to cut him down..."[101] Karloff's levity was demonstrated during Poelzig's introduction. "One

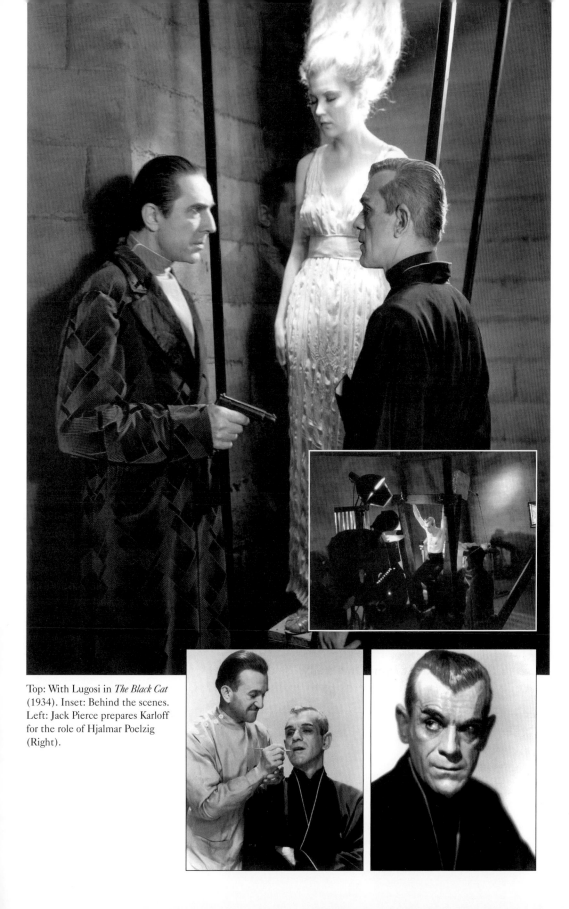

Top: With Lugosi in *The Black Cat* (1934). Inset: Behind the scenes. Left: Jack Pierce prepares Karloff for the role of Hjalmar Poelzig (Right).

of the nicest scenes I had with him," said Ulmer, "he lies in bed next to the daughter of
Lugosi; and the young couple rings, down at the door, and he gets up and you see him the
first time in costume, in that modernistic set. I explained the scene to him and he said,
'Aren't you ashamed to do a thing like that – that has nothing to do with acting?' So I told
him to be nice, and do it: he got into bed, we got ready to shoot, and he got up, he turned to
the camera after he put his shoes on, and said, 'Boo!' Every time I had him come in by the
door, he would open the door and say, 'Here comes the heavy.' He was a very lovely man."[102]

In another scene – his final in the picture – Lugosi, too, proved problematic. The script called
for Werdegast to wreak his revenge and skin Poelzig alive.[xix] Yet, as the scene was shot, Lugosi
repeatedly fluffed his lines. Karloff remained half-naked and tethered to an embalming rack
until Lugosi was word perfect. "Poor old Bela… It was a strange thing," Karloff recalled. "He was
really a shy, sensitive, talented man who had a fine career on the classical stage in Europe. But
he made one fatal mistake. He never took the trouble to learn our language. Consequently, he
was very suspicious on the set, suspicious of tricks, fearful of what he regarded as scene stealing.
Later, when he realised I didn't go in for such nonsense, we became friends."[103]

During his usual 4 p.m. tea break Karloff would relax, smoke a cigarette or talk with
the director. "Karloff was a very charming man," Ulmer recalled. "Very charming – and
he never took himself seriously."[104] There was no small talk, however, between the two
stars. This also extended beyond the set. "I worked with Bela Lugosi in, oh, three or
four pictures,[xx] but outside of the studio we didn't meet," Karloff said. "You know it's an
enormous, rambling big place spread out all over southern California. You perhaps do a
picture with somebody, and your paths don't cross again for a year. It depends what your
individual tastes were… I used to play a lot of cricket, for years – which I don't think
would have appealed a lot to Bela."[105]

The picture was completed on 17 March, less than three weeks after filming
had begun. The studio, however, was not happy at the picture's content as Ulmer's
daughter, Arianne Ulmer Cipes, recalled. "The front office was appalled at what they
were getting," she said, "especially since Papa Laemmle was away… This was not what
they expected at all!"[106]

To downplay the satanic element of the picture, and placate the studio executives,
Ulmer removed some scenes and reshot others. Poelzig's Black Mass[xxi] was toned down
from its original, more orgiastic, treatment. The retakes were shot between 25 March and
27 March. Yet the additional footage included a scene that was more subtly disturbing than
any of the excised footage. Poelzig wanders the bowels of the old fort and gazes at the
preserved bodies of women suspended in glass cases, adding the suggestion of necrophilia
to Poelzig's other evils. It was a scene that pleased Ulmer. "My father was always very proud
of the fact that he pulled a fast one," said Ulmer's daughter. "He got that scene in, in the
reshoot. They never understood how wicked and marvellous that scene was."[107] The final
cost of the picture, including reshoots, was $95,745.

---

xix In the original shooting script this scene was far more explicit: "The wall. The shadow of Werdegast and Poelzig. An
effect as if Werdegast was splitting the scalp slowly, pulling the sheath of skin down over Poelzig's head and shoulders.
Poelzig, *sans* skin, is struggling on the rack. By a superhuman effort, he frees himself and falls expressionlessly, on Joan. He
laboriously, painfully, crawls towards her." Even toned down *Variety* baulked at the scene. "Its inclusion in a motion picture
is dubious showmanship," it claimed.
xx Karloff and Lugosi appeared in eight pictures together, although in *Gift of Gab* (1932) they shared no scenes.
xxi The first line of the black mass – *Cum Grano Salis* [*With a Grain of Salt*] – may have been a surreptitious tribute to
Karloff's playlet of the same name, penned with Margot Beaton and copyrighted in 1913.

The Black Cat premiered at Pantages Theatre in Hollywood on 3 May 1934. In attendance were the Karloffs, the Lugosis and Jacqueline Wells. A little over two weeks later, on 19 May, the picture opened at the Roxy Theatre in New York.[xxii] *Variety* was unimpressed. "Because of the presence in one film of Boris Karloff, that jovial madman, and Bela Lugosi, that suave fiend, this picture probably has box office attraction," it wrote. "But otherwise and on the counts of story, novelty, thrills and distinction, the picture is sub-normal... Story is confused and confusing, and while with the aid of heavily-shadowed lighting and mausoleum-like architecture, a certain eeriness has been achieved, it's all a poor imitation of things seen before... Karloff and Lugosi are sufficiently sinister and convincingly demented."[108]

The *New York Times* considered the picture, "A clammy and excessively ghoulish tale of hi-jinks in a Hungarian horror salon, *The Black Cat* is more foolish than horrible. The story and dialogue pile the agony on too thick to give the audience a reasonable scare."[109]

Although the reviews were unenthusiastic, business was excellent and, with reported box office receipts of $236,000, *The Black Cat* became Universal's top moneymaker of 1934. Yet despite the picture's success it was to be the last film Ulmer would make at the studio. During shooting Ulmer had fallen in love with his script assistant, Shirley Castle Alexander. Unfortunately Alexander was not only married but her husband was Max Alexander, a nephew of Carl Laemmle Sr. The relationship effectively ended Ulmer's Hollywood career. Alexander divorced her husband and married Ulmer. The couple left Hollywood to settle in New York where Ulmer made low-budget independent pictures.

In Britain problems with the censor meant *The Black Cat* opened in London ten months after its American premiere. Retitled *The House of Doom* the picture also suffered various cuts. All references to Satanism were removed and Karloff and his coven became sun worshippers. "Boris Karloff and Bela Lugosi piling horror upon horror," wrote *Film Weekly*, "until it all becomes just silly. Lots of screams, but neither rhyme nor reason. You'll need to be very indulgent to enjoy this one. In the opening scenes it is almost funny to watch Karloff and Lugosi trying to outdo one another for the horror honours. Lugosi, however, gives up the struggle halfway through and turns into quite a benevolent kind of menace, leaving Karloff in full possession of the honours, such as they are."[110]

Following the box office success of *The Black Cat* Universal announced further Karloff-Lugosi teamings including *Dracula's Daughter* and the inevitable *Frankenstein* sequel, *The Return of Frankenstein*. Despite these announcements the next picture to feature Universal's greatest horror stars, albeit briefly, was the musical comedy *Gift of Gab*.

Directed by Karl Freund the picture concerned an egocentric broadcaster Phillip Gabney [Edmund Lowe] who is fired when he fakes an interview. Gabney turns to drink but, having learned his lesson, finally regains his job and marries the Program Controller, Barbara Kelton [Gloria Stuart]. The picture also featured musical numbers performed by Ruth Etting, Ethel Waters and the Downey Sisters.

Inexplicably, and contrary to some publicity shots which showed Karloff and Lugosi together, the two shared no scenes in the finished picture. Both made brief appearances in a comic murder mystery 'broadcast' at the beginning of the film for which Karloff and Lugosi were paid $500 and $250, respectively. Karloff, bedecked in a top hat, featured as 'the Phantom' while Lugosi, as a flat-cap wearing, gun-toting French Apache dancer, was

---

xxii To publicise the picture Universal had held an outdoor 'Black Cat Show'. Dozens of children paraded their family pets before Karloff and Lugosi, who were suitable attired in their costumes from the picture.

relegated to standing in a closet asking, "What time is it?" The picture was released on 24 September 1934.

Gift of Gab was Karloff's last picture of 1934. The rest of the year was spent at leisure at the couple's new home at 2320 Bowmont Drive in Coldwater Canyon. The canyon, journalist Jonah Maurice Ruddy wrote, "is a quiet section running north of Beverly Hills. A mile from the main road is a winding street called Bowmont Drive. It curls up the hillside and loses itself in a maze of oak trees. Near here is a rambling Mexican-style of home, very hard to see from the road. Growing in wild abandon around it are masses of morning glory and honeysuckle."[111] The house had been purchased from Virginia Barnard, a friend of Dorothy's, on 31 March 1934 while Karloff was filming *The Black Cat*. It had once belonged to Katherine Hepburn who claimed the property was haunted.

During his time away from the studio Karloff put pen to paper and the resultant article, *Cricket in California*, was published in the Screen Actors Guild magazine, *The Screen Player*, on 15 May. Karloff began:

> IN ADDITION to having a most conservative nature. I am also a stickler for the plain, unvarnished truth, so I feel quite safe in prefacing my remarks by the simple statement that cricket is the finest game in the world…[112]

The magazine also included information on the upcoming 'Film Stars Frolic', the Guild's second fundraising event. "Jimmy Cagney is handling the reins in connection with the arena activities," it reported. "Then there's Boris Karloff, who has been placed in charge of special events. Not only these events, but also on the radio and in innumerable ways, Karloff is busy spilling the news about the Frolic."[113]

Karloff and Lugosi's appearance in the short *Columbia Snapshot #11* also referred to the forthcoming event. "It is an historic occasion whenever Boris Karloff and Bela Lugosi confront each other," stated the announcer. "Their very presence weaves a spell of mystery and horror." Sitting either side of a chessboard the two stars confront each other.

> Karloff: Are you ready for the test, Dracula?
> Lugosi: I'm ready, Frankenstein.
> Karloff: Then… let us begin.
> **Both laugh**
> Karloff: You understand, Bela, don't you, that the one who wins this little game of chess is to head the parade at the 'Film Star's Frolic'?
> Lugosi: O.K. Boris. Your move.
> Karloff: Right.

The 'Frolic' was held at the Gilmore Stadium from 18 to 20 May and had a programme that included a chariot race, a rodeo, and circus acts. It also featured appearances by such stars as Claudette Colbert, Jimmy Durante, W.C. Fields, Carole Lombard, Bela Lugosi, Jeanette MacDonald, Edward G. Robinson and Spencer Tracy.

Unfortunately, of the Guild's membership of 4,000, less than two hundred showed for the event and the failure depleted the Guild's treasury. Only the loans of $1,000 each from President Eddie Cantor, Vice Presidents Robert Montgomery, Ann Harding, and James Cagney and board member Fredric March kept the Guild afloat. The

Guild held another ball before the year was out. This time the event, which featured performances by Jeanette MacDonald, Joe E. Brown and Bill 'Bojangles' Robinson, was an unqualified success.

Although Karloff was taking time out from making pictures the studio continued to announce pictures intended for the star. In early June the *Los Angeles Times* announced that Karloff and, possibly, Lugosi would star in *The Raven*, a tale fashioned from Edgar Allan Poe's famous poem. In addition the pair might also co-star in the horror story *Yahgan* to be directed by Irving Pichel. A month earlier the same newspaper had announced Universal would make an adaptation of Charles Dickens' final (and unfinished) novel *The Mystery of Edwin Drood*. Heather Angel would feature alongside Frank Lawton and, possibly, Boris Karloff. In mid-August it seemed likely Karloff would star in the picture as John Jasper. Yet two weeks later the situation had changed and, instead, Claude Rains took the role. The film began shooting in mid-November. Still, Universal had alternative plans for Boris Karloff – a science-fiction picture entitled *A Trip to Mars*, to be directed by James Whale.

The project, though, had its origins several years earlier. On 18 March 1932 Universal had purchased a 27-page story by *The Lost World* (1925) director, Harry O. Hoyt, then working as a staff writer at the studio. Several treatments followed including one by Ralph Parker and another, on 20 May, by Richard Schayer and Tom Reed. This was followed by a full screenplay on 13 June before the project was shelved. It was only revived following the success of the effects-laden *King Kong* and *The Invisible Man* (both 1933).

In September 1933 *Frankenstein* director James Whale agreed to direct the picture upon the condition that Universal optioned John Galsworthy's new novel, *One More River*. Three months later he left Hollywood for his native England where he arrived on the 12 December. Whale and R.C. Sherriff then began working on the screenplay for *A Trip to Mars*, which was almost complete when the director left for his hometown of Dudley a week later. In 1973 Davis Lewis recalled, "It was a brilliant script... The blast-off, everything, was as it finally happened. It wasn't exactly as it happened, but it was damn close!"[114]

The screenplay told the tale of Professor von Saxmar, who launches an unmanned rocket bound for Mars.[xxiii] When the rocket explodes upon the planet the Martians retaliate by sending their own missile, which destroys half of Europe. Saxmar, along with his daughter, a reporter and the Professor's dog (an Irish Terrier), journey to Mars to stop the Martians. The red planet, they discover, is home to a race of intelligent giant insects, the rulers of a race of giant ants. Bizarrely, the reporter falls in love with Meera, the Queen of the Martians, who becomes more human as a result of the reporter's affection. The ants, however, rise up against their insect masters and Saxmar and his daughter are killed. The dog, who had learned to talk on Mars, dies 'with a cheerful wisecrack on his lips'.[115]

While Whale was in England scenarist Philip MacDonald was preparing a 36-page synopsis for another Karloff picture, *The Return of Frankenstein*. However, when Whale returned to America the following February the *Frankenstein* sequel was postponed so the director could concentrate on *A Trip to Mars*. Yet, as with *The Invisible Man*, time again became a factor. The stop-motion animation that Whale declared would "soar higher still into the realms of trick photography"[116] would take time to produce. Instead, Whale began to work on *One More River* and (according to *Variety*) intended to return to *A Trip to Mars* at a later date. Despite

---

xxiii According to both R.C. Sherriff and David Lewis the rocket's destination was changed from Mars to the Moon – although publicity continued to refer to the picture as *A Trip To Mars*.

Universal Weekly's September 1934 announcement that it was 'highly possible' the picture would be produced in the 1934/35 season, the project never materialised.

Karloff's final radio engagement of 1934 was broadcast on 11 October when he made his second radio appearance that year playing Death/Prince Sirki in a scene from Alberto Casella's play *Death Takes a Holiday*.[xxiv] In August he had presented a scene from the drama on *The Show*. Now he revisited the role on Rudy Vallee's variety show *The Fleischmann Hour* on NBC. He would play the part again two years later.

Three days later the Karloffs attended the Loyala Lions-Santa Clara football game at the Gilmore Stadium. Then, in mid-November, Karloff returned to the stage for a one-off event. *The Los Angeles Times* wrote, "What with the Little Theatre of the Dominos positively bulging from the pressure of overflow audiences… the Dominos' Revels took on the outlines of decidedly cosmopolitan entertainment."[117]

The evening's bill consisted of Maude Fulton in the playlets *Scenario* and *The Last Act*, Willie Collier and Sam Hardy in a satire called *Ripping and Rapping*, Kitty Kelly in *Hard Hit*, and Robert Emmett O'Connor in *Our Little Hollywood*. Karloff appeared in a piece called *Mud, Blood and Kisses*. "It was an exposé of radio station methods in play production," explained the *Los Angeles Times*. "Boris Karloff and H.B. Warner were the stars, with Edward Ellies, Inez Regan and Matt McHugh running close for honours."[118]

On 14 December 1934 Karloff's engagements for the year came to an end with an appearance at an annual benefit at the Shrine Auditorium. The star joined other Universal players at the event (including Bing Crosby who, naturally, sang), which was sponsored by the *Examiner* newspaper. The Christmas season signalled the end of Karloff's respite from pictures and, as the year drew to a close, he began to prepare for his role in, arguably, the greatest horror movie of them all – *Bride of Frankenstein*.

xxiv A movie version, starring Fredric March as Death/Prince Sirki, had opened in February.

Chapter 9

BRIDE OF FRANKENSTEIN

(1935)

"The producers realised they'd made a dreadful mistake. They let the Monster die in the burning mill. In one brief script conference, however, they brought him back alive. Actually, it seems, he had only fallen through the flaming floor into the millpond beneath, and could now go on for reels and reels!"[1]

Boris Karloff (1962)

A sequel to *Frankenstein* had been years in the planning. Originally announced for production during the 1932-1933 season, director Robert Florey had submitted a seven-page treatment entitled *The New Adventures of Frankenstein – The Monster Lives!* in February 1932. It proved no more successful than his 1931 efforts to bring Mary Shelley's characters to the screen and the studio rejected it.

James Whale, however, was not happy to continue the tale and instead prepared *The Old Dark House* for production. When his following picture, *The Invisible Man*, ran into script problems, the director persuaded Universal to contract his old friend, the playwright R.C. Sherriff, to supply a script. Sherriff signed his contract in February 1932 and presented Whale with a completed screenplay a few months later.[i] The studio, concerned over the ongoing script problems with the Wells story, requested Whale drop the project and prepare the *Frankenstein* sequel instead. "They're always like that," Whale told Sherriff. "If they score a hit with a picture they always want to do it again. They've got a perfectly sound commercial reason. *Frankenstein* was a gold mine at the box office, and a sequel to it is bound to win, however rotten it is. They've had a script made for a sequel and it stinks to heaven. In any case I squeezed the idea dry on the original picture, and never want to work on it again."[2] Sherriff's literate script for *The Invisible Man*, however, meant that the Wells project was once again given the green light and the *Frankenstein* sequel passed from Whale's hands.

---

i Sherriff's final script for *The Invisible Man* was submitted to MPPDA on 12 June 1933. It was passed without any changes.

Left: With Ernest Thesiger. Right: With Elsa Lanchester.

In June 1933, while Karloff was having his altercation with the studio, the project was revived. Tom Reed submitted a treatment on 10 June and followed this with three drafts of a screenplay. "Decision to make a sequel to the blood-chilling *Frankenstein*, with Karloff playing the role of the man created by science," wrote the *Washington Post*, "was made after Tom Reed, Universal scenarist, found the inspiration for the new story, with even greater thrill possibilities than the original, in a certain chapter of the Mary Shelley novel written 100 years ago."[3] After receiving MPPDA approval for Reed's draft, which had been submitted on 25 July, Laemmle Jr. assigned the project – then titled *The Return of Frankenstein* – to director Kurt Neumann. The studio's 1933 deficit of $1,062,216 meant, however, the project was subsequently postponed until that December.

Following the success of *The Invisible Man* in November, Laemmle once again pursued James Whale to helm the *Frankenstein* sequel. In December, however, Whale returned to England to work with Sherriff on *A Trip to Mars*. Nevertheless, the search for a suitable *Frankenstein* script continued and writers Lawrence G. Blochman and Philip MacDonald both attempted versions.

In Blochman's treatment, submitted on 5 December, Henry and Elizabeth had joined a travelling carnival and, travelling under the surname Heinrich, were working as puppeteers. The Monster finds them and demands that Henry create him a mate. Although he does the Monster's bidding Henry's new creation does not live long. The Monster also perishes – in a fight with a lion. In contrast, Philip MacDonald moved the story (submitted on 26 December) to a contemporary setting. In his 36-page treatment Frankenstein creates a death-ray, which he tries to sell to the League of Nations. The invention re-animates the Monster and is later used to destroy it. Perhaps unsurprisingly neither treatment was acceptable to Whale when he returned to California in mid-February 1934 with his screenplay for *A Trip to Mars*. When his Martian picture was shelved he began work on *One More River* and the *Frankenstein* sequel was again postponed.

In June 1934 Whale asked John L. Balderston to work on a treatment, requiring the picture to begin where the last left off. Balderston introduced the prologue with Mary Shelley and fashioned a screenplay in which the female creature is created from variety of cadavers including train wreck victims and the body of a circus giantess who had committed suicide. On 8 June the *New York Times* revealed that the sequel would now be entitled *The Bride of Frankenstein* although the original title of *Return of Frankenstein* was bandied about in the press (including the *New York Times*) until January 1935.

Concerns over the violent and sexual content of motion pictures had led, on 13 June 1934, to the establishment of the Production Code Administration (PCA). Approval under the code, which had until then been voluntary, now became a requirement. As a result only pictures passed by the PCA would display a certificate of approval. Now the Administration would rigidly uphold its three general principles, as stated in the original Production Code of 1930:

> 1. No picture shall be produced which will lower the moral standards of those who see it. Hence the sympathy of the audience shall never be thrown to the side of crime, wrong-doing, evil or sin.
> 2. Correct standards of life, subject only to the requirements of drama and entertainment, shall be presented.
> 3. Law, natural or human, shall not be ridiculed, nor shall sympathy be created for its violation.[4]

While *Frankenstein* had not been subject to any compulsory censorship under the Code the picture had suffered cuts from state censors who felt its content was both horrific and sacrilegious. With the creation of the PCA the sequel would now be subject to even greater restrictions.

On 9 June Balderston submitted a treatment for the sequel. On 23 July a copy of his fourth and final draft was submitted to the PCA. The PCA's director Joseph Breen responded with his objections. "Throughout the script there are a number of references to Frankenstein which compare him to God and which compare his creation of the monster to God's creation of Man," Breen wrote. "All such references should be eliminated."[5] Breen also opposed a scene in which the Monster watches a courting couple through a window and recommended the removal of any material which suggested the monster desired a sexual companion.

Although, by September, Balderston had been working on the picture for three months James Whale found the results disappointing. R.C. Sherriff, then back in Hollywood, was now asked to write a treatment. "They fished out the sequel to *Frankenstein*, the old bogy that had bedevilled Whale. They suggested calling it *The Bride of Frankenstein* and were sure that I could do something very exciting with it. But it was dreadful stuff. I should have spent the summer writing pulp, and been ashamed of every page I wrote. So I suggested that we should cut the third assignment[ii] and call it a day. This they agreed to, and I went home relieved, but out of work."[6]

In November playwright William Hurlburt and writer Edmund Pearson began work on the script and on 30 November a screenplay constructed from elements of previous attempts was submitted to the PCA for consideration. Breen responded with requests for some changes of dialogue and a reduction to the number of deaths. "We counted ten separate scenes," he wrote, "in which the Monster either strangles or tramples people to death – this in addition to some other murders by subsidiary characters. In a picture as basically gruesome as this one, we believe that such a great amount of slaughter is unwise

---

ii Sherriff's first two assignments for Universal were James Whale's pictures *One More River* (1934) and *The Road Back* (1937).

and recommend very earnestly that you do something about toning this down."[7]

Breen also complained about a scene where the monster, fleeing the villagers, enters a cemetery: 'Long shot… an imposing monument… night… set against the sky – a huge Christus. The Monster comes upon it suddenly. In the dim light, he sees it as a human figure, tortured as he was in the wood. He dashes himself against the figure, grappling with it. The cross is overturned. He tries to rescue the figure from the cross…'

"Although this scene," Whale wrote in explanation, "including the figure of Christ on the cross, as I explained to Mr. Shurlock,[iii] was meant to be one of supreme sympathy on the part of the Monster, as he tries to rescue what he thinks is a man being persecuted as he was himself some time ago in the wood, if you still find this objectionable, I could easily change it to the figure of death…"[8] Breen did, indeed, find it objectionable and Whale later amended the scene. He replaced one potentially sacrilegious image with another and had the monster topple a statue of a bishop instead.

Following Breen's letter Whale met with the PCA to personally discuss their concerns. He defended the work by citing instances in the script that questioned the morality of Frankenstein's actions. Whale also reminded the PCA that the principal characters atone for their actions when they are destroyed in the climactic explosion. The PCA's concerns remained however and on 10 December Whale wrote to them with amendments to the script.

> December 10, 1934
> Dear Mr. Breen,
> Herewith are the proposed changes, which deal with your letter of Dec 5th, and also your letter of December 7th. As, however, the former letter is fuller, I think it best to send on the letter I had written immediately after the conference, as in your letter of December 5th there are several points about God, entrails, immortality and mermaids which you did not bring up again, and I am very anxious to have a script meet with your approval in every detail before shooting it.
>
>   All best wishes,
>   Yours sincerely,
>   JAMES WHALE[9]

The final approved storyline began with a prologue. On a stormy night in a castle (presumably a stylised Villa Diodati) Mary, Percy Shelley and Lord Byron[iv] discuss Mary's novel. Mary then reveals her story did not end with the fire at the mill and begins her tale.

The Monster is alive, having fallen through the wreckage of the burning mill into the pond beneath. The body of Henry Frankenstein is taken home where it is discovered that he still lives. The old Baron has died and as the new Baron recuperates he is visited by his old teacher, Dr. Septimus Pretorius. Expelled from the University for "knowing too much" Pretorius tries to persuade Henry to join him in his work. At his home Pretorius reveals the results of his experiments at creating life – seven miniature people, or homunculi, that

---

iii Geoffrey Shurlock of the PCA.
iv David Niven was tested for the role of Lord Byron.

he keeps in jars: a King,[v] Queen, Bishop, Ballerina, Mermaid, Baby and a Devil. "While you were digging in your graves, piecing together dead tissues, I, my dear pupil, went for my material to the source of life. I grew my creatures like cultures; grew them, as Nature does – from seed…" he tells Frankenstein. "Our mad dream is only half realised. Alone, you have created a man. Now together, we will create his mate."

The Monster, meanwhile, makes his way through a forest. There he meets a young shepherdess who, shocked by the Monster's appearance, falls into a pool. The monster saves her but the girl's screaming alerts some hunters who shoot him in the arm. The Monster escapes but the burgomaster is alerted to the situation and a search is initiated. The Monster is pursued and captured. Tied to a pole, he is removed to the town dungeon and shackled to a large chair. He soon escapes, however, killing several of the villagers, and sending the townsfolk into a panic.

The injured Monster comes upon a forest hut and enters. Its occupant – a kindly blind old hermit – befriends him and teaches the monster some rudimentary speech. Their friendship is shattered, however, when the two hunters, having lost their way in the forest, enter the hermit's hut and discover the Monster. A struggle ensues and the hut is set ablaze. The Monster escapes and, once again pursued by the villagers, enters a graveyard. He descends into a crypt where he finds Dr. Pretorius and his assistants, Karl and Ludwig, indulging in a spot of grave-robbing. The assistants leave complaining, "This is no life for murderers." Pretorius remains to have a meal, however, and the Monster approaches him. Unafraid, Pretorius feeds the Monster. "You make a man like me?" the creature asks. "No. Woman. Friend for you," the doctor replies.

Pretorius again visits Henry. "All the necessary preparations are made," he says. "My part in the experiment is complete. I have created by my method a perfect human brain, already living but dormant. Everything is now ready for you and me to begin our supreme collaboration." However, the Baron has now changed his mind and refuses to help. Pretorius then reveals the Monster. "Must do it!" the Monster growls. Henry still refuses. The Monster leaves and, on Pretorius' orders, kidnaps Frankenstein's wife, Elizabeth. Henry is forced, therefore, to agree to Pretorius' demands.

In the laboratory in the old watchtower the scientists create their female monster, the 'Bride', who is brought to life during a thunderstorm. When the Monster approaches his mate, however, she is repelled by him and screams. A despondent Monster pulls a lever, destroying the watchtower and its occupants – the 'Bride', Pretorius, Frankenstein and himself.

Although the script had been approved, a few were unhappy with the end results. Laemmle Jr. had wanted the picture to contain less humour and more horrors and had repeatedly asked Whale to comply. He was ignored. John L. Balderston, conversely, annoyed that his satire had been ruined by the added horror elements, later disowned the picture and requested his name be removed from the credits.[vi] Even Boris Karloff had objections. Although the concept of a talking monster had been Mary Shelley's the manner of his speech belonged firmly to the screenwriters. In Shelley's novel the monster had learned to speak and became fluent. The speech of Karloff's monster would be restricted to a few words and phrases. Karloff felt that even the simplified speech was inappropriate for

v The King, a miniature King Henry VIII, was an in-joke. Elsa Lanchester's husband, Charles Laughton, had won an Academy Award the previous year for his portrayal of the monarch in *The Private Life of Henry VIII* (1933).
vi Balderston's final screen credit read '… adapted by William Hurlbut and John L. Balderston.'

Above: Hiding in the crypt. Below Left: The Monster attacks the Burgomaster (E.E. Clive) in a deleted scene. Below Right: With the villagers in another deleted scene.

the picture. "They made a great mistake about which I also complained, but, you know, you don't have much say in it," he said. "The speech… stupid! My argument was that if the Monster had any impact or charm, it was because he was inarticulate… this great, lumbering, inarticulate creature. The moment he spoke you might as well take the mick or play it straight."[10]

Whale, however, ignored Karloff's protestations and the Monster was fated to speak. Jack Latham, employed by Whale as a stand-in, would talk to Karloff between takes. "He most certainly wanted the drama and seriousness of the Monster… I don't think Mr. Karloff had much humour about him. He was a hearty tea drinker, and that was about as much humour as he could conjure up."[11]

To shoot *Bride of Frankenstein* Whale gathered a familiar crew. Charles D. Hall, who had worked as art designer on all the director's pictures from *Waterloo Bridge* onwards, would design the sets and scenery. Hall's sets included a forest, a cemetery, Pretorius's abode, the hermit's hut and a dungeon. Hall also re-imagined some of the sets from *Frankenstein*. Frankenstein's castle became more elaborate with gothic architecture and vaulted ceilings. The watchtower laboratory was redesigned and, at 70 feet, was much higher than in the previous picture.

John J. Mescall ASC, was engaged as director of photography. Mescall had worked with Whale on several pictures including *The Invisible Man*. Although a self-confessed alcoholic, Mescall's addiction did not seem to affect his work on the picture. The only problem the condition caused for the studio was ensuring Mescall got to work in the morning and home at night.

Mescall shot the picture in a 'Rembrandt' style – a contrast of light and dark. He later described his technique on the picture. "It involves neither a straight cross light from the side nor a flat light directly from the front," Mescall explained, "but rather a combination of the two, with the light originating mainly from a point in front and to one side of the objects to be photographed. With one side of the faces thus placed in partial shadow, the style tends to impart a roundness to the features, and this pseudo stereoscopic effect is heightened by arranging for a dark background behind the bright side of the face, and vice versa." The picture's editor, Ted Kent, had also worked with the director before. *Bride of Frankenstein* would be his fifth picture with Whale.

To supply the picture's special effects Whale once more relied upon John P. Fulton, who had worked on *Frankenstein* and had been lauded for his effects in *The Invisible Man*. Fulton's special effects can be seen to best effect[vii] in *Bride of Frankenstein* in the famous 'Homunculus scene'. To achieve this affect the actors were filmed inside giant jars against back projection and were later matted into the scene. Fulton and optical effects expert David S. Horsley were on set for two days during shooting so they could plan the scene. They took measurements of the giant jars and props as well as the camera angles, elevations and distances which they used to calculate the effects.

While the original *Frankenstein*, as was then the norm, had no musical soundtrack except for opening and closing music, *Bride of Frankenstein* would contain a full score. James Whale personally chose the composer. Whale had met Franz Waxman, recently arrived in California, at a party at the home of the German actress/screenwriter Ms. Salka Viertal.

---

vii A lesser effect can be seen during the final creation scene. When the monster pursues Fritz, before throwing him from the top of the watchtower, both become transparent.

Having admired Waxman's score for the picture *Liliom* Whale approached the composer and told him about his film. "Nothing will be resolved in this picture," Whale explained, "except the end destruction scene. Will you write an unresolved score for it?"[12]

The shooting script made it clear that the end for the protagonists was final: "With the lightning and thunder of the heavens for accompaniment, the structure that was the laboratory collapses into a burning heap, the cloud of smoke and dust disperses a little and settles over the scene, and the thunders of a jealous and triumphant Jehovah roll for positively the FINAL FADE OUT."[13] Whale, appropriately, suggested Waxman end the score with "a big dissonant chord."[14] Having accepted Whale's offer the composer visited the soundstage to watch the picture being shot. "It was a 'super horror' movie," Waxman said, "and demanded hauntingly eerie, weird and different music."[15]

The recording of the score, played by a reduced 22-piece orchestra and conducted by Mischa Bakaleinikoff, was made in a single nine-hour session attended by Waxman and Whale. The success of Waxman's score, which would later be adapted and used in the serials *Flash Gordon*, *Buck Rogers* and others, ensured the composer's appointment as the studio's music director.

Whale had begun casting the picture while the script was being written, which therefore allowed the script to be tailored to the individual actors. In addition to Karloff only two of the main actors from the original *Frankenstein* would appear in the sequel. Colin Clive was borrowed from Warner Brothers to return as Henry Frankenstein. Since the original picture Clive had appeared in Whale's *One More River* (1934), played Edward Rochester in Monogram's *Jane Eyre* (1934) and had appeared in *Clive of India* (1935) with Ronald Colman. Clive's health, however, had deteriorated since the first *Frankenstein*. By now he was an acute alcoholic having originally started drinking to abate his nerves prior to appearing on stage in *Journey's End*. His condition would contribute to his premature death by tuberculosis on 25 June 1937, aged only 37.

Although Dwight Frye's character, the hunchbacked Fritz, had been hanged by the Monster in *Frankenstein* Whale insisted the actor take a role in the sequel and cast him as Karl, a combination of two roles in the script: Karl – "a bit of a village idiot", and Doctor Pretorius' assistant, Fritz. Frye had appeared in several films since *Frankenstein* such as *The Vampire Bat* (1933) with Lionel Atwill and Fay Wray, and had also appeared (uncredited) as a reporter in *The Invisible Man*. Mae Clarke's star had faded since *Frankenstein*. Despite receiving the famous half-grapefruit in the face from James Cagney in Warner's *Public Enemy* (1931) the quality of Clarke's pictures had declined. Her personal life had also suffered. In 1933, while on a date with actor Phillips Holmes, she was involved in a car accident that left her with a broken jaw. In place of Clarke, 17-year-old English actress Valerie Hobson was engaged to play Henry's wife, Elizabeth.

Whale had originally wanted his star of *The Invisible Man*, Claude Rains, for the Mephistophelian Dr. Septimus Pretorius. Rains had a two-picture contract with Universal and having starred in *The Man Who Reclaimed His Head* (1934) still owed the studio a picture. Instead of appearing in Whale's picture, however, Rains received an assignment to play the murderous John Jasper (a role originally intended for Karloff) in the studio's adaptation of Dickens' *The Mystery of Edwin Drood* (1935). Whale, therefore, offered the role to Ernest Thesiger who returned from England to take the part.

Two of Whale's supporting players from *The Invisible Man* were cast in his new picture. Welshman E.E. Clive was promoted from his bumbling policemen in the

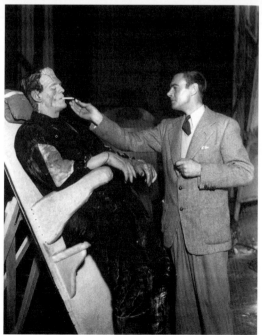

Top: The Monster's sanctuary is disturbed. Above Left: The Frankenstein Monster at rest. Above Right: Taking a cigarette break with Colin Clive during production.

Wells film to the pompous burgomaster in the Frankenstein sequel. Irish born Una O'Connor was assigned the role of Frankenstein's maid, Minnie.[viii] It was O'Connor's first picture after having suffered fractures to five vertebrae after having been thrown from a horse.

In a pre-production publicity campaign for the picture Universal had begun releasing the names of various actresses who, it claimed, may possibly play the Bride. German actress Brigitte Helm, who had played Maria and her robot double in Fritz Lang's *Metropolis*, was revealed to be in the running for the role. Model Phyllis Seller and Arletta Duncan, who had played one of the bridesmaids in *Frankenstein*, were other, apparent, considerations. Duncan was even despatched to the Karloff residence for publicity purposes, sharing a picnic with the star. Seller, signed by Universal in August 1934 and renamed Phyllis Brooks, was even announced for the role. "Phyllis Seller formerly posed for cigarette ads, and a few days ago she arrived here for pictures, under contract to Universal," wrote the *Los Angeles Times*. "And that isn't all. She is to play a lead in her very first film. This will be *The Return of Frankenstein*, in which Boris Karloff is featured."[16] Despite such announcements Whale had already decided upon his old friend Elsa Lanchester for the role. Her name was suggested for the Bride in Balderston's script of 9 June 1934. In the script of 23 June, Lanchester is listed against both roles of Mary Shelley and the Bride.

Whale had first met Lanchester in 1926 when he stage-managed a revue in London called *Riverside Affairs* at the Lyric Theatre. Lanchester had arrived with her husband, Charles Laughton, in Hollywood in March 1932. While Laughton had appeared in *The Old Dark House*, *The Barretts of Wimpole Street* (1934) and others, Lanchester had been on contract to MGM where she had appeared in *David Copperfield* and *Naughty Marietta* (both 1935). "It was a little nothing of a contract just to keep me busy, since Charles was here,"[17] she later said.

Whale was intent on using Lanchester and MGM agreed to loan the actress for the picture. "I do have an odd face," she later said, "and James was absolutely dead set that my face was the face for the Bride of Frankenstein!"[18] Whale had also decided that whoever played the Bride should also play Mary Shelley. "James's feeling was that very pretty, sweet people, both men and women, had very wicked insides… evil thoughts," Elsa Lanchester later said. "These thoughts could be of dragons, they could be of monsters, they could be of Frankenstein's laboratory. So James wanted the same actress for both parts to show that the Bride of Frankenstein did, after all, come out of sweet Mary Shelley's soul."[19]

To complete the cast Whale chose 58-year-old Australian O.P. Heggie to play the old blind hermit who befriends the Monster. Whale's insistence to cast the actor, however, caused a lapse in production. On 19 February, with nothing but Heggie's scenes left to shoot, production temporarily shut down. It resumed ten days later when the actor became available.

Although Karloff's status had changed considerably since *Frankenstein* few concessions were afforded during the make-up process.[ix] The rigours of the role remained even

viii O'Connor can also be seen briefly as Mary's Shelley's maid in the prologue, walking the dogs from the room.
ix One concession was the supply of a 'Monster Chair' for Karloff's use. This device – in effect a large slantboard with armrests and a seat – allowed the star to relax between takes.

though make-up man Jack Pierce[x] had replaced the cotton and collodion application process with a less time-consuming rubber headpiece. "Since shooting starts promptly and early in the day, Karloff has had to arrive at the studio in order to be ready for work when the company was assembled and the cameras ready to grind," the *Washington Post* reported. "Even the four-hour session hasn't been the end of Karloff's tribulations in this picture. The devices, which give him extra height and breadth, have to be fastened on. To date those contrivances are a state secret guarded by Universal, probably for Karloff's exclusive use in future films based on monsters of one sort or another. But it isn't a secret that Karloff, whose working days were close to 16 hours during the production of his new film, had to be handled as gently as possible to insure against a breakdown under the strain of the monstrous affair. A plaster duplicate of Frankenstein's head was made and mounted on a tripod to save Karloff's strength in setting lights and arranging the thousand other details for which a star must be on hand unless a 'stand-in' is available."[20]

Once again the order came for Karloff to cover his face when made up as the Monster. In this instance Universal's publicity campaign was somewhat redundant, as the *New York Times* pointed out. "That this device has not caused more talk and speculation among the typewriting fraternity," it wrote, "may be attributed to the fact that every one knows what he looks like, the make up being identical with that which he wore in the first Frankenstein film made two years ago [*sic*]."[21]

In fact, Pierce's make-up for the monster had been amended although, it is true, not by enough to warrant such an air of secrecy. Burns were added to the Monster's face as a result of the fire in the mill. His hair, which grows throughout the picture, was also shorter having been singed in the flames exposing a second clamp on his forehead. Artist Rolf Armstrong was permitted to visit the studio to paint the Monster's portrait with this revised make-up.

Even though the monster's face was now well known, the make-up could still be alarming if caught unawares. Actress Sally Eilers was one such victim. Having entered the make-up room Eilers heard a groan and was shocked to see Karloff, in his Frankenstein make-up, sleeping as his make-up dried. Another incident occurred to the wife of actor Henry Hull. Hull was then filming *Werewolf of London* on another soundstage. As Valerie Hobson was appearing in both pictures a corridor was built between the two sets for Hobson's use. One day, Hull's wife decided to use the corridor as Hull's great nephew, Cortlandt Hull, recalled. "Henry's wife came to visit him on the set," he explained, "and she was directed to the Bride set by mistake. A technician told her, 'You don't have to go around the buildings. There's a connecting corridor between the two stages.' The corridor was dimly lit. As she proceeded toward the other end, she heard 'thump! thump! thump!' Halfway through, she saw Boris Karloff coming down the corridor in full Frankenstein make-up, smoking a cigar. As they met, he said, 'Good morning, Mrs. Hull.' She shrieked, 'Aiee! Aiee! Aiee!' She knew Boris, but in the dark corridor she didn't recognise him."[22] Valerie Hobson had a similar experience despite careful precautions. "We were all kept rather apart so that it would all be shocking. For instance, I wasn't allowed to see – and did not see – the Monster until he came toward me, ready to put me over his shoulder, so that I would be duly shocked. And most unfortunately, I met him in the passageway! I had all my shock long before, but I had to do it all over again. They were quite angry about all of that."[23]

x Pierce was assisted on the picture by make-up man, and sometime actor, Otto Lederer. Lederer would later assist Pierce with the make-up on the Karloff pictures *The Raven* (1935), *The Invisible Ray* (1936) and *Tower of London* (1939).

The monster make-up did not, however, scare everyone. "I remember, during the early days of the picture, that there were ten small girls working in one of the sequences," Karloff said. "These children were most friendly. They gathered round me, lifting my enormous shoes, pinching my padded legs and trying to find out just what the Monster really was. Youngsters are thrilled but not frightened by my fantastic get-up. It seems to be the adults who are scared."[24]

The colour of Karloff's make-up required special considerations. "Karloff's make-up was blue-green in colour," Mescall explained, "and to register this photographically, the light on him was projected through blue filters... the make-up of the others were pink or reddish in tone, and lights of a corresponding shade had to be trained on their faces, while the blue lights had to be shielded from them... no matter where the characters moved in the scene, each constantly had to be in the rays of lights of the proper colour."[25]

The European village on the Universal backlot in the 1930's.

On Wednesday, 2 January 1935, and with a budget of almost $300,000, filming began on *Bride of Frankenstein*. Except for the street scenes, which were to be filmed on the European village set back-lot, the picture would be shot entirely on Universal's soundstages. Within a week, however, the production was in trouble. Karloff had been filming the Monster's re-appearance in the millpond scene, as he recalled. "The watery opening scene of the sequel, *Bride of Frankenstein*, was filmed with me wearing a rubber suit under my costume to ward off chill," he said. "But air got into the suit. When I was launched into the pond, my legs flew up in the air, and I floated there like some sort of obscene water lily while I, and everyone else, hooted with laughter. They finally fished me out with a boat-hook, and deflated me."[26]

Soon after, however, Karloff suffered a fall back into the pond and dislocated his hip. It was feared that the production would shut down while the star recuperated. However, Karloff, regardless of the discomfort, visited the studio doctor and had his hip bound so he could return to work. The pain of his injury only added to the discomfort already caused by the daily application, and removal, of the Monster's make-up.

Karloff was not the picture's only casualty. Colin Clive also suffered a fall early in production and tore the ligaments in his knee. As a result he spent the rest of the production either shot in close-up while on crutches, or sitting down. On-set the accident was generally attributed to the actor's now acute drinking problem fuelled, perhaps by his unhappy home life. "Charles and I stayed in the country with Colin Clive and his wife, Jeanne de Casalis, once or twice," Elsa Lanchester later said. "Theirs wasn't a very happy marriage. She was very precious, very affected... He was very nice, an English gentleman..."[27]

Clive's personal problems also caused some difficulty on set. "He was very excitable," Whale's friend Jack Latham recalled. "Whale had to be careful so that Colin wouldn't shoot his mouth off – about Whale or anything else. He would go off to his own little dressing room and they'd call him and he'd come out and do the 'it's alive' thing and then go back. We didn't see him very much."[28]

The cast relax on the set.

Valerie Hobson's introduction to Colin Clive was on her first day on set. "The first scene I had in the film was the scene where I'm just about to get into bed in a rather pretty pink number and my husband is sitting up in bed," Hobson recalled. "I remember Jimmy introducing me and saying, 'You haven't met Colin Clive. Colin, this is Valerie Hobson.' I was in the negligee – almost in the bed – and I hadn't even met him! That, I do think, was done as a tease, to possibly see if I would be shocked by it."[29] Hobson soon also witnessed the troubles with Clive. "People had to watch him like a hawk to see that he shouldn't drink and that made one a bit nervous. I remember that he had a dresser who stuck very close to him, and maybe he was a paid dresser who made quite sure he didn't have a nip."[30]

Despite the problems Whale suffered no pressure from the picture's producer, Carl Laemmle Jr. "He left Jimmy alone," said Jack Latham. "I don't remember him ever coming down to the set."[31] In fact, Whale received no outside interference at all during production. "He had complete control from beginning to end," said editor Ted Kent. "I don't believe he could have worked any other way."[32]

Whale concentrated, initially, on the scenes concerning the Monster. "Jimmy had a great deal to say to Karloff about the intimate scenes," Latham explained. "They rehearsed, and when he finally got what he wanted, he usually printed the first take."[33] Sometimes, however, Whale's shooting methods could cause difficulties, as Kent explained. "Whale shot only what he felt he needed," he said, "and sometimes he would get caught without enough footage; there were times when he wished he had more. Often, when I'd get stuck on something, I'd go to the set and tell him I had a situation that wouldn't match. He'd think for a moment, and if he didn't have a quick answer, he'd say, 'Do the best you can' or 'Go ahead and jump it – it'll only hurt for a moment.' Fortunately, I always had something I could jump to, if only for a split second – someone raising their eyebrows or the like. He was never terribly concerned about matching shots, but had faith in my ability to always get him out of trouble – or so he thought."[34]

Although Whale and Karloff worked closely together on the Monster's scenes some evidence of the director's animosity towards his star remained. The usually reticent Whale seemed to vie for the limelight, posing on the set for photographers, and flicking dust onto Karloff's plaster monster stand-in. "James Whale was a very strange personality," Elsa Lanchester later said. "He was a bitter man – very bitter. I think it was because he had been in love with a lady painter, named Zinkheisen, whom he'd bring with him to the Cave of Harmony. They didn't marry, and I think that was to blame for his not having a normal life… James had an Italianate Gothic house near the ocean, and he always had the portrait of that lady painter in his dining room. He *was* brilliant – such an imaginative mind – but so bitter. And, of course later, he just retired completely from life, save for a few friends – young men and such."[35]

The cast enjoyed the customary tea-breaks. Ernest Thesiger, or "the stitchin' bitch" as he had christened himself, would spend the time between takes indulging in his hobby of needlepoint. "Ernest Thesiger was a delightful laugh for anybody who saw him or talked to him," Lanchester later said. "[A] weird, strange character! Very acid-tongued – not a nasty person at all, just *acid*!"[36] Jack Latham also liked Thesiger. "He was charming," he said. "He was, of course, ugly as sin, which he resented, but God knows he was great in the part."[37]

Whale enjoyed working with his friend, particularly on the scenes between Pretorius and the Monster. "I think he had great fun with it," said Jack Latham. "He was very amused by Boris and Ernest Thesiger and their characters; they amused him very much."[38]

While shooting a scene in the crypt, however, Karloff suffered another fall. "In the part where I clattered downstairs into the crypt I fell over a box by accident and wrenched my back and tore several ligaments," he said. "It could have happened to anybody."[39] Curiously, Karloff stated that his was his "only injury" while working on the picture, ignoring his earlier mishap.

His daily regime was gruelling. Karloff would be awoken at 4:30 a.m. then take a cold shower before having infra-red treatment for his injured hip. After taking breakfast, consisting of toast and black coffee, he would drive the 15-miles to the studio where, at 5:50 a.m., Jack Pierce began to apply the monster make-up. At 1:30 p.m. Karloff had tea and a sandwich and half an hour later started filming.

The strain of wearing the costume and makeup, though, meant the actor was obliged to lie down and rest between scenes. The days filming would end around 6:30 or 7 p.m. and for the next hour the makeup was removed using oils and acetic acid. At 8 p.m. Karloff would take another cold shower, then have tea and a light dinner before leaving the studio. Arriving home half an hour later he would have a massage to assist the circulation in his arms and legs followed by more infra-red treatment. At 9:30 p.m. Karloff would retire to bed to study his script for the next day.

As shooting progressed Karloff was afforded a few Saturdays off to attend the cricket. "I met him at the Hollywood Cricket Club during one of his rare week-ends away from the studio," wrote Jonah Maurice Ruddy. "He was not playing because he was still suffering from a dislocated hip."[40] Ruddy also met the star at the studio. "During the filming of *Bride of Frankenstein*, I went on to the set on two or three occasions to see the shooting and to chat with Boris Karloff," he wrote. "What an extraordinary transformation was there! Here was this cultured, quiet-spoken Englishman changed into a terrifying monster by the use of skilfully applied make-up."[41] Even in make-up, however, Valerie Hobson found Karloff endearing. "It was Boris's kind eyes – he had the kindest eyes!" she said. "Most monsters have frightening eyes, but Boris, even in make-up, had very loving, sad eyes. The thing I remember best about him was his great gentleness… he was awfully quiet, softly spoken, and always interested in one's problems, but still had his reserve. He was a dear man…"[42]

Whale left the shooting of the prologue until towards the end of production. Ted Kent believed its inclusion was a mistake. "As far as I was concerned it was a horror picture and I wanted to get on to the Monster," he said. "The Shelley sequence was unnecessary."[43] Elsa Lanchester, however, enjoyed working on the sequence and was particularly impressed by her costume. "The dress I wore cost a fortune," she recalled. "For weeks and weeks, they had 17 Mexican ladies creating it completely by hand. It had the finest possible net, and a train at the back which you don't get to see (I don't think I stood up in the scene). It was embroidered with pearl sequins in the figures of stars and moons and butterflies. It was a beautiful work, all done by hand – and it hardly shows in the film."[44] Moviegoers did, however, get the opportunity to view the costume later on when, during the picture's run, the dress was displayed in the foyer of some of the bigger theatres.

For the climactic creation sequence the studio had again leased Kenneth Strickfaden's laboratory equipment. They had the pieces transported from storage in their creator's garage to the Universal lot. The paraphernalia was then enhanced by additions from the studio technicians. "The special effects and electrical departments made up numerous meaningless gadgets, switches, and indicators," recalled Ted Kent, "and Mr. Whale chose the most interesting."[45]

To prepare for the creation scene Lanchester, like Karloff before her, placed herself in the hands of Jack Pierce. Lanchester's feelings for the make-up man were, however, less reverential than that of her co-star. "Jack Pierce did really feel that he *made* these people – like he was a *God* who created human beings," she later said. "In the morning he'd be dressed in white, as if he were in a hospital to perform an operation. He'd say 'Good morning' perhaps – but you shouldn't say it first. You didn't bounce in and say 'Hello' – oh no! As for the Bride make-up… he took *ages* to make a scar that hardly shows under my chin. For a whole hour he would draw two lines of glue, put a red line down the middle, then start making up the white edges of the scar – *meticulously* done. Well, frankly, I'm sure he could have bought such a scar for ten cents in a joke shop! But he started fresh every morning, drawing in that scar which is rarely even seen. After the scar came the eyebrows, and the hair. It's my own hair. I had it lifted up from my face, all the way around; then they placed a cage on my head and combed my own hair over this cage. They then put the grey-streak hair-pieces in afterwards."[46]

The process took between three and four hours to apply. "He took so long to make Karloff up and so long to make me up, we'd only have an hour or two together."[47] The costume also caused problems. "I was tied up in those bandages, so I had to be carried to and fro, once or twice, to a wicker lounge. There my feet would be untied, and I could relax for tea."[48] Even this small pleasure, though, was restricted. "I drank as little liquid as possible – all those bandages – and having to be accompanied by my dresser."[49]

James Whale contributed to the Bride's design – described as an 'Egyptian mummy' in the script – as he had with the Monster in 1931. Ted Kent saw evidence of the director's involvement. "I know the Bride's make-up was Whale's conception," he said. "He was very clever with his pencil and I saw several sketches he made showing details such as how her hair should look."[50]

The final iconic make-up is revealed when the living Bride is unveiled and introduced to the Monster. Repelled by her 'intended', the Bride hisses in disgust. Lanchester later revealed her inspiration for the Bride's distinctive sound. "Charles and I used to go to Regent's Park in London to feed the swans," she said. "Swans get very, very angry. If you throw them food, that's all right, but if you walk too near then, they *hiss*. It's like a noise through the nose and there's nothing in it."[51] The technique did, however, prove painful. "So I practised these hisses," she said, "and I did a very large hiss from my throat… I did get a very sore throat, what with the long shots, medium shots, retakes and so forth. With the hisses and the screams, I lost my voice. It hurt very much, and I had codeine. Charles finished the same day on *Les Misérables* at Fox. We got on the train the next day,[xi] after we were sure we were free from retakes, departed for New York and London – and *slept!*"[52]

Like Karloff, Lanchester would for evermore be associated with her monstrous role. "I have so many fan letters now – more than I used to receive," she said in her later years.

---

xi Lanchester and Laughton sailed from New York for England on the French Liner *Champlain* on 23 February 1935.

"Little children who have seen *Bride of Frankenstein* recognise me in grocery stores! I've changed, of course, after all these years, but I still have a lot of hair, and it blows around, and I'm still recognisable. Whatever James Whale saw in my face, it didn't leave me.'[53]

The Monster's scenes with the blind hermit were the last to be filmed. Free from his prior commitments at RKO, O.P. Heggie joined Karloff on the Universal soundstage. *Variety* later said of the scenes, "Karloff manages to invest the character with some subtleties of emotion that are surprisingly real and touching. Especially is this true in the scene where he meets a blind man who, not knowing that he's talking to a monster, makes a friend of him."[54]

By the time production ended, on 7 March, Karloff had sweated off 20 pounds. The picture was ten days over schedule and more than $100,000 over budget. Ted Kent then went to work with Whale assembling a print. "His scenes would start out simply enough – he didn't like to get things all jumbled up at once – and then we would build them as we went," Kent explained. "He would say, 'That two-shot plays too long. I think we'd better use some close-ups there', and it would get more complex. By the time a scene was finished with, there was very little film left in the can; he would have used every angle he had shot. He prided himself on using it all – he didn't waste a thing."[55]

Echoing the Monster's billing in the original picture Elsa Lanchester did not receive screen credit for her role as 'The Monster's Mate' which was shown, instead, with a '?' Lanchester's name did, however, appear on the cast list against the role of Mary Shelley.

On 20 March the finished picture was shown to Geoffrey Shurlock and Islin Auster of the PCA. Unhappy with the picture however they sent another three PCA representatives to view the picture the following day. The resulting comments were passed to Joseph Breen who then wrote to James Whale with the bad news. Breen was, he wrote, "gravely concerned"[56] over *Bride of Frankenstein*. "This picture seems to us definitely to be a violation of our Production Code because of its excessive brutality and gruesomeness."[57] The PCA's objections were not only confined to the macabre elements of the film. "The shots early in the picture," wrote Breen, "in which the breasts of the character of Mrs. Shelley are exposed and accentuated, constitute a code violation."[58] On 25 March Whale met with Breen to discuss the PCA's concerns. This resulted in a number of concessions by Whale who agreed to remove some of the objectionable footage.

On 6 April *Bride of Frankenstein* was previewed with, according to *Variety*, a running time of 90 minutes. That same day Joseph Breen wrote to Dr. James Wingate of the MPPDA. "*The Bride of Frankenstein* [sic] is now being re-cut," he wrote. "We saw the picture twice and asked for eliminations, which the studio is now making."[59]

Whale re-edited the picture addressing the PCA's concerns. He then went on to make some unprompted cuts of his own. When finished, Whale had reduced the running time of his picture from 90 minutes to 75. All close-ups of Lanchester's décolletage were removed. Some of Mary Shelley's dialogue was also trimmed from the prologue: "… We are all three infidels, scoffers at all marriage ties, believing only in living fully and freely in whatever direction the heart dictates. Such an audience needs something stronger than a pretty little love story. You say look at me; I say look at Shelley – who would suspect that pink and white innocence, gentle as a dove, was thrown out of Oxford University as a menace to morality, had run away from his lawful spouse with an innocent me but 17, that he was deprived of his rights as a father by the Lord Chancellor of England, and reviled by society as a monster himself. I am already ostracised as a free thinker, so why shouldn't I write of monsters?"[60]

The homunculus scene was trimmed to remove a seventh jar. "In the jar is a baby," the shooting script revealed, "already as big as the Queen and looking as if it might develop into a Boris Karloff. It is pulling a flower to pieces." The jar's occupant, Pretorius thinks, "will grow into something worth watching."[61] Although the majority of footage featuring this seventh homunculus, a baby played by ten-year-old midget Billy Barty, was cut some shots of it can still be glimpsed in the final picture.

To Dwight Frye's dismay the entire subplot in which his character, Karl, murders his uncle and blames the deed on the monster was excised. Also cut was a scene were Karl sees the homunculi. A mortuary scene, which took place after the Monster escaped the dungeon, was removed, as was a hearing in which the burgomaster disputes the existence of the Monster. Moments later the Monster pulls him through the window and attacks him.

The excision of these scenes left a hole in the picture that needed to be bridged. To serve this purpose Whale shot a scene in which the Monster stumbles upon a gypsy encampment. To play the old gypsy woman Whale used Elspeth Dudgeon, his 'great joke' from *The Old Dark House*. As this scene was shot at the last moment it is the only scene in the picture totally devoid of music.

On 11 April Whale's revised picture was shown to Shurlock, Auster and Karl Lischku of the PCA. Four days later *Bride of Frankenstein* was issued with its Certificate of Approval. An accompanying note from Joseph Breen, however, warned the picture may "meet with considerable difficulty at the hands of [state and local] censor boards both in this country and abroad."[62]

Only days before the picture opened Whale decided to make one final amendment. To Colin Clive's displeasure the director decided the ending should be changed so that Henry and Elizabeth survive the climactic explosion. Karloff, Hobson and a disgruntled Clive were recalled to shoot additional footage. The complex and expensive set-up had ruled out a reshoot of the explosion so in the release print Clive can still be seen inside as the watchtower collapses.

Although some stills of the excised scenes remain, the fate of the missing footage is unknown. "In 1985, because of the success of the videos of the restored *Frankenstein*, MCA made a worldwide search for any prints of *Bride* that might exist," explained Universal Home Video technical director Ron Roloff. "It drew a blank. In 1992 it was rumoured that the Library of Congress had unearthed a complete nitrate print that had been copyrighted in 1934. Before these rumours started, we had the print measured and compared it to what we had on the lot, and they were the same."[63]

Bride of Frankenstein opened on Good Friday, 19 April 1935 in San Francisco to capacity business and long queues. The LA opening was held at the Pantages Theatre at noon the following day. A midnight matinee followed that night. "Young children and grown-ups with weak nerves are advised to shun Pantages during the screening of this super-thriller," advised the *Los Angeles Times*.[64] Despite the warnings the clamour for tickets was such that the 2,812-seat theatre was forced to hold eleven screenings a day to meet the demand. The picture took more in its first day than the theatre usually took in a week and went on to break the cinema's two-year record.

Whale's picture opened at the Palace Theatre in Chicago on 22 April. "It's a film that, from opening to closing scenes, never stops trying to scare its audience to death… It will curl the hair of the thin-skinned and imaginative," wrote the *Chicago Herald Tribune*. "Hardier souls will respond to it with interest… As in *Frankenstein*, Boris Karloff portrays the monster who, this time in the woodland home of a blind hermit, learns to talk. And, I think, it is in the nature of an achievement that he manages to make you feel desperately sorry for the horrible creature he depicts… Thunder and lightning, graveyards, crypts, lonely castles, gruesome woods – and gruesome acting – all combine to make *Bride of Frankenstein* a blood-curdling thriller that no child should be taken to see.[65]

It previewed at the Roxy Theatre in New York on Thursday, 9 May and opened there at 10:30 the following morning.[xii] The *New York Times* wrote:

> In **Bride of Frankenstein** Boris Karloff comes again to terrify the children, frighten the women and play a jiggling tune upon masculine spines as the snarling, lumbering, pitiful Thing that a scientist formed from grave-snatched corpses and brought to life with the lightning…
>
> The picture again ends with the apparent demise of the Monster–and his mate–but Mr. Karloff's best make-up should not be permitted to pass from the screen. The Monster should become an institution, like Charlie Chan.
>
> Mr. Karloff is so splendid in the role that all one can say is "he is the Monster." Mr. Clive, Valerie Hobson, Elsa Lancaster, O.P. Heggie, Ernest Thesiger, E.E. Clive and Una O'Connor fit snugly into the human background before which Karloff moves. James Whale, who directed the earlier picture, has done another excellent job; the settings, photography and the make-up (contributed by Universal's expert Jack Pierce) contribute their important elements to a first rate horror film.[66]

Bride of Frankenstein opened at the 1,000-seat Strand Tivoli in London on Thursday, 27 June. The picture, the *Kinematograph Weekly* wrote, was a "spectacular thriller, a macabre morality play."[67] Still, the picture did not escape the British censors. The crypt scene, where the Monster gazes at the face of a dead girl, was removed due to its necrophilic undertones. In Birmingham the picture was banned altogether.

The film suffered the same fate elsewhere. "The Lieutenant-Bailiff of Jersey, Jurat P. de C. Le Cornu, has banned the film *The Bride of Frankenstein* [*sic*] which was to have been shown in Jersey this week," *The Times* reported.[68] Merely being a horror picture was enough to ensure a ban in Hungary, Palestine and Trinidad. The picture suffered cuts in China and Singapore. In Japan the scene where Pretorius lifts the miniature King with a pair of tweezers was found to be offensive as it ridiculed royalty and was summarily removed.

Regardless, *Bride of Frankenstein* had been a critical and commercial success. Wherever the picture was shown Karloff was acclaimed for his portrayal. "His Monster was a marvellous creation," agreed Elsa Lanchester. "That *gentleness!*"[69] Karloff, too, was full of praise for his co-stars. "Elsa Lanchester as Mrs. Shelley, the author, in the first part of the story, is, I think, excellent," he said. "As the bride, I thought her performance excellent, too. O.P. Heggie, as the hermit, impressed me greatly. The casting of the mad doctor, Pretorius, was a sheer bit of good luck for us. He made the atmosphere of the picture."[70]

Although Karloff would later say he preferred the original *Frankenstein*, in May 1935 he said, "I feel proud of my recent picture, *Bride of Frankenstein*. In many ways it is much better than *Frankenstein*."[71] Even so, it would be another four years before Karloff would don the monster's make-up, one last time, for a Universal picture.

On 19 March, the day before *Bride of Frankenstein* was screened for the PCA, the *Los Angeles Times* revealed a new *Dracula* picture was being planned. "Carl Laemmle, Jr.," it announced, "has decided soon to produce *Dracula's Daughter* with a cast composed of Lugosi, Boris Karloff, Claude Rains and Colin Clive, and feels he will be able to secure all those players, famous in one respect or another from their horror impersonations... It was because of results attained in *Bride of Frankenstein*, which is now completed, that Laemmle decided to produce the new thriller film."[72] When the picture went into production the following February, however, none of the four stars were involved. Instead Karloff and Lugosi would star in a picture that would drive one more nail in the horror genre's coffin – *The Raven*.

Chapter 10

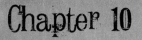

HOME AGAIN

(1935-1936)

"The vogue for monstrous men in the movies can't last forever.
When it ends, where will I be if I specialised in them? Out in
the well-known cold."[1]
Boris Karloff (1935)

The success of *The Black Cat* had prompted Universal to once again team its two horror stars in another picture inspired by the writings of Edgar Allan Poe. The project had initially been announced as a possible vehicle for Karloff back in June 1934 when the *Los Angeles Times* reported, "While no actors have been chosen as yet for *The Raven*, which Universal is to produce, it seems likely that Boris Karloff will have a part in this new horror film… The new story as fabricated for the screen will be a combination of the poem by Edgar Allan Poe, and also *The Gold Bug*. This makes the third Poe thriller produced there… Bela Lugosi may also be in *The Raven* as he was in *The Black Cat*."[2]

In November the newspaper announced that Chester Morris would also appear in the picture alongside the two horror stars. Jim Tulley, the newspaper revealed, had scripted the picture. Tulley had been assigned to salvage the story after several writers had failed to win approval with their attempts to transfer Poe's poem to the screen. In all eight writers (including Tully, Guy Endore and Dore Schary) worked on the screenplay although only one, David Boehm, received final screen credit.

Poe's treasure-hunt tale, *The Gold Bug*, was not included in the final script. Instead the screenplay told the story of a retired surgeon, Dr. Richard Vollin, whose obsession with the writings of Edgar Allan Poe has extended to the creation of a torture chamber complete with a blade-edged pendulum, beneath his house.[i] Vollin is persuaded to come out of retirement to

---

i Vollin's entire house is bizarre – with steel shutters on the windows, trap doors in bedroom floors, entire descending rooms, and an enormous basement to house his instruments of torture. It is never explained how this all came to be constructed.

Left: Karloff and Lugosi 'asleep' on the set of *The Raven* (1935). Right: Learning lines.

operate on a young dancer, Judge Thatcher's daughter, Jean. The operation is successful and Jean makes a full recovery. However, Vollin soon becomes obsessed with the dancer and, when her father warns the surgeon off, Vollin plots a revenge of 'torture and murder' aided by an escaped murderer, Edmond Bateman.

Production on *The Raven* began on 20 March 1935 with a budget of $109,750. Although Karloff's contract ensured him top billing it was Lugosi's role as the Poe-obsessed Dr. Vollin that received more screen time. Despite this Lugosi received only $5,000, half of his co-star's fee. Joining the two stars were former Miss America, Irene Ware, as the object of Vollin's desires, Jean Thatcher, and Samuel Hinds as her father, the Judge. Chester Morris was initially considered (and announced) for the role of Jean's fiancé, Jerry Halden, but was replaced by British actor Lester Matthews. According to the *Washington Post*, "173 actresses besieged director Louis Friedlander[ii] to fill the three feminine roles. Only 27 actors applied for the five supporting male parts."[3] The reason for the female's interest in the picture was, claimed the newspaper, Bela Lugosi's female fan base, which was responsible for most of the 200 letters he would receive daily.

Karloff was given the role of the escaped killer, Edmond Bateman, but was not happy with his assignment, the picture or the studio. This quickly became evident to Ian Wolfe who appeared in the picture as Colonel Grant. While wandering lost through the corridors of the studio one day Wolfe encountered the star. He asked Karloff if he could direct

---

ii *The Raven*'s director Louis Friedlander later changed his name to Lew Landers.

Above Left As Edmond Bateman in *The Raven*
(1935). Above Right: Publicity shot with Lugosi.
Right: Poster for *The Raven*.

him to the toilets and was told, in
reply, that the whole studio was a toilet.
Although Wolfe had little contact with
Karloff during production he witnessed
"enough to know that, indeed, he was thoroughly disgruntled."[4] Karloff's disaffection
with the studio did not extend, however, to his fellow actors. "Karloff was a very
kind and cooperative big pussycat," Wolfe later said, "and always defended actors in
general."[5] Yet on this occasion this congeniality did not appear to be tendered towards
his co-star. During the picture, Wolfe claimed, Karloff "had no contact whatsoever with
Bela Lugosi."[6]

To prepare for the part Karloff once again placed himself in the hands of (an
uncredited) Jack Pierce. Although the resultant make-up, which covered only the right
side of Karloff's face, was a lesser effort from the make-up maestro the MPPDA took
the unusual measure to approve the make-up prior to production.

The Raven was shot on the soundstages at Universal and wrapped in a little over two
weeks, on 5 April. It opened at the Roxy in New York on Thursday, 4 July where Bela
Lugosi made a personal appearance at the evening's performance.

The *New York Times* unflatteringly ascribed the picture "the distinction of being the
season's worst horror film. Not even the presence of the screen's Number One and Two
Bogeymen, Mr. Karloff and Bela (Dracula) Lugosi, can make the picture anything but
a fatal mistake from beginning to end."[7]

Critics were little kinder elsewhere. When the picture had opened in Boston at the end of June the *Christian Science Monitor* wrote, "It is an unpleasant yarn about a mentally unbalanced physician who delights in torturing people, and it displays his chamber of horrors in detail. For adults, the terrors are merely ludicrous, but children should by all means be kept away from the picture."[8] Karloff was later to concur. "Poor Poe," he said. "The things we did to him when he wasn't there to defend himself."[9]

By the time *The Raven* reached the screens Karloff had already completed work on another picture and had signed up for another to be made back in England. On 12 April, a week after *The Raven* had wrapped, Michael Balcon, the head of Gaumont British Pictures, announced an arrangement for the exchange of talent on loan between England and Hollywood. This exchange would include actors, writers and directors. "I am happy to say that the producing heads of Hollywood have recognised the value of talent loans," Balcon said. "The added exploitation of an American player appearing in British films is of immense value to the players, just as our British players have added to their popularity by appearing in American pictures."[10] Balcon left Hollywood with signed contracts for C. Aubrey Smith, Richard Dix, Madge Evans and Helen Vinson. Negotiations continued for Karloff, Maureen O'Sullivan, Peter Lorre and Walter Huston. By the time Balcon and his wife sailed for England from New York on 19 April Karloff and the others, plus two scenarists, Arthur Caesar and Rian James, had signed up. Lorre's contract, the *Washington Post* joked, had the clause, "Each day, before work, he has the right to go into Karloff's dressing room and frighten him."[11]

Four days after *The Raven* finished shooting the *Washington Post* revealed producer Darryl F. Zanuck's top ten British actors. He chose George Arliss, Charles Laughton, Ronald Colman, Robert Donat, Leslie Howard, Clive Brook, Herbert Marshall, Sir Cedric Hardwicke, C. Aubrey Smith and Karloff.[iii] "Boris Karloff," explained Zanuck, "is without a peer in the type of horror roles in which he specialises. A great individualist, a master of make-up, he possesses remarkable interpretation qualities."[12]

It was just these 'type of horror roles' that Dorothy Karloff felt had been beneficial to her husband's nature. "Before Boris began playing such sinister parts," she said, "as the monster in *Frankenstein*, the title role in *The Mummy* and that hideous creature of [*The*] *Old Dark House* and *The Ghoul*, he was a much more irritable person than he has ever been since. Whether or not these roles give him the opportunity of purging himself of any latent streaks of malevolence he might ordinarily possess, I cannot say. But I do know that since he has been doing the type of role that made him famous, he is a much sweeter person at home than before. He really is a lamb."[13]

Karloff's next picture, *The Black Room Mystery*, was set to commence at Columbia Studios in early May. He had been announced for the lead the previous October when Garrett Fort, a screenwriter on *Frankenstein*, was reported as working on the screenplay. The following March director Roy William Neill was assigned to the picture and two months later Marian Marsh was announced as the picture's "menaced heroine".[14] Also in the cast would be Robert Allen, Thurston Hall, John Buckler and director Cecil B. DeMille's adopted daughter, Katherine.

The screenplay, written by Henry Meyers and Arthur Strawn, told the story of 19th century twins, Gregor and Anton de Berghman, who live in the shadow of a prophecy

---

iii Zanuck deliberately excluded Charlie Chaplin from the list "because," he explained, "there is only one Chaplin – and he's in a class by himself."

which states their dynasty will end as it began – with the slaying of the older twin by the younger in the castle's 'black room'. The prophecy is reflected in the de Berghman family motto *Principio et Finem Similia* – 'I end as I began'. In an effort to escape the prophecy the black room is sealed.

Years later the kindly Anton, born with a paralysed right arm, returns to the family estate. He finds unrest among the people who hate his brother, the Baron, a cruel, murderous tyrant who has caused the disappearance of local girls. When the villagers rise up against the Baron, he suggests he renounce his title and estates to his younger brother, Anton.

Unknown to all Gregor has discovered a secret entrance to the black room. He invites Anton into the room and pushes him into a pit. Before he dies Anton swears that the prophecy will be fulfilled "even from the dead". Gregor takes the place of his twin realising that to affect the charade he can never again move his right arm. Gregor now intends to marry Colonel Hassel's daughter, Thea [Marian Marsh] but when the Colonel discovers the true identity of the new baron Gregor kills him and allows the blame to fall upon Albert Lussan [Robert Allen], a young lieutenant who is in love with Thea. The lieutenant is imprisoned for the murder and Thea agrees to marry the baron. At the wedding, however, Anton's dog attacks the false Baron and Gregor's charade is revealed when he raises his 'paralysed' arm to strike the hound. Gregor makes for the castle and hides in the black room. When Anton's dog reveals the secret entrance to the room the villagers gain access. Gregor, knocked backwards by the dog, falls into the pit and is impaled on a knife held in the dead Anton's paralysed arm. The prophecy has been fulfilled.

Despite taking two roles in the picture the make-up was far simpler than he had been accustomed to at Universal. "I don't know if it's an artistic advantage; that is highly questionable," Karloff remarked. "My make-up for this role will consist of only a wig with the ordinary facial make-up. It's quite unusual for me to be able to get my make-up on in less than an hour as I can in this role."[15]

Production on *The Black Room Mystery* began at Columbia Studios on Monday, 6 May 1935. As usual Karloff got on well with the rest of the cast. Marian Marsh and her husband were occasional guests at the Karloff home for dinner. Torben Meyer, who played the servant Peter in the picture, also became good friends with Karloff. Sometimes they would lunch together. "I remember once we talked about misuse and overwork of actors... by the studios... He said in a very subdued way: 'Yes, I hate them'."[16] Despite his animosity towards the studios ill treatment of actors Karloff remained grateful for the opportunities offered by one. "He was thankful for the chance he got at Universal," Meyer recalled. "He said to me, 'Torben, I never thought I'd be a star'."[17]

Production on the picture ended on 7 June which by the end of the month had been renamed *The Black Room*. It opened at the Warner's Downtown Theatre in Los Angeles on Thursday, 15 August in a double feature with the drama *Jalna*. "At least Boris wears his own face in this one," one reviewer wrote. "His acting, of course, is adequate."[18] Dorothea Lewis of the *Washington Post*, however, thought the picture "an intelligent horror play, rather more interesting than scream-at-able, but with fine regard for sinking feelings and excellent climaxes."[19] The newspaper thought the picture benefited from good direction and "really superior acting by Karloff, who provides two vivid characterisations."[20] More importantly, the audience liked the

As the villainous Gregor de Berghman in *The Black Room* (1935). Inset: With Katherine DeMille and Marian Marsh.

picture. "Last night's audience had lots of fun hissing the villain and cheering the dog-hero," wrote Lewis, "but that's probably just Roadside influence. *The Black Room* deserves more than being kidded – it's extremely good and just about shivery enough for a summer night."[21]

Although the picture still had its horrific elements *The Black Room* was a change from the pictures he had been making for Universal. Karloff was conscious of the limited appeal of the horror pictures and, although it had made him a star, had determined to move away from the genre. "I can't wear a false face all the time," he explained. "I do not in the least object to being a heavy, but a masked heavy…! I am trying to establish myself as a character player – without make-up – and since the termination of my original contract [with Universal] I have been quite successful."[22]

Karloff's colleagues at the Screen Actors Guild agreed. On Sunday, 15 September they awarded him an honourable mention in the category 'best performance in August'.[23] The joint winners were Henry Fonda in *The Farmer Takes a Wife* and Will Rogers, posthumously, for *Steamboat Round the Bend*.

As always, Karloff's filming commitments did not impinge upon his social life and he was often spotted dining out. Gossip columnists regularly reported his culinary sightings – dining at Sardis, taking tea at the New Rendezvous café at the Biltmore Hotel, or enjoying something stronger at the Hollywood Knickerbocker cocktail lounge.[24]

On the evening of 6 May the day production of *The Black Room* commenced, Karloff attended a ball to celebrate the Silver Jubilee of King George and Queen Mary at the Fiesta Room of the Ambassador Hotel in Hollywood. The event, which included a "massing of the colours" by the Canadian Legion Post, was also attended by, amongst others, Mary Pickford, Charlie Chaplin, Maureen O'Sullivan, Ida Lupino, Una O'Connor, Ronald Colman and Lionel Atwill. The proceeds of the event went to the British Old People's Home in Sierra Madre.

On 24 May, three weeks into production, actor Chester Morris and his wife entertained the committees of the Screen Actors Guild in the garden of their home. In addition to the Karloffs the long list of guests included Joan Crawford, Bette Davis, Ginger Rogers, Fredric March, Bing Crosby, Edward G. Robinson and the Gleasons. Two days later the Gleasons held a party of their own in the garden of their home in Beverly Hills to jointly celebrate James Gleason's birthday and the twenty-fifth wedding anniversary of Gleason's cousin Gladys Tyler and her husband Harry. "The feature of the afternoon," reported the *Los Angeles Times*, "will be a re-enactment of the Tyler wedding with Jimmy and Lucile Gleason acting as attendants."[25] The wedding ceremony, which was held at three o'clock, was followed two hours later by James Gleason's birthday party. Birthday guests included the Karloffs, Clark Gable, James Cagney, Pat O'Brien and Jimmy Durante.

May was a busy time for Lucile Gleason and many other members of the Screen Actors Guild. In addition to the socialising that went with the attending (and hosting) of parties, Gleason was also engaged as the 'Chairman' of the Hollywood Exhibit at the California-Pacific International Exposition. In all, 33 Guild members, including Karloff, James Cagney, Joan Crawford, Bette Davis, Clark Gable, James Gleason, Fredric March and Robert Montgomery, sat on the Hollywood Exhibit committee.

The $15,000,000 Exposition was designed to trace "man's spectacular conquest of the West"[26] and suggest "the accomplishments of tomorrow".[27] Set in the 300 acres of San Diego's Balboa Park, the Exposition opened on Wednesday, 29 May 1935.[iv]

That same day the *Los Angeles Times* announced that Karloff was to play a new role. "Bayard Veiller, formerly with Paramount, has been signed to do the screenplay of *Bluebeard*, which will be taken from an original by Stuart Palmer. Karloff is endeavouring to delay the two pictures he is to do for them until November or December because he wants to see the Rugby tournament in England at that time."[28] Karloff was also slated for the lead in *Dr. Nikola*, one of 11 pictures Gaumont-British planned to make.

A week later Universal announced its own list of 42 features for production in the 1935-36 season. This list included remakes of Lon Chaney's silent pictures *The Hunchback of Notre Dame* (at one time linked to both Karloff and Peter Lorre) and *The Phantom of*

---

iv The Exposition ran five and a half months, concluding on 11 November.

the Opera. At the time Karloff's name was attached to a single picture – Bayard Veiller's script, now entitled *Bluebeard's Eight Wives*. The picture was later postponed before being dropped from the studio's schedule.

As the studios pondered possible vehicles for the star, Karloff and Dorothy spent time in their two acres of garden tending to the pets and plants. "There are fruit trees by the dozen," reported Jonah Maurice Ruddy. "... Mrs. Karloff told me that they grow their own vegetables and flowers, and they have oranges, grapefruit, limes, lemons, peaches, apricots, plums and avocados during the season... Most of the trees, especially the tall hedges of laurels and eucalyptus, have been put in by Boris and his wife."[29] That year's harvest proved so successful that the Karloffs were left with such a surfeit of fruit they were able to sell 900 pounds of plums from their orchard.

Their horticultural skills, however, were not confined to fruit and vegetables. "There is something chaste and virginal about Boris Karloff's garden," Alma Whitaker wrote in the *Los Angeles Times*, "radiant with 30 or 40 varieties of luscious flowers, all white. Gladioli, oleandor, hibiscus, heather, lantana, begonias, iris, lilies, narcissi, hyacinths, camellias, anemones, gorgeous white blossoms everywhere. Even the geraniums are white, great tall bushes laden with snowy blooms. Now wouldn't a chap who specialises in horror pictures go in for virginal purity?"[30]

"We could easily be self-supporting here," Karloff said, "and that is something to be considered in these changeable times... The remarkable thing, living in the country as we do here, is the sense of being away from all things connected with films. We are 15 minutes from any studio, yet it is so completely in the country. The dogs love it as much as we do, even the little Bedlington who is called Agnus Dei. I suppose one's ambition is economic freedom and running one's life unhampered and unhindered by worry of the future."[31]

The dogs especially kept Karloff busy. "As a matter of fact," Dorothy Karloff told the journalist, Henry M. Fine, "he enjoys an international reputation as a breeder and trainer of setters. He loves dogs and, by that very token, dogs love him."[32]

Karloff also enjoyed books, especially the novels of the Polish-born author, Joseph Conrad,[v] whose tales of sea voyages may, possibly, have influenced a young Karloff in his desire to emigrate. "Boris reads omnivorously," Dorothy said.[33] He also enjoyed sports, despite his bowed legs and recurrent back problems. "He is a typical outdoor man. His years of training on the sports fields of England have left indelible marks on his tastes and nature," Mrs. Karloff explained. "Karloff is a great soccer player, and if the stage hadn't lured him away he might have become a player of international note. This I learned, not from my husband, but from players around here. You see, he just can't keep away from the grounds, even at this stage of things. He's always arranging games and playing in them. His friends tell me when he deserted shin guards for grease paint, a grand footballer, if that's what you call them, was lost."[34]

Cricket, though, remained his sporting passion. "The man just loves the game," Dorothy said, "and never lets his interest in the sport dwindle. When visiting teams from Australia and New Zealand come through here on their way East, Karloff is always playing host to them and arranging exhibition matches for them here."[35] His hospitality often extended beyond the playing fields. "If he hears of a sportsman who happens to be up

---

v Curiously, Conrad (born Józef Teodor Konrad Korzeniowski) had two sons, one of whom was named Borys (born 1898). It is possible that this may have influenced Karloff in his choice of forename.

against it, his cheque is always in the mail," Dorothy revealed, "and this is done without solicitation, either."[36] Dorothy, too, had her hobbies. She enjoyed her frequent games of bridge with friends and for the Dominos Club (the female equivalent of the actors' club The Masquers) and was often a guest, and sometimes the host, at the club's luncheons. Dorothy often dined out with her husband at such establishments as Sardis, Al Levy's Tavern and the Brown Derby as well as the numerous Screen Actors Guild functions. Both enjoyed the horses and on Saturday, 22 June they went to the races at Agua Caliente where they were spotted along with Mr. and Mrs. Stan Laurel and Wallace Beery. The next day the Karloffs, along with the Gleasons, comedienne Pert Kelton and actresses Adrienne Ames and Binnie Barnes visited the Motion Picture Hall of Fame at the San Diego Exposition.

In mid-July Karloff attended a party given by director Herman Biberman and his wife, the actress Gale Sondergaard. It was here Karloff met Peter Lorre and Claude Rains for the first time. Lorre, reported the *Los Angeles Times*, "looked up with a seraphic smile and assured the company, 'We are just trying to outcharm each other'."[37]

A week later, Karloff appeared in the national press in an advertisement for Dodge Cars. It was an early, if not the first, example of the use of the star in advertising. It was an avenue of income he would continue to benefit from throughout his career and attested to the selling power of the internationally famous star.

On 1 August the Screen Writers Guild held its annual summer dinner-dance in the Fiesta Room of the Ambassador Hotel. Karloff, recently elected to a one-year term as the Guild's assistant secretary, reserved a table. Then, towards the end of the month, Nigel Bruce held an all-day party at his Malibu Beach home. At the barbecue dinner that evening the guests were required to cook their own steaks. The list of guests who, according to the *Los Angeles Times*, "swam, romped on the sand and exercised in general" included Karloff, Brian Aherne, Merle Oberon and David Niven.[38]

On 28 August Karloff attended a *bon voyage* party hosted by his co-star from *The Raven*, Lester Matthews and his wife, Anne Grey, in honour of the British director Arthur Woods[vi] who was soon to depart for England. The list of guests included Robert Montgomery, Ernst Lubitsch, Ian Hunter, Nigel Bruce, James Whale, Thelma Todd and Frances Drake who, according to the *Los Angeles Times*, was "quite the centre of masculine attention..."[39]

Three days later, on Saturday, 31 August Karloff made his first radio appearance in almost a year when he appeared on Al Jolson's radio show *Shell Chateau*. The hour-long show included songs by Jolson and Maxine Lewis, music by Victor Young and his orchestra, comedy from George Jessel and an interview with golfer Joyce Wethered. Karloff, supported by Margaret Brayton and Crawford Kent, appeared in a 12-minute long dramatic scene from William Archer's stage play *The Green Goddess*.

Karloff played an Indian Rajah who, like Fu Manchu, was educated in England but hated the English. The Rajah plans to execute three British subjects (Lucilla Crespin, her husband, Major Crespin, and her brother, Dr. Basil Traherne) whose plane has crashed in his territory, in retaliation for the capture and impending execution of his three half-brothers, held by the British for murder.

The Rajah is, however, enamoured of Lucilla and wants her to be his bride. She refuses even when the Rajah threatens the life of her children back in England. After the Major is

---

vi Nine years later Woods was killed while serving as a night fighter pilot. He was 43 years old.

killed trying to send a radio message Lucilla and Dr. Traherne are taken to be sacrificed. Once again the Rajah offers Luvilla marriage but before she can decide she and the doctor are rescued by British troops, summoned by the Major's successful radio transmission. The Rajah is taken into custody. One reviewer thought "Boris Karloff passable as the Rajah in the rather antiquated Here-comes-the-Marines plot of *The Green Goddess*."[40]

Two weeks later Edwin Schallert of the *Los Angeles Times* reported Karloff was to become "a mere shadow of a shade in his next picture",[41] *The Invisible Ray* to be directed by Lambert Hillyer. Karloff, Schallert continued, "will impersonate a scientist who searches for Radium in Africa, and absorbs so much of it that he eventually becomes a dim manifestation of light."[42]

The studio had originally chosen *Werewolf of London* director Stuart Walker to helm the picture but, having read the script, Walker was unhappy with the tight time schedule imposed by the studio and passed. The project then fell into the hands of Lambert Hillyer. Primarily a director of westerns, Hillyer would later direct Universal's *Dracula* sequel, *Dracula's Daughter*.

Having decided to team Karloff and Lugosi again, the studio cabled Bela Lugosi, then in England filming *The Mystery of the Mary Celeste*, the second picture from Hammer Films. Lugosi had planned to travel with his wife to Hungary following the completion of the picture, but on receiving Universal's offer of the role of Dr. Felix Benet in *The Invisible Ray*, he returned to Hollywood, arriving in late August. Lugosi would receive $4,000 for his role, considerably less than his co-star's fee of $15,625 for the five-week shoot. Also appearing in the picture would be Frances Drake, Frank Lawton and Violet Kemble Cooper.

The Invisible Ray told the story of Dr. Janos Rukh [Karloff] a scientist who discovers a new element, 'Radium X', in a fallen meteorite. However, Rukh is contaminated by the element, which causes him to glow in the dark. Worse, he discovers that his touch can kill. He asks Benet for help and is given a serum that he must take in order to stay alive.

Rukh returns to his Carpathian home to use his discovery to cure his mother's blindness. Meanwhile, Benet and his colleague, Stevens, present the discovery to the scientific community and use it to help the sick at Dr. Benet's clinic. Rukh feels betrayed and determines to kill those whom he feels are responsible. He fakes his own death and begins murdering several members of the expedition. Rukh is finally confronted by his mother [Violet Kemble Cooper] who destroys the serum. Rukh leaps from the window and disintegrates in a ball of flame. Filming began on Tuesday, 17 September 1935.

Karloff's dissatisfaction with the studio appeared to have eased since working on *The Raven*. His make-up requirements were simpler this time – just a moustache and curly hair. Frances Drake, who played Rukh's wife Diane, recalled, "Boris was a very intelligent, rather serious man, and a very effective actor. During the making of *The Invisible Ray*, he was interested in establishing the Screen Actors Guild. Very pleasant to work with, no temperament on the set, and seemed to get on well with Bela Lugosi."[43]

His affability allowed the star to become the brunt of some good-humoured japing on the set. Affected by a superstitious streak, the star later confessed to columnist Hedda Hopper that before shooting a scene he would knock on wood and whistle twice.[vii] Aware of the star's foibles George Robinson, the picture's cameraman, hid everything with wood on it "to give vent to his superstition".[44] On another occasion, while filming Rukh's

---

vii Karloff also told Hopper he carried a Chinese coin for luck, and liked everything in multiples of three – "so," wrote Hopper, "his phone number, auto licence, home, even social security card bear multiples of three."

descent by bosun's chair into the meteor crater, Karloff was left dangling while the technicians broke for lunch. Co-star Marian Marsh later said that the star was a good sport and took the prank well.

Karloff's commitment to increasing the Guild's membership was in evidence throughout the production. On 22 September, a week into filming, Karloff wrote to the Screen Actors Guild secretary, Kenneth Thomson, enclosing a cheque and completed SAG application form from cast member Frank Lawton. "His wife, Evelyn Laye, undoubtedly will follow," Karloff added.[45] Having requested the status of the other cast members Karloff's recruiting skills were

With Lugosi in *The Invisible Ray* (1936).

put into force and two weeks later he was able to report that he had successfully signed up all of *The Invisible Ray* company.[viii] "I have found no resistance at all from the people I have worked with," he wrote, "and I believe that by studying the casts as published in the Reporter, selecting some real member of the cast who is also in the Guild, firing them up and arming them with applications for immediate action, we can make each working unit 100% by working from within."[46]

Three days later the Karloffs attended a party at the house of actress Marian Marsh, Karloff's co-star in *The Black Room*. At 5 p.m. on Thursday, 26 September the two-hour-long tea and cocktail soirée was held in honour of Lord Stonehaven's second son, Greville Baird. Baird was on leave from the Gordon Highlanders stationed at the lonely outpost of Landi Kotal in Afghanistan. In addition to the Karloffs the long list of guests included the Gleasons, Cary Grant, David Niven, Mr. and Mrs. Nigel Bruce and Mr. and Mrs. Peter Lorre.

Shooting on *The Invisible Ray* ended on 25 October, 12 days over schedule. Despite the cost-cutting decision[ix] to utilise some sets from the *Flash Gordon* serial, then being shot at the studio, and using shots of Kenneth Strickfadden's electrical equipment from *Frankenstein* and *Bride of Frankenstein* in Rukh's laboratory, the picture came in at $235,000, more than $68,000 over its $166,785 budget. Some, if not most, of the additional funds had been spent on John P. Fulton's impressive optical effects, which included a voyage through the solar system, following the ray's path past the planets and out into the Andromeda nebula. The meteor's fall through space, its landing in Africa, and the luminosity of an infected Karloff (an effect which, alone, took weeks to perfect) all added to the increasing costs.

The Invisible Ray opened at the Roxy in New York on Friday, 10 January 1936. The *New York Times* wrote, "Universal, which seems to have a monopoly on films of this sort, has made its newest penny dreadful with technical ingenuity and the pious

---

viii Karloff had also attempted to recruit the cast of *Bride of Frankenstein* earlier that year. His only success on that occasion, however, had been Colin Clive.

ix In another cost-cutting exercise Universal later used footage from *The Invisible Ray* in episode 3 of its 1939 serial *The Phantom Creeps*, starring Bela Lugosi. Footage of Karloff descending into the crater was used to represent Lugosi although, somewhat incongruously, a close up of Karloff's eyes was used.

hope of frightening the children out of a year's growth. There is evidence, too, that Carl Laemmle wanted to say 'boo' to maturer audiences. In a printed forward is the legend, 'That which you are now to see is a theory whispered in the cloisters of science. Tomorrow these theories may startle the universe as a fact.' Boo right back at you, Mr. Laemmle!"[47]

It had originally been envisioned that Karloff would, following his work on *The Invisible Ray*, make the picture *Dr. Nikola* in England for Gaumont-British producer Michael Balcon. After reading the script, however, the British censors deemed the picture unsuitable for production. "It is too horrible, they claim," journalist Dorothy Dix reported, "and would offend people's finer senses."[48] Although the studio initially intended to pay Karloff off the star's agent, Myron Selznick, negotiated instead another picture for his client. In early November, while this new British picture was being prepared, Karloff signed with Warners for *The Walking Dead*.

"The film concerns the scientific resurrection of those who have passed on, and also involves gangsters and a murder trial," revealed the *Los Angeles Times*. "It will start filming in two weeks. The story of *The Walking Dead* was written by Ewart Adamson and Joseph Field."[49] A little over a week later Marguerite Churchill and Richard Cortez, both of whom had been linked to the picture since August, were confirmed in the cast. Filming began in late November.[x]

The Walking Dead had a budget of $200,000 and would be directed by Michael Curtiz. Curtiz, who had recently completed *Captain Blood* starring Errol Flynn and Olivia DeHavilland, was not a novice in the horror genre. In 1932 he had directed Lionel Atwill and Fay Wray in *Doctor X*. A year later he reunited those same two stars in Warner's *House of Wax*, filmed in early two-strip Technicolor.

It would be the second time Karloff had worked with the director – for it was Curtiz who had employed Karloff five years earlier for his picture, *The Mad Genius*, under the misapprehension that the actor was Russian.

Karloff would receive a guaranteed $3,750 per week for his role as John Elman, an ex-convict who is framed for the murder of an incorruptible judge. Elman is tried for the murder, found guilty and sentenced to the electric chair. However, only hours before the execution is due to be carried out, two witnesses, Nancy [Marguerite Churchill] and Jimmy [Warren Hull], come forward. Elman's lawyer, Nolan [Ricardo Cortez], is informed but stalls calling the district attorney as Nolan is, in fact, responsible for the judge's death. When the stay of execution finally comes through it is too late. Elman has already been executed.

However, the witnesses, Nancy and Jimmy, are lab technicians who work for Dr. Beaumont [Edmund Gwenn]. Beaumont is a scientist who experiments in reviving dead animals and he successfully restores Elman to life. At first Elman remembers nothing but soon gains a supernatural awareness of the injustice done to him by Nolan and his gang. When he confronts each of the gang in turn they mysteriously meet with accidents and are killed.[xi]

---

x It has often been claimed that *The Walking Dead* began shooting on 23 December. However in mid-December the Mayor of Syracuse, Roland B. Marvin, and his wife met Karloff and Marguerite Churchill on the set of the picture. The couple toured the Warner Brothers Studio at Burbank and watched scenes being shot for the pictures *Colleen*, *The Walking Dead*, *Anthony Adverse*, *The Singing Kid* and *The Man With the Black Hat*.

xi One falls and accidentally shoots himself. Another tumbles from a window while backing away from Elman.

Top: Watching Ray Romero make preparations for *The Walking Dead* (1936). Middle Left: As John Elman. Bottom Left: With Edmund Lowe, H.G. Wells and Jack Warner on the set.

When Elman goes missing Nancy goes to the Jackson Memorial Cemetery – the only place Elman feels at home – where she finds him. She leaves to telephone Dr. Beaumont and in the interim Nolan and his sidekick arrive. As Elman approaches them they fire seven shots into him and make their escape. Dr. Beaumont, Nancy, Jimmy and the District Attorney arrive and tend to the dying man. Although Beaumont is still determined to find the answers to death's secrets Elman entreats him, "Leave the dead to their maker. The Lord, our God, is a jealous God." Meanwhile, Nolan's car skids in the rain and, crashing into an electrical pylon, the occupants are killed. With the last of the guilty parties now dead, Elman finally succumbs to his wounds.

The script required Karloff to submit to another 'creation' scene and the star was duly strapped to a tilting table for the set piece. This table was, in fact, a medical reality and was a replica of the one used by Dr. Robert Cornish, the Berkeley scientist who, in 1934, claimed to have revived a dead dog. The scene also featured the 'Lindbergh heart', a device created the previous year by the famed aviator Charles Lindbergh and Nobel Prize winner Dr. Alexis Carrel of the Rockefeller Institute. The device, scientifically referred to as a 'perfusion pump', was designed to keep organs alive indefinitely. Warner Brothers obtained permission to duplicate the device and Dr. Stanley Fox, pathologist of Western Scientific Research Laboratories, created it for the picture. "The heart itself is a complicated series of glass test tubes and rubber piping with small reservoirs of saline solution pumped by a small electric motor," wrote journalist Henry Sutherland. "One of the tubes contains a turkey heart, hooked up with the pump so that it expands and contracts and propels the fluid as it would blood in a living gobbler."[50]

If the resurrection scene had echoes of the creation scene in *Frankenstein* Karloff's make-up was also reminiscent of his most famous role. Karloff removed his bridge and sucked in his cheek, as he had in *Frankenstein*. A single eye was fitted with a heavy lid, and a streak of white was added to his hair. Karloff also affected a limp and a withered left arm, which only seemed to come to life when he plays the piano.

The star maintained his union duties during filming by actively recruiting new members. Soon after filming began in late November Karloff received a letter from the Guild informing him that cast members Eddie Acuff, Warren Hull, Joseph King, Addison Richards, and Ruth Robinson had not joined. "Mike Morita… has never paid a penny," the letter added. "Ricardo Cortez, as you know, has resigned."[51]

Karloff and other members of the cast took a break from filming one day when they paid a visit to a neighbouring soundstage to visit Leslie Howard, Bette Davis and Humphrey Bogart who were filming *The Petrified Forest*. On another day they received a special visitor of their own. Author H.G. Wells, then visiting Hollywood, met studio head Jack Warner, Curtiz, Edmund Gwenn and Karloff on the set of *The Walking Dead*. Warner pointed out the bow of a galleon used in *Captain Blood* that protruded onto the set. "Right here, Mr. Wells, within a foot of each other you see yesterday and tomorrow." "Yes," Wells replied, "the inaccurate past gazing into the incredible future!"[52]

Karloff finished his final scene – the dénouement at the Jackson Memorial Cemetery – at 2:30 a.m. on the morning of 21 December. The picture was completed in January, coming in at $217,000. Of this Karloff had earned $18,750.

The Walking Dead opened at the Strand in New York on 1 March 1936. "Karloff is another boo-boo-bogey man [in a] story about a man who is brought back to life after being electrocuted for a murder he did not commit," wrote the *New York Times*. "Only second-degree goose flesh, at that."[53]

The picture opened in Los Angeles at the Warner Brothers' Hollywood and Downtown theatres on 2 April. "The picture may be just what the doctor ordered for Karloff fans," wrote the *Los Angeles Times*, "although at that there's probably not quite enough horror for them."[54] Despite such criticisms the public liked the picture and *The Walking Dead* took an initial $300,000 at the box office.

On Sunday, 1 December, during the production of *The Walking Dead*, Karloff joined another 85 stage, screen and radio stars to celebrate the life of the comedian Will Rogers. Rogers and his friend the aviator Wiley Post had been killed on 15 August when the engine on their monoplane misfired and they crashed into an icy river near Point Barrow, Alaska.

A memorial benefit, entitled *Show of Shows*, was to be held at the Shrine Auditorium and all of the major studios in Hollywood participated by contributing artists and technicians. The final rehearsals were held all day on 1 December and at 8:15 p.m. that evening the three-hour show, which consisted of musical numbers, vaudeville skits, dance numbers and comedy acts, began.

MPPDA President Will Hays opened the benefit with a tribute to his friend. This was followed by George Stoll and his orchestra playing one of Rogers' favourite tunes, *The Last Round-Up*. Mme. Ernestine Schuman-Heink sang *The Star Spangled Banner* and Bing Crosby sang *Home on the Range*. In addition to Karloff, other stars who had volunteered their services included Clark Gable, Spencer Tracy, Mae West, Barbara Stanwyck and Fredric March. This concentration of stars resulted in a deluge of autograph hunters who flocked to the stage door. The crowd was so large extra police had to be called to keep the entrance clear. Still, the event, which played to a sell-out crowd of over 6,000, was a complete success and raised more than $15,000 for the Will Rogers Memorial Fund.

The Christmas season brought an invitation for the Karloffs to attend Basil Rathbone's festive party. The celebration, on 29 December, was an elaborate affair given in honour of the Dowager Countess Poulett and her daughter Lady Bridget. "Arriving at the gates of the Rathbone home in Beverly Hills," wrote journalist Isabel Sheldon, "guests advanced to the house along a driveway picturesquely converted into a glistening snow scene in yuletide spirit. There were Christmas carols sung beneath the windows while inside the candlelighted [*sic*] ballroom an orchestra played for dancing and groups gathered for eggnogs and cocktails from 5 until 8 in the evening."[55]

On 16 January Karloff typed a letter to his brother Charles informing him of the impending trip to England:

> My dear Charles:
> The glut of contradictory cables you have received from us must have made you think that we are completely insane. Thank goodness the arrangements are definitely made now, and we will be in London on or about the 25th of February.
>   As you know, I was to have been home in November, but the censor intervened on the score that the type of entertainment I furnish was corrupting the youth of the Empire. Fortunately for me, I had Gaumont British tied up on a very tight contract, and after a good deal of uproar the picture has finally been passed by the authorities. I'll be in London the end of February. It doesn't

leave me a great deal of time to get things fixed up at this end, so you'll have to excuse a rather short note.

It's not really forty years since we saw each other. I left Uppingham in 1906 and it was either just before or after that that we saw each other in Enfield. Anyhow, don't boast about your gray beard; wait until you see mine – in case I have to let it grow for the picture.

I am terribly glad to hear how comfortably and happily situated you are in Guernsey, and as you know, my own fortunes have taken an upward turn in the last five years after lying perilously close to the bottom of the sea – for what seemed to be forever. The ups and downs of life are curious uncontrollable things, but one thing is sure: the later in life that the "ups" come, the more one appreciates them.

I hope… that we will have a chance to see you when we get there. If not, we'll do our level best to get over to Guernsey this time.

Love from us both.

Your loving Brother,
Billy.[56]

At the end of the month Karloff prepared to leave for England to fulfil his contract with Gaumont-British. He would be paid $30,000 and afforded a few days paid holiday in New York. While they were away Dorothy's mother Louise would housesit for them at Bowmont Drive. So at 5 p.m. on Thursday, 30 January the Gleasons held a farewell party at their Alpine Drive home for the departing Karloffs. The long list of guests, which included Mr. and Mrs. Murray Kinnell, James Cagney, Pat O'Brien, Kenneth Thomson, Nigel Bruce, Rolf Armstrong, Basil Rathbone and Russell Gleason's girlfriend, Cynthia Hobart, gathered for drinks before they all transferred at 7 p.m. into a bus to drive to the station for the final farewell. There the Karloffs took a berth on a train to New York and upon arriving at the Grand Central Station took a taxi through the snowy New York streets to the Algonquin Hotel at 59 West 44th Street.

There Karloff found a telegram waiting for him. It was from his representatives, the Joyce-Selznick Agency. Impressed by the favourable results of *The Walking Dead* studio head Jack L. Warner wanted the star to sign a three-year contract to make a series of pictures for his studio. These movies would be made when the star was not busy with his Universal contract, which would take precedence. "A nice jump in salary too," commented Dorothy. "Wasn't that a pretty greeting to N.Y.?"[57]

Soon the couple were socialising and partying, often until the early hours. "Have cirrhosis of the liver, *delirium tremens* and nervous exhaustion," wrote Dorothy.[58] In their quieter moments they went to the theatre and, during their stay in the city, saw eight plays. It was not all recreation, however. On 5 February Karloff rehearsed for his appearance the following evening on Rudy Vallee's radio show *Vallee's Varieties*. The show featured Bohemian folk tunes played by the Kazanova Tziganes String Orchestra, songs from the Brown Sisters and comedy from Frank Fay, and the double act Anne Butler and Art Landry. Karloff appeared in a scene from *The Bells*, the drama he had filmed with Lionel Barrymore as a silent a decade earlier.

A week later the Karloffs were on the move again. At 11 a.m. on Wednesday, 12 February they boarded the liner *S.S. Washington*. "It was so cold," the star later wrote, "that Dorothy and I ached all over."[59] Before they could rest, however, the couple were requested to pose for photographers both at the rail and on the gangplank. The ship sailed at noon and the tired Karloffs took lunch before falling into bed. Their time in New York had taken its toll and, as Karloff later related, "had practically killed us."[60]

The sea voyage, however, presented an opportunity for rest and recuperation. The following day was spent half-dozing in deck chairs, broken only by an excursion to the ship's theatre to see *The Petrified Forest*. On Saturday they received an invitation to a cocktail party from fellow passenger Mrs. Wallace Beery, where they danced, and played the horse races.

At 7 a.m. on Tuesday the ship arrived at Cobh, Ireland. Due to fog, however, the ship could not enter the harbour until four hours later. According to *The Times*, the *S.S. Washington* was due to reach Plymouth at 6:50 p.m. that evening but due to the delays docked at 3 a.m. the following morning.

When Karloff disembarked he was met by photographers, reporters and representatives from Gaumont-British. Also waiting patiently were two girls who had made the trip from Torquay in Devon just to meet the star. The delayed arrival of the ship had proved no deterrent and the girls stayed up all night in order to get Karloff's autograph. Having graced the fans with his signature he passed through immigration where, he recalled, they got through "without one trunk or bag being opened!"[61]

They boarded the train and arrived at Paddington station to be met by yet more photographers and autograph hunters. From there the Karloffs transferred to the Berkeley Hotel in London's Knightsbridge where their rooms, they discovered, had been filled with flowers for Dorothy. They then spent time taking calls and, after lunch, took a brief walk in Green Park where the first thing they heard, Karloff later related, "was a delivery boy whistling *The Music Goes Round*, which we'd just escaped in America!"[62] Later that day the couple attended a press cocktail party at the Savoy before going to the Theatre Royal, Drury Lane to see *Jack and the Beanstalk*, the first pantomime Karloff had seen in 30 years.

On Thursday, 20 February Karloff met with his brother Sir John Pratt, then adviser on Far Eastern Affairs at the Foreign Office. They had lunch at Sir John's club where, to Sir John's horror, all the little pageboys asked for the actor's autograph. After lunch, as they were leaving, a waiter rushed up to Sir John. "Oh, Sir John," the waiter said, "just to think I've known you for years and never realised you were really Boris Karloff, the great star in disguise!"[63] This time, Sir John was amused. "It's the funniest thing that ever happened to Jack," Karloff later said, "or me."[64]

Within days of Karloff's arrival in England his new picture, *The Man Who Changed His Mind*, was in trouble. Unhappy with the screenplay the front office requested a rewrite and with no material to shoot Karloff's pay was suspended. A series of meetings with Harry Ham, the London representative of the Joyce-Selznick Agency, followed to discuss the situation. With nothing but time on their hands the Karloffs decided to vacate their suite at the Berkeley and move to the Dorchester. They would soon move again, preferring to return to the flat at 1 Duchess Street, where they had stayed during their previous visit to England three years earlier. The meetings with Ham continued, punctuated by additional meetings with Gaumont-British. Yet the problems did not abate and many involved with the picture came to believe it would never be made. Dorothy, too, had her doubts. Having read the script she declared it "rotten".[65]

While Karloff awaited the studio's 'green light' he and Dorothy embarked on a spate of visits and socialising. On Saturday, 22 February – after spending the morning flat hunting – they met Sir John and drove with him to Essex. When they returned Karloff set off for the BBC to record a broadcast for the radio programme *In Town To-night*, which was broadcast at 7 p.m. that evening. Leaving the building after the session he was once again mobbed by autograph hunters.

After lunch at the Grosvenor House Hotel the Karloffs were guests of Sir John at the *International Exhibition of Chinese Art* at the Royal Academy in London's Piccadilly.[xii] When they later returned to their accommodation they found a barrel-organ playing in the street under their window. "That's an English sound if ever I heard one," Karloff wrote. "Dorothy and I just threw him some pennies and he's giving it the works."[66]

The following day they had dinner at the Ivy. There they spent a pleasant evening talking with Laurence Olivier and his wife Jill Esmond who were seated at the next table. Then it was back to the hotel for an early night. On Monday the Karloffs dined at the home of Robert Stevenson. Stevenson was set to direct Karloff's picture for Gaumont-British and his wife, Anna Lee, was to co-star. "Their home is so lovely that Dorothy honestly covets it," Karloff said. "It is Queen Anne… and right across the river from St. Paul's Cathedral. Sir Christopher Wren lived in it while St. Paul's was being built. There's a Queen Anne staircase from the ground to the third floor."[67]

On Wednesday, 26 February the couple visited Harrods to buy a percolator and some American coffee. "The shock of English coffee in the mornings is too great for our systems," Karloff wrote. "But it's better than it was three years ago, and we have hopes."[68] The next evening they had supper at the Dorchester where *The Hollywood Beauties* were dancing. "Aside from them, the floor show wasn't bad," Karloff commented, "but those girls certainly weren't up to the Hollywood standards of beauty!"[69]

On Friday the Karloffs bought a new dog to add to their menagerie. It soon became apparent, however, the purchase was not a wise choice. "He didn't like me," Karloff explained. "I couldn't get used to him and, after all, we have five dogs at home in Beverly Hills, which ought to be enough for any one family."[70] According to Karloff he returned the dog the following day. However, on 17 March an advert appeared *The Times*. "Mrs. Boris Karloff," the advert ran, "wishes to SELL her long-haired red DACHSHUND Dog by Champion Jager of Dilworth, seven months old. Seen at Mayfair Dogs, Ltd., 45, Curzon Street, W.1. Gros. 1527."[71]

On Saturday evening it was off to the Palladium to see the Crazy Gang in the revue *Round about Regent Street*. Karloff's presence was noted and the star was announced from the stage. "Then everyone knew where Dorothy and I were sitting," he said, "and was there a rush for autographs afterwards!"[72]

The delay before filming had allowed the star to indulge his love of the theatre. In a week the Karloffs saw half a dozen productions ranging from the pantomime *Forty Thieves* at the Lyceum, *Out of the Dark* at the Ambassador, *Anthony and Anna* at the Whitehall, Fay Compton in *Call It a Day* at the Globe, and Cedric Hardwicke in *Tovarich* at the Lyric. Sometimes, however, these excursions caused some problems, as Karloff later recounted.

xii The exhibition ran from November 1935 to March 1936.

Above: With Anna Lee in *The Man Who Changed His Mind*
(1936). Inset: A scene from the movie.

"English fans are rabid!" he said. "I've been carried in and out of theatres by policemen
and commissioners. I've spent whole nights at the theatre waiting to escape. Once I was
seized by two burley commissioners, pushed into a car, only to be trailed by a covey of kids
on bicycles."[73]

On Sunday, 1 March the Karloffs dined at Scott's. "When we walked in," Karloff
recounted, "the waiter said, 'Would you like the same table you had last time, Mr. Karloff?
Three years ago, wasn't it?'"[74] Then, while the couple were dining, Dorothy heard an
American voice at a nearby table. It was *The House of Rothschild* director Alfred Werker.
With him was the American critic Alexander Woollcott and the ex-president's eldest son,
Theodore Roosevelt Jr.

On Tuesday, Karloff was visited by some movie cameramen who wanted to take footage
of "the monster eating breakfast".[75] Their ideas, however, did not go down well with the
star. "They had dialogue ready for me to say what a sweet soul I really am, at which I
rebelled," he said. "So they have to 'dub in' the continuity."[76] Later that day the couple
went shopping and looked for gifts for the Gleasons.

That same day Karloff was finally put back on salary by Gaumont-British and, according to his newspaper article *Diary of a Monster… By Boris Karloff*,[xiii] he began work on *The Man Who Changed His Mind* a little over a week later, on Thursday, 12 March.

The script by L. du Garde Peach, John L. Balderston and Sidney Gilliat told the story of Dr. Laurience [Karloff], a scientist who has discovered a method to extract and store the mind – or "thought content". He is aided in his work by a young scientist, Clare Wyatt [Anna Lee], and his wheelchair-bound assistant Clayton [Donald Calthrop].

Laurience is offered funding by newspaper magnate Lord Haslewood [Frank Cellier] but, when the scientific community dismisses Laurience's claims, Haslewood withdraws his funding. The scientist extracts his revenge by transferring Haslewood's mind into Clayton's crippled body. However, when Clayton discovers his new body has a defective heart he asks Laurience to transfer his mind into Haslewood's son, Dick [John Loder]. Instead, Laurience kills him and swaps his own body with Dick's. However, when Laurience's body falls from a window Clare reverses the procedure. The dying Laurience asks Clare's forgiveness and requests she destroy his work.

As Gaumont's main Lime Grove studio in Shepherd's Bush was unavailable, the picture was relegated to the company's Islington studio. The soundstage used for filming there was, Dorothy wrote, "a foul filthy hole if ever I saw one."[77] Located deep inside the studio, the soundstage had little access to fresh air. The chimpanzees that featured in the picture did nothing to add to the already stale atmosphere, which did not endear them to the star. "He wasn't too happy about the monkeys – the chimpanzees – that we had," Karloff's co-star Anna Lee recalled. "They were not at all well trained. I know they inhabited the dressing room next to mine and they used to make an awful smell."[78]

As the studio's canteen was so poor Dorothy bought her husband's lunch every day, which she would sit and share with him. Yet if the conditions at the studio were unpleasant, there was some compensation to be gained by the growing friendship between Karloff and his co-star, Anna Lee. The two often spent lunch and tea breaks together. "I remember him as a very kind and gentle man," Lee later said.[79] "We shared a great love of poetry. We used to have 'jam sessions' together – he would start a poem: 'Between the dark and the daylight…' and I would continue 'When the night is beginning to lower…' and go on until one of us got stuck! I forgot who usually won!"[80]

On Sunday, 15 March the Karloffs drove to Southwold in Sussex. The day, Karloff recalled, was "as cold as anything I want for a long time."[81] The purpose of the journey was to see his niece, Diana. She had been born in China in 1918 while her father, Sir John Pratt, was in the consular service there. Now she was attending St. Felix School some 30 miles south of Norwich. After a day with Diana, which involved lunch and a boat trip to the Suffolk coastal village of Walberswick, the Karloffs drove down to Brentwood, Essex to have dinner with Diana's parents.

The stay in England had allowed Karloff to catch up with, at least, some of his family. He saw much of Sir John during the stay and even spent some time with his brother, Frederick. Fred, as he was known, had retired from his position as the Commissioner of the Northern Division in India. During the Karloffs stay in England in 1936 Fred, then 66 years of age, suffered from a bout of flu and Dorothy visited him, taking him some fruit.

xiii Karloff's article is not entirely accurate. While some of the dates given are correct, others are not. For example, Karloff claims he left New York on 20 February when, in fact, he departed over a week earlier, on 12 February.

Karloff, too, was later able to visit his brother. The two trips to England, made three years apart, had presented Karloff with a treasured opportunity "for," he later wrote, "it was then that I really saw more of [Fred] and got to know him better than I ever had before. He was a strange mixture at that. I remember going to Simpson's with him for a late dinner, quite forgetting his eating habits, and he remarked that I was taking a tiger to a greengrocer's shop!"[82]

The trip to England also gave Karloff the opportunity to help develop relations between the British and American actors' unions. He met Alfred M. Wall, executive secretary of the London Trades Union Council and lunched with actor Godfrey Tearle, the President of the British actors' union, Equity. Equity wanted to formalise the demands they wished to make to the British producers, as the Screen Actors Guild had done in 1933.

A typical working day at a London studio, Karloff found, was similar to a Hollywood one. "The pressure to keep up the schedule and the hours are fantastic," he explained. "It's a business of nine to six… and there's no 12-hour rest period."[83] Karloff, with his detailed knowledge of SAG, was enlisted to help. "I was invited to sit in on a committee to talk over the preliminary steps with English producers, but the meeting did not eventuate," he said. "Anyway, I left some copies of the Guild's NRA brief with Equity and I do know they were greatly interested in what we considered fair working conditions."[84] It was an issue Karloff had strong views on. "With the growing interchange of talent between countries," he said, "I believe it is most important that working conditions be put on an international basis – that is, made the same for all countries."[85]

Before he left England Karloff had a final meeting with Equity to discuss an agreement with the Guild. "I found them most eager for such an arrangement," he said. "My first idea was merely to acquaint them with the Guild, its history, its administrative set-up, and what we are working for. You know the English do things slowly, and I didn't want to seem in a hurry. But I soon found I was the slow one. They were anxious for affiliation with the Guild as soon as possible."[86] Karloff went home and, from memory, drew up an agreement similar to the one the Guild had with American Equity, merely substituting the word 'British' in place of 'American.' Although he left England before the agreement could be ratified Karloff was told Equity was definitely in favour of an agreement with the Guild. "So," he reported, "the day cannot be far off when such a pact will be working to our mutual advantage. In the meantime, I think that Guild members who work in England should immediately join British Equity – to show our willingness to go half way."[87]

On Wednesday, 18 March the star had a day off from the studio. "Sir John Pratt took me through the Temple," Karloff recalled, "which is a sort of legal fastness, and Jack, being a 'bencher', took me through all kinds of places where no one but 'benchers' can go. We spent about an hour in the Great Hall, where I saw a table made from the wood of the Golden Hind – the boat in which Drake sailed around the world. Then into a Norman round church which is kept in perfect condition. The Temple has belonged to the members of the bar since 1600, and before that to the Templars and the Knights of St. John."[88]

On Friday – a "nasty, cold, wet day"[89] – the Karloffs attended the London premiere of the Irene Dunne/Robert Taylor picture *Magnificent Obsession*. A large crowd had gathered hoping to catch sight of the stars in attendance, which included Constance Cummings, Nils Asther and George Arliss. This congregation, however, caused some problems. "Police had to fight every inch of the way and still could not hold back the crowd," Karloff said.[90]

On the following Wednesday Dorothy had lunch with her husband at the studio and stayed all afternoon to watch him at work. "We had dinner alone," Karloff wrote, "and went for a long walk around London this evening in the fog – both a bit lonesome for our friends back in Hollywood."[91] The following evening the couple dined at Bentley's Oyster House in Piccadilly where they were introduced to a 'Black Velvet' – a beer cocktail made of equal measures of Guinness and champagne. It was, Karloff said, "something to dream about".[92]

On Friday, 27 March they attended a party in the country. As it was the day of the famous horse race, the Grand National, the partygoers listened to the event on the radio. "I bet on three horses," Karloff said. "One broke his neck at the first jump; another fell at the second jump, and the other didn't even finish. So I went back to the studio for some night work."[93]

In late March he signed with producer Julius Hagen for another British picture – *Juggernaut* – this time for Twickenham Pictures. The new contract would require the Karloffs to stay in England for, perhaps, another three months. As a result, they began their search for a suitable home.

On Sunday, 29 March the couple joined Sir John and Lady Pratt on a drive through Surrey and Sussex. They arrived at an old inn in Mayfield, East Sussex, some nine miles south of Royal Tunbridge Wells. "We sat before a roaring fire toasting ourselves, and drinking good English Ale," Dorothy wrote. "It was a *real* English Inn – the kind you read about – and they are truly hospitable and filled with the atmosphere of good comfort."[94] The following day, while her husband was at the studio, Dorothy dined with the actress/comedienne Joyce Grenfell. "She is delightful company," Dorothy wrote, "and Lady Mary Campbell joined our table for a chat as well. I liked them both tremendously."[95]

On Tuesday, Karloff was afforded a lie-in. "I didn't have to be at the studio until 10:30 this morning," he said, "and was that a break! First time in four weeks that I haven't been there before 8."[96] In the evening Karloff and Dorothy had dinner at the Ivy. "Then," Karloff revealed, "to a Mickey Mouse and newsreel theatre."[97]

On a rainy April Fool's Day, the Karloffs drove out into the countryside for a spot of house hunting. They had little success, "perhaps," mused Karloff, "because nothing looked attractive in such weather."[98] That weekend they had better luck when they stayed with friends, Gordon Walker and George Simpson, at Moyleen Farm in Berkshire. During their stay they drove on to nearby Hurley, "which," wrote Dorothy, "is the loveliest, tiniest village you can imagine."[99] There they found their perfect home, The Old Malt House, a large 17th century building set in eight acres of gardens. As soon as they saw it, wrote Dorothy, they "both fell in love[xiv] with it at once."[100]

---

xiv According to the *Los Angeles Times*, the Karloffs admired the building so much they planned to reproduce it on their Coldwater Canyon estate when they return to Hollywood.

On Wednesday, 8 April Karloff, accompanied by a publicity man, visited The Ideal Home Exhibition where the star was seated with other actors on a large platform. For a fee the stars would sign autographs with all the proceeds going to the Actors' Relief Fund. "I signed for over an hour," Karloff explained. "There were at least 3,000 people watching in addition to all those in line with their sixpence."[101]

The Old Malt House, 1936. Opposite page: Lobby card for *Juggernaut* (1936).

Two days later – Good Friday – the Karloffs began a long-weekend at the 12th century inn 'The Old Bell' in Hurley. Over the Easter holiday they took long walks through the snowy countryside, watched a point-to-point meeting of the Berkshire Hounds, and played darts in the pub. "I put a lot of time playing darts with the local worthies, and I'm afraid it costs me quite a bit," Karloff said. "The only man I could beat was my chauffeur, and I suspect him of allowing me to win."[102]

Sunday was the couple's wedding anniversary and Karloff presented his wife with a solid silver George IV wine cooler. The following day they signed the lease for the house, complete with three gardeners and three indoor staff. They moved in later that week.

The new tenants soon settled in. "Malt House grows on you," Karloff wrote, "we like it better every day. We are taking miles of colour film. Our first roll was very successful: we were off in a blaze of glory taking everything we see. This, billiards and punting on the river just about complete our present activities."[103] On Sundays the couple would have breakfast in bed followed by a long walk – "too lazy even to play tennis," Dorothy said.[104] Then, at teatime, their friends would appear. "Last Sunday," Dorothy recorded, "four men came in for tea, making me the only female with eight men – which is all right too!"[105]

The house was often busy with guests. The Karloffs friend Eb Morgan stayed with them for a time and could often be found pitting his skill against Karloff in the billiard room. "My high point," wrote Dorothy, "was reached when I found myself playing bridge with Lady Mary Montague, who went to New York last year to stay with the Culbertsons[xv] just for some bridge – which may give you a rough idea of the way she plays. However, I was the only one at the table who held any cards, and the only winner – even Boris was unusually unlucky – so I had a real break that night."[106]

On another occasion royalty came to dinner. "The owner of a film company here in London arrived with Princess Toubitsky and Prince and Princess Lowenstein," Dorothy explained. "Then, after dinner, we all went to the local or village 'pub' called 'Chequers' where we were entertained after hours by the proprietors. I can't describe what fun it was or how different from anything in America. All eight of us and an ancient dog sitting around the parlour of an old pub with special police permission for late hours, eating cheese and watercress and drinking ale. We didn't get home until the wee hours, and I claim it to be a perfect night's entertainment."[107]

---

xv Mr. and Mrs. Ely Culbertson were well-known bridge experts.

The Old Malt House was also the focal point for a female devotee. "When I got home today," Dorothy wrote, "I found one of Boris's most ardent admirers waiting with flowers, which she brings three times a week and sits until he comes home. How is that for a nice gesture? All the fans are so friendly and courteous over here."[108]

Karloff began work on the new picture *Juggernaut* on Saturday, 25 April at Twickenham Film Studios in St. Margaret where, claimed one reporter, "he is much sought after by the ragged little boys of the district, who he requites with autographs and pennies."[109]

Based on Alice Campbell's novel of the same name, *Juggernaut* told the story of a scientist, Dr. Sartorius [Karloff], whose research is jeopardised when his funding runs out. Unable to continue he leaves Morocco and returns to general practice in France. There he meets Lady Clifford [Mona Goya] who asks him to kill her ill millionaire husband, Sir Charles [Morton Selten], so she can inherit his money and live with her lover. For performing this task Sartorius is offered half of Sir Charles's legacy, some £20,000. The doctor agrees, hoping to use the money to fund his work.

Sartorius then begins a series of injections that will slowly kill Sir Charles. When the patient becomes suspicious he transfers his will to Roger [Arthur Margetson], his son by a previous marriage. On Lady Clifford's orders Sartorius now kills Sir Charles and the two plan to murder Roger to complete their scheme. However, when the doctor's nurse, Eve Rowe [Joan Wyndham], discovers the plot the doctor kidnaps her. She escapes in time to warn Roger. Sartorius, ashamed of the depths to which he has fallen, injects himself with the lethal cocktail and Lady Clifford is arrested.

Filming was expected to end on 6 June. The shooting schedule, however, was haphazard and, although this allowed Karloff the odd day off, it meant that when he was at the studio he would invariably work a long day, usually finishing at 8 p.m.

Although many miles from home, and now for an extended period, the Karloffs maintained their staff at the Coldwater Canyon house in order to look after the pets. Once a week they phoned home to check that the dogs – the five Bedlingtons and the two Scotties – were all right. "And each mutt must bark into the receiver to prove he's OK," claimed the *Los Angeles Times*.[110]

On 4 May the Karloffs attended the premiere of director Robert Stevenson's picture *Tudor Rose* (about Lady Jane Grey) at the New Gallery Cinema. Two days later they took a drive to Oxfordshire where they had lunch and watched the first day of a three-day match at the University Parks between Oxford and the Indian team, then on an England tour. When the actor Murray Kinnell and his wife arrived in London a week later, the Karloffs were able to spend time with them, playing tennis, watching cricket and sampling the delights of the local pubs and hostelries.

On 19 May Dorothy wrote to her mother informing her that the couple planned to extend their time in England and acquire a six-month residency. Without it Karloff would be required to pay U.S. state and federal tax on his British earnings, even though he had already paid tax on the same monies while in England.

Karloff had been troubled by his back and one of his legs during the stay but by the end of May had declared himself "feeling awfully fit".[111] Although his work on *Juggernaut* had come to an end, he was now required to return to Gaumont for retakes on *The Man Who Changed His Mind*. When both films were finally completed the Karloffs made plans for a trip abroad.

On Tuesday, 14 July they took the ferry at Dover bound for Calais for the start of a touring holiday in France. They would, Dorothy wrote, "just turn the nose of the car loose for four weeks."[112] They spent a night in Amiens before travelling on to Rouen and then driving west, on to Brittany. There they stayed at the Hotel de l'Univers in the walled seaport of St. Malo.

After a tour of the region the couple headed southeastwards, down into the Loire Valley, stopping in the town of Tours. That night, as they were leaving a restaurant, Karloff was approached by two sailors seeking the star's autograph. "When you realise Tours is miles inland – and isn't exactly the place you'd expect to find anything in a sailor suit," Dorothy said, "then to have these two off the *U.S.S. Wyoming* waiting there was a shock – and a very funny feeling it was."[113]

It had not been the only time the star had been recognised in France. One day, while driving through Brittany, Karloff had got lost. "In the dreadful remains of my schoolboy French, I inquired in a tiny village butcher shop," he explained. "The proprietor looked me in the face and exclaimed, 'Frankenstein's Monster!'"[114] This encounter, Karloff later revealed, had a profound effect on him. "'Good heavens,' I thought, 'do these people out here see my pictures?' I went away muttering to myself, 'My God – I've *got* to do better next time. That last thing [*Juggernaut*] was *awful!*'… I had to go to Brittany to get a shock which made me want to do better work. When I saw with my own eyes a little man in a hide-away town in a foreign land who knew me because he had watched me act on the screen, I was ashamed. Yes, ashamed. My perspective returned, and I knew when I got back to a Hollywood set, I would remember the little man in the Brittany butcher's shop."[115]

The trip away from Hollywood had, he felt, opened his eyes. "We completely lose the breadth of view which makes for fine performances," he explained. "Somehow we forget that the picture, which to us is a daily routine, is sooner or later going to travel all over the world, going to reach the millions we've forgotten all about. And that, I say, is too bad. Getting away from Hollywood for a time, leaving behind all the familiar faces and schedules, restores your vision. Your mind is jolted out of its customary groove and, by Jove, you begin to realise again that, after all, Hollywood and its studios aren't the sum and substance of existence. And believe me, it's a great awakening!"[116]

On 27 July they were on the road again, heading towards Paris. There they took a top floor suite at the Hotel George V, just off the Champs-Élysées. For the next nine days the couple toured the city before heading back to Calais, via Rheims, to catch the return ferry to England. Reaching Dover on 9 August, the bad weather forced them to forgo a trip to Cornwall and instead they made straight for the Washington Hotel in London's Mayfair.

Before returning to America, however, Karloff had an engagement to fulfil in Canada. He had agreed to appear on the radio show *Vallee's Varieties* to be broadcast from the Canadian National Exposition in Toronto. So, on 22 August, the couple boarded the liner *Empress of Britain* bound for Quebec. It was the second time Karloff had boarded a ship of that name to take him to Canada. On the first occasion, 27 years earlier, he had been an unknown, alone and with few prospects. Now he was an internationally famous horror movie star. But the times were changing, and the horror movie's days were numbered.

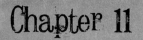

Chapter 11

A LULL IN THE MONSTROSITIES

(1936-1938)

"I'm anxious to do away with the word 'horror' in connection with my roles. But… odd or strange characterisations really are much more interesting to play."[1]

Boris Karloff (1937)

K arloff's stay in Canada was brief, staying only to fulfil his final commitment before returning to Hollywood after almost seven months away. On 3 September he appeared in a dramatic sketch on Rudy Vallee's radio show *Vallee's Varieties*. Broadcast at 8 p.m. the show included the singer Arline Jackson, the comedy team of Tom Howard and George Shelton, actor Eddie Green and comedian Doc Rockwell.

Following the show the Karloffs left Canada and arrived back in Los Angeles upon the passenger train *The Chief* on 7 September. Karloff was glad to be back in Southern California after the terrible weather he had experienced in England. "It rained constantly," he told reporters. "So I'm not expressing a mere pleasantry when I say that I am glad to be back in the sunshine."[2]

Hollywood had changed during Karloff's absence. His staple genre, the horror movie, had gone into decline. There had been mounting pressure, both at home and from abroad, to curb the tide of such pictures. Censor groups in Britain had long objected to the genre's supposed damaging effects on children. In January 1933 the 'H' [Horrific] rating was introduced to identify 'films which are likely to frighten or horrify children under the age of 16 years'. The first picture to receive the rating was Carl Theodor Dreyer's *Vampyr* (1932). However, at that time the rating was merely advisory and children could still see the picture if accompanied by a parent or guardian. In June 1937 the 'H' rating was made official and children under the age of 16 were prohibited entrance to such films. Yet, by this time, Universal – the home of the horror picture – was in new hands.

The studio had been losing money. At the end of fiscal 1935 Universal had lost $677,185 and 125 studio workers were laid off. When the studio urgently needed money to complete the pictures *Show Boat*, *Magnificent Obsession* and *Sutter's Gold*, which had already been scheduled by the distributors, Laemmle sought the funds from J. Cheever Cowdin, the president of the Standard Capital Company, and independent movie producer Charles R. Rogers.

The $750,000 loan, provided by Standard Capital, the Eastman Kodak Company and Electrical Research Products Inc., was secured on 1 November 1935. The terms of the loan required the monies to be repaid within three months at seven percent interest. At the end of the 90 days, if the terms were not met, Capital could purchase Laemmle's 80% interest in the film company for $5.5 million. When the studio's receipts failed to cover the loan, however, Laemmle was forced to sell out.

On 14 March 1936 – the 21st anniversary of the founding of Universal City – Carl Laemmle Sr. sold his controlling interest in the studio. General Film Distributors, a syndicate headed by C.M. Woolfe, J. Arthur Rank, Lord Portal, Paul Lindenberg and L.W. Farrow would take over the studio's British holdings for £1,225,000. With the sale Laemmle Sr. retired and Cowdin became the new chair of the board. The company's vice-president, Robert H. Cochrane, was promoted and became the studio's new president. "The harmonious and industrious co-operation given me by Mr. Cochrane during the thirty years of Universal progression has made me extremely happy to learn that he will guide the future destinies of the company," said Laemmle Sr.[3]

Cowdin then sacked 70 employees, mostly relatives of the Laemmles, and placed Charles R. Rogers in charge of production. There was no place for Laemmle Jr. within the new regime and with his departure the golden era of the horror picture came to an end. Rogers did not share his predecessor's enthusiasm for the horror picture. Instead 'New Universal', as it soon came to be called, would aim to produce more family-orientated productions.

The success of *The Invisible Ray* had prompted Universal to plan another feature for their two horror stars and *The Electric Monster*, a story of a man who feeds on electricity, was hastily announced. Originally entitled *The Man in the Cab* Universal had purchased the property in August 1935 and Karloff signed for the picture before he left for England in February 1936.

"The character I play," Karloff revealed, "is a chap named Jean Dumarque, who works in the laboratory of one Professor Einmetz, an electrical wizard who uses me as a sort of human guinea pig for his experiments in the interests of science. He charges me up with electricity like a storage battery. In the course of the story I am innocently accused of murdering the professor and am condemned to the electric chair. It wouldn't be cricket, as we Englishmen say, to tell you what happened after I am fastened to that uncomfortable piece of furniture, but I can assure you the results will be one surprise after another."[4]

As always, Karloff was interested in the studio artists' preliminary drawings. "This make-up is going to be the most ponderous I've ever worn on the screen – 15 pounds heavier than the monster rig-out which weighed over 80 pounds. But very little of the 'Man in the Cab' make-up is to be visible. It will be worn mostly underneath my clothes and is to be made chiefly of metal and insulation. Some of it will be aluminium, other parts will be glass and still others, rubber and steel. This is because it must carry electrical equipment, so I can shoot sparks in every direction, like the rays of the sun."[5] Karloff

Left: As Gravelle in *Charlie Chan at the Opera* (1936). Above: Peter Lorre visits Karloff during filming of *Charlie Chan at the Opera*.

estimated it would take around two hours to be made up for the role – "shorter than usual for me, because this time I shan't be remodelling my face with my usual beauty-clay."[6]

However, the picture became one of the casualties following the sale of Universal and was cancelled. It was later resurrected and finally went into production in late 1940 as *The Mysterious Dr. R* without either Karloff's or Lugosi's involvement. It was released as *Man Made Monster* in March 1941 and starred Lon Chaney Jr. and Lionel Atwill.

In June 1936 it had been announced that Universal had purchased pulp writer Fred MacIsaac's detective tale *Murder on the Mississippi* as a starring vehicle for Karloff. A month later the *Los Angeles Times* revealed the star would 'abandon' his usual horrific make-up when he plays a detective in his next film, the mystery *The Case of the Constant God*, also for Universal. "Just because he is escaping a disguise on this occasion does not mean that Karloff is avoiding the thriller atmosphere," the newspaper asserted. "Dire happenings eventuate in *The Case of the Constant God* which was written by Rufus King, with screenplay by Lewis R. Foster. Foster may co-direct the picture with Milton Carruth."[7]

In late August it was also announced that Karloff was to star in a picture for Warners that would "combine the supernatural with science."[8] The picture would be called *Hell Is Above*. In the event, the horror star would not appear in any of these pictures. When *The Case of the Constant God* went into production in early September it featured Ralph Forbes and Harry Hunter. It was later released under the title *Love Letters of a Star*. Instead, in mid-August, it was announced that Karloff would co-star with Warner Oland, at Fox, in the detective story *Charlie Chan at the Opera*. It would be Oland's 13th Charlie Chan picture for Fox.

The Chan pictures were a lucrative series for the studio. Costing around $125,000 each to make they often took $500,000 at the box office. Although the series was successful their star did cause the studio some trouble. Oland had a drink problem of 20 years' standing and was prone to partake during filming. One day, while shooting the racetrack sequence at the Santa Anita track for *Charlie Chan at the Racetrack* (1936), Oland went missing. The crew searched for him and he was found, fast asleep, in the track restaurant. Despite such occurrences the picture's director, H. Bruce Humberstone, was not opposed to the star's drinking. On the contrary, he felt it actually aided Oland's performance. On viewing the rushes Oland was forced to agree. While sober the actor spoke his lines too quickly. After a few drinks he slowed down and hesitated and mumbled as he was forced to recall his lines through an alcoholic haze. Despite an inebriated star *Charlie Chan at the Race Track* proved successful at the box office and the studio wanted more. Humberstone was, therefore, signed to direct the following Chan picture, *Charlie Chan at the Opera*.

It was Humberstone's idea to cast Karloff. Producer Sol Wurtzel initially rejected the idea due to the added expense of hiring the star but later changed his mind. "Real build-up is in sight for the 'Charlie Chan' films," wrote the *Los Angeles Times*, "and why shouldn't there be such a boost given this remarkably popular series? Warner Oland... will have none other than Boris Karloff as a team-mate."[9] Production on *Charlie Chan at the Opera* began on 7 September 1936, the same day Karloff returned to Hollywood. He began work on the picture eight days later.

Karloff played Gravelle, an amnesiac opera singer, who escapes from the Rockland State Sanatorium when his memory is jogged by a newspaper picture of his wife, the opera singer Lilli Rochelle. When Rochelle subsequently receives a death threat she enlists the help of the police.

Gravelle has been presumed dead, the victim of a fire in the Chicago Opera House that raged on 15 September 1923. The blaze, it transpires, was set by Lilli and her paramour, the opera singer Enrico Barelli, who had locked Gravelle in his dressing room. When Lilli and Enrico are found murdered at the theatre during preparations for the opera *Carnival*, Chan investigates. As would often be the case, Karloff provided the picture's red herring. As the star's mere presence in a mystery picture implied guilt the studios would often cast him in an attempt to mislead the audience.

The role of an opera singer required Karloff to appear in a segment of the opera specially written for the picture by pianist/composer, and sometime actor, Oscar Levant. "20th Century-Fox had just completed an elaborate spectacle with Lawrence Tibbett, of which one of the high spots was a Faust scene in which the star wore a magnificent Mephistophelian costume," Levant later wrote.[i] "One of our first problems arose when the costume was assigned to *Charlie Chan at the Opera*, with instructions for us to put it to work. I had heard of music being written around a singer, but never for a costume. Nevertheless, determined to become a cog in the wheel, I set myself to writing an operatic sequence in which the big aria found a baritone wearing this elegant Mephistopheles costume."[10] Having had little experience in writing opera Levant sought the advice of his mentor, the composer Arnold Schoenberg. "He advised me to study the score of Beethoven's *Fidelio*," Levant explained. "Since this is one of the most unoperatic of all operas it was just what I didn't need."[11]

The opera's libretto was written in English by William Kernell and translated into Italian. Although baritone Tudor Williams provided Gravelle's singing voice, Karloff was required to mouth the words. According to actress Nedda Harrigan, who played Anita Barelli in the picture, it was this libretto that gave the star some trouble. "Boris could never master the Italian so he bellowed away – 'SAN FRANCISCO! SACRAMENTO! SANTA BARBARA!'"[12] Although a charming anecdote, a viewing of the picture reveals that Karloff is, in fact, 'singing' the correct words.

---

i The costume appears to have come from Tibbett's film *Under Your Spell* (1936) although only the headpiece is similar in both pictures. In addition, there are actually *two* Mephistopheles costumes in the Charlie Chan picture. In one scene Gravelle confronts Enrico Barelli [Gregory Gaye] while they are both wearing the same attire.

To cut costs Humberstone utilised sets from D.W. Griffith's latest picture *Café Metropole*. When studio head Darryl F. Zanuck saw Humberstone's movie he remarked, "This son-of-a-bitch, Humberstone, is making my 'A' directors look sick turning out a 'B' that looks like this. Put him under contract."[13]

The picture wrapped towards the end of October. It had been a fun shoot with Karloff at his most genial. "He was a joy," Harrigan recalled, "every moment of the shooting was fun – so much so that we occasionally broke up... he knew he could break me up so he did – constantly."[14]

The picture opened at the Palace in New York on Friday, 4 December 1936. "The news from the Palace this morning," wrote the *New York Times*, "is that *Charlie Chan at the Opera* is by far the best of the recent crop of Chan pictures turned out by 20th Century-Fox... Once the story gets under way, it flows smoothly and swiftly... Warner Oland, the perennial, who has just signed for ten more Chan pictures, performs the title role with his customary dexterity. He is assisted herein by Boris Karloff (who has a knack of chilling audiences without benefit of a cooling system) as the supposed lunatic."[15]

The picture's title card misleadingly read "20th Century-Fox presents Warner Oland vs. Boris Karloff in *Charlie Chan at the Opera*." This deception was noted by some. "Mr. Oland, as it turns out, isn't really 'versus' Mr. Karloff – but beyond this I won't tell you anything," wrote Philip K. Scheuer of the *Los Angeles Times*.[16]

Following his work on the 'Charlie Chan' picture in October, Karloff had a three-month break from making movies. He still had a single picture outstanding from his contract with Universal and it was originally envisaged that this would be *The Man in the Cab* (a.k.a. *The Electric Monster*). Instead, he would make the crime drama *Night Key* for the studio.

In the meantime Karloff appeared, albeit briefly, on the Los Angeles theatre stage. William H. Smith's 1844 temperance melodrama *The Drunkard; or, The Fallen Saved* opened at the Theatre Mart on Clinton Street in Hollywood on 6 July 1933. "Though the actors are playing it straight," one reviewer wrote, "to our modern sense it gives the effect of a riotous burlesque, and by the same token the audience reaction is hilarious."[17]

To present the play the theatre had all its seats removed and replaced with tables and chairs. Once seated the audience were served free beer. At the end of the play free coffee and sandwiches were available. Then there came the olio, or after-show. While the play remained the same each night the after-show would often change. Members of the cast and audience would sing old songs, tell amusing stories or make recitations. There were also musical skits and communal singing.

Originally only intended for a short run the play soon gained an audience and was championed by such Hollywood stars as W.C. Fields, Gloria Stuart, Lew Ayres and Boris Karloff. The play eventually ran for 20 years, chalking up 7,510 performances.

Karloff saw the show almost 30 times. He was also personally responsible, early in the run, for the inclusion of several old music hall songs in the after-show: *Minnie the Old Mermaid, Nana of the Manor, The Bushes in the Bottom of the Garden* and *Ada, Pin a Rose In Your Hair*. This last song was presented as an animated curtain. The song, the *Los Angeles Times* reported, had "naughty insouciant lines pinned on everybody from the scantily clad Monsieur Gandhi down to Moses and even Cleopatra."[18] These animated paintings, like the inclusion of the songs, were Boris Karloff's idea. On Monday, 19 October the star appeared as the guest of honour on the night of the 1200th performance.

On 8 December Karloff appeared on the radio show *Camel Caravan* along with Benny Goodman and his Orchestra and soprano Olga Albani. The star featured as 'Death' in a presentation of Alberto Casella's *Death Takes a Holiday*. The play told the story of 'Death' who takes a three-day holiday in an attempt to discover why he is feared. He takes the guise of Prince Sirki and spends the time at the estate of Duke Lambert where a young princess falls in love with him.

It would be Karloff's third radio appearance in the role. This time he asked Russell Gleason's girlfriend, Cynthia Hobart, if she would like to play the young princess, Grazia, opposite him on the radio. Hobart agreed. "Boris would pick me up and take me to rehearsals," she later wrote, "work with me over the script,

put his arm around me, and draw me closer to the microphone if I backed away."[19] All was going well until the final rehearsal. During the love scene when Death reveals his name is 'Boris' Hobart was supposed to repeat the name, but no sound came. The reality of her venture had struck and she could not speak. "Boris read the line again," Hobart explained. "He had put his arm around my shoulder. He pressed it tightly. I just stood there."[20] Despite Karloff's protests Lindsay was replaced. "Come on, love," Karloff said. "I'll take you home."[21] As Hobart sobbed in Karloff's car the star remained philosophical. "All will be alright," he told her. "There's always a standby actress dying for a chance. This just wasn't the right corner or the right time for you."[22]

Night Key had been announced as a Karloff vehicle in mid-October. The star would play Dave Mallory, a genial old inventor[ii] with failing eyes, whose alarm system was stolen and patented 20 years earlier by his previous partner, Steve Ranger. Mallory has now invented a new system, an invisible beam alarm that would put Ranger

Poster for *Night Key* (1937).

out of business if purchased by a rival company. Ranger, therefore, agrees to purchase the new system from Mallory but, after signing the contract, the inventor discovers Ranger has no intention of implementing the new system; he merely wants to stop its sale to anyone else. Incensed, Mallory begins a crime spree. Assuming the moniker 'Night Key' he breaks into establishments protected by the Ranger Protection System. He steals nothing, wishing only to discredit Ranger's company. However, a gang of thieves led by

---

ii Early announcements mistakenly claimed Karloff would play a 'night watchman' in the picture.

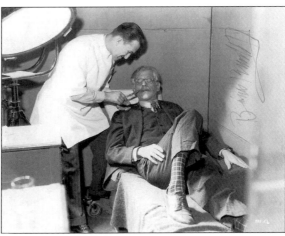

As Dave Mallory in *Night Key* (1937).
Jack Pierce tends to Karloff's makeup on *Night Key*.

Alan 'the Kid' Baxter discover Mallory's new device and kidnap his daughter, Joan, forcing Mallory to comply. Mallory seeks out Ranger's help in stopping the criminals. Ranger agrees, fearing the crime spree will ruin the reputation of his company. When the crooks are apprehended Ranger agrees to install Mallory's new system.

As with *The Black Room*, Karloff seemed pleased to be moving away from the more monstrous roles. "I've always wanted to portray a role in which I did not have to resort to grotesque make-up," he said.[23] However, the film had a troubled history. The original director, Arthur Lubin, was replaced by Sidney Salkow who was, in turn, replaced by Lloyd Corrigan. The picture also went through various re-writes and in November was postponed due to "story trouble".[24] To assist Universal borrowed Jack Moffitt from Paramount to work on the script.

There were also some problems with the casting. J. Carrol Naish, who was originally cast as the mobster John Barron, was replaced by Alan Baxter. Further misfortune occurred when Hollywood was hit by a flu epidemic. Actress Polly Rowles was originally cast as Dave Mallory's daughter, Joan, until she was struck down with the virus. The picture's director, Lloyd Corrigan, waited a week for Rowles to recover but, when this did not happen, was forced to replace her with Jean Rogers. Karloff, too, had been struck by the bug and required a brief stay in hospital.

Karloff decided to model the role of Dave Mallory on his gardener and began shadowing the man, writing notes all the while in a little black book. One day, however, the gardener caught site of Karloff peering at him from a bush and almost jumped out of his skin. "I went away saying nothing," Karloff recounted, "and resumed the shadowing later. But it was no use after that. The gardener just wouldn't be natural any more. He was watching for me. I thought I had lulled him once, but he was only playing 'possum'. He edged around the back gate then bolted as if the devil were after him."[25]

Shooting finally commenced, with a budget of $175,000, on Monday, 18 January 1937 at Universal. Despite the fact that Karloff was still recuperating from his recent bout of flu he was required to work in an environment that visiting reporter Robbin Coons described as "a draughty, clammy frigid sound stage".[26] Karloff was given a canvas dressing hut to rest in but it offered little refuge from the cold. During his interview with Coons, Karloff spotted Robert Presnell. "Ah, but there's the villain of the piece, the producer," Karloff told Coons. "Excuse me. I'm going to speak to him about this cold stage."[27] While Karloff was in conference attendants deposited an army cot in Karloff's tent. They then set up an arc light to keep the star warm between takes. Having spoken to Presnell, Karloff shot a scene. "After it, he joined me in the hut, where the heat was good but dangerous – when you left it," Coons wrote. "He wouldn't lie down, although he was supposed to. He insisted on being courteous, which was more than I'd have been, wheezing and sniffling and make-up forbidding a handkerchief. There ought to be a limit to this show-must-go-on thing."[28] There was. When the studio required Karloff to work for more than the normal eight-hour day, the star complained. When they ordered him to attend a night shoot he refused to show up the following day.

Karloff had also been concerned about the picture's ending. In December the *Los Angeles Times* had asserted that Karloff's character in *Night Key* "comes to a sticky end"[29] but the following month its denouement remained unwritten. The star had his own ideas on what his characters fate should be, favouring the 'sticky end'. "He's got to die," Karloff told Coons. "He's a sympathetic character – sniff – old and nearly blind. He's honest, and the things he does are not intended to harm anyone but merely to get back his rightful share from the man who robbed him of his invention. It's not his fault that gangsters step in. And if he doesn't die – sniff – what can be done with him? Have him shake hands with his old enemy and live happily – sniff – ever after?"[30] Karloff was to be disappointed, for this is exactly what the screenwriters did.

Shooting was completed on 16 February, six days over schedule and $17,000 over budget. *Night Key* opened in New York on Saturday, 17 April at the Central, replacing *Racketeers in Exile*, a crime drama that had been previously intended for that spot. The *New York Times* thought the picture, "in the polished manner of the traditional Universal thriller, capably served throughout by enjoyable players."[31] The picture opened at the RKO Hillstreet and Pantages Hollywood theatres in Los Angeles on 16 August. It was shown as the companion feature to Joe E. Brown's comedy *Riding on Air* and the Bing Crosby short *Blue of the Night*.

With the completion of *Night Key* Karloff's contract with Universal had come to an end. He was now scheduled to return to Warners to star in the picture *Black Widow* for the studio. The story, by Crane Wilbur, concerned a scientist who discovers an invisibility drug. The star had been announced for the picture the previous November when, it was claimed, he had "rebelled so strenuously against hideous make-up and horror pictures."[32] Karloff would play the straight role of the scientist. Yet by the following February these plans had changed. "Preferring something more than the scheduled mystery yarn *Black Widow*," the *New York Times* explained, "the Warners today shifted Boris Karloff to headline story, *China Bandit*. Crane Wilbur is writing the screenplay and John Farrow will direct. Beverly Roberts and Ricardo Cortez will provide the romantic interest."[33]

Then, on 16 February, three weeks before production began on the picture, Dorothy Karloff was admitted to the Good Samaritan Hospital to undergo a major operation. Although the nature of Dorothy's complaint was not revealed, Dr. William E. Branch, who performed the surgery, told reporters Mrs. Karloff was expected to make a full recovery. While Dorothy recuperated her husband returned to Warners to make his latest picture.

China Bandit was a remake of *The Bad Man*, a play and subsequent novel set in Mexico. Events in China at the time, however, persuaded the studio to change the story's location. The unstable political relations between China and Japan would, in July, develop into full-scale war between the nations (the second Sino-Japanese war). This conflict would only end with Japan's surrender to the Allies in August 1945.

Shooting on *China Bandit* began in the first week of March.[iii] Before the week was out the picture had been renamed *War Lord*. In mid-April the press announced the picture was renamed again – this time to *The Adventures of Fang*, although *War Lord* was still used in the press.

The picture told the story of an American, Jim Hallett [Gordon Oliver], who has discovered oil in the bandit-ridden territories of northern China. To finance the venture Hallett borrowed money from businessman Myron Galt [Douglas Wood] who, along with his daughter Lola [Sheila Bromley] and Gordon Creed [Ricardo Cortez], travel by train to see the American. Hallett, however, has defaulted on the loan and Galt intends to take possession of the oil fields. Creed also plans to become a partner in the fields and has travelled on the pretence of visiting his estranged wife, Jane [Beverly Roberts]. Jane works as a medical missionary in the village of Sha Ho Shei, close to the oil fields. She, it becomes apparent, is in love with Hallett.

Rebel leader General Wu Yen Fang [Karloff] – "The White Tiger" – has taken control of the region, and the general and his troops arrive in the village. They set up their headquarters in the mission where the occupants are kept prisoner. Fang and Hallett, it transpires, are already acquainted for, before the general's rise to power, Hallett had saved his life. Fang determines to repay the debt and destroys Galt's foreclosure notice. He also makes a deal with Galt and Creed to the effect that they can have the oil fields in exchange for $50,000. Fang is given the money unaware that Galt and Creed plan to double-cross him and have Hallett murdered. Fang, however, foils the plot. Government troops arrive and surround the town. Fang shoots Creed, leaving Hallett and Jane free to marry. The general is taken prisoner and led away to be shot.

West of Shanghai (1937).

Karloff's make-up for the role of the bandit general was simpler than he had been accustomed to at Universal. Although it still took make-up artist Perc Westmore three hours to apply, Karloff was afforded a 'lie-in' being required to report to the studio at 6 a.m. instead of his normal 4:30–5 a.m. start. The make-up applied to Karloff's eyes, however, proved troublesome. The invisible tape

iii Although it is often claimed the picture began production on 8 March 1937, the previous day's *New York Times* stated shooting began earlier in the week.

used caused the lower eyelids to press against his eyeballs, which had the effect of badly blurring his vision.

One evening, during production, cast members Richard Loo and James Leong entertained their colleagues at a Chinese dinner. The guests, which included Karloff, Ricardo Cortez, Gordon Oliver, Marcia Ralston, Tetsi Konai, Phil Harris, Gordon Hart, the picture's director John Farrow and his wife, the actress Maureen O'Sullivan, were entertained by Beverly Roberts who regaled them with an oriental song she had learned from cast member Chester Gan. She was accompanied by Eddie Lew on a Chinese guitar.

West of Shanghai was previewed at the Warners Beverly Hills Theatre on Saturday, 3 July. The *Los Angeles Times* thought the picture an "unusually good orientalised version of *The Bad Man*".[34] The picture was only let down, the reviewer felt, by its ending which "draws to such an abrupt close that the effect was lost. With the quality of the Karloff portrayal more attention could well have been given to the subject."[35]

The picture opened on Thursday, 7 October at the Warner Brothers Hollywood and Downtown theatres with the Pat O'Brien and Joan Blondell picture *Back in Circulation*. It previewed at the Criterion in New York on Thursday, 28 October and opened the following day. B.R.C. of the *New York Times* wrote, "After all these humourless, if not outright horrendous, years (even the advertisements proudly proclaim him as 'baby-scarer'), Boris Karloff admirably acquits himself as a comedian in *West of Shanghai* at the Criterion. With infinite gallantry and urbanity, Mr. Karloff plays a Mongolised version of the old Holbrook Blinn 'Bad Man' role – a loveable, charming and ridiculous Chinese war lord who bumps off the villain and sets matters right for the nice people in the cast, then gracefully eliminates himself before a Nanking firing squad."[36]

While Karloff was shooting *West of Shanghai* for Warners, Universal announced their intention to feature the actor in the picture *Armoured Car* in which, an informant told the *Washington Post*, Karloff would play "kind of a nutty guy – who is a musician in the day time and a bandit at night."[37] Within days, however, it was decided Cesar Romero would play the role instead. Karloff would move to an "untitled mystery melodrama".[38] In the end neither happened. Irving Pichel played the role intended for Karloff in *Armoured Car* while Romero was moved to the role of the Pichel's henchman. Karloff's mystery melodrama never materialised.

On 9 April Karloff's home at 2320 Bowmont Drive was the site of a terrible tragedy. Ricardo Salazar, the four-year-old son of Karloff's washwoman, Mrs. Concha Salazar, fell into the swimming pool and drowned as his mother worked only a few feet away. Sadly, it would not be the only tragedy involving children that would touch Karloff's life.

At Bowmont Drive, 1937.

At that time all was not well in Hollywood. On 4 April the Screen Actors Guild had issued a statement to the effect that there would be strike action by its members unless the studios formally recognised both the Guild and its right to collective bargaining. The next day a committee of motion picture producers agreed a 10% pay rise to the industry's craftsmen, including joiners. This agreement would affect some 20,000 workers in the industry. The Brotherhood of Painters, Decorators and Paperhangers, however, had not participated in the agreement due to the studios refusal to recognise the union's jurisdiction of hairdressers, make-up artists, scenic artists and art directors.

The Screen Actors Guild grievances also remained unresolved and there was soon talk of strike action. At 2 p.m. on 11 April a Guild meeting was held in the Hollywood Legion Stadium to discuss the situation. On 30 April a further meeting with studio representatives to discuss the union's demand for a closed shop broke down. Then, at noon, president of the Federated Motion Picture Crafts, Charles Lessing, issued a strike call and workers in the four crafts (scenic artists, hairdressers, painters and draftsmen) went on strike.

That evening the senior executive board of the Screen Actors Guild held a meeting at its headquarters to discuss what part its members would take in the strike. In London British Equity announced that, should the Guild go on strike, it would instruct its members to boycott Hollywood film studios in support. In Hollywood it was feared the walkouts would paralyse the film industry.

On 2 May the Screen Actors Guild decided to defer action on a walkout until they could confer with the producers. It was also decided that players should continue to pass through the federation picket lines until final action was decided upon. On 8 May the Guild's business agent, Aubrey Blair, announced scores of renowned Hollywood screen players, including Karloff, would join the picket lines at the nine major picture studios.

The following day six of the major studios (Columbia Pictures, RKO, Paramount, MGM, Universal and 20th Century Fox) verbally agreed to the Guild's demands. These included: an increase of $15 to $25 a day for bit players, a minimum of $50 a week for stock players, abolition of the $3.20 standard wage for the most lowly class of extra players, compensation for all players while riding to and from location, a 10% increase for all extras earning up to $15 per day with a $5.50 minimum, an increase from $20 to $33 a week for stand-ins or a daily wage of not less than $6.50 a day plus overtime. SAG's demands to be granted a Guild Shop were also met. "Guild Shop does not mean closed shop, as so many people believe," the Guild's Executive Secretary, Kenneth Thomson, explained. "Guild Shop merely means that no one may work before the camera who is not a Guild member in good standing. The Guild agrees with the producers that new talent, new faces, are necessary and we do not intend to restrict those seeking opportunity on the screen. We merely insist that they join the Guild and be governed by the same rules that apply to other players."[39] This agreement meant that stars such as Lionel Barrymore, Norma Shearer, Marlene Dietrich and Wallace Beery would be forced to join the union.

At a meeting at the Hollywood Legion Stadium SAG president Robert Montgomery announced the victory to 4,000 members who cheered and applauded the news. The news was disappointing for the studio craftsmen who had counted on the Guild's members to join them on the picket lines outside the studios and major picture theatres. Instead, with its demands met, the Guild voted not to assist. Charles Lessing called the move "a dirty double cross".[40] However, high-salaried movie stars contributed "substantial financial support"[41] to the striking studio craftsmen.

On 15 May a contract was agreed between the Guild and the studios formally agreeing to the Guild's demands. For its part, the Guild agreed a ten-year ban on its members from striking – for any reason. The craftsmen's strike finally ended on 1 June when it was agreed the craftsmen's unions should be admitted to April's studio-union basic agreement, under closed-shop conditions and with a 10% salary increase. Following the end of the strike the Federated Motion Picture Crafts union was dissolved.

As the Screen Actors Guild's assistant secretary, Karloff was concerned by the climate of strikes in the movie industry. However, he still found time to lend himself to other good causes. On 30 April the Philadelphia Symphony Orchestra, under its new conductor Jose Iturbi, played the first of two concerts at the Shrine auditorium in Los Angeles. Many local groups, including the Hollywood community, sponsored the event. Karloff served on the motion picture committee, along with such stars as Charles Chaplin, Paulette Goddard, Edward G. Robinson, Deanna Durbin, Joan Crawford, Irene Dunne and Nelson Eddy.

Back in England on 12 May King George VI was crowned in Westminster Abbey. That evening, in Hollywood, a Coronation Ball was held in the Fiesta room of the Ambassador Hotel to celebrate the event. Many of the so-called 'British colony in Southern California'[42] were in attendance and the proceeds for the evening were donated to several charities caring for people of British origin. The Karloffs were joined at their table by the Gleasons, Mr. and Mrs. Sidney Brown, Miss Vickrey and Miss Mumford.

The following day Karloff umpired a benefit match at Laguna Beach between the Hollywood cricket squad, captained by C. Aubrey Smith, and the San Diego team. Eugene Walsh of the Hollywood squad was the man of the match scoring 29 runs before the large crowd and helping the team to win by 131 runs to 59.

In July Warners purchased Ralph Spencer Zink's mystery play *Without Warning* as a vehicle for Karloff. The play had opened at the National Theatre in New York on 1 May 1937 but had run for only 17 performances. Jane Wyman, it was rumoured, would play the female lead in the picture version while *West of Shanghai* director John Farrow would helm the project. By early August, however, Marie Wilson was confirmed in Wyman's place.

The final draft of Crane Wilbur's screenplay, dated 27 July 1937, told the tale of Private Eddie Pratt [Eddie Craven] who smuggles his new wife, Sally [Marie Wilson], onto the army base. While attempting to hide her in a disused armoury they discover a body pinned to the wall with an army bayonet. Colonel Rogers [Cy Kendall] is sent to investigate the murder. Karloff appeared in another red-herring role as Jevries, an embezzler suspected of the murder. His make-up for the role required little more than a grey wig.

In August the filming of the picture's dénouement caused some amusement. Regis Toomey, who played the murderer Lieutenant Matthews, stood at the top of a staircase holding an automatic pistol and using Marie Wilson as a shield. The director, John Farrow, told Wilson he wanted her to emit a horrified shriek in the scene. "Don't worry," Wilson told him, "I will when I hear that gun."[43] The crew, and visitors to the set, laughed before bracing themselves for the gunshot that would follow. Some even placed their hands over their ears to dull the sound. Farrow called "Action!" and the scene began. "All right, you asked for it," Toomey told an approaching Karloff. He squeezed the trigger but, instead of a load retort, the gun issued forth a feeble cap pistol 'pffft.' The actors finished the scene despite the laughter. Farrow then asked Wilson why she did not scream. "I didn't scream," she explained, "because the gun didn't make any noise."[44]

An alternate version of events appeared in the press a month later. According to that article the scene was rehearsed several times before the cameras rolled, with Toomey saying "boom" in place of the gunshot. The gun was loaded with blanks and filming began. However, when Toomey tried to fire the pistol it jammed. He tried again and again without success. Exasperated, Toomey turned to the crew and asked, "For Pete's sake, isn't there a knife in the house?"[45]

In mid-December the picture was retitled *The Invisible Menace*. It opened across cities in America on Friday, 21 January 1938, usually as a second feature. The *Hartford Courant* thought the picture "a mediocre murder mystery on which the talents of Boris Karloff are entirely wasted."[46]

In the months that followed his work on *The Invisible Menace* Karloff spent much time socialising and attending functions, hosting dinner parties and dining out with friends. On Labor Day – Monday, 13 September – with the movie studios closed, members of the Screen Actors Guild were driven in the grand parade with Guild president Robert Montgomery at the head. Next came Edward Arnold, followed by Boris Karloff who sat with Russell Gleason and actress Elizabeth Risdon. Then, on Thursday, the Karloffs attended the star-studded premiere of Paul Muni's picture *The Life of Emile Zola* at the Carthay Circle Theater.

With William S. Hart and Rudy Vallee on radio's *Rudy Vallee's Varieties*, 11 November 1937.

On the afternoon of 11 November Karloff appeared on the radio show *Rudy Vallee's Varieties* along with western star William S. Hart. Karloff read an Armistice Day soliloquy, *Resurrection*, by Horace Brown. Later that evening the Karloffs attended an Armistice Day ball in the Fiesta Room of the Ambassador Hotel.

On 23 November Karloff celebrated his 50th birthday with a party at his home with 20 close friends, which included the Gleasons and Murray Kinnell. Two weeks later, on 9 December, Karloff was driven down Hollywood Boulevard (nicknamed 'Santa Claus Lane' for the occasion) in the tenth annual Hollywood Christmas Parade. His year concluded with a party at his home where a pair of pipers, complete with kilts, heralded in the New Year.

Boris Karloff's first professional work of 1938 would also prove to be one of his most controversial. At 5 p.m. on 30 January Karloff appeared on *The Chase and Sanborn Hour* radio show to recite *The Evil Eye*, an adaptation of Poe's tale *The Tell-Tale Heart*. However, Senator Clyde L. Herring of Iowa, who was campaigning to introduce a bill governing the censorship of radio programmes, took exception to the broadcast. "The fact that the poem [*sic*] is a classic does not make it satisfactory for broadcasting on a 'children's hour' programme," he said. "It is all right for the book to be on the shelf to be read when anyone desires, but I don't think it should be broadcast just before children go to bed."[47] Three days after the broadcast the Senator informed the United States Senate that he had written to the sponsors of the show for a copy of the script. It would, said Herring, provide evidence of the "harmful effects of that sort of thing".[48] Although the senator was reliably vocal in his opposition to such broadcasts he was, ultimately, unsuccessful in his campaign.

On 4 March Warners announced Boris Karloff would appear in *The Witches Sabbath*. The star would play a 17th century German robber baron who sells his soul to the Devil. Dr.

Manley P. Hall and Anthony Coldewey were scripting the story, which would include "a cast of witches, sorcerers and other fantastic characters".[49] Despite further announcements, including assertions in February 1939 that the picture would be made, it never went into production.

On Sunday, 13 March Boris Karloff and Bela Lugosi appeared together on radio. The pair appeared on *The Baker's Broadcast* (a.k.a. *Seein' Stars in Hollywood*) joining the show's host, the cartoonist Feg Murray, Ozzie Nelson's orchestra and Harriet Hilliard. Karloff read Rudyard Kipling's poem *The Supplication of the Black Aberdeen* and joined Lugosi in a duet, singing a short ditty entitled 'We're Horrible, Horrible Men'. It was the beginning of what would be a busy year on radio.

Soon Karloff prepared himself for a trip to Chicago where he would appear in a series of five radio dramas on the horror show *Lights Out*. The show had been created in 1934 by 36-year-old Willis Cooper who also wrote, produced and directed the dramas. Initially only 15 minutes long, the shows were later extended to 30 minutes. *Lights Out* was billed as 'the ultimate in horror' and it lived up to its claims. In a first for radio, the show featured graphic sound effects – an array of maimings, decapitations, garrottings, the rendering of limbs and, as one critic at the *Radio Guide* described, "the most monstrous of all sounds, human flesh being eaten".[50]

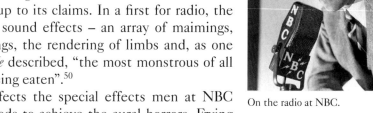

On the radio at NBC.

To create these effects the special effects men at NBC used a variety of methods to achieve the aural horrors. Frying bacon was used to simulate an electrocuted body, spare ribs were snapped with a wrench to simulate the sound of human bones being broken, and that 'monstrous' sound of cannibalism was effected by the sound effects men slurping down spaghetti and smacking his lips. The chopping of cabbages took the place of the chopping of heads while sliced carrots substituted for sliced fingers.

In May 1936, after Cooper had left to pursue a Hollywood screenwriting career, Arch Oboler took over the reins. His first play *Burial Service*, about a paralysed girl who is buried alive, caused outrage from the listening public. Over 50,000 letters of complaint were received by NBC. Nevertheless, over the next two years, Oboler penned and directed over 100 plays for the show.

For the fourth anniversary a special treat was arranged for the show's fans. "Here's an item that will make you *Lights Out* fans shudder for weeks to come," announced the press. "Boris Karloff, who specialises in horror roles in pictures, is coming here March 23 and will remain for five weeks to be the headliner on this macabre Wednesday night show on NBC. Arch Oboler, who arranged with Karloff to do the guest appearances, will write a group of plays specially suited to his talents."[51] In addition to Karloff, the plays would also feature Mercedes McCambridge, Templeton Fox, Arthur Peterson, Ray Johnson and Bob Guilbert.

Karloff left Dorothy in Los Angeles where she would enjoy a skiing holiday at the Village Inn, Lake Arrowhead and, along with Arch Oboler, took the train east. At Wickenburg, Arizona, they picked up actress Betty Winkler who had been vacationing there. They arrived in Chicago on Sunday, 20 March and went straight to work, beginning rehearsals that same day.

Although Karloff had worked on radio before the show's rehearsal regime was a surprise to him. "There is nothing like that on the coast," he said. "You are lucky if you know by Wednesday what the vehicle is that you are to do on the following Sunday. Then there are one or two brief rehearsals and on you go."[52] The director, G.P. Hughes, also had a unique method to instil the mood of the play into the cast during rehearsals. The actors would rehearse in a darkened room with only the light from shaded stand lamps to read their scripts by.

Karloff's first show for Oboler was broadcast at 11:30 p.m. on Wednesday, 23 March. *The Dream*[iv] told the story of a murderer, Darrell Hall, who sits in a courthouse awaiting the verdict for his murder trial. As he waits for the jury's verdict he recalls the events that led him there. For Hall is a man who had never experienced a dream. Then, one night, he experiences his first – a terrible nightmare in which he hears a terrifying murmuring and sees the visage of haunted faces. A woman [Templeton Fox][v] with "a face from hell" tells him to kill. He later begins to see her during his waking hours, always at 7 o'clock, when again she orders him to commit murder. She continues to visit, goading him until Hall kills his beloved Mary. He is now visited again by the murmuring voices who tell him they too had obeyed the voice. But now they are damned, slaves to the woman for all eternity. The only escape, they tell him, is to pay for his crimes. Hall, therefore, confesses to the murder, is tried and found guilty. Yet, as he celebrates in the dock he suffers a heart attack and dies. His face, it is remarked, looks "as if he was looking at the devil himself". Hall's death has prevented him from paying for his crime – the woman has won.[vi]

Journalist Larry Wolters, who watched the broadcast, found the event disillusioning. "There is nothing horrible or frightening about the setting. Karloff, coatless and with shirt loosened at collar, sits on the floor running over his lines. He simply doesn't look the part of the insane murderer he is about to portray. Once he is on the air you quickly become absorbed in his powerful characterisation. He becomes utterly convincing. The role is almost a monologue. To appreciate the horrible role played by Templeton Fox, the fiendish 'voice' which insists that Karloff 'kill, kill, kill', it is much better not to look at her. She is too young, too beautiful, too vibrant to be in any way related to those chilling words that come out of the microphone… But it is disillusioning to have a man[vii] 30 feet distant fall to the floor when a young lady is murdered, and to see her trip blithely away from the microphone, script still in hand. To get the full macabre effect, stay home and put all lights out!"[53]

The following week Karloff appeared in *Valse Triste*, "a story of death, and a revenge beyond death" suggested by Sibelius' composition of the same name. The play told the story of an Englishman unjustly imprisoned for life on Devil's Island. "His suffering," one newspaper reported, "and attempts to escape to wreak vengeance on the person responsible for his imprisonment form the subject matter of the drama."[54]

The third of Karloff's appearances has become one of the most highly regarded broadcasts in the show's entire run. In *Cat Wife*, broadcast on 6 April,[viii] Karloff played John Taylor – a man who, during an argument, brands his neurotic wife Linda [Betty Winkler]

---

iv Although entitled *The Dream*, the show has also been referred to as *Darrell Hall's Thoughts*.
v Betty Winkler was initially announced for the role before it passed to Templeton Fox.
vi Karloff makes a minor error in the show, saying "eternities" instead of "attorneys".
vii The show's special effects were provided by Bill Joyce and Tommy Horan.
viii *Cat Wife* had been presented twice before and in both instances Betty Winkler had played the role of the wife. The second recording was produced at the request of fans of the show.

"a cat." Soon his wife inexplicably changes, taking on the form of a large feline. Horror-struck, Taylor kills those who discover his wife's transformation. But when John tries to keep his wife away from one of his victims, Linda attacks and blinds him. John finds his gun and shoots her. As she dies her speech returns. Horrified, John shoots himself. "Wait for me, Linda, my beloved," he says with his dying breath, "Wait!"

The episode's director, Maurice Lowell, was surprised at how much Karloff differed from his expectations. Lowell had feared the actor would prove to be a temperamental film star and was surprised by his affability and professionalism. His colleagues on the show agreed and Karloff was dubbed a 'trouper'. "This is high praise in the theatrical world," one reporter remarked.[55]

On 11 April Karloff appeared on the radio variety show *For Men Only* with John Ringling North, Head of Ringling Brothers and Barnum and Bailey Circus, Dorothy Rodgers and the Van Steeden Orchestra. Two nights later he starred in the next episode in the *Lights Out* series. *Three Matches* told the story of a man [Karloff] who is haunted by the memory of a girl [Mercedes McCambridge] he sent to her death. She returns to haunt the man, appearing in the blaze in his fireplace and the flame of his match. Karloff completed his five-week contract with *Night on the Mountain*. The tale, which Karloff helped Oboler to develop, was of a convicted murderer who escapes from his cell an hour before his execution. Unfortunately this episode, like *Valse Triste*[ix] and *Three Matches* (and all of Willis Cooper's early *Lights Out* shows), appear to be lost.

Towards the end of April, before he returned to Hollywood, Karloff appeared in a short-lived touring production. Although it a had a running time of only 55 minutes the show managed to incorporate acts by singers, dancers, acrobats and even a psychic. Karloff appeared in an adaptation of an Edgar Allan Poe tale. One reviewer thought the star, "A bit disappointing, chiefly through unfortunate selection of dramatic vehicle, Edgar Allan Poe's *Tell-Tale Heart*. Characterisation is far from being the grotesque stuff patrons would naturally expect, but Karloff does nicely with that at hand."[56]

On Thursday, 5 May the star appeared on *Rudy Vallee's Variety Hour* along with the Colgate University Glee Club, Irving Caesar and his 'Songs of Safety' and show regulars Tommy Riggs and Betty Lou. Karloff appeared in a one-act play, *Danse Macabre*, specially written for the programme by Arch Oboler.

Three days later Karloff arrived in Albuquerque on his journey homewards. Alighting from the westbound *Chief* he told reporters he had needed to block out the thought of the listening public when making the *Lights Out* broadcasts. "I play to just two or three people, sitting in a living room by the radio," he said. "If I remembered that there are perhaps fifteen million people listening to me, I'd find myself shouting louder and louder into the microphone until Esquimos [*sic*] at the North Pole could hear me."[57]

Back in Hollywood later that month, Karloff and other stars, such as Basil Rathbone, Herbert Marshall and Ronald Colman, helped in arranging an Empire Day charity ball. The event, held under the auspices of the Council of British Societies of Southern California, was held at the Ambassador Hotel on the evening of Tuesday, 24 May. The proceeds from the ball, the *Los Angeles Times* reported, went to "needy persons of British birth in Southern California".[58]

Four days later the *New York Times* announced Warners had purchased *I Spy* by Lee Katz. The story of a contemporary international spy ring would, it was asserted, be Karloff's next

---

ix This show is often confused with the later *Lights Out* episode *Valse Triste* which starred the singer Dinah Shore.

vehicle at the studio and would co-star Kay Francis in her final role before leaving pictures to marry Baron Erik Barnekow. Karloff would play a munitions manufacturer in the picture while Francis would play a spy. By mid June, however, the picture had been cancelled as Kay Francis, it was alleged, did not want to work with the horror star. However, Karloff was not without work for long for, on 22 June, work began on *Devil's Island* at Warners.

Back in mid-February the *New York Times* had revealed Warners were planning a sequel to its 1932 horror picture *Dr. X*. Michael Curtiz, who had shot the original, would also direct the Technicolor follow-up, *The Return of Doctor X*. When the idea was eventually shelved[x] Karloff was moved to *Devil's Island*.

Karloff would star as Dr. Charles Gaudet, a surgeon who is sentenced to ten years on the infamous penal colony for tending to an escaped prisoner. While incarcerated on the island Gaudet and several other men are held responsible when a prisoner attacks a guard and, as a consequence, are sentenced to death. When the young daughter of the island's director, Colonel Armand Lucien [James Stephenson], is injured in an accident, Gaudet agrees to tend to the child on condition that the men's lives are spared. Lucien agrees and Gaudet successfully operates. When Lucien reneges on the deal his wife helps the men escape. They are recaptured but not before they discover that Lucien has been embezzling funds. The escapees once again face the death penalty but Mrs. Lucien goes to the mainland and successfully appeals to the Governor. The men are spared, Gaudet is freed and Lucien is arrested.

Nedda Harrigan, who had worked with Karloff on *Charlie Chan at the Opera*, played Mrs. Lucien in the new picture. She enjoyed working with the star again. "I made two films with him," Harrigan later said, "and seem to remember howling with laughter through both of them... Any work with Boris was a joy. I loved him."[59]

Despite the laughter, however, the production had more than its share of mishaps. In early July, the script girl, Alma Dwight, struck a match on the bottom of a canvas chair. She lit the match but also set both the chair and her slacks alight. Karloff leaped to the rescue and beat the fire out. A few days later, on 9 July, two visitors to the studio – Mrs. Eva Raymond and Mrs. Myrtle Fleischer of Chicago – were allowed access to the *Devil's Island* soundstage. There they watched Karloff performing the operation on the seven-year-old child [Rolla Gourvitch].[xi] The sight of the fake blood, however, proved too much for the visitors and both passed out. They were carried off to be tended at the studio hospital. "With film production rated at about $10,000 an hour, it is easy to see why Warners have finally put up the bar against tourists," one journalist commented.[60]

For the role of Dr. Gaudet, Karloff was required to report to make-up to have his hair curled by a lady beautician. Any mention of his hairstyle was, claimed one newspaper, the only thing that could anger the mild-mannered star. The star also required nine costumes for his role in the picture. Each had to be aged, soiled, ripped, and sewn to accurately represent the ragged attire of a Devil's Island prisoner. The suits required cleaning after each wearing and then had to be resoiled to ensure continuity with previous shots. The cost of maintaining Karloff's costumes totalled $165, three times the cost of an average tailored suit.

---

x Edwin Schallert of the *Los Angeles Times* claimed *The Return of Doctor X* was retitled *Devil's Island*. *The Return of Dr. X* was finally made in 1939 and starred Humphrey Bogart in his only horror role.
xi The operation scene took three days to shoot, with doctors in attendance to ensure accuracy.

One day during production Karloff received an unexpected visit from an avid fan. Harvey Lindstrom, a youth from Chicago, had hitchhiked to Hollywood with his collection of 450 Karloff photographs packed inside his knapsack. His intention was to visit Warner Brothers and pay his idol a visit. Unable to gain entry to the studio Lindstrom obtained Karloff's home address from a movie home guide and walked to Coldwater Canyon. There he encountered the star. "To think that I should be standing here talking to you,"[61] Lambert said before promptly fainting. Karloff took the boy inside, fed him and listened to his story. The star offered to pay Lindstrom for the collection of photographs. Lindstrom refused although submitted to 'a loan'. Karloff let the youth stay the night and the next day Lindstrom, his dream realised, left for home.

Later in production the pregnant wife of Warner Brothers still photographer, Mickey Marigold, was admitted to hospital. Karloff stayed with the expectant father all that evening and night – some 13 hours – until the baby boy was born at 7 a.m. the following morning. A grateful Marigold wanted to name his son after the star but Karloff insisted the child should be named after his father. The boy, who weighed six pounds, was called Patrick Michael Marigold.

Devil's Island opened at the Warner Brothers Hollywood and Downtown theatres in Los Angeles on New Years Eve, sharing the programme with musical comedy *Going Places*, starring Dick Powell. "*Devil's Island* holds up its end satisfactorily," wrote Philip K. Scheuer of the *Los Angeles Times*. "A portentous air hangs over all… The plot doesn't develop any startlingly new angles, but it does exert a spell of sorts in the old, grim way. Karloff is passable. He can't seem to break himself of the Frankenstein's monster, or acting, habit."[62]

Devil's Island was due to open at the Globe in New York on 25 February but, instead, Warners withdrew the picture from circulation. During its production, it was revealed, the French Embassy, through the French Consul in Los Angeles, had voiced its objections to the movie's portrayal of the French administrators in charge of the penal colony. When the French Government threatened to ban all Warner Brothers pictures the studio took action and pulled it. "We had no intentions of showing the picture in France," a Warner representative said. "But we are good sports and have withdrawn the picture entirely. It won't be seen anywhere from now on."[63]

Devil's Island (1939).

However, it was already too late. On 5 April, as a penalty for releasing *Devil's Island*, the French Government announced a two-month ban on the studio's pictures and applied the ban by cancelling Warners' film visas for the period. The Quebec board of censors soon followed the French Government's lead and also banned the picture.

Devil's Island finally reached New York on 11 July 1940 when it opened at the Globe. By this time France was too involved with the war in Europe to be concerned with a motion picture. After viewing the controversial picture the reviewer for the *New York Times* could understand, if not condone, the protests the picture had incurred from the French. "For *Devil's Island* pulls no punches," he wrote, "in its portrayal of the barbarous conditions popularly supposed to prevail in the French penal colony... Mr. Karloff contributes a sterling characterisation, and James Stephenson succeeds admirably in arousing hatred for the sadistic commandant, who clips off the tip of his cigar by placing it in a miniature guillotine."[64]

Towards the end of August 1938, having completed *Devil's Island*, Karloff began work on *Mr. Wong, Detective* – his first movie for Monogram Pictures Corporation. Monogram was one of the independent 'B' movie studios whose reputation to produce fast and cheap pictures earned them the collective moniker of 'Poverty Row' studios.

In September 1937, encouraged by the success of Fox's Charlie Chan and Mr. Moto series, Monogram had purchased the rights to Hugh Wiley's Mr. Wong detective stories. Wiley's oriental detective, James Lee Wong, had first appeared, albeit in a minor role, in *Collier's Weekly* on 10 March 1934 in the story *Medium Well Done*. It was the first of a dozen Wong stories Wiley would pen over the next four years.

The studio initially tested several character actors, including Harold Huber, for the role of Wiley's detective. Then, possibly prompted by his portrayal of the Chinese general in *West of Shanghai*, Monogram producer Scott Dunlap approached Boris Karloff. In early April 1938 the press announced the star had signed with the studio to make a series of four Mr. Wong pictures. Four months later it was announced Grant Withers and Maxine Jennings would play the romantic leads in the picture. Evelyn Brent, whom Karloff had worked with in the silent picture days, would also appear.

Once again Karloff was involved in the development of his character's look. "I spent more than a week trying to obtain the correct make-up," he explained. "I visited public libraries and did research, but finally discovered quite accidentally what I thought Mr. Wong should look like. I was going through a photo album and ran across a picture of a Chinese servant my sister in Shanghai had sent me. He looked exactly like the Mr. Wong that author Hugh Wiley had described."[65]

Once again, however, the application of the make-up was a painful affair. Karloff would report to make-up man Gordon Bau for the three and a half hours it took to be transformed into James Lee Wong. "It's lovely," Karloff told reporters, "to get up and go to the studio at 6 a.m., stretch out in a barber chair and have somebody with hobnailed boots crawl in and out of your eyes."[66] After the make-up had been applied, Karloff explained, "my eyeballs are pressed, my vision is off focus and I walk around all day in a haze"[67] According to the star, make-up man Bau was proud of his work. "He thinks it is a work of art," Karloff said. "He hates to wash the stuff off at night. He is even trying to get me to sleep in it."[68]

Mr. Wong, Detective told the story of the oriental sleuth's investigation into the death of the chemical manufacturer Simon Dayton [John Hamilton] and his associates. Wong discovers the killer is using a poison gas to dispatch his victims. The gas, he deduces, is encased within a glass sphere which shatters at the sound of a police siren. During the case the detective also foils a gang of international spies intent on obtaining the gas formula, before finally unmasking the killer.

True to Monogram's ethos the picture was shot and released in double-quick time. It opened at the Orpheum in Los Angeles on 12 October – less than two months after shooting had begun. "[Karloff] enacts a Chinese detective… in a splendid fashion," wrote the *Los Angeles Times*. "He completely immerses himself in the role with very little make-up. Evelyn Brent, Grant Withers and others are good."[69] After the picture opened at the Globe theatre in New York on Saturday, 19 November B.R.C. of the *New York Times* wrote, "Next to having the detective himself turn out to be the murderer, we like the solution in *Mr. Wong, Detective* at the Globe…"[70] The reviewer then, somewhat inconsiderately, revealed the killer's identity to the readers.

Despite Karloff's positive reviews some, however, found it difficult to separate the star's latest role from his popular screen persona. A reviewer for the *Christian Science Monitor* remarked, "Occasional flashes of expression reminiscent of Frankenstein and his other horrific characterisations make it a trifle difficult to bear in mind that he has become thoroughly beneficent."[71] It was a criticism that would often be repeated when Karloff undertook non-horror roles. Yet those unable, or unwilling, to disassociate the actor from his horror roles may have been pleased to know Boris Karloff would soon return to the horror genre.

On 5 August 1938 the public's interest in horror pictures had been rekindled when exhibitor Emile Euman had decided to exhibit three horror pictures – *Dracula*, *Frankenstein* and *Son of Kong* – in a triple bill at his 800-seat Regina Theatre in Wilshire, Hollywood. "We dare you to sit through four hours of horror,"[72] the show's adverts ran. As the rentals were small ($99 per week), the risk was minimal. Although Euman had expected some interest he was surprised when the demand was such that long lines could be seen, both day and night, queuing for tickets.

The horror picture was popular once more. Universal quickly re-issued 500 prints of *Dracula* and *Frankenstein* to capitalise on the renewed interest and soon turned its attention to thoughts of a new picture, the next in the saga of Frankenstein's creation – *Son of Frankenstein*.

Chapter 12

SON OF FRANKENSTEIN

(1939)

"I would rather be a monster than be President!"[1]
Boris Karloff (1936)

By 1938 Universal were in desperate need of hits. The studio was consistently losing money – $1,835,419 in 1936 and $1,084,998 the following year. 1938 was faring no better. In February the studio's president, Robert Cochrane, resigned and was replaced by Nat Blumberg of RKO. The rumour was that Cochrane had, in fact, been fired. On 19 May the studio's vice-president in charge of production, Charles R. Rogers, also resigned and left his $2,000 per week job. The word, though, was he, too, had been ousted. Rogers was replaced by Cliff Work, another ex-employee of RKO.

The unexpected success of the horror reissues, though, had proven timely for the studio and they quickly put the second *Frankenstein* sequel into action. This picture would, by necessity, differ from the first two in the series. Unlike its predecessors, which had been carefully considered and nurtured projects, this new horror picture would be a somewhat hurried affair, rushed into production, riding on the wave of renewed interest in the genre. It would also be missing two of the previous movies' key personnel.

The actor Colin Clive – Baron Frankenstein himself – was dead. On 25 June 1937 Clive had died of tuberculosis, possibly hastened by his heavy drinking. He was 37 years old. For three days his body remained on display to the public at the Edwards Brothers Colonial Mortuary in Venice Boulevard, Los Angeles before being taken away for cremation at Hollywood's Rosedale Crematory. His ashes remained unclaimed for over a week until an Edwards Brother undertaker removed them. Their final fate remains uncertain, although it has been claimed the ashes stayed in the basement of the funeral parlour until 1978 when they were removed and scattered at sea.

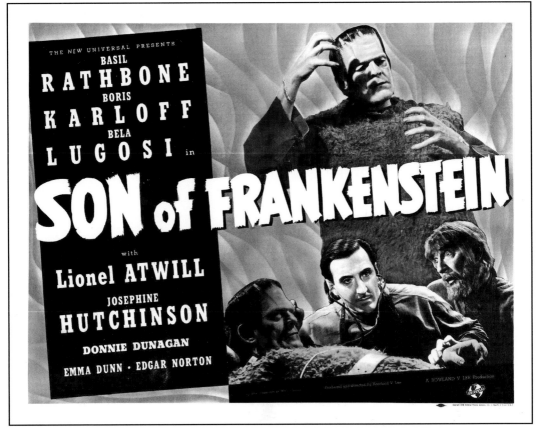

James Whale, who had developed and directed both *Frankenstein* and its sequel, was not approached to helm the third. By late 1938 the director's career had gone into decline. Although his picture of the musical *Showboat* (1936) had been successful his later films had not fared so well. His historical comedy for Warners, *The Great Garrick* (1937), about the 18th century actor, had fared poorly at the box office. The studio head, Jack Warner, was so incensed by the picture he reportedly banned the director from the lot. Whale had also had problems back at Universal. To appease German sensibilities his WWI picture *The Road Back* (1937) had been recut and partially reshot on the orders of the studio. Even so, the picture went on to be one of the biggest earners of the season. Nevertheless, Whale was disappointed with Universal's handling of his picture and refused to watch the studio's final version.

The *Frankenstein* director no longer received the same support he had enjoyed under the Laemmles. So when his five-year contract with the studio expired he signed a new non-exclusive contract with Universal giving him the freedom to make pictures for other studios. Whale made three more films for Universal ending with the jungle adventure *Green Hell* in 1940. He made a single film for MGM, *Port of Seven Seas* (1938), and *They Dare Not Love* (1941) for Columbia. But of these post-*Showboat* movies only *The Man in the Iron Mask* (1939) was successful. He made a short piece, *Hello Out There* (1949), before retiring from the movie business. This piece, which was intended as part of an anthology picture, remained unshown until 1967.

In 1957, after several strokes and periods of depression, James Whale committed suicide by throwing himself headlong, and fully dressed, into his swimming pool. He was 67 years old. For 30 years his death was assumed to have been an accident until

1987 when, shortly before his own death, Whale's partner David Lewis made public the director's suicide note. It read:

> To ALL I LOVE,
> Do not grieve for me. My nerves are all shot and for the last year I have been in agony day and nights – except when I sleep with sleeping pills – and any peace I have by day is when I am drugged by pills.
> I have had a wonderful life but it is over and my nerves get worse and I am afraid they will have to take me away. So please forgive me, all those I love and may God forgive me too, but I cannot bear the agony and it [is] best for everyone this way.
> The future is just old age and illness and pain. Goodbye all and thank you for all your love. I must have peace and this is the only way.
>
> Jimmy[2]

In 1938, with Whale no longer a consideration, the new *Frankenstein* picture was assigned to director Rowland V. Lee, one of 'New' Universal's top directors. On 25 October Edwin Schallert of the *Los Angeles Times* announced the engagement of the 47-year-old moviemaker to direct *Son of Frankenstein*.

The studio hired *Lights Out* creator Willis Cooper to write the screenplay for the new movie. In early September the *Los Angeles Times* announced the writer's appointment and revealed the picture would be called *After Frankenstein*. Cooper set to work after viewing a print of *Bride of Frankenstein* and on 20 October presented his first draft of *The Son of Frankenstein* – a hefty 195 pages. He later refined the script but even then it still ran to a lengthy 138 pages.

Reflecting the real life death of 'the Baron' the screenplay focused instead on the scientist's son, Wolf, who arrives at his father's estate with his wife Else and young son Erwin. In the castle library Wolf discovers his father's diary and reads the account of the creation and destruction of the Bride. Intrigued, he visits the ruined laboratory and there finds the remains of Dr. Pretorius and the Bride. The Monster, however, had escaped the explosion and commits a series of murders in the village. Wolf's childhood friend, police inspector Ewald Neumüller, believes the killings to be the work of the Monster and asks Frankenstein to help. Wolf agrees. "Well," he explains, "a Frankenstein created the curse. A Frankenstein will end it."[3] However, Wolf is soon confronted by the Monster who wants the scientist to build him a friend. Frankenstein acquiesces only when the Monster threatens to kill his wife and child.

The murders continue and Neumüller requests military backup. Lorry loads of troops arrive who set up machine gun nests in the neighbouring hills. They prove of little use and one of the soldiers, Lieutenant Ott, is killed by the Monster to supply a brain for his new 'friend'. However in slaying the soldier the Monster has rendered the brain useless. A new one must be found.

After Neumüller sends Else and Erwin away the Monster catches up with their car and kidnaps Erwin, carrying him to the ruined laboratory. There Wolf finds the Monster preparing to operate on the boy. "Friend," the Monster explains. "Good – brain!"[4] Wolf, however, stabs the monster with a scalpel and, as the shocked creature repeats his entreaty, a volley of shots rings out. Neumüller and the troops have arrived and continue firing until the Monster falls backwards into a long, dark pit. Neumüller tosses a grenade after it for good measure.

Karloff was, naturally, engaged to return to his role as the Monster in a picture that would reunite him with Lee, his director from *The Guilty Generation* (1931). He would receive second billing – as 'Boris Karloff' – and earn $3,750 per week. Star billing would be reserved for Wolf – the son of Frankenstein himself. Initially, Universal had wanted Peter Lorre for the role but the actor, then working for 20th Century Fox, turned the picture down. He had moved away from those types of roles, he explained, "and doesn't want to take a chance on another meanie."[5] Instead the studio hired Basil Rathbone, whom Lee had directed in the Agatha Christie mystery *Love From a Stranger* (1937). Rathbone was then the highest earning freelance actor in Hollywood and would receive $5,000 per week for his work in the picture.

Philip St. John Basil Rathbone was born in Johannesburg, South Africa on 13 June 1892 to English parents. During the Boer War, however, his father was accused of being a British spy and the family fled to England. Educated at Repton School Rathbone first took to the stage in 1911 with Sir Frank Benson's No. 2 Company as Hortensio in Shakespeare's *The Taming of the Shrew*. The following year he accompanied the troupe to America and, in July 1914, made his first London appearance at the Savoy Theatre.

In 1916 he enlisted as a Private with the London Scottish Regiment where he served alongside Ronald Colman, Herbert Marshall and Claude Rains. In September 1918 Rathbone was awarded the Military Cross for a trench raid – while disguised as a tree. "All I did," he later explained, "was to disguise myself as a tree and cross no man's land to gather a bit of information from the German lines. I have not since been called upon to play a tree."[6]

After the war Rathbone returned to the stage. In 1921 he made his first movie appearance in the silent *Innocent*. With the coming of sound Rathbone's appearances in such films as *Anna Karenina*, *David Copperfield*, *Captain Blood* and *The Adventures of Robin Hood* (both with Errol Flynn) secured his reputation as one of the silver screen's most urbane villains.

In October 1938, in an attempt to move away from this type of role, Rathbone signed with Universal to star as Sherlock Holmes in a new adaptation of Arthur Conan Doyle's 1902 novel *The Hound of the Baskervilles*. Production on the picture was due to start on 1 December, once Rathbone had completed his work on *Son of Frankenstein*.

In accepting the role of Wolf the actor had, reportedly, defied a Hollywood jinx. When it was pointed out both portrayers of the previous male members of the Frankenstein family – Colin Clive and Frederick Kerr – had since died, Rathbone merely laughed at the suggestion. Still, *Son of Frankenstein* was Rathbone's introduction to the horror genre and, although he would later dismiss the venture as a "penny dreadful,"[7] at the time he had no qualms about appearing in a picture of this type. The picture's press book even claimed Rathbone was a stickler for costume authenticity and went to great lengths to obtain a Bavarian cape to wear in the picture. Yet despite his alleged efforts, and the cape's prominent appearance in publicity materials, the garment would not appear in the final cut.

In order to reunite once again its two horror stars Universal engaged Bela Lugosi for a role in the picture. For Lugosi, who would receive third billing, *Son of Frankenstein* provided both a professional, and financial, lifeline – as well as a renewed source of irritation. The picture would be his first movie work in two years. His continual attempts to secure a non-horror role had all proven unsuccessful. "I was a fine actor in the Hungarian theatre,"

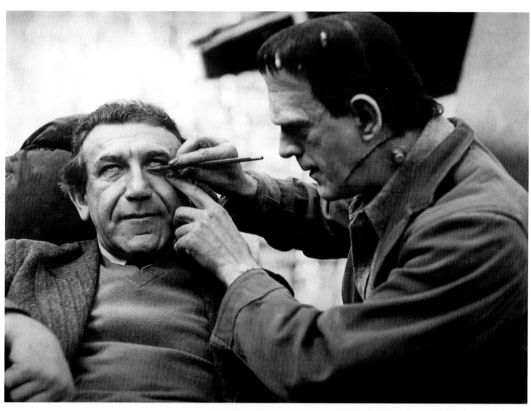

Above: Karloff clowning with Otto Lederer. Below: Taking a tea break during filming (Courtesy of Dwight Kemper).

he had told the studios. "You're a bogey-man," they had replied, "and we have nothing for you today, or tomorrow, or the next day."[8] During his absence from the screen Lugosi's only professional work had been a stint playing Commissar Gorotschenko in a 1937 touring production of the comedy *Tovarich*. Following the play's closure he appeared in a 12-chapter serial *S.O.S. Coast Guard* as the villainous scientist Boroff.

The lack of steady work had, the same year, forced Lugosi to remortgage his home with the Citizens National Trust and Savings Bank. The actor had to resort to borrowing money from friends to try to keep his head above the water, but to no avail. The house was lost and the Lugosis were forced to relocate to rented accommodation in the San Fernando Valley. Then one day Lugosi received a phone call from Emile Euman, the owner of the small Rialto Theatre. Euman told Lugosi about the triple bill of *Dracula*, *Frankenstein* and *Son of Kong* he planned to exhibit. "I think they will do some business," Euman explained, "because movie audiences are fed up with the stuff they're getting now, and a new generation of fans never saw those pictures."[9] When asked if he would be willing to make a personal appearance Lugosi agreed. Euman's venture had renewed Universal's interest in the horror genre,[i] and was a move that would give Lugosi's movie career a renewed lease of life. "I owe it all to that little man at the Regina theatre," the actor later said. "I was dead and he brought me to life."[10]

Initially it was Universal's intention to cast Lugosi as Inspector Neumüller and the actor's participation was announced in the press in late October. However, Rowland V. Lee had other plans. Instead, Lugosi would play one of his greatest roles – Ygor, the broken necked blacksmith, a character absent from Cooper's drafts. Even so Lugosi later told the journalist, and later television presenter, Ed Sullivan he would have turned down the work on the picture had he not been desperate. "He is very bitter at the 'typing' which has short circuited his career," Sullivan wrote, "and which put him out of work from 1936 to 1938. 'I played every type of role in Budapest,' he (Lugosi) explains wearily, 'but here they only think I can scare children. It is very discouraging.' His wife nods in assent."[11]

To round out the main members of the cast Josephine Hutchinson was engaged to play Wolf's wife, now named Elsa, while the English actor Lionel Atwill (known as 'Pinky' to his friends) would play the inspector originally intended for Lugosi. Now, however, the character would be a one-armed policeman named Krogh.

Four-year-old Donnie Dunagan, who had recently debuted in *Mother Carey's Chickens* (directed by Rowland V. Lee), was chosen to play Wolf and Elsa's son. As Dunagan was, at that time, contracted with RKO Lee personally requested Universal borrow the boy for his picture. Dunagan would be paid $75 per week to play little Peter von Frankenstein.

Dunagan had never heard of Boris Karloff and was introduced to his co-star in Universal's cafeteria. They subsequently met there several times and on one occasion the actor presented Dunagan with an ice-cream cone. It was then explained to the child who Karloff would be playing in the picture. "That disarmed *every*thing," Dunagan said. "Later, when I first saw him in his Monster make-up, he laughed at me – 'What do you think about me now?'"[12] Asked years later if he had been afraid of the Monster Dunagan replied, "*No*. I had a *ball*! Boris Karloff was a wonderful man."[13]

---

i The revivals netted Universal almost $500,000 in receipts. Instead of expressing any gratitude to Emile Euman the studio raised the rental costs forcing the entrepreneur to pull the films from his cinema after five weeks.

Many of the assembled cast had already been professionally acquainted. Rowland V. Lee had already worked with both Dunagan and Karloff on separate occasions. Atwill had directed Basil Rathbone on the Broadway stage in December 1930 in the short-lived comedy *A Kiss of Importance*. Emma Dunn, who played the housekeeper Amelia, had coached Josephine Hutchinson ten years earlier for a stage role. One of the town's councillors, Gustav von Seyffertitz, had previously worked with Rowland V. Lee in *Barbed Wire*, and had appeared in *The Bells*, which had also featured Boris Karloff.

The picture also boasted cast and crew that had worked on previous *Frankenstein* films. Dwight Frye, who had appeared prominently in both pictures, was given the minor role of a villager. *Frankenstein* players Lionel Belmore (Burgomaster Vogel) and Michael Mark (little Maria's father) would now play two of the town's councillors. Special effects wizard John P. Fulton, who had worked on both of Whale's previous movies, and *Bride of Frankenstein* editor Ted Kent would also work on the new picture.

On Thursday, 20 October the *New York Times* reported production on *Son of Frankenstein* would commence the following Monday. Basil Rathbone's engagement as Wolf was also announced. Meanwhile, construction was underway on Universal's stage nine as workmen prepared Art Director Jack Otterson's expressionistic sets. Despite the press announcements the cameras finally stated rolling on production No. 931 on Wednesday, 9 November.[ii]

To shoot the script the studio had proffered a budget of $250,000, some $12,000 less than the initial budget of *Frankenstein* seven years earlier. According to the press Lee was unhappy with the figure and was able to persuade the front office to double the budget. Still, the studio was not always so generous when it came to money matters. They took advantage of Lugosi's well-publicised financial difficulties and cut his salary by half from $1,000 to $500 per week. Then, to add insult to injury, the front office determined to shoot all Lugosi's scenes within a single week. When the director found out he was outraged. Lugosi's wife, Lillian, later told film historian Gregory William Mank, "When Rowland V. Lee heard about this, he said, and I quote, 'Those God-damned sons of bitches! I'll show them. I'm going to keep Bela on this picture from the first day of shooting right up to the last!' And he did!"[14]

Throughout production the script constantly changed. Although the Monster retained his powers of speech in Cooper's original script, by the time the cameras rolled the monster had lost this ability – a development that no doubt pleased Karloff who had always preferred his Monster to be mute.

In the final script Wolf returns to his father's estate with his wife and child. He is soon approached by Ygor, a broken-necked blacksmith the villagers had hanged for graverobbing. Believing him to be dead they had cut Ygor down and thrown his body into the ruins of Frankenstein's laboratory. Ygor now wants Wolf to resurrect the Monster who lies in the Frankenstein crypt in a coma. Overcome by curiosity Frankenstein attempts the resuscitation but to no effect. However, the Monster does later revive and is sent out by Ygor to kill those men that had condemned him to the gallows.

With the villagers up in arms, Inspector Krogh investigates the murders and rumours of the Monster. It is not, however, his first dealings with Frankenstein's creation. As a child

ii It had been a consideration to shoot *Son of Frankenstein* in Technicolor. Some colour test footage was shot of Karloff in costume but the plans were abandoned, probably due to the added expense rather than any problems with the Monster's make-up. Karloff's own colour home movies taken on the set clearly attest to the acceptability of Pierce's colour make-up.

the Monster had entered his home and, in the fracas that followed, pulled the boy's arm from his body. "One doesn't easily forget, Herr Baron," Krogh tells Frankenstein, "an arm torn out by the roots!"

When Wolf confronts Ygor, the blacksmith attempts to attack Frankenstein with a hammer but is shot and mortally wounded. The Monster is incensed when he discovers the body of his friend and kidnaps Wolf's young son Peter, taking him back to the ruined laboratory. Krogh, however, attempts to stop the Monster and once again has his arm, albeit his wooden one this time, ripped from him. Wolf swings down and knocks the Monster into the sulphur pit. Frankenstein bequeaths the castle and estate to the villagers to do with what they will, and he and his family depart.

Posing with guests.

Left: With Donnie Dunagan. Right: Ygor and the Monster.

The continual script changes allowed Lugosi to develop his role into one of the greatest in the classic horror cannon. "We gave him his sides as Ygor and let him work on the characterisation;" Lee later explained, "the interpretation he gave us was imaginative, and totally unexpected. It wasn't Dracula at all, in fact, quite the opposite. He played Ygor as a rogue, but one that evoked sympathy. There was warmth in his voice and a twinkle in his eyes that made him almost lovable. His eyes were like prisms that caught and reflected the light in a most unusual way."[15] Lugosi loved the role. "God, he was cute!" he later said.[16]

To prepare for the role Lugosi required a four-hour stint in the make-up chair. Ygor's shaped rubber 'broken neck' was applied to the left side of the actor's neck and fastened with an elastic strap, which passed under Lugosi's right arm. Yak hair was then glued to the actor's face and trimmed to shape and a wig was fitted and styled into a suitably bedraggled state. A set of misshapen teeth completed the ensemble. The rigours of wearing the rubber neckpiece, however, caused Lugosi some discomfort. "My wife's nightly job is rubbing the kinks out of my neck with liniment," he complained. "I don't expect to be comfortable until this picture is through."[17]

An early start was required to prepare both Karloff and Lugosi. "We all have to get to the studio no later than five o'clock each morning in order to be ready by nine o'clock for the picture," Jack Pierce explained.[18] Karloff would be up at four and in the make-up chair an hour later. "I've been making up Karloff since his first horror picture," Pierce said. "Me and Lon Chaney – we used to have adjoining dressing rooms. I never got away from his influence. The monster Frankenstein gets the credit for what it takes me four hours daily to create. Another hour to change 'it' back to Karloff, at night. I let my assistants handle the rest of the cast, like puncturing Bela Lugosi's neck with a rubber spine and pulling Lionel Atwill's arms out by the roots. Good realistic jobs, too. Karloff wears 65 pounds

With Bela Lugosi Jr.

of make-up and padding, poor fellow. There's 12½ pounds of lead in each shoe and weights on each eyelid. He can't help but look and walk like a synthetic man."[19] "Karloff and I don't talk much while I'm making him horrible," Pierce explained, "but he tells me about his garden and his cricket playing… It's weird, sometimes, to hear his quiet English voice coming out of a scary green face. You ought to see him politely lift a cup of tea each afternoon. Polished manners, no less. He isn't any boogey man."[20]Although, physically, the Monster looked the same, this time he had a new costume, to Karloff's dismay. "In the third one," he later said, "I didn't like it because they changed his clothes completely… wrapped him in furs and muck, and he became just nothing. I mean the make-up, like the clothes, had become part of him. If you accepted the convention that he lived or came to live, as it were, at the end of the film… after practically being destroyed… you could accept that he wore the same clothes to meet the script."[21]

Under the hot studio lights the wardrobe soon took its toll on Karloff, as Donnie Dunagan witnessed. "The costume was punishing him," Dunagan said. "His costume was heavy and it really hurt him, he was in pain with that. But he wasn't a complainer… he was constantly fidgeting, and once in a while he would mumble to somebody something like, 'I gotta get *out* of this thing…' When we had a break sometimes Mr. Karloff would take off some of that costume – he'd take off the vest, which was killing him, and those awful, heavy, lead-weighted boots. That's when I became aware that that stuff was punishing him."[22]

12-year-old contractee Gloria Jean was at Universal making her first movie when she had an unexpected encounter. "I was on my way to my dressing room, which was at the end of a very dark hall, when I noticed a horrific monster coming my way," she said. "It was Boris Karloff in his *Frankenstein* make-up. My heart stopped when he spoke to me in a very gentle manner, telling me not to be frightened. We became friends from then on and I watched Jack Pierce spend hours making him up for the *Frankenstein* role and other roles. To this day, I think his Frankenstein movies surpassed anything that we see today… We were friends all the while I was under contract to Universal. My parents were worried my baby sister, Bonnie, would be frightened by him, but she loved him and would run up to him whenever she saw him. He was the kindest, most gentle man I ever met. I will always remember him as a superb actor and a great friend."[23] Their friendship continued over the years. "One of his hobbies was raising orchids and I'll never forget the day I turned 18 (14 April 1944)," she said. "I received a long white box on the set. It was filled with white orchids, signed, *Love and Happy Birthday, Boris Karloff*."[24]

Top Left: Hiding Karloff's birthday cake. Top Right: Eating the cake on the set (Courtesy of Dwight Kemper). Bottom Left and Right: With Rathbone, Lugosi and Rowland V. Lee.

The front office had expected *Son of Frankenstein* to wrap on or before 10 December. Soon it became clear, however, that such plans were optimistic. Rowland V. Lee had decided to dispense with the script using it, instead, merely as a template for his picture. "I do remember that the director had a theory that dialogue learned at a moment's notice would be delivered more naturally," Josephine Hutchinson recalled. "For actors like Basil and Pinky (Atwill) and myself, trained in the theatre technique, this is not true. Nevertheless, Mr. Lee did some rewriting on the set. We spent a lot of time in separate corners pounding new lines into our heads, which, of course, one can do, but it adds pressure."[25] These unorthodox methods were, for some, an irritation. "I didn't care for it," Hutchinson later said. "But Atwill and Rathbone were real pros to work with."[26]

The Studio Production Manager, Martin F. Murphy, was fully cognisant of the problems Lee's methods created, which he noted in a memo of 12 November. "Operating under conditions like we are," Murphy wrote, "without script, it is extremely difficult for all departments concerned in physical production and, more important, most expensive. We have no way of determining just how long this picture will take in production and nothing concrete upon which to substantiate any detailed figures we might attempt to compile as an estimated budget..."[27]

Despite such difficulties the front office was awash with requests to visit the set, often from the studios' own pool of starlets. This prompted Rowland V. Lee to have a 'No Visitors' sign posted on the soundstage door. However, Deanna Durbin was granted access, as was ventriloquist Edgar Bergen and his dummy Charlie McCarthy, who posed for photographs with Karloff and Lugosi. John J. Raskob, the builder of the Empire State Building, was also a guest and he, too, was photographed with Karloff.

Meanwhile, Dorothy Karloff, who had fallen pregnant earlier in the year, was nearing the end of her term. Her husband, excited at the prospect of being a father, was keen to be present at the birth of his child and, he told reporters, had arranged he would rush from the soundstage to a standby car the moment the call came through. Should he receive the call while filming, a make-up man would accompany him on the dash to the Hollywood Presbyterian Hospital and begin the lengthy process of make-up removal in the vehicle.

The call came on Karloff's 51st birthday – Wednesday, 23 November. At 10:50 a.m. Karloff's daughter, Sara Jane, was born by Caesarean section. Her father was naturally anxious to see his wife and child and visited the hospital. Dorothy had lost a lot of blood during the operation and had required a transfusion. Sara recalled that, in the end, her mother stayed in hospital for about two weeks before being allowed home with her daughter. Karloff later confessed he had been of little use to his wife during the late stage of her pregnancy. "Instead of comforting Mrs. Karloff during the time when I thought she needed it most she bolstered up my courage," he said. "How unreal her nerve makes all the characters I've ever played in pictures seem."[28] Dorothy was finally able to leave the hospital in mid-December and she and little Sara Jane came home. A proud father reportedly took to showing pictures of his daughter's 'lovely hands' which he said was a sign of a born actress.

Top: Karloff sees his daughter for the first time. Bottom: With his baby daughter, Sara Jane.

The birth of Karloff's daughter led several newspapers to print erroneous accounts of the star's visit to the hospital. Many claimed he had seen his newborn while still caked in his monster make-up. One went even further. "Karloff drove to the hospital in the gruesome make-up he uses in the picture," reported the *Washington Post*. "His appearance in the maternity ward caused temporary alarm, but the infant daughter, brought to the mother's bedside, turned to Karloff – and yawned."[29]

"That was just a Hollywood legend," the star later explained. "When I asked the director how much longer we should shoot and told him why I was so interested, he merely said, 'Shooting for the day is over, go down to the hospital and meet your new master.'"[30] According to the studio's records, however, it was a different story. "This unit was forced to change plans last Wednesday, due to the absence of Boris Karloff because of the birth of his first born," Studio Production Manager Martin F. Murphy wrote. "Fortunately, the company was able to carry on without Karloff and Dan Kelley has made arrangements to obtain the gratis services of Karloff on the last day of the engagement in lieu of the one day he was absent…"[31] While Murphy's memo suggests Karloff was away from the studio for the whole of 23 November, newspaper reports told a different story.

On Karloff's birthday the company prepared to shoot the scene in which the reanimated Monster meets Frankenstein for the first time. Climbing up from a sulphur pit he approaches the unsuspecting Wolf. At 4 p.m. Lee told Karloff they had completed the setup and were ready to shoot the scene. Karloff was to climb down into the pit. "Now you stay there until I give the word," Lee instructed the star. "Then come up with menace written on your face, sneak across to Rathbone and scare the living daylights out of him."[32] Karloff duly climbed down into the pit and waited beside the steam pipes that filled the set with its atmospheric 'sulphur vapours'.

Unknown to Karloff, however, Rowland V. Lee had arranged a joint surprise birthday party and baby shower for the star. With Karloff safely out of the way in the pit the director cleared the stage and had a birthday cake and a large box of baby clothes brought in. Basil Rathbone stood in position, blocking the cake from Karloff's view behind his outstretched cape.[iii] Karloff meanwhile – oblivious to the preparations – waited in the pit and complained about the heat.

When Lee finally called "Action!", Karloff climbed from the pit and approached his co-star. Rathbone then dropped the cape revealing the cake, which was duly cut and shared amongst the cast and crew. Karloff even took the opportunity to smear some of the icing on his despised sheepskin jerkin. In addition to the cake he also received congratulatory telegrams and a special additional gift – a small pair of monster boots for his baby.

On 28 November, Lugosi bought his wife Lillian and 11-month-old son, Bela Jr. to the set with a present for Karloff's new daughter. Lugosi even told reporters how he and Karloff "often get together and talk about when our children grow up and how nice it would be if they fell in love with each other."[33] According to Lillian Lugosi, however, such pleasantries belied her husband's true feelings towards his actor colleagues. Although Lugosi enjoyed the role of Ygor – his best since *Dracula* – Lillian later claimed her husband found his co-stars insufferable. "Basil Rathbone was *verrrry Brrrritish*," she later said. "He was a cold fish, and Karloff was a cold fish. Bela, who actually was very warm, couldn't tolerate either one of them!"[34] Karloff, in contrast – never one for professional jealousies – thought Lugosi, "a kind and lovable man."[35]

Rathbone, it was reported, was something of a joker on the set, a characteristic far removed from the 'cold fish' Lillian Lugosi purported him to be. Having called for silence on the set prior to shooting Rowland V. Lee was often forced to add "Quiet, Rathbone!" to stall the actor's antics.[36]

During those tedious times between scenes when the actors were not required Karloff taught Donnie Dunagan to play checkers. They would play between rehearsals and scenes and eventually began betting on the outcome of each game. The loser would pay the winner a quarter. The first time they played for money Dunagan won. "He (Karloff) got to talking, having some fun with people, lost his concentration, and I double-jumped him

---

iii Although the cape is clearly shown in pictures and publicity materials it does not appear in the final film.

and I had him locked up!… When I won, he was surprised," Dunagan explained. "I put my hand out. I wanted my quarter! I knew I was making a ton of money but nobody ever *gave* me any money, so I wanted my quarter! He went 'Rrrr! Rrrr! Rrrr!' (like the Monster)… then he alibied that he was in costume and didn't have any money on him. 'I'll give it to you later.'"[37]

The next time they played Dunagan won again. "The people around were again laughing and having a good time about this," he recalled, "and he again went 'Rrrr! Rrrr! Rrrr!' I think he really meant it this time – he did not like losin' for poop [*laughs*]! But he was in costume again, and 'I'll give it to you later.'"[38] This time, however, Dunagan would not be swayed and demanded to go with Karloff to fetch his winnings. "So he took me by the hand… and we went over to what looked like a small trailer inside of the stage," Dunagan said. "He went inside, 'Rrrr! Rrrr! Rrrr!', he came back out and he gave me a half dollar… And after that, he wouldn't play me for quarters no more [*laughs*]!"[39] Still, there were no hard feelings. Karloff took the youngster to lunch a few times and they could often be seen walking together across the set, hand-in-hand and still in make-up – the Monster and the curly-haired boy. "They curled my darn hair twice a day," Dunagan later explained. "What a pain in the neck. I *hated* that, just hated it."[40]

Once the pair's antics resulted in a reprimand from the director. In the Monster's final scene young Peter is lying on the floor of the laboratory while the Monster stands over him, pinning him to the ground with his foot. "Anyway," Dunagan said, "we got to laughing in this scene because he was ticklin' me with his darn boot [*laughs*]! I was lying down and Karloff had his boot on me, and I could tell he was trying to keep it from pressing on me. His boot was heavy and he was very sensitive to hurting me – for which I'm grateful! But until they said, 'Roll 'em!', he would wiggle his boot and *tickle* me."[41] Of course, Dunagan began to laugh. Then Karloff began to laugh. "At *this* point I don't think Mr. Lee was too happy, because he scolded both of us."[42]

Lee was, however, often 'aided' in his directorial duties by the boy. When the setups were complete and the cast and crew were ready Lee would tell Dunagan, "All right, Donnie; it's up to you."[43] Dunagan would then call "Roll 'em, Bill!"[iv] If a line was fluffed during a scene the child would halt the proceedings by yelling, "Cut!"[44] Dunagan was also prone to ad-lib a line or two in his scenes, a method surely in tune with Rowland V. Lee's style of shooting the picture.

In early December, Lee began to shoot the scenes of Frankenstein's attempts to raise the Monster from its coma. Once again Karloff was strapped to an operating table and surrounded by Strickfaden's electrical equipment. This apparatus, it was reported, used 50,000 volts of electricity and was, therefore, very dangerous. 'Caution – High Voltage' warning signs were placed on the equipment when not in use on the set. These were removed at the start of each scene but replaced as soon as Lee called "Cut."

To offer some protection Boris Karloff wore a large rubber apron. Still, according to one press account, this scene caused the star some agitation. When the electrical equipment was switched on the high voltage burned the oxygen and the resultant smell of ozone filled the air. As Rathbone tried to revive the Monster one journalist quoted Rathbone as saying, "He lives! My father's reputation will be saved."[v] "But it'll be lost again if you

---

iv It is unclear to whom this quote refers for the production's camera crew included no person named Bill, or William.

v No such line appears in the final movie.

don't get me out of this thing pretty quick," Karloff replied. "I'm smothering."[45]

Karloff, however, was not the only one to suffer. Both Rowland V. Lee and Basil Rathbone caught colds, the ever-present hazard of a winter shoot. Rathbone, it was noted, suffered from a high temperature and "a touch of the flu."[46] When, in early December, it was suggested to 'shoot around' the actor so he could recuperate Rathbone refused, not wishing to disrupt the already fragile shooting schedule. Instead he would wait until the following week, when the schedule concerned only those scenes with Karloff and Lugosi, and take the opportunity to go to a nearby desert resort and "bake it out in the sun."[47]

A few days later journalist Sheilah Graham was given access to the set to watch the shoot. That day they were filming the Monster as he carries the lifeless body of Ygor down to the crypt. In her article Graham recounted how, during one take, Karloff looked at her full in the face. At that same moment Basil Rathbone tapped her on the shoulder. The unexpected contact caused Graham to scream thereby ruining the shot. "I say, what is the time, old boy?" Karloff asked Rathbone.

"Four o'clock," Rathbone replied.

"Tea time," Karloff said gleefully.[48] Karloff, Lugosi, and Rathbone then adjourned for several cups of tea accompanied by chocolate-covered cookies. A mischievous Graham then asked Rathbone to tickle Karloff's tummy as, she told Rathbone, she wanted to see how the monster would react. Rathbone complied and Karloff squealed, "Oh, my goodness."

"Oughn't that be 'Oh, my badness'?" Graham asked.[49]

Another amusing incident occurred during filming, as Karloff later recounted. "In the scene where Bela slowly tells Basil, 'He – does things for me', and there I am, all stretched out on this dais – well, we all just doubled up, including everyone else on the set, the entire cast, crew, and even Rowland, who said he didn't mind the extra takes for the chuckles it gave everyone."[50]

As filming progressed Rowland V. Lee informed the front office that he would complete the production by Christmas Eve. Martin F. Murphy, however, had his doubts and noted in a memo, "We cannot help feeling a little dubious on the possibility of accomplishing this, considering we have two weeks left from today. Of course, we still have no script upon which to base this contention, and unquestionably Lee should be in a better position than we are to know just how much he has left to do because the story appears to be altogether in his mind."[51] Still, Murphy placed the new estimated cost of production at $347,100.

Christmas Eve came and still *Son of Frankenstein* was not near completion. Traditionally on that day the studio would stop shooting at noon. Lee, however, kept his company working until 6:15 p.m. Only then were the cast and crew allowed home to spend the Christmas holiday with family and friends. On Christmas Day the Karloffs settled for a family dinner, and were joined later on by the Gleasons.

The yuletide bought with it an extra seasonal gift for little Donnie Dunagan, for Karloff had bought his small co-star a toy train. When the boy later requested a signed photograph Karloff happily complied. "Dear Donnie," Karloff wrote. "I am so glad you like the train & that you are having fun with it. Thank you for asking for my picture[vi] which I am enclosing. I do hope we work together again soon & this time maybe I won't have to be a giant."[52]

On 26 December, after the brief seasonal respite, the cast and crew of *Son of Frankenstein* reassembled to continue production. Basil Rathbone completed his work on the picture

vi Karloff inscribed the photograph, *Donnie With love from the Giant! Boris Karloff* two days later – Martin F. Murphy's new completion date. Rathbone began work on *The Hound of the Baskervilles* at 8 a.m. the following morning. "For the last month I've been out at Universal working with monsters inside of dungeons in *The Son of Frankenstein*," the actor said. "I didn't finish up until last night at 9 and all these people here with normal bodies and faces that aren't colored blue, simply don't seem real to me yet."[53]

As at 29 December only Karloff, Lugosi and Dunagan had scenes left to shoot and Murphy duly supplied yet another completion date – this time Wednesday, 4 January. Again, however, Lee overran the schedule, albeit this time by only a matter of hours. Filming finally concluded at 1:15 a.m. the following morning.

Meanwhile the editing, music and sound departments scrambled to ready the picture for its fast approaching release date of Friday, 13 January 1939. Hans J. Salter, who worked with the film's composer, Frank Skinner, recalled the hectic schedule. "I remember there was one stretch," he said, "pretty close to the recording date, where we didn't leave the studio for 48 or 50 hours. He (Skinner) would sit at the piano and compose a sequence, and then he would hand it to me. I would orchestrate it and he would take a nap on the couch in the meantime. Then, when I was through orchestrating, I would wake him up, and he had to go back and write another sequence while I would take a nap. And this went on for 48 hours or so, so that he could make the recording date."[54]

Amazingly *Son of Frankenstein* was previewed on Saturday, 7 January – only two days after Lee had called his final "Cut!" Martin F. Murphy called it an "unbelievable accomplishment."[55] However, there was still work to do. The picture ran to 100 minutes – too long for the front office. Cuts had to be made and in the process Dwight Frye's entire role hit the cutting room floor. When completed the final cost of production was estimated at approximately $420,000.

The final cut opened on Friday, 13 January on the screens of the Pantages Hollywood and RKO Hillstreet theatres in Los Angeles with the Lucille Ball comedy *Next Time I Marry*. The next day Edwin Schallert of the *Los Angeles Times* wrote:

> **Son of Frankenstein** is a first-class successor to the original **Frankenstein**. Of course due allowance must be made for the fact that it is pretty high keyed at times in the playing, and this is liable to evoke laughter, or other distracting outbursts from the audience.
>
> But the plot is pat enough and the Monster as impersonated by Boris Karloff is a horror personality in earnest, with a bit of tragedy about him as well. He can roar like a bull too. And when he doesn't roar Ygor (Bela Lugosi) growls. So everything is lovely…
>
> Rowland V. Lee directed the picture and in settings and atmosphere it is a triumph.[56]

The *New York Times* agreed when the picture opened there on Saturday, 28 January. "No beating around the razzberry (*sic*) bush; if Universal's *Son of Frankenstein*, at the Rivoli, isn't the silliest picture ever made, it's a sequel to the silliest picture ever made, which is even sillier," it wrote. "But its silliness is deliberate – a very shrewd silliness, perpetuated by a good director in the best traditions of cinematic horror, so that even while you laugh at its nonsense you may be struck with the notion that perhaps that's as good a way of enjoying oneself as any."[57]

The picture was a success wherever it played and was often held over. In Oakland one newspaper reported, "That the famed screen monster, Frankenstein's creation, is still a box office magnet is being amply proven at the Franklin this week where, all through the holiday, standees attested to the pull of *Son of Frankenstein*."[58]

During production Rowland V. Lee had been asked why there had been such an enthusiastic reception to the recent horror picture revivals. "They're 'audience stuff' for the same reason that a murder or a kidnapping or a major accident or a great catastrophe is always front news," Lee mused. "Morbid curiosity, which cause people to be interested in traffic accidents, to look at 'X-marks-the-spot' pictures and to read the details of a lurid trial, is the explanation."[59]

The public's interest in the new *Frankenstein* picture helped push the studio back into the black, giving Universal a profit of $1,153,321 for the financial year 1938/39. The success of *Son of Frankenstein* also prompted the studio to green light further tales in the monstrous saga.

Despite his initial protests Lugosi had proved he was still a bankable horror star. However, his treatment by the studio did not improve. While Ygor would return in *The Ghost of Frankenstein* (1942) the character would be effectively killed off after his brain is transferred into the Monster (Lon Chaney Jr.). In the following picture, *Frankenstein Meets the Wolfman* (1943), Lugosi got to play the Monster – "And," as Karloff later stated, "was rather good at it, I remember."[60]

Yet, here again, Lugosi would suffer under the studio's aegis. Lugosi's Monster was blind – an effect of the brain transplant – but could now speak with Ygor's voice. When the picture was screened, however, the Monster's speech was met with laughter. As a result all his dialogue was cut. When a scene could not be excised the Monster's voice was simply removed from the soundtrack leaving Lugosi mouthing silent words. In addition, all references to the Monster's blindness were cut leaving the creature inexplicably lumbering through the picture, a stance the Monster continued to maintain throughout the following pictures. It was a sad comedown for Lugosi, and a terrible slight by Universal after the actor's excellent performances as Ygor. "Bela was greatly underestimated by the studio," Rowland V. Lee later remarked. "When we finished shooting, there was no doubt in anyone's mind that he stole the show. Karloff's Monster was weak by comparison."[61]

Karloff was fully aware of the direction his Monster was now taking and, despite the favourable reviews, decided not to play the role again. The reason, he later explained, "was because I thought I could (and I was right as it turned out) see the handwriting on the wall as to which way the stories were going... that they would go downhill. There was not much left in the character of the monster to be developed; we had reached his limits. I saw that from here on, he would become rather an oafish prop, so to speak, in the last act or something like that, without any great stature, and I didn't see any point in going on."[62] Although, as Karloff later claimed, Universal would seek the actor to play the Monster in three more pictures he steadfastly refused. "I owe him so much," Karloff explained, "that I owe him a little respect, a little rest."[63]

"WHY SHOULDN'T I KILL YOU . . . IF IT WILL HELP MILLIONS TO LIVE?"

BORIS KARLOFF

in

THE MAN WITH NINE LIVES

with

ROGER **PRYOR** · JO ANN **SAYERS** · STANLEY **BROWN**

Screen Play by Karl Brown
Directed by NICK GRINDE

DISTRIBUTED BY **FAVORITE FILMS**, INC.

BORIS KARLOFF
BELA LUGOSI

BLACK FRIDAY

WITH **STANLEY RIDGES** · Anne Nagel · Anne Gwynne

Original screenplay by Kurt Siodmak & Eric Taylor
ASSOCIATE PRODUCER · BURT KELLY
DIRECTED BY ARTHUR LUBIN

TRADE SHOW
PARIS CINEMA
Lower Regent Street. S.W.I.
(PICCADILLY CIRCUS)
WEDNESDAY · MAY 22ND
2·30 P·M

GENERAL FILM DISTRIBUTORS LTD. 127 - 133 WARDOUR ST. LONDON, W. I. Telephone: GERRARD 7311

A NEW UNIVERSAL PICTURE

Chapter 13

MYSTERIES, MEDICINE & MURDER

(1939-1940)

"The scriptwriters had the insane scientist transplant brains, hearts, lungs and other vital organs. The cycle ended when they ran out of parts of anatomy that could be photographed decently."[1]

Boris Karloff (1962)

The horror picture was back and Boris Karloff, 'the screen's number one bogeyman,' as the press would refer to him, was much in demand. His continuing popularity was in evidence when, in early January 1939, the Karloffs paid a visit to their friends, Mr. and Mrs. Sidney Brown. During the evening approximately 20 children from the neighbourhood were spotted sneaking a peek at the star. When Brown's son was questioned he duly confessed. He had received five cents a head from his friends for a look at Boris Karloff.

Over the next two years the star would appear in 13 features. Despite his renewed success as the Frankenstein Monster none of these pictures could, strictly speaking, be classified as horror movies. Several genre pictures were announced as Karloff vehicles but none came to fruition as originally planned.

The previous November, during production of *Son of Frankenstein*, it was announced Karloff and Claude Rains would appear in *Dark Tower*, an adaptation of the play by George S. Kaufman and Alexander Woollcott. This melodrama concerned a promising young actress named Jessica Wells whose manipulative husband re-appears to exert his Svengali-like influence over her – until he is murdered.

The picture had been filmed before as *The Man with Two Faces* (1934), starring Edward G. Robinson. This time the scenario, by Anthony Coldewey, would be rather different. "Plot of this," Edwin Schallert wrote, "concerns a circus trainer who disguises himself to commit a murder and is known to incorporate quite a few thrilling angles."[2] Then, in early January 1939, days before the shooting of *Son of Frankenstein* came to an end, the newspapers announced Karloff would team with Deanna Durbin in a remake of *The*

Phantom of the Opera. Both plans, however, came to naught. Instead, Karloff would embark on what became known as his 'mad doctor' phase for Columbia, portraying a series of scientists whose good intentions are waylaid, by accident or design, ultimately leading to tragedy. First, however, he would revisit another non-horror role, that of the Oriental sleuth, James Lee Wong.

In late January 1939 Karloff returned to Monogram for *The Mystery of Mr. Wong*. The picture concerned Wong's investigations into a series of murders and the theft of the world's largest star sapphire – the 'Eye of the Daughter of the Moon.' The picture premiered at Monogram's headquarters, the Talisman Studios on Sunset Boulevard, before going on general release on 8 March. The *Los Angeles Times* wrote, "The story is absorbingly and smoothly told. Karloff manages a surprisingly Oriental appearance with little make-up and with no over stressing of Oriental characteristics."[3]

Production on the star's next feature, *Enemy Agent*, began in mid-March[i] when he returned to Warners to fulfil his single picture commitment for the studio. In this movie, a First World War spy drama based on Anthony Paul Kelly's play *Three Faces East*, Karloff appeared as Schiller, a German spymaster, in a role that required little make-up save a large scar on the left side of his face.

The picture was a low budget affair and the studio utilised already existing footage, most notably for the sequence when the Allied planes destroy an ammunition dump. This was lifted from Warner's WWI picture *Dawn Patrol* (1930).[ii]

As Valdar in *British Intelligence* (1940).

Although shot in March Karloff's picture was not released until the following January. By this time it had gone through a few name changes – from *Enemy Agent* to *Secret Enemies*, and then to its final release title of *British Intelligence*.

The picture opened at the Warners Downtown Theatre on 18 January 1940 as a companion feature to the comedy *Brother Rat and a Baby*, starring Priscilla Lane. Philip K. Scheuer, writing for the *Los Angeles Times*, thought the picture "one of the poorest of the Warner semi-documentaries and its title almost a libel... A good deal of the war stuff has done service in other, better pictures."[4] When the picture opened at the Capitol Theatre in Washington on 30 January 1940 critic Nelson B. Bell was equally unimpressed. "This obviously 'C' subject embodies little that will appeal to the intelligence," he complained.[5] Karloff, however, Bell wrote, "turns in a typically fine performance in a role that is largely denatured by the conspicuous ambiguity that characterises the developments of the entire film."[6]

---

i It has been incorrectly claimed this picture was rushed into production after the outbreak of the war in Europe that September.
ii The same footage also appeared in the war picture's remake (also entitled *Dawn Patrol*) starring Errol Flynn, David Niven and Basil Rathbone which hit the screens in December 1939.

While making *British Intelligence* Karloff was awarded an honorary membership to the French Society of Mental Sciences. This had been prompted by his agreement two-years earlier to complete an elaborate questionnaire at the request of a group of psychiatrists. This paper required the star to analyse both his horror and non-horror roles to determine how they affected his off-screen life. Karloff's 58-page submission, the scientists concluded, showed that portraying the 'villain' roles "is a healthy pastime that improves the mind and moral fibre!"[7]

Socially, the year so far had seen the Karloffs mixing in their usual circle of friends, dining out with the Gleasons, attending various soirees and functions. On the evening of Thursday, 16 February Karloff was a guest speaker at a special dinner at the Masquers clubhouse to celebrate W.C. Fields' 40th anniversary in show business. Joining Karloff on the speakers' table were Master of Ceremonies Harold Lloyd, Jack Benny, Joe E. Brown, Ken Murray, Eddie Cantor, the Marx Brothers, Bing Crosby, Frank Morgan, Andy Devine and Jesse L. Lasky.

Later that month the Karloffs, the Gleasons and Murray Kinnell joined a large congregation for dinner at the home of the Sidney Browns to celebrate their host's silver wedding anniversary. Then on Sunday, 26 February they attended the England vs. California polo match at Midwick where Karloff was seen cheering on his countrymen alongside cricket team-mates Nigel Bruce and Leslie Howard. On Sunday, 7 May the husbands and members of the Domino Club gave a benefit garden party at the Gleasons. The entertainment included fortune tellers, games, swimming and exhibition dancing. The event was organised by a committee that included James Gleason, Edward G. Robinson and Karloff.

There were also the occasional radio appearances – only three that year – and all were completed by early April. On 16 January Karloff was a guest on the *Eddie Cantor Show* during which he was interviewed by Cantor's sidekick, Bert 'The Mad Russian' Gordon. Then, on 5 March, he appeared on *Gateway to Hollywood* in a half hour radio play entitled *Empty Coffin*. His third, and final, radio broadcast of 1939 was on 6 April when Karloff appeared on *Vallee's Varieties* performing in a drama entitled *Resurrection*.

Throughout all his work since the previous November, Karloff's main topic of conversation was his young daughter Sara Jane, as Read Kendall of the *Los Angeles Times* revealed. "Boris Karloff," the journalist wrote, "will talk for hours about the new baby at his home to any and all who will listen."[8] A perfect opportunity to do just that occurred on 9 April – Easter Sunday – when the Karloffs were joined by 30 of their closest friends for the occasion of Sara Jane's christening.

May began with an announcement that Monogram planned to make another four Mr. Wong pictures – all to star Boris Karloff. Over the next season they would, the studio asserted, produce *Mr. Wong Vanishes*, *Mr. Wong in Havana*, *Mr. Wong's Chinatown Squad* and *Mr. Wong in New York*. According to the *New York Times* production on the first of the proposed Monogram pictures, now entitled *Mr. Wong in Chinatown*, began on Saturday, 10 June.[iii]

The picture followed the detective's efforts to solve several murders – including that of the Princess Lin Hwa – and recover the murdered Princess's money. While production

---

iii Although the *New York Times* announced filming of *Mr. Wong in Chinatown* would begin on 10 June, the film industry magazine *Boxoffice* claimed production on the picture was "well along" by this date.

on the picture was typically speedy and efficient, one incident during its making found its way into the newspapers – Boris Karloff's brush with the law.

According to columnist Jimmie Fidler, Karloff's make-up man, Newton House, had gone to the star's home early in the morning to prepare him for the day's shoot. That done the two got into their separate cars and began the drive to the studio. House drove a block ahead but when Karloff reached the intersection of La Brea and Sunset he saw the make-up man had been pulled over at the side of the road and was in the process of being ticketed by two motorcycle cops. Amused by House's misfortune Karloff blew a loud raspberry – a 'Bronx cheer' – as he drove past. But his humour quickly dispelled when he, too, was pulled over. The star, it transpired, had been too absorbed in jeering House to notice he had driven through a red light.

Mr. Wong in Chinatown premiered at Monogram's Talisman Studios in mid-July before going on general release on 1 August. The *Los Angeles Times* called the picture, "without doubt the best of the James Lee Wong series... Boris Karloff manages an amazingly Oriental characterisation, chiefly through suave mannerisms and intelligent conceptions, with very little make-up."[9]

While the reviewer for the *New York Times* found the movie to be "pretty good"[10] he complained about the current surfeit of Oriental detectives. "There must be hundreds of good American sleuths out of jobs or on job relief because of pictures like *Mr. Wong in Chinatown* in which Boris Karloff nabs the real murderer while the San Francisco Police Department... plays around with small fry. In fact, the Occidental part of the proceedings this time is even harder to bear than usual... This subtle discrediting of the West, this constant insistence on the superior fitness of the yellow races in the presence of homicide, is something which every red-blooded American should resent."[11]

As Karloff worked at Monogram *The Old Dark House* was re-released, hitting the screens on 22 June. Two days earlier the film had been paired with the William Powell/Carole Lombard comedy *My Man Godfrey* in a 'Laugh-and-Shiver Show' at the Paramount Theatre in Los Angeles. The screenings were accompanied, on stage, by a Fanchon and Marco review. It was another in a series of re-issues of Karloff's old pictures, following on the heels of the February re-release of *The Lost Patrol*.

On 23 June the *Los Angeles Times* announced Karloff had signed with Columbia to make *The Man They Could Not Hang*. Production on the picture, the newspaper stated, would begin on Monday, 26 June – although the 24 June edition of *Boxoffice* claimed production had already begun.

Karloff starred as Dr. Henryk Savaard, a scientist who has designed a mechanical heart capable of restoring life. To test his device Savaard puts a volunteer student to death. However, his assistant Betty Crawford [Ann Doran] informs the police and the doctor is arrested before the experiment can be completed. Condemned to death for the murder of his student Savaard is hanged. His body is returned to his assistant Lang [Byron Foulger], who is able to revive the Doctor. Savaard, now legally dead, then sets about his plan to kill those who convicted him.

Interviewed on set during the making of the picture Karloff explained the repercussions of his years in the horror genre. "Monster roles may have made me a star," he said, "but I can't sleep after seeing myself in pictures. Every time I appear in a new picture, people turn pale when they meet me. I've even caught my wife wearing a peculiar expression when she thought I wasn't looking… You know… every one of my screen roles evokes a barrage of blistering letters from indignant fans who all agree on one thing – they would like to inflict terrible punishment on me. I'm a quiet citizen. I have my home, my dogs and my orchids. I vote and pat little children on the head – if they haven't seen me in pictures. I'm peaceful and harmless. What does it get me? Queer stares from strangers and even more unusual glances from my friends. Every time I walk into a room, there is a noticeable lull in the merrymaking."[12] Despite such claims Ann Doran later remembered Karloff with affection. "Boris was such a gentleman," she said. "A gentle man, a great person. He told me they always had him playing weird characters, 'I guess because I'm weird looking!'"[13]

Lorna Gray, who played Karloff's daughter in the picture, also recalled working with the star. "We were supposed to shoot just outside the studio, in the New York street," she said. "All of a sudden it started to rain and we had to come inside. They decided to do a scene in the courtroom with Karloff on the witness stand. He had at least two pages of dialogue. He looked at it and did it. He was one of those wonderful instant studies, a remarkable man. We had English tea every afternoon with the monster."[14]

Production lasted only a few weeks during which the cast and crew was often required to work long hours. Karloff was, Doran recalled, "the sweetest man that God ever made on this earth… We worked very, very late hours on that one, and he never lost his good humour. It didn't bother him to go over and over and over something, because he always wanted to do a good job."[15]

The Man They Could Not Hang went on national release on 17 August 1939 to generally good reviews. Pennsylvania's *Titusville Herald* thought the picture "Weird and fascinating… sufficient to satisfy the most hardened horror fan. Starring Boris Karloff in a tale which makes the flesh creep and at the same time emerges as a dramatic triumph, the new melodrama is compelling film fare. Boris Karloff, through his performance, proves conclusively that his title of 'King of Horror' is not a misnomer. He is superbly cast… It is a tribute to Karloff's acting that he makes the character-change of the scientist so real when he is restored to life after his execution. Rarely has there been as thrilling a portrayal as that of the inhuman ghoul who leaves a trail of cruel revenge."[16]

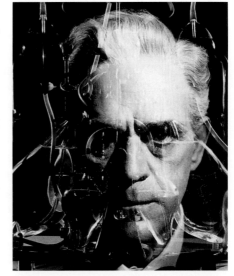

To help attract custom some exhibitors had gone onto the streets to sell the picture. In a publicity stunt for the Capitol Theatre in Philadelphia a tall, white-faced man wearing a black shroud was seen greeting passers by on Market Street. Around his neck hung a hangman's noose and a sign: "I am the man they could not hang." Still, the picture clearly held no appeal for columnist Walter Winchell who wrote, "Hanging is too good for the film."[17] However, the picture was successful enough to urge Columbia to continue in that vein and employ Karloff for more of the same. First, though, the star had commitments elsewhere

As Dr. Henryk Savaard in *The Man They Could Not Hang* (1939).

Left: A little light reading during *Tower of London* (1939). Right: As Mord in *Tower of London* (1939).

and, after a few weeks break, Karloff returned to Universal for the medieval melodrama *Tower of London*.

In April Universal had announced the picture as one of the studio's 44 large-scale productions it would produce during its 1939-40 season. These movies would benefit from an increased total budget of $5,000,000 in what the studio hoped would be its most ambitious season to date. Two months later the newspapers reported a 1st August start date for the picture, which would be helmed by *Son of Frankenstein* director Rowland V. Lee and written by the director's brother, Robert. The brothers had collaborated several times in the 1920s beginning with the silent *Shirley of the Circus* (1922) but had not worked together professionally in over a decade.

Rowland had originally wanted to make a picture set in the Stuart era – the era of the English Civil War. His brother, however, persuaded him an earlier period – that of the War of the Roses – was a tougher age. "Men of the 15th century lived in the last remnants of the Dark Ages," the director explained. "Perhaps more than any other time survival of the fittest was a vital rule. These were the men who managed to escape the executioner's axe or an equally bloody death on a battlefield. They lived and died by the sword, and the annals of their careers make dramatic reading and potentially action-filled screen drama."[18] Having decided upon a synopsis Lee gained studio approval and the picture was allocated a $500,000 budget and a 36-day shooting schedule.

Although Robert was primarily concerned with writing the screenplay his brother's input was necessary. "Many people think research experts do all the work on historical films, but the directors must study intensely themselves," Rowland said at the time. "The director can't achieve the correct historical tone unless he makes himself an authority on his subject. I know English history quite well except for the 15th century. I'm learning about that now for work on *Tower of London* which deals with the period from 1475 to 1485, sometimes

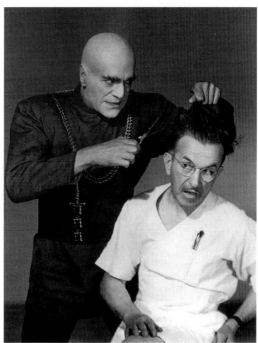

Left: Karloff feeds a visitor to the set – Baby Sandy (Sandra Henielle). Right: Clowning with Jack Pierce.

known as the horror decade…[iv] The metabolism of people must have been different in those days. Those cruelties that amused them then – we just couldn't take them today."[19]

Lee's new picture would use many of his crew from *Son of Frankenstein*. George Robinson (Director of Photography), Jack Otterson (Art Director), Richard Riedel (Associate Art Director), Fred Frank (Assistant Director), Bernard B. Brown (Sound Supervisor), William Hedgcock (Sound Technician), Russell A. Gausman (Set Decorations) and Vera West (Gowns) would all work on Lee's new picture.

Jack Otterson was given the task to design and construct a replica Tower on the back lot. Aided by Richard Riedel, Otterson designed all interiors and exteriors including, at 75 feet high, a slightly reduced White Tower, the most famous building in the fortress. In some instances the standing sets would also be combined with matte paintings by Jack Cosgrove and Russell Lawson. Newspaper reports of the time also claimed the British Government had given its permission for the studio to pick up background material at the real Tower on the north bank of the River Thames.

Basil Rathbone was announced as the lead in mid-April 1939 and a month later the press revealed Karloff would play Mord, the Tower executioner. In August it was announced Nan Grey had been assigned the role of Lady Alice Barton, John Sutton would play John Wyatt and George Sanders would portray Richard's brother, King Edward IV. Within days, however, Sanders was out, possibly to make *Green Hell* at the same studio. Instead, Universal borrowed Ian Hunter from MGM to fill the role. Hunter later said of Karloff, "It was a pleasure to know such a charming man…"[20]

Also included in the cast were five-year-old Donnie Dunagan and Basil Rathbone's

---

iv The picture actually spans the years 1471-1485.

son, Rodion, who was featured in the brief role of Lord DeVere. Cast as Richard's doomed second brother, George, in only his third movie, was 28-year-old Vincent Price.

Vincent Leonard Price Jr. was born in St. Louis, Missouri on 27 May 1911. After graduating from Yale University he spent some time teaching before he left for England to study for a master's degree at the University of London, "and there," Price later told Lawrence French, "I fell in love with the theatre, which was very easy to do in England, particularly at that time [1934], because it was very cheap."[21] Price made his theatrical debut in May 1935 at the small Gate Theatre in Villiers Street (off the Strand) as Prince Albert in Laurence Housman's play *Victoria Regina* – a role he would play later that year, with great success, alongside Helen Hayes on Broadway.

In July 1938 the actor signed a 12-picture, five-year contract with Universal, and the following year was loaned to Warner Brothers to appear as Sir Walter Raleigh in *The Private Lives of Elizabeth and Essex*, starring Bette Davis and Errol Flynn. Price would now return to Universal to shoot two pictures concurrently. He would appear with George Sanders and Douglas Fairbanks Jr. in *Green Hell* (for *Frankenstein* director James Whale) while also playing the squint-eyed George, Duke of Clarence, in *Tower of London*.[v]

As in *Son of Frankenstein*, Rathbone and Karloff would receive first and second billing respectively. Working at Universal, though, had cost Rathbone a key role in another prestigious production. For at that time RKO was casting for its new version of *The Hunchback of Notre Dame*, which would star Charles Laughton as Quasimodo and Maureen O'Hara as the gypsy Esmeralda. The studio originally wanted Rathbone as the archdeacon's wicked brother Frollo, and in July some newspapers even announced the actor had been engaged for the role. However, scheduling conflicts with the drama *Rio* at Universal resulted in Cedric Hardwicke's casting in Victor Hugo's tale. As it was, the production of *Rio* overlapped with *Tower of London* and, as a consequence, Basil Rathbone spent a week working on both films at the same time. Unlike the historical Richard, Karloff's character, the bald-headed, club-footed executioner Mord, was a wholly fictitious creation. To achieve the look Karloff once again reported to the studio's head make-up man, Jack Pierce. After having his head shaved Karloff's ears were taped back and glued flat against his head. His nose was built up into a hawk-like beak while his eyebrows were waxed and curled. His right leg was padded and, to affect the appearance of a clubfoot, he wore a large built-up shoe.

Rathbone had an easier time in make-up, which consisted of little more than sharp eyebrows and a wig (a red one according to columnist Erskine Johnson) that required constant combing by hairdressers. The combination of the wig, the silk tights and

---

v *Green Hell* went into production on 21 August 1939.

leather shoes prompted Rathbone to comment, "I know now what it's like to be a glamour girl!"[22]

Production began on Friday, 11 August 1939 but the problems soon began. The first of the battle scenes – the Battle of Bosworth (1485) – was shot on Saturday, 19 August on a ranch in Tarzana, some 20 miles north of the studio. Over three hundred extras were issued with a 4 a.m. call to supply the picture with its opposing armies – but the shoot proved to be a disaster. As the engagement was to be shot in fog,[vi] fog-machines were available for the day's filming. However, the wind that day proved too strong to use the machines effectively and so the director chose to shoot the movie's first engagement, the Battle of Tewkesbury (1471), instead.

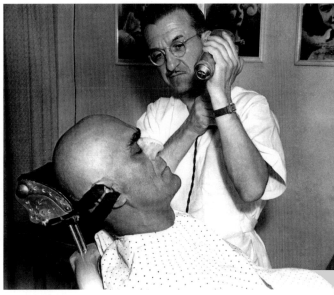

Opposite: Poster for *Tower of London* (1939). Above: Jack Pierce prepares Karloff for *Tower of London* (1939).

This encounter was to be shot in rainfall, so rain-machines had to be set up. However, filming soon came to a halt when the water pump broke down and, while attempts were made to fix it, the extras were left sweltering in a summer heat wave that had already claimed several lives in the state. Then, when the pump was fixed and the artificial rain fell upon the field, the extras' cardboard 'armour' began to disintegrate. Once again, as on *Son of Frankenstein*, Lee was falling behind schedule. Three days later Lee tried again but once more the heat proved too much. As a compromise, and to speed up production, it was decided to shoot groups of soldiers in front of process shots.

Concerned at the delays, the studio reacted by trying to cut corners and removed the marriage scene between the baby Prince Richard and Lady Mobray, thereby shaving $10,000 off the costs. Lee, however, fought to keep the scene but in doing so had to agree complete the scenes for the higher-paid cast members, including Boris Karloff, first.

Karloff is first seen in the picture sharpening his axe in the tower's dungeon. Upon his shoulder sits a raven – a bird that also caused some trouble during production. Four-year-old Jimmy, as the raven was known, had from the age of seven months been trained by his owner, Curly Twiford. By the time of the *Tower of London* shoot, the bird was earning $50 a day. In the dungeon scene Jimmy was required merely to sit on Karloff's shoulder but when Rowland V. Lee called "action" the bird flew up to a

Shooting *Tower of London* (1939).

---

vi In fact, the contemporary sources indicate the Battle of Bosworth was fought on a sunny summer's day.

The Karloffs with Russell Gleason at the Pacific
Southwest tennis matches, Los Angeles, 1939.

corner of the soundstage where he remained for sometime, holding up production. The reason for Jimmy's disobedience, his owner claimed, was professional jealousy.

During rehearsals another bird of Twiford's, a five-year-old raven called Koko, was used as a stand-in as Jimmy sat on the sidelines – apparently much to the latter's displeasure. Twiford had used Koko as a stand-in to give it experience before the camera. Now filming was halted as the bird's owner climbed to the catwalks to cajole Jimmy down. This proved unsuccessful, however, and Jimmy would only return to his position on Karloff's shoulder after Koko was returned to his cage.

Despite the difficulties and the pressures there was still fun to be had, as Hedda Hopper noted. "Funniest sight of the week," she wrote in her column, "was Basil Rathbone running out to meet the rain from the *Tower of London* set in his short-shorts."[23]

Rathbone, who had been something of a joker on the *Son of Frankenstein* set, was up to his old tricks again on his latest picture, as Vincent Price recalled. "We had this scene where Basil and I had to drink for the kingdom of England," he said. "Rowland Lee, who directed the picture, didn't like the dialogue, and neither did we, because the more we drank, the less we could remember. It was only Coca-Cola, but Coke is stimulating too. Well, over in one corner was a huge vat of Malmsey wine, in which I was to be drowned. Boris and Basil, knowing I was new to the business, thought it was great fun to throw everything they could into that vat of wine, which was actually just water. You know, old Coca-Cola bottles, cigarette butts, anything they could find to dirty it up, because they knew at the end of the scene I had to get into it! They had fixed a handrail at the bottom of it, so I could dive down and hang onto it. I had to stay under for a full ten counts, and then I was yanked out by my heels. Well, when I came out I got a round of applause from the crew, but was disappointed not to see Boris and Basil. Then a few minutes later they re-appeared and were very nice to me. They congratulated me on playing the scene so well for a newcomer, and then presented me with a case of Coca-Cola [*laughs*]!"[24]

Tower of London officially wrapped on 4 September, ten days over schedule and almost $80,000 over budget. When it was found, however, there were still some incomplete shots the studio assigned serial director Ford Beebe[vii] to gather together the necessary members of the cast – many of whom had since gone on to other projects – and finish the film.

Yet even with a completed film the front office was not happy. After previewing the picture the studio found fault with the movie's soundtrack. Unhappy with the historically accurate medieval music the studio demanded a more conventional score. When the picture hit the screens in mid-November little of the period music remained. In its place were selections from the score of *Son of Frankenstein*.

---

vii Beebe had directed many serials including *Flash Gordon's Trip to Mars* (1938) and *Buck Rogers* (1939).

By the time production was over Karloff, it was reported, had had his head shaved 44 times. On Sunday, 3 September he attended a Screen Actors Guild meeting at the Hollywood Legion Stadium and could be seen, bespectacled and bald-pated, amongst his fellow actors. This bald state, however, would inspire him to commit a curious act and shave his daughter's head. Dorothy was, naturally, far from happy as Cynthia Lindsay (née Hobart) recalled. "She was furious," Lindsay wrote. "She said, 'Boris, how dare you? It's going to take years to grow out.' Well, it didn't… but it wasn't really the thing to do – but it amused him to do so. Whether he'd done it to annoy Dorothy, or to make her laugh – she did not laugh – I don't know."[25]

Tower of London was previewed at the Alexander Theatre in Glendale, California on the evening of 16 November 1939. A review appeared in the *Los Angeles Times* the following day. "A somber study it is of murders and tortures, and the darker pages of history," it read. "It may be roundly hailed as one of the most unusual features ever produced – even though it may prove repellent to some audiences… This solemn processional will meet an engrossing test, one may well say, at the box office of the country… A singular brooding and haunting atmosphere overhangs this production, the events of which are well delineated under the direction of Rowland V. Lee… The progression, at times, is a little tedious… Rathbone is the star and gives a stellar performance in fine classic style as the ever-menacing Richard. Karloff manages well his impersonation of the hangman… Settings are splendid."[26]

The picture opened at the Paramount Theatre in Los Angeles on 7 December with entertainment by Glen Gray and the Casa Loma orchestra. Philip K. Scheuer of the *Los Angeles Times* remarked, "Automatically, I think, Shakespeare is called to mind when one speaks of Richard III. And this Rowland V. Lee film does bear certain resemblances to the Bard's historical plays… The metered verse is, to be sure, missing, the language being semi-colloquial and largely expository – but even the absence of long speeches does not keep one from the consciousness that a certain static quality has intruded at moments… In all this it is natural to find Boris Karloff alive and active. Still with the monster's tread, he goes around chopping off people's heads. His Mord (an imaginary figure?) is Richard's closest ally. As for Rathbone himself, he is again the master villain, but not too exuberantly so. The crook in his back is more talked about than seen."[27]

Tower of London opened at the Rialto in New York on Monday, 11 December, following upon the heels of Laurel and Hardy's *Flying Deuces*. When the picture premiered at the Warfield Theatre in San Francisco four days later Karloff, Nan Grey and John Sutton were in attendance. To emphasise the horrific nature of the picture Universal also arranged for Bela Lugosi to be present.

Even though Karloff was clearly added to supply the picture's horror he was still able to imbue his character, however loathsome, with a modicum of humanity. Sent to kill the two young Princes in the Bloody Tower there is a moment when Mord contemplates, and almost seems to regret, his heinous task. It was these moments that Karloff savoured. "There is one thing about my characterisations that is important," he had said in 1935. "No matter how bad I am, I always try to obtain just a bit of sympathy, generally by showing some feeling for the most helpless of my intended victims, and none for the others. The public reacts just as I want it to. In fact, after one film, a storm of protest came in because a member of the cast struck me in one scene."[28]

On the evening of Wednesday, 11 October the premiere of James Cagney's latest gangster picture – *The Roaring Twenties* – was held at the Warner Brothers Hollywood

Theatre. The attendees listed like a veritable who's who of the industry's stars. In addition
to the Karloffs and the Cagneys, the list included Clark Gable and Carole Lombard, Errol
Flynn and Lili Damita, Robert Taylor and Barbara Stanwyck, George Burns and Gracie
Allen, Pat O'Brien, Bing Crosby, Groucho Marx and Spencer Tracy.

Two weeks later a new Karloff picture was announced as being on the drawing board.
Monogram announced the star would feature in a picture called *Haunted House*, in addition
to three more Mr. Wong pictures. While Karloff never made *Haunted House* the first of the
Oriental detective pictures went into production the following month.

Originally announced as *Mr. Wong at Headquarters* the picture's title was subsequently
changed to *The Fatal Hour*. It would be the third and final Wong picture scripted by Scott
Darling. Darling would go on to write *The Ghost of Frankenstein*, the first of Universal's
Frankenstein series not to feature Karloff as the Monster.

The Fatal Hour, the *Los Angeles Times* reported, would begin production on 27 November.
This time Wong is asked to investigate the murder of a detective killed while working on
a smuggling case. The picture opened at the Pix Theatre on West 42nd Street in New York
on Friday, 12 January 1940 and three days later went on national release. "Despite the fact
that the film gives away its solution long before its Chinese detective… gets around to
it," wrote the *New York Times*, "we enjoy Mr. Wong too much to object… The calibre of the
performances matches that of the film itself, except for Mr. Karloff, who, as usual, is a few
millimeters better."[29]

The reviewer for the *Dallas Evening News* was not so keen. "Boris Karloff," he wrote,
"is taking another of those occasional vacations from his regular business of horrifying the
customers, and comes up again at the Capitol in *The Fatal Hour*, wherein he reprises his
role of Mr. Wong, the Chinese detective. But he might just as well have kept on with his
boo-work for us all… Mr. Wong goes about ignoring the murderer until he has all the clues
neatly catalogued, then springs his solution."[30]

In the closing months of 1939 Karloff had some time on his hands and was able to
spend it with his family. On 23 November, he had turned 52. More significantly it was also
his daughter's first birthday and the event was marked by a gathering of friends.

It would be a celebratory few months for little Sara Jane. Her first tooth had broken
on 19 August during the filming of *Tower of London* and Karloff had received a telegram
after lunch informing him of the fact. "Upper or lower," he wired back. "Suspense holding
up production. Congratulations and love, Daddy."[31] Then, that Christmas, Sara took her
first steps. Within days, though, Karloff was back at the studio. On Saturday, 28 December
1940 production began on his next picture for Universal which, with *Tower of London*, was
made under his two-picture extended contract with the studio.

Almost a year earlier, in January 1939, the *New York Times* had revealed Willis Cooper
was preparing a horror story entitled *Friday the Thirteenth* which was expected to feature
both Karloff and Lugosi. Then, that April, Universal announced the picture as one of the
40 feature-length films it would release in the 1939-40 season. Two months later *Boxoffice*
reported Rowland V. Lee had been assigned to direct Cooper's screenplay – a story of a
genial man who commits a murder every Friday the 13th.

Then, by late August, all had changed. Cooper was out of the picture and instead
Kurt (later Curt) Siodmak and Eric Taylor would write a scenario. In mid-December
Arthur Lubin was assigned to direct the picture – now entitled *Black Friday*. Lubin's
appointment, it was said, was on the strength of his work on the recent crime drama *Big*

Guy. Throughout all the changes however, the assertion remained that the picture would star both Karloff and Lugosi.

The screenplay told the story of George Kingsley, a mild-mannered college professor who is injured when the car of the notorious gangster, Red Cannon, is forced off the road. Cannon and Kingsley are rushed to hospital where Kingsley's friend, Dr. Sovac, attends them. To save the professor's life Sovac performs an illegal brain transplant using Cannon as the donor. Kingsley recovers, but when Sovac discovers Cannon had hidden away $500,000, he re-awakens Cannon's identity in the hope this will lead him to the money. The professor unknowingly begins to lead a Jekyll-and-Hyde existence, switching between the personalities of the mild professor and the violent gangster. As Red Cannon, the professor embarks on a killing spree, hunting down his old gang members who had tried to kill him by forcing him off the road. The gangster recovers his money but falls asleep in the back of a taxi. When he awakes he is the professor again and Sovac takes the money. The professor returns to teaching but one day during class Cannon's psyche resurfaces. He goes to Sovac's house believing the doctor to be in possession of his money. There he attacks Sovac's daughter, Jean, but is shot dead by Sovac who is then sent to the electric chair.

Initially Karloff was scheduled to play the dual role of Professor George Kinsley and the hoodlum Red Cannon, while Lugosi was set to play the surgeon Ernst Sovac. However, the production suffered a setback when Boris Karloff switched roles. Although Universal made no statement why the change occurred, screenwriter Curt Siodmak had his own opinion about what had happened. "Karloff didn't want to play the dual role in *Black Friday*," he said. "He was afraid of it: there was too much *acting* in it, it was too intricate… Karloff was smart enough to know that he might not come off too well in the role."[32] Although Karloff and Lugosi would both be credited above the title, and would feature together in publicity shots, the recasting of roles meant the two horror stars would now not share even a single scene in the picture.

Whatever the reason for the change the front office obviously thought Lugosi was not up to the role vacated by Karloff and, instead, looked elsewhere. In an interview with Keith Alan Deutsch several years later Siodmak elaborated. "He [Karloff] was highly intelligent and not conceited… He thought he wasn't a good enough actor for the lead and took a secondary part, suggesting Stanley Ridges, a very good stage actor to play the part," Siodmak said.[33]

The 50-year-old Englishman, Stanley Ridges, arrived in Hollywood on Wednesday, 27 December and shooting began the following day. Lugosi, meanwhile, was relegated to the role of Eric Marnay, one of Cannon's ex-gang members who also seeks the hidden money. "That didn't turn out well at all," Siodmak later commented. "Bela never could act his way out of a paper bag. He could only be *Mee-ster Drac-u-la* with that accent and those Hungarian movements of his."[34] It was a claim that has infuriated Lugosi's fans.

Black Friday was given an 18-day shooting schedule and a budget of $130,750, a small amount when compared with the usual 'A' feature budgets, which were often in excess of $500,000. The front office was eager the production should meet its deadline and put pressure on the director to deliver. As a result the cast and crew would often work late – all save Boris Karloff, who steadfastly refused to work over the regulation eight hours a day. It seems an obvious slight towards the studio from the actor who had, six months earlier, been happy to work long hours at Columbia.

On Saturday, 13 January 1940 Studio Production Manager, Martin F. Murphy, reported the position to the front office. "With weather conditions very much against us during the past two weeks – Karloff refusing to work over eight hours in any one day – and the constant changing of pace in progress shown by Lubin, this picture has been a somewhat problem child," he wrote. "They will finish up tonight running about a ½ day behind schedule. We believe if weather holds out Monday our revised schedule will be possible to fulfil by next Thursday night, the end of their 18-day schedule…"[35]

Pressured by the front office the cast and crew, excluding Karloff, worked the last four nights of production and finished on schedule on Thursday, 18 January. The shoot had taken the 18 days expected by the front office although, to meet the deadline, the cast and crew had worked late on half of those days, often shooting until 10 p.m. and once to 3:15 the following morning. More pleasing to the studio was the fact that Lubin had bought the picture in at $7,000 under budget.

Anne Gwynne, who played Karloff's daughter in the picture, recalled working with the star. "What an actor; what a man!" she said. "I had a key scene with Boris, the one where I'm urging him to take Stanley Ridges back home from New York. Well, we shot the entire scene with the camera on Boris. Arthur Lubin was the director, and for some reason I've always felt that he didn't like me. He said, 'Wrap!' but Boris came to my rescue and said, '*Don't do this to her*. Give Anne a close-up.' Which is exactly what Lubin had to do, and it's in the picture! Now that is a really terrific guy. Most actors wouldn't think of it, or do it if they *did* think of it, but Boris Karloff I'll always admire. He was not only a fine actor who could play just about anything, but a really terrific human being."[36]

As Dr. Ernest Sovac in *Black Friday* (1940).

The picture's trailer opened with a bizarre statement. To prepare for the scene when Marnay is trapped in a closet and, implausibly, suffocates Lugosi was, the trailer claimed, hypnotised by his friend, Dr. Manley P. Hall (the co-author of the unrealised Karloff picture *Witches Sabbath*). Before this scene was shot 25 reporters gathered on Soundstage 14 at Universal City to witness the process and were introduced to the actors by director Lubin.

Dr. Hall then proceeded to 'hypnotise' Bela Lugosi. "Hypnotised, Lugosi made his way to a two-sided set which was the closet in which the actor was locked and in which he was to suffocate," journalist Douglas W. Churchill explained. "Hall went over the script once with the hypnotised man, the cameras turned, Hall whispered, 'Now you're suffocating', and

Lugosi began to nose the cracks in the door… His voice became shrill as he screamed his lines. With his shoulder against the door, the set began to give, and then he slumped to the floor. A doctor who was in attendance stepped in, took his pulse, which had increased from normal to 160 which, the physician said, would be actual in a suffocating person."[37] The actor was then carried to a chair where Hall roused him. Lugosi's pulse was then taken again and this time registered as normal.

Arthur Lubin told those present the scene was 100% better than it had played that afternoon, when Lugosi had acted without hypnosis. However the actor's scene of suffering was very brief in the final cut due to the fact, it was later revealed, the cameraman had run out of film half way through. For those present who doubted the veracity of the situation Boris Karloff, Churchill wrote, "stated he was positive Lugosi was hypnotised because he had never seen his fellow-actor keep his back to the camera for so long."[38] Years later, however, Arthur Lubin came clean and admitted the whole thing had been a publicity stunt.

Black Friday premiered at the Alexander Theatre in Glendale, California at the end of February. Philip K. Scheuer of the *Los Angeles Times* thought the picture "a fair enough shocker of its type."[39] In Chicago on 1 March the picture was half of the 'first DOUBLE WORLD PREMIERE in screen history!'[40] as the newspapers reported it, when it opened with *The House of the Seven Gables* starring George Sanders, Margaret Lindsay and Vincent Price. "Stanley Ridges does an impressive job of personality switching," wrote one reviewer. "He certainly can look like two different persons. I did think, though, that having the colour of his hair change from grey to black and back again was going a bit too far… Karloff makes a believable medical man, and Lugosi plays a very tough egg as he so well knows how."[41] When, on 14 March, the double-bill had its west coast premiere at the Orpheum in San Francisco the stars of both films – Karloff, Lugosi, Price and Sanders – were in attendance.

The picture reached New York three weeks later opening at the Rialto on 21 March. "Lugosi's terrifying talents are wasted in the role of a mere gangster, an unsupernatural mugg [*sic*]," complained the *New York Times*, "but Karloff is in exquisite form as a surgeon who 'transplants' the brain of a killer…"[42]

The picture had given Lubin the opportunity to work with his old acquaintance, Bela Lugosi. The two had met in 1922 when Lubin had worked as an assistant stage manager in New York. Lugosi had been hired to play the Spaniard Franco in the comedy *The Red Poppy* at the Greenwich Village Theatre, alongside Estelle Winwood. However, when hiring the Hungarian actor the management had neglected to ask the Hungarian if he spoke English. Lubin was therefore required to coach Lugosi in the language. The two would later be re-acquainted and become close friends at Universal although *Black Friday* would be the only time Lubin would make a picture with Lugosi, or Boris Karloff. "He was a real gentleman," the director later said of Karloff. "He was a scholar – he was high class! Both Bela and Boris were gentlemen. They were both fine men… and I don't remember anything unpleasant ever happening with either one of the two boys. They were just wonderful, wonderful guys to work with."[43]

On the evening of 13 January 1940 – during the production of *Black Friday* – columnist Hedda Hopper interviewed Karloff and Lugosi at the former's home in Coldwater Canyon. Approaching the Karloff residence Hopper heard a dog howling. "But the whine of the hound brought my host to the gate," she wrote, "and the warmth of the crackling fire, the tumbler of sherry from a vat on the bar, and broad smiles from Karloff and Lugosi made me feel at home."[44] Karloff's home, she noted, was devoid of wallpaper or stucco work with walls of plain white brick. "Incongruous are the nursery touches trailing through living room, sun parlour and bar – rattles, dolls and hobby horses," Hopper noted.[45]

As the columnist spoke to the stars she felt something brushing against her ankles. Looking down she saw it was a duck. "Don't let Abigail get you," Karloff told her. "Abigail was a birthday present and she's so tame she eats out of my hand. I leave water in the pool all winter so she'll have a place to sleep and she gets along beautifully with my 11-year old Persian cat, Whiskey and the parrot."[46] When Hopper asked who Whiskey was Karloff whistled and in came the black Scottish Terrier. "Is that the wolf who yelped when I breezed in?" Hopper asked. "Sure," Karloff replied, Whiskey's the only dog I have left."[47]

Hopper noted that Lugosi had taken out American citizenship ten years earlier. He felt, he told the columnist, he was lucky to be an American, "and thinks," Hopper wrote, "every naturalised American and every person born here should kneel every morning and utter a prayer for being an American."[48] Of course Karloff, too, had come to America from Europe. "This was the land of opportunity for me," he said, "but it never occurred to me to take out papers."[49] And it never would.

Karloff's next picture was *The Man with Nine Lives* which went into production on 16 February. He would play Dr. Leon Kravaal, a scientist whose research into cryogenics, or 'frozen therapy,' had convinced him that therein lay a cure for cancer. However, the scientist has been mysteriously missing for a decade.

When it is erroneously announced that Dr. Tim Mason [Roger Pryor] has, in fact, discovered a cure for the disease while following in Kravaal's footsteps, he is sent on holiday to avoid the media spotlight. Mason and his fiancée Judith Blair [Jo Ann Sayers] travel to Kravaal's home on Crater Island where they stumble upon the doctor in his underground laboratory, a facility carved into the ice of a giant glacier. Mason resuscitates Kravaal who then relates his story.

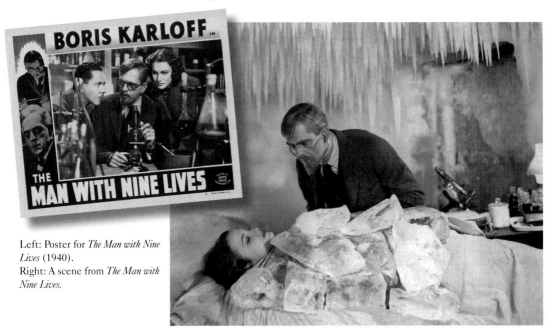

Left: Poster for *The Man with Nine Lives* (1940).
Right: A scene from *The Man with Nine Lives*.

Kravaal had been using his formula treating Jasper Adams, a millionaire dying of cancer. However, the glacial laboratory is invaded by Adams' nephew Bob and his entourage: the District Attorney Hawthorne, Sherriff Stanton and Dr. Bassett. In the fracas that follows Kravaal's drug is dropped, rendering everyone unconscious.

Mason and Kravaal now revive the others but an angry Bob Adams destroys the formula. Kravaal now determines to keep them all prisoner until he can recreate the potion. Adams, however, is shot trying to escape, while Hawthorne and Bassett die during the tests. Kravaal realises the men had died due to overexposure to the formula and now plans to experiment on Judith. His scheme is foiled, however, when a search party arrives. Kravaal is shot and mortally wounded. As he lies dying he hands his notes to Mason, entreating him to carry on his work.

The picture wrapped on 5 March and went on general release on 18 April. It opened at the Globe in New York nine days later. One critic commented on the similarity between this and another recent Karloff effort. "When Karloff, the benefactor of mankind… comes through with a discovery that will revolutionise the treatment of cancer… you can safely predict that his motives will be completely misunderstood," he wrote. "Wasn't that the case when 'Dr.' Karloff produced last Autumn an artificial heart to enable physicians to perform operations more efficiently in *The Man They Could Not Hang*?… Being a great Karloff admirer anything he does is all right, but for casual and literal-minded moviegoers *The Man with Nine Lives* may seem hard to take."[50] Karloff would later concur. "The formula was successful, if not original," he explained. "The scientist would set out to save mankind. His project would sour and he with it. In the end he'd have to be destroyed regretfully, like a faithful old dog gone mad."[51] Still, the *Los Angeles Times* called the picture, "a first class shocker."[52]

After finishing the picture Karloff was afforded time off and spent that spring and summer with his family. He also continued raising funds for the war effort. On 21 April Karloff, a committee member for the British War Relief fund, supported the cause by taking a box at the exhibition tennis matches held at the Ambassador courts. Many Hollywood stars, including Charlie Chaplin, Gary Cooper, Ronald Colman, Alfred Hitchcock, Maureen O'Hara and Nigel Bruce, also lent their support by taking boxes at the event.

The following month the Karloffs attended a party at the Florentine Gardens given by Louis Ghiradelli of the famous chocolate company. Then, in the middle of the month, Dorothy packed and left for a holiday in Oregon, staying at the Timberline Lodge on the slopes of Mt. Hood. While there she sprained her ankle, causing her husband to feel the need to explain the injury to columnist Hedda Hopper. Karloff had approached her, she said, in the hope she could nip in the bud any rumours that he was beating his wife. "That sprained ankle she's wearing," Karloff explained, "she got while skiing up in the mountains near Timberline, Oregon."[53]

While Dorothy was away her husband returned to Monogram for another Mr. Wong picture. *Doomed to Die* would be Karloff's fifth and final performance as the Chinese sleuth. This time he would investigate the slaying of shipping magnate Cyrus Wentworth. Captain Street [Grant Withers] soon arrests Dick Fleming [William Sterling], the son of a rival magnate. It is only after Dick's father is also killed does Wong unmask the murder.

The picture opened at the Rialto in New York on Monday, 29 July and went on national release five days later. "As is usual in this Monogram series," wrote the *New York Times*, "suspicion is cast about freely, and Mr. Karloff and the audience are the only ones who are not at all surprised when the real culprit is uncovered. For you can be sure that every time Captain Street of the homicide squad makes an arrest he's bound to have the wrong party. And that makes identifying the guilty one a comparatively easy matter for armchair sleuths."[54] *Boxoffice* put it more succinctly. "It's the stock approach to a murder mystery, with a heckling female reporter, a dumb detective and the discovery of the real criminal as the attorney."[55]

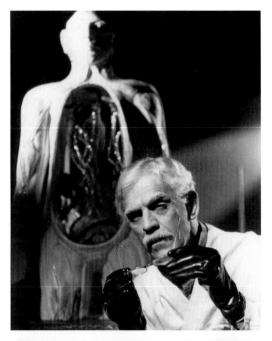

On 28 June, directly after completing his work for Monogram, Karloff returned to Columbia to start work on *Wizard of Death*, the third of his recent 'mad doctor' pictures for the studio. Karloff would be re-united on the picture with Nick Grinde, the director of both earlier offerings. This time he would play Dr. John Garth, a scientist who searches for an elixir to restore youth and prolong life. When Dr. Garth performs a 'mercy killing' on an elderly, and suffering, test patient he is tried and condemned to be hanged. The prison governor, however, is sympathetic to the doctor's cause and allows him to continue his experiments until the execution. He is successful in discovering the elixir but unfortunately mixes it with the blood of a killer, giving him the killer's lust for murder.

When Dr. Garth's sentence is commuted to life imprisonment he kills the prison doctor (*Frankenstein* co-star Edward Van Sloan). Another inmate is blamed for the

Top: As Dr. John Garth in *Before I Hang* (1940). Bottom: Karloff with Gloria Jean.

crime and the doctor is pardoned. Returning to his practice Dr. Garth tries to convince his ageing friends to try the serum. When they refuse, his murderous tendencies return. "I'm a cross between a ghoul, a zombie and a vampire," Karloff remarked on his role.[56] In a scene late in the picture Karloff was required to wear a tuxedo. He referred to it as his 'Little Lord Fauntleroy' suit.

The picture – now entitled *Before I Hang* – went on national release on 17 September. It opened at the Bryant in New York two weeks later on Wednesday, 2 October. "If you're taken in by reels and reels of test tubes, mechanical hearts and other scientific gadgets," wrote one reviewer, "or the brooding atmosphere provoked through the use of murky photography, then *Before I Hang* should prove to be moderately entertaining. It's strictly a one-man show – Mr. Karloff's as far as performances go, but Pedro de Cordoba manages to get off a pretty good imitation of a piano maestro."[57]

Once again there were theatre owners who would promote the picture in their own unique ways. In Worcester, Massachusetts, Robert Portle of the Plaza hung two dummies from the flagpole over the theatre's marquee. He also had another dummy borne on a stretcher outside the theatre with a sign: "Before I Hang, I want to see Boris Karloff at the Plaza."[58] In New Haven the manager of the Bijou, Bill Reisinger, and his assistant, Vernon Burns, contrived an even more macabre stunt. They placed a white-lettered

Lobby Card for *The Ape* (1940).

black coffin on the theatre's marquee and hung two dummies from a scaffold from an upper storey window. In addition, alarm clocks were placed in several local store windows with the sign: "When the alarm rings it will be time to see Boris Karloff."[59]

On 29 July Karloff again returned to Monogram to make *The Ape*, one of the 50 features the studio planned to release in its 1940-41 season. The director of the studio's *Mr. Wong* series, William Nigh, would helm the picture. Although publicity stated the movie was 'suggested from the play by Adam Hull Shirk' the picture bore no relation to the play, which had premiered in Los Angeles in 1926. Shirk's play told the story of an Englishman who, while in India, kills one of a temple's sacred apes. 30 years later the man, now a nervous wreck, is living in Los Angeles. Then a series of murders occur, apparently perpetrated by an ape. Shirk's tale, however, would not be used in the new picture, despite the screen credit. Instead, screenwriters Kurt Siodmak and Richard Carroll would fashion a new story. "In *The Ape*," Siodmak later explained, "Boris Karloff played a scientist who discovers that fluid taken from the human spine can be used to cure a crippled girl, played by Maris Nixon. That was an idea which *I* had."[60]

In the Siodmak/Carroll script Dr. Bernard Adrian [Karloff] seeks a cure for the paralysing disease that killed his wife and daughter. Unable to save them he now seeks a cure for Francis Clifford [Nixon], a crippled young woman who reminds him of his daughter. After a travelling circus comes to town the ape's sadistic trainer is mauled and the dying man is taken to Dr. Adrian. The doctor extracts the man's spinal fluid – an essential ingredient for his cure – and injects it into Clifford. However, more fluid is needed to affect a complete cure. A means is provided when the circus gorilla escapes and breaks into Adrian's laboratory. The scientist kills it and dresses in its skin to search for victims.[viii]

The Ape had its world premiere with a midnight showing at the Pastime Theatre in Iowa City on Saturday, 21 September. It went on national release nine days later. "Boris

---

viii The actor in the ape suit was serial star and stuntman Ray "Crash" Corrigan.

The Monster scares Buster Keaton at a 1940 charity baseball game.

Karloff's films come so thick and fast that critics can rarely remember which they have not seen," one reviewer wrote. "Hence their ordinary comments are apt to be vague. This week, however, they've nothing better to do than dissect *The Ape*, and discover with no surprise at all that it is just like every other Karloff made."[61]

The critic for the *New York Times* thought even less of the picture. "Perhaps," he wrote, "if you are under 12 or just like to be frightened and try very hard, *The Ape*, now at the Rialto, will scare daylights out of you. Otherwise we think [this] newest growl-and-glower epic is apt to seem merely quaint... Mr. Karloff, both in his gruesome disguise and in mufti, is properly baleful... Maybe this is an age of lost innocence or perhaps it is because even horror follows the law of diminishing returns, but from where we sat we couldn't count half-a-dozen goose pimples in the house."[62]

On the evening of Thursday, 8 August the 'Comedians vs. Leading Men' charity baseball game was held at Los Angeles' Wrigley Field ballpark to raise funds for the Mt. Sinai Hospital. The game began at 8 p.m., announced by Milton Berle. The umpires for the evening were James Gleason, Kay Kyser, Thurston Hall and Chico Marx. The two teams included such stars as Fred Allen, Jack Benny, Jerry Colonna, Buster Keaton, the Keystone Cops, the Ritz Brothers and the Three Stooges on the Comedians team, and Fred Astaire, Gary Cooper, Errol Flynn, Cary Grant, Peter Lorre, Tyrone Power and John Wayne for the Leading Men.

'Trouble' erupted when Jack Benny approached the mound accompanied by two bodyguards and two scriptwriters. When Fred Allen asked if Benny had warmed up Benny answered he had. "I thought I smelled ham burning," Allan replied. This light-hearted banter resulted in a comic altercation involving another 50 bodyguards. The face-off was finally broken up by the Keystone Cops.

Later, Boris Karloff made a surprise appearance striding onto the field in full monster garb supplied, once again, by Jack Pierce. The Monster played, somewhat incongruously, on the side of the leading men. "I strode up to the plate for the occasion in my full make-up as Frankenstein's Monster – whereupon Buster Keaton, who was catching for the comedians, promptly shrieked at the sight of me, did a backward somersault, and passed out cold behind the plate," Karloff later explained. "I waved my bat. The pitcher tossed the ball in my direction, and I swung it as best I could, encumbered as I was with the Monster's metallic overalls. Luckily enough, I managed to tap the ball, which bounced crazily in the general direction of the pitcher's box. It should have been an easy out at first. But as I approached each base the opposing player fainted dead away. And the Three Stooges, who were playing second, all passed out cold. It was a home run – though horrible!"[63]

Despite the Monster's success the evening ended with the Comedians triumphant, beating the leading men 5-3. The event was a great success and broke the stadium's attendance record. It was, Karloff later revealed, "the only time I really enjoyed playing the Monster."[64]

That same day production had begun on Karloff's next picture, one that would team him for the only time with Peter Lorre and Bela Lugosi – *You'll Find Out*. This venture,

however, would not be a starring vehicle for
any of the trio. Instead, this accolade was
reserved for bandleader Kay Kyser.

By 1940, Kay Kyser had one of the most
popular bands in the country. Their radio
show *Kollege of Musical Knowledge* was a great
success and, as a result, the band had already
starred in RKO's musical comedy *That's
Right – You're Wrong* (one of Kyser's catch-
phrases) with Adolphe Menjou and Lucille
Ball. The success of this picture prompted
the studio to plan a second feature for Kyser
and his band. The new picture, originally
entitled *The Old Professor*, would be directed
and co-written by David Butler. When he
requested that the studio provide him with
"three notable heavies"[65] for box office
value, RKO's front office chose Karloff,
Lugosi and Lorre.

In the picture Kyser and his band arrive
at Bellacrest Manor to play at heiress Janis
Bellacrest's 21st birthday party. There they

Triple Trouble: Karloff, Lorre and Lugosi in *You'll Find Out*
(1940).

meet Janis's guardian Aunt Margo, a lady who claims she can commune with the dead.
Other guests at the party include Judge Mainwaring [Karloff] and the mystic Prince
Saliano [Lugosi]. Also present is Carl Fenninger [Lorre], a professor hired by Janis to
expose Saliano for the charlatan she believes him to be.

During the evening Janis is almost killed by a falling chandelier. However, it later
transpires the judge, Saliano and Fenninger are in league with a plan to kill the debutante
for her money. Exposed by Kyser, the trio try to destroy the band with dynamite but,
instead, are killed when Kyser's dog returns the explosives to them.

Karloff had signed for the picture on 20 July for a salary of $4,166.66 per week with
guaranteed work for three-weeks. He would also receive 'special billing.' Once again
Lugosi would receive only a fraction of Karloff's salary – $1,250 per week with the three-
week guarantee. His contract, which he signed on 23 July, would give him 'best billing
possible.' Peter Lorre's contract, however, gave him primary billing – that is, the highest
billing of the trio. He would receive $3,500 per week, with a four-week guarantee. The
picture's final billing read: Kay Kyser in *You'll Find Out* with Peter Lorre, Boris Karloff and
Bela Lugosi. Kay Kyser meanwhile received a $75,000 advance for him and his 'associates.'

Shooting began on Thursday, 8 August and lasted for two months, concluding on 11
October, some 13 days over schedule. The picture had cost $367,689.90 (excluding Kyser's
$75,000). Still, according to the director, David Butler, it was a happy set. "The picture
was one of the happiest I ever did," he said. "Everybody simply had fun making it."[66]
Louise Currie, who played Marion, a society girl, agreed. "*You'll Find Out* really was fun;
it was light-hearted, the whole idea was a spoof, and everybody was happy… I remember
meeting all the girls (we were all supposed to be debutantes) – a nice group of girls. As for
the horror men… Boris Karloff, interestingly enough, was very quiet. He didn't participate

on the set too much – he was, I'd almost say, rather a recluse. I distinctly felt you just didn't run up and start chatting with him! Nor do I remember having too much contact with Peter Lorre, who, as I recall, was a strange little fellow – much the sort he portrayed on the screen! But Bela Lugosi was different. I remember long chats with Lugosi: he was a very educated, polished, interesting man."[67]

On Wednesday, 25 September the three 'horror men' joined Kyser on his radio show. They were not present, however, on 4 November when Kyser and his band made a personal appearance at the Roxy in New York for the opening of *You'll Find Out*.

Bosley Crowther of the *New York Times* found the picture disappointing. "Apparently the script writers were scared out of their wits by their own ideas, for the dialogue and plot developments indicate that little was devoted to them," he wrote. "With three of the most calculating villains *vis-a-vis* Mr. Kyser in one film, you would think that something more original than shrieks in the night and sliding panels and hidden passageways could have been contrived to confound them. Some of the incidents are amusing, mainly because of Mr. Kyser's frightened-rabbit attitude when in the midst of them. But, on the whole, the picture is just routine and dull."[68]

In mid-July Columbia had purchased William Sloane's novel *Edge of Running Water* – the story of a man who constructs a machine to communicate with the dead – as a possible vehicle for Boris Karloff. The resulting picture, *The Devil Commands*, would be his last serious entry in the 'mad doctor' series for Columbia. "I must confess that I didn't accept this constant and continual madness quite placidly myself," Karloff admitted. "Once, during the crazed-scientist cycle, I said wearily to the producer: 'These things are all right, but don't you think we should perhaps spend a little more in the writing, or change the format?' He was in an expansive mood. He opened his desk drawer and pulled out a great chart. 'Here,' he said, 'here's your record. We know exactly how much these pictures are going to make. They cost *so* much. They earn *so* much. Even if we spent more on them, they wouldn't make a cent more. So why change them?'"[69]

Left: As Dr. Julian Blair in *The Devil Commands* (1941). Right: With Anne Revere in *The Devil Commands*.

Production began on *The Devil Commands* on Friday, 22 November. Karloff would play Dr. Julian Blair, a scientist who is developing a machine to record people's thoughts. However, when his wife dies in a car crash Blair adapts the device in the hope it will allow him to communicate with his dead wife. Ignoring pleas from his daughter Ann [Amanda Duff] to discontinue the work Blair hires a medium, Mrs. Walters [Anne Revere], to aid him. After an experiment using his servant Karl [Ralph Penney] goes badly wrong, Blair relocates to New England where he continues his work, reverting to grave-robbing to provide corpses to use in his research. Eventually the townspeople rise up against him and storm his house, just as he finally makes contact with his deceased wife. The mob destroys his laboratory and Blair is killed when his machine explodes.

The picture's director, Edward Dmytryk, was pleased to be working with Boris Karloff. "He was one of the gentlest men I have ever known," the director said. "Very gentle, very sweet – *sweet* is the word. (In a *masculine* way, of course!) He was really such a nice guy in every possible way – every other word was 'God bless you'."[70] Amanda Duff, who played the scientist's daughter, Anne, also enjoyed working with the star. "He was simply charming," she explained, "very elegant and such a sweet, sweet man... Karloff never gave the impression that he had been dissatisfied with doing this type of film... and Boris, aside from being an absolute gentleman and professional, valued not only having the work but having the chance to perform and develop into the fine actor that he was. I thought his most outstanding feature was his genuineness as a person."[71] Duff found Karloff just as charming away from the studio. "One time," she explained, "he had been visiting us at home and when he learned that our daughter, Philippa, who was just a small child at the time, was sick, he asked me if could go upstairs and read to her. So he did. It was these things that made Boris so dear to me."[72]

Production on the picture ended on 7 December and, after a period of post-production, was tested at the El Capitan in Inglewood, a suburb of Los Angeles. Edward Dmytryk was present at that screening. "*The Devil Commands* had been advertised – not *what* the picture was, but just A PREVIEW TONIGHT, the way they usually did," he explained. "The theatre was full, and when the main feature was over, ours came on and it said, COLUMBIA PICTURES PRESENTS BORIS KARLOFF. And half the people got up and walked out [*laughs*]! I thought, 'My God, how do they know that it's lousy this early?' I was *so* let down! Then I recognised that a lot of people in the United States didn't want to see a Karloff picture, no matter what. Those that stayed, *liked* it [*laughs*]! I was always learning something about people, and I learned something about audiences then."[73]

The Devil Commands was released nationally on 3 February 1941. It opened at the Rialto in New York ten days later. The critic for the *New York Times* was less than impressed. "Never have we witnessed upon the screen such a hodge-podge of scientific claptrap,"[74] he wrote. It is unlikely Karloff would have been fazed by such a review. For by now he had embarked upon a new project, one that was far closer to his heart.

In mid-1939, during the making of *The Man They Could Not Hang*, Karloff had revealed a desire to take his career in a new direction. "Whenever a story is written in which a particularly loathsome creature plays the principal part a howl goes up for Karloff, and the meaner the man, the louder the howl," he said. "But if the studio executives chuckle while reading a screen script concerning a light-hearted, whimsical character, do I ever get a thought? Not a chance."[75] The bitterness many comedians expressed about their own lot, he added, proved a constant source of amazement for him. "Imagine anyone being upset because he catches a custard pie with his face or slides into a picture on his head," he commented. "I wonder how they would feel if an iron spike were driven through their head or their limbs twisted out of joint, or some new torture devised by make-up artists applied to their physiognomy... Some day, someone will take pity on a lonely old ghoul. I'll get a chance to play a comedy part. And do you know what will happen? I'll be hissed every time I crack a joke."[76] Then, one day, he received an invitation to lunch by playwright Russel Crouse that would see his wish fulfilled and result in a self-imposed absence from the big screen and a return to his first love – the theatre.

Chapter 14

BACK TO THE BOARDS

(1940-1944)

"And for 10 more years I made these horror films. They were of little importance in anybody's scheme of things, including my own, and though I did earn a disgraceful amount of money, I was getting nowhere. Then out of the blue, three years and one month ago, came this incredible play."[1]

Boris Karloff (1944)

Despite his successful film career Karloff still preferred working in the theatre. "It's live, it's immediate," he later explained, "it's a sustained effort and it's in continuity. It's much harder work than films and much more difficult because films aren't shot in continuity… they're spread over so long a time. It's hard to sustain a thing in film – especially when it's not known in which order it's going to be shown."[2]

Time and circumstance had resulted in Karloff's long periods of absence from the stage. His last major stage work was back in 1930, the year before *Frankenstein*, as the convict Galloway in the Los Angeles production of *The Criminal Code*. "I sneaked into films that way through the back door," Karloff said. "I felt I never knew anything about pictures and always intended to return to the stage. But before I knew it, the years began piling up and [the] next peek I took at that back door, it was slammed close behind me."[3]

In his post-*Frankenstein* days Karloff had, several times, been offered the chance to return to the stage but had so far rejected all offers. Then, at a Hollywood party in mid-1940, Karloff met the playwright Russel Crouse who, with his writing partner Howard Lindsay, had penned the 1946 Pulitzer Prize winning play *State of the Union*. In June 1940 their comedy *Life With Father* was successfully playing on Broadway with Howard Lindsay in the lead role. Now they had a new play – and a proposition for Boris Karloff. So, with Lindsay unavailable due to his New York commitment, Crouse alone invited Karloff to lunch at Lucey's restaurant in Hollywood.

At the lunch Crouse asked if Karloff would like to appear in a play in New York. His question was answered with a resounding "No!" It would be very presumptuous on his part, the star told Crouse, to try to act on Broadway. "I explained," Karloff said, "if he had a play with a good part for me and two parts better than me for which he had good actors I'd go. I wasn't going to lead with my chin on Broadway."[4] Crouse had just the play – a comedy by the playwright Joseph Kesselring.

Kesselring was a former teacher who had shunned an academic career to write short stories and plays. His first play on Broadway, the comedy *There's Wisdom in Women*, opened in October 1935 but ran only until that December. Another comedy, *Cross-town*, opened in April 1937 but had only five performances. Undeterred by his limited success Kesselring took up his pen and began to write a new play – a macabre piece entitled *Bodies in Our Cellar*. He originally intended to write the piece as straight drama until a friend pointed out the story's comic potential. The finished product far surpassed the playwright's previous works. Such was the improvement that many later suspected the involvement of Lindsay and Crouse. It was an accusation the pair strenuously denied.

The play concerned the Brewster sisters, Abby and Martha, who invite lonely old men into their house and, under misguided acts of kindness, dispatch them with a glass of home made elderberry wine laced with arsenic. The sisters' equally deranged brother, Teddy, buries the bodies in the cellar believing them to be yellow fever victims and the cellar to be the excavations for the Panama Canal. Teddy, who also believes himself to be Theodore Roosevelt, punctuates his time in the play with shouts of "Charge!" before rushing up San Juan Hill (i.e. the stairs).

Mortimer, the nephew of this unbalanced trio, stumbles upon his aunts' secret. To make matters worse, his brother Jonathan reappears after 20 years absence and enters the house with his colleague, Dr. Einstein. Jonathan too, it transpires, is a murderer and is on the run from the law. To escape detection Dr. Einstein has changed his face.

Jonathan and Dr. Einstein also discover the old ladies' secret. Jonathan now plans to use the Brewster house as his base of operations – once he has disposed of Mortimer. However, Jonathan's plan is foiled and he and Dr. Einstein are arrested. Mortimer arranges for Teddy and his aunts to be committed to a mental institution and is relieved to discover he was adopted. Realising he is no longer subject to the Brewster's genetic lunatic tendencies he is free to marry his fiancée, Elaine. However, before the sisters depart for their new home they offer a final glass of their homemade wine to Mr. Witherspoon, the man from the institution. The curtain falls as he raises the glass to his lips.

Kesselring sent his finished play to the home of the actor/playwright Howard Lindsay in the hope that his wife, the actress Dorothy Stickney, would be interested in playing one of the sisters. Lindsay passed the manuscript to his wife telling her he did not have time to read it. Stickney began to read and could soon be heard laughing at the material. This aroused Lindsay's curiosity and he asked his wife's opinion of the piece. Stickney told him that nobody could get away with presenting such a subject of somewhat dubious taste on the stage. But, she added, it was very, very funny. Lindsay then read the play and agreed with his wife's assessment. He wired his writing partner, Russel Crouse. "Shake your head, take a cup of coffee and read further," the wire read. "Have just read a play about two charming old ladies who go around murdering old men. Very funny. How would you like to be a producer?"[5] Crouse wired back, "Buy it."[6]

Having reached terms with Kesselring, Lindsay and Crouse began selecting a cast and crew. The French-born Bretaigne Windust had recently directed *Life With Father* and so was engaged to provide his services for the new play. Josephine Hull and Jean Adair were signed to star as the pleasant, but murderous, siblings. Allyn Joslyn would play Mortimer, with John Alexander as Teddy Brewster. The producers had set aside a special role for Karloff, that of the psychotic sibling Jonathan Brewster.

Hearing the plot at Lucey's, Karloff, like Stickney, Lindsay and Crouse before him, was intrigued. "What really sold me on taking the part was a line of Jonathan's in his first scene," he later explained. "He'd just murdered a kindly motorist. Another character says, 'He was a nice chap, that man who gave us a lift. You shouldn't have killed him. Why did you do it?' And Jonathan replies, 'He said I looked like Boris Karloff.' I expected that a line like that, spoofing me so early in the play, would disarm any New York audience."[7]

Karloff's interest led to what Crouse later described as a second "slightly more expensive luncheon"[8] at the end of which the producers had secured the star's services, entering into a professional relationship that would last over three years. Karloff's contract provided a straight salary of over $2,000 per week plus 10% of the box office. In addition, he would receive an additional percentage through any sale of the play's movie rights.

Press reports originally stated there were 21 backers. This was later revised upwards to 23, with donated funds ranging between $250 and $7,500. Karloff, it was reported, invested $6,000. It had not been an immediate decision, though. While he remained undecided the playwrights offered the star a unique opportunity. They would withhold a batch of shares until after the play's first night. This would enable the cautious star to read the reviews before deciding.

Before rehearsals could begin though, Karloff had first to complete work on *The Devil Commands* at Columbia. The picture's director, Edward Dmytryk, accommodated the star by shooting into the night to complete his final scenes. Karloff finished in the early hours then rushed to the airport to catch his plane to New York. The trip, though, gave him the opportunity to mull upon the enormity of his undertaking. "By the time I arrived in New York, I was almost shaking from sheer fright," he said. "I'd rushed through a hard week at Columbia studios, then taken an all-night flight East."[9]

Russel Crouse met Karloff at the airport and accompanied him to the Algonquin Hotel on West 44th Street where Howard Lindsay was waiting. Upon arrival the three immediately engaged in a discussion regarding the play's first rehearsal, scheduled to take place that very afternoon on the empty stage of the Fulton Theatre. The prospect was an unsettling one and Karloff's doubts increased. Later that day he made his way to the Fulton. "At the theatre they handed me a script," he recalled, "and we did something I'd never done in stock or repertory – we sat down, cast and director together, and read cold turkey. I was so tired, and so frightened of my New York role, that I began to stutter – something that always besets me when I'm tired."[10] It was an inauspicious start for the Hollywood movie star. Bruce Gordon, who was cast as Officer Klein, recalled that first read-through. "I was sitting on a bench," he said, "and he was sitting on the other end with people in between, and this bench would be shaking. Quivering. This man was so frightened. He'd light a cigarette and his hand would be shaking. When he got nervous, his stammer would become very pronounced. We would kid about it later, saying, 'This man's a big Hollywood star and he's so nervous. What's he so nervous about?' We were nervous about his being there, and he about not having been on the stage for a long time. He was with New York actors and was scared to death."[11]

The early rehearsals were a trial for Karloff. "I rehearsed in stutters for three days," he explained, "continually thinking that it would cure itself. But instead it grew."[12] His predicament made him anxious and unable to sleep. "I was rotten and I knew it," he said. "I wanted to say, 'I can't go through with it – let me get back to Hollywood.' And I almost did go back."[13]

On the third night he took a long walk up Fifth Avenue to contemplate his predicament. "I thought I'd have to walk up to the management and say, 'I'm very sorry. I've made a mistake, and so have you. I've got to get out of your play. Do I owe you anything?' I walked some more and thought, *If I do that, honest though it is, I've certainly had it in New York and haven't done myself an awful lot of good in Hollywood either. Somehow I've got to go through with the play*."[14] Karloff returned to his hotel at 5:30 a.m. and, after a brief catnap, set off for the rehearsal. "I'd always stuck on the word 'Come' in my first line," he said. "Now I walked on, took a deep breath and said, 'Come in, doctor.' Not a stutter. By that evening all was OK."[15]

The rehearsals improved until, one day, Karloff discovered to his horror he was losing his voice. The oral techniques required in the theatre were playing havoc with his vocal chords. The play's director, Bretaigne Windust, came to the rescue with a homemade cure: a corncob pipe, the bowl of which was filled with cotton soaked in eucalyptus oil. By puffing upon this device and breathing in the soothing vapours Karloff's voice soon returned.

The play was set to open in Baltimore on Thursday, 26 December. The company would have a two-week tryout in the city before opening in New York, but time was running short. One Sunday Howard Lindsay came to watch a run-through. He "tore us apart, we were so terrible," Bruce Gordon recalled. "Oh, it was awful, and he set us on the right path."[16]

Karloff spent part of Christmas Day dressed as Santa at a party in Baltimore for children with disabilities. The next day *Arsenic and Old Lace* opened at the Maryland Theatre. Donald Kirkley of the *Baltimore Sun* called it "the funniest play about murder in the history of the stage",[17] even if, he added, some members of the audience were "somewhat bewildered by the multiplicity of the corpses."[18] These performances, and the seven-days-a-week rehearsals, were the company's final chance to iron out any wrinkles before opening at Broadway's Fulton Theatre, which Lindsay and Crouse had hired for $850 per week. As this figure covered only the building's rent the producers also paid all operating costs.

Following the Baltimore shows the company returned to New York. Dorothy Karloff arrived from California, having left Sara Jane with her nanny, and joined her husband in a rented apartment in the Lombardy Hotel on East 56th Street. Her presence at the play's opening night, however, did nothing to alleviate her husband's first night nerves. "I only hope I can stagger through," Karloff had told journalists. "Ever since last June, when I first got the part, I've been living in fright. Why, I haven't faced a real live audience in 10 years – and I've never been on the New York stage before."[19]

The curtain rose on *Arsenic and Old Lace* at the Fulton Theatre in New York at 8:35 p.m. on Friday, 10 January 1941. While the theatrical critics took the first few rows celebrities, including Charlie Chaplin, could be spotted in the auditorium. Lindsay and Crouse had also extended an invitation to the entire staff of the theatrical union Equity to attend the opening. It was the first time the organisation had received such an offer.

As Howard Lindsay was appearing in *Life With Father* that night he could not be present at *Arsenic*'s premiere. Instead Crouse kept him informed between acts with bulletins as to how the audience was receiving the play. Crouse had also received a telegram of his own, a

Left: Karloff and Edgar Stehli make their entrance in *Arsenic and Old Lace*. Right: Menacing Allyn Joslyn later in the play.

customary first night message 'from' one of his house cats, 'Miss Frothingham'. "Tell me if it's a hit," the wire read. "Curiosity is almost killing me."[20]

Initially the producers had been concerned about the play's reception. "It is my studied conviction that we either have a very big hit or we'll be run out of town,"[21] Lindsay told Crouse on opening night. However, any fears over the plays macabre subject matter were quickly dispelled as the audience could soon be heard roaring with laughter. "From the moment the curtain went up you knew it was going over," Dorothy Karloff wrote to her mother. "The audience started to laugh – and it just never stopped. They were the most wonderful audience I've ever seen – they applauded and cheered and yelled, 'Bravo' and 'Speech' – and after about 15 curtain call, Boris and the two old ladies had tears streaming down their face – and I was weeping – and it was just colossal – the whole thing."[22]

An after-show party was held at the apartment of one of the show's backers. When Josephine Hull went to a midnight dinner at Sardi's she was greeted by a standing ovation led by actor Henry Hull. As the cast and crew celebrated Brooks Atkinson of the *New York Times* penned his review. "Although there have been some other good plays recently, this is the freshest invention," he wrote. "It is full of chuckles even when the scene is gruesome by nature... There could hardly be sweeter ladies than the two played by Josephine Hull and Jean Adair. Allyn Joslyn gives an amazingly humorous and resourceful performance as the frightened drama critic. As the evil one, Mr. Karloff moves quietly through plot and poison without resorting to trickeries, and Edger Stehli is light footed in the part of a satellite."[23] Atkinson was not alone in his praise. "Messrs. Lindsay and Crouse have waved their wand again, and produced a masterpiece," wrote the *Wall Street Journal*.[24]

For Karloff it was the icing on the cake – the best possible result after so much worry and self-doubt. In fact, such was his anxiety throughout the rehearsal period, and the first night performance, Karloff claimed to have lost 25 pounds. "It was sheer terror for me," he later admitted.[25]

The good news travelled fast and the next day a steady line of people could be seen outside the Fulton queuing for tickets for that evening's performance. By the early afternoon all available tickets had been sold. In fact, such was the demand for future bookings a third treasurer, Dan Melnick, was transferred from the Cort Theatre to assist the box

Top: Karloff at home at 124 East 62nd Street during the New York run of *Arsenic and Old Lace*. Opposite: Father and daughter in New York.

office staff, Harry Martin and Leo Miller. Still it was not enough and a fourth treasurer, Cora Gibbs, was enlisted to help out temporarily by filling mail orders. A second box-office window was also installed on Monday, 20 January.

Initially, though, there had been some complaints about the ticket prices. For despite the advertisements stating tickets would be available at 55 cents the price list hanging in the Fulton Theatre's lobby included no such ticket price, the cheapest ticket on sale being $1.10. To rectify this Russel Crouse announced immediate action had been taken and two rows of balcony seats would be available for the promised 55 cents for the duration of the play's run.

On Sunday, 12 January – Karloff's first day off – he took Dorothy to meet actor/producer Maurice Evans at his country home. This may possibly have been to discuss Evans' revival of *Macbeth*, which would open that November with Karloff as one of the play's backers. While Karloff's association with Evans would later bear theatrical fruit it would also provide a more significant impact upon his life – by introducing Karloff to a woman who would become increasing important in his life – Evans' assistant Evelyn Hope Helmore.

Evelyn, or Evie as she was known, was born in Putney, South West London in 1904. After leaving school she got a job working at a London dry cleaning establishment owned by struggling-actors Maurice Evans and Tom Helmore. Soon Evie was managing the business and her relationship with Helmore blossomed. In 1931 the two were married and when Tom's career finally took off the couple moved to America. Evie later became Evans' assistant, and through him met Boris Karloff.

From all accounts the backstage shenanigans of the *Arsenic and Old Lace* cast and crew almost matched the onstage antics. Lindsay and Crouse were in the habit of sending jokey telegrams to the play's backers. Within weeks of the New York opening the first cheque went out to the backers with a letter from the producers. "Dear Angel," it read. "Enclosed you will find our first statement. We think it is a charming document and hope that others more charming will follow. If there is anything in this about which you want to complain, we shall be glad to hear from you. Just address us care of the Dead Letter Office, Washington D.C."[26] More would follow.

After his initial indecision over whether or not to invest in the play Karloff became the focus for Lindsay and Crouse's teasing. Once the 'Beamish Ones' as Karloff referred to them,[i] arranged to have the star's weekly salary delivered entirely in nickels. The accusation of 'penny-pinching' was one that has often been levelled against Karloff. Cast member Bruce Gordon, however, was one of many who had the opposite experience. After the play's run had ended Karloff and Gordon kept in touch. "I was in boot camp in Idaho,"

---

i According to the Oxford English Dictionary 'Beamish' is a 16th century word meaning 'shining brightly, radiant.'

Gordon later told Gordon Shriver, "and he made it possible for me to come to Los Angeles on my liberty by sending me $50. Not that I had any money. We were only getting about $60 a month maybe. That was something. Bowled me over."[27]

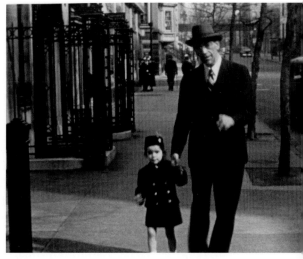

Karloff's skin tone also became a target for Lindsay and Crouse. "We're not playing *Uncle Tom's Cabin*," the producers once wrote him. "If I were earning a decent salary I could afford some powder," the star wired back.[28] The producers' assistant, and Crouse's later wife, Anna Erskine later described how this developed. "During the first summer the play ran, Boris got even darker," she said, "and Howard and Russel told him he was going to have to purchase some white powder to look less healthy. He objected that it wasn't called for in his contract, so I was sent out to buy every form of powder on the market – foot, roach, baby, tooth, baking, gunpowder, Seidlitz powders and powdered eggs. I remember wrapping it all in a Bergdorf Goodman dress box and delivering it to the Fulton Theatre."[29] It was certainly a fun working relationship. "We spent all out spare time exchanging insulting telegrams," Karloff later said.[30] The star also became the focus for other mischievous members of the troupe. To ascertain Karloff's sense of humour Bruce Gordon, in collaboration with the play's stage manager Walter Wagner, drafted a light-hearted rebuff aimed at the star. "[We] devised a long letter with a legal stamp at the end as to why Boris Karloff should not be permitted in the city of New York or in the theatre," Gordon recalled. "He was all wrong for the part, and there were other actors who could have played the part."[31] The letter was pinned to the callboard where Karloff soon posted a response. Gordon and Wagner then posted a new diatribe. This continued until Karloff triumphed. "Finally," Gordon explained, "he sent his secretary down to Chinatown, and had an answer written in Chinese red. That, of course, was the clincher because nobody could translate it."[32]

However, Karloff too could be the instigator of such japes. In mid-June 'Chubby' – a member of the backstage crew – had all his teeth removed and was fitted for a set of upper and lower plates. The day after he had his new teeth installed Chubby received a gift – a large crate – and packed inside was a side of beef weighing over 80 pounds. A note accompanied the gift. "Try them on these – Boris," it read.[33]

Arsenic and Old Lace had brought to the public eye another aspect of Boris Karloff – people now realised the horror star could be funny. His humorous side could also be witnessed when, on Friday, 24 January 1941, the star made his first appearance on the radio quiz show *Information Please*. Hosted by Clifton Fadiman the show featured a panel of experts who would attempt to answer questions submitted by members of the public. Should the experts fail the questioner would earn a cash prize (at that time $25) and a complete set of the Encyclopaedia Britannica. Each week a guest would join the resident experts; columnists John Kieran, Franklin P. Adams and composer Oscar Levant. As Levant was absent from the show Karloff was joined for his first appearance by Lewis E. Lawes, the long-standing warden of Sing Sing Prison. The half-hour show was broadcast from 8:30

p.m., which allowed Karloff fifteen minutes to get to the theatre to prepare to make his first entrance at 9:15 p.m. This gave him plenty of time to prepare for a role that required only the usual stage make-up – plus the occasional trip to Elizabeth Arden's salon on Fifth Avenue to have his hair dyed to remove the traces of grey.

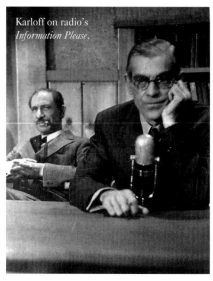

Karloff on radio's *Information Please*.

On *Information Please* that evening Karloff successfully answered questions on the tales of *Mother Goose*, the play *Charley's Aunt* and correctly identified scenes from *Paid in Full* and *Bought and Paid For*, plays he had appeared in during his touring days in Canada. However, it was his very first answer, during a pre-quiz chat, which caused some contention. Fadiman began by asking Karloff how many murders the play *Arsenic and Old Lace* contained. "26," came the reply. Fadiman's answer card, however, stated there were 25 murders – an assertion supported by Franklin P. Adams. "I have a perfect tally of 13," Karloff countered, "the old ladies have 12 and at the end of they play they get Mr. Witherspoon – which makes 13 for them. It's a tie still, that makes a grand total of 26."

Brooks Atkinson addressed the thorny subject the following month in his article for the *New York Times*. "In *Arsenic and Old Lace* they [the murders] achieve a fantastification that is wholly uproarious. As a matter of fact, they are so prodigal that the final score is in doubt," he wrote. "To settle that minor dispute, this column is in the fortunate position of being able to present the official finding. Here it is: the lovable aunties have poisoned 12 homeless gentlemen,[ii] and they poison their thirteenth in the last scene. Jonathan Brewster, who is really Boris Karloff, has an undisputed score of 12, which makes a total of 25. But Karloff also claims for his side a case in South Bend, which his associate assassin insists on writing off as death from natural causes. Whether the total carnage of the play is 25 or 26 depends, therefore, upon your faith in Karloff's judgment, experience and principle."[34]

In early February Howard Lindsay held a supper party at his house to which Boris Karloff was, naturally, invited. When Lindsay's sister-in-law asked the star if he would like to look around the house Karloff readily agreed. A group of guests assembled and the impromptu tour began. "What made you suggest this tour?" Dorothy Stickney whispered to her sister. "I just want to hear what my friends will say when I tell them I went upstairs with Boris Karloff," came the reply.[35]

As the New York show was such a hit Lindsay and Crouse decided to create a second company to take the play on the road. The only question was who to cast as Jonathan Brewster. "I wish we could perform a Karloff horror operation on Boris to split him in two so we can have two Karloffs – one for the road show," joked Russel Crouse.[36] On 18 February the producers officially announced that the role had been filled by actor/director Erich von Stroheim and Karloff was soon photographed with his road show counterpart. A letter from Crouse to the investors joked about the new production. "We have a Chicago

---

ii In fact – and to make matters more confusing – the first of the spinster's victims also died of natural causes. It was that peaceful death that inspired the sisters to embark on their murderous cause.

company in rehearsal with Erich von Stroheim in the lead," it said. "We wanted Al Capone, but couldn't afford to pay the back taxes. I might also add, to be on the safe side, we are holding two tickets at the Fulton Theatre every night in the name of Adolf Hitler. However, wait 'til he sits in them! You need not reply to this letter, but if it comes to our ears that you have any objections to the way this office is being operated, we will be glad to send you, free of charge, one bottle of Aunt Martha's elderberry wine."[37]

In the first summer of the Broadway run Lindsay, Crouse and Karloff received a telegram from one John Reinhardt in Buenos Aires. "I went to South America to direct a couple of movies," Reinhardt explained. "In the evening I went to the theatre for relaxation, but instead of having any fun I was bored to death. You could hear the audience yawning and snoring. There was no enthusiasm. Something completely new and dynamic was needed. The most original play I could think of was *Arsenic and Old Lace*. I decided to put it on."[38]

Having received the producers' agreement Reinhardt set about assembling a cast. To play Jonathan Brewster Reinhardt found Marciso Ibanez Menta, an actor with a natural resemblance to Karloff. Menta had played the Phantom of the Opera in a stage version of the tale and claimed to have taken make-up lessons from Lon Chaney Sr. himself.

The Argentinean production of *Arsenic and Old Lace* opened in November 1941 at the Astral Theatre. The house was packed that night, for the first time in years. When the play ended the auditorium rang with applause. There were no less than 37 curtain calls. At the end of the first week the play had taken 44,000 pesos ($10,000), an unheard-of sum for that theatre. Following this venture's success Lindsay and Crouse sent news to the backers: "You heard the good news from Buenos Aires, where we were terrificos! We are negotiating some South American bookings if we can find a guy who looks like Karloff and does the conga."[39]

Other companies followed suit and productions of *Arsenic and Old Lace* sprang up around the globe, from Montevideo (also staged by Reinhardt) and Mexico City to London and Gothenburg in Sweden. "We get no money," Lindsay and Crouse told the press, "but we get good notices."[40] However, the producers refused to allow productions in Spain and Denmark. "It's too good for Fascists," they explained.[41] There would be a children's version of the play, performed by a cast that ranged in age from seven to twelve and, on the evening of Sunday, 10 May 1942, a production by the deaf, the first public presentation of the play in sign language.

Lindsay and Crouse had received a request from the dramatic club of Gallaudet College, Washington – the only college for the deaf in the United States – to perform their version of the play. The producers agreed and, in addition, donated the use of the theatre, the set, transportation for the troupe, "and other items so that the receipts may go to the dramatic club of the college, to be used in furtherance of its work in the drama."[42] In addition, following two weeks of rehearsal in Washington, Bretaigne Windust would direct the cast for three days prior to the performance. Karloff visited the troupe during rehearsals and was photographed helping the make-up girl, Julia Berg, preparing student Eric Malzkuhn for his role as Jonathan Brewster.

The production was an enlightening experience, as Karloff recalled. "We went along for politeness' sake," he admitted, "expecting to creep out after a few minutes. But I have never seen anything so fascinating in my life. It's a beautifully written play, with witty, economical dialogue, but the *speed* of that production, the short cuts they could take playing it completely in mime and lose nothing – even in the dark scenes, where all you could see were two pairs of disembodied luminous hands conversing on the darkened stage! It was a real lesson in dramatic expressiveness to me, and one I've never forgotten. I think we tend to forget that stage, film and television are all visual media, and that for most of the time words alone are so much less important than we take them to be."[43]

Karloff's time in New York also gave him the perfect opportunity to engage in more radio, most notably in the new series *Inner Sanctum*, which was broadcast on Sunday evenings when there was no show of *Arsenic and Old Lace*. Created by Himan Brown the series would tell stories of suspense, thrills and the macabre. Karloff's first appearance in the series – in *The Man of Steel* – was broadcast at 8:30 p.m. on Sunday, 16 March 1941.

Even with the steady income from the play Karloff still actively sought work as Brown recalled. "Whenever he was between pictures, he would call me and I'd fit him in. He was very popular with my audience and I didn't always play him to 'type'… He was the easiest actor to work with and he could play anything."[44]

Following each broadcast Karloff and Brown would dine together. "In those days," Brown said, "we had no tape and the repeat performance for the Coast, which came three hours later, had to be live. I always looked forward to those dinners before we returned for the repeat performance."[45] Over the time Karloff was in New York with *Arsenic and Old Lace* he would appear in 18 episodes. Unfortunately, only a handful of these recordings are known to survive.

Karloff made other radio appearances during his New York stay, occasionally appearing on talk shows such as *The Voice of Broadway*, where he often discussed *Arsenic and Old Lace*. Other times he was a guest on the variety shows of stars like Eddie Cantor and Groucho Marx – or supporting the war effort by appearing on programs such as *Bundles for Britain*.

In early March 1941, with the play now looking set for a long run, Karloff rented a large furnished apartment at 45 East Sixty-Sixth Street. The following month Dorothy had a brief holiday when she and a friend took a 1,900-mile road trip down the East Coast. When she returned Dorothy and Sara Jane joined Karloff at 'Blue Spruce', a stone house he had rented in the Tokeneke section of Darien, Connecticut.

A journalist who went to the house to meet Karloff found the star "in blue slacks and mussed white linen shirt, a pair of white 'sneakers' and white socks."[46] At the time of the visit Karloff was found pondering the problem of his daughter's dolly's pushed-in face. First the star tried a remedy used to take dents out of ping-pong balls, and immersed the doll's head in a glass of hot water. When this process proved to be too slow Karloff resorted to using the heat from a lighted candle – with disastrous results. The doll's head went up in smoke. Sara Jane, who had been watching her father's efforts, picked up her celluloid duck and, after telling him the duck had a little dent declared, "See, there? But the duck is alright, Daddy."[47]

The house's location in the Connecticut countryside meant a train ride each night after the show. The curtain came down each evening at 11 p.m. and Karloff would then go to dinner, usually at Sardi's, before taking the midnight train home. He originally walked the two blocks from the theatre to the restaurant but was soon forced to start taking cabs due to the number of autograph hunters that would regularly accost him. When, in mid-1941, he attempted once more to walk the route he was followed by two drunks who shouted after him, "We're not afraid of you. Boo!"[48] He reverted to taking cabs. Karloff would arrive back at 'Blue Spruce' at about 1:30 a.m. He would then rise late – often past noon – before making the return journey back to New York and the Fulton Theatre.

Even when Karloff was not due at the theatre he had little respite for now, with the war raging in Europe, fund-raisers had become a constant feature during the star's stay in New York. In January he had been one of the stars of stage, screen and radio that had conducted a variety of games in the Monte Carlo Room of the Waldorf Astoria as part of the evening's 'Scotch Ball'. The event, with its Scottish pipers and dancing, raised funds for the war effort under the auspices of the British-American Ambulance Corps for four Scottish war relief organisations. Dorothy, too, aided the causes and the following month became a member of the committee of the 'Soldiers and Sailors Club of New York' and helped organise the supper and entertainment held on 19 February at the Algonquin Supper Club.

On 9 April, the Karloffs attended a benefit for British Naval Officers in the Rainbow Room of the Rockefeller Centre. They were back in the Rainbow Room on 8 October, this time supporting the American Theatre Wing of the British War Relief Society. Other times Karloff had a more hands-on approach, serving food at the American Canteen, or raising money for the American Theatre Wing.

In May, Karloff, along with Victor Mature, had sold tickets for the 'Greek Fashion festival' held at the St. Moritz for the Greek War Relief Association Inc. The following month he joined other *Information Please* regulars John Kieran, Franklin P. Adams and Deems Taylor in a game of doubles tennis at the West Side Tennis Club, Forest Hills for the benefit of the War Relief Fund. They were introduced onto the court by *Information Please* host Clifton Fadiman. In early July Karloff was announced as the divisional chairmen for 'drama' for the newly organised artists' 'Auxiliary of Bundles for Britain, Inc.'

Then, at the end of the month, the production was shaken by the sudden death of cast member William Parke. The actor had come out of retirement to play the spinsters' final victim, Mr. Witherspoon, the superintendent of the asylum. On 28 July Parke suffered a fatal heart attack at his home. He was 68 years old. The funeral was held on 30 July at the Church of the Transfiguration (The Little Church around the Corner) at One East 29th Street. Boris Karloff and Allyn Joslyn were among the honorary pallbearers while other members of the cast and crew also attended the service.

The success of *Arsenic and Old Lace* naturally drew the interest of Hollywood and in early February 1941 columnist Louella Parsons revealed Warner Brothers had purchased the film rights for $100,000 – a figure that was later revised upwards to $175,000. Karloff, Parsons added, was being sought to recreate his role on screen along with, possibly, Marjorie Rambeau and May Robson as the murderous spinsters. Later that month Hedda Hopper claimed it was Edward G. Robinson who had persuaded Warners to buy the play after he saw it in New York. According to the columnist, Robinson was even lined up for the role of Jonathan Brewster. However, none of these casting assertions panned out.

Instead, Warners arranged with Lindsay and Crouse to use only certain members of the stage company in the film – the Brewster siblings, Josephine Hull, Jean Adair and John Alexander. Karloff, unfortunately, did not get the opportunity to commit his role to film and was replaced by Raymond Massey. This appears to have rankled with the star, although Anna Crouse (née Erskine) believed it was all due to a misunderstanding. "There is one strange conflict in a story about Boris and the film of *Arsenic*," she later said. "Howard and Russel always credited him with being a sweetheart and a gentleman in allowing Josephine and Jean to play the picture while he stayed in New York and kept the play going. 'What a saintly thing to do for two old ladies,' they said. I have heard rumours that he was bitter he did not make the picture and somehow blamed Howard and Russel. I know they went to their deaths believing that Boris offered to stay with the play."[49]

The film version went into production on 20 October 1941 under the direction of Frank Capra. Shooting lasted until mid-December during which time the three members of the stage company absent in Hollywood were replaced by Patricia Collinge, Minnie Dupree and Harry Gribbon.

Karloff's replacement in the movie, Raymond Massey, was apparently not too keen on being made up to look like his co-star from *The Old Dark House*. The studio had reportedly sent make-up men to New York to make a plaster cast of Karloff's head for reference and the resultant make-up took two hours to apply to Massey's face. Instead, Massey allegedly tried to have the play's Karloff reference changed to Abraham Lincoln – whom Massey had already portrayed on film. The front office refused. Although the film version of *Arsenic and Old Lace* ended production in-mid December 1941 a clause in the contract with Lindsay and Crouse prevented the picture's release until the stage play of *Arsenic and Old Lace* had finished its run. Capra's movie finally opened at the Strand in New York on Friday, 1 September 1944.

On 6 November 1941, with the replacement members of the cast in place, a special matinee was held at the Fulton Theatre. The event was part of the Control Board of the New York City School Program which arranged showings at a reduced cost (in this instance, ten cents) enabling students to attend the theatre. The performance that afternoon received 12 curtain calls and the invitation to the students to come backstage and get Karloff's autograph was answered with a stampede.

The 23rd of November was Karloff and Sara Jane's birthday and to celebrate a party was thrown at 'Blue Spruce'. For her third birthday, Sara Jane received a playhouse from her parents. Three days later the Karloffs attended a literary breakfast at the Waldorf Astoria held by the Limited Editions Club. The event was arranged to present a gold medal to the author whose book, published within the last three years, the judges felt, would most likely "attain the status of a classic."[50] The award went to Ernest Hemingway's novel *For Whom the Bell Tolls*.

That evening, Karloff was back on the benefit circuit, this time appearing as one of the stars at the eighth annual *Night of the Stars* at Madison Square Gardens for the benefit of the United Jewish Appeal. Joining him at the event were many other celebrities including Groucho Marx, Eve Arden, Ray Bolger, Lillian Hellman, Danny Kaye, Sophie Tucker, Errol Flynn and Lana Turner.

The next day – Thanksgiving Day – Karloff bought two tickets for the annual Army-Navy college football game at the Municipal Stadium in Philadelphia. Knowing when he purchased the tickets that his *Arsenic and Old Lace* commitments excluded him from going, Karloff suggested his wife go with family friend, Bob Beckham. To avoid the crowds expected for Saturday's parade Dorothy and Beckham left New York on Friday night – but Dorothy had planned on more than just seeing the game, as Beckham later revealed. "We went to Philadelphia on the train to see the Army-Navy football game the big weekend in November. And, lo and behold, as we got into the lobby of the hotel where we were staying, Dorothy said, 'Well, what a surprise! There's Edgar Rowe, of all people!' So they had a very nice rendezvous in Philadelphia. Obviously, it was all arranged. I was the escort for Dorothy, and probably the excuse so she could get out of town and meet Edgar for a little rendezvous in Philadelphia."[51]

Edgar Rowe had been introduced to Dorothy by one of her long-standing bridge partners, Bob Beckham's mother, Mae. Over the following years Dorothy and Edgar's relationship would deepen, and with hindsight it seems apparent their affection grew as the Karloff marriage began to fail, possibly due to the actor's insistence on continual work.

One can only speculate why Boris Karloff continued to work as much as he did, especially with a wife and young daughter waiting at home. Perhaps it was a reaction to the hard times he had been through in his youth. Maybe the fickle nature of the movie business urged him to make hay while the sun shone. Of course it may just be he simply loved to work.

Now he was earning a steady income, more than enough to live comfortably on. *Arsenic and Old Lace* was paying dividends. In May 1941, only four months after opening, the play was reported to have earned Karloff $50,000 (excluding his salary) from his initial $6,000 investment. Whatever his reason, it seems to have had a detrimental effect on his marriage. Dorothy, perhaps lonely, forged her friendship with Edgar Rowe and, while any surreptitious meetings between the two appear to have been chaperoned, things would soon develop. However, in the early years of the play's run in New York, at least, all seemed calm. There would soon be bigger concerns for all.

On the morning of Sunday, 7 December 1941 the Japanese attacked the American fleet at the Hawaiian Naval Base on Pearl Harbor. It was a date President Roosevelt later announced would "live in infamy". America was now in the war and the country began to mobilise. Karloff and Dorothy were both keen to enlist their services. They had already been involved in raising funds for various causes. Now Dorothy sold defence bonds and even took a course in aircraft spotting.

The Karloffs would spend that Christmas at 124 East 62nd Street, a house they had leased for the remainder of the play's New York run. Then, on 23 December, Karloff once again donned a Santa suit for the benefit of children. He arrived at the Beekman Hospital on the lower East Side to pay a visit to two hundred underprivileged children. Aided by the former Governor, Alfred E. Smith, the star handed out gifts to the children – either patients or outpatients – aged between five and twelve years old.

While every child received a stocking filled with small toys and sweets Karloff presented each with an additional, bigger, toy. However, this benevolence caused a small riot as the clinic was swamped by the enthusiastic children who nearly upset the large Christmas tree. Four policemen from the Oak Street station had to be recruited to help the staff in restraining the children. Karloff then took a tour of the wards wishing the patients a merry Christmas. It was "very exciting",[52] he said, to see the children's eyes light up as he walked the wards although, he added, "I think they were much too interested in the Christmas tree to notice me very much."[53]

On the evening of 10 January 1942, the *Arsenic and Old Lace* company celebrated their first anniversary on Broadway with a party at the Cottage Club. During the evening the cast did turns. Even Lindsay and Crouse rose to the occasion and sang a comedy song about the show's backers. Karloff, Stehli, Adair and Hull performed a scene from the play, but mixed up the parts. The men took the roles of the two aunts while Hull and Adair portrayed Jonathan and Dr. Einstein respectively. Dorothy Karloff thought the whole evening "lots of fun".[54]

Ten days later the Karloffs reported to a New York police station to be fingerprinted and photographed for Civilian Defence work. Dorothy would soon begin work as a secretary at Air Warden Sector Headquarters. Karloff, meanwhile, would become an air-raid warden and was required to be on duty from midnight till 8 a.m. on every third Thursday.[iii]

That evening, Karloff made a return appearance on *Information Please*. Originally he had been scheduled for the 13 February show but had cancelled citing a fear of that date. Although the excuse was fake, his trepidation over the second appearance was not. "What an ass I am," Karloff wrote. "I was so lucky the last time that I swore I'd never do it again, but Russel Crouse talked me into it, the scoundrel."[55] When he made this second appearance a week later the show's host, Clifton Fadiman, mentioned the previous cancellation due to the star's alleged fear. "I made a mistake, Mr. Fadiman," Karloff joked. "I meant the 20th." Joining Karloff on the show this time was his old stage and film acquaintance John Carradine, who punctuated the proceedings with recitations from his beloved Shakespeare.

In early March Karloff's commitment to the war effort saw him donate a pint of blood at the Red Cross. When he explained where he had been Crouse asked, "What are they planning to do with your blood – give it to a Jap?" Karloff replied, "They're saving it for the day when the zoo is bombed. Then they'll give it to the gorilla."[56] Then, on the evening of Tuesday, 10 March Karloff joined stars of stage, screen and radio when he appeared in the Navy Relief Show at Madison Square Garden. Before a crowd in excess of 20,000 Karloff, Eddie Cantor, Danny Kaye, Vincent Price, Clifton Webb and Ed Wynn took the stage in drag as the 'Floradora Sextet' in a number conceived and directed by Kaye's wife, Sylvia Fine. Karloff wore a yellow-sequin dress and a large yellow hat for the skit, while Price sported the beard he had grown for the play *Angel Street*, then playing at the Golden Theatre.

Another of the evening's comedic highlights came from an unexpected source, as journalist Dorothy Pratt later explained. "All the other film celebrities contributed turns except one," she wrote. "A famous star who was capable of only looking decorative. So when her turn came, she walked over to the microphone swathed in mink and glittering in diamonds and said in honeyed tones, 'I just wanted to tell you how happy I am to be here to bring relief to the Navy.' There was an instant's stunned silence, then a roar went up from the huge audience that nearly took the roof off. 'The poor girl couldn't think what they were laughing at,' says Karloff, 'which of course only made everyone laugh the more!'"[57] The show was a great success and made $156,000 for the fund.

There were further antics on Friday, 13 March when the company staged a midnight horror party for the press in, what *Life* magazine called "a ghostly brownstone mansion near Gramercy Park, in Manhattan. Through a cellar door and up a creaky staircase trooped members of the cast of *Arsenic and Old Lace*… There were John Kieran and F.P.A. [Franklin P. Adams], Howard Lindsay and Russel Crouse… Frank Sullivan and Lucius Beebe, many other Broadway characters who had fun talking shop, being scared, drinking, gossiping with Beebe. Notably, no-one was camera shy."[58]

On that following Thursday air-raid warden Karloff made his way to the sector headquarters, situated in the basement of the Hotel Beekman. At 1 a.m. the next morning, while still on duty, he put pen to paper and wrote a letter to his mother-in-law, Louise Stine. "Good morning, or rather, good afternoon Mother, how are you," he wrote. "I'll give you ten guesses as to where I am writing from. Down in the basement of the

iii The Karloffs had already made provision for the eventuality of a blackout by hanging torches around their house.

Karloff and Evie leaving a show.

Hotel Beekman, just round the corner from the house!.. Wadeah [Karloff's housekeeper] has put up a lunch for me that would feed an army & I'm as comfortable as can be & a wonderful chance to write letters."[59] Karloff then informed Louise he was currently reading *Mission to Moscow* by former Ambassador Joseph E. Davies. He planned to follow that with Steinbeck's *The Moon is Down* and then *Mr. Lincoln's Funnybone*, an anthology of the president's best 'yarns and fables'. Then there was word of Dorothy and Sara. "Really good news about the family at last," he continued. "They are all leaving for home the last of April to open up the house etc & I'll be home the end of June to do the Columbia Picture [*The Boogie Man Will Get You*] & then take a three weeks vacation & could I use it! After that back to the play most likely on the road & perhaps opening in San Francisco, so you'll have a chance to see it at last in Los Angeles! Honestly I'm so homesick I could burst & the closer it gets to seeing all of you again the harder it is to wait. Dorothy & Sara Jane are fine. The last one knows so much & talks so much – she springs a new surprise every day! It's been a very mild winter & she has come through beautifully. The cold has been good for her but I do want her to be running around in some of that good sun!"[60]

That month Karloff had also played host to almost one hundred young high school magazine editors who convened at the Fulton Theatre one Saturday afternoon to interview the star. The young reporters asked him if he preferred the theatre to movies. "Hollywood work is easier," Karloff told them. "You can have a very pleasant time on the set between takes. You can relax and forget about your role until the director calls 'Camera! Action!' On the stage you cannot relax for one minute. You have to maintain your own interest in the play or you are sunk with an audience. Yes, it's quite a strain. But the work is really more enjoyable. Nothing can take the place of an audience. It's fun to see and hear them."[61]

A long run in a play, though, was dangerous, Karloff told them. Such familiarity with the work could easily result in your walking through the play. "I have to pretend each time that it is the first performance," he explained.[62] Karloff was then asked whether he preferred to live in New York or Hollywood. "I lived in the country last summer," he replied, "but when the weather turned cold I brought the family to the city. You see, I have no understudy: If I failed to arrive for the show, it would be called off. I felt that in fairness to the other players and the management I could not risk being snowed up in the country."[63]

On 3 May, Karloff made another appearance on radio's *Inner Sanctum*. This time he played a psychiatrist, Herbert Large, who seeks to discover the psychological reasons for murder, hoping, by doing so, to help others avoid such a terrible course of action. To aid his research he surrounds himself with underworld associates but soon finds himself spiralling downwards into a life of crime – and murder.

Two weeks later, on Saturday, 16 May, he tackled the macabre in a different way when he penned the forward to the first anthology of cartoonist Charles Addams' works, *Drawn and Quartered*. "Addams seems to me to be the one comedic artist today whose drawings need no letterpress at all," Karloff wrote. "Supremely he has achieved the primary and essential purpose of any drawing, serious or comic, which is to tell a story graphically in one blinding flash without a single written word of explanation... Perhaps Mr. Addams is happiest in his dealing with the macabre. His preoccupation with hangman's nooses and lethal doses is always innocent and gay. He has the extraordinary faculty of making the normal appear idiotic when confronted by the abnormal, as in his scenes of cannibals, skiers and skaters. Somehow one never dreams of questioning his premise, but only the rather childish alarm of the onlookers."[64]

The next day, as their time in the city neared its end, the Karloffs held a farewell party for 30 guests in the Victorian suite of New York's prestigious Carlyle Hotel. Dorothy now prepared to leave for their home back in California and on Sunday, 31 May, she and Sara Jane left New York on *The Chief* bound for Los Angeles.

After the curtain fell on Saturday, 27 June 1942 Karloff left *Arsenic and Old Lace*, albeit temporarily, in order to return to Hollywood to make his long-planned final picture from the Columbia contract, the comedy *The Boogie Man Will Get You*. On the following Monday Erich von Stroheim made his Broadway debut when he took the stage as Jonathan Brewster at the Fulton Theatre.

Karloff's contract with Columbia had given the studio the right to make the picture anytime between 1 June and 1 October 1941. Originally, he was scheduled to leave the play in June to make the picture. To keep Karloff in the play, however, Lindsay and Crouse, it was reported, made a cash settlement "to another actor"[65] who was to have appeared in a picture with the star. Although the report lacked further details it most probably referred to Peter Lorre and the picture *The Boogie Man Will Get You*. Columbia later postponed the picture again, this time until the following February, and after further negotiations with Lindsay and Crouse revised the picture's start date once more, to 15 June.

The Boogie Man Will Get You was a thinly veiled attempt to recreate the success of *Arsenic and Old Lace*. In it Karloff played Professor Nathaniel Billings, a scientist who conducts experiments in the basement of his dilapidated old Colonial Inn. Billings sells the building to Winnie Layden [Jeff Donnell] on condition he can continue his experiments in the cellar. The scientist, it transpires, is trying to transform men into supermen for the war effort but each of his attempts has, so far, met with failure. Taking the local doctor and lawman Lorentz [Peter Lorre] as a partner, the pair persuade a gullible door-to-door salesman, Maxie [Maxie Rosenbloom], to be their next subject. However, when Winnie and her ex-husband Bill [Larry Parks] find the bodies they call the police. Then, somewhat bizarrely, an escaped fascist aviator enters the basement, but his plan to blow up a local munitions plant fails when the 'bodies' – not dead, but in suspended animation – rise up. The police arrive and determine to take Billings and the rest of the household to the local asylum. Dr. Lorenz, however, tells Billings not to worry, for he is the Chairman of the asylum's Board of Directors.

Production began on Monday, 6 July 1942 under the direction of Lew Landers.[iv] Production seems to have been a light-hearted affair. 21-year old actress Jeff Donnell

---

iv The director had worked with the star before. In 1935 Landers, then credited as Louis Friedlander, directed Karloff and Lugosi in *The Raven*.

was, it was reported, often the focus of the cast and crew's teasing. One day, during a lull between set-ups, Karloff was sitting with Peter Lorre and Donnell. Around Karloff's middle was tied a dainty pink apron. "You know," he said, shaking his head. "I don't know what the films are coming to. I kill six people in this picture but none of the killings take. What kind of business is that for a man who slaughtered a score of victims and thought nothing of it?"[66]

Peter Lorre grinned. "This is a real holiday for me," he said. "I do carry a gun, but I don't have to kill anyone."[67] As Lorre suddenly whipped out his revolver, Donnell jumped and screamed. "It isn't loaded," he assured her and pulled the trigger six times.[68]

"Imagine," Donnell replied, "an unloaded gun that lives up to its reputation."[69]

"It's just like this picture." Karloff added. "A lot of killings, but they're all blanks."[70]

Director Lew Landers then arrived with a glass of milk for Karloff. The gruelling regime of playing in *Arsenic and Old Lace* had caused the star to drop 31 pounds in weight, from his normal weight of 180lbs down to 149lbs. Physicians had prescribed him a build-up diet and, as a result, the star was to consume milk and other fatteners every quarter of an hour. Peter Lorre was dismayed by the sight. "What would the public think if they knew Boris Karloff was actually drinking milk?' he asked. "I'm just surprising my liver," Karloff quickly replied. "Things are coming to a pretty pass," Lorre moaned, "when the greatest ghoul of them all drinks milk." Then, looking at his revolver he muttered to himself, "It isn't the same old Hollywood. Milk – and an unloaded gun!"[71]

Jeff Donnell had other troubles when it came to shooting a scene in which she was required to kiss Larry Parks. Foolishly she confessed that she had never been kissed by an actor. Stage kisses, she said, could be faked. So when it came to filming the scene the cast and crew crowded around and stared. During the first take of her first screen kiss Donnell broke up. "Hey," Landers said. "No giggling."

"Well, it isn't very romantic," the actress replied. "Besides, Mr. Parks has a cold!"[72] The next take, however, was fine. "In fact," one witness wrote, "they got almost enough for the whole picture. With a sort of do-or-die desperation Miss Donnell grabbed Mr. Parks and – not forgetting the ecstatically lifted left foot – hung on like a vampire." The company applauded. "Ghouls!" remarked Donnell.[73]

Ex-prizefighter Maxie Rosenbloom also had some difficulties on the shoot. In one scene he was required to sit in Professor Billings' invention, which had a frosted glass window and door. It was hot in the cabinet and perspiration was soon pouring down his forehead. Nearby, Karloff was bending over the control panel, while Lorre looked on waiting for the shoot to begin. Landers, however, was still pottering about the set. "Hey, Lew," Rosenbloom yelled. "I'm dying! Will you get to a neutral corner and start this thing?"[74] Landers called for the side of the cabinet to be closed, completely encasing Rosenbloom within. Columnist Harrison Carroll, who was visiting the set, asked if a double could be used since the ex-boxer's face could not be seen. "Impossible," Lorre replied. "That carcass of Rosenbloom's is unmistakeable, even through frosted glass."[75]

The Boogie Man Will Get You opened at the Rialto in New York on Saturday, 10 October. To herald the occasion the theatre held a midnight 'Boogie Man Preview' and invited along famous 'boogie-men' of stage, screen and radio. Among those in attendance were Erich von Stroheim, Vincent Price, Joseph Schildkraut and the voice of radio's *The Shadow*, Bill Johnstone. A reviewer for the *New York Times* wrote, "For Boris Karloff's return to the screen after a long absence on Broadway as the murder specialist of *Arsenic and Old Lace*,

Columbia Pictures has thrown together the wackiest homicidal comedy of Mr. K's diabolical screen career in *The Boogie Man Will Get You*. The formula for a Karloff exercise in spine-chilling hasn't changed one iota, even though the scenarists had more than a year in which to prepare for the "'boogie man's' return."[76] Still, after the picture went on national release an exhibitor in Medicine Hat, Alberta, Canada commented on how the picture had played there. "The picture went over big," he wrote. "Some were a little

With Peter Lorre in *The Boogie Man Will Get You* (1942).

disappointed because it wasn't a horror picture, but as it was a comedy it kept patrons laughing all the way through."[77]

After concluding his work at Columbia Karloff was afforded his three-week rest prior to rejoining *Arsenic and Old Lace*. During this time he did little but relax, and continued in his attempt to regain the weight he had shed during the New York run by consuming six quarts of milk a day.

At 8:30 p.m. on Monday, 17 August 1942 the curtain rose on the much-anticipated[v] Los Angeles production of *Arsenic and Old Lace* at the Biltmore Theatre. Again, the pre-show tensions loomed large, "And I'm nervous as a lost kitten about the opening night here," Karloff confessed. "It will be the biggest thrill of my life to appear in that show before the Hollywood folks."[78] He had trod the boards in Los Angeles before, of course, but that was over a decade earlier – before he was a star.

Although Karloff gave a "good realistic sinister performance" *Los Angeles Times* critic Edwin Schallert's praise was reserved for Josephine Hull who, he said, almost stole the show, "particularly when she discovers a strange corpse in the window seat. This is one of the big laughs of the play."[79] The play stayed in Los Angeles for two weeks grossing over $40,000 before closing on Saturday, 29 August. Then it was on to the Curran Theatre in San Francisco for a four-week stint where the play performed even better, taking $86,000.

Earlier in the run, and as a joke, Lindsay and Crouse had presented a new replacement contract to Karloff. Under the new terms the star would have a reduced salary – $25 per week – *but* could keep any monies thrown onto the stage. The high returns on tour now prompted Karloff to send his own telegram to Russel Crouse. "Women are stripping themselves of their jewels and throwing it on the stage," the message read.[80]

While *Arsenic* was still playing in San Francisco it was booked for a return two-week engagement at the Biltmore in Los Angeles to commence on Monday, 28 September. While this was good news for theatregoers who were unable to get tickets during the original run it meant the entire route of the subsequent tour had to be amended with the eastern city bookings having to wait an additional month. Following the return visit to Los Angeles the play then revisited San Francisco – this time at the Geary Theatre – for an additional two weeks.

---

v The play took $20,000 in advance ticket sales.

Karloff and Dorothy stayed at the Hotel Sir Francis Drake for the duration of that stint in San Francisco. One evening they attended a party at the Nob Hill apartment of Bob Beckham's parents, Mae and Rob. As well as being a long-standing bridge partner of Dorothy's, Mae was also godparent to Sara Jane and had stayed for a while with the Karloffs at 'Blue Spruce', keeping Dorothy company while Boris trod the boards. It was also Mae and Rob who had first introduced Dorothy to San Francisco attorney Edgar Rowe who, along with his wife Sara, were also at the Beckham's party that evening.

Dorothy would later take the opportunity to see Rowe again during her stay in the city, playing bridge with him one afternoon at the San Francisco Bar Association and again that evening, while accompanied by her friend Ruth Swaney, at Rowe's home. This was followed by another game the next day, back at the Bar association. The two obviously enjoyed each other's company.

On Monday, 26 October, *Arsenic and Old Lace* opened at the Oakland Auditorium Theatre for a single night before moving eastwards, through Chicago, Boston and Washington. Everywhere the play met with success. According to the show's publicist Richard Sylvester Maney, as at Saturday, 28 November 1942, the production had taken $2,389,348.69. This figure, Maney pointed out, did not include any monies from the various versions that played in Santiago, Buenos Aries or Gothenburg and excluded the $175,000 paid by Warners for the screen rights – and still the play had 19 months to run. When it reached Hartford, Connecticut in February 1943 for a single night's performance the show was quickly sold out and hundreds of disappointed theatregoers had to be turned away. Advance bookings for the play's run in Seattle in March exceeded the $20,000 mark.

In 1943, while touring with the play, Boris Karloff received an interesting offer. "It all started out in a spirit of good clean fun," he explained. "Or, so I thought. An old friend of mine, Edmund Speare, a college professor of English letters and now, to my undoing, a publisher's editor as well, suggested I help in compiling an anthology of terror tales."[81] Karloff agreed and was soon set to work. "The publishers sent me boxes of books while we moved from town to town on the tour – and I would read through a volume and select a story to go into my collection," he said. "It was quite a task but great fun. I think we raised a few goose bumps with that book."[82]

Karloff chose 14 tales from such authors as Edgar Allan Poe, Bram Stoker, O. Henry, William Faulkner, Ambrose Bierce and his personal favourite – Joseph Conrad. In Beverly Hills in August 1943, during a break in the tour, Karloff penned his introduction in which he explained his admiration for the novelist. "All my reading life I have been devoted to this great master of English prose," Karloff wrote. "He too had the power of creating suspense and terror through suggestion. But he added one ingredient which drives his story home. Compassion. He knew that compassion is the touchstone of our common humanity, and he never fails to make us share and understand the sufferings of his characters persevering hopelessly but gallantly in an unequal struggle."[83] It was just this 'ingredient' Karloff tried to imbue in his own characters.

The resultant book – *Tales of Terror* – was published that November by the World Publishing Company. "Somebody thought it would be a bright idea to let Boris Karloff, the werewolf of the films, select an anthology of frightening short stories," wrote Charles Collins of the *Chicago Daily Tribune*. "The book contains 14 tales, most of which may be found in similar collections… No matter; Karloff's taste in the literature of cold shudders is sound."[84] The book was a success and would sell out through four printings.

On Tuesday, 18 January 1944, while touring with the play, Karloff paid a visit to the Schick army hospital in Clinton, Iowa where he entertained the servicemen. In the evening he took to the stage in Davenport. The following day the company played in Des Moines and on Thursday opened at the Music Hall in Kansas City. When the curtain came down on that final performance on Sunday 23 January Boris Karloff left the play. He had been with the production for three years. On the afternoon of Saturday, 29 January *Arsenic and Old Lace* opened at the Shrine Auditorium in Oklahoma City with a new Jonathan Brewster – Bela Lugosi.

Lugosi had been offered the role in the road show production two years earlier and was ready to sign until he noticed a clause compelling him to stick "for the run of the play."[85] He therefore turned the offer down, fearing it would keep him from making pictures. However, he later appeared in the role in the West Coast touring production, opening at the Tivoli Theatre in San Francisco on 5 August 1943. He stayed with the production in Los Angeles and left in late September. Like Karloff before him, Lugosi would frequently revisit the role until his final appearance in St. Louis in January 1954.

Throughout the play's run the producers, Howard Lindsay and Russel Crouse, had proved to be sympathetic, caring and trustworthy – the antithesis of the stereotypical Broadway producer. They happily allowed many other productions of the play to be staged – for which they received no recompense – and permitted their own company to give benefit shows such as the one in October 1941 in aid of the Stage Relief Fund.

Another had occurred five months earlier, on Easter Sunday, 13 April, when the company had travelled by bus on the 50-mile journey to West Point Military Academy to give the cadets and officers a special free performance of *Arsenic and Old Lace*. The cadets had built the set for what was the first Broadway play to be performed at the Academy in its 139-year history. The production was met with such adulation from its audience, who stomped and cheered, the cadets had to be quietened by the police. "I imagine they liked it," Karloff said.[86]

In Philadelphia on Thursday, 23 September 1943 the company gave another benefit performance – this time for defence workers. Aimed primarily at those on the 4 o'clock shift the curtain rose at 11 a.m. Many workers attended in their work clothes, bringing their lunch with them. The performance took $2,000.

It seemed as though Lindsay and Crouse genuinely enjoyed sharing their success. On one occasion they distributed notes to the stagehands and lesser members of the cast that said, "Starting Saturday your salary will be increased 50%."[87] The main earners, of course, were the play's backers. Towards the end of the run the producers sent a cheque to each one with an accompanying note. "Sweetheart," the message read. "Enclosed you will find a check for the amount of your original investment and 25% more. This is absurd."[88] "They were four very happy and pleasant years," Russel Crouse later remarked.[89]

By now Karloff had not made a movie in two years. "Of course it's fun kidding the spine-ticklers," he had said during the tour, "but don't think I'm escaping from something I don't like doing in playing this role. I love taking those scream-and-scram parts."[90] Now, with *Arsenic and Old Lace* behind him, Karloff would return to Universal to do just that.

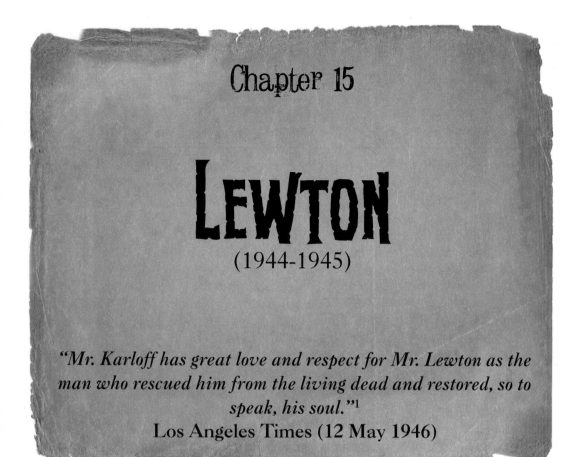

Chapter 15

LEWTON

(1944-1945)

"Mr. Karloff has great love and respect for Mr. Lewton as the man who rescued him from the living dead and restored, so to speak, his soul."[1]
Los Angeles Times (12 May 1946)

When Karloff arrived back in Hollywood he found things had changed. Since the outbreak of war the studios had begun to move away from the production of the cheaper 'B' pictures. With the conflict raging overseas there was, naturally, a diminished market for their movies. Instead, they would concentrate on making the more prestigious, often morale boosting, 'A' pictures. Karloff returned to Universal under a two-picture contract for a salary of $5,000 a week for 13 weeks work. The first picture – his first in Technicolor – would be *The Climax*, a thriller based on Edward Locke's 1909 play of the same name.

Locke's play told the story of Adelina von Hagen, a girl from Ohio, who has come to New York to study for a career as an opera singer. However, a doctor who loves her, Dr. John Raymond, attempts to save her from the temptations he believes such a career can bring, and so hypnotises her to believe she can no longer sing. To make his deception secure he prescribes a medicine for her throat which she must use daily. She becomes suicidal at the loss of her voice but later promises to wed the doctor. However, shortly before the wedding she forgets to take the medicine and the doctor's scheme is discovered. She then continues her lessons and Dr. Raymond realises the errors of his ways. The story had been filmed several times before, most recently in 1930 with Jean Hersholt and Kathryn Crawford. To fashion a new version producer George Waggner handed the project to scriptwriter Curt Siodmak.

Originally Universal had planned the picture as a sequel to *The Phantom of the Opera* made the previous year with Claude Rains in the title role. In September 1943, only one month after *Phantom* went on release, the press announced the follow-up would be called *The Climax* and would star the *Phantom*'s romantic leads, Susanna Foster and Nelson Eddy. However, despite securing Foster for the sequel, Universal's negotiations with Eddy and Claude Rains came to naught. So, when the sequel failed to materialise, the project was instead adapted as a vehicle for Boris Karloff.

With Susanna Foster in
The Climax (1944).

Karloff would play Dr. Hohner, the house physician for the Royal Theatre. He is a man with a terrible secret, for ten years earlier he had killed the opera singer Marcellina when she did not return his love, and now keeps her embalmed body in a shrine in his house. When a young singer, Angela [Susanna Foster], arrives at the opera house Hohner is struck by the similarity between her singing voice and Marcellina's. He determines to put an end to her singing and, under the pretence of examining Angela's throat, hypnotises her, willing her voice to fail. However, his scheme fails and the doctor flees taking refuge in Marcellina's shrine. When the police attempt to gain entry Hohner accidentally knocks over a lit torch and perishes in the flames. Production began on 1 February 1944 with a budget of $750,000.

On Universal's soundstage 28 stood, and still stands, the old Paris Opera set that had been constructed for Lon Chaney's *The Phantom of the Opera* (1925). The set had been used in the picture's recent remake and would now be featured in *The Climax*. It was here Susanna Foster would sing the picture's musical numbers, adapted by Edward Ward from themes by Chopin and Schubert. The English lyrics were supplied by producer/director George Waggner.

Unusually for a Universal picture Karloff wore very little make-up this time, requiring only the application of a waxed moustache. Once again, this was provided by Jack Pierce. "I have spent," Karloff estimated, "at least two-thirds of my life stretched out in that barber chair at Universal studios, looking straight up at the face of Jack Pierce. The wonder of it is that we're still friends."[2]

Although Waggner wrapped the picture on Saturday, 1 April, the picture sat on the shelf for over six months while Universal worked through its backlog of unreleased pictures. *The Climax* finally opened at Keith's Memorial in Boston on Wednesday, 11 October with a companion feature, the musical *Babes on Swing Street*. "The film has been well photographed and provided with attractive settings," one reviewer noted. "The acting makes as much as possible of artificially written parts."[3]

The Climax opened at Loew's Criterion in New York on 13 December 1944. Bosley Crowther of the *New York Times* found the whole thing rather predictable. "However," he added, "the brooding malevolence of Mr. Karloff as the hypnotic doc and the vocal displays of Susanna Foster as the singer have their entertaining points… As a matter of fact, if you take this film as flim-flam, you may find it rather crude but colourful fun."[4]

Three days after production ended on *The Climax* the cameras started rolling on the second of Karloff's pictures under his two-picture contract. This would be his final entry in Universal's Frankenstein saga, the monstrous mélange – *House of Frankenstein*.

Since Karloff had been away Universal had made two more pictures in the Frankenstein saga: *Ghost of Frankenstein* (1942) and *Frankenstein Meets the Wolfman* (1943). Press reports back in November 1941 claimed the studio had 'desperately' wanted Karloff to reprise the role of the Monster in the former. When this did not happen Universal cast Lon Chaney Jr. Then, when the studio made the second of these pictures the following year, the front office was faced with a problem – for Chaney also played the Wolf Man. Initially, the picture's producer, George Waggner, planned to have the actor in both roles and use stunt doubles in the scenes that featured both creatures. However, the time, effort and, most importantly, cost of such an endeavour soon put paid to Waggner's plans and the search began for an actor to play the Frankenstein Monster. The studio chose Bela Lugosi. Having seen a decline in his fortunes since the days of *Dracula* and, no longer in the financial position to turn down the role he had rejected 11 years earlier, Lugosi signed on the dotted line.

Curt Siodmak had ended his screenplay of *Frankenstein Meets the Wolf Man* with the apparent death by drowning of both monsters. "We finished the picture in such a way that the next writer couldn't revive the characters," he later explained. "We'd freeze them in ice, cremate them, whatever. It was a *game*."[5] Unfortunately for Siodmak in this instance he also got the job of bringing them back. Once Siodmak had written the storyline it was passed to Edward T. Lowe to fashion a screenplay.

The picture followed the exploits of Dr. Gustav Niemann, an admirer of Dr. Frankenstein's, who escapes with his assistant Daniel from Neustadt prison. They kill a travelling sideshow owner, Professor Lampini, and his driver and assume their identities.

Niemann resurrects Count Dracula (one of Lampini's exhibits) and uses the vampire to despatch Hussman, one of the three men who caused his imprisonment. Later, after causing the Count's death, Niemann and Daniel continue towards to the ruins of Frankenstein's castle. En route the pair rescue a mistreated gypsy dancer, Ilonka, and Daniel soon begins to fall in love with her. Arriving at the ruins they discover both the Wolf Man and the Frankenstein Monster still alive and encased in ice. The Wolf Man is revived and returns to his true form of Lawrence Talbot.

Talbot helps the scientist find Frankenstein's notes in the hope they will provide a cure for his terrible malady. Niemann, however, has his own agenda and plans instead to transplant Talbot's brain into the Monster. He therefore transports Talbot and the Monster to his laboratory in the village of Vasaria. There he and Daniel kidnap Ullman and Strauss, who are informed of Niemann's plan for revenge. Strauss' brain will be swapped with that of the Wolf Man while Ullman's will be transplanted into the Monster.[i]

When Ilonka falls in love with Talbot a jealous Daniel tells her of the werewolf curse. After the Wolf Man kills again the gypsy tells Talbot she wants to help him. The only way he can be killed, he informs her, is with a silver bullet. That night, however, Talbot transforms and attacks Ilonka. She shoots him and they die together.

Enraged by the death of the gypsy, Daniel attacks Niemann in the laboratory. The assault finally raises the Monster who tosses the hunchback through a window to his

---

i Curiously, aside from references to the pair by the villagers, Ullman and Strauss are not seen again in the picture.

Dr. Niemann finds the Monster in *House of Frankenstein* (1944).

death. The villagers now enter the building and the Monster flees carrying Niemann with him. The mob follows and set fire to the marsh grass, forcing the pair back into the swamps. "Not this way," Niemann implores. "Quicksand!" His words go unheeded and the villagers watch as the doctor and the Frankenstein Monster sink beneath the surface.

The picture had been announced under various titles starting life in mid-1943 as *Chamber of Horrors*. Eight months later the title had been changed to *Destiny*. Then, when Universal announced its new horrors for the 1944-45 season (which included such tantalising, and unrealised, titles as *Dracula vs. the Wolf Man* and *The Mummy's Return*), the title had been amended to *The Devil's Brood*. Although originally envisaged as a vehicle for a multitude of monsters – Dracula, Frankenstein's Monster, The Wolf Man, The Invisible Man, The Mummy and The Mad Ghoul – ultimately only the first three would appear.

The completed script was sent to the MPPDA for approval and, on 27 March 1944, Joseph Breen penned his reply. "We have read the script, dated March 23, 1944, for your production *THE DEVIL'S BROOD* (formerly *DESTINY*)," he wrote, "and are happy to report that the basic story seems to meet the requirements of the Production Code."[6] However, there were some concerns. "We urge you strongly," the letter continued, "to avoid all unnecessary gruesomeness, brutality, or horror in accordance with the requirements of the code."[7] Scenes of stranglings – including the sounds of such acts, Breen urged, should be handled with care. Ilonka's dance, too, should refrain from containing "any unacceptable movements."[8] Even the villagers crossing themselves, Breen warned, should not be "overemphasised".[9]

With Lon Chaney happy to reprise his role of the Wolf Man, Lawrence Talbot, the front office now had to cast its other monsters. Lugosi, now aged 61, was passed over for the role of Dracula. Instead, the studio turned to John Carradine. "When they asked

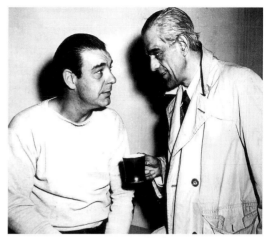

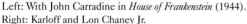
Left: With John Carradine in *House of Frankenstein* (1944).
Right: Karloff and Lon Chaney Jr.

me to play Dracula, I said yes," he recalled, "if you let me make him up and play him the way Bram Stoker described him – as an elderly, distinguished gentleman with a drooping moustache."[10] However, when the studio objected Carradine was forced to compromise. "They didn't like a big moustache, so I had to trim it and make it a very clipped, British moustache," he said. "It wasn't really in character."[11]

Karloff was still adamant he would not revisit his most famous role. "I will never play Frankenstein's monster again," he had re-iterated only months earlier. "Other people have taken similar roles and the edge is off of it. I am through with it."[12] With Chaney cast as the Wolf Man, and Lugosi already excluded, the problem remained – who could Universal cast in the role?

The studio had already been on the look out for a replacement and had tested western actor Lane Chandler. Then one day the 6' 5" tall, 43-year-old western actor Glenn Strange went to Jack Pierce to have a facial scar applied for a role. "I didn't know Jack; this was the first time I had ever met him," Strange explained. "He said, 'Just a minute', and went over to the phone and called Paul Malvern. Well, I knew Paul very well. I'd made a lot of Westerns for him. Paul was on the lot and was going to produce [*House of Frankenstein*]. He came down and Jack said, 'Here's the contour we've been looking for. Right here.' And Paul said, 'That's fine with me. Do you want to put [the make-up] on him and try it out?' So… they put it on me. I went out and did a few little walk-throughs in the Monster get-up and they said, 'okay'. And that was it. That's the way I became the Frankenstein Monster."[13]

Karloff's presence in the picture gave Strange the unique opportunity to be instructed in the role by its originator. "Nobody ever helped anybody as much as Boris Karloff helped me," Strange later said. "I'll never forget that. I asked him for advice because I wanted to do this thing as near as he did. He was very kind about it. He would stay on set and coach me."[14]

Production on the picture began on Tuesday, 4 April 1944 with a budget of $354,000 and a 30-day shooting schedule. To stretch the picture's budget further, sets from other recent Universal pictures were used. The Neustadt prison scenes were shot using scenery from *Tower of London* and James Whale's *Green Hell*, while the underground tunnels were remnants from the Marlene Dietrich picture *Pittsburgh* (1942).

According to the casting budget, Karloff would earn $5,000 per week for four weeks work. Chaney, a contract player, would receive a flat fee of $10,000. Carradine came next in the list of earnings and would take $3,500 per week for two weeks on the picture. Both

J. Carrol Naish and Lionel Atwill would earn $1,750 per week for three weeks' and one week's work respectively. George Zucco followed with $1,500 for his single week on the picture. At the bottom of the list, earning $250 per week, would be Elena Verdugo (3 weeks) and the new Monster, Glenn Strange (1 week).

Karloff's *Son of Frankenstein* co-star Lionel Atwill had gone through a change of fortunes since they had last worked together. In May 1941 a 16-year-old "film-struck Minnesota girl",[15] Sylvia Hamalaine, made assertions that would later bring Atwill to trial. Hamalaine claimed she had attended several parties at Atwill's home during which the guests watched bawdy motion pictures before indulging in "lewd orgies".[16] Atwill appeared in court in May 1941, denying all charges. He was lying.

In June 1942, and again that September, the actor was indicted on charges of perjury resulting from his testimony of the previous year. On 24 September, during the production of *Frankenstein Meets the Wolf Man*, Atwill changed his perjury plea to guilty, admitting that he had owned and shown the motion pictures. He had, he told the court, "lied like a gentleman to protect friends".[17] The actor was given five years probation.

Then, on 23 April, the case reached an unusual dénouement when the Judge, William R. McKay, gave Atwill permission to change his plea from guilty to not guilty – and then promptly dismissed the perjury indictment against him. Atwill was exonerated. He had, in the Judge's view, been sufficiently punished. "You are now in the position where you can truly say you have not been convicted of a felony," the Judge told the actor.[18]

Time for celebration was short, however, for the following month Atwill's wealthy wife, Louise, sued for divorce charging desertion and misconduct. They had, she said, separated back in 1939. The divorce was granted in June 1943, ten months before Atwill started work on *The Devil's Brood*.

The picture was, by all accounts, a happy set. Carradine could be heard reciting his beloved Shakespeare, and Lon Chaney would often cook lunch in his dressing room for his fellow artists. When journalist Edward J. Eustace visited the lot during production he found the cast, all in make-up, sitting together and chatting. Karloff was still eating crackers and drinking milk to get his weight up after *Arsenic and Old Lace*. "I see you're wearing my old black Frankenstein suit," Karloff said to Glenn Strange. "I remember when they fitted me for it back in 1931 when I created the monster you are now playing. The idea was to make me look gigantic and gawky, like a big boy who had outgrown his rompers. So they made me that black suit, much too small. Then, when we tried it on, it still looked too good, so they cut the sleeves off halfway up my arms and the pants off above my ankles. Then they soaked it in acid to rot it and kicked it around the floor to make it dirty. How does it fit you, Glenn?"

"They had to take it in a little in the back," Strange replied while eating a piece of coconut cake, "otherwise it's all right. It's these shoes that are killing me. My feet feel like I was a letter carrier after the Christmas rush. These brogans weigh 21 pounds – and that's apiece, brother, not a pair."

"Don't tell me," Karloff sighed, "I'm the chap who broke them in 13 years ago. When I walked across this set with them for the first time, I kept thinking of those gangsters they used to throw in the river with their feet in a tub of hard cement."[19]

Removing his wolf fangs from his mouth Lon Chaney Jr. joined the conversation. He, too, had experienced the discomfort of playing the Monster. Indeed, the task had become so tiresome during his time in *Ghost of Frankenstein* he had, in a fit of frustration, ripped off the square topped headpiece, tearing his forehead in the process. "I used to say," he told his colleagues, "just kidding, that the Frankenstein monster used those studs in his neck to hang his collar on. That was before I had to play him and watch those electric sparks snapping off those studs in the recharging scene. After that, playing this Wolf Man with a face full of yak hair is a cinch."[20] After discussing Chaney's father – "A great actor and a great chap. He helped me get a job in pictures when he hardly knew who I was," Karloff told the ensemble – Karloff proposed a toast to the deceased actor. "Here's to his memory," he said, raising his glass of milk.[21]

Having finished their night scenes Anne Gwynne and Elena Verdugo passed the ghoulish group on their way home. "Girls," John Carradine asked them, "how does it feel to work all day with a gang of banshees?"

"I don't know," Gwynne replied, "it's kind of thrilling. I get a kick out of it."

"Well, why not?" Chaney said. "After all, we made the girls swoon before Sinatra."

"But not for the same reason," added Glenn, licking a strand of coconut from his lip.[22]

Elena Verdugo later spoke of her time with the picture's 'monsters'. "Working with Boris Karloff, I had an intense awareness that I was working with a 'great'," she said. "He was a serious actor but never unkind. Lon Chaney was a lovely, friendly man. I remember often sitting and chatting with him. I had met J. Carrol Naish on the set of my first picture, *Down Argentine Way* [1940] when I was 15. He loved working. I simply loved him. He helped, he supported, he gave so much. I'd see Glenn Strange in the make-up department every a.m. Glenn was dear, and Jack Pierce, his make-up man, was a genius... All in all, I enjoyed making the picture very much. I was a still-growing teenage girl, and ALL those fine actors were kind, considerate, and made me feel part of everything."[23]

Although Karloff's return to the Frankenstein franchise was affable enough, it would have serious medical repercussions for the star. He had already suffered back pains while making *The Climax*, and now the demands of his new role would exacerbate the problem. Still, he soldiered on as Peter Coe, who played Karl Hussman – the grandson of Dr. Niemann's first victim – observed. "Boris Karloff was an amazing man... There seemed times, between the scenes," Coe explained, "when he looked very tired and he had trouble with his legs, but when the director called for action he would straighten up, and an inner energy force could be seen taking over his body. His eyes would just radiate and it looked as if he became 15 years younger to become the sinister, mad doctor while the cameras kept rolling."[24]

Karloff, though, was not the only one to suffer during the shoot. Glenn Strange found the make-up for his new monstrous role very restricting. It took Jack Pierce and his assistant, Otto Lederer, 3½ hours to transform him into the Monster. Karloff's invention of the wax eyelids, especially, gave Strange some trouble as he could not see where he was going. In addition, the headpiece was tight and after several hours under the studio lights it would fill with sweat which would slosh around inside. Like Karloff before him, the make-up also rendered him *persona non grata* in the commissary and, instead, had his lunch brought to him in a paper bag. The difficulties inherent in wearing the costume and make-up caused some trouble during the filming of the climactic sequence, which was shot at 3 a.m. on Tuesday, 25 April. "If you recall the picture," Strange later said, "I had to come out of the castle where Karloff had brought me back to life. I had a big strap that went underneath my coat, with a ring or snap on it. His [Karloff's] double wore a belt around himself, and I'd snap into the ring and then put mine around him, 'cause nobody can walk around with a guy hanging under your arm. And coming down those steps, besides. There must have been 30 or 40 of those steps. They were chasing me with these torches. Somebody whizzed one of these torches – they were big, with a long club, and all that burlap on them – and hit me right between the shoulders, and almost knocked me off one of those steps.

Then we went down into the swamp thing, where we went into the quicksand. That's where they lined up this big ring of tumbleweeds, then a little clear spot, and then another ring. They were dousing this with some sort of chemical; I don't know what it was. I said to the special-effects man that I couldn't move very fast with those boots, and carrying this guy besides. And now he's really just out, and I had to carry his whole weight. He said I had plenty of time to get across there. But actually, I didn't. That was just one flash, and burning all around there. I went straight through it, kicking the stuff out of my way as I went. It singed his [Karloff's double's] hair. I almost lost that camera, I got in the water so fast, carrying him with me."[25]

At the scene's conclusion Niemann and the Monster were to disappear into the quicksand. Karloff and Strange duly climbed into the water and stood on the platform of a hydraulic lift. When the platform was lowered Niemann and the Monster would disappear beneath the surface. By the time the scene was concluded Karloff had put in a 14-hour day. Still, that evening he made an appearance on the radio in another episode of *Creeps by Night* and was back on set the following afternoon to shoot the scenes in the ice caverns beneath the ruins of Frankenstein's ruined laboratory.

Boris Karloff concluded his work on *House of Frankenstein* at 4:30 p.m. on Saturday, 29 April with the scene where Niemann unveils his 'Chamber of Horrors' to the townsfolk of Reigelberg. Production came to an end at 5 p.m. on Monday, 8 May 1944 after a final week of filming the Dracula segment of the picture. After post-production was completed, however, the movie sat on the shelf while the studio released its backlog of pictures.

House of Frankenstein was finally previewed at the studio on Thursday, 14 December 1944. It opened at the Rialto in New York the following day. "Universal, generous to a fault," announced the *New York Times*, "has presented as complete a gallery of ghouls as ever haunted a Hollywood set in *House of Frankenstein*... And, although they all finally fade into celluloid limbo, it's a safe bet they'll return."[26] The picture opened at the Hawaii Theatre in Los Angeles a week later, on 22 December, in a double-bill with another Lon Chaney Jr. picture – *The Mummy's Curse*.

Strange proved successful enough to reprise his role as the Monster in its final two incarnations for Universal – *House of Dracula* (1945) and the comedy-horror *Abbott and Costello Meet Frankenstein* (1948). Over 20 years later, when Karloff was asked what he thought of Strange's monster, he replied, "Well, he wasn't as lucky as I was. I got the cream of it, being the first. I know I wished him lots of luck... hoping it would do as much for him as it did for me, but..."[27]

If Karloff's return to the Frankenstein series had not been particularly auspicious things were about to change. While the cameras rolled on *House of Frankenstein* he received an invitation to the offices of RKO Radio Pictures to discuss the prospect of making pictures for the studio under the aegis of the head of the 'B' picture unit, producer Val Lewton.

Back in February 1944 the newspapers had announced Boris Karloff would probably return to New York after completing the Frankenstein picture to do another play for Lindsay and Crouse. The playwrights planned to write a psychological melodrama for the star but the piece never materialised. Instead, on 18 May, Karloff signed with RKO.

By the mid-1940s RKO – the studio that had produced such notable pictures as *King Kong* (1933), *Top Hat* (1935), *The Hunchback of Notre Dame* (1939) and *Citizen Kane* (1941) – had, on the whole, turned its attention to the production of 'B' pictures. In charge of the studio's horror unit was Vladimir Ivan Leventon, known to all as Val Lewton.

Born in Yalta, Russia in 1904, Lewton had emigrated to America with his mother, Nina, and sister, Lucy, five years later. Through her sister, the actress Alla Nazimova, Nina obtained work at MGM. This later proved beneficial for Lewton who, after writing several novels, was asked to pen an adaptation of *Taras Bulba* for the studio. Lewton moved to California and, although his script was never filmed, he continued to work as David O. Selznick's story editor and assistant. Then, in 1942, Val Lewton was offered the position of head of RKO's new horror unit.

His first production, *Cat People*, was a great success earning the studio almost $4,000,000 against its original budget of $134,000. Of course, the studio wanted more of the same and so Lewton produced *I Walked With a Zombie*, the 1943 horror picture inspired, in part, by Inez Wallace's *American Weekly Magazine* article of the same name and Charlotte Brontë's classic novel *Jane Eyre*. He followed these with the horror pictures *The Leopard Man*, *The Seventh Victim* and *The Ghost Ship* (all 1943), a sequel to his first picture entitled *The Curse of the Cat People* (1944), and two dramas, *Mademoiselle Fifi* and *Youth Runs Wild* (both 1944), which performed poorly when compared against Lewton's horror pictures.

Lewton's success had meant that, on the whole, the studio left him to his own devices. However, in 1944 Jack G. Gross, Universal's executive producer of such genre pictures as *The Wolf Man* and *Son of Dracula*, joined RKO. It was a change that did not sit well with Val Lewton.

Gross wanted to utilise the screen's most famous bogeyman, Boris Karloff, and it was arranged for the star to come to the studio to meet with Lewton and directors Mark Robson and Robert Wise. Lewton, though, was not enthused by the prospect of working with the star. However, the meeting soon changed his mind, as Robert Wise recalled. "When [Karloff] first walked in the door I was startled by his colouring," he said, "the strange bluish cast – but when he turned those eyes on us, and that velvety voice said, 'Good afternoon, gentlemen', we were his, and never thought about anything else."[28]

In Lewton Karloff had found a man of like mind, a producer intent on portraying horror in a more cerebral, less visceral, manner. It was an approach the star heartily approved of. "Val," Karloff later explained, "was the first person to realise consistently that the unspeakable terror behind the door remains terrifying only as long as the door isn't opened, and all his films were based on the principle of making the audience do most of the work, using hints and suggestions which each spectator's imagination could play round to the maximum effect."[29]

Unfortunately Jack Gross held an opposing view and wanted his horror pictures to be truly horrific. It made for a fragile working relationship. The two men, Robert Wise later explained, were "miles apart in terms of quality and being – Lewton being very, very well-educated, a very sensitive man, a very tasteful man, and Mr. Gross a little bit like his name, a little bit out-spoken and not very much taste, and a little bit of a loudmouth, let's say, and Lewton worked with him but didn't, in a matter of fact, have *any* respect for him."[30]

On 18 May 1944 Boris Karloff signed with RKO Radio Pictures. He would make two pictures for the studio and receive a salary of $6,000 per week – a healthy 20% increase

The third version of Arnold Böcklin's painting, *Isle of the Dead* (1883).

on his last salary at Universal. Initially it was envisaged Karloff's first starring role for the studio would be in *Carmilla*, an adaptation of J. Sheridan Le Fanu's 1872 tale of vampirism. Although Le Fanu's story was set in Austria the new version, the *New York Times* revealed, would be "about vampires in America during colonial times".[31] However, for reasons unclear, the picture was never made. Instead, Karloff would star in *Isle of the Dead*.

The movie took its inspiration from the 1880 painting of the same name by the Swiss artist Arnold Böcklin.[ii] Lewton's interest in the picture began as a boy when he saw it hanging on the wall in the country home of his aunt, Alla Nazimova. It both fascinated and frightened the boy and he would spend hours concocting tales around the image. When Lewton made *I Walked With a Zombie* he had featured the painting on the bedroom wall of Jessica Holland [Christine Gordon], but now an entire movie would be based upon it. Lewton's initial treatment was passed to two of the studio's screenwriters, Ardel Wray and Josef Mischel, to flesh out the script. Then, as was usual, Lewton wrote the final draft.

The picture told the story of Nikolas Pherides [Karloff], a Greek General serving in the Balkan War of 1912. During a lull in the fighting Pherides and an American reporter, Oliver Davis [Marc Cramer], row out to a lonely island in order for the General to visit the grave of his wife. On the island they hear the sound of a woman's singing and follow it to the home of Hugo Albrecht [Jason Robards], a retired Swiss archaeologist who lives in the house with his Greek housekeeper, Madame Kyra [Helene Thimig]. Albrecht also plays host to several guests, refugees from the fighting on the mainland: British Consul Mr. St. Aubyn [Alan Napier], Mrs. St. Aubyn [Katherine Emery] and her companion Thea [Ellen Drew], and a seller of tinware named Henry Robbins [Skelton Knaggs]. Madame Kyra, however, is a superstitious woman and warns the General the house may be harbouring a vorvolaka, a vampiric undead creature from Greek folklore. She tells Pherides that Thea may, in fact, be this evil spirit in human form. The General, however, dismisses her superstitions and he and the reporter agree to spend the night in the house.

---

ii Böcklin (or Boecklin) painted five versions of the picture. Adolf Hitler once owned one.

Left: As General Pherides in *Isle of the Dead* (1945).
Right: Poster for *Isle of the Dead*.

In the morning, however, Albrecht finds Robbins dead. Fearing the plague Pherides sends to the mainland for his military doctor, Drossos. The doctor confirms the worst – Robbins was a victim of septicemic plague, a highly infectious, always fatal, disease transmitted by fleas. Only the arrival of the warm southern sirocco wind can destroy the pestilence. The doctor is the next to succumb and the General begins to believe Madame Kyra's claims – perhaps Thea is a vorvolaka after all. Davis begins to fear for Thea's safety and tries to escape the island with her. However, their plan is thwarted when they discover Pherides has destroyed the only boat.

When Mrs. St. Aubyn is found 'dead' Pherides has her immediately laid to rest in a crypt. The remaining inhabitants are saved when the wind changes and the hot sirocco blows across the island, destroying the plague-carrying fleas. However, Mrs. St. Aubyn, a cataleptic, awakens in her coffin and, now deranged by her experience, kills Madam Kyra and stabs the General before fleeing and falling from a cliff to her death. The dying general warns Oliver he has seen the vorvolaka. "She came out of the darkness," he says. "She must be destroyed." When the reporter tells Pherides it is done, the General dies. "Back of his madness, there was something simple, good," Davis tells Thea. "He wanted to protect us."

Isle of the Dead went into production on Thursday, 13 July 1944 with the picture's opening scenes of the aftermath of battle. However, it was soon clear that all was not well. Karloff's back troubles had resurfaced, probably exacerbated by his recent tribulations during the making of *House of Frankenstein*. "Between shots, he was in a wheelchair but he made no complaints," Ardel Wray later said. "He managed to be wryly humorous about it – not falsely, in that obnoxious 'see how brave I'm being' way. Everyone liked and respected him."[32]

Although Karloff tried to continue to work as long as possible the pain soon became too much to bear and Lewton shut down production. On 21 July Karloff was admitted to the Good Samaritan Hospital in Hollywood and was soon scheduled for a spinal fusion to relieve his "chronic arthritic condition".[33] The star's physician, Dr. Raymond L. Jeffries, told reporters Karloff would be unable to work for at least a month.

While he lay in his hospital room Karloff received regular visits from Maurice Evans' assistant Evelyn Helmore who would play the star at gin rummy. Meanwhile, as Karloff recuperated in hospital, Val Lewton turned his attention to his next picture, an adaptation of Robert Louis Stevenson's short story, *The Body Snatcher*.

Written in 1881, Stevenson's tale opened with a group of four men sitting in a tavern in the town of Debenham, England. One of the four is Fettes, "an old drunken Scotchman, a man of education obviously, and a man of some property, since he lived in idleness."[34] One night a man is taken ill in the tavern and his London doctor is summoned by telegraph. However when the doctor, Wolfe Macfarlane, arrives there is an altercation between the medical man and Fettes which ends with the Scotsman asking, "Have you seen it again?" Fettes' drinking companions determine to find the cause of the confrontation and the findings are related to the reader.

Fettes, it transpires, was once a medical student in Edinburgh. While there he was entrusted with the job of paying grave robbers for their supply of corpses. One morning, however, he recognises a body as that of a young woman he had known to be alive the previous day. He relates his suspicions to the young doctor Macfarlane who suggests the best course of action is to ignore it. Fettes takes Macfarlane's advice and the girl's body is dissected.

One afternoon Fettes enters a tavern and finds Macfarlane speaking to a stranger [Gray]. "This was a small man," Stevenson wrote, "very pale and dark, with coal-black eyes. The cut of his features gave a promise of intellect and refinement which was but feebly realised in his manners, for he proved, upon a nearer acquaintance, coarse, vulgar, and stupid. He exercised, however, a very remarkable control over Macfarlane…"[35] Fettes joins the two men for an evening of drinking but early the next morning he is roused from his bed by a banging on the door. It is Macfarlane who has brought with him a cadaver. It is the odious Gray.

Three days later, with Gray now well and truly dissected, Fettes and Macfarlane take a gig and drive out to a lonely graveyard. In the falling rain they disinter the recently buried corpse of a woman. Placing it in a sack they prop it between them in the gig and turn for home. As they drive through the rain and the darkness, the body keeps falling against them. The wet sack is clinging to the cadaver and the body now seems to have changed. They stop the coach and, fetching a lamp, Macfarlane uncovers the dead face. "The light fell very clear upon the dark, well-moulded features and smooth-shaven cheeks of a too familiar countenance, often beheld in dreams of both of these young men." Stevenson wrote. "A wild yell rang up into the night; each leaped from his own side into the roadway; the lamp fell, broke and was extinguished; and the horse, terrified by this unusual commotion, bounded and went off toward Edinburgh at a gallop, bearing along with it, sole occupant of the gig, the body of the dead and long-dissected Gray."[36]

Val Lewton had thought the story ripe with possibilities and on 10 May 1944 he sent a memo to Jack Gross proposing the tale as a suitable vehicle for Boris Karloff. The star, Lewton explained, would portray the odious Gray. Although the character only appeared briefly in Stevenson's original Lewton believed it could be expanded into "a truly horrendous person".[37] The memo then laid out Lewton's reasons for choosing the story:

1) The title seems good to us.
2) There is exploitation value in the use of a famous Robert Louis Stevenson classic.
3) There is a ninety percent chance that this is in the public domain. The legal department is now searching the title.
4) The characters are colourful. The background of London medical life in the 1830s is extremely interesting. The sets are limited in number but effective in type. The costumes are readily procurable and no great difficulties of any sort so far as production is concerned are evident.
5) There is also an excellent part for Bela Lugosi as a resurrection man.[38]

After the story was approved Lewton wrote an initial treatment, which he then passed to Philip MacDonald to fashion a screenplay. In conference with Lewton, MacDonald removed the beginning of the story with its altercation and set the story completely in Edinburgh and its environs. He also added a sub-plot of a little girl who needs MacFarlane's[iii] skills as a surgeon to restore her ability to walk. A slew of new characters were added – MacFarlane's housekeeper (and secret wife) Meg, the girl Georgina and her mother Mrs. Marsh. MacDonald also changed the story's ending. Now, after revealing Gray's face, the gig would speed away and crash, killing Doctor MacFarlane. When Fettes rushes to help he now finds the bodies of MacFarlane and the exhumed woman lying in the rain.

To appease Jack Gross's desire for more horror Lewton and MacDonald fashioned scenes that had little, if any, chance of being passed by the censor. This proved to be the case. On 8 September Lewton sent a working draft of the screenplay to the Breen Office. Their reply came back later that month. "We have read with close attention your estimating script… and regret to advise that this story is unacceptable under the provisions of the code," it said, "because of the repellent nature of such matter, which has to do with grave-robbing, dissecting bodies, and pickling bodies… the undue gruesomeness which would unavoidably be attached to the picturisation of such scenes could in no wise be approved."[39] The studio acquiesced and the offending scenes did not appear in the final picture.

Following the Breen Office response Lewton set about revising the screenplay and changed it to such an extent that Philip MacDonald insisted the producer share screen credit with him. The reason, however, seems unclear. Some have claimed MacDonald was unhappy with the new script and did not want sole blame if the picture failed. Others have said MacDonald's insistence on a co-credit was in due recognition to Lewton's contribution. Whatever the case the final screen credit went to MacDonald and Lewton's *nom-de-plume*, Carlos Keith.

With Karloff already cast as the cabman John Gray, Lewton began filling the other roles. He had requested these be taken by 'moderate stars' to increase the picture's

---

iii The spelling of Macfarlane's name was slightly amended for the movie.

bankability and cited Universal's *The Wolf Man* (1940)
– with Lon Chaney Jr., Claude Rains, Ralph Bellamy,
Maria Ouspenskaya and Bela Lugosi – as an example of
the potential success of such an approach.

Aside from Lugosi, however, Gross made only one
other concession to Lewton's request and the English
character actor Henry Daniell was signed for the role of
Dr. Wolfe MacFarlane. Even then Daniell had not been
a clear choice for the role – George Coulouris, Albert
Dekker, John Emery and Alan Napier had all been
considered by Lewton and Wise before they settled on
the Englishman.

By this time 50-year-old Daniell had become
known chiefly for his villainous roles. He had been
the traitorous Lord Wolfingham dispatched by Errol
Flynn in *The Sea Hawk* (1940) and, more recently, Mr.
Brocklehurst, the cruel schoolmaster in RKO's version
of Charlotte Brontë's *Jane Eyre* (1944).

The remainder of the cast was filled primarily from
the pool of the studio's contract players. Russell Wade
would play Fettes with Edith Atwater as Meg and
Rita Corday as Mrs. Marsh. Robert Wise had originally
considered using Ann Carter from *Curse of the Cat People*
for little Georgina but ultimately decided against it.
"She just didn't have the right look for the little girl,"
Wise later explained. "I needed somebody who looked
a little more wan, somebody who looked a little sickly,
and Ann was too healthy for that."[40] Instead Wise
chose eight-year-old Sharyn Moffett whose casting
was announced in the *New York Times* on Saturday, 21
October 1944. Production on *The Body Snatcher* officially
began four days later.

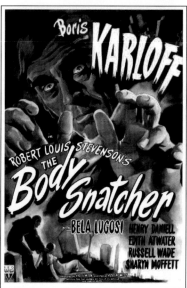

Top: As Cabman Gray in *The Body Snatcher*
(1945). Bottom: Poster for *The Body
Snatcher*.

As usual, Lewton would utilise sets and dressings
from other pictures. It was an effective way of
maximising the budget. The exteriors were shot at the
RKO ranch in San Fernando Valley where some of the sets from *The Hunchback of Notre
Dame* (1939) – primarily the cobbled square and the archway – were used. Interiors were
shot on soundstage four at RKO's studio on Hollywood's Gower Street. Here the anatomy
room was a redressed set from Jacques Tourneur's picture *Experiment Perilous* (1944).

The shoot, however, had its share of problems. Lugosi had been added to the picture
under the express wish of Jack Gross. Although a grave-robber role had originally been
muted for the actor the part of MacFarlane's caretaker Joseph was written especially for him
instead. The character's slight hunchback was added at the specific request of Jack Gross.

Lugosi had signed his contract on 25 October, the day that filming began. He would
receive $3,000 per week with one week's guaranteed work. He would also receive second
billing behind Boris Karloff, despite Daniell's role being far more significant. By now,

however, Lugosi was in poor health and required special treatment. "He was not well at all," Robert Wise recalled. "It was a small part and didn't require too much of him but I had to, kind of, nurse him through the whole role, such as it was. And I always appreciated Karloff's sensitivity when it came to the scene where they played together in the film – where the Lugosi character came to see the Karloff character. Boris was very, very gentle with him… and was very patient with him… I always respected Karloff for that – for the sensitivity in that situation. I have heard that he [Lugosi] was on drugs at the time but I think it might have been drugs because he was in pain – but he got through it – it was alright – but Karloff was very, very helpful in getting him through the sequence that I had to do with him."[41]

The rumours of Lugosi's dependency on drugs were true. For years he had been suffering from pains in his legs. "I had a very painful ailment," he later told a reporter. "My sciatic nerves bothered me terribly. I suffered very much, and so I went to the doctor and he gave me some narcotics to kill the pain."[42] Aspirin was the usual medication in such cases but Lugosi's stomach ulcer had precluded that. Instead he was prescribed morphine, to be administered by injections. "That happened about every week once," Lugosi explained, "and it helped me so much – it put me so much in a state of feeling that I later [used them] myself, even if I didn't have pain."[43] Lugosi had become an addict.

His health was such that he required to rest between scenes, as Robert Clarke, who played a medical student in the picture, later revealed. "During the time that I was involved on *The Body Snatcher*, he hardly came out of his dressing room unless the assistant director called him," Clarke said. "They had a day bed in there, and he was flat on his back on that couch nearly all the time. He talked very little to anyone, and obviously, he wasn't at all well. It was very difficult for him to perform."[44]

Karloff, too, still had his health problems although, as usual, he made the best of it. "Karloff was marvellous to work with," Wise said. "He was… very professional – very good, although he was having back problems in a serious way, he never complained about them. He just gritted his teeth and did it."[45] Wise – like so many before him – found the star the antithesis of his usual screen persona. "He was very educated and had a pleasant and friendly attitude to all his co-workers," the director recalled. "However, he did not single out any one relationship but was cordial to all on the set of the movie."[46] Working with the star, Wise later said, was, "one of my very best experiences."[47]

The Body Snatcher was an important film for Karloff. Although he had recently proved he could hold his own on the New York stage, cinema audiences still saw him primarily as a horror star. "Boris was very keen to do this film because he felt it gave him an opportunity to show that he could act as well as play the monster," Robert Wise said. "He was fascinated by the duel between him and Henry Daniell,[iv] one of the great character actors of the time. This pleased Boris very much and he worked hard on his performance. He was not feeling well during the shooting; he had back problems, but he never let that interfere a bit and was determined to show that he could hold his own with Henry Daniell… We had very good meetings with Boris before we started to shoot… His role in *The Body Snatcher* meant a lot of him."[48]

The picture also provided Henry Daniell with his best movie role. "Henry was a lovely man… he was one of the best actors I ever worked with," Wise later said. "He was

---

iv The short scene when Gray and MacFarlane are joined in the tavern by Fettes used much of Stevenson's original dialogue from the story.

just excellent. He and Karloff got along fine off the set... there was no problem there... Henry was an excellent trouper, very professional, very good, always right there and always contributing and helping."[49]

Production ended on Friday, 17 November 1944. Roy Webb, who had composed the scores for all of Lewton's RKO horror pictures, supplied a score that drew on a number of traditional Scottish folk songs, including *Will Ye No Come Back Again*, *We'd Better Bide a Wee* and *Bonnie Dundee*. The most memorable use of music in the picture, however, is the murder of the street singer, played by Donna Lee. One night she passes under the arch singing the 18th century ballad *Huntingtower (When Ya Gang Awa, Jamie)* and is followed by Gray's cab. The girl's singing and the beat of the horse's hooves on the cobblestones can still be heard as both go out of shot. Then the sound of the hooves stop and the singing is abruptly halted. Penned by Val Lewton, the scene is simple, subtle and chilling – a perfect example of the understatement preferred by Karloff and the producer.

The picture also gave Karloff his sympathetic moment. Cabman Gray transports Mrs. Marsh and her crippled daughter, Georgina, to the house of Doctor MacFarlane. Gray is friendly towards the child and as he carries her from his cab and places her in a wheelchair tells her, "You watch sharp, little miss, for my horse to give you a 'hello'." Later it is the prospect of seeing Gray's horse over the parapet that induces the child to rise from her wheelchair and walk again. Ironically, it is also the Cabman's hectoring of MacFarlane that persuades the surgeon to perform the operation that restores the girl's ability to walk – and the surgeon's self esteem.

Production of *Isle of the Dead* resumed on 1 December 1944, exactly two weeks after work on *The Body Snatcher* had ended. By now, however, Val Lewton had lost heart with the project. He wrote to his mother and sister telling them the picture was "a complete mess".[50] Filming concluded on 12 December and after the usual post-production work the picture was ready for exhibition. Lewton, however, felt it best to release *The Body Snatcher*, the stronger of the two pictures, first. It opened at the Hawaii and Elite theatres in Los Angeles on 10 May 1945 in a double feature with *The Brighton Strangler*.

"Boris Karloff as the cabby purveys plenty of soft-spoken villainy," wrote the *Los Angeles Times*, "while Henry Daniell gives an equally interesting portrayal as the doctor."[51] The picture opened at the Rialto in New York two weeks later, on Friday, 25 May. The *New York Times* critic thought it, "eerie business".[52] "This new gloom-lodger," he added, "though not as nerve-paralysing as the performers might lead you to expect, has enough suspense and atmospheric terror to make it one of the better of its genre... *The Body Snatcher* is certainly not the most exciting 'chiller-drama' – the Rialto has often done much better – but it is somewhat more credible than most and manages to hold its own with nary a werewolf or vampire! But then, with Karloff on the prowl, what chance would a blood-thirsty hobgoblin stand?"[53]

When the picture opened in London – at the Odeon Marble Arch on Monday 19 November 1945 – it was in an altered state. All the picture's references to the notorious Burke and Hare had been excised. Unfortunately, it is not known why this decision was made as J.L. Green of the British Board of Film Classification (BBFC) later explained. "Our records prior to WW2 and in the immediate post-war period are scanty, if not non-existent in some cases," he said. "For example, our offices were bombed in 1941 and very little survives pre-1950s. According to the old register we still have, the entry for *THE BODY SNATCHER* is annotated with the letter 'D'. This usually indicates 'Deletions' (i.e. cuts) as with other similar entries. There is a further annotation, 'Resubmitted', which would corroborate this assumption."[54]

Despite their long-lived reputation as grave-robbers, Burke and Hare never actually robbed a grave. After they had received monies from Dr. Robert Knox of the Edinburgh Medical College for the body of an old army pensioner who had died of natural causes while staying at Hare's lodging house in the city, the pair had concocted a diabolical scheme. Instead of haunting the graveyards at night they took a more direct course and simply resorted to murder. Each of their 17 victims was sold to the college for dissection.

When a lodger discovered a body under a bed the police were informed and Burke, his mistress, Hare and his wife were arrested. Hare was offered immunity if he would give evidence against Burke, which he duly did. On 28 January 1829 Burke was hanged. His body was then publicly dissected at the Medical College. Hare was released and he, like the two women, faded from the history books, their fates unknown. Doctor Knox was never brought to trial but eventually left the city for London where, in 1862, he died.

It is hard to see why the mere mention of Burke and Hare, in a picture made over a century after the crimes were committed, could prove in any way contentious. Still, it did and *The Body Snatcher* could not be seen in its original uncut state in Britain until the picture's second outing on home video in 1998.

Isle of the Dead finally hit the screens four months after the U.S. release of *The Body Snatcher*, opening at the Rialto in New York on Friday, 7 September 1945. The *New York Times* called the picture, "more horrible than horrific and poor Boris Karloff, who must be pretty tired of this sort of monkey business by now, stumbles through the picture with a vacant, tired stare... That Mr. Karloff eventually loses his mind is small wonder indeed."[55]

The picture opened in Los Angeles on 22 November at the Vogue and Million Dollar theatres in a double-feature with the Lugosi comedy-horror picture *Zombies on Broadway*. John L. Scott of the *Los Angeles Times* thought the Karloff movie, "exciting enough for any devotee of macabre film fare."[56]

Early in 1945 Maurice Evans' assistant, Evie Helmore, paid a visit to the Karloff home. An American citizen since 1941, Evans was now a major in the U.S. army and had been put in charge of troop entertainments in the central Pacific. He now planned to produce a touring

The *Arsenic and Old Lace* Pacific cast.

production of *Arsenic and Old Lace* and required a photograph of Boris Karloff to use as reference for the Jonathan Brewster character. Evie Helmore was, therefore, dispatched to the Karloff home to procure the picture. After listening to the request, however, Karloff wrote to Evans proposing another idea. "If he could stand it," Karloff later explained, "I would be pleased to come out and do it myself. So, out I went. It took a bit of arranging – not easy."[57]

In February, with the war still raging in Europe and the

Pacific, Karloff arrived in Honolulu[v] and was issued with army fatigues. Although a civilian, his presence in a war zone required he be subjected to a simplified version of basic training and the star was therefore put through his paces in weapons training and amphibious manoeuvres.

His position in the troupe was unique as he later explained. "I was not merely the only actor," he said, "except for George Schaefer, who directed it – he played the Teddy Roosevelt part – he was good, too – but he and I were the only civilians outside of three local women. The others were all boys in uniform."[58] Schaefer, though, also had a third duty. "He drove the bloody truck," Karloff explained, "which put us on the horns of a dilemma. Schaefer loved Gilbert and Sullivan and the only way we could keep him awake while he drove was to bellow out Gilbert and Sullivan at the top of our lungs."[59]

For almost four months Karloff and the troupe toured the Pacific islands entertaining the troops with Kesselring's play. "I had the most wonderful time," he later said. "We played every camp and air strip there was... We were on Oahu, then up to Midway, to Canton, and to the Marshalls, and camped on Christmas Island. Then we went to Johnson's [sic Johnston] Island, my favourite. It's virtually just a landing strip, about a thousand miles from Hawaii. The island is only about three hundred yards long and a hundred yards wide."[60]

Top: Amphibious Training. Above Left: Karloff signs autographs for troops in the Pacific. Top Right: Addressing the troops on Kwajalein, 1945 (Courtesy of Frank E. Acker). Bottom Right: Signing on Kwajalein, 1945 (Courtesy of Frank E. Acker).

v During his stay in Honolulu Karloff met *Tarzan* author Edgar Rice Burroughs, who came to see one the shows.

On Johnston Island the play was presented in a small makeshift theatre next to the aeroplane's loading zone, where the aircraft would rev up before taxiing to the runway. It was a noisy spot to place a theatre. "Always on your best lines, there'd be a blast of engines – talk about point killers," Karloff later said.[61] Then one day, while still on the island, the star was recognised by a young marine. "He asked me what the hell I was doing there – a good question if you think about it – and I told him,"

With Robert Karnes and George Schaefer.

Karloff recalled. "He said, 'And are you playing here tonight?' I said, 'Yes.' He said, 'Well, I think I'll just take it in – you know, I haven't been downtown in two weeks.' Just marvellous. He was perfectly serious."[62]

There was another memorable moment on the island of Kwajalein. "The Sea-Bees had asked us to play their end of the island and said they'd built us a stage," Karloff explained. "They were marvels. They built a stage in a couple of hours and erected the set – a Victorian living room. And then the most astounding thing happened – on that dreary, wasted island. A cat emerged from the kitchen door of the set. He looked around the living room – and, bless me, walked calmly out of the living room door as if he'd lived there all his life."[63]

When not performing, Karloff would visit the troop hospitals to chat with the sick and the wounded. He also had RKO ship out a print of *The Body Snatcher* to play for the troops. The play's director, Sergeant George Schaefer, later remembered the star with affection. "I've never seen such enthusiasm," he said. "He was in and out of everything. The men were crazy about him… He never complained and we were pretty uncomfortable at times. Boris treated the whole thing like a picnic."[64]

After the performances Karloff would invariably mingle with the troops. "I'd get out and tell jokes to the boys," he explained, "just to show them I'm a human being. Many of them, having seen me as a monster so often, apparently had begun to have their doubts."[65] Later, he said, "The whole trip was a wonderful experience. I wouldn't take anything for it."[66]

In July Karloff returned to Val Lewton's fold at RKO and started work on *Bedlam*. Set in London in 1761, the picture would star Karloff as Simms, the corrupt apothecary general in charge of the inmates of St. Mary's of Bethlehem Hospital – or 'Bedlam' as it was commonly known.

Appointed to the position by the stout Lord Mortimer, Simms is constantly challenged by Mortimer's protégé, Nell Bowen. When she plans to reform the asylum Simms has her committed to Bedlam. However, there she befriends the inmates who later rise against their sadistic keeper. They submit him to a mock trial and, although they set him free, Simms is stabbed by one of the inmates. Believing they have killed him, and fearing for the consequences, they wall him up. But as the last brick is being placed, unseen by the inmates, Simm's eyes flicker open. They have walled him up alive.

Again, Karloff would play a reprehensible character, which he would try to approach with some understanding. "All the famous men of that age had to have sponsors," he explained. "They couldn't make a living in the arts. Therefore, there were toadies, foot-kissers and all around scoundrels and hypocrites – like this chap I'm playing – a poet who

Left: As Master Sims in *Bedlam* (1946). Right: Poster for
Bedlam (1946). Top: With Anna Lee. Inset: Karloff and Val
Lewton.

has charge of that notorious insane asylum. There he takes his spleen out on the loonies in his charge, in sadistic cruelties and graft at their expense."[67]

Karloff would arrive at RKO at 7:30 a.m. to prepare for the day's filming, which would continue until 6 p.m. However, despite the long day it was reported Karloff would only manage an average of 35 minutes before the camera each day. "That's because low-key lighting, which results in dense shadows, is used in his films to enhance dramatic effects," revealed the *Hartford Courant*. "Time required to set the lights is 150 percent longer than needed for normal set lighting."[68]

To play the role of Lord Mortimer's protégé, Nell Bowen, the studio engaged Anna Lee, Karloff's old friend from *The Man Who Changed His Mind* (1936). Lee also enjoyed working for Lewton's unit. "After *How Green Was My Valley*, I think *Bedlam* is my favourite picture," she later said. "I loved it. I knew Val Lewton quite well, because I had been close friends with Val and his wife Ruth – I used to go to dinner with them all the time. Val told me he was writing this story, this historical picture... but I forget exactly how I became involved. I suppose it would have been Val who wanted me to do it. I know Mark Robson, the director, had other ideas; he wanted Jane Greer for the part and Val wanted me. And finally I did it, on the condition that I change my hair from blond to dark, which is nothing unusual."[69]

Production began on Wednesday, 18 July 1945 with a budget of $350,000. Again, to spread the budget further, Lewton used sets and costumes from other pictures. "I know that my costumes were not made for me," Anna Lee later explained. "The green velvet riding habit that I wore was Vivien Leigh's dress, the one she makes out of curtains in *Gone With the Wind*. I was always very happy about that [*laughs*]! And the lovely ball gown that I wore in the gardens was Hedy Lamarr's [from *Experiment Perilous*]. So I wore all hand-me-downs from various actresses."[70]

The asylum set had originally been the church in the Bing Crosby/Ingrid Bergman picture *The Bells of St. Mary's* (1945). Likewise, the Quaker's meeting room was the redressed dining room from an Edgar Kennedy comic short. Even sound effects were re-used. The scream, early in the picture, as the man falls from the window was lifted from the soundtrack of the studio's 1933 hit *King Kong*.

Karloff was interviewed during the shoot by journalist Victor Gunson and revealed he had refused a role in Universal's next Frankenstein picture (presumably *House of Dracula*). "It may mean that I'll not do a picture there at all," he told Gunson, "and I'm supposed to do three... I am pursued by a monster. I created a Frankenstein monster and so far I haven't escaped from him. Maybe this picture will do it. Who knows?"[71] Unfortunately, Karloff's mere presence in a picture automatically earned it the label 'horror picture'. "It's not a horror picture," Mark Robson declared. "Boris is getting away from horror pictures. His last three have been historical suspense films, that is, counting this one."

"Here's what happens," Karloff added. "They put me in this picture, no more a horror picture than, let us say, *The Story of Emile Zola*. But, originally it was called *Chamber of Horrors*. Now, couple that title with my name on the theatre marquee, and what does the public think?"

"Horror picture," Gunson proffered.

"Of course," Karloff replied. "And even with the new title [*A Tale of Bedlam*] they're liable to think the same thing. But we have here a quality film, based on the stirring events and personages of a remarkable period in English history. So I hope at least it keeps out of those theatres which specialise in chiller-dillers."[72]

This kind of pigeon-holing proved irksome for the star. "Boris used to get quite annoyed when people referred to *Bedlam* as a horror picture," Anna Lee explained. "He said, 'It's not a horror picture, it's a *historical* picture', and he was right, absolutely dead right. There was never any thought of making it into a so-called horror picture; it was exactly what happened at St. Mary's of Bethlehem, so much so that it was not allowed to be shown in England for a long, long time. They felt it was a true but rather melancholy description of St. Mary's of Bethlehem."[73]

During the shoot – as they had on *The Man Who Changed His Mind* set nine years earlier – Karloff and Lee competed in their 'poetry jam'. "So always, on *Bedlam*," Lee said, "we'd recite poetry to each other, for hours – poems I hoped he *hadn't* remembered, but he always *did*! The reunion with Boris was wonderful, as was the atmosphere on the set of *Bedlam* – because Boris had a great sense of humour, and he used to laugh about everything."[74]

Robert Clarke, who had appeared in *The Body Snatcher*, now played an inmate of Bedlam. Of course this brought him into contact, once again, with Boris Karloff. "He had a very gentlemanly attitude," Clarke said, "and in working in a scene with him, he never tried to upstage you or to get the best of the scene. He was awfully kind, and his dressing room door was always open to anyone who wanted to say hello or chat with him. I never worked with any man for whom I had more admiration."[75]

The picture was completed on Friday, 17 August 1945, two days after WWII was effectively brought to a close by the Japanese surrender. *Bedlam* opened at the Rialto in New York eight months later, on Friday, 19 April 1946. "This is a production," wrote the *New York Times*, "several cuts above the average run of so-called horror films... Anna Lee gives a fine performance here, bringing a spark and compassion to her role of the crusading young girl, and even putting life into the eighteenth-century rhetoric that frequently handicaps the script. As the sadistic chief warden of Bedlam, Boris Karloff is completely at home and is his usual sinister self... While the film has a tendency to wander into unadulterated Hollywood-isms in spots, it is a generally straight-forward and imaginative estimate of a two-century-old sociological theme."[76]

Working at RKO had been a satisfying experience for all involved. Val Lewton, who had initially been reluctant to work with Karloff, now planned to work with the star again. On 24 September 1945 the *New York Times* announced Karloff would star in *Blackbeard* for the producer. The picture would be written and directed by Mark Robson. While that project remained in development Karloff returned to work in a period that would provide new pictures, new challenges – and a new wife.

Chapter 16

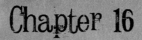

Moving On
(1945-1950)

"I usually wait a year before seeing one of my pictures. It's the only way I can learn anything about my acting. It's like reading something you've written. The next day it sounds pretty good. But a year later it stinks."[1]
Boris Karloff (1946)

"If you take a walk through a graveyard in the dead of night," Karloff told the *Los Angeles Times* in 1946, "and the wind howls, a mist rises and the clock strikes twelve, it inevitably follows that a white form will rise from a grave and tap you on the shoulder. What did you expect to confront you in such a place and at such a time – Mary and her little lamb? But if you are dining at home and are promised a dish of cabbage and you lift the cover from the pot and see there the head of your best friend, to the element of terror is added the element of shock. You did not expect it – that is, unless you put the head there yourself."[2]

Karloff had hoped his association with Val Lewton would lead to his continued involvement in a better class of genre pictures – the psychological horror. It was not to be, however, and in the films that followed Karloff would instead be relegated to supporting roles. None would reach the aesthetic heights of the Lewton pictures or present him with a role as rewarding as that of *The Body Snatcher*'s Cabman Gray. Still, new challenges lay ahead. There would be the rewards offered by his first love, the theatre, plus his introduction to the new rival to motion pictures – television. But first he returned to radio, the medium that continued to provide a welcome source of income.

On Friday, 19 October 1945 he appeared as a guest on the comedy series *Those Websters*. Then, four days later, he began a short season of *Inner Sanctum* mysteries. Broadcast on Tuesday, 23 October at 9 p.m. Karloff's tenure began with *The Corridor of Doom*. He starred as John Clay, a wealthy man who wakes one day in a mysterious hospital. While sleeping he dreams he is walking down a long corridor lined on each side with an endless expanse of doors. Upon each is a single surname, one door representing each surname that has ever been. Clay finds himself inexorably approaching the door marked with the surname 'Clay'. When he awakens from the dreams he finds his feet are dirty. Perhaps it was not a dream after all.

Recording radio's *Inner Sanctum*.

30-year-old Richard Widmark was featured as Clay's son-in-law, Alec Bartlett, only a few years before he found movie fame as the psychotic killer Tommy Udo in *Kiss of Death* (1947). He was already a fan of the star. "When I was a kid," he later said, "I loved *Frankenstein* – I thought Boris Karloff was great."[3]

On 6 November, Karloff appeared on the series in *The Wailing Wall*, a loose amalgam of Poe's tales *The Black Cat* and *The Tell-Tale Heart*. When Gabriel Hornell [Karloff] is saved from a fire at his home he is taken to hospital but disappears. He leaves a note telling his terrible tale. The paper relates how he had strangled his wife before walling her up in his home. Yet he begins to hear a moaning from behind the wall. When he reports his wife as missing the policeman hears the wailing too.

Soon the police fish a woman's body out of the river and Hornell intentionally misidentifies it as his wife. However, his lover Dorothy suspects him of killing his wife and breaks a hole in the wall, revealing the corpse. When she then tries to blackmail the killer she too is murdered.

To avoid discovery Hornell determines never to leave his house and, as a result, spends the next 40 years without going outside. Now, with all his money gone, he is offered $250,000 for his home. But that evening, on hearing the wailing again, he opens up the wall. It is only then he discovers the source of the terrible noise – not a supernatural cause, but a small hole through which the wind has been blowing. In despair he burns the building down but is rescued and taken to the hospital. There he writes the letter from his room on the 18th floor – before leaping to his death.

On 11 November Karloff appeared on *The Theatre Guild on the Air* in a double feature of Eugene O'Neill's works, *The Emperor Jones* and *Where the Cross Is Made*. The first play told the tale of the African-American Brutus Jones [Canada Lee], a former Pullman porter who escaped to an island in the West Indies after murdering two people. Within two years he had risen to become the Emperor of the island, perpetuating a myth that only a silver bullet could kill him. When cockney trader Henry Smithers [Karloff] informs Jones of an impending rebellion he flees to the forest where he is finally shot and killed by the superstitious rebels – with a silver bullet made from melted coins.

In *Where the Cross Is Made* Karloff played Captain Isaiah Bartlett, a whaling captain who paces his room at the top of the house waiting for the return of his shipmates, gone on the ship *Mary Allen* to retrieve treasure, the captain claimed, they had found on an island after being shipwrecked. The captain's story, however, has tormented his son who wavers between acceptance and disbelief. Finally, he determines to have his father committed to the asylum. But, that night, the three arrive with the treasure – ghostly, decomposing figments of both the captain's, and his son's, imagination. Only the captain's daughter fails to see them. Isaiah Bartlett accompanies his ghostly colleagues up to his room where he succumbs to heart failure.

Karloff returned to radio drama on Saturday, 8 December when he appeared opposite Helen Hayes in a half-hour abridgement of Patrick Hamilton's hit play *Gas Light* which, retitled *Angel Street* for American audiences, had closed on Broadway a year earlier.[i] Karloff took Vincent Price's stage role as the psychotic murderer Jack Manningham. On 23 December he starred in a yuletide fantasy entitled *The Baffled Genie* on the radio programme *Exploring the Unknown*. Then his Christmas Eve appearance on the quiz show *Information Please* – his second in as many months – rounded off Karloff's radio work for 1945. However, the holiday soon took a tragic turn for the worse, for the very next evening Karloff's family friend Russell Gleason died. He was 36 years old.

Christmas, 1945.

Gleason, an Army Sergeant, had been billeted at the Hotel Sutton on 6th Street with other personnel of the Army Signal Corps photographic centre of Long Island City. On Christmas night the police received a phone call reporting a man standing on the hotel's rain-swept fourth floor ledge. Before they could reach the building, however, Gleason had fallen, breaking his back when he landed on the second floor extension. His wife, Cynthia, was already in New York with her six-year-old son, Michael, at the time of her husband's death. "My husband died under heartbreaking and public circumstances: 'Fell or Jumped?' the headlines read," she recalled. "My son and I were with the Golenpauls for Christmas. They and all my other friends were magnificent and one friend, Boris, particularly. He talked to the press. He comforted my little boy. He sat with me at the terrible funeral and drove me through freezing weather to the bleak, frozen burial ground.[ii] He stood beside me staring at the Fellini-like scene. It was a military burial and at the incredibly ludicrous moment when the funeral director said, 'There will be a two-hour delay – the firing squad is out to lunch', Boris stormed like an avenging angel at the frightened man, *'Get on with it! Now!'* He got on with it – it was awful. As we drove home, Boris took my hand and said, 'Full marks, old girl – full marks'. Somehow it made everything better."[4]

Russell Gleason's death was a tragic end to an already emotionally trying year for Karloff. While the star's professional life remained buoyant his private life – his marriage – had gone into decline. In early December Dorothy Karloff had sued her husband for divorce charging him with 'cruelty'. She asked he be restrained from threatening or injuring her or attempting to remove their seven-year-old daughter from her custody. She

---

i The play had also been filmed twice before under the title *Gaslight*, firstly in Britain and starring Anton Walbrook and Diana Wynyard in the leads. In 1944, the picture had been remade by MGM and starred Charles Boyer and Ingrid Bergman in an Oscar-winning role. However, fearing the earlier British version would prove stiff competition, MGM reportedly tried to have the negatives of the British picture destroyed. Thankfully, they were unsuccessful.

ii Russell Gleason's funeral was held on the morning of 28 December at the Riverside Memorial Chapel.

also requested $2,000 monthly alimony, plus $500 monthly for support of their daughter, declaring her husband's income from motion pictures and radio to be some $150,000 annually. The couple, Dorothy added, had community property worth nearly $300,000 including an interest in the stage play *Arsenic and Old Lace* in which her husband had appeared. She asked the actor be restrained from disposing of any of it. "Our married life has reached a state of incompatibility," Dorothy announced. "Under the circumstances, the next step is to be divorced."[5]

Dorothy had now been living apart from her husband for some time. On 1 May 1945 Karloff had sold the family home at 2320 Bowmont Drive, the place they had lived in for over a decade, to director Robert Siodmak. Dorothy took Sara and moved into rented accommodation at 714 North Foothill Road in Beverley Hills. They would soon relocate to number 503.

However, in late February 1946, Dorothy had an apparent change of heart and dismissed the suit for divorce against her husband. Her attorney, S.S. Hahn, announced a property settlement had been agreed but refused to issues details. He also would not say whether the couple had been reconciled. They had not. Despite Dorothy's announcement the marriage was over and Karloff went to Boulder City, Nevada to get away from it all. "I am tired," he said. "I just want to rest for a while."[6]

In early April 1945 columnist Hedda Hopper had announced the rights to James Thurber's short story *The Secret Life of Walter Mitty* (published in *The New Yorker* magazine on 18 March 1939) had been purchased as a vehicle for Danny Kaye. Originally planned to go before the cameras the following March production finally began in April 1946.

Ken Englund and Everett Freeman's screenplay told the tale of Walter Mitty [Danny Kaye], a proofreader for a pulp-magazine publishing company. Harassed by his boss, his mother, his fiancée and her would-be suitor, Mitty escapes temporarily into daydreams where he becomes a sea captain, a surgeon, an RAF fighter pilot, a Mississippi riverboat gambler, a milliner and a cowboy.

Then one day Mitty meets Rosalind Van Hoorn [Virginia Mayo] who is the image of the woman who frequents all his dreams. She tells him of a villain nicknamed 'The Boot' who is trying to obtain a little black book containing the details of the whereabouts of art treasures,

Karloff (alongside his wife) in test makeup for *The Secret Life of Walter Mitty* (1947).

taken from the Royal Netherlands Museum in Rotterdam and hidden prior to the German's invasion of Holland.

Although the story's author, James Thurber, later expressed his dissatisfaction with the picture he had, prior to filming, been consulted at length and approved Ken England's adaptation – his only stipulation being Danny Kaye's hands should always be full of packages.

Karloff appeared in only a handful of scenes in the Technicolor feature playing one of The Boot's cronies, Dr. Hugo Hollingshead. His character makes his first appearance with the words "I know a way to kill a man and leave no trace" some 50 minutes into the picture.

During the shooting of this scene Karloff was visited on the set by journalist Erskine Johnson who asked the star where his monster make-up was. "Please," Karloff replied. "Today I am the new Boris Karloff. I left the old one under a wet rock in the Universal prop department." He then left Johnson to continue with the

With Danny Kaye in *The Secret Life of Walter Mitty* (1947).

scene – and pushed Danny Kaye from his office window. "See," Karloff said returning to talk to Johnson, "I'm still a menace. But I don't scare people with neon lights sticking out of my skull, two heads, or eyeballs that pop out every time the heroine looks at me. I'm just Boris Karloff. Not Boris Karloff, horror man."[7]

Johnson took the opportunity to ask the star about his divorce. Karloff's revelation in court that his wife was 'cruel' to him, Johnson noted, had given Hollywood "quite a chuckle".[8] Karloff replied, "Please, let's not go into that. It was purely a technical charge."[9]

In October the picture's title changed, albeit briefly, to *I Wake Up Dreaming*. The change came about when George Gallup's Audience Research Institute convinced Samuel Goldwyn the new title was a stronger selling point. However, within a month Goldwyn gave orders the picture should revert to its original title. The reason, Goldwyn said, was "due to insistent pressure".[10]

The Secret Life of Walter Mitty had its world premiere on 4 August 1947 at the Woods Theatre in Chicago, almost a year after its completion. "While only the basic idea of the original James Thurber story has been retained for film use," wrote the *Chicago Daily Tribune*, "and it has of necessity been enlarged and embroidered, Walter Mitty's wool gathering is excellent for comedy purposes... it is just very, very funny from beginning to end. If you're looking for laughter, you'll find your money's worth at Woods."[11]

The picture opened at the Astor in New York ten days later, on Thursday, 14 August 1947. The *New York Times* thought the picture, "a big, colourful show and a good one. Perhaps it is just a little too big, for it is difficult to sustain a comedy for close to two hours without a letdown every so often."[12]

When the picture went on release, however, it was shorn of at least one daydream sequence. Shot but not used was a sequence in which Irish rebel Mitty is pursued by a policeman through the Dublin night. He finally arrives at his beloved Molly's house to find her mother in tears. Molly has gone.

In mid-2007, 60 years after the picture's release, a photograph surfaced that brought with it the possibility of the existence of another excised daydream – this time featuring Boris Karloff. When film historian Scott McQueen noticed the intriguing picture for sale on eBay, the Internet auction site, he alerted fellow film historian/author Tom Weaver and comic artist Kerry Gammill. Gammill purchased the photograph, which showed Jack Pierce, Boris Karloff – in Frankenstein's Monster make-up – and an unidentified man. The picture's existence was posted on the Internet's fan based *Classic Horror Film Board* and the discussions began.

The picture was obviously taken at the same time as another, previously published, photograph of Karloff, in the same make-up, standing alongside Evie. It had been assumed that that this photograph had been taken at the time of the monster's appearance at the Wrigley Field celebrity baseball game in 1940. However, this second photograph would disprove that theory.

In mid-June 2007 MacQueen posted on the Board a copy of an interesting memo from Universal to A.R. Evans of Samuel Goldwyn Productions. The memo of 30 August 1946 read:

> Gentlemen:
> Enclosed for your records is an agreement dated August 1, 1946 between us concerning your use of the character of the Frankenstein Monster.

When *CHFB* member Robert James Kiss proposed the missing person as director Norman Z. Macleod the mystery was solved. It now seemed clear that Karloff had been made-up as the Monster once more with the intention of making an appearance during a daydream sequence in *The Secret Life of Walter Mitty* – the Danny Kaye picture directed by none other than Norman Z. Macleod. What remains uncertain, however, is whether any Monster footage was shot. No screenplay or additional paperwork has been uncovered that makes mention of this sequence. Still, it is a tantalising prospect that perhaps somewhere there exists an unused colour sequence of the Frankenstein Monster in action.

On Thursday, 11 April 1946 Karloff telephoned Russell Gleason's widow, Cynthia, from Boulder City, Nevada. He wanted a favour. "I would be forever grateful if you would go down to the Miramar Hotel in Santa Monica and fill our room with flowers," he said. "I'm bringing my bride home and I'd hate to have Evie come into a room with no flowers when I carry her over the threshold."[13] The request came as a big surprise. "I nearly dropped the telephone," Cynthia recalled. "I didn't even know Boris and Dorothy were divorced. I just sat there with the telephone in my hand."[14] Karloff explained his divorce had been granted the day before. "And you were married today?" she asked.

"Right. No point in wasting time, Cyn?" Karloff replied. "I'd appreciate it if you keep this our secret," he added. "The papers will get it, but I don't want anyone nosing around. I have been married four times before – they didn't matter really, mostly, but it would be nicer for Evie not to have it mentioned." Gleason agreed to do as her friend asked. "I went to the hotel," she said, "fixed the flowers, put a bottle of champagne, a pot of caviar and a Gideon Bible in the refrigerator, and left."[15]

By this time Evie's ex-husband actor/writer Tom Helmore had also married again – this time to writer Mary Drayton. In April, at the time of Karloff and Evie's wedding, the Helmores were sent to California on a contract with MGM. By co-incidence they were booked into the Hotel Mirimar in Santa Monica – the same hotel where the Karloffs were staying on their honeymoon. Not only that, they would occupy room 602 – next door to the newlyweds. "When we got to our room," Drayton recalled, "we talked it over and decided that since no one had any rancour against anyone it would be silly not to behave in a normally friendly way, and both felt Evie and Boris would agree with that attitude. Still, we couldn't be sure and decided it would be less awkward to let them know we were there than to run into them in the lobby. So Tom called on the house phone..." Evie then relayed the information to her husband. "Great!" replied Karloff. "Ask them to dinner with us. I know a good place near the hotel."[16] That evening saw the beginning of some long-lasting friendships.

Sara was told of her father's divorce and re-marriage on the afternoon of the wedding. At home from school due to illness she was in her room when her mother delivered the news. "I have some good news and some bad – which do you want first?" she asked her daughter.[17] "Your father and I are divorced. Your father married Evie this afternoon," she added, then turned and left the room.[18]

"My mother seldom, if ever, spoke about my father," Sara recalled. "I do believe that the cause for the divorce was that Evie had been a 'family friend' for years and had pretty much set her cap for my father. She divorced Tom at the same time or a bit earlier than my father divorced my mother. At the same time I know my mother had been seeing Edgar and my father found out about it."[19]

Returning from their honeymoon the Karloffs moved into their new home. Set in an acre of ground, Karloff had recently purchased the property from Gregory Peck. Evie quit her job working for Maurice Evans and would now devote her time to looking after her husband. She became, in effect, his driver, nurse, secretary, confidant and adviser. She also began to manoeuvre some of her husband's long-standing friends into the periphery. Bob Beckham, who had been a friend of both Karloff and Dorothy's, recalled, "I remember Evie as being a little bit cold to me. She was not overly friendly, because of course I was involved with Dorothy in the old days, and my mother was a good friend of Dorothy's. So I was not particularly a favourite of Evie's. She was cordial and pleasant, but not overly friendly. And Boris seemed happy. She took very good care of him. She was very possessive, and also very supportive of him. And I thought they were a great pair."[20]

Sadly, Evie's coolness would even extend to Karloff's only child, his daughter, Sara Jane. Sara was now no longer part of Karloff's life. That was in the past, and Evie desired her to remain there. Evie wanted her husband to belong to her, and her alone.

On Thursday, 26 April 1946, two weeks after Karloff's marriage, the star's second editorial effort, *And the Darkness Falls*, hit the shelves. Featuring some 72 stories and poems the book was, like its predecessor *Tales of Terror*, published by the World Publishing Company. A heftier tome than Karloff's previous book, this new anthology ran to over six hundred pages and contained works by such luminaries as Edgar Allan Poe, Ambrose Bierce, Somerset Maugham, Dorothy L. Sayers and inevitably, Karloff's favourite, Joseph Conrad.

For each selection Karloff had written introductory notes as well as a forward. "The collection is broad enough for almost any taste," wrote C.V. Terry of the *New York Times*. "There's enough guignol for the addicts – and enough good writing for those who insist on polish as well as punch. The editor, one might add, is a discerning student of literature, as well as a dependable performer in Hollywood terror specials: his paragraphs of comment preceding each story make first rate reading. When he is discussing the techniques of such writers as Maugham and Galsworthy, Mr. Karloff speaks with authority. On the other hand, when he notes that 'the odd angle of the corpse's head is provocative, to say the least', one is just as positive that he knows whereof he speaks."[21]

Soon Karloff would return to pictures, albeit in another supporting role. This time, however, it would be for the renowned director Cecil B. DeMille who, for the past few years, had been making preparations for his latest picture, the Colonial epic *Unconquered*.

In March 1946 Gary Cooper had been announced for the lead role in the picture and a month later it was revealed Paulette Goddard would star opposite him. Then, shortly afterwards, Boris Karloff received a telephone call from the director. DeMille asked if Karloff would be interested in playing an important role in his next picture. "It's the part of a Seneca Indian chief," the director explained. Karloff laughed. "It will be a slight variation from my usual type of role," he said. "Instead of just raising people's hair, I'll be able to go out and lift their scalps!"[22]

In a hark back to his early days in silent motion pictures he would appear, stripped to the waist, in the supporting role of the Indian Chief Guyasuta. Karloff signed for the picture in mid-May. He would receive fourth billing behind Cooper, Goddard and Howard De Silva.

Originally scheduled for a May 1946 start *Unconquered* went before the cameras a month later. DeMille's crews had spent eight weeks in forests near Pittsburgh filming backgrounds

and action sequences, while other external shoots were made at Idaho's Snake River. In all the picture's crews travelled some 5,000 miles setting up and shooting in eight locations from Pennsylvania to California.

DeMille's 2½ hour long tale told the story of Abigail Martha Hale [Goddard] who, in 1763, is sent to America to be sold into servitude after killing a royal officer. On board ship she is bought by Captain Christopher Holden [Cooper] who then sets her free. However, after Holden disembarks, a rival bidder, Martin Garth [Howard Da Silva], takes

With Gary Cooper in *Unconquered* (1947).

possession of the slaves, including Abigail, and takes her to Fort Penn where she is later reunited with Holden.

Garth has been illegally trading weapons with the Indians and is married to Hannah [Katherine DeMille], the daughter of Chief Guyasuta [Karloff]. With Garth's encouragement the Indians attack the Fort. However, Holden organises a successful ruse, which convinces the Indians a relief column is on its way. After they flee Holden finds Garth trying to escape and, in self-defence, kills his rival. Holden and Abigail are reunited and marry.

In pursuit of realism the director requested Karloff learn his lines in the authentic Seneca language. His 1944 spinal fusion meant he was required to wear a brace, which had to be disguised during filming by his loincloth and fur wrappings. An Indian expert, who was also a deaf mute, supervised Karloff's daily make-up regime and was impressed by the star's attitude. He wrote a note to his assistant, which somehow fell into Karloff's hands. "This man is as patient as a horse," the note read.[23]

According to press reports *Unconquered* took two years of research and almost one hundred days to shoot. Excluding promotion and publicity costs the picture cost close to $4 million, of which $1 million had been the combined costs of the principal and supporting players' salaries. These salary costs had been the largest in DeMille's 34 years as a producer and director.

The picture received its premiere at Loew's Penn Theatre in Pittsburgh on Thursday, 3 October. While DeMille and Howard De Silva were in attendance, Cooper, Goddard and Karloff were not.

Unconquered opened at the Rivoli in New York on Friday, 11 October. A reviewer for the *San Antonio Light* stated the following month, "*Unconquered* is THE Indian picture of all time, and it'll keep you gripping the arm-rests (or your escort) until the very last redskin bites the dust."[24] This sentiment was echoed by Olga Ann Pinette, the reviewer for the *Portland Press Herald*. "The long-awaited and much-heralded *Unconquered* which opened at the State Theatre Thursday, was loudly acclaimed by Thanksgiving Day audiences as one of the most magnificent movies yet to come out of Hollywood. It's been three years since the movie-going public thrilled to a Cecil B. DeMille picture and on this one DeMille has outdone himself... And if you miss *Unconquered* you'll wait a long, long time for a movie that will equal it, for it is truly the greatest of all the great DeMille films."[25]

In October 1946 the *Los Angeles Times* announced Karloff would appear in Paul Osborn's play *On Borrowed Time* alongside Beulah Bondi,[iii] Ralph Morgan, Margaret Hamilton, Joseph Crehan and ten-year-old Tommy Ivo.

Julian (Gramps) and Nellie (Grandma) Northup look after their young grandson John (Pud) after his parents are killed in a car accident. After the funeral of Pud's parents Gramps makes a donation to the church. Pud tells him that, according to his storybook, such a good deed is repaid with a wish. Gramps, frustrated at the local boys stealing his apples, wishes that anyone who climbs his apple tree will be stuck there until he releases them.

One day a Mr. Brink visits Gramps and tells him that soon the old man will need to go with him – for Mr. Brink is, in reality, Death. Not long after, Grandma dies and Pud is left solely in the charge of his grandfather. However, the boy's shrewish aunt Demetria Riffle wants to the raise the boy against Gramps' wishes. When Brink returns to take the old man Gramps requests an apple from his tree so he can taste the fruit one last time. Brink obliges but is trapped in the branches, unable to get down. Now death only comes to those that touch the tree.

Then, one day, Brink encourages Pud to climb the high fence around the tree, hoping the boy will touch the tree and die. Instead, Pud falls, severely injuring himself. The doctor examines him and concludes the boy will never walk again. Gramps releases Brink from his captivity who then takes the old man and Pud, who are reunited with Nellie.

On Borrowed Time would be presented by the Players' Productions in Los Angeles. "A lot of actors were trying to get legitimate theatre out here and got together at the El Patio Theatre on Hollywood Boulevard near La Brea," Tommy Ivo later explained. "One would be a director one time or a stage hand. On ours, Keenan Wynn was running the production end. But they wouldn't have a kid in every show, though they needed one for that one. That's where I really got a love for the stage. I wish I had done a lot more because it was so much fun to do. That catapulted my career because with all the actors in there, everybody in town came to see the thing; when I read for it I read with Keenan Wynn. I thought, 'Gee, he's really great,' but he said Boris Karloff was going to play the grandfather. 'Boris Karloff? You got to be kidding me!' So the first day we were rehearsing I was sitting there

---

iii Beula Bondi had also played Nellie Northrup in the 1939 film version of *On Borrowed Time* starring Lionel Barrymore.

just glued to the door waiting for this guy with a square head and pegs coming out of his neck to come walking in… But of course Boris Karloff was very much different than that."[26] Like many others, Ivo found the star to be the exact opposite of his horrific screen creations. "He absolutely couldn't have been nicer," Ivo later said. "He used to call me his walking script because, if he couldn't remember something while we were doing the show, I'd whisper the line to him."[27]

The play opened at the El Patio Theatre on Hollywood Boulevard on Tuesday, 5 November 1946. *Billboard* found the play "a rare treat", and praised the star's acting. "As

Gramps in *On Borrowed Time* (1946).

the kindly, profane and colourful Gramps of *Time*," it said, "Karloff proved that his versatility and talent extend far beyond the scope of restricting screen roles. Working with a good supporting cast, Karloff made his role a vivid portrayal, full of pathos and humor which the character demands… *On Borrowed Time* should rank at the top of Hollywood's recommended plays to see."[28] The play was a great success and, entering its second week, broke the theatre's box office records. It closed at the El Patio on Sunday, 24 November then moved on for a stint in San Francisco.

Karloff later called Gramps his favourite role. "But even then," he added, "I felt that the audience was waiting for me to unmask and exterminate the rest of the cast."[29] He was able to attempt just that when, on 25 November, he appeared in another radio adaptation of *Arsenic and Old Lace*, this time for the *Lady Esther Screen Guild Players*, opposite Eddie Albert as Mortimer.

Karloff's next film work would be a small role in the murder mystery *Personal Column*, a remake of the French picture *Pièges* (1939), to be directed by Douglas Sirk. Karloff would join Lucille Ball (on loan from MGM), George Sanders, Charles Coburn and Sir Cedric Hardwicke. The picture concerned the search by the London police to find a killer who lures his female victims through his messages in newspaper personal columns. Ball would play an American showgirl enlisted by Scotland Yard to help catch the killer.

Pre-production had begun in October 1946 when camera crews were dispatched to London to take background shots. Principal photography began on 4 November. Exactly one month later Lucille Ball was taken ill for several hours due, it was reported, to her close-fitting costume. As Ball recuperated the tight garment was altered.

Two months later, in late January 1947, Hedda Hopper announced Karloff had been engaged to appear in the picture. Executive producer Hunt Stromberg explained the star had been sought to play the role of a dress designer who "goes mad when someone steals his favourite pattern and makes for the horror in the picture…"[30] His role in the finished movie lasted only eight minutes.

The picture, now retitled *Lured*, opened in New York on 28 August. "A good cast has been assembled by Hunt Stromberg for his production of *Lured*, which opened yesterday

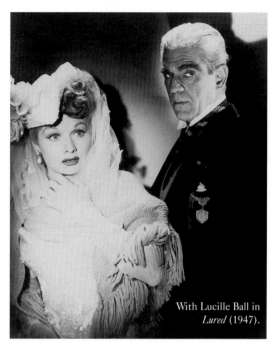

With Lucille Ball in
Lured (1947).

at the Victoria," wrote *The New York Times.* "Unfortunately, the whodunit tale that goes with it has not been so inspired. It is a rather routine piece of story-telling in the mystery genre, decked out with lavish backgrounds and good acting that are not warranted by some of the aspects of the story. For one thing, the film is about a half an hour too long and a number of extraneous and rather absurd sequences could have been omitted."[31]

While *Lured* was in production Karloff's ex-wife, Dorothy, issued another suit, suing on the ground that the monthly $250 support her ex-husband was paying had become inadequate for the proper care of their daughter Sara Jane – now eight years old. Dorothy wanted the payment increased to $600 per month.

Answering the charge Karloff insisted the allowance he provided was more than sufficient. He admitted his gross income for 1946 had been $67,797 but added his taxes would amount to $30,400. Dorothy, he pointed out, had received more than $100,000, including the $75,000 home at 714 North Foothill Road, Beverly Hills. For six months after the settlement, Karloff added, he had paid her $1,000 a month as rent for the house. During 1946 he had paid Dorothy $6,000 alimony in addition to making continuous contributions toward a trust fund, then valued at $28,288, for his daughter.

In her suit Dorothy had also demanded exclusive custody of the child. In answer Karloff said, although he had joint custody of Sara Jane, she had continued to live with her mother with his consent. If any change was to be made, he added, Sara Jane should be placed in *his* care.

On 7 January 1947 Karloff and Dorothy appeared in the domestic relations court where Dorothy's counsel, Martin Gang, argued that all of the money would be utilised in the care of the child. With assets totalling over $100,000 and earnings of $90,000 in the previous year Karloff was, Gang claimed, more than able to support his child. In reply Karloff's attorney, Frank Belcher, presented an affidavit from the star stating that Dorothy, too, had assets in excess of $100,000.

Belcher also informed the court that, at the time the divorce settlement was signed, Dorothy had asked for $200 per month but Karloff, not wishing to appear 'niggardly', raised the amount to $250. This sum, Belcher maintained, was ample for the care of an eight-year-old girl. After deliberation Superior Judge Fred Miller ordered the star to increase his monthly payments to $350. It would not spoil the child, Judge Miller told the court, to raise Sara Jane according to living standards set by her father's income.

On 4 January 1947, while the lawsuit was in progress, Karloff's sister, Julia, died, aged 72. She was the third of the star's siblings to pass away, following George's death in 1904, and his half-sister Emma's death in 1924. Julia's grand-daughter, Elisabeth Crowley, later remembered her as "a very formidable woman."[32] In 1924 Julia had made overtures to find a husband for her daughter, Dorothea – even if this meant sending her overseas. This attitude brought her into some conflict with her brother John, as he related in a letter to Emma. "She [Julia] is taken a little against me at present," he wrote, "because I would not have Dorie [Dorothea] here after she left China – but she doesn't realise that Dorie's chances of finding a husband in Bombay were practically nil!"[33]

Despite Julia's interference Dorothea was married on 16 May 1930 to Percy Edwin Read. Dorothea's father, Reverend Arthur Donkin, performed the ceremony in Semer Church in Suffolk and Karloff's brothers Charles and John were present for the occasion. Julia, however, had never been pleased with the arrangements. "The sad thing is that she was not at all pleased when my parents got engaged," Elisabeth Crowley later explained. "I suspect it was because she didn't think an organ-builder of modest means was an acceptable son-in-law."[34] Dorothea and Harold would go on to have two children, Elisabeth and Jeremy. Of the two Julia clearly had a favourite, as Elisabeth recalled. "She didn't have much time for me either when my brother and I were sent to stay with her at Westerfield during the war, on account of the bombing which affected Enfield," she explained. "She had me learning the psalms at the age of six and tied woollen gloves on my hands at night to stop me sucking my thumb, not to mention closing the bedroom door so that I was totally in the dark, and forcing me to eat fish which I hated! My brother, on the other hand, could do no wrong, even when he threw a stone into a cow-pat and covered me with manure!"[35]

While between pictures, keeping busy as usual, Karloff returned to the radio, a medium he had already graced that year. On 19 January 1947, he appeared on *The Jack Benny Show* in a skit entitled *I Stand Condemned*. Benny, in prison awaiting execution, relates his story – how he had met a man [Karloff] who buys Benny's cigarette lighter for $20,000. Over the next few days the stranger buys the comedian's clothes for more ridiculous sums. Soon the stranger is living with Jack Benny and his family, but the now fabulously wealthy Benny goes money mad. Yet after his family leaves him he discovers the stranger had been printing the money himself. Mad with rage Benny strangles him. "Oh, why must I always die in the end?" Karloff asks.

In March Karloff opened in *On Borrowed Time* at the Irish Theatre in Mexico City. His weeklong tenure was part of the city's theatrical season known as 'Teatro Americano'. The 11-week season opened in February with Gertrude Lawrence in *Pygmalion*. This was followed by a variety of plays including *Night Must Fall* (starring Dame May Whitty), *Springtime for Henry* (with Edward Everett Horton), and Eddie Albert in *Boy Meets Girl*.

The following month Boris Karloff returned to RKO to fulfil his contract for the studio. Although Val Lewton had planned to feature the star as a pirate named Captain Aguilar in a film biopic of the notorious Blackbeard the project failed to materialise and instead Karloff's talents were put to use in *Dick Tracy Meets Gruesome*, a crime picture based upon the comic strip characters of Chester Gould. Receiving top billing, Karloff would play the villain of the title opposite Ralph Bird's crime fighter.

During production Karloff was visited on the set by journalist Inez Wallace who recorded that, at the time of her visit, the picture was called *Dick Tracy vs. the Gruesome Gang*. "The set on the RKO lot was as bad as the name of the film," she wrote, "a cheap cafe, red tablecloth, a gaudy bar – all the atmosphere of the waterfront. As the director started to shoot, Karloff's valet stepped up and took the star's eyeglasses, also lighted a cigarette for him. Karloff is a chain-smoker on and off the screen."[36]

Dick Tracy Meets Gruesome (1947).

After the scene was in the can Karloff retired to his dressing room where Wallace asked how he managed to appear in so many pictures. "Because I'm a freelance," he replied, smiling, "and therefore I can pick my own vehicles. This way, too, I only work when I want to and can spend more time in my garden in Beverly Hills. We've moved into town, you know, from the San Fernando Valley. I have a little girl of eight, and the Valley was too far for her to come to the school we wanted. She always wants to come to the studio to watch me work, but I never permit it. Take, for example, a look at the name on the window of this set. 'Hangman's Knot Café', it says. Wouldn't that be wonderful for a girl to find her father associated with? And, of course, she is never permitted to see any of my pictures."[37]

Asked if Karloff intended to continue playing monsters alongside the character roles Karloff replied, "Probably. I don't object to doing heavies but don't want to do two-headed monsters. Anyhow, they are outmoded. I don't mean to be ungrateful, but there is still a wide field for work without a third arm. I do want to do a play called *On Borrowed Time*, the story of a man over 80. As to my character roles, I feel that anybody can shout. So I play my roles very quietly and let the audience use their own imagination. They will always imagine more than I can do."[38]

Wallace then asked if Karloff was disturbed by being constantly cast as a heavy. "Not at all," he replied. "It's LUCKY to be typed because this is the day of specialists. Be known for a certain thing – be good at it. The comedian who plays Hamlet usually dies in the attempt. But I feel the word 'horror' is a mistake. The right word is 'terror'. Horror is nauseating. The more normal circumstances you present the term in, the more you heighten the effect. I do want to get away from the obvious and the charnel houses. What I would like is a 'reasonable terror'. You know, we all like to pretend there is something behind the door, but we should never show it – ."[39] But where, Karloff was asked, would he find such a role? "Ah, that's just it," he replied, "WHERE? My dear, I've looked everywhere – and am still looking. Right now I'm reading plays in an effort to find such a one. I doubt greatly whether I shall find it in a motion picture – they are all too obvious. The ones they offer me on the radio make my hair curl, and I'm not speaking of this wig I have on, either. I just have to find something subtle, that's all, and shall keep on looking until I do."[40]

Life as a cinematic villain was not easy, he explained, "and for just one reason. It's these awful make-ups. This horrible looking make-up I'm wearing right now makes me almost hate myself. I look into the mirror at myself and think, 'Good Lord, do I have to do this to make a living?' Yet such a make-up is essential to this type of role. Actually, it's half the battle – to have moviegoers hate you before you open your mouth, just by your appearance. But there is consolation to that, too. It is the fact that, so long as time goes on, this sort of role will always be in demand. Goodness may cease to attract or change its style. But down-to-earth just plain devilish villains always will have a place in the public's affection. By the way, who do you suppose is my greatest audience – children and men? Not at all. The ladies, so help me! They have a sadistic streak which is simply incredible."[41]

Dick Tracy Meets Gruesome opened in New York on Friday, 26 September 1947. Bosley Crowther's review for the *New York Times* was short and to the point. "*Dick Tracy and Gruesome*, at the Rialto, is precisely what it says it is," he wrote. "Dick Tracy – and gruesome. Any questions? No? Then, dump it in the incinerator, boys."[42]

On 12 June 1947, within months of completing his work on the Dick Tracy picture, Karloff signed once more with Universal – now known as Universal-International after its merger with International Pictures – for the Civil War picture, *Tap Roots* starring Van Heflin, Susan Hayward and Julie London. Once again Karloff would play a Native American, this time a sympathetic Choctaw Indian named Tishomingo.

Shooting began in early June, over a week before Karloff had signed for the picture. During production the company went on location to shoot near Asheville, North Carolina. Karloff arrived there in the midst of a terrific storm. The wind howled and the sky was black, broken only by flashes of lightning. The cast and members of the press were waiting at a country inn when a car pulled up and Karloff got out, stepping into the storm. "Oh, brother," a reporter was heard to say. "What an entrance!"[43]

Tap Roots premiered at the Goldman Theatre in Philadelphia on 14 July 1948 and opened at the Criterion in New York on 25 August. Bosley Crowther called the picture, "a tedious attempt at duplication of the sweep and romance of *Gone With the Wind* with busty Susan Hayward and Van Heflin in the counter to the Scarlett and Rhett roles, and with rugged Ward Bond as the king-pin of an anti-Confederacy schism."[44]

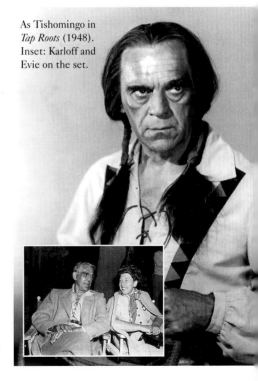

As Tishomingo in *Tap Roots* (1948). Inset: Karloff and Evie on the set.

That month the newspapers announced it was expected Karloff would play the wicked king of the Philistines, the Saran of Gaza, in Cecil B. DeMille's forthcoming picture, *Samson and Delilah*. However, for whatever reason, this did not transpire and George Sanders eventually played the role.

On Wednesday, 16 July Karloff returned to radio's *Lights Out* for a short season, scheduled as a replacement for the Henry Morgan Show while Morgan was on holiday. In the first episode, *Death Robbery*, Karloff played a scientist who brings his wife back to life after a fatal car accident. His wife lacks a soul, however, and is now no more than a fiend. When she kills her husband's friend the scientist is forced to shoot her. "It's an expertly done thriller backed by a long successful tradition," wrote *Billboard*. "Now it's got the sepulchral Karloff in the lead, and if you'll take my advice you won't extinguish those lights – just dim 'em somewhat… It's all effectively done, and those ghoulish actors, led by Karloff, and the writers and directorial talent, deserve kudos."[45]

Soon, however, it was reported that Karloff was unhappy with the show and intended to quit as soon as the sponsor, Eversharp, could find a replacement. The scripts, he said, were "too gruesome".[46] Then, in early August, it was reported Karloff's show had been cancelled. Until Morgan returned in the autumn the time would be given over to a variety music show.

Between pictures again, Karloff revealed he now hoped to be rid of the monstrous roles. "As a matter of fact," he said, "there is nothing more to be done with Frankenstein," he said. "He's been played to the saturation point. Frankly, I doubt if he frightens anybody any more. What I want now are good parts, even though they may be minor parts. I intend to pick and choose very carefully."[47]

On 29 October, to celebrate Halloween, Karloff appeared on Bing Crosby's show *Philco Radio Time*, during which he joked and sang with Crosby and fellow guest, actor/comedian Victor Moore. Karloff told Crosby he had had to get away from Los Angeles. "I just had to get away from Hollywood, Bing," he said. "My nerves are completely shattered... I've been working in a picture with Danny Kaye!" Working on *Unconquered*, too, had had its downside, Karloff told the crooner. "Having to run around with feathers stuck in my head I felt like Hedda Hopper," he joked. Then, later in the show, when Victor Moore suggested the trio go out for Halloween and stick pins in doorbells, Karloff had a better idea. "Stick pins in doorbells!?" he exclaimed. "What's the fun in that? Stick 'em in people!"

On Halloween two days later Karloff was a guest on Burl Ives' radio show singing *You Are My Sunshine* and *The Girl That I Marry* from *Annie Get Your Gun*, retitled for the occasion *The Ghoul That I Marry*. Then, on 10 December, he appeared on *The Jimmy Durante Show* as radio host Happy Sam, the record man. "Girls, are you neglected?" he asked his radio audience. "Do you have a winning smile and a losing face? When you walk into a room do mice jump up on chairs? Mmmmm? Then there's only one solution for your face – 'Pickle It', the cucumber beauty cream!"

"I'm not a horror man," Karloff told Durante during the show. "I'm a gentle soul. I hate horror but nobody believes me. Nobody believes me," he sobbed. It was a sentiment he reiterated on Christmas Day when he appeared on Al Jolson's *Kraft Music Hall* – as Santa Claus. Challenged by Jolson, Karloff admitted being the horror star. He had only dressed as Santa, he explained, because he wants to be loved.

Before the year was out Karloff received an interesting proposal from actor/producer Maurice Evans. Evans planned to produce J.B. Priestley's play *The Linden Tree*, then enjoying a successful run in London with Sir Lewis Casson and his wife Dame Sybil Thorndike. Now Evans planned to produce the play on Broadway and wanted Karloff to play the lead.

The play told the story of Professor Robert Linden, a history teacher at an English University, whose three grown children return home to celebrate the professor's birthday with their mother and younger sister. "At heart, *The Linden Tree* is a conversation piece," explained critic Brooks Atkinson. "Professor Linden, sixty-five years of age, and a history professor, speaks for wisdom and probity. His wife speaks for weariness. His son speaks for cynicism and despair. One daughter speaks for the peace of retreat into religion. Another daughter, who is a scientist, has no concrete program, although she discusses one. The only member of the Linden family who shares her father's native faith is the youngest daughter, who is a musician. As one of Mr. Priestley's spokesmen declares, the young and the old were always the best. The cheap stuff lies in the middle."[48]

Karloff was immediately interested. The role was the antithesis of the type of characters he was generally known for. With Karloff's participation assured Evans contacted Priestley to ask for his casting approval. "Good Lord, not Karloff!" Priestley replied. "Put his name up on the marquee and people will think my play is about an axe murder."[49] Evans contacted Karloff by telephone and told him the bad news. Disappointed, Karloff sent the playwright a telegram. "I PROMISE YOU I WOULD NOT HAVE EATEN THE BABY IN THE LAST ACT," the message read.[50] "Upon that solemn assurance," Karloff later said, "he withdrew his objections. The part was mine."[51] He later added, "A sly cable, wasn't it? You see, there really isn't any baby in *The Linden Tree* for me to eat!"[52]

In the New Year Karloff and Evie arrived in New York in time to start rehearsals, which were scheduled to begin on Tuesday, 13 January 1948. Joining the star, who had grown a moustache for the role, were Barbara Everest, Cathleen Cordell, Marilyn Erskine, Halliwell Hobbes Jr. and Viola Keats as the professor's family. Karloff's *Bride of Frankenstein* co-star Una O'Connor would also feature as the Linden's housekeeper, Mrs. Cotton. Directing the play would be a more recent acquaintance of Karloff's, George Schaefer, who had directed the star in the U.S. Army Special Service touring version of *Arsenic and Old Lace* in the Pacific.

Before opening in New York the play would have tryouts in New Haven, Philadelphia, and Washington. After three weeks of rehearsals *The Linden Tree* opened at the Schubert Theatre in New Haven, Connecticut on Wednesday, 4th February where it played the rest of the week.

"*The Linden Tree* is a wordy, very slow moving, dull piece with no saving grace," wrote Sydney Golly of *Billboard*. "But there's a fine characterisation by Boris Karloff, its star... Karloff, alone of all the cast, gave a sincere reading. His characterisation of the kindly, understanding old prof was a good job... He underplayed the role to perfection, and stood out significantly because of silent movie interpretations by the others."[53]

The play opened at the National in Washington on Monday, 23 February where it played until that Saturday. His brief tenure in the city allowed Karloff to visit his new grandnephew, Stephen, the second son of Sir John Pratt's daughter Diana and her husband Tom Bromley, who was then on the British Embassy Staff in the city. It was a happy time for the Bromleys. No one could have foreseen the terrible tragedy that would befall them a decade later.

The Linden Tree opened at the Music Box Theatre at 239 W. 45th Street in New York at 8 p.m. on Tuesday, 2 March. The play would run six days a week with matinee performances on Thursdays and Saturdays. Ticket prices ranged from $1.20 to $3.60 for matinees and $1.80 to $4.80 for evening performances. The *New York Times* critic Brooks Atkinson wrote:

> Mr. Priestley is a solid citizen of the world, but his prose style is solemn and his set speeches of wisdom sound like sanctimonious phrase-making... **The Linden Tree**, like most of his plays, looks as though it were written with his left hand between more important engagements.
>
> Give it credit for one achievement. It proves that Boris Karloff, made up to look like a human being, is an extraordinarily winning actor. He plays the venerable academician with attractive, humorsome conviction. Shaggy, tweedy,

grey-haired, he has warmth and magnetism; and those beetling brows, which can scare you in his shiver-plays, can soothe you with wisdom when he is in a benevolent mood…

Although Mr. Priestley earnestly argues for faith in **The Linden Tree**, he does it with words. Spirit is the seed of faith. But there is very little spirit in this dull play.[54]

Everywhere the reviewers were in agreement – the play simply did not hold the same relevance to American audiences as it had to English ones. With consistently poor reviews it was decided to cut their losses and on 6 March, after only seven performances, the final curtain came down on *The Linden Tree*. It was a disappointing return to Broadway after the great success of *Arsenic and Old Lace*. Over a decade later Karloff reflected on the playwright's initial misgivings and the play's subsequent early closure, "and," he said, "I've always been haunted by the thought that possibly Priestley was right after all."[55]

According to Ralph Edwards – the creator and host of radio's popular quiz show *Truth or Consequences* – Boris Karloff appeared, albeit briefly, on stage in New Mexico that July. In association with his radio show's stage manager, Al Paschall, Edwards was in the process of opening a new summer theatre in New Mexico – *El Teatro de Santa Fe*. "We petitioned all of our acting friends to be apart of it," Edwards later explained. "I opened the season with a week of *Goodbye Again*. Boris came the next week, and my mind fails for his vehicle… Boris and Evie stayed on for another week and then returned for the end of season party at our house."[56]

However, Edwards was mistaken. The nine-week season did open on 4 July 1948 with Edwards' play. However, this was followed by the comedy *John Loves Mary* which starred Jeffrey Lynn, not Boris Karloff. Although Karloff and Evie did arrive in Santa Fe they merely attended the Saturday evening performance of *Goodbye Again* (10 July) before making their way to New York.

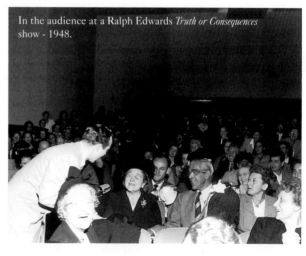

In the audience at a Ralph Edwards *Truth or Consequences* show - 1948.

Following the *Tap Roots* premiere on 14 July 1948, Karloff, Evie and members of the cast embarked on a weeklong tour to promote the picture. Universal representative Philip Gerard found Karloff to be a calming presence. "When tempers flared and patience wore," he recalled, "it was always Boris's good humour which brought our little troupe around… Van Heflin constantly worrying about photographers and his hairpiece – sulky Julie London – and affable Richard Long… I remember each town on that tour. Frantic schedules, the trains, the planes and the rain. There was lots of rain."[57]

Then, towards the end of the month, the Karloffs arrived in New York at the behest, and expense, of Universal-International. According to Hedda Hopper the star had come east to speak to John C. Wilson about a potential play. Ever mindful of a photo opportunity, Universal wanted Karloff to help promote what would be its final picture to feature the

Frankenstein Monster – *Abbott and Costello Meet Frankenstein*. Karloff agreed to have shots taken of him buying a ticket and gazing at the marquee of Loew's Criterion when the picture opened there as long as, he said, he did not have to see the picture. "I'm too fond of the monster," he explained. "I'm grateful to him for all he did for me, and I wouldn't like to watch anybody make sport of him."[58]

On 4 September, however, Karloff himself would parody the monster when he joined over two hundred Hollywood actors and the performers of Ringling Brothers and Barnum & Bailey Circus in a benefit to raise funds for a new 100-bed wing for St. John's Hospital. At one point during the three-hour event Karloff was joined by Harpo Marx and actor Jack Norton in a 'Frankenstein comedy act'.[iv] Ex-circus performer Burt Lancaster got loud applause that evening flipping on parallel bars with his partner Nick Cravat. Gregory Peck, Bing Crosby, Van Johnson, and Frank Sinatra all appeared as clowns, and the new Tarzan, Lex Barker, rode round the ring on an elephant. Gary Cooper paraded around as Robinson Crusoe with Buster Keaton as his Man Friday. Nelson Eddy entered the ring as a Northwest Mounted policeman and Lucille Ball did a bareback riding act.

Between acts Harpo Marx chased Danny Kaye. Marx carried a watering can while Kaye held a small pot plant. Each time Kaye re-appeared he was short by one piece of clothing while the plant he was carrying was noticeably bigger. By the end of the evening Danny Kaye staggered out in only his shorts, carrying an eight-foot aspidistra. The event raised $175,000 for the hospital.

A week later, on 12 September, Karloff returned to radio on *Guest Star*, appearing in a skit entitled *The Babysitter* as an escaped convict named Spider Parsons. The following month brought more respectable fare when, on 17 October, he appeared as the title character in an hour long radio adaptation of H.G. Wells' novel *The History of Mr. Polly*. Then, at the end of the month (29 October), he revisited the role of Gramps in a half-hour abridgement of *On Borrowed Time* for radio's *Great Scenes from Great Plays*. The following day Karloff was in Milwaukee, Wisconsin, having flown in on a TWA Constellation especially to make an appearance on Ralph Edwards' *Truth or Consequences* Halloween show.

On the broadcast Edwards introduced one of the contestants, housewife Mrs. Peterson. "Why would anybody bring a bottle of milk to a poker game?" he asked her. When she failed to give the correct answer – "To feed the kitty" – she had to pay the consequences. Mrs. Peterson would have her fortune told.

When she was sent offstage to fetch the crystal ball Edwards informed the audience that Mrs. Peterson would now be told the fortune teller is really her husband in disguise. She would also be instructed to give the swami a kiss each time he is correct in his assertions. Then Edwards revealed the fortune teller would not be Mr. Peterson – he would be Boris Karloff.

The announcement was met with applause and screams of delight from the Milwaukee audience. "Lovely…" Karloff told them as he walked on stage. "I've always wanted to play a tender love scene." Then, as the audience laughed, Karloff put on a black beard, dark glasses, turban, robe and gloves. He then turned, looked in the mirror at himself, and screamed. Now he would disguise his voice and answer Edwards' questions with answers provided by the real Mr. Peterson.

---

iv Unfortunately the press failed to record the content of the Frankenstein skit, so it is not known if Karloff appeared as the Monster.

When Mrs. Peterson planted the first kiss the audience went wild. "The swami just about passed out!" Edwards announced. With each subsequent answer Mrs. Peterson went to town kissing her 'spouse', much to the audiences delight. "Do you think your husband would mind you kissing this stranger?" Edwards asked. "Not at all," she replied, "I knew it was him all the time… I knew those lips." Again the audience erupted. Then the swami was asked to remove his disguise. With his back towards the contestant he complied and, turning towards her, Karloff growled like the Frankenstein Monster. Mrs. Peterson screamed, and then began to roar with laughter. "Brother, have I been kissed!" Karloff told the audience.

The following month, undeterred by the failure of *The Linden Tree*, Karloff agreed to return to the New York stage. On 24 November he signed an *Actor's Equity Association/Standard Run-of-the-Play* contract to appear in Edward Percy's play *The Shop at Sly Corner*. The play had been produced in London in 1945 and had enjoyed a successful two-year run. It was naturally hoped the play would fare just as well on Broadway. Karloff signed to play the lead role for in the new production for $1,000 a week and 10% of the play's gross receipts.

Percy's play told the story of Descius Heiss, a Frenchman who, following the death of his wife, moved to London with his daughter Margaret [Mary MacLeod] and sister Mathilde [Ethel Griffies]. There he owns and runs a respectable antique shop which, in fact, serves as a front for Heiss's criminal activities. For, unbeknown to his daughter, the Frenchman is a criminal fence dealing in stolen gold and diamonds.

When his shop assistant, Archie Fellowes [Jay Robinson], discovers his secret the youth attempts to blackmail him. To protect his daughter Heiss embarks upon a course of action that includes murder and, ultimately, suicide. "In it," Karloff explained to Hedda Hopper, "I play the part of an old Alsatian fence for thieves. The man commits a few murders, but he's such a nice old dear that you just can't help hoping that he gets away with it all."[59] Karloff grew a beard for the role, which opened on Christmas night at the Wilbur Theatre in Boston for a two-week, pre-Broadway try-out.

The play opened in New York on 18 January 1949. "Boris Karloff, the illustrious shudder man, is stalking ominously through *The Shop at Sly Corner*, produced at the Booth last evening," wrote Brooks Atkinson of the *New York Times*. "This just about concludes the bill of virtues for the occasion… Mr. Karloff is too good a man to waste on so much domestic banality… Under Margaret Perry's workmanlike and appreciative direction, the performance is enjoyably animated… But Mr. Karloff is capable of much finer slaughter than anything *The Shop at Sly Corner* has dreamed of."[60]

Karloff later agreed. "It was the usual actor's trap," he said, "a jolly good part in a very bad play. I fell into the trap. No excuse. I should have known better."[61] So, despite some good reviews, the final curtain came down on *The Shop at Sly Corner* on 22 January 1949 after only seven performances. Once again the early closure of a play meant Karloff was now available for work. He would find much of it in television.

On 7 February he appeared in his first drama on that medium when *Chevrolet on Broadway* presented *Expert Opinion*, a drama by True Boardman. Karloff was joined on the live broadcast by Dennis King and Vicki Cummings. Three days later production began on his latest picture, *Abbott and Costello Meet the Killers*. The picture had a budget of only $685,000 and, of this, Abbott and Costello received $113,750. Boris Karloff, who had signed for the picture on 5 February, received $20,000 for his work.

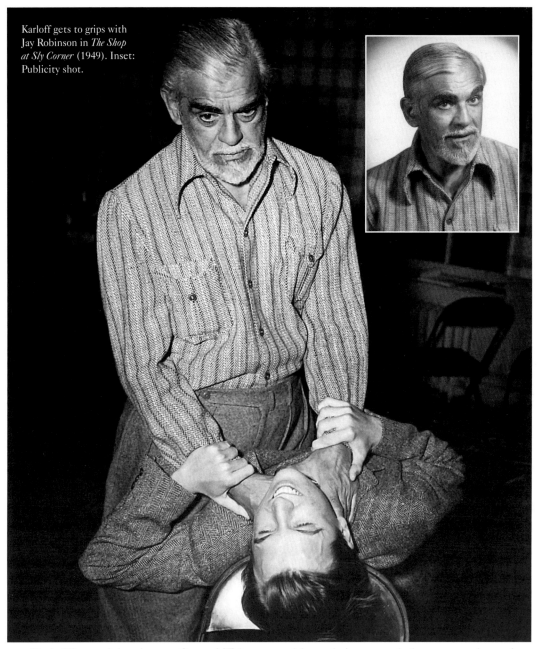

Karloff gets to grips with Jay Robinson in *The Shop at Sly Corner* (1949). Inset: Publicity shot.

Karloff's participation, as Swami Talpur, would result in several changes to the script. Initially his role was to have been a woman, a character named Madam Switzer. More significantly, though misleadingly, the picture's title was changed. Now it would be called *Abbott and Costello Meet the Killer, Boris Karloff*.

When a famous criminal lawyer is murdered at Crandall's Lost Cavern Hotel a band of the lawyer's criminal clients, headed by Swami Talpur [Karloff], attempt to pin the blame on the bellhop, Freddie Phillips [Lou Costello]. They hope to bring a swift resolution to the case thereby keeping secret their previous associations with the dead man. However, more murders follow.

After Freddie inadvertently destroys a vital piece of incriminating evidence – a handkerchief – Inspector Wellman [James Flavin] seizes the opportunity. As they are the only ones who

Abbott and Costello Meet the Killer, Boris Karloff (1949).

know the fate of the piece he instructs Freddie to try to sell the handkerchief to each of the guests. Whoever wishes to buy it will be the killer. The killer is, indeed, keen to retrieve it but, after making several unsuccessful attempts on Freddie's life, he is captured.

Karloff's first picture with the comedy duo was, apparently, a rather sombre affair – for the duo was living in the shadow of a tragedy from five years before. On 4 November 1943 Lou Costello's son, Lou Jr. ('Butch') was drowned in the swimming pool at his home. He was two days short of his first birthday.

In May 1947 Abbott and Costello opened the Lou Costello Jr. Youth Foundation, a playground and medical clinic for underprivileged children. It was later reported that the comedians had paid 75% of the $350,000 cost to erect the main building, its pool and playing fields from their own pockets. But, at the time of making *Abbott and Costello Meet the Killer, Boris Karloff*, they had concerns they would not be able to pay off the remaining $80,000 mortgage on the building. While most of the cast relaxed between scenes Costello could usually be found on the phone trying to raise the necessary funds.

The legacy of the tragedy was still in evidence during the shoot as actress Donna Martell recalled. "Lou Costello was a fine person," she said, "but he was still trying his best to get over the death of his infant son, so his actions were indeed acting, and nothing more. After his son's death, something died in him, and I think it was apparent to just about everyone who worked with him. Still, despite his sorrow, Lou managed to muster up some high jinks, and he would often play practical jokes. Bud Abbott would play cards with me from time to time, and I became friends with Bud's sister, Olive."[62] Martell also came to know Karloff during the shoot. "Boris was just the opposite of the characters he played," she said. "There was no killer or monster in this man. He was the perfect gentleman; sweet, calm and even-keeled."[63]

Production on *Abbott and Costello Meet the Killer, Boris Karloff* ended on 26 March, 14 days over schedule and $52,000 over budget. It opened at Keith's in Washington on Wednesday, 10 August and in Chicago a week later. On Saturday, 3 September the picture opened at United Artists' Ritz, Vogue and Studio City theatres in Los Angeles. "Maybe Lou Costello has never been as funny as he is in *Abbott and Costello Meet the Killer, Boris Karloff*," wrote the *Los Angeles Times*. "He plays a hotel bellboy accused of three murders and floundering in bewilderment… Bud Abbott plays the house detective who doesn't believe Costello guilty… Probably the most hilarious scenes occur when Karloff tries to get Costello to commit suicide,[v] first hypnotising him."[64]

The picture opened at the Globe in New York on Saturday, 17 September. Bosley Crowther of the *New York Times* felt it necessary to point out the picture's titular misnomer. "According to that compendious title," he wrote, "one is led to assume that the ultimate villain in this nonsense will turn out to be Mr. K. And since it is virtually impossible to follow the plot as it transpires, that one clarifying assumption is something, at least, by which to go. But (big switch!) the authors trick us – or maybe someone has tricked them: when the pinch is finally put on the villain, Mr. Karloff is in the clear. Wearing a very long face and a turban, he is merely one of several suspects in a room who are brusquely eliminated by the detective sifting the crime. This is plainly the last straw of confusion – and, from the look on Mr. Karloff's dismal face, he is quite as surprised and bewildered as you unquestionably will be. Obviously he, too, figured that he had done it all the time."[65] The critic found the whole thing rather unfunny. Still, despite some lacklustre reviews the picture went on to make $1,850,000, placing it eighth in the list of Universal's top earners for 1949.

On 11 April 1949 Karloff's role as Jonathan Brewster was finally made available to a wider audience when *Arsenic and Old Lace* aired as part of television's *Ford Theatre Hour* season. Karloff was joined by original cast members Josephine Hull and Edgar Stehli, as well as William Prince (Mortimer), Ruth McDevitt (Aunt Martha) and Bert Freed (Teddy). Two weeks later (26 April) he graced the television screen again in *A Night at an Inn*, his first appearance in an episode of the series *Suspense!*

Karloff played Arnold Everett Scott-Fortesque ('The Toff'), the leader of a band of sailors who have escaped from India with a ruby stolen from the forehead of an idol. Two of their band, however, were killed in the escape and the remaining four are now holed up in a rural English inn awaiting the arrival of their pursuers. The Toff, however, proves too clever for them and sets a trap, killing all three. But as the thieves celebrate their victory the idol itself appears and calls each of them to their deaths.

On 9 May Karloff made his second appearance on *Chevrolet on Broadway* (a.k.a *Chevrolet Tele-Theatre*) in *Passenger to Bali*, alongside Vicki Cummings and his *Black Friday* co-star Stanley Ridges. Then, on 17 May, he returned to the *Suspense!* series, and joined Mildred Natwick in an adaptation of W.W. Jacobs' classic story *The Monkey's Paw*. The two played Mr. and Mrs. White, a couple who are presented with a monkey's paw – a talisman with the ability to grant its owner three wishes. Mr. White wishes for £200. The next day, however, the couple's son, Herbert, is killed – mangled in the machinery at his factory. The Whites are awarded £200 in compensation. After Herbert's funeral Mrs. White convinces her

---

v Karloff tells Costello, "You're going to commit suicide if it's the last thing you do!"

husband to make a second wish and bring their son back to life. "I wish my son alive again," he says. Soon there comes a knocking at the front door and Mrs. White rushes to answer it. But as she struggles with the lock her husband realises that their son will still be in a terrible state – mangled and ten days dead. He makes the third wish and when his wife opens the door their late night caller has vanished.

On 29 May Karloff returned to radio drama on *Theatre Guild on the Air*, playing an ex-convict in an adaptation of A.A. Milne's detective-comedy drama *The Perfect Alibi*. This was followed, on 7 June, with Karloff's third *Suspense!* appearance – in *The Yellow Scarf*.

On television with Mildred Natwick in *The Monkey's Paw*, 17 May 1949.

Set in 1897, Karloff played Bronston, a mysterious scientist who takes in a drunken young woman named Ettie. He feeds her, clothes her, and keeps her on condition that she doesn't leave his house, except when she goes shopping for food, and always keeps the front door locked. She is also forbidden from entering his laboratory where only himself, his hunchback assistant and his clients go.[vi] To further the illusion of respectability he marries the girl but she soon falls in love with Tom, a young man from the mission who gives her a yellow scarf as a token of his affection. Aware of his wife's dalliance, Bronston confiscates the gift and places it in a jar of powder which will slowly destroy the material. One day Tom is invited for dinner and, while Bronston is out, retrieves the scarf from the jar. However, at dinner, Bronston makes veiled threats towards his guest and cuts his hand. Although her husband tries to stop her, Ettie wraps the scarf around Tom's wounds. Bronston reveals the powder was poisonous and fatal if brought into contact with an open wound. Tom dies and in revenge Ettie cuts her husband's hand and thrusts the scarf onto his wound, condemning him to a painful death.

Although relatively new to the medium Karloff was quickly taken with the immediacy of a live broadcast. "Television has tremendous charm," he explained. "It requires a continued, sustained effort like a play... In that half hour you are absolutely on your own. Nobody can help you. There are eight million eavesdroppers but you are alone in the world for half an hour."[66] Live television, he felt, had a frisson missing from film work. "The clock is ticking and there's no stopping it," he said. "If your head falls off at five minutes to nine you have to find a way to screw it back on. It's a hideous kind of excitement, a terrific stimulus."[67]

Over the following months the radio and television work continued. Usually these were inconsequential guest appearances but in mid-July he signed with ABC for a new half-hour anthology series entitled *Starring Boris Karloff*. The show would tell "exciting, offbeat stories" for, as Karloff explained, "I don't think the public ever wants me to play Little Lord Fauntleroy."[68]

On Wednesday evenings, commencing on 21 September, Karloff would present these tales on the radio. Then, using practically the same scripts, he would repeat these roles on television the following evening. "I'd cut that [radio] show on a record Saturday morning and then go to the television rehearsal in the afternoon," he told Sonia Stein of the *Washington Post*. "I'd just leave the radio head behind and bring the television head with me."[69] Being a fast learner helped. "Having a quick study is like having big feet or small

---

vi The nature of Bronston's business is never revealed.

feet," he said. "You have it or you don't."[70] Karloff would start studying the television script at 1 a.m. on the Sunday morning and work for the next 2½ hours. "The lines are still there in the shower Sunday morning," he said.[71] Then, following a quick run through that evening with Evie, his lines would be committed to his memory.

The show, Karloff explained, gave him the chance "to flex [his] muscles".[72] In 13 weeks he would play 13 different parts including, on 8 December, Descius Heiss in an abridgement of his last Broadway failure, *The Shop at Sly Corner*. "I'd wait 10 years for that in Hollywood," he said. "An actor should be constantly working at his trade… I must have developed myself as an actor during this series."[73]

Much of the credit for Karloff's enjoyment on the series was, he said, due to the show's director, 34-year-old Alex Segal. Although this was Segal's first attempt at directing for television he soon found approval with his star. "I can't say enough about him," Karloff enthused, "He knows the medium inside and out, has everything prepared for us before the first rehearsal. Actors who've never worked with him before and are used to the frightful frantic business common on other shows say, 'This is like dying and going to Heaven'. Alex does everything. I think he sweeps up after we go home."[74]

Segal was as equally impressed with Boris Karloff. "He had such respect – such total respect for the craft we shared and a love of art," Segal said. "Boris was willing to take chances – so many actors play it safe... He was always cheerful – he had the vision to see and recognise talent in others long before anyone else even sensed it. Our relationship started with this show – it was an MCA package – they were representing him as well as the show – David Susskind was his agent. This was no ordinary show – we did plays of all varieties – classic and otherwise. Boris always gave me unlimited credit for running things – it meant a great deal to me. I was young, inexperienced, he made the whole thing possible. Television was in its infancy – really none of us knew what we were doing, so when Boris gave out interviews expressing his appreciation for my running things smoothly, it was marvellous for me. I remember one – he said, 'This man does everything – he's both a director and an engineer – as a matter of fact I think he sweeps up after we go home'."[75]

When MCA insisted Karloff also be credited as the show's producer Karloff baulked, as Alex Segal later explained. "He called in Susskind and said, 'This is preposterous – I'm not producing this show – Alex is. Get rid of this title and put it where it belongs – with Alex.' MCA refused, and I heard no more about it until next payday – I was getting 75 dollars a week at the time. This week the check was 125 dollars. I went to the powers-that-be and said there had been a mistake. 'No mistake,' they told me. 'Boris was furious you weren't properly credited. You didn't get the credit he wanted you to, at least take the money. It comes out of his salary, incidentally.'"[76] For three months Karloff starred in the series, and enjoyed every moment of it. "I'm back in stock again," he told Segal, "I love it – a new play every week – it keeps you on your toes – lucky for me I'm a quick study.'"[77]

On 6 October, two weeks after *Starring Boris Karloff* hit the screens, Karloff's brother, Frederick Greville Pratt, died at the Queen Victoria Hospital in East Grinstead, West Sussex. He was the second of Karloff's siblings to pass away that year, coming only three months after Edward's death on 28 June. Following Frederick's death Sir John wrote to his brother of the news and on 6 November Karloff wrote in reply from his rented New York apartment at 40 Central Park South. "I had already heard of old Fred's death through the Westminster Bank at the request of a 'Mr. Raymond' who is, they said, Fred's son in law," he wrote. "Fred and I had as you know kept up a desultory sort of correspondence but it became increasingly difficult as time went on and his letters became a bit rambling and there was really not much to talk about except politics! What a scattered lot we have been... Well, there it is, the Pratts are beginning to drop like flies."[78]

On 17 October an obituary had appeared in *The Times*, which read in part:

> With his keen critical mind, radicalism, love of philosophy, and his own "experiments in truth" – dietary and other – he could better appreciate the questings and heart searchings of the Mahatma [Gandhi] than most of his official contemporaries. By an irony of fate during Lord Lloyd's Governorship he was administratively responsible on one celebrated occasion for the arrest of the Mahatma... His eccentricities and odd theories endeared him to many friends, and he was a gay and delightful companion in their homes. For several years past he had lived at East Grinstead the life of a recluse, happy with his books, his well-stored memories and the studies, strangely varied, to which he was attracted. In 1903 he married Miss Enid Blanche Malet St. Lo, and had a family of three sons and a daughter, the latter well known on the stage as Gillian Lind.[79]

Karloff thought the piece, "was really charming and had quite caught him, whoever wrote it obviously knew him well and appreciated him."[80] He added, "The television series goes on, and in combination with a radio show really keeps me hopping which I like. November 22 will tell the tale of whether we are renewed or not. There is a fair prospect of a film in the offing at home in the spring and I am dying for it to come off."[81]

However, the news regarding the television show *Starring Boris Karloff* was not good. On 5 December the *New York Times* announced the American Broadcasting Company had decided to discontinue the series after the 15 December broadcast. "Because an AM production is less costly than video," the newspaper explained, "there is a possibility that Mr. Karloff's radio series will remain on the air on Wednesday nights, provided he and the ABC executives can come to terms."[82] Apparently they could not, for a week after the first announcement came a second – Karloff's radio show, too, was cancelled. So, on Thursday, 15 December 1949, he closed the series with a piece entitled *The Night Reveals*.

Regardless of ABC's decision, Karloff had already decided he would remain in New York that winter so he could be available for other television and theatre work. When the decision to cancel both his radio and television series was finalised Karloff returned, albeit briefly, to the theatre with *On Borrowed Time*.

This time the play would be presented in Atlanta, Georgia in the Penthouse Theatre situated on the top floor of the Ansley Hotel. The staging for this production, however, was different – presented in arena style, or 'in the round', where the audience surround the play on all sides. The theatre accommodated 445 people who sat around the stage in rows seven seats deep. "I loved that arena staging, except for opening night," Karloff later said. "I paced out my entrance in the dark, groped for a chair and sat, but when the lights came up, I was sitting in the lap of a woman in the third row!"[83]

On Borrowed Time opened on Monday, 16 January 1950. All tickets cost $3 and the production took $7,800 that week. Such was the success of Karloff's brief tenure he was soon asked to return. "It was a most exciting experience and proved so successful that we are on the way in the morning for a return visit for a week," he wrote to Sir John at the end of the month. "It was particularly interesting and revealing to me that, in spite of the many years I have lived in America I have never before penetrated into the jungles of the central, let alone the deep, south. I had the opportunity of seeing the Assembly and the Senate in session (and even mentioned a few words to them!) and met the Governor of the sovereign state of Georgia. All of which confirmed and explained a lot of what I already knew. The corruption and know-nothingness is unbelievable. And the shocking thing is that the Southern democrats in conjunction with the Northern Republicans largely control American politics and consequently call the tune for the whole world."[84]

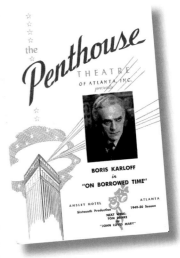

That second stint at the Penthouse Theatre in Atlanta concluded Karloff's work commitments for the time being. But he would soon return to the stage. For, in January 1950, he had received an exciting proposition, to return to Broadway as the greatest fictional pirate of them all – Captain James Hook – in a new production of J.M. Barrie's play, *Peter Pan*.

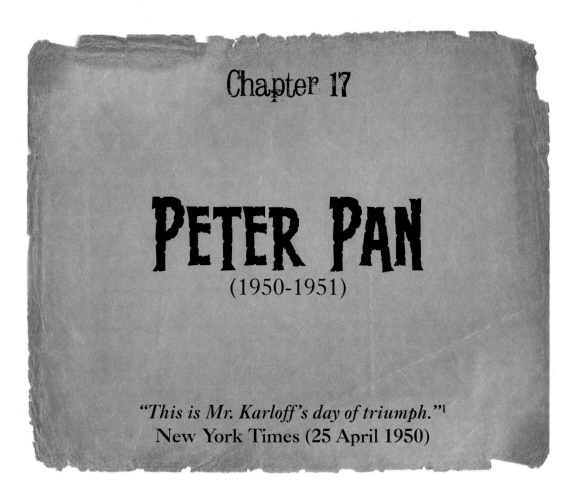

Chapter 17

PETER PAN

(1950-1951)

"This is Mr. Karloff's day of triumph."[1]
New York Times (25 April 1950)

In 1929 the Scottish playwright and novelist Sir James Barrie presented the copyright to his most famous literary creation, *Peter Pan*, to the Hospital for Sick Children, Great Ormond Street in London. Barrie's gift meant all royalties from his character would go to the institution and, as a consequence, all new productions of *Peter Pan* would require the approval of the hospital's board of directors.

In 1948 the 29-year-old New Yorker Peter Lawrence made plans to stage the first American production of Barrie's play in over 20 years. He entered into negotiations with the hospital's board and that December successfully convinced them he was a suitable person to produce the work. Under the agreement 9% of the gross earned by the production would go to the children's hospital. Lawrence's success in obtaining the rights also put paid to Richard Rodgers and Oscar Hammerstein's own proposed revival of the play which, they had planned, would star Mary Martin.

Although Lawrence had previously been Executive Manager of the Ballet Theatre and had stage-managed three shows on Broadway, *Peter Pan* was to be his first show as producer. The production was originally intended as a vehicle for Joan Fontaine who had expressed an interest in playing the title role, but when this fell through Lawrence spent a year interviewing alternatives that included Mickey Rooney and Beatrice Lillie. However, the ballerina Vera Zorina quickly became Lawrence's new preference to star in the play that he hoped would be ready for the Christmas 1949 season. Zorina, however, had already committed to appear with the Boston Symphony Orchestra and so would not be available for *Peter Pan*. Fortunately, Lawrence then discovered Jean Arthur was

As Captain Hook.

interested. "I planned to do another play which didn't turn out right," Arthur later said. "I had been reading articles in the paper about Peter Lawrence trying to find someone to do Peter Pan – and suddenly Tink's bell rang in my head, and I knew it was time to pay attention. I called Mr. Lawrence up..."[2]

Although still under contract to Paramount the studio held no objection to Arthur taking the role and she signed at Christmas. It was a dream come true for the 49-year-old actress. "The role of Peter Pan has been one so close to me for so many years," she said. "I have wanted to do Peter Pan all my life, just as some actors, I suppose, hope to do Hamlet. In the seasons I had been playing on Broadway, most of my roles were wisecracking comedies, and I had always dreamed of and studied Peter Pan, both the character of the boy who was determined to never grow up and the play as a whole."[3]

It would be Arthur's first play in four years. Her last theatrical engagement had been in Garson Kanin's comedy *Born Yesterday* in 1946. However, during its road break-in engagement her nerves got the better of her and she withdrew. Judy Holliday successfully took over the stage role and was offered the subsequent film role, for which she won an Academy Award.

Despite the lack of an actor to play Captain Hook, and with incomplete funding, rehearsals were set to begin on 13 February 1950 with opening night planned for Easter Sunday, 9 April. The financial problem was soon resolved. Following Jean Arthur's acceptance of the role Lawrence was able to raise $110,000 – some $10,000 over the initial budget – in only three months. The theatrical producer Dwight Deere Wiman contributed a large sum while Detroit businessman Roger L. Stevens alone provided $30,000. As a result of his contribution Stevens would co-produce alongside Peter Lawrence. Stevens had made his producing debut the previous year with a production of Shakespeare's *Twelfth Night* on Broadway. It had starred Henry Brandon and Nina Foch and ran for 48 performances.

In January 1950 Peter Lawrence approached Boris Karloff to see if he was interested in appearing in the play in the traditional dual role of Mr. Darling and Captain Hook. At the end of the month the star wrote enthusiastically to his brother, John. "The television is over for the time being," he wrote from his rental apartment at 40 Central Park South, "but there is a sporty chance that at long last I will play Captain Hook in a revival of *Peter Pan* in New York. That would be wonderful. I saw Du Maurier do it the first year when I was a small boy in Enfield!!"[4]

20-year-old Marcia Henderson was cast as Wendy Darling in her first Broadway role, having graduated the previous spring from the American Academy of Dramatic Arts. Peg Hillias would play Mrs. Darling, having recently completed a two-year stint as Eunice Hubbard, the upstairs neighbour of the Kowalskis [Marlon Brando and Kim Hunter] in the Broadway production of *A Streetcar Named Desire*. Joe E. Marks would play the Captain's sidekick, Mr. Smee. To direct the play Lawrence secured the services of the 39-year-old English director, John Burrell.

In 1937 Burrell had been appointed director of the London Theatre Studio and eight years later, along with Ralph Richardson and Laurence Olivier, he was made resident director of the Old Vic Theatre Company where he directed Olivier in *Richard III*. The following year he took the company to Broadway for the productions of Shakespeare's *Henry IV Parts I and II* and Chekhov's *Uncle Vanya*. *Peter Pan*, however, would be his first directorial effort in America. To assist Burrell Lawrence appointed the English actress, dancer, director, choreographer and producer Wendy Toye as Associate Director in what would also be her first American production.

Lawrence had decided upon a background score for the play and contacted his friend, the successful 31-year-old composer/conductor Leonard Bernstein. In 1944 Bernstein had conducted the premiere of his score for the Ballet Theatre's *Fancy Free* at the Metropolitan Opera House and won the New York Music Critics Circle Award for his 1st Symphony (*Jeremiah*). Later that year he composed the score for the musical *On The Town* and in 1946 conducted his *Facsimile* ballet in New York. The following April he premiered his 2nd Symphony (*The Age of Anxiety*).

The composer welcomed Peter Lawrence's offer. "First time in five years someone hasn't called me to say he has a wonderful show for me to do – all about subways, skyscrapers and New York's crowds," he said. "I'm very flattered to be thought of for this kind of play."[5] After receiving the script Bernstein suggested adding musical numbers. Lawrence agreed and Bernstein wrote seven songs for the play. Originally it was planned that Wendy would sing four (*My House, Dream with Me, Who Am I* and *Peter, Peter*), one – *Never Land* – would be sung by the mermaids, while the remaining two (*Drink Blood* and *The Plank*) would be performed by Captain Hook and his pirates.

Despite the addition of songs the play would, it was hoped, still appeal to purists. "Not a musical version," Lawrence later told the press, "this fantasy with music is exactly as Barrie wrote it, with the added stimulation of several lovely songs written by Leonard Bernstein for Wendy, and some rousing pirate songs. The play is essentially a magic one which will utilise many theatrical effects that are comparatively rare these days. The children fly through the air, the pirates and Indians fight, the boys live under the ground, and it promises again to be the exciting experience *Peter Pan* always has been."[6] Even so, the inclusion of songs would be a new experience for Karloff who later confessed he had, "Never sung a note before in my life outside the shower."[7]

To manage the essential element of the stage-flying Peter Lawrence turned to the London firm of Joseph Kirby Ltd., the sole proprietor of Kirby's Flying Ballets. Kirby had provided the flying effects for the original production of *Peter Pan* at the Duke of York Theatre in London in December 1904. Lawrence, therefore, entered into months of negotiations to arrange for Peter Foy, a representative of the firm, to come over from London to take charge of the flying.

It originally seemed, however, that Foy would not be allowed into America. The problem was a 1907 Act of Congress which stated an artisan might only enter the country if there were no similar artisan already there who could do the job. It took the combined efforts of Lawrence, two Government departments and several unions to resolve the matter.

Having been postponed for two weeks, rehearsals finally began on Monday, 13 March 1950. Karloff's wife, Evelyn, accompanied him to the daily sessions. "They were always together," Peter Foy recalled. "They were lovely, calm people... Just nice."[8] Fortunately, Leonard Bernstein was available to coach the singing members of the cast. Still, it was an anxious time for Karloff as Wendy Toye recalled. "I remember how nervous and insecure Boris was about it," she said, "but he had a great untrained voice, and Lenny [Bernstein] and all of us were delighted with it... Boris sang this with a great twinkle in his eye. His comedy was delicious."[9]

Despite the initial hiccup, Peter Foy was finally allowed to travel to New York and within days of his arrival was flying Jean Arthur across the stage. Although Foy later developed more sophisticated methods of stage flying, or 'aerography' as he liked to call it, in 1950 the mechanics consisted of a hemp rope attached to a steel cable. The cable passed through a pulley system and was attached at the other end to a harness that was worn under the performer's costume.

An enthusiastic Jean Arthur had her hair cropped for the role. "When I started to rehearse Peter Pan I thought... Well, I thought about, you know, what a child's first laughter sounds like... It sounds like anything is possible in this world and that is how I wanted to do Peter Pan."[10] During rehearsals, however, it soon became apparent to Foy that the actress had troubles. "She was a problem," he later explained, "because she had some upsets in her love life."[11] Her husband, the film producer Frank Ross Jr., had left Arthur for the young starlet, Joan Caulfield. Although Ross divorced Arthur in March 1949 and would marry Caulfield on 29 April 1950 – five days after the opening of *Peter Pan* – all was not as it seemed. "Her husband was gay," Foy later revealed. "I don't like even talking about it."[12]

Arthur's troubled personal life had made her withdrawn and unsure of herself with others. Her self-confidence, Foy recalled, was "very low".[13] This was most evident when the actress attempted to converse with members of the cast and crew. "For instance, the sort of thing that would happen," Foy explained, "[was that] she'd be standing there and there was somebody, we'll say, from the cast that she saw and you can imagine the process of her thoughts was, 'Oh, there's a new member of the company. I must go over there and talk to him.' And she would rehearse what she was going to say to him… She'd go up and say, 'How do you like it here?' and she'd expect him to say, 'Oh, it's fine' but he'd say something like, 'I'll be glad when we get off the road' or something, which had nothing to do with what she wanted him to say – and she'd freeze and walk away."[14]

Arthur's insecurity was reflected in her refusal to give interviews prior to the opening of the play. She would first, she insisted, have to prove her mettle in the part. This attitude was reflected in the actress's biography that appeared in the play's theatrical programme. Unlike the page afforded to Karloff, Jean Arthur consented to the publication of a mere four lines:

> Miss Arthur is one of the best-known actresses on the American screen. Her present contract with Paramount Studios permits her to do plays and pictures independently of this studio. Her favourite picture of all time is Mr. Smith Goes to Washington and she is glad to have been a part of it. She feels the same way about Peter Pan, the play.[15]

Shortly before the play opened Lawrence decided to remove one of Wendy's songs which, he felt, was not right for the show. Leonard Bernstein, who was then in Rome and would be absent from the play's opening night, was in full agreement and wrote as such to his sister, Shirley. "Do send me all the news, including that of *Peter Pan*," he wrote. "Write me to Israel, as I fly on 24 [April]. And, apropos, tell Peter Lawrence… that I thoroughly agree with the deletion of 'Dream With Me': from this perspective it looked weak anyway, & out of style with the rest of the score… Cable me to Israel about the opening!!!"[16]

Karloff with two of the Lost Boys.

Following a week of previews *Peter Pan* opened at the Imperial Theatre at 249 W. 45th Street on Monday, 24 April 1950 with curtain up at 8 p.m. First nights were always a worrying time for Karloff. "Terrifying, simply terrifying," he later admitted.[17] "I'm always nervous every time the curtain goes up, no matter how long a play runs. But it's the first night that really petrifies me."[18] Regardless of any first-night nerves the evening's performance proved to be a great success. "On opening night it had about 20 curtain calls and really caught fire," Roger L. Stevens recalled. "Once you've had a lot of curtain calls and great praise, it's like heroin. You're hooked for life."[19]

Brooks Atkinson's review appeared in the *New York Times* the following day.

"Although the world may have grown old and cynical, *Peter Pan* is still a thing of delight," he wrote. "… Miss Arthur is ideal as Peter."[20] Karloff, too, garnered praise. "As the father of the Darling children and the pirate King, he is at the top of his bent… His Captain Hook is a horrible cut-throat of the sea; and Mr. Karloff does not shirk the villainies… There is something of the grand manner in his style and the role of his declamation; and there is withal an abundance of warmth and gentleness in his attitude towards the audience… Miss Arthur, Mr. Karloff and their associates have brought a purity of style and genuine affection to Barrie's winged fairy story. They have recaptured something that is priceless in the workaday theatre. You would be surprised how touching some of it is."[21]

As Captain Hook.

John Chapman of the *Chicago Daily Tribune* concurred. "To a time and a town which badly need it," he wrote, "J.M. Barrie's *Peter Pan* has bought the sweet, sentimental and complete enchantment of Never-Never land… Miss Arthur's Peter Pan is in all ways splendid – boyish and cocky, yet one to tug at the heartstrings. And Boris Karloff's dual roles of Mr. Darling and Capt. Hook are a triumph of comedy – a performance of high style and sly humour."[22]

The youngsters, especially, were enchanted with the production and it became common for the children to urge their parents to see the show again. This young audience, often so small that they had to stand on their seats to see the stage properly, would scream, laugh and climb on the backs of the seats whenever Pan and Tinker Bell appeared.

Karloff would peek from behind the curtains at the end of the first act at matinees to watch the children, "leaping hopefully off their seats, trying to fly like Peter Pan".[23] This was, for the actor, a highlight of the production. "The children in the audience," he said, "they are the stars now of *Peter Pan* – and they devour the parts, they act them out *for* you, they keep one step ahead of you all the time. For a perfect example of that, just watch what happens when Tinker Bell, the fairy, is dying – and the only way to save her is to *believe* in her. Peter Pan turns to the audience and says – 'Do *you* believe in fairies' – and every time, children yell back, 'YE-E-E-E-SSSS! WE DOOOOOO!' To me, that is one of the most thrilling moments in the theatre!"[24]

After each show Karloff could be found in his dressing room, still in costume, granting an audience to any child brave enough to venture in. "Children were there with their parents and their parents were trying to push the child towards Boris and they didn't want to go," Peter Foy explained. "They wanted to hide behind their mother or father. And he always used the same line. I think he played it saying [*deeply*] "Here, boy." [*laughs*] It was wonderful."[25] The star would ask if the children wanted to try on his double-pronged hook. "Even little blond angels would reply, 'Yes, sir'. They'd turn on the mirror," Karloff recalled, "put on the most terrible face they could make and, without fail, take a terrific swipe at themselves in the glass."[26] It was all, he maintained, "just good, scary fun".[27]

Sadly, this sentiment was in contrast to the current climate. To some, America in 1950 had seemed an unlikely place to present a play such as *Peter Pan* with its tale of fairies, mermaids and pirates – for as these characters took the stage the country was in the grip of internal anti-communist investigations.

In 1938 the House Un-American Activities Committee (HUAC) began its career by investigating subversive activities that supported the Nazis. The focus soon shifted towards the perceived threat of communism and in 1945, in the new Cold War era, the committee was made permanent. Its investigations continued and in 1947 the committee turned its attention to the Hollywood movie industry. On 24 November ten writers and directors[i] were cited for contempt of Congress when they refused to testify before the committee – an action that would later result in jail sentences of a year apiece. The Hollywood blacklist had begun.

That December Eric Johnson, the president of the Motion Picture Association of America, issued a two-page statement following a meeting by 48 motion picture executives at New York's Waldorf-Astoria Hotel in New York. The press release – The Waldorf Statement – condemned the actions of the Hollywood Ten. The release continued:

> We will not knowingly employ a Communist or a member of any party or group which advocates the overthrow of the government of the United States by force or by illegal or unconstitutional methods. In pursuing this policy, we are not going to be swayed by hysteria or intimidation from any source. We are frank to recognise that such a policy involves dangers and risks. There is the danger of hurting innocent people. There is the risk of creating an atmosphere of fear. Creative work at its best cannot be carried on in an atmosphere of fear. To this end we will invite the Hollywood talent guilds to work with us to eliminate any subversives, to protect the innocent, and to safeguard free speech and a free screen wherever threatened.

Over the coming years more than three hundred people within the motion picture industry were blacklisted. Some writers continued to work, writing under assumed names or using 'fronts' to take the credit. Many, though, were simply left without work with no possibility of employment within the industry.

In February 1950 Senator Joseph McCarthy made a speech to the Republican Women's Club of Wheeling, West Virginia in which he produced a piece of paper on which, he claimed, was a list of names of known communists working for the State Department. Although the claims remained unsubstantiated the media circus had begun. Following the Senator's claims a new investigation, unconnected to the HUAC, was initiated to conduct "a full and complete study and investigation as to whether persons who are disloyal to the United States are, or have been, employed by the Department of State".[28]

For Karloff, things seemed gloomy. "It's very sad," he wrote to his brother that May, "but this is not the America [in which] I found myself in 1913. A fearful sickness seems to have overtaken the country or perhaps it is only the logical result of the ghastly immorality

---

i The 'Hollywood Ten', as they were known, were Alvah Bessie, Herbert Biberman, Lester Cole, Edward Dmytryk, Ring Lardner Jr., John Howard Lawson, Albert Maltz, Samuel Ornitz, Adrian Scott and Dalton Trumbo.

that, with very few exceptions, has always marked public life. Taft, who at least has had a semblance of respectability, is now openly backing McCarthy for possible partisan political advantage in the November elections, and to hell with what it may do to the country and the whole world in the process. It's depressing and more than a bit frightening. A brand new technique has evolved. Instead of shooting or imprisoning people who don't think as you do, you simply let them live on but take away their means of livelihood! This is literally true… I often think of what you said that time in Boston about the danger of Dollar Imperialism. How right you were. That, coupled with the psychopathic hatred that seems to be engendered in official quarters at the mere thought of doing something for one's less fortunate neighbour, makes for a sad and depressing world."[29] Karloff penned this letter from his apartment at the Navarro, a small hotel on the south side of Central Park. "Evie is on her way on Thursday and will be home by the time you get this," he added. "It makes me very sad to send her off again alone, but when you are working you can't go and when you are not you daren't!! That is the actor's lot!"[30]

Peter Pan, however, provided more cheerful news. "We were very lucky in the reception of the play," Karloff wrote, "as *Peter Pan* 1950 in New York might very easily have gone down the drain. But just enough was done to it in the matter of new music, boys playing the little lost boys instead of great strapping wenches. However there is still the small but faithful band of puritans who rather frown on what has been done, but not enough of them to hurt. John Burrell of the Old Vic directed and did a very good job and of course I fared miraculously well at the hands of the critics so it looks like a run. I have only signed until September first and have just lunched with my agent who is on his way to London for a four months stay and he is going to try to dig up a film or a play for the autumn. If nothing happens I will of course stay with this if we are still running. Summer is a chancy thing in the New York theatre… However I am thoroughly enjoying Darling and Hook even though it does entail a fearful lot of skipping around and my knees go off like revolver shots when I crawl in and out of the dog kennel."[31]

Although busy with the daily routine of appearing in the play Karloff was still committed to union activities as Nehemiah Persoff, who played the pirate Cecco in the play, later recounted. "During our run of *Peter Pan* AFTRA [American Federation of Television and Radio Artists] was not yet in existence and a meeting was called for – I think it was 11:30 or 12:00 midnight – at the Malin studios," he said. "I decided to attend and was surprised to find the hall empty except for Boris Karloff who was patiently sitting there."[32] Karloff was both annoyed and disappointed at the pitiful turnout. It was a far cry from the dedication he had witnessed during the formation and early days of the Screen Actors Guild.

After waiting for half an hour Persoff wondered if they had made a mistake. Karloff checked the circular. There was no mistake. Although Persoff then decided to leave, Karloff felt it was an important matter and chose to stay on. The following day he expressed his disappointment. "He said he could understand established, successful actors not showing up," Persoff explained, "but he could not understand the fear or lack of courage that young actors had about standing up for their rights."[33] Unfortunately, it was a sign of the times.

While news of the anti-communist witch-hunts made the headlines, an older, more deep-rooted prejudice still prevailed in America, as Peter Foy later explained. "You know the big thing, though, in 1950 was there was still a colour problem and their company was foremost against the colour problem," he said. "But when we went on tour that's when we ran into big problems, because it was like – water fountains, when we were going by trains – different ones for the blacks… I'd never seen anything like that. When the understudies sat out front they could not sit downstairs if they were coloured. They had to go up into the 'gods'… And when you travelled in a train the black people went to their separate toilets if they wanted to relieve themselves. I didn't understand it. It seems so unnecessary. And, of course, it doesn't exist now."[34] Karloff was appalled by such bigotry. "He was against it, terribly," Foy later said. "Because that's what the company was composed of, people that were completely against the colour bar."[35]

Foy, a foreigner, had been unprepared for the situation. "My problem was a little odd as I wasn't aware of this as in England we didn't have that," he later explained. "I just didn't understand it at all, and people warned me because if there was a meeting of the cast to do with 'what stand shall we take against this?' and I went into these meetings and then I'd go out and talk to some of the stage hands and they'd say, 'Don't mix with those people!' (the cast) – because they were activists against the colour bar. The whole company was like that… It was a shock to me… [It was] a very tight group that was almost isolated from the rest of theatre because they were afraid that they would be judged as being on the side of the blacks. And they were. So, it was a very, very tight group. Most other companies were afraid to do what we did in that production."[36]

The group was, therefore, naturally cautious. "They had meetings and meetings where, some of them, I wasn't invited to because they weren't sure of me at the beginning," Foy said. "Later on it was fine. It was a little core of people who were, kind of, branded as Communists."[37]

Although Karloff was not a Communist (in a private letter he dismissed the ideology as "nonsense"),[38] as a well-known unionist he may have seen himself as a potential target of the HUAC. "He was slightly left wing, if you call being democratic left wing," Karloff's friend Cynthia Lindsay later said. "And everybody then who wasn't a straight Republican in the industry was a 'pinko' and he was definitely known as a pinko. He was not a pinko, but he was on the liberal side."[39] Even so the spectre of the witch-hunts hung over Karloff. "We were very, very conscious of it," Evie later remarked.[40]

In June actor Nehemiah Persoff took ten weeks out to study theatre developments in Israel and was replaced by Dan Walden who also soon witnessed Arthur's curious temperament. "Jean Arthur was a great actress," Walden later said. "On stage she was magic. Off stage she never talked with anyone. At the end of the show she did not take her make-up off. She didn't want the kids who came backstage to see how old she was, she stayed in her Peter Pan make-up."[41]

Karloff, however, was more accessible. "Unlike Jean Arthur he was open and warm and loved talking about his past," Walden recalled. "His door was always open. He especially spoke of his one-nighters in Canada in a touring company – which is where he said he learned his craft."[42] Nehemiah Persoff also recalled Karloff with affection. "I have fond memories of him as Captain Hook," he wrote. "I did the role years later and was much influenced by his performance. Mr. Karloff was a calm unassuming man. To me he was a big movie star and I often stopped to say hello when I passed his dressing room. He was always warm and friendly."[43] Peter Foy too remembered Boris Karloff with fondness. "Just a kind, kind, kind man," he later said. "And a great actor – a great actor. And wonderful family man… I mean just a *good* person that you'd love calling a friend. Never any problems. You know, once or twice things would go wrong with the flying. He didn't say, 'What the hell was that!?' He said, 'That wasn't supposed to happen, was it?' I'd say, 'No, Boris.' He'd ask, 'It won't happen again, will it?' [*laughs*] It was that kind of level."[44]

On Saturday, 17 June the cast assembled at the CBS 30th Street Studios to record two versions of *Peter Pan* to be issued by Columbia records. One contained a narration by Torin Thatcher and, running over 50 minutes, was issued as a long player. The second, a heavily abridged version complete with story booklet, was narrated by the dog Nana (voiced by Miriam Wolfe) and was intended for the four-to-eight year old age group. Curiously, Leonard Bernstein's incidental music from the play was not used for the recordings but, instead, was replaced with a score by Alec Wilder.

After the curtain descended on Friday, 11 August Jean Arthur unexpectedly quit the show. She was suffering from laryngitis, she told the producers, and her doctor had suggested she get some rest before returning. Three days later, however, Arthur declared – from her hotel room – she was tired. "I want to have a few weeks to rest," she said.[45] As a temporary measure Arthur's understudy, Barbara Baxley, stepped into her shoes and took to the stage as Peter Pan. Meanwhile, Lawrence and Stevens contacted the Actors' Equity Association concerning the matter and received permission to cancel Jean Arthur's contract. Incensed by this action, the actress fired off a telegram to the Union's council:

> Have been informed of today's council action cancelling my contract with Peter Pan under ten-day clause. Feel such arbitrary action grossly unjustified and unfair.
>
> I am due representation at any meeting concerning action of such vital importance to my entire career. My only representation at today's meeting was a doctor's letter, the contents of which I had already withdrawn in verbal agreement with the producers.
>
> I demand my side of whatever disagreement there may be between me and Peter Pan management be heard at an emergency meeting of council before another actress is signed to succeed me. Will attend emergency council meeting at any time it is called. Please wire.[46]

Although the producers had by now asked Betty Field to take over the role they had a long meeting with Arthur's acting attorney, Morris L. Ernst, to discuss the matter. Jean Arthur, it transpired, had left town after requesting no information about her activities be issued. However, the parties reached an agreement. Arthur would return to the production under a new standard minimum contract which contained a four-week cancellation clause, as opposed to the original run-of-the-play contract. Barbara Baxley continued in the role until her final performance on Friday, 24 August. Before curtain up that evening the cast presented her with a bouquet of flowers in appreciation of her efforts. Jean Arthur returned to the production the following evening.

In September Nehemiah Persoff returned from Israel and rejoined the play. While abroad he had received letters from Karloff who had taken the time to write and keep Persoff up to date on the happenings at the Imperial Theatre. Soon after returning to his piratical role, though, Persoff fell ill but still made his way to the theatre for the evening's performance. It was an act that met with Karloff's approval. However, the next day all was not well. "I overslept and missed my half hour call for a matinee," Persoff recalled. "Mr. Karloff took time to explain gently to me how theatre was a group effort and that everyone had a responsibility to do his share. I was always thankful for that little talk, as a rebellious young man it was a great help. The man exuded kindness."[47] Yet, ironically, by this time Karloff, too, had also missed two performances and had required a replacement. "His understudy was Bill Marshall,"[ii] Dan Walden explained, "a tall African American with a deep voice, who got to go on one Saturday, for the matinee and evening performance. I recall Karloff had been out that day in a boat and gotten sunburnt."[48]

At the end of the month, after the curtain came down on Friday, 30 September, the play transferred to the St. James Theatre, a block away at 246 W. 44th Street where it would stay for the final months of the New York run. It was here on 20 December Marcia Henderson gave her last performance as Wendy. Her replacement was the 25-year-old Jennifer Bunker who would stay with the play until the end of its run.

Yet all was not well at the St. James, as Karloff revealed in a letter to his brother. "I've been meaning to write you for so long but I simply haven't been able to settle to anything," he wrote. "I've been so depressed at the hideous drift to catastrophe which is being forced upon us by the 'know-nothings' over here. But enough of that. The play miraculously is still running in spite of the most amateur management which makes one tear one's hair out by the roots! However we take to the road the end of January, opening in Boston... and then going on for three or four months. We may close for the summer or even before that and, unless something definite happens to hold us here, I have promised myself a trip home for a couple of months... that is, unless the worst has happened in the meantime."[49]

The 'worst' was the proposed use by the American Government of the atomic bomb in Korea and the feared consequences of such an action – retaliation by the Russians who had tested their own nuclear weapon the previous year. "And even if it has, we might still come," Karloff continued, "as I have a feeling that if we are all going up in smoke I'd rather do it at home than over here!! This is a filthy depressing Christmas letter, I'm afraid, but the savour has gone out of a lot of things perforce. A tide of irresponsible madness seems to have swept over the country and there seems to be no way of stopping it. Well, anyhow, here's all our love not just for the appropriate season but continuously and we hope to get a look at you this year. Evie joins me in all good wishes."[50]

Although committed to the run of *Peter Pan* the lack of shows on Sunday and Monday evenings allowed Boris Karloff to accept other work in other mediums. While the majority of this additional work consisted of guest appearances or radio interviews a few provided more dramatic roles. On 3 September he appeared with Eva Gabor and Walter Abel in a live hour-long adaptation of Chekhov's *Uncle Vanya* on the short-lived series *Masterpiece Playhouse*. Two weeks later it was more familiar ground when he appeared in the suspense drama *Leopard Lady*, part of the *Lights Out* television series.

On Christmas Eve Karloff appeared on the radio as the scheming Uriah Heep in an hour-long adaptation of Charles Dickens' *David Copperfield* for *The Theatre Guild on the Air*. The drama also featured Flora Robson, Cyril Ritchard, Hugh Williams and the 25-year-old Richard Burton, as the adult David. After several rehearsals that week the play was broadcast live at 8:30 p.m. from the Belasco Theatre at 111 W. 44th Street. Playwright Robert Anderson, who wrote the adaptation, recalled, "It was a great experience working with the likes of that cast. Boris was a charmer. He was great as Uriah Heep, and whenever

---

ii William Marshall is probably best known for starring in the blaxploitation horror picture *Blacula* (1972) and its sequel, *Scream Blacula Scream* (1973).

I saw him after, he would always greet me with a line from that show."[51] Karloff's favourite radio work of this period, however, was a simple show that had its origins months before.

In April, shortly after *Peter Pan* had opened, Dick Pack, the programme director of New York's independent radio station WNEW, was passing the theatre when he stopped to listen to the children waiting to be admitted for the matinee. Pack realised that most of the youngsters were excited because they were going to see Boris Karloff. So, a few days later, Pack asked the star if he would like to be a disc jockey. When he explained that the show would be entirely for children Karloff agreed immediately. "I've been working for years in horror films," he explained, "and I knew that kids loved them. It really isn't horror to them, you know, it's exciting adventure. I've had mail from children for years – actually there were only three of those Frankenstein things, and I discovered that the highest compliment one of them could pay me was to say, 'Dear Mr. Karloff, your picture has kept me awake for a week!' I think it's true that all children – and grown-ups – have fun pretending there's something hiding just behind the door. It compensates for a life that can get pretty dull sometimes."[52]

At 7 p.m. on Sunday, 17 September the first show in his new series *Boris Karloff's Treasure Chest* went on the air. It would run for the rest of the year. The star entertained his audience with stories and riddles,[iii] and played his own selection of records. The show was an immediate success with the young listeners and the day after the first show was broadcast the radio station was overwhelmed with fan mail. Although intended for a younger audience it was quickly found that people of all ages were tuning in. As a consequence the show was soon no longer referred to as 'a programme for children'. Now it was 'a programme for children of all ages'.

This additional work, however, did not exclude Karloff from more social events. On 15 November he paid a visit to the fourth annual Boys and Girls Book Fair in the American Museum of Natural History where he was photographed, surrounded by fifth grade students of the Thornwood School of Westchester, as he read them chapters of *Peter Pan*. That month Karloff was also photographed purchasing the first ticket for Errol Garner's Town Hall concert, to be given on 3 December in aid of the American Negro Theatre. It would, it was hoped, be the first of a series of events to help build a legitimate theatre in Harlem.

Then, on 23 November – Karloff's 63rd birthday – the star donned his Captain Hook make-up and costume and climbed aboard the Pirate Ship float, along with his piratical crew, for the annual Macy's Thanksgiving Day parade. Jean Arthur, however, was not featured. By now news of the actress's behaviour was spreading and in December Walter Winchell was prompted to write in his column, "Jean Arthur and Boris Karloff of *Peter Pan* only speak on stage."[53] Peter Foy later confirmed this was true. "On the stage, obviously, they were fine but she was a loner," he said.[54] Even Karloff was disposed to make comment. "She was a great 'Peter'," he later said of his co-star. "But when a person thinks only of himself or herself, there's bound to be some confusion. There are so many other people in the world."[55] Her antics had obviously become tiresome.

The Broadway run of *Peter Pan* ended on Tuesday, 27 January 1951 after 321 performances – a record for Barrie's play. After the curtain came down the costumes, sets and props were packed away ready to be transported by train to Boston for the first date in the *Peter Pan* tour. As was often the case Evelyn Karloff accompanied her husband on the

iii One of the riddles Karloff posed was – "He wears a hat stuck on his neck because he has no head, and many times his hat comes off because we're sick in bed. What is it?" The answer was "a bottle of medicine".

venture. "His wife was with us all the time on tour,"[56] Peter Foy said. The play opened at the Opera House three days later, on 30 January, for the start of a two-week engagement. Then it was on to Philadelphia where the troupe would stay for a three-week stint.

On Sunday, 17 February Karloff wrote to his brother, Sir John, from his rooms in Philadelphia's Warwick Hotel. "So the New York run of *Peter Pan* finally came to an end after 40 weeks," he wrote, "which is a record run for the play anywhere and we are now touring at least until Easter and possibly a little longer, with even a short trip to the Pacific Coast in the offing, which would be wonderful as Sara Jane could then see it... We have just taken a small unfurnished apartment in New York, for a more or less permanent *pied-à-terre* there, as it is pretty obvious that most of my time will be spent in New York and not on the coast. It's a wise move, we think, as apartment hotel living is ruinous and most unsatisfactory. We hope to move most of the coast furniture here and either let the house unfurnished or sell. This turns out to be just a gossip about trivia as it seems hopeless to write about anything else at the moment, things look so dark. But I can tell you this much. If you don't keep your name out of the American papers, and our relationship becomes known, I will inevitably wind up at Ellis Island awaiting deportation! Jokes aside it is extraordinary how many subjects one must not talk about now in this climate without provoking a deep and uneasy silence of suspicion. It's amazing."[57] The new permanent New York address, Karloff added, would be the famous Dakota building at 1 West 72nd Street.

From Philadelphia the tour moved to Cincinnati, Cleveland and Detroit, playing a week in each city. Yet it was not all work. "We had several parties," Peter Foy recalled. "Even on the road. Because people tend to get together a lot more when they're on the road than when they're playing in New York or London."[58]

On 27 March *Peter Pan* opened at the Civic Opera House in Chicago. "Miss Arthur's Peter is quite her own," wrote Claudia Cassidy of the *Chicago Daily Tribune*, "perhaps a cross between a leprechaun and Huckleberry Finn. She has cropped hair that sticks up at the crown, a hoarse little cracked voice, and an air of desperate eagerness to be happy. She looks vulnerable, and you care, or at least I do. I like this Peter."[59] Cassidy's praise did not extend to Karloff, however. "As the fatuous Mr. Darling and the horrendous Captain Hook, Mr. Karloff is among those present, but not very convincingly so," she wrote. "Joe E. Marks as Smee is more fun to watch."[60]

It was in Chicago that Karloff's daughter, Sara Jane, finally got to see the show, having recovered from a broken ankle which had kept her from travelling to New York to see the play there. After one performance of the play Sara Jane was put in the harness and flown across the stage. "I certainly do remember flying across the stage and it was wonderful," she recalled. "I believe it was at an evening performance. I was there for a week so I saw many performances."[61] This was not, however, special treatment for the star's daughter. "I did it with everybody like that that I knew. It was a little thing," Foy later said. "I was king then. Kirby was in England. If they said 'Can my daughter fly?' I'd say 'No problem!'"[62] However, despite Sara Jane's enthusiasm for the flying, it was apparent to Karloff that the daughter did not share the father's passion for acting. "My father always said I paid more attention to Nana the dog and the Lost Boys than I did to him during the visits to the theatre," she later said.[63]

After the curtain descended at the Chicago Civic Opera House on Saturday, 14 April Jean Arthur left the show. In March she had announced her intention to depart at the end of the Chicago engagement. After this she would return to California in preparation to appear in the western *Shane* for Paramount. To replace her the producers engaged the 33-year-old actress and dancer Joan McCracken. However, with Jean Arthur's departure, Karloff reportedly insisted on sole-billing, feeling the new replacement did not warrant co-star billing. It was only, McCracken alleged, when the producers pointed out how ridiculous the legend 'Boris Karloff *in* Peter Pan' would be did the star relent.

McCracken had gained recognition in 1943 when she played the dancing, non-speaking role of Silvie in the musical *Oklahoma!* on Broadway. Then in 1949, while Peter Lawrence was searching for a Peter Pan, McCracken had expressed an interest in playing the role. Although she had been unsuccessful at the time, on 23 March 1951 the actress finally got her wish and signed to replace Jean Arthur. Three weeks later, on 15 April, after only a week of rehearsals McCracken opened in the role in a special matinee performance that had been added to the end of the Chicago engagement. Although her stint would last for only two weeks *Peter Pan* became McCracken's favourite role.

Richard Knox, who, at the age of 13, played the Lost Boy Slightly, recalled, "Joan did a fine job and was a joy to work with… and I'm sure felt she was stepping into big shoes when she took over Jean's role. Jean had a deep, throaty voice that everybody loved and that was sort of her trademark. Joan didn't have that voice, but having been a dancer, she was a much more physical Peter than Jean had been… Joan was very sweet, she was not a prima donna or anything like that, and I think everyone in the company really cheered her on and wanted her to succeed."[64] And succeed she did.

"Gone was Jean Arthur of the crew-cut and the hoarse, cracked little voice," wrote Claudia Cassidy, "but in her place, or rather in the place she instantly made her own, was Joan McCracken. When Joan flew in, regret flew out the window… Where Jean's Peter Pan was a leprechaun lodged in Huck Finn, Joan's is a boyish, sometimes an impish, elf. Tiny in her green jerkin, her dark hair in a ruffled crop, she moves with a good dancer's silky simplicity, and when she flies she makes you catch your breath."[65]

After Chicago the show played weekly stints at the American Theatre in St. Louis and the Lyceum Theatre in Minneapolis where, on 29 April 1951, the final curtain descended on *Peter Pan*. The play's run had been an unqualified success and, according to John Byram of Paramount (which controlled the Barrie plays), had earned the Hospital for Sick Children, London $105,000 in royalties.

With this success under his belt Peter Lawrence began to plan for an additional tour. In early April Lawrence and Stevens had considered two West Coast bookings for *Peter Pan* – in Los Angeles and San Francisco – to precede a trans-continental tour starring McCracken and Karloff, which would arrive in New York for Christmas. Although this never transpired plans for a second tour remained. In July Lawrence once again applied to the Hospital for Sick Children for the rights to the play. He also purchased the scenery and costumes from the previous tour in readiness for the new endeavour.

Although McCracken had been successful in the role Lawrence, curiously, now decided he wanted a bigger 'name' for the new tour and began a search for another Peter Pan. Although he was interested in Shirley Temple taking the role the producer finally settled upon Veronica Lake. "One of the theatre's more serious injustices," Claudia Cassidy later opined, "was letting [McCracken] cut that sleek black hair for *Peter Pan*, then robbing her of a role she played bewitchingly to give it to Veronica Lake, who didn't."[66]

Lawrence's decision also cost him Karloff. "I have decided not to tour with Peter Pan this season," the star wrote to his brother in July, "as they couldn't get a good enough replacement for Jean Arthur who had to leave on account of picture engagements."[67] Peter Lawrence, therefore, hired the opera singer and actor Lawrence Tibbett to star alongside Lake. The new tour of *Peter Pan* began in Baltimore that October. However, it was not the success Peter Lawrence had hoped for and the play closed in Chicago six weeks later.

Peter Pan had been a personal triumph for Boris Karloff. "I hated to give it up," he later admitted, "as it was such a rewarding job… outside of being a mankiller… playing to thousands of children who were seeing their first live theatre."[68] As to the future, Karloff wrote, "There is a faint chance of being in another film for Universal… but nothing definite. In the meantime the garden grows and I am sunning my arthritic bones which were sadly in need of a rest after more than a year of Mr. Darling and Captain Hook."[69]

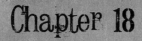

Chapter 18

THE RETURN OF THE GHOST
(1951-1955)

"I do have a good time... I enjoy myself enormously. I think a man who is well paid for doing what he thoroughly enjoys is very fortunate – and very rare."[1]
Boris Karloff (1955)

Peter Pan had been a success. The dual role of Mr. Darling and Captain Hook had proved gruelling but, not one to rest on his laurels, Karloff would continue to look for, and accept, work elsewhere. In January 1951, while still starring in Barrie's play on Broadway, he had signed to provide the English narration for the Czech picture *The Emperor's Nightingale*, a stop-motion animation based on Hans Christian Andersen's tale *The Nightingale*. The picture opened at the 60th Street Trans-Lux in New York on 12 May. Bosley Crowther thought it was, "A beautiful, delicate little picture... and Mr. Karloff recites it like an amiable uncle telling a fascinating tale to his favourite nephews and nieces. And a fascinating tale it surely is, created in a medium that is ideal for this sort of thing."[2]

Then in mid-May, within weeks of *Pan*'s end, Karloff signed for a picture back at Universal. He would receive $6,000 a week for 'not less than two weeks work' to appear in the supporting role of Voltan in an adaptation of Robert Louis Stevenson's *The Sire de Maletroit's Door*. He would take second billing in the new film (provisionally entitled *The Door*) behind his co-star from *The Old Dark House*, Charles Laughton. Also joining the cast would be Sally Forrest (on loan from MGM) and Richard Stapley. The picture, which began production on 15 May, would be Stapley's first under his new contract, shared by Universal-International and Hal Wallis.

The picture told the story of the aristocrat Alan De Maletroit [Laughton] who, for 20 years, has been planning revenge. Two decades earlier, Alan had been abandoned by his fiancée who instead married his brother Edmond. The union produced a daughter,

Blanche [Forrest], but after the mother died in childbirth Edmond is imprisoned in the dungeon of his brother's chateau. Alan raises the girl himself and now, all these years later, plans to ruin her life by having her marry the wastrel Denis de Beaulieu [Stapley]. However, the unforeseen occurs and Blanche and Denis fall in love. They are imprisoned in the dungeon where Blanche is reunited with her father. Alan's plan to crush his captives to death in Edmond's cell is foiled by his servant, Voltan [Karloff], who kills his master and sets the prisoners free.

Australian born actor Michael Pate, who appeared in the picture as Laughton's crony Talon, recalled working on the picture. "Boy, that *was* a strange film, and a strange experience," he said, "Charles Laughton was an actor that I'd seen in any number of films, a person that was highly thought of... But by 1951, I would say that a *little* bit of the aura of Charles Laughton 'the star actor', had diminished... I never felt quite comfortable with Laughton, because you really couldn't be sure whether he was genuine when he said, 'You were very good in a scene', or if he was 'sending you up gutless'. It was difficult to know – Laughton was a 'cutie', and he liked to have his jollies by playing around with people mentally. He had quite a few shots at the juvenile lead [Stapley], and a couple of other people in the cast. I don't remember him ever having a go at me; he wouldn't have lasted or got very far if he *had* [*laughs*]! I watched him have a very sarcastic dig at certain people, and cut other people off, and isolate himself. I thought it was very sad, it was a shame,

Top: *The Strange Door* (1951). Bottom: Signing autographs during the promotional tour for the film.

because it could have been a rollicking kind of a fun picture and it turned out to be a little like treading on eggshells. But I certainly had great admiration, if not *total*, respect for him."[3]

Boris Karloff, however, was another matter. "I thought Boris was one of the loveliest people that I'd ever come across," Pate said. "We had many a chat over a cup of coffee, a cigarette or a pipe. I'd seen his work in any number of things, but I had no idea what kind of a *man* he was. He turned out to be such a charming, laid-back, relaxed Englishman, just a marvellous person. He was always considerate, always charming; he had a nice attitude toward 'being Boris Karloff'. I think, generally speaking, he was just a little tired of playing 'the Boris Karloff part', but he never showed it all that very much. He just went about his work, did his business as it was expected of him, in the style that people had become accustomed to. Very contained, a little avuncular. That's a professional attitude. He was in a situation where you take the money and run, and I guess somewhere in the back of his mind he figured that that was the most secure way to do his work, and continue to live as comfortably as he'd always liked to."[4]

The Strange Door opened on 8 December at the Criterion in New York. "Perhaps *The Strange Door* might have been a genuinely suspense-filled film if Maletroit simply were characterised as a nasty man. In Charles Laughton's portrayal, he is merely an oily, petulant and flamboyant nobleman, more farcical than evil. Although he is [a] varsity villain from way back, Boris Karloff is more woebegone than menacing as the retainer of Sally Forrest, the pretty and put-upon maiden of this chamber of horrors. Richard Stapley is properly energetic as her romantic *vis-à-vis*. And in scoffing at his host by saying 'I'm not impressed', he speaks the film's most prophetic line."[5]

At the end of May Karloff had announced his intention to make his home in New York once he had finished working on *The Strange Door*. "There are more things to keep an actor busy in New York," he explained. "You have the stage, television and radio. Out here it's mostly pictures. If you're not working, there's not much else to do but garden. I like gardening, but not as a full-time job."[6] The plans for the move were, however, temporarily put on hold when he received an interesting proposition.

Charles Laughton had created the Drama Quartet, a troupe consisting of himself, Agnes Moorehead, Cedric Hardwicke and Charles Boyer. The quartet had been giving readings of *Don Juan in Hell* – the often excised part of Act III from George Bernard Shaw's play *Man and Superman* – and planned to sail to England to give readings as part of the Festival of Britain celebrations. However, the plans were put in jeopardy when Cecil Hardwicke was restricted from leaving the country due to tax troubles. Laughton, therefore, asked Karloff to step in.

It would be Karloff's first professional engagement on the British stage. However, it was not to be, as he later explained when he wrote to his brother from his home at 12750 Mulholland Drive, Beverly Hills. "We damned nearly came to England this summer with the Drama Quartet," Karloff wrote. "Hardwicke was in income tax trouble over here (as usual), and I signed to take his place and was within three days of flying over when somehow or other he got it all straightened out… How he did it, God only knows, he owed $54,000… so I had to bow out of the picture. The whole thing was pretty shabby but that is another and long story. Thank goodness we didn't get buck fever and cable you that we were coming and cause no end of confusion. For the rest, I have finished the film at Universal that I came out to do and we are just marking time for the moment trying to sell or lease the house as I am going back to New York in September for television and, who knows?, another play."[7]

By now Karloff had decided against returning to *Peter Pan* on tour. With only the faint chance of another picture at Universal he decided to stay in Los Angeles and rest until August after which, he said, he would return to New York. But while Karloff rested in Hollywood his brother, back in England, was causing a stir in Parliament.

In late July Sir John Pratt gave a speech in which he claimed the Communist Soviet-backed North Korea was a victim of Nationalist South Korean aggression. It was, he claimed, the South Koreans who had fired the first shots that sparked the Korean War. Although he denied he was a Communist Sir John had also stated, "the only country which committed aggression in the Far East is America."[8]

There was disapproval in the House of Commons. Conservative M.P. Mr. Vaughan-Morgan asked, "As Sir John Pratt's views on far eastern affairs at present are exactly contrary to what are alleged to be those of the Government and the United Nations, does the Minister not think it time that a change was made in the Foreign Office representation on this committee?"[9] Minister of State Kenneth Younger replied. "The position which the gentleman has held was concerned with essentially non-political activities," he said. "The Foreign Secretary was very reluctant to connect that with Sir John Pratt's recently expressed political opinion. At the same time, it is now a very long time since Sir John left China, and taking that in conjunction with recent events, he has decided that there should be a change in representation."[10] In effect, Sir John had been ousted from his (non-paying) job as Foreign Office representative on the Universities of China Committee.

Within days Karloff broached the subject in a letter to Sir John. "Evie's mother sent me a cutting from *The Telegraph* reporting your speech at Holborn," he wrote, "and I must say that your argument that the South Koreans started the fighting confused me, as all the evidence, at least as it is reported to us, is to the contrary. Then a few days ago I read in a local paper of your removal from the Universities of China Committee. Of course, being a Hearst paper, the reason given for your removal was that you had 'rapped the U.S.'!! I am terribly sorry that such a thing could have happened. While I know you will ride out whatever storm there may be, it is nevertheless appalling to think that witch-hunting is starting at home. I think that Younger's statement in the House that 'it is a long time since he (Pratt) has been in China' is snide to say the least, as it completely ignores your long service at the F.O. in the capacity of advisor of Chinese affairs, which puts a very different light on the matter. I agree with all you say except about the South Koreans starting the shooting, and on that matter you obviously have sources of information which I don't. But I just had to write and tell you how grieved and disgusted I am about the whole affair. So that's that."[11]

On 11 August 1951, two weeks after Karloff wrote the letter, his brother Charles Rary Pratt died. Charles, a widower, had retired in 1924 and left South America, settling on the Channel Island of Guernsey. There, in 1932, he set up a money-lending business – the Mutual Benefit Supply Company Limited – with his landlord, Percy Reginald Smith. But when the war came his fortunes began to change.

On 30 June 1940 Guernsey surrendered to the Germans and began almost five years of occupation. Charles' landlord was deported to Germany along with his wife and two daughters. Charles, however, was permitted to stay on the island as he was over 70 years old. Then, on 14 June 1942, now aged 73, Charles walked into a door in a blackout and lost an eye. He was nursed back to health by the nuns of Blanchelands Convent and was eventually fitted with a glass eye, which his great-niece Elisabeth Crowley later said, "I found fascinating as a child! During the Occupation my mother [Dorothea] kept in touch with him through the Red Cross and they were allowed to exchange brief messages. He was back in [his home] Campbell Lodge by 17 July 1943 and helped by German soldiers billeted there. He and the other remaining residents were saved from starvation by the arrival of Red Cross parcels towards the end of the Occupation. At some time between 1948 and 1951 he moved to the hostel of St. John, Sausmarez Park. On 31 July 1951 he suffered serious burns as the result of scalding while having a bath. He was taken to the Town Hospital, St. Peter Port where he died on 11 August."[12]

In the autumn of 1951, following a period of rest and relaxation, the Karloffs relocated to New York, moving into their apartment on the top floor of the famous Dakota building. With the move to New York Karloff's long-standing acquaintance with the Screen Actors Guild came to an end. In Los Angeles, on 11 November, Ronald Reagan was re-elected, unopposed, as president of the Guild at that evening's annual membership meeting in the Hollywood Legion Stadium. William Holden was elected vice-president, Walter Pidgeon as second vice-president with John Lund as third vice-president.

At that time the Guild was negotiating a new basic labour contract with the studios and was committed, it said, to the principle of obtaining extra payment for actors for the re-use of their films in television. There was, however, other business. "The meeting was highlighted," the *Los Angeles Times* reported, "by the awarding of a gold life membership card to Boris Karloff, one of the Guild founders in 1933."[13] In New York the city's SAG Council presented the golden membership card to a teary-eyed and grateful star.

On 20 November Karloff put pen to paper and wrote a note of thanks to the Guild's Board of Directors:

Ladies and Gentlemen:

You have just done me the greatest honour that any actor could receive from his fellows, and I am humbled and deeply grateful. I was only luckier than most in that I happened to be around when things got started. My best love to those who are serving now, but most of all to those who have gone ahead and those who will follow on… God bless you all.[14]

By now Karloff was fully ensconced in the world of television. Although he would continue to make appearances on radio the frequency would decline as the popularity of television increased. On 21 October he had made his first appearance on the musical variety television programme *The Fred Waring Show*. However, after the show was broadcast in Chicago, one disgruntled viewer, L.L. Bomberger, complained in the local press. "Ordinarily, Fred Waring's programme is quite worthwhile," he wrote, "but last night he fell down very sadly. He put on a skit by Boris Karloff, which was not only moronic but absolutely criminal. I did not watch it to the end, but nothing could have redeemed the deliberate planning to murder one's wife, which he [Karloff] revealed in the skit."[15]

On 19 November, the day before penning his note to the SAG Directors, Karloff had appeared on the television drama show *Robert Montgomery Presents* in the episode *The Kimballs*. He played an embittered father whose actions jeopardise his unhappy daughter's [Vanessa Brown] chance to find a happier life through love. In the *Studio One* episode *Mutiny on the Nicolette*, broadcast on 3 December, Karloff played a crew member on a tramp steamer, pressed into service by the U.S. Navy to carry munitions from Panama to North Africa – until his character incites mutiny. "The settings on the deck of the merchantship were extraordinarily lifelike and vivid," wrote the *New York Times*, "and the camera work was further evidence of the remarkable ability of Mr. Miner and his associates to expand TV's scope and still stay within the studio. Mr. Karloff and Anthony Ross were fine in the leading parts."[16]

Christmas Day brought the fourth of Karloff's six appearances on television's anthology series *Suspense!*. Although this series was usually broadcast live Karloff's contract for this

Shooting at CBS – 1950's

Christmas Day edition – *The Lonely Place* – suggests the show had been pre-recorded for transmission during the festive period. Karloff was required to attend three days of rehearsals at CBS's New York studios. At 2 p.m. on 12 December rehearsals began in the Oak Room and lasted for three hours. The following day, in Studio B, they continued from 8 p.m. to 10 p.m. The busiest day, though, was the last, the 15 December. Rehearsals began in Studio 41 at 11 a.m. and lasted until 12:30 p.m. After an hour for lunch they resumed and continued until 6:30 p.m. Karloff was back in the studio for an hour, from 8 p.m. to shoot the show. He was paid $1,000 for his services.

He ended the year on New Year's Eve with an appearance in Lord Dunsany's play *The Jest of Hahalaba*. In the live broadcast Karloff played Sir Arthur Strangways, a London businessman who uses a mystic to produce a future copy of *The Times*. Wishing to make a fortune on the stock market, Strangways reads the paper but discovers it contains his own obituary. To prepare for the half hour long broadcast Karloff attended six days of rehearsals with its final day of rehearsals and the live broadcast taking place at CBS Studio No. 41 at 15 Vanderbilt Avenue. He received $1,500 for his work.

Two weeks later, on 13 January 1952, Karloff appeared in the premiere of the short-lived drama series *CBS Television Workshop*, receiving $1,000 for his work. In this opening episode he starred as Cervante's chivalric hero in an abridged adaptation of *Don Quixote*, co-starring Grace Kelly as Dulcinea. Jack Gould of the *New York Times* thought the project was overly ambitious. The decision to dramatise the book in only 30 minutes was, he wrote, "a little like compressing *Götterdämmerung* into a set of station chimes... Boris Karloff had the role of Quixote, and it was an unusual bit of casting; unfortunately, it did not work too well. While Mr. Karloff was burdened with cumbersome armour and amateurish make-up, he played the central figure in a very somber and depressed key. Where elements of true inspiration and lofty purpose... were needed, Mr. Karloff's interpretation was drawn in terms of an errant Pagliacci."[17] Still, *Don Quixote* was the start of a busy year for Boris Karloff. He would make a dozen television appearances and ten radio appearances – an average of almost two per month.

At the end of January he gave his first television interview on the CBS talk show *Stork Club*. He followed this, on 22 February, with his first appearance on ABC's live television science-fiction series *Tales of Tomorrow*, joining Barbara Joyce in an episode entitled *Memento*. Then, two days later, he was back on the radio joining his *Son of Frankenstein* co-star Basil Rathbone in the *Theatre Guild on the Air*'s hour-long radio adaptation of Dickens' *Oliver Twist*. Karloff played the brutish Bill Sikes alongside Rathbone's Fagin. Leueen MacGrath played Sike's doomed girlfriend, Nancy, while nine-year-old Martin Friend appeared as Oliver.

A signed photograph for his daughter - 1952.

The drama, broadcast live from Constitution Hall in Washington, served to open the 1952 Red Cross fund appeal which aimed to raise a total of $85 million. Within weeks of the broadcast, however, Karloff was be back in Hollywood to start work on his only picture of 1952 – Universal-International's *The Black Castle* – which had begun production on 12 February. Karloff, though, was not required from the outset. Instead, he and Evie made their way to Hollywood in mid-March.

The Black Castle told the story of Sir Ronald Burton [Richard Greene] who arrives at the castle of Count von Bruno [Stephen McNally] to avenge the murders of two of his friends. There he falls in love with the count's wife, Elga [Paula Corday]. When their romance is discovered Von Bruno has them imprisoned in the dungeons until he can do away with them.

The Black Castle (1952).

Dr. Miessen [Karloff], however, gives the couple a potion that will feign death for ten hours but is later forced to reveal his deceit. The count therefore plans to bury them alive but, as they are about to be interred, Burton awakes and, using the pistols placed in his hands by the doctor, shoots Von Bruno.

Once again Karloff was joined by Michael Pate who found this experience a distinct improvement over *The Strange Door*. "That was a *much*, much more enjoyable film for me to do," he later said, "because I had settled into Hollywood better then; certainly I rather enjoyed doing the film more than I had enjoyed the adventure with Charles Laughton. Plus, I knew Richard Greene and Stephen McNally, and of course Boris Karloff from *The Strange Door* already…"[18] Lon Chaney Jr. also appeared in the cast as the Count's mute manservant, Gargon, but curiously never shared a scene with Boris Karloff.

Following a Halloween pre-release *The Black Castle* opened on 20 November 1952 at the Downtown Paramount Theatre in Los Angeles in a double-feature with *The Raiders*, starring Richard Conte.

The picture opened in New York on Christmas Day. The *New York Times* called it, "a Christmas day offering of questionable taste… [It] is one of those dreary 'horror' tales manufactured to shiver the souls of the space-suit set… To open Universal-International's *Black Castle* at any time is a mistake, but to tender it to the public on Christmas Day is remarkably indiscreet."[19]

Actor Michael Pate did not agree. "I think that *Black Castle* was an infinitely better picture than *Strange Door* all around," he later said, "it had a more interesting story and it was a more vigorous type of film. There were a lot of good things in it. And I think that Nathan Juran's direction of it was very good; it was the first picture that he directed… Nathan was a very highly talented man."[20]

Returning to New York after completing his work on *The Black Castle*, Karloff continued to split his time between radio and television. On 18 April he was the guest on Dean Martin and Jerry Lewis's radio show where he once again lamented his public persona. "In spite of the fiendish parts that I play in pictures," Karloff told Dean Martin, "I'm really a kind and mild-mannered man. In fact, I'm as soft-hearted and gentle a man as you could ever meet. Don't I appear that way? Dean – why don't you answer?"

"I can't," Martin replied. "You're choking me!"

Nine days later (27 April) he joined Burgess Meredith and Margaret Phillips on another of radio's *Theatre Guild on the Air* literary adaptations, this time in a version of Jack London's novel *The Sea Wolf*. Another appearance on Milton Berle's television show *Texaco Star Theatre* followed two days later then, on 19 May, Karloff played the king alongside Thomas Mitchell in a television adaptation of Mark Twain's novel *A Connecticut Yankee in King Arthur's Court* for *Studio One*.

On 25 May Karloff could be seen alongside host Conrad Nagel and fellow guests Vivian Blaine and Dorothy MacKaill on the television quiz show *Celebrity Time* and a week later (1 June), in the drama anthology series *Philip Morris Playhouse on Broadway*. This episode, *Outward Bound*, was an adaptation of Sutton Vane's popular 1923 play about seven passengers who meet in the lounge smoke-room of a liner. No one knows how they got there or why they are on board. They later discover they are all, in fact, dead and will have to face 'the Examiner' who will determine whether they are bound for Heaven – or Hell.

Less than three weeks later, on 19 June, Karloff was a guest on the premiere episode of the game show *I've Got a Secret* where the panellists attempted to guess his secret – he was afraid of mice. It was an admission one journalist felt, "added absolutely nothing to the overall production. It was difficult to understand why such [well] known people as those who sat on the panel would agree to take part – unless it was $. I know most of us can find better ways to occupy a half-hour than to witness such trite and foolish 'entertainment'."[21]

On 22 June he made his first appearance in over six years in the first of a new season of the radio show *Inner Sanctum*. The episode, *Birdsong for a Murderer*, was a re-recording of a 1949 episode that had starred Ted Osborn. Now Karloff took Osborn's role of Carl Warner, a man who may be an escaped killer – a madman whose murderous impulses can only be kept in check by the birdsong of canaries.

Five days later he was back on television in *The Soul of the Great Bell*, an adaptation of Lafcadio Hearn's 1887 story. Karloff played the Chinese official Kouan-Yu, who receives orders from 'the Celestially August, the Son of Heaven, Yong-Lo'[22] to have a great bell forged whose voice 'should be strengthened with brass, and deepened with gold, and sweetened with silver…'[23] Twice, however, the metals refuse to merge and the casting fails. The Son of Heaven becomes angry and threatens to have the official beheaded if he fails a third time.

Kouan-Yu's devoted daughter, Ko-Ngai, seeks the advice of an astrologer. "Gold and brass will never meet in wedlock, silver and iron never will embrace, until the flesh of a maiden be melted in the crucible, until the blood of a virgin be mixed with the metals in their fusion," he tells her.[24] As the bell is about to be cast in the third and final attempt Ko-Ngai flings herself into the furnace and the bell is successfully cast. Ballerina Raimonda Orselli appeared alongside Karloff as his daughter in this dramatisation that included songs and ballet. One reviewer thought the production "a charming Chinese fable, with Boris Karloff giving it the correct chop-suey tang."[25]

Days later Karloff revisited the role of Jonathan Brewster in his third appearance in *Arsenic and Old Lace* on radio. Joining him were Jean Adair (as Martha Brewster) and Edgar Stehli (Dr. Einstein) – two of the cast from the Broadway run over a decade before. Evelyn Varden took the role of Abby Brewster while Donald Cook played Mortimer. This hour-long adaptation was recorded at New York's NBC studios on 1 July and broadcast five days later. Karloff was paid $500.

In *House of Death* (broadcast on 4 July), part of the *Schlitz Playhouse of Stars* television series, Karloff appeared as a cantankerous, wealthy recluse who begins to receive anonymous death notes. A week later (13 July) he returned to radio's *Inner Sanctum* in the episode *Death for Sale*. He played Mark Deevers, a man who plans to defraud an insurance company of $50,000. Deevers had paid one Elliott Starr $5,000 to marry Deevers' partner, Cora, then disappear. For seven years the couple wait for Elliott Starr to be legally declared dead so Cora can claim the insurance. However, only days before the deadline, Starr re-appears and demands more money – with murderous results. It was Karloff's final appearance on the show, which would come to an end on 5 October after 11 years on the air. By the time the radio show hit the airwaves Boris Karloff was back in England, this time to make a new television series – *Colonel March of Scotland Yard*.

Karloff had received the job offer from American television producer Hannah Weinstein, a known left-wing activist, who had left the U.S. in 1950 to escape the questioning of the HUAC. After moving to Paris she finally settled in London where, in 1952, she founded Atlas Productions, reportedly using funds supplied by the Communist Party of the United States of America (CPUSA).

For her first English venture Weinstein chose the stories of John Dickson Carr, an America-born Anglophile who specialised in the so-called 'locked-room' mysteries, stories of seemingly impossible crimes. "Edgar Allan Poe invented the whole thing and put into his stories every single device that has since been used," Carr later observed. "Arthur Conan Doyle owed a lot to Poe and said so."[26]

Writing as Carter Dickson, Carr's stories concerned Colonel Perceval March, the eye-patch wearing detective from Scotland Yard's department D-3 – the Department of Queer Complaints. It is March's remit to investigate the seemingly impossible crimes, as he would explain to Detective Ames [Ewan Roberts] in the first pilot, *Hot Money*. "Now if that fellow had robbed a magic lamp to disappear in a puff of smoke, that would be *my* department," March explains. "But he robbed the bank, killed the commissionaire and just ran out – that's *your* department." Initially there would be three pilot episodes which would serve as examples to sell the potential series to the television networks.

While in New York, Weinstein contacted blacklisted writer Walter Bernstein. "She wanted to use blacklisted people and had called me to work on it… She was a small, indomitable woman who had too much impatient drive to set policy but was wonderful at carrying it out."[27] Weinstein wanted the writer to work on *Colonel March of Scotland Yard*, adapting Dickson Carr's tales. "The stories themselves were thin and more cerebral than dramatic," said Bernstein, "but Hannah didn't care. They could easily be rewritten, or new stories created; it was just a matter of writers. She also didn't care what name anyone used."[28] As a result Bernstein's name is not featured in the credits of any of the *Colonel March* episodes.

Because of the cryptic nature of the tales Bernstein though it would be easier to work in collaboration. He was joined by Abraham Polonsky, the blacklisted writer/director who had been Oscar nominated for his screenplay for *Body and Soul*, the 1947 boxing picture starring John Garfield. "We told Hannah, who also knew Polonsky, and it was fine with her. She was happy another blacklisted writer was getting work. She took off for England, but first she asked if I would meet Karloff and see what ideas he might have. I leaped at the chance, wondering if I should tell him how I had dived under the seat when he came to life in *The Mummy*."[29]

Bernstein went to the Dakota building and took the elevator. Then he climbed a winding set of iron stairs upwards towards the Karloffs apartment. Ringing the bell Bernstein waited in nervous anticipation. "The door was opened by a tall, elderly English gentleman wearing fawn-coloured trousers and a houndstooth jacket," Bernstein said. "He had a clipped white moustache and the familiar stoop, and when he opened his mouth, there was the familiar lisp. It was Karloff all right. I felt as I had on meeting Bette Davis, that I already knew him. The movies had performed another one of their miracles; Karloff and I were old friends without having met. He invited me in and sat me down and offered tea. His manner was pleasant and courtly. His wife brought the tea and then left with a smile. They were both charming and very English. The apartment was like a small, neat upper-class English cottage. The rooms were bright and cheerful and had eaves and leaded windows. The sofa and chairs were covered with floral patterns. There were hunting prints on the walls. You were in the presence of a lot of chintz. It was like walking on to the set of an old MGM movie about Little England."[30]

The two discussed the series and Karloff offered some ideas about his character. "He was modest about them, offering them merely as suggestions, but they were good suggestions," said Bernstein. "He knew what he was talking about."[31] They discussed how to keep the drama moving, how to avoid bringing the story to a halt as the detective explained the crime and identified the murderer. Then, drinks in hand, the conversation turned to other matters. "I kept pumping Karloff about his career, whom he had worked with, the pictures he had made. He answered willingly; he was humorous, knowledgeable and self-deprecating and gave me more time than I deserved. I could have stayed there forever," Bernstein said.[32]

Later, while working on the episodes, the writers were presented with a problem. "Our puzzles were so good they were unsolvable," Bernstein explained. "The question was not how to make the endings more active but how to end them at all. No one else seemed to worry about this, least of all Hannah. So long as she got something to shoot, she was happy. If the endings made no sense, that did not bother her. It didn't seem to bother Karloff, either. His part was not demanding and he performed it professionally and without complaint."[33]

On 28 June 1952, as he prepared for the trip to England, Karloff wrote to his brother and sister-in-law, Sir John and Dorothy.

> Just a quick one to let you know that everything is all set and we DO sail on the third on the *Italia* and arrive at Plymouth on the eleventh. You are not to think of doing anything about getting a car or nonsense of that sort to meet us. I don't know the hour of arrival and we have made arrangements at this end for a car which we will get in a couple of days. How is Jack getting along? I do hope he will be well enough to be kidnapped to Lords for I'll be heading in that direction as soon as possible! We've had the most appalling heat wave in New York the past few days, over one hundred at night, the worst I've ever

known and will we be glad to get on the boat next Thursday! We still have our reservations at Old St. James house but I still don't know where the films will be made and that will have an effect on where we finally dig in. Some bitter is on the way and I hope it does the trick. Our love to you both and we'll see you so soon I can hardly believe it![34]

Stepping off the ship with Evie at Plymouth Karloff was once again met by the press. "Let's forget Frankenstein," Karloff announced, "this is just the weather for cricket."[35] "You might call it The Return of the Ghost," he added. "But… it's grand to be back after 16 years. I'm looking forward to Lord's and Denis Compton. I've given up playing now – I'm 65, you know. Poor old Aubrey Smith and I introduced cricket to Hollywood. Now there are six teams there."[36]

Karloff, it was noted, was sporting a grey moustache. "This is for some TV pictures I hope to make for the American market while I'm in England," he explained. "I expect to play the role of Colonel March, special investigator… I shall be tackling very odd assignments in a rather light-hearted manner. In fact, the role may be a little too benign."[37]

Karloff and Evie were expecting to stay in England for four months and would live in London for the duration. He also intended to visit relations, including Sir John, and pay a visit to his old school, Uppingham. "The last time I was at Uppingham, it was the summer vacation," Karloff said. "I walked round like a ghost… a great school. I remember seeing a fellow hit 303 against Repton."[38]

Asked if he ever intended applying for American citizenship Karloff replied, "No, sir – I've been nearly 40 years in the States. I owe my success and my money to America, but I would be a hypocrite if I became anything but British."[39] After startling a newspaper boy by asking for a copy of the daily news Karloff perused the headlines. "I wonder how the Republican Convention is going?" he said, before turning to the sports day. "Must keep up with the cricket scores, you know."[40]

The three *Colonel March* pilots were filmed at Nettlefold Studios, in Walton-on-Thames in Surrey. All were adaptations of Carr's original stories and were produced and directed by Donald Ginsberg. Curiously, when the three pilots were later edited together and released as the feature *Colonel March Investigates* (1952), blacklisted Cy Endfield, who later made *Zulu* (1964), was credited as director.

The pilot episodes were shot economically, mainly inside the studios with only a few exterior shots. March is seen outside only once in each episode; approaching a bank in the Kings Road in the first, crossing the forecourt of the British Museum in the second, and talking to witnesses in a London Mews in the third.

In the first of the trio – *Hot Money* – a masked man robs a bank and, while escaping, shoots the commissionaire dead. However, while fleeing the bank he is followed by a clerk, John Parrish, who tails him to the office of a solicitor, Mr. Boulder. The teller informs the police and the solicitor's office is thoroughly searched, but the police fail to uncover the money. Instead, they begin to suspect the teller is the culprit. Colonel March, however, proves the solicitor's guilt when he correctly deduces the money's hiding place – secreted in the solicitor's false radiator.

22-year-old Joan Sims, who would later become a regular on the popular *Carry On* team, appeared in the episode as Marjorie Dawson, the robber's unsuspecting secretary. She later recounted her experience of working with Boris Karloff in her autobiography *High Spirits*. "I was very nervous before the filming and went over my lines again and again and again," Sims wrote. "Not that I had many lines to learn… My nerves were not helped by the fear that the real Boris Karloff might be like the on-screen Boris Karloff and start doing unspeakable things to me, but he turned out to be very docile and sweet, more inclined to talk about gardening than wander round the countryside terrorising the natives."[41]

Sims also erroneously claimed to have played the detective's secretary. "And my few moments on screen," she wrote, "were mostly spent taking calls from clients anxious to have the intrepid Colonel March set about solving the latest supernatural mystery haunting London."[42] In fact, Colonel March had no secretary.

In the second tale, *Death in the Dressing Room*, March investigates the death of Javanese dancer, Francine Rapport who, during her display at the Embassy nightclub, uses the 'torture movement' – a sequence that should not appear in the dance. When she is then found dead March investigates and discovers Rapport was killed by her lover, the nightclub's owner D.W. Cabot [Richard Wattis]. His new love, Paula, had then danced in Rapport's place, but had made that fatal error in her dance by including the erroneous movements.

In the third, *The New Invisible Man*, a prying neighbour is disturbed when he sees a pair of floating hands wield a gun and seemingly shoot a man dead in a mews cottage. March investigates and discovers the floating hands were an illusion designed to put a stop to the neighbour's snooping. He is, however, almost killed when he uncovers a plot to steal valuable artworks.

Away from the studios Karloff made time to watch his beloved cricket. Unable to play any longer he had requested someone be found who could accompany him to the matches. The person who got the 'job' was 28-year-old Bernard Coleman who recalled the circumstances behind his first encounter with the star:

> I had a phone call from a young journalist who'd worked on the **Streatham News**, and he'd got a job working for Universal Films in London doing the handouts about their latest films. And he was frantic, really, because they'd had a cable from America to say that Boris Karloff was coming back to England for the first time in many, many years and he wanted to go to a cricket match. He loved cricket and he wanted to go – and I was the only chap this fellow knew who knew anything about it. So, I was a member of Surrey County Cricket Club, and he [Karloff] asked if I'd meet him at a flat they'd got in Brompton Square. So I duly arrived there and was met by Boris and Evie and they were very courteous – quiet, nothing much was said.
>
> I took him up to the Oval and we sat on what was then the upper tier looking down right over the wicket where I always sat. And it was a lovely sunny day, Alec Bedser was bowling and plenty of time had gone by – he hadn't said very much – and suddenly in this voice which seemed to come from somewhere deep below the belt, this voice said, "This is like dying and going to heaven." And I've heard it quoted since then by many people, but Boris was the man who first said it, in my view. And… gradually we chatted and I said to him, "I know Alec Bedser. Would you like to meet him?" So, he said, "Yes, that would be very nice. I would like to." So I went down to the dressing room. I'd met Alec on a number of occasions that particular season, so I knocked on the door and they came out. "Can I speak to Alec?" – and I said to Alec "I've got a very famous film actor

sitting upstairs," so Alec said – in his usual manner – "I don't know **anything** about films." Then I said, "His name's Boris Karloff," and Alec said, "Well, even *I've* heard of *him*!" So I duly took Boris down and met him and they became, over the years, great friends. And Boris would go and sit on the players' balcony and watch the cricket quite often, when he wasn't sitting with me.[43]

On 25 November 1952 the Karloffs (and 13 pieces of luggage) boarded the liner *S.S. America* at Southampton and sailed for New York. They arrived in the city on 2 December, and, within a week of his arrival, Karloff was back on television.

On 8 December, he appeared alongside Gene Lockhart on *Lux Video Theatre* in *Fear*. The drama told the story of two men – one a millionaire philanthropist, the other an ex-convict – who have a reunion after 25 years. Two days later he was on the radio in another piece for the *Philip Morris Playhouse on Broadway*. In this story, *Man Versus Town*, Karloff played a man falsely accused of murder. Then, on 16 December, he made another appearance on Milton Berle's *Texaco Star Theatre* appearing on the same show as Don Ameche and singer Monica Lewis. With it Karloff's professional work for the year was over but, on 26 December, Hedda Hopper revealed he would soon reunite with Abbott and Costello for the comedy duo's next feature, *Abbott and Costello Meet Dr. Jekyll and Mr. Hyde*. It would mark Karloff's first return to a monster role since *Son of Frankenstein* 14 years earlier. Originally the studio had wanted Basil Rathbone to play the dual role but when he proved unavailable the picture's director Charles Lamont suggested Boris Karloff instead.

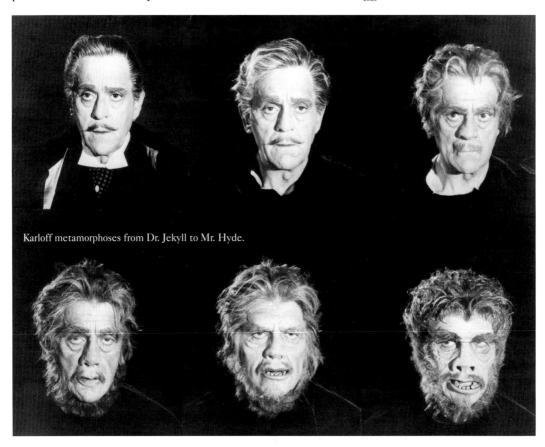

Karloff metamorphoses from Dr. Jekyll to Mr. Hyde.

Karloff's second film with Abbott and Costello told the story of two turn-of-the-century American policemen, Slim [Abbott] and Tubby [Costello], who are in London to study the city's police methods. There they meet music-hall singer Vicky Edwards [Helen Westcott] and her guardian, Dr. Henry Jekyll [Karloff]. Jekyll, however, has been injecting a serum, which transforms him into the monstrous Mr. Hyde, and in this guise he has committed a series of murders in the capital.

When Vicky falls for journalist Bruce Adams [Craig Stevens], the jealous doctor plans to be rid of him. Tubby, though, discovers Jekyll and Hyde are one and the same, yet nobody believes him. However, Jekyll later confesses his love for Vicky but when she rejects him he turns into Mr. Hyde. Hearing Vicky's screams Bruce, Slim and Tubby chase the monster but during the fracas Tubby sits on the hypodermic containing the formula. While chasing Hyde through the London streets Tubby, too, transforms into a monster.

He is captured but Hyde escapes and returns to his house where he tries to abduct Vicky. Bruce saves her and when Hyde tries to escape by climbing through an upper storey window he falls to the ground and is killed.

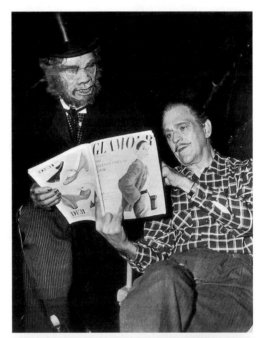

Although stuntman Eddie Parker played Mr. Hyde in his more physical moments Karloff was still required to submit to the make-up men, Bud Westmore and Jack Kevan. "He had to spend days before the cameras in a rubber headpiece made hideous with wolfish features and long hair," wrote journalist Ben Cook. "So much time was needed to fit the headpiece that Karloff could not remove it between scenes. He employed an extra-long cigarette holder when he felt the need for a smoke, and long straws when he took a drink of water or coffee between meals. The headpiece was removed only at lunchtime. 'I should acquire a very thin face by the end of the picture,' Karloff said. 'They use rubber girdles for taking off weight in the middle, you know. My face has perspired enough to take off all plumpness. Who knows but that I shall gain a new look?'"[44]

Abbott and Costello Meet Dr. Jekyll and Mr. Hyde opened at the RKO-Boston, on 30 July 1953. "Co-starring Boris Karloff as a moustachioed version of Stevenson's classic dual personality, this latest bit of nonsense from A. & C. is among their best," one critic wrote.[45]

The picture opened in Los Angeles on 12 August at RKO-Hillstreet and Hollywood Pantages Theatres. The *Los Angeles Times*

Top: Karloff and Hyde (Eddie Parker) relax on set of *Abbott and Costello Meet Dr. Jekyll and Hyde* (1953).
Bottom: Meeting a familiar face.

described the picture as, "a real giggle getter, despite many of its many ancient gags, for it has some that even old Maestro Mack Sennett himself may wish he had thought of…

Boris Karloff of course is perfect as the temperamental pair, Jekyll and Hyde."[46]

In February columnist Hedda Hopper had announced Karloff would, following his second pairing with Abbott and Costello, return to England to star in a "Jules Verne story for Michael Powell and Emeric Pressburger; then plunge into a series of television films."[47] For whatever reason this unnamed Powell/Pressburger project failed to materialise and, instead, Karloff embarked on a less prestigious production entitled *Sabaka*.

This picture was written and directed by television and radio producer Frank Ferrin who had originally planned to call it *Gunga Ram* after the movie's young hero. However, following complaints from RKO who insisted Ferrin's title was too similar to their own picture *Gunga Din* (1939) the

With Jack Kevan (with moustache) and Bud Westmore.

picture was renamed, briefly, *The Hindu* until its final release title was settled upon.

Sabaka told the story of Gunga Ram [Nino Marcel], a young elephant trainer whose sister and brother-in-law are killed by members of a fire-worshipping cult. When the authorities dismiss his story the youth embarks on his own path of vengeance and wipes out the cult with the aid of a tiger and an elephant named Sabaka.

While the majority of the picture was shot in India, Karloff's handful of scenes as the Indian Army General Pollegar (alongside his old-friend, and *The Lost Patrol* co-star, Reginald Denny) were shot on a Hollywood soundstage. Despite Karloff's brief appearance in the picture his worldwide fame ensured him top billing. *Sabaka* went on general release almost two years later, in February 1955.

After finishing his two pictures Karloff and Evie decided it was time to take a holiday. "After the work in Hollywood we took a week and came back to New York by way of Mexico," Karloff wrote to his brother, Sir John. "Friends of ours from the coast were vacationing there so we flew down to join them in Acapulco far down on the Pacific coast and Evie landed

a 90 pound sail fish and I got a 110 pounder and the excitement was terrific. We will show you pictorial proof when we see you this summer. Then we drove back to Mexico City to fly back here. Mexico City was simply marvellous, a beautiful handsome city, old and new side by side and in many ways like Paris. The new extension of the University of Mexico which is being built on the outskirts is really magnificent and some of the most exciting buildings I have ever seen."[48]

Karloff was back in New York by 17 March when he appeared in

Fishing in Acapulco - 1953

another episode of the television series *Suspense!* While the episodes were usually original tales or adaptations of classic stories this episode, *The Black Prophet*, was based upon a real event – the assassination of Grigori Rasputin in St. Petersburg's Yusupov Palace in December 1916.

At 65 Karloff was almost 20 years too old for the role (Rasputin was 47 when he was murdered). Still, sporting a long matted wig and beard, he starred as the famous 'mad monk'. Appearing alongside him as conspirator Prince Yusupov was 27-year-old Leslie Nielsen who would go on to star in the sci-fi classic *Forbidden Planet* (1956) and the later comedies *Airplane!* (1980) and *The Naked Gun* trilogy (1988, 1991 and 1994). "Boris Karloff was an easy man to work with," Nielsen recalled, "and was just as bowlegged (if not more) as I was!"[49]

Two days later Karloff and Evie attended the 25th Academy Awards ceremony at the NBC International Theatre at Columbus Circle in New York. This event was the first to be held simultaneously in Los Angeles and New York, and the first to be televised gaining an estimated viewing audience of 40 million. Although Karloff would later vilify the event, he and Evie were in the audience that night to watch Cecil B. DeMille's *The Greatest Show on Earth* take home the statuette for best picture. John Ford won for directing *The Quiet Man* while Gary Cooper was awarded the best actor Oscar for *High Noon*. In New York an eager Shirley Booth tripped on her way to the stage to collect the best actress Oscar for her performance in *Come Back, Little Sheba*.

At the end of the month (30 March) Karloff was featured in an episode of the television drama series *Robert Montgomery Presents* in *The Burden of Proof*, a tale of an English murder trial involving, as one newspaper put it, "a shrewish wife, spoiled son, misunderstood father and compassionate daughter".[50] Then, in the *Tales of Tomorrow* episode *Past Tense*, televised on 3 April, he played a time traveller who attempts to make his fortune selling penicillin years before its 1928 discovery by Alexander Fleming.

Two days later (5 April) he returned to the radio in another adaptation of a Charles Dickens novel, this time *Great Expectations* for *U.S. Steel Hour*. Karloff appeared as the convict Magwich in the drama, joining Melville Cooper, Margaret Phillips and Estelle Winwood. The play also featured Evie Karloff's ex-husband Tom Helmore. In the radio drama *Dead Past*, broadcast on 15 April, Karloff starred in a sympathetic role as a man suspected of murder. It was a busy time.

The following day Karloff wrote to his brother with news of a forthcoming trip to England:

> My dear Jack,
> My God, where does the time go? Here it is in the middle of April and I am just getting around to yours of February 23. But honestly I think I have been up to my ears in work almost as much as you and that is going some!! I've made two films in Hollywood so far this year and last week had to fly out and back for one day's reshooting sandwiched in between TV and radio shows here. It's getting that I am [a] public scandal to my friends here, doing as much work as I do and I couldn't enjoy it more!! But then I know we both feel alike about that, apart from any monetary considerations, which too are not to be despised. Awfully good news about Tom [Sir John's son-in-law Tom Bromley] and his promotion at the embassy, he and Diana must be a jolly good team and

that is what it takes. We plan to come home the end of June for a few weeks anyhow, whether the TV films that I did in London [**Col. March**] sell or not... and at the moment it looks very much as if they will, but nothing has been signed as yet. However, we will come… for one thing, when one is as active as I am, it is a very good thing to give the customers a complete rest for a while, and the time to do that is in the summer when it is too hot for comfort here and work falls off anyhow.[51]

Again, Karloff commented on the political climate:

I can't say that I admire [Malcolm] Muggeridge[i] as he reveals himself to me in Punch. The annoying thing about all "reformed" communists is that they assume such an air of superiority and presume to lecture us who never swallowed the nonsense that they did. Over here before the investigating committees, etc., the only man whose word is worth a damn is the ex-communist. It's fantastic! I'm glad you feel that people at home are waking up to the true facts of what is going on on one side of the so-called curtain but I see very little signs of it here. And that makes the outlook for peace depressing in spite of the developments of the last few weeks... I've been keeping my eyes peeled for any articles on Korea and China that might interest you or be of any value but I've drawn a blank. It's no use sending you all the old hashed-over stuff. Well, that seems to be all the gup for the moment. I have high hopes that within the next two weeks we'll know something definite about the English TV but in the meantime expect us the end of June anyhow. Our best love to you and Dorothy.

as ever,
Billy[52]

On 23 April Karloff was back on the radio in *Plague*, "a story of man's fight against epidemics and plagues since the Middle Ages, during *Heritage* on KECA at 8 o'clock tonight," one newspaper explained. "Drama concerns itself with man's increasingly successful battle against disease from the time of the Black Plague. Karloff will narrate part of the story and will also play several roles."[53] Two weeks later (7 May) he joined Laraine Day, Leo Durocher and June Lockhart on the television panel game *Quick as a Flash*. Karloff had been on the show before when, in 1952, he and actress Wendy Barrie had appeared on the pilot episode.[ii]

On 24 May Karloff was back on television in the series *Plymouth Playhouse*. That evening's episode featured four short plays: John Collier's *The Chaser* (with Karloff and Philip Truex), Dorothy Parker's *You Were Perfectly Fine* (with Kyle MacDonnell), *Nightmare Number Three* by Stephen Vincent Benet (with Walter Matthau) and Saki's tale *The Reticence of Lady Anne* (Karloff, again).

i Journalist/author Malcolm Muggeridge was the editor of *Punch* magazine from 1953 to 1957. In the early 1930s Muggeridge had been an advocate of Communism but later changed his political views.
ii The pilot episode of *Quick as a Flash* was hosted by Bob Cullen who also served in that capacity on the show's radio version. However, when the television series began in March 1953 Cullen was replaced by Bobby Sherwood and, later, Bud Collyer.

A week later, on a rainy Tuesday, 2 June 1953, Queen Elizabeth II was crowned in Westminster Abbey in London. In his apartment in the Dakota Building Boris Karloff tuned in. "All this last week has been devoted to the Coronation of course, which received wonderful coverage here," he wrote to Sir John four days later. "I heard the whole ceremony from the Abbey on the wireless and at four-thirty p.m. of the same day I was watching the films on the TV here in my room! It really was a miracle technically... but the bloody weather, of course!"[54]

By now it had been confirmed there would be further episodes of *Colonel March of Scotland Yard*, as Karloff mentioned in the letter to his brother:

> Well, we are finally all fixed up and are flying BOAC on June 26th arriving early June 27th and will be home until some time in October at least. We are going to Old St. James' House, 7 Park Place where we were before for a week or two, and then I believe something in the nature of a real flat for housekeeping has been fixed up. Needless to say we can't wait to get home and already dread the thought of having to return perhaps in October. But our stay may be longer as there seems to be a more than even chance that the TV films will continue. It should be fixed by the time we leave at the end of this month... which would of course mean that we would be home much longer... Anyhow we'll see all of you early in July and, by the way, what news of Jeremy [Read]? He's such a fine lad and I want to see something more of him this time... always avoiding Dorrie [Karloff's niece, Dorothy] of course!![55]

Before he left the country, however, Karloff had a few more work commitments to attend to. On 17 June he revisited his brief Broadway role of Descius Heiss in a radio adaptation of *The Shop at Sly Corner* for the *Philip Morris Playhouse*, alongside Charles Martin. Then, on Tuesday 23 June, he played the title role, alongside Alan Webb, on the 200th episode of *Suspense*, in a live television adaptation of Charles Dickens' famous ghost story *The Signalman*. Then, three days later, Boris Karloff flew to England where he would once again don his eye-patch and return to the role of Colonel March of Scotland Yard. He would make an additional 23 episodes, bringing the total to 26.

Away from the studio Karloff made time for his cricket. Unable to play anymore he would often watch the matches, although he sometimes became involved in a more official capacity as Bernard Coleman recalled. "He used to umpire," Coleman said. "In the days before Sunday cricket started officially, they used to play matches for the beneficiary – each county has a beneficiary for the year, raises money on the Sunday matches – so he did Alec Bedser's [in 1953]. He [Boris] went and umpired for these Sunday matches. He'd always enjoy that and he'd meet all the players and he loved it all and he did that a lot of the time... he was very keen on that."[56]

Karloff's stints as a spectator could sometimes be quite lengthy. "We would go to Lords and the Oval and watch cricket for days – literally – for *days*," Coleman explained. "And I would bring some sandwiches and veal-and-ham pie – which he *loved*. He had a little old rucksack in which he would have a bottle of Tollemache bitter beer, and tonic water for me. And we would go to all these cricket matches and in '53 we'd gone to Lords for the test match there and we looked like losing it – we'd lost three wickets overnight – and so it looked as though we were out of the game and I said, "Shall we go tomorrow?"

Relaxing and fishing during production of *The Monster of the Island* (1954).

and he said, "Well… we'll go." So we duly arrived on the Mound Stand and the ground was virtually empty and Trevor Bailey and Willy Watson – it was one of the great stands of English cricket – they batted most of the day and saved the game, and the ground filled up and we had been the first people in the ground! So we were *highly* delighted and we managed to get a draw and then the match at the Oval – the last test – we won the Ashes back! And so Boris and I went down to what was a rickety old bar under what was then called the 'Ladies Pavilion' which would have been a disgrace for a doss-house, that's how bad it was, but we had a drink there – we had a few drinks – and I was going back to work! And I wasn't much of a drinker. When I arrived back at work everybody said 'What's the matter with you?' I was well gone!"[57]

On 2 September 1953 the *New York Times* announced Karloff's next picture, an Italian venture entitled *Il Mostro dell'Isola* would soon get underway. "Another Italian project," it wrote, "*The Monster of the Island*, which is scheduled to go before the cameras this week, will have Boris Karloff as the featured player, I.F.E. announced yesterday. The Romano Films production is being directed by Roberto Montero."[58] The Karloffs, therefore, flew to Rome where the picture would be shot at the city's Paolis Studios. Location work would be filmed on Ischia, the volcanic island in the Gulf of Naples.

The picture's title proved to be misleading though, for despite the presence of Boris Karloff, it was not a horror movie and contained no monster. The monster of the title was, in fact, Karloff's character Don Gaetano, an outwardly philanthropic man who secretly runs a band of smugglers.

Despite the pleasures of filming in Italian locations the shoot proved to be something of a trial for Karloff. "I haven't the least idea what it was like," he later admitted. "Incredible! Dreadful! No one in the outfit spoke English; I don't speak Italian. Just hopeless. I had a very good time, but that's beside the point."[59]

The stay in Rome, too, had its problems, all due to the manager of the Hassler Hotel where the Karloffs were staying. Actor Henry Brandon, who had appeared with Karloff in the Mr. Wong picture *Doomed to Die* (1940), was in Rome at the time of the shoot and paid the Karloffs a visit. Some time later Brandon spoke with Karloff of this. "I reminded him and Evie of the time I had visited them at the beautiful old Hassler at the top of the Spanish Steps in Rome," he explained. "The pompous old fool of a manager behind the desk had sent me to the wrong suite. I surmised that it was his way of demonstrating that he was unimpressed by his illustrious guest. Boris sat up and shouted, "They're *venal*, the Romans are *venal, venal, venal*!" I had lived there for a year and a half and was in complete agreement."[60] *The Monster of the Island* was completed by early November and released in Italy two months later. When the picture was finally released to English-speaking audiences Karloff's voice was dubbed by an impersonator.

On 2 December British radio broadcast Raymond Massey's play *The Hanging Judge*, itself an adaptation of Bruce Hamilton's novel *Let Him Have Judgement*. Karloff starred as Sir Francis Brittain who, to uphold the law, passes a guilty verdict on an innocent man believing no one who was innocent would panic when accused of a crime he did not commit. Brittain, however, harbours a dark secret – for many years ago he fathered a son out of wedlock. However, he never supported the mother or the mentally unstable son, Ted, who continued to live in poverty. When the judge finally visits his deranged son Ted kills himself, having arranged for the death to look like murder. Brittain is tried for the crime and condemned to hang.

1954 was a leaner year, work-wise, for Karloff. Residing back in New York, he made no films that year and, in fact, would not appear in another film until *Voodoo Island* two years later. Even so, this did not mean Karloff would be absent from the public eye. In mid-January his television series *Colonel March of Scotland Yard* was purchased for local release by Dick Moore, the vice-president and general manager of KTTV (Channel 11).

The detective series hit the television screens at 9:30 p.m. on Thursday, 11 February 1954 when it opened in Chicago with the episode *The Invisible Knife*. In it March tries to prove the guilt of a suspected multiple murderer but almost becomes a victim. "There is really nothing startlingly new in the Karloff series," wrote one reviewer. "Yet television's whodunits are so sterile [of originality] and stereotyped that by comparison this one stands out. *Dragnet*, while not a conventional whodunit, still falls in the general category and is almost everybody's choice as No. 1. The likes of *Martin Kane, Boston Blackie, Mr. and Mrs. North* and *Man Against Crime* wallow on the same level of mediocrity. Somewhere between these two extremes belongs *Col. March of Scotland Yard*."[61]

Viewers in California had to wait another month before the series was screened there, commencing on Saturday, 6 March. New Yorkers could not see the series until exactly four months later, on Tuesday, 6 July. British audiences did not get to see the detective in action until *Col. March* was aired by the Associated Broadcasting Company at 7:45 p.m. on Saturday, 24 September the following year.

Later in 1954 Karloff made yet another trip back to England and this time was able to visit his great-nephew Jeremy Read, the grandson of Karloff's sister, Julia. During the war

Read and his family had received gifts sent from their famous relative in Hollywood. "We got food parcels sent across," Read recalled, "and they were the sort of things one didn't get at that time. The thing I particularly remember is some very rich fruitcake, which was absolutely brilliant! Heck, I must have been about ten at the time, or a little under – eight

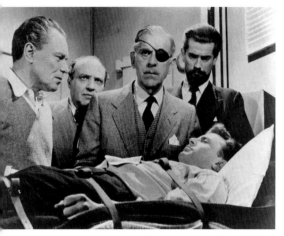

On television in *Colonel March of Scotland Yard* (1954).

to ten. I certainly remember that vividly, and it was all a part of my feeling – when I did meet him – that he was somebody who was very kind. Very kind, very good-natured and I thought also very modest. Nice is a much misused word but the quality struck."[62]

The visit to London would allow Read to repay, in some measure, his great-uncle's kindness. "I was a sub-lieutenant undergoing a training course at the Royal Naval College, Greenwich," he explained, "and my great-uncle and his wife were in London, for, I think, a comparatively short time. I invited him to a Mess Dinner which was held in the Painted Hall at the College when the principal guests were members of the City Livery Companies.

He was there as my private guest, but I remember the Commander of the College, as Mess President, mentioning him in his speech of welcome. I had invited him because we were very grateful to him for the parcels that he sent from time to time from California during the war. I went to tea, I think, with him and his wife during his visit, but I think that was all. My memory of him is of a friendly, gentle man, with quite a soft voice and a twinkle in his eye, and his kindness was very evident."[63]

On 15 June Boris Karloff opened a crime book exhibition in the gallery of the National Book League in London. The event had been arranged by the Crime Writers Association who were hoping to raise "the prestige and the fortunes of crime writing and writers generally."[64]

Opening the exhibition Karloff told those assembled that all of them, whether authors or readers, were partners in crime. Looking around it struck him, he said, how absurd was the saying 'crime does not pay'. At this point, however, crime writer Bruce Graeme spoke up. If Karloff really thought crime did pay, the author said, he would introduce the star to every publisher present and disenchant him.

Being in England during the cricket season meant, for Karloff, the almost obligatory days at the matches with Bernard Coleman who would be informed of the star's visits. "He always let me know," Coleman said. "And we'd go out for dinner. We became very, very firm friends. It wasn't just the cricket. And he was always interested in what I was doing and any new business that I was getting involved in and things like that."[65]

Sitting in the stands at Lords or the Oval the two would often spend time chatting. "He would ask questions," explained Coleman, "and I would ask him stories and you gave him a cue line and you'd get a story about an actor or a film he'd been in or a play he'd been in. And he was absolutely marvellous."

The tales were usually humorous in nature. "He told me a marvellous story about Groucho Marx," Coleman said, "when they were negotiating with Louis B. Mayer – who was the legendary head of MGM films – and they'd had great success with *A Night at the Opera* and things like that. And Louis B. Mayer was a very tough operator. Now their fourth brother Zeppo was the world's worst actor – he wasn't funny – and he'd been the juvenile lead. But he had become their agent rather than playing – and he was a good agent. But Louis B. Mayer wouldn't accept the terms. Everytime they went back for more money [Mayer said], "No!" So eventually Groucho said to Louis B. Mayer, "Alright, we'll accept your offer but Zeppo comes back into the act." And Mayer said, "Anything but that!" and pushed their money up [*laughs*]. This was the great story he told me.

"Then there was another beautiful story about this actor. The big theatrical people in London were H.M. Tennent who put on all the plays – Gielgud, Richardson, Olivier – they all worked for Tennent's. They were huge. They were the 'Andrew Lloyd Webber' [of their day] but they owned the theatres and everything. And he told me the story about this young actor – and they were all a little bit... er... they were gay but that wasn't the word that was used in those days. But apparently this man [Binkie] Beaumont dominated it all [at Tennent's] and they were auditioning a young actor. He went through his piece. 'Yes, yes, that'll be quite alright,' said Beaumont. So the young actor said, 'Oh, I have to tell you, Mr. Beaumont, I'm not queer.' And Beaumont said, 'Never mind, never mind, it won't notice from the front!' [*laughs*]. And Boris used to tell this story with great glee."[66]

Sometimes Karloff would discuss his own roles and once expressed his disappointment at being excluded from the movie version of *Arsenic and Old Lace*. "He was terribly upset – bitterly, bitterly disappointed that he didn't get it," Coleman said. "They wouldn't release him. He had the contract and they wouldn't release him to do the film because they wanted the show to run and if they had let him out of it the show might have come off, so he had to stay. And Raymond Massey did it. Oh, very upset – he was very upset."[67] Still the play was still paying dividends after all these years. "Every so often we'd be sitting at the cricket and he'd say, 'The pension cheque arrived this morning!' and that was his royalty," said Coleman. "The other thing he loved doing was *Peter Pan* because the royalties go to the Great Ormond Street Hospital and that thrilled him. He loved that. That was marvellous. The thing about Boris was his enormous interest in *everything*. If he met somebody he'd be interested in *them* and what *they* did. He didn't talk about himself – unless you gave him the line to actually talk about himself, in which he was fine. He was excellent company always and we'd have lots of laughs. He took me to Twickenham and to the rugby. I'd never ever been to Twickenham. He loved rugby. Oh, yes – he was a great rugby man."[68]

The Karloffs remained in England until Tuesday, 28 September when they boarded the liner *S.S. Ile de France* at Southampton. They arrived in New York six days later, on 4 October.

In the closing months of the year Karloff would make only a few television appearances. On 6 November he was a guest on comedian George Gobel's show. Then, on 16 December, he appeared alongside Teresa Wright in another dramatic role in Dorothea Carousso's psychological drama *The White Carnations*. Broadcast live from Television City in Hollywood the story, one paper revealed, concerned a wife who, "cannot remember a song but when she receives a bouquet of white carnations, a flower she detests, she links the melody with her husband's European colleague in psychology. Karloff is the menace and there is certainly a climax."[69]

On Wednesday, 22 December he made his first appearance on the television quiz show *Down You Go*. His participation had made the news weeks earlier. "Boris Karloff, Laura Z. Hobson and Leonora Corbett will alternate as panellists for future telecasts of *Down You Go*," the item read. "Fitting role for horror expert Karloff: *Down You Go* is based on a game called *Hang the Butcher*."[70] The panellists were required to guess a word or phrase in a game similar to *Hangman*. The show was hosted by Dr. Bergen Evans and featured – in addition to Karloff – actress Elizabeth Montgomery, cartoonist Walt Kelly and baseball star Phil Rizzuto.

The New Year brought Karloff's second appearance in a live television broadcast of *Arsenic and Old Lace*. On Wednesday, 5 January 1955 he revisited the role of Jonathan Brewster in this hour-long adaptation by Howard Lindsay and Russel Crouse. This time he was joined by his old friend Peter Lorre (as Dr. Einstein), Orson Bean as Mortimer Brewster, with Helen Hayes and Billie Burke as the murderous siblings, and Edward Everett Horton as the ill-fated Mr. Witherspoon.

Karloff was happy to appear again in the play, which he maintained was one of the best-written plays in American history. "I love the way the audience finds out for itself, without being told, that we're all dotty in the show," he explained. "Take John Alexander, who played Teddy Roosevelt. Nobody really knows he's off-centre until, while taking tea, he remarks, 'Personally, I've always enjoyed my talks with Cardinal Gibbons – or have I met him yet?'"[71] Jack Gould of the *New York Times* thought the broadcast, "easily the best of this star-studded series, presented once a month in colour."[72]

On Saturday, 19 February Karloff appeared as Donald O'Connor's guest on *Texaco Star Theatre*. Journalist Jack Gould thought it a pity that Karloff's name was still synonymous with horror. "How silly and short-sighted this abuse of Mr. Karloff has been... For 15 minutes it was Mr. Karloff's lot to be back in the usual laboratory with usual corny props. But for much of the balance of the programme he was relieved of the chore of being a king-sized menace and finally allowed to play something different... Freed of the gobs of make-up, Mr. Karloff was not only a strikingly handsome man but an individual of genuinely engaging charm... After Saturday evening some imaginative soul in TV is going to come up with a sympathetic assignment for Mr. Karloff and capitalise on his warmth and ability. It is certainly high time."[73]

On 22 February, and as if to address Gould's concerns, Karloff joined Robert Fleming, Hermione Gingold and Martyn Green on the *Elgin TV Hour* in *The Sting of Death*, an adaptation of H.F. Heard's novel *A Taste for Honey*. Karloff played Mr. Mycroft,[iii] a bee-keeping sleuth who investigates the death of another bee-keeper's wife, the apparent victim of multiple bee-stings.

Karloff's next television appearance was almost three weeks later, on Saturday, 12 March, when he appeared in another adaptation of Mark Twain's novel *A Connecticut Yankee in King Arthur's Court*. This 90-minute live broadcast, however, was a version of the 1927 Broadway musical featuring songs by Richard Rogers and Lorenz Hart. Again, Karloff was called upon to play the king – "a sort of Blimp", he said, "a pompous ass who is absolutely gullible"[74] – but this time he would also be required to sing. "Eddie Albert and I will have a duet," he explained. "It comes at the beginning of the third act. It's called *You Always Love the Same Girl*. In a way it's terrifying. It's a new wicket for me. I did two short songs when I was with Jean Arthur in *Peter Pan* but this will be much more elaborate."[75]

---

iii The character was known as Mr. Mycroft only in the U.S. edition of Heard's novel. In the U.K. version he was named Mr. Bowcross. Although the author never confirmed or denied the speculations it is generally supposed that Mr. Mycroft/Bowcross is, in reality, Sherlock Holmes himself, having retired to live in Sussex to keep bees (as he had in Conan Doyle's story *His Last Bow*).

With Donald O'Connor on television. 19 February 1955.

Rehearsals began in early March and journalist J.P. Shanley visited Karloff in his dressing room. The room was filled with the scent emanating from a vase of fresh flowers. "It smells a bit like an undertaking parlour, doesn't it?" Karloff remarked.[76]

Television was now becoming the star's most consistent source of employment. It was a medium Karloff enjoyed. "The wonderful thing about television," he explained, "is that it gives you an opportunity to do things that you normally wouldn't do – certainly not in films. I'm all for live television. It's much more exciting from the actor's point of view. In film you get a chance to rectify mistakes. On stage you can look forward to an improvement the next night. But on live TV you are on, and if you make a muck of it, you just make a muck of it. There's a great challenge in it."[77] Discussing his career with Shanley, Karloff once again expressed his gratitude to the Frankenstein Monster. "In a sense he's been a handicap to me but because of him I've been able to work right along. Now that I'm being called on for other kinds of parts, like King Arthur, it's most satisfying."[78]

On 1 May Karloff graced the television screens again when he appeared with Susan Strasberg, Anthony Perkins, Haim Winant [H.M. Wynant], Eli Wallach and Bramwell Fletcher[iv] in the Oriental love story *Mr. Blue Ocean* on *General Electric Theatre*. Karloff starred as the title character, a lonely man since the death of his wife and the departure of his two sons. To combat his loneliness he courts the young, but tempestuous, Rain Drop but has competition from two young men, Earth Quake [Winant] and West Wind [Perkins]. Susan Strasberg had taken the role, she said, because she liked the play. "After all," she explained, "how often will I get a chance to play a character named Rain Drop."[79]

Within weeks the Karloffs were back in England on a visit that gave the star his sole opportunity to work, albeit briefly, on the London stage. In the early hours of Saturday 25 June, Boris Karloff stepped onto the stage of London's prestigious Palladium Theatre as part of *Night of 100 Stars*, an event organised in aid of the Actors' Orphanage, a charity for children 'made destitute by the profession'. According to a journalist for *The Times* the show provided, "a treasure trove full of almost as many memories. The galaxy shone resplendently, but – thanks to careful planning – not overpoweringly or even exhaustingly. When into the small hours of yesterday, Sir Laurence Olivier bade the house a farewell good-morning, it was clearly in the mood for yet another encore."[80]

---

iv Bramwell Fletcher had played the archaeologist Ralph Norton, who had read the Scroll of Thoth and awakened Imhotep in *The Mummy* over two decades earlier.

The entertainment had begun at midnight with Beatrice Lillie, and in the hours that followed the audience was treated to a variety of skits, scenes and songs. Danny Kaye had joined Olivier and John Mills to sing a Noel Coward song about three 'Teddy Boys'. There were scenes from *Kismet*, *The Jazz Train*, *Jokers Wild* and *Talk of the Town*. Richard Attenborough played a schoolboy opposite Bernard Lee in a scene from *The Guinea Pig*. Hermione Baddeley and Michael Somes appeared in *The Creaking Princess* while Michael Redgrave sang a song from *Carmen Jones*.

Karloff was joined on stage by Hermione Gingold. "And he did the sketch which is a very famous sketch done every Christmas – there's a film of it, a German film of the butler and the lady of the house," Bernard Coleman explained. "And he played the butler. And he gets more and more tiddly as he's talking to her, and he escorts her up to her room. It was a very famous film and sketch of it, and Boris did it and it was the only time he'd ever appeared on the stage in London. He never worked there, but he did this charity night."[81]

Marlene Dietrich closed the evening after Flanagan and Allen and the rest of the Crazy Gang lead a long line of the evening's performers – including Karloff – in a rendition of *Underneath the Arches*. This must have been a highlight for Karloff who had last seen the comedy group at that same theatre back in 1936. "He loved the Crazy Gang," Bernard Coleman said. "He thought they were marvellous."[82]

While in England the Karloffs often spent time with Ralph and Barbara Edwards. Edwards had been the creator of the popular show *This Is Your Life*, which had first aired on American television in 1952. Now Edwards was in England to promote a British version.

The first episode was televised on the BBC on 29 July 1955, presented by Ralph Edwards. "British viewers are in for a shock," wrote journalist Clifford Davis from America. "I have seen this programme here and know what's coming. The programme recreates the life of someone in the studio audience – but right up to the moment the show is on the air the victim has no idea what's happening. The victims – on whom secret research has been carried out – are specially invited to the show as members of the audience."[83]

The first guest on the show was 32-year-old broadcaster Eamonn Andrews who, that September, would be chosen to front the British version. He would continue in that capacity for the following 32 years until his death in 1987. In the early days of the show Karloff and Evie would occasionally be seated in the audience as Edwards pounced on his 'victim'.

In August James E. Lynch, then a member of the faculty of the Television Centre at the State University of Iowa, was invited to New York to witness, first hand, the process of television production. He would see everything from the first reading up to the on-air performance. The programme Lynch observed was a show for *The United States Steel Hour* named *Counterfeit*. Its star was Boris Karloff. Lynch's subsequent article, published in *The Quarterly of Film, Radio and Television*, gives an insight into the processes Karloff was continually involved in.

The Theatre Guild had selected J.B. Priestley's 1933 play *Laburnum Grove* as a suitable subject for their show. It told the story of the North London family, the Radferns. As the father, George [Karloff] pottered happily in his greenhouse and garden while his wife looked after the house. When their daughter complains about the boringly tranquil nature of their lives George tells them he is, in fact, the leader of a counterfeiting ring. They think he is joking until, one day, a police inspector calls.

The rehearsal period covered nine days commencing at 10 a.m. on Tuesday, 23 August in a conference room at the Theatre Guild building on West 53rd Street. It was the first time the cast had been called together and the morning's schedule consisted of a first read-through of the script, during which the director explained movements and the major camera shots. For the afternoon session the cast and crew reconvened, now at the Central Plaza building at 111 Second Avenue. The sets had been taped out on the floor and the cast began to familiarise themselves with the surroundings. Now the director began the blocking of the show, running through the position of the actors for each scene. After Act I was blocked the cast ran through the entire act. This process was repeated for Acts II and III and by the end of the day the entire show had been blocked.

The next day was taken up with scene-by-scene rehearsals. The director, Norman Felton, would occasionally suggest ideas for interpretation and characterisation but was reluctant to impose too many ideas on his cast. "Offer suggestions and bits of business," he explained, "but generally let them figure things out for themselves. If they can't do that, then, of course, you have to move in. But, in general, when you see the plot and characterisations rigidly, you find your actors following your every suggestion – and they automatically stop thinking."[84]

After a free Thursday the cast and crew reconvened on Friday to iron out any difficulties that had so far presented themselves. This was followed by two complete run-throughs of Acts I and II. At 4 p.m. Felton decided on a complete performance, this time without scripts. Although there were numerous dropped lines during that run-through these were ignored as the actors ploughed on.

Saturday's rehearsal began with a run through of Act II. This was followed by a discussion to identify the scene's weak spots. The short speeches, Felton found, had posed a problem, as the actors were still not familiar with their cues. The director, therefore, held a rehearsal for just this portion of the show. This time the rehearsals were timed. Musical director Harold Levey was also present and played the theme, bridge and background music on the piano during the run-throughs. This also gave the director the opportunity to discuss any amendments to the music. Finally, Felton talked his associate director through each of the planned shots.

On Sunday the cast and crew re-assembled and began by working through any remaining trouble spots. Then the acts were run through, this time with music. By now, Lynch noted, the line troubles had virtually disappeared and the actors were beginning to enjoy themselves.

The next day began with another run-through. This was followed, at 11:30 a.m., by a dress rehearsal before the Theatre Guild's production staff, the advertising agency representative and the show's technical staff. A conference was then held to discuss any changes the Theatre Guild staff had suggested and at 1:30 p.m. the final dry rehearsal – in effect, a full performance – began.

On Tuesday, 30 August the production moved to CBS TV Studio 61 at 1456 First Avenue for the beginning of camera rehearsals. With the sets and lights in place the camera rehearsal began at 2 p.m. The planning of each camera shot was a long but necessary process. It was finally completed at 7:45 p.m. This was followed by a re-run of the final three scenes so Boris Karloff had the opportunity to rehearse some fast costume changes. At 8:10 p.m., following a short break, the first camera run-through began and at 9:30 p.m. the cast was released while the director, associate director, and production assistant conferred with the Theatre Guild staff.

At 3:30 p.m. on the final day – Wednesday, 31 August – the cast met with the director to go through any minor line changes and bits of business. At the same time, in a side room, the musical-director and his 12-piece orchestra rehearsed. That afternoon's run through, however, went badly. The actors were continually dropping their lines and two big blow-ups stopped the rehearsals. The many last minute dialogue changes were causing some of the cast problems. Even so, at 7:45 p.m., after dinner, Felton met with the actors and presented them with yet more line changes. A full dress rehearsal followed half an hour later, complete with music, commercials and sound effects. At 9:30 p.m. the rehearsal ended and the cast and crew were given a 20-minute break. It was now half an hour to the broadcast.

At 9:50 p.m. the cast and crew took their places, waiting tensely for the 10 p.m. set-off. Then, at 9:59 p.m. the director, Norman Felton, spoke over the intercom. "In television as in crime," he said, "it's all a matter of time!"[85]

"A roar of laughter followed," Lynch wrote, "and the tension was released. There was silence again, and then the assistant director's voice called out 'Stand by!' The second hand on the control room clock read 9:59:50. The assistant director counted "ten-nine-eight-seven-six-five-four-three-two, roll film, track up, announcer."

"*The United States Steel Hour*… Live from New York."'[86]

J.P. Shanley of the *New York Times*, however, thought all the effort had gone unrewarded. It was, he wrote, "for the most part, a dull production. The plot moved sluggishly and most of the performances were uninspired. There was only one scene in which the play acquired real vitality. It was a brief sequence in which Mr. Karloff was confronted with evidence against him by a relentless Scotland Yard inspector… It is to be hoped that Mr. Karloff soon will see the light and mend his ways. A good script would not be a bad idea, either."[87]

In early September the Karloffs returned to England. Their stay was brief – only a few weeks – and on 27 September they left Southampton on the French liner *S.S. Flandre*. They arrived in New York on 3 October and Boris Karloff immediately began rehearsals for a new Broadway production – *The Lark*.

Chapter 19

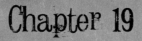

THE LARK

(1955-1957)

"I have a theory that when an actor gets to the point where he may choose his own parts, nine of ten times he is in a very dangerous position. For myself, I know what I can't do, but I have no idea what I can do. That is rather putting the cart before the horse."[1]
Boris Karloff (1956)

In 1953 the French playwright Jean Anouilh wrote *L'Alouette* (*The Lark*), a play concerning the trial of the French national heroine Joan of Arc. In doing so he followed in the famous footsteps of George Bernard Shaw's *Saint Joan* (1923). Unlike Shaw, however, Anouilh took a less political approach. "You cannot explain Joan," he wrote, "any more than you can explain the tiniest flower growing by the wayside. There's just a little living flower that has always known, ever since it was a microscopic seed, how many petals it would have and how big they would grow, exactly how blue its blue would be and how its delicate scent would be compounded. There's just the phenomenon of Joan, as there is the phenomenon of a daisy or of the sky or of a bird. What pretentious creatures men are, if that's not enough for them. Children, even when they are growing older, are allowed to make a bunch of daisies or play at imitating bird-song, even if they know nothing about botany or ornithology. That is just about what I have done."[2]

An English adaptation, by the poet and playwright Christopher Fry, opened at the Lyric Theatre in London on 11 May 1955. The play was produced by Peter Brook and featured Dorothy Tutin as Joan, Laurence Naismith as Cauchon, Richard Johnson as Warwick and Donald Pleasence as the Dauphin. In New York the theatrical producer Kermit Bloomgarden had already been preparing a version of his own.

In the summer of 1954 Bloomgarden had turned to the playwright Lillian Hellman to adapt Anouilh's *The Lark* for American audiences. "At first I said yes – well, semi-yes," Hellman

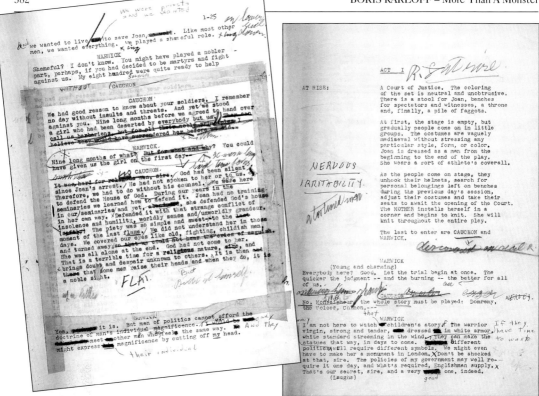

Karloff's script annotations for *The Lark*.

explained, "Then, very fast, I said no. Then I read the play and said yes. You know, you keep thinking that you can do these things in a month or so, while gambolling on the grass with ribbons in your hair."[3]

The first draft was completed in around four months and although, as Hellman recalled, "everybody was satisfied",[4] she continued to tinker with it before eventually deciding to type a new version. The rewrites, additions and deletions, however, would continue into rehearsals. Later, when asked if she would repeat the experience she replied, "Never again… I'll have to be terribly hungry before I do another adaptation… And I don't ever expect to get that hungry."[5]

The final result, Hellman later said, had become "such a mish-mash that I can't tell which is Anouilh's Joan and which is mine."[6] She was conscious, however, that she had removed some of the French nationalism present in Anouilh's play. "Joan is not just a French girl," Hellman explained. "She is everybody's girl. She belongs to the world."[7]

On 22 March 1955 the *New York Times* announced Boris Karloff would star in the play alongside 29-year-old Julie Harris. Lillian Hellman, it was noted, was "well-along" in her adaptation of Anouilh's play, having completed the first act. Rehearsals were expected to begin on 29 August.

Initially the newspapers had announced Karloff would play the Inquisitor, although Bloomgarden later admitted his office had erred in making that announcement. Karloff would, in fact, play the role of Pierre Cauchon, the bishop of Beauvais, the man who had presided over Joan of Arc's trial.

In late June Bloomgarden made a trip to California to search for an actor to play the Inquisitor and engaged Canadian actor Joseph Wiseman.[i] Now the producer announced the play would open at the Longacre Theatre in New York on 24 October. Rehearsals, he said, would begin on 12 September under the direction of Denis Carey. Neither statement, though, would come to fruition.

In late July the *New York Times* announced Jay Robinson, who had worked with Karloff in *The Shop at Sly Corner*, was up for the role of the Dauphin. The actor had read Hellman's adaptation and called it "tremendously exciting".[8] It was, however, another non-starter and the role went to Paul Roebling. Karloff alerted his *Arsenic and Old Lace* colleague Bruce Gordon to the role of Captain La Hire that was being cast and Gordon successfully auditioned for the part, being presented also with the additional role of Monsieur de la Tremouille.

Also joining the cast, as the Englishman Warwick, was the 28-year-old Canadian actor Christopher Plummer. "Chris saved the day," Julie Harris later declared. "We would have gone down without him… Chris saved the day because we had had two Earls of Warwick,"[9] neither of which, the actress recalled, were "very compelling".[10] Plummer was even personally vetted by Lillian Hellman. "Lillian," Plummer recounted, "who was smoking thousands of cigarettes all at once, out of the corner of her mouth said, 'He'll do fine'."[11]

Hellman was also present during at least some of the casting process. "I was delighted when my agent arranged a meeting for me with the play's producer and director," Theodore Bikel later wrote, "and came in for a mild shock when I saw the third person present at the meeting: Lillian Hellman, a legend to me in more ways than one."[12] Bikel's meeting was successful and he was cast as Robert de Baudricourt, the captain of the garrison of Vaucouleur – the man whom Joan persuaded to escort her to see the Dauphin at Chinon.

Leonard Bernstein, who had provided songs and music for *Peter Pan*, was now asked to compose incidental music for *The Lark*. For his three French choruses – *Spring Song*, *Court Song* and *Soldier's Song* – the composer used as a basis medieval French folk songs, and utilised text from the Roman mass in his five Latin choruses – *Prelude*, *Benedictus*, *Sanctus*, *Requiem* and *Gloria*. The score was then recorded by the choral septet New York Pro Musica Antiqua, and used throughout the run of the play.

Rehearsals finally began in early October 1955 in the New Amsterdam Roof, the small theatre situated on top of the New Amsterdam theatre at 214 W. 42nd Street. "We got in on the third of October and I literally went from the dock straight to rehearsal," Karloff wrote to his brother, Sir John.[13]

It soon became clear, however, that Hellman's involvement in the production would extend further than the mere adaptation of the play. "The director was Joe Anthony," Theodore Bikel explained, "a gentle and considerate man, perhaps too gentle for the buffeting that theatre politics can subject you to. It was also his first Broadway directorial job. Little wonder that the constant presence of Lillian Hellman found him under more pressure than he should have been. It was a tense atmosphere that none of us managed to escape. My earlier admiration for the formidable Miss Hellman soon gave way to exasperation as she insinuated herself into a process that by rights should be the sole province of actors and their director. Playwrights as a rule do not interfere in this

i Joseph Wiseman would later play the first cinematic Bond villain, *Dr. No* (1962).

process; if they have comments about the work, they are voiced outside of rehearsals during production conferences. And this was not even Hellman's own play! Still, she was there, often interrupting the rehearsal with criticisms that more often stifled rather than encouraged any creative processes."[14]

Hellman's constant rewrites were also causing problems. The changes meant the cast had to amend their copies by hand, sometimes having to tape larger tracts of revised text over the old. Not all of these revisions, however, were considered improvements. Following one amendment Karloff scribbled in his script, 'The guts of the scene are gone.'

With Julie Harris in *The Lark* (1955).

Of course, these changes did nothing to alleviate the already tense atmosphere of rehearsals. Sometimes the pressure became too much. "Oh, yes, we've all lost it," Christopher Plummer later admitted. "We have to lose it. Because you have to shed some tightness."[15] Even Julie Harris (who, according to Plummer, rehearsed in her armour) had exploded when a lighting cue kept going wrong. "I was so glad," Plummer later told Harris. "You were so sweet otherwise."[16]

Things were not made easier by Lillian Hellman's continual interference. Unfortunately for Bikel one of the playwright's criticisms was directed at him. At the end of Bikel's long scene where he is persuaded by Joan to accompany her to Chinon, Bikel grabbed the sides of his head and let out a sigh in exasperation. Suddenly Hellman's voice boomed forth. "What was this supposed to mean?" she asked. "Don't do that – I don't like gestures."[17] Bikel stopped and, trying to remain calm, responded. "Miss Hellman, I cannot accept such a statement," he said. "If you do not like a particular gesture, then we might discuss it with the director and, if we should all agree that it is wrong or inappropriate, then we might consider changing or eliminating it. But to have you say to me, categorically, that you do not like gestures – in the plural – directly attacks one of the principal things my profession is all about. Words are your department, Miss Hellman, gestures are mine. I wish you would realise that my work starts where yours ends."[18]

Infuriated, Bikel left the stage and sat in the wings. He knew, though, his outburst would likely result in his exit from the play. "While they did not fire me, my life was made more than a little difficult for the next few days," he said, "with extra rehearsals called just for that scene. But as we opened in Boston for the play's tryout, my scene – including the gesture – received prolonged applause from the audience. Hellman, clearly miffed, never talked to me again, and while she seemed to have backed down, she never apologised, either."[19]

Bikel, though, was not the only object of Hellman's criticisms, as he would soon witness. One night after the show, he was waiting for Christopher Plummer to join him for dinner. While waiting Bikel saw the director, Joseph Anthony, enter the dressing room Plummer shared with Joseph Wiseman. There Anthony, somewhat unwillingly, told Wiseman of Hellman's 'suggestions' for his performance. "Why?" Wiseman was heard to say, "Why is everybody – allowed – to – make – pauses – except – me? Oh – shit!"[20] Hellman's antics, though, did not seem to faze the production manager, Bill Ross, who seemed mostly amused by them. When Hellman once enquired of him, "If I were an actor, what role do you think I should play in this play?" Ross immediately replied, "The Executioner".[21]

Julie Harris faced a different problem during rehearsals. Having caught a cold the actress lost her voice. Karloff came to the rescue, prescribing her the treatment he had found so successful during his time in *Arsenic and Old Lace* – the trusted corncob pipe with cotton soaked in eucalyptus oil.

"It was *wonderful* working with Boris," Harris later said. "He was a dream of a man – kind, humorous, gentle, and very, very strong... He was a tireless worker – knew his lines backwards and forewards – was patient and giving to everyone. I thought he was a glorious actor, and wanted him to play King Lear, but he told me he had never played Shakespeare and now it was too late. I loved him as a man and as an actor."[22]

The play opened at the Plymouth Theatre in Boston on the 28 October 1955 for a two-week pre-Broadway tryout. The *Christian Science Monitor* called it "an intriguingly staged production... skillfully directed by Joseph Anthony... Joan herself is admirably played by Miss Harris. She wears the plainest of costumes until the final scene of the coronation. Her hair is short and combed straight down all around in irregular fashion. But she has an intensity that lifts her above her surroundings. She conveys to the audience a feeling of unquenchable inner fire. Mr. Karloff as Cauchon mingles compassion for Joan with determination to carry out his duty as he sees it. Christopher Plummer is a somewhat cynical but likable Warwick. Joseph Wiseman gives a cutting edge and almost fanatical zeal to the Inquisitor, and Roger de Koven is a less subtle and more pugnacious Promoter. Michael Higgins portrays Ladvenu as a kindlier member of the court, eager to intercede for Joan. Theodore Bikel depicts an earthy and not too bright de Baudricourt and Bruce Gordon a bluff but considerate La Hire."[23]

"We got unanimously good notices there," Karloff later wrote, "but the wise management never stopped working on the play and we were hard at it the two weeks there."[24]

The play closed in Boston on Saturday, 12 November and opened at the Longacre Theatre in New York five days later. According to Louis Calta of the *New York Times* the applause when the curtain fell was "thunderous and unbroken. There were many curtain calls and they were brought to a halt only when the house lights were turned on."[25] During the curtain calls the cast, unexpectedly, turned in unison towards Julie Harris and joined the applause for the star of the play.

Her colleagues always found one of Harris's scenes, in particular, extremely effecting. It was, Plummer explained, "when she stood up on her little stool, and she screamed for her soldiers, and the tears ran down her face. And, oh, boy, every night, we stood behind her, bawling... I think I told Julie that once during the run... She said, 'Please don't talk to me about moments!' And I remember I went away thinking, 'Hey, I could really ruin a lot of great actors by telling them how wonderful they were in certain moments.'"[26]

Still, after leaving the theatre that night Julie Harris went home, she later admitted, feeling "suicidal".[27] At home she climbed into bed only to be roused some time later by a telephone call informing her of the play's rave reviews. Harris rose, dressed and left for the party at the Plaza Hotel.

The next day the theatre's box office was a hive of activity as patrons queued from 10 a.m. to purchase tickets. Later that day, however, Kermit Bloomgarden announced the price of tickets would have to be raised. From 26 December, he said, the price of orchestra seats for Monday to Thursday performances would be increased. It was not as a result of the play's excellent critical reception but was, he explained, "because of the exceptionally heavy operating costs... It needs a weekly box-office gross of $22,000 to break even at the Longacre," he said, adding, "at its presents scale of prices it would require six months of capacity trade to recover the initial cost of $100,000."[28] The ticket price would rise by $1.15 – from $4.60 to $5.75.

It was gratifying for Karloff to be in another Broadway hit, especially as his last ventures in the city had not lived up to expectations. "It looks as if the play will run the balance of the season and we are all very happy and grateful," Karloff wrote to Sir John that December. "It has been particularly interesting to me after having seen it at the Lyric this summer, where I frankly thought it very bad. Lillian Hellman's adaptation as opposed to Fry's translation is simply superb and Julie Harris as Joan is really brilliant. The whole scheme of the production is so simple and yet so rich and beautiful and it has been splendidly directed. Altogether it is by far the best thing I have ever had in New York and I couldn't be happier. We are all just now catching our breath and settling down to the job of keeping it intact and really enjoying playing it."[29] It was an important play for Boris Karloff. "That was the part he loved," Bernard Coleman later said, "he told me that."[30]

According to Bill Ross, Karloff would arrive at the theatre early, clearly enthused by each day's entry into the theatrical world. This was, after all, his passion, his first love. After all the movies, after all the television and radio appearances, this – the theatre – was the reason he had longed to be an actor.

In his dressing room Karloff would prepare for each performance by pulling himself up to a bar he had installed for this purpose. This exercise, he found, helped to alleviate both his troublesome back and his arthritis. Julie Harris had been cognisant of her colleague's medical problems and had graciously swapped her stage-level star dressing room with Karloff's, which had been situated on another floor.

Although they never socialised off stage – or even discussed their craft – a bond of mutual respect grew between the two. The role of Cauchon was, Karloff told the press, "the most tiring and exacting"[31] of his career. Every night, for the entire length of the play – some two hours and ten minutes – Karloff kept his eyes fixed on his co-star. It was, he said, "something that grew"[32] between them during rehearsals. "Every so often she throws me a little look," he explained, "and I've got to be there to catch it."[33]

One night, early in the run, Julie Harris had an accident, falling on stage in the first act. "Well, really," she later said, "I was supposed to fall but I misjudged the distance, and as I went down to my knees, my head – my mouth – grazed the side of the bench I sat on and I hit it with some force. I heard Boris behind me say – in a very low voice – 'J-U-L-I-E!' And the next thing I knew, I felt something drip into my hands – my own blood, as I discovered a few moments later. I had split my lower lip open rather badly. I staggered through the next scene, spraying blood all over Joe Mielziner's blue carpet. I'll never forget how Boris said my name at that moment – full of such concern."[34]

As much as Karloff enjoyed the play the work was not, however, without its problems, as he later explained to Bernard Coleman. "He said there was this young actor who everybody said was going to be the new Olivier and he had come down from Canada and his name was Christopher Plummer," Coleman explained. "And he was always late, very undisciplined and used to arrive just as the curtain was going up – always, always. So the cast said, 'Look, Boris, you've got to talk to him. You're the senior member. You've got to talk to him and tell him about this.' So he said, 'Alright.' So, one evening, he said to Plummer, 'I want to see you. I'd like to have a chat with you in the dressing room after the show.' So after the show he explained to him about the courtesy to your fellow actors and he gave him a very courteous lecture about disciplines and things you should do. And Plummer thanked him very much and said, 'Very kind of you.' So, he [Boris] said, the following night, when they were doing the play, Plummer, as he walked by, said 'Silly old bastard!' [*laughs*]. Boris said it was so funny and he said, 'It was all I could do not to laugh!' He always tickled me with that story."[35] This was not, however, the only occasion Karloff almost 'corpsed' on stage during the run.

Often the cast and crew would play games backstage. "We would make up rhymes, poems, limericks, and play games that twisted the text of the play," Bikel later explained. "I am afraid I was the culprit one evening when, fooling around backstage, I turned some of the inquisitors' phrases around. The scene in question occurs when one of the priest inquisitors grills Joan on whether she was aware of the ways the devil had of ensnaring souls. 'When the devil wants a soul for his own, he appears in the shape of a beautiful girl with bare breasts.' Whereupon the cardinal cautions, 'Let us keep our own devils to ourselves.' That night the inquisitor, played by Roger de Koven, thundered, 'Do you know what the devil does when he wants a soul for his own? He appears in the shape of a beautiful *bear* with *girl* breasts!' Even Boris Karloff, usually so very solid and serious, was hard-pressed to keep a straight face as he admonished the priest to keep his own peculiar devil to himself."[36]

According to Christopher Plummer, Karloff soon became a kind of 'Father Confessor'[37] for the troupe and every night, as they left the theatre, each member of the cast would call out 'goodnight' as they passed his dressing room. Such was the depth of feeling Karloff instilled in his colleagues there was genuine concern one night when he was uncharacteristically absent when the half hour call was made. 15 minutes later Karloff had still failed to arrive at the theatre and, as he was usually so prompt, his colleagues began to worry. As the stage manager paced the alley outside every member of the cast, spread over the theatre's four landings, eagerly watched over the balustrades waiting for the star to appear. "Boris was our tower of strength, you see; we not only needed him, we already missed him," Plummer later wrote. "Just then he lumbered in through the stage door and, as one man, we gave him a rousing welcome ovation. He looked up at us, beaming, with that wonderful twisted smile of his, and we all went back to our rooms as if we'd just been given a present. As I was struggling into my armour it came to me like a ray of truth that there are only the rarest few born into this world who are truly good humans and, I realised, with a sharp pang of sadness and envy, I could never be one of them."[38]

On Easter Sunday, 1 April 1956, the annual Tony Awards ceremony was held in the Grand Ballroom of the Plaza Hotel. Both Julie Harris and Karloff were present having been nominated in the categories of Best Actress and Best Actor (in a dramatic play) respectively. While Harris won the award Karloff did not, losing out to his *Scarface* co-star Paul Muni for *Inherit the Wind*. Also nominated was *The Lark*'s director Joseph Anthony, scenic designer Jo Mielziner and costume designer Alvin Colt.

The final curtain descended on the New York run of *The Lark* two months later, on Saturday 2 June 1956, after 229 performances. That same day Julie Harris penned her co-star a letter:

Dearest Boris – I have never been so happy acting with someone as I have been with you – I love you and am grateful for the unspoken help and encouragement you have given me. I hope in my heart we will work together again and that the next time it will be a perfect experience. I realise that this time there were disappointments but I know that you have made The Lark a beautiful and happy run for me.

All my love, Julie[39]

As was often the case when appearing on stage, Karloff would accept short-term commitments on the side. In 1955, while still treading the boards in *The Lark*, he entered into what would be a fruitful relationship with Caedmon Records.

In 1952 Barbara Holdridge (then Cohen) and Marianne Roney contacted the Welsh poet Dylan Thomas and invited him to record some of his works. The resulting record *Dylan Thomas Reading* was released in April 1953 and went on to sell 50,000 albums. Hoping to repeat this success the women now began to contact other authors, actors and poets to record popular works. Writers such as Thomas Mann, Tennessee Williams, Sean O'Casey and Ogden Nash soon gave readings for the company. Then, in December 1956, Caedmon Records released three children's albums; two of these, [*Oscar*] *Wilde Fairy Tales* and *Edgar Allan Poe* (containing the stories *The Red Death* and *The Black Cat*) were read by Basil Rathbone, the third – Rudyard Kipling's *Just So Stories* – was narrated by Boris Karloff. "There's no reason why a kiddie package cannot be distinguished," *Billboard* wrote. "The Rudyard Kipling stories are great, and the reading by Boris Karloff is wonderful. It's plain that Karloff loves the stories himself. The album is excellent inventory for good shops, and is an item the literate buyer will want to add to his permanent collection."[40]

Although this period saw no radio appearances by Karloff there was still the television work. On 3 April 1956 he signed a contract to appear on *The Alcoa Hour* in *Even The Weariest River*, a western written entirely in blank verse by Alvin Sapinsley. Karloff would receive second co-star billing and $4,000 for his services. Joining him in the programme were Franchot Tone, Lee Grant and *The Lark*'s Christopher Plummer. Sapinsley later told Gordon Shriver, "Boris was one of the two hardest-working actors I was associated with during the days of live television; hard-working in the sense that he rehearsed assiduously, studied his role and his lines unceasingly, made effort upon effort to sharpen, improve and hone the part. During rehearsal breaks, while the others sat around drinking coffee, Boris would be off in a corner, working on his character."[41]

The drama was broadcast live on Sunday, 15 April and told the story of the death of a western town, Weary River, whose only purpose is to serve as a waypoint for the stagecoach. With the expansion of the railroad, however, the town's days are numbered. Franchot Tone played the sheriff whose best days seem to be behind him. He has been unable to catch a bandit who has robbed the stagecoach five times, killing five men in the process. When a wounded stranger [Plummer] enters town the sheriff quickly establishes the man to be innocent of the robberies. However, when his daughter and the townsfolk demand the stranger be arrested, the sheriff acquiesces – with fatal results. Karloff played the narrator, the town's doctor. "Our country's history is simply told," he said. "The land grows up – the people just grow old."

John Crosby of the *Hartford Courant* called it "a sort of Shakespearean western... It was one of those big gambles that only television seems prepared to make, something that could have been just awful and turned out to be perfect… There were genuinely fine performances by all four principals – Mr. Tone, Mr. Karloff, Miss Grant and Christopher Plummer who played the stranger – and a great job of directing by Robert Mulligan."[42] Jack Gould of the *New York Times* agreed. "It was one of the season's fine achievements," he wrote.[43]

Sometimes potential Karloff projects of this period never came to fruition. One of these was announced in mid-May. "Mary Martin's next project will undoubtedly be a two-hour version of *Jack and the Beanstalk*," wrote the *Los Angeles Times*, "with Boris Karloff playing the giant, for NBC TV."[44]

On 18 July Karloff appeared on *The Amazing Dunninger* where he presented the master mentalist, Joseph Dunninger, with a mind-reading problem. This was followed, two weeks later, by the first of two consecutive weeks as a guest on *Frankie Laine Time*. Then, on 13 August, he appeared on *The Ernie Kovacs Show*. Three days later, on 16 August 1956, Bela Lugosi died, the victim of a heart attack. He was 73 years old.

The years had not been kind to Lugosi. After completing his work alongside Karloff in *The Body Snatcher* (1945), he had been presented with a series of mediocre movie roles. Only *Abbott and Costello Meet Frankenstein* (1948) had given him a worthy role, and he revisited the role of Dracula in that picture to fine effect. In the last decade of his life the actor made only six films, half of which were for writer/producer/director Edward D. Wood Jr., and although many of Wood's pictures have since taken on the status of cult classics it is generally acknowledged the quality of these efforts was poor.

On Friday, 22 April 1955 Lugosi was, at his own request, committed to hospital in an attempt to cure him of the narcotics addiction that had plagued him for 20 years. In 1935 he had begun taking morphine to relieve pains in his legs, before later switching to methadone. Now, too ill to go to court and weighing only 125 pounds, Lugosi was granted a hearing in a ward at General Hospital. "I need help to overcome the drug habit," he told Superior Judge Wallace L. Ware. "I'm dependent on the goodness of friends for my food. I get a small old-age pension that takes care of the rent."[45] Wallace ordered Lugosi be committed to the Metropolitan State Hospital at Norwalk for a period of not less than three months, but no more than two years.

On 2 August, after three months of treatment, Bela Lugosi was subjected to a staff examination at the hospital and "passed with flying colours".[46] As a result he was granted a leave of absence and left the hospital that Friday. He would, however, remain under the jurisdiction and supervision of the Department of Mental Health for the period of one year.

Three weeks later, on 24 August, the actor was married for a fifth time, after being both widowed and twice divorced. His new bride was 39-year-old Hope Lininger, a studio cutting-room clerk who had written to the actor in hospital on a daily basis, signing each 'just a dash of Hope'. "I've been a fan of Bela's ever since I was a kid," she said.[47] The ceremony was performed before a dozen guests (including Ed Wood) by Lugosi's long-standing friend, Manley P. Hall – the man who had 'hypnotised' Lugosi for his suffocation scene in *Black Friday* (1940).

The following February Lugosi played Basil Rathbone's mute valet in *The Black Sleep* then, returning to Wood's fold, he began work on *Tomb of the Vampire*, a picture that was subsequently scrapped when its star died. In true Ed Wood style the director incorporated the Lugosi footage in his new picture *Grave Robbers From Outer Space*, and replaced his now deceased star with his wife's chiropractor, Tom Mason, who spent the rest of the picture masked by his cloak. The picture opened two years later as *Plan 9 From Outer Space*.

On 18 August 1956 Bela Lugosi was laid to rest in the Holy Cross cemetery in Hollywood. He was buried, according to his wishes, wearing his *Dracula* cloak. His death, Hope Lugosi had explained, had been unexpected. "We have been very happy together," she told the press. "He seemed to be getting better month by month, and it was a great shock to me to find him dead when I entered the house. He didn't answer me when I spoke to him, so I went to him. I could feel no pulse, but apparently he must have died a very short time before I arrived."[48]

In the years that followed, stories emerged that Karloff, Vincent Price and Peter Lorre had all attended the funeral. When viewing the body Lorre, it was claimed, turned to Price and asked, "Do you think we should drive a stake through his heart just in case?" Another story had Lorre, accompanied by Karloff, viewing the body and saying, "Come now, Bela, quit putting us on!" All, however, are purely apocryphal for neither Price, Lorre nor Boris Karloff were present at Lugosi's funeral.

Despite the tales of rivalry Karloff later stated he had enjoyed working with Lugosi. "Very much indeed," he said. "Bela was a great technician – he was worth a lot more than he got. Poor Bela, he had a very tragic life, you know. A very sad life. He was a charming man but in some ways a fool to himself... But Bela was a kind and lovable man and I remember our work together with affection."[49]

Lugosi's troubles, Karloff said, had all stemmed from the Hungarian actor's troubles with the English language. "He refused to learn the language," Karloff later explained. "Once when we were doing a picture together, he asked me to help him with some lines. I learned to my horror that he was saying his lines almost phonetically... He never learned, and so he limited his own career."[50]

On 14 August 1956 *The Lark* had opened in Central City, Colorado at the beginning of a four month long tour. While Harris recreated her Broadway role many, including Karloff, had not. Instead, Sam Jaffe took the role of Bishop Cauchon. Karloff did, however, rejoin the play when it opened in San Francisco on 5 September allowing his daughter, Sara, to see him in the role. He left the play at the end of the month, this time for good. The play, however, continued on tour, opening in Los Angeles on 1 October with Sam Jaffe reinstated as Cauchon.

Both Julie Harris and Christopher Plummer would go on to have long and distinguished careers in the theatre. Each, like Boris Karloff, would have only one child – a son and a daughter respectively. "I will always remember Boris Karloff saying to me, 'Only have one child'," Harris recalled.[51] The nature of the business, he felt, would make it unfair to have more children. "I think families suffer," Harris agreed. "In my life, I never could sustain that. I would have loved to have had more children. But I just found it so difficult to manoeuvre all of those complicated relationships."[52] "It is a selfish profession," Plummer added. "You can't avoid that."[53] Plummer's chosen career meant he would never consider having a second child. "It would have to be brought up by a nanny," he said, "and what the hell is the point of that?"[54]

The night after *The Lark* opened in San Francisco Karloff appeared on television in another episode of the *Climax!* series. *Bury Me Later* was adapted by Jean Holloway from F.F.M. Prescott's mystery novel *Dead and Not Buried*. Karloff played a gentle English vicar who, believing an accused man to be innocent of the crime of murder, investigates and unmasks the real killer.

Left: The Karloff's in Hawaii for *Voodoo Island* (1957. Right: Paddling his own canoe with Evie in Kauai.

By now Karloff had been engaged to appear in a new film – *Voodoo Island*. He would be joined by Beverly Tyler, Murvyn Vye and Elisha Cook Jr. According to newspaper reports Peter Lorre had turned down a starring role opposite Karloff (probably the role taken by Cook Jr.), explaining it was not the kind he wanted to do now.

Karloff would play Phillip Knight, a famous writer and exposer of hoaxes who is employed by a hotel magnate, Howard Carlton, to investigate rumours of voodooism on a Pacific island where Carlton plans to build a hotel resort. After a series of deaths on the island, however – including two by carnivorous plants – Knight is forced to re-evaluate his beliefs.

Filming began on the island of Kauai in Hawaii on 26 October 1956 and, although his role was by no means as challenging as that of *The Lark*'s Bishop Cauchon, Karloff appeared to enjoy the experience. "He had a ball, he really did," the pictures co-producer, Howard Koch, later said. "Again, he was the opposite of everything he was on the screen: He was very congenial, worked hard and loved it... We lived very well over there in Hawaii. We stayed at the Cocoa Palms, on the island of Kauai, and Karloff had a nice bungalow. We did all the interiors there, too, because we couldn't afford to do it any other way – coming back and forth was out of the question, we couldn't afford the travel time between."[55]

The picture's shooting location was important to the budgetary considerations. The weather was very mild and Koch was already familiar with the locale having shot the Tony Curtis war picture *Beachhead* (1954) on the island. "There was a strip of land in a certain garden there where the flora in each direction was different," the picture's director, Reginald LeBorg, explained. "All we had to do was turn the camera, and there was a different location. So it was done very economically and efficiently. The budget was, I think, about $150,000."[56] Filming had completed by mid-November and *Voodoo Island* opened in Los Angeles on 13 March 1957 in a double bill with the horror picture *Pharaoh's Curse*.

Howard Koch later called the picture the favourite of his early horrors. "Oh, I liked *Voodoo Island* the best," he said. "I enjoyed the experience, and the dealings with Karloff. And I liked the picture's ambience – the background of the Hawaiian Islands. I just liked the look of it, and thought Reggie LeBorg did one hell of a job. I *love* that picture. I

think it's a classic."[57] However, fellow co-producer, Aubrey Schenck, did not agree. "Oh, *that* picture didn't come through," he said. "You see, you can't put Karloff doing a good-guy part – he has to be the heavy or it's wrong. That was a lost cause. Making those man-eating plants the heavy, that didn't make any sense. But, hell, you take a chance. With Karloff's name, we thought we had a good chance, but it didn't work out. I'm not proud of that picture at all."[58]

Returning to Los Angeles Karloff appeared, on 25 October, in the 90-minute *Playhouse 90* drama *Rendezvous in Black*, a murder mystery based on Cornell Woolrich's 1948 novel. "A fine cast in this weird mystery about a series of unrelated murders in which the victims are all women," revealed one reviewer. "The acting of Franchot Tone, Laraine Day, Boris Karloff and Viveca Lindfors are strong points, along with a top-flight production. Also notice the hand of talented director John Frankenheimer, responsible for the good camera work on *Forbidden Area*."[59]

On 27 November, four days after his 69th birthday, Karloff was seen in a less challenging role, appearing for the first time on the *Red Skelton Show*, joining the host in a skit entitled 'Atomic Sailor'. Then, for three consecutives weeks, commencing on Thursday, 11 December, Boris Karloff appeared on the television quiz show *The $64,000 Question*.

The object of the quiz was to answer a series of increasingly difficult questions on a chosen subject. Each correct answer would double the prize money for the next round. Karloff's chosen subject was 'Children's Stories', and on his first appearance he won $8,000. On the second he successfully increased his winnings to $32,000. Then, on his return visit, broadcast on Christmas Day, Karloff was asked by quizmaster Hal March if he wanted to go for the $64,000 prize. To everyone's surprise he turned the offer down. It later transpired he had a considered reason for stopping at $32,000. Should he win the top prize, his lawyer had informed him, he would be required to pay so much tax it would reduce his winnings below the $32,000 he had already won.

Karloff's first television work of the New Year occurred on 18 January 1957 when he appeared on *The Rosemary Clooney Show*. "In the mornings when I look into a shaving mirror I frighten myself," he told Clooney on the broadcast. "Well, how would you react to the sight of a razor held against your throat by Boris Karloff?" He then revealed his longing to do something different – something, perhaps, for children. So, in a piece entitled *Storytime*,

Karloff appeared as 'Uncle Boris', and began to read the story of *Little Red Riding Hood*.[ii] The story was then enacted on screen with Clooney as Red Riding Hood and Karloff as the Wolf. Later, still in character, Karloff joined his host in a rendition of the Irving Berlin song *You'd Be Surprised*.

A month later, on 10 February, Karloff was reunited with Julie Harris to revisit *The Lark*, this time in a live colour 90-minute television abridgement, as part of *The Hallmark Hall of Fame* series of dramas. The show was produced and directed by Karloff's old acquaintance George Schaefer who, over a decade earlier, had directed, and appeared with, the star in *Arsenic and Old Lace* in the Pacific.

Karloff and Harris were two of only five of the original Broadway cast to recreate their roles in the television version; the others were Bruce Gordon, as Captain La Hire, Michael Higgins [Brother Ladvenu], and Ralph Roberts [the Executioner]. Denholm Elliot would now play Warwick, and Karloff's old acquaintance Basil Rathbone would take the role of the Inquisitor. Eli Wallach played the Dauphin. "Boris Karloff, in the mind of the general public, was Frankenstein – a monster," Wallach later said. "Actually he was a friendly, mild-mannered theatre and film professional. He talked frequently about the sport he loved – cricket. At work he was always co-operative and attentive. Rehearsals [for *The Lark*] took 2 weeks. In those days the cast and camera crew spent several days marking out the positions. Today with special equipment and lenses it is much easier to do the show... Sometimes an actor is strongly identified with one particular role – like Frankenstein – or Tarzan – or in my case as a Mexican Bandit in Spaghetti Westerns. But Mr Karloff – above all was an actor – devoted to his craft."[60]

Jack Gould of the *New York Times* wrote, "Last night's presentation of *The Lark*, with Julie Harris portraying Joan of Arc, was a superb television accomplishment... Miss Harris, playing the role which she enacted in the Broadway production, gave a performance of deep beauty, inspiration and excitement; the other parts were perfectly cast; the production had a majestic simplicity and cleanness of pictorial line that were striking. It was an evening in which all the elements of true stagecraft fitted together magnificently... *The Lark* was true theatre brought to television."[61]

The broadcast concluded Karloff's association with the play he had called the "high point of my career as an actor".[62] Soon he would be asked to return to another cherished and familiar role – that of the villainous Jonathan Brewster in *Arsenic and Old Lace*. This time, however, the play would not be performed in Boston, San Francisco or on Broadway. Boris Karloff would now star in *Arsenic and Old Lace* – in Alaska.

---

ii At one point in the narration Karloff looks into the camera and directly addresses a child watching at home, referring to the child as Sara Jane – the name of his own daughter.

Top: Socialising at Anchorage International Airport, 1957. Bottom: On their way to the hotel in Anchorage. (Both Courtesy of Pat Christensen).

Chapter 20

ARSENIC IN ALASKA

(1957)

"Three years ago I played it in Anchorage, Alaska, a place so remote the people have to create their own entertainment. The local group rehearsed two months in their school auditorium; we did three performances which were a roaring success. I wouldn't exchange anything that's ever happened for that experience."[1]

Boris Karloff (1960)

In early 1957 the production staff of the Anchorage Community College Theatre Workshop in Alaska was in a quandary. Their next production, it had been decided, would be Joseph Kesselring's comedy *Arsenic and Old Lace*, which the college had last presented a decade earlier. The funds raised by the production would contribute to the construction of an 'intimate theatre' close to the high school auditorium. The work was scheduled to begin in 1959 and was estimated would cost between $30,000 and $40,000.

The first auditions began at 8 p.m. on Thursday, 10 January in Room 223 of the high school. Originally these were planned to last for two nights but an additional night was later added to cast those roles that remained unfilled. "All seven parts as yet uncast are male character parts," the Workshop's Executive Committee member and production co-ordinator, Bill Trotman, announced. "They range in age from 21 to 75 years old."[2] To ensure as large a pool of talent as possible personnel from both Elmendorf Air Force Base and Fort Richardson Army Base were invited to audition alongside the residents of Anchorage. Private First Class Trotman, who was also in charge of radio and television for the U.S. Army in Alaska, would take the role of Mortimer in the production.

Frank Brink, the Head of the Speech and Drama Department, would direct the play. "He was a very good director," recalled the stage-manager, John Elliott, "but he'd apparently not quite made it on Broadway as a director, so he went back to where his wife was and eventually became the drama teacher at the Anchorage Community College. He was quite a persuasive person, and when they started the Anchorage Community Theatre, which was an adjunct to the college, they wanted something to really make an impression on the community."[3]

The stories behind Karloff's involvement vary. According to the theatre's publicity director, Pat Christensen, there was some disagreement how to cast Karloff's role of the murderous Jonathan Brewster. No one could agree which of the drama students, after an appropriate application of make-up, would best resemble the famous movie star. Christensen, however, disagreed with the entire prospect. What the production needed, she said, was "something special," although what that was she could not say. If that was the case, she was told, she had until the next meeting to come up with an alternative. Pat Christensen, therefore, left the meeting pondering the problem.

Christensen had a keen interest in the theatre and, as a result, regularly purchased theatre magazines to keep up to date with the American theatre scene. She recalled reading Boris Karloff was working on a project in New York and decided to bite the bullet and try to contact the star direct by telephone. Using her title of 'Publicity Director' she managed to obtain Karloff's personal telephone number. It was only when she later started to receive publicity packets, negatives and materials from Universal Studios that she realised contacting a major star directly to invite them to appear in an amateur production was, by no means, standard practice. At the time, however, and in her ignorance, Christensen picked up her telephone and dialled the actor's number.

Boris Karloff listened politely to Christensen's offer but as she recalled, "Mr. Karloff apologised and said that he was so busy and literally buried in his work that he would not be able to come."[4] Christensen pleaded. "There was silence on Mr. Karloff's end of the line," she said. "He finally asked what he would be expected to do."[5] She told him he would "come in a few days ahead of time, go to receptions, hit some points of interest and wave at people and do three shows at the end of the week."[6] Again there was silence. "He finally said that he did have some free time coming up and maybe he needed a change of scenery," Christensen said.[7] Karloff told her when he was free and was assured that the Theatre Workshop would schedule around him.

Christensen informed the committee of the good news and went to work, flooding the newspapers with articles. "The news was received in Anchorage with as much enthusiasm as V-day," she recalled.[8] Television in Anchorage, which then consisted of a single channel available for only a few hours in the evenings, carried the story on the news, counting down the days until the star's arrival in the city.

Christensen was unrelenting in her duties. She had 'Arsenic Cocktail' cards printed and handed out to every restaurant in the town. She made signs for bars announcing these special drinks and had little folded cards advertising the play, complete with a picture of Karloff, placed on every available table. To aid her in the execution of her work she enlisted the help of her seven-year-old daughter, Marcie. "I remember going from bar to bar, restaurant to restaurant and placing the recipe cards and cards on every table while Mum talked to the proprietors," Marcie recalled.[9]

Karloff's engagement was a real coup. It was, Frank Brink said, the first time any recognised Broadway star had come to Alaska to act in an amateur production. In February the Workshop's President, Don Gretzer, confirmed he had received Karloff's Actors' Equity contract confirming the star would appear in the play. Meanwhile everyone was preparing for Karloff's arrival. The cast had rehearsals at the Anchorage High School Auditorium several times a week with Karloff's understudy, Errol Brown, in the role of Jonathan

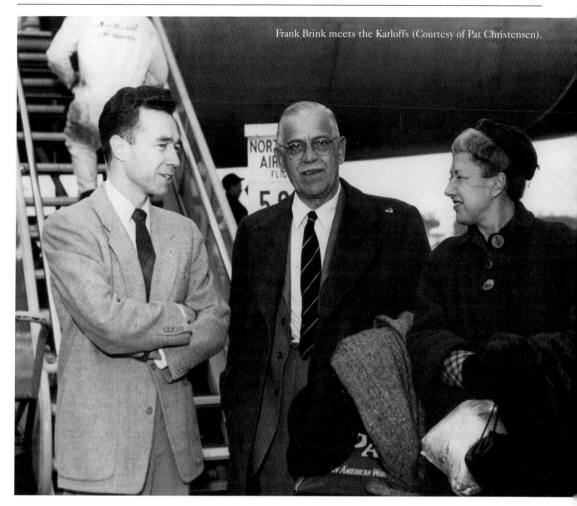

Frank Brink meets the Karloffs (Courtesy of Pat Christensen).

Brewster. As time was short the cast would also join the technical crew in backstage work, collecting props and building and painting scenery. It was all hands to the wheel. "With Karloff arriving in a few days," Bill Trotman said, "and rehearsal time running out, the cast and technical crews… hardly have time to draw a breath."[10]

On Monday, 25 February tickets went on sale at the Anchor Book Shop at 420 Fourth Avenue. The demand was such that within a week the bookshop's owner/manager, Mrs. Jane Reed, was forced to recruit a full time ticket seller, Mrs. Irene Roscoe, to handle the sales. "On Saturday the counter space was so jammed people could not get in the door," Mrs. Reed told a reporter. "The ticket selling space has been moved to another part of the bookshop to reduce congestion."[11]

On the 10th March, less than a week before he was due to arrive in Anchorage, Karloff spoke to the play's director, Frank Brink, over the telephone. "Frank, please listen!" he said. "You need not prepare any reception. I would prefer not. There will be plenty of time for that after you fit me into the play, for I want to give you the best performance I can."[12] Karloff also said he would fit in with Brink's vision. "I want to do your show, not mine," he said. "Whatever you decide, let me know. I will adapt. There's no sense in your forcing the others to do anything, except perhaps to learn their lines."[13] When, the next day, Brink told the cast of Karloff's wishes the cast applauded and cheered.

Left: A float announces the imminent arrival of Boris Karloff (Courtesy of Pat Christensen). Right: Downtown Anchorage, 1957.

The Karloffs had originally been scheduled to arrive shortly after midnight on Friday, 15 March but bad weather had resulted in the flight being changed. They had flown in from a rain-soaked Seattle where they had spent a day visiting friends. As it had been Evie's first visit to the city she and her husband were taken sightseeing, driven around in the wet weather. "We don't mind the rain though," Evie said later, "like the people who live there."[14] At 1:15 p.m. the following afternoon the Karloffs landed at Anchorage International Airport on Northwest Orient Airlines flight 583.

Upon arrival in Anchorage the Karloffs were met by a delegation, as Marcie Christensen later explained. "Pat and the main officials from the theatre and college went to meet Mr. Karloff's plane," she said. "Pat was impressed with the Karloffs. Mrs. Karloff was elegant and refined. Mr. Karloff was kind, considerate, and Pat thought he was the sweetest, most charming man she ever met. Since this was the 50s everyone was addressed by their title. There were few people that Pat addressed by a given name so we knew them only as Mr. and Mrs. Karloff... They were escorted around Anchorage as royalty."[15] After being the focus of the usual press attention the Karloffs were driven to their accommodation at the Travelers Inn on Gambell Street. Then, only two hours after landing, Boris Karloff began rehearsals.

From the outset he made a lasting impression, as John Elliott recalled. "I was stage managing the show," he said, "and the way he treated me probably influenced me to work in theatre more than anything ever has. For example, there's a scene where... Karloff is going to make Mortimer tell him some information and also make him ugly... We had gotten a roll of surgical tools from the Civil War, and they are some of the most grotesque pieces of equipment you've ever seen in your life. The first rehearsal he unrolled this, and he kinda fussed around with the stuff, and after, he came to me and said, 'Joooohn, can you get me a knitting neeeedle?' I said, 'Yes, sir, yes sir!... Grandma! Grandma! I need a knitting needle!' So the next night, when he turns to look at Mortimer, he takes out this needle and measures the distance between Mortimer's ear and his eye – and when he did that in performance you had people [*simulates the audience's horrified reaction*]... That was probably the biggest influence on me."[16] Elliott also observed, "He was incredibly sincere and patient. But above all, in my eyes, he was professional... He treated me exactly as he would have a professional stage manager in a New York Theatre."[17]

Evie, as always, would be a constant presence at rehearsals. "To the best of my knowledge she was at every one," Elliot said.[18] "Mrs. Karloff was at the theatre during rehearsals," Pat Christensen confirmed. "She made sure that props were placed properly so that everything would be just where Mr. Karloff was used to having it in his 1000 performances on stage and everything would go smoothly and Mr. Karloff wouldn't have any surprises."[19] Evie also kept a watchful eye on her husband. "He seemed to tire easily," Elliott observed, "but his wife seemed to know his limits, and carefully steered him to take breaks and rest."[20]

Pat Christensen's young daughter, Marcie, was also often in attendance. "When the Karloffs were on the set, I was usually in tow of Mrs. Karloff and my little brother, Roger, was being toted around by Mr. Karloff. They loved children and the actors' kids that were there during rehearsals learned quickly that Mr. Karloff kept candy in his pocket. They were the substitute grandparents for a lot of the kids. Most of the kids were up there for military or other temporary reasons, and had left their extended families far away in Nebraska, Texas, New York or other far points."[21]

Evie enjoyed accompanying her husband on his professional engagements. "I settle down wherever I go," she explained. "I always feel at home."[22] While they were in Hawaii for the *Voodoo Island* shoot she had gathered driftwood, shells, stones and "even sand".[23] However, her favourite things to collect, she told the Alaskan press, were antiques, especially old wood, pewter and mâché items. Yet despite their frequent international travels, there was still one place she longed to see – Asia. "We keep getting on planes going to the Orient," Evie said, "but we have to get off."[24] Asked if she liked the snow she replied, "We got here just in time... I've been so hot ever since I came to Alaska. It's much hotter than in New York. I like it because there's no wind and New York is so windy."[25] The next trip, she revealed, would be a return to England in May where her husband was scheduled to start his next picture – *Stranglehold* – on 3 June.

At 6:45 p.m. that first evening the Karloffs were collected from their accommodation and driven to take dinner with Lt. General Frank A. Armstrong Jr., the commander of the joint Alaskan Command, headquartered at Elmendorf Airforce Base.[i] It was at that dinner with the Lt. General, his wife 'Fluffy' and twenty other guests that the Karloffs first sampled the delights of the large Alaskan king crab, a delicacy they would partake of often during their stay.

At 1:45 p.m. the following afternoon, Sunday, 17 March, the couple were collected by the Workshop's business manager, Fannie L. Hoopes, who drove them to a 2 p.m. public reception at the Z.J. Loussac Public Library. For two hours the Karloffs, along with members of the Workshop's committee and the Anchorage Symphony, as well as *Arsenic*'s cast and crew, met over three hundred members of the public. "Most of the members of the Anchorage Community Theatre and the college were invited as well as the mayor and other city officials," Marcie Christensen later explained. "Pat was not invited. When the Karloffs heard that the one person responsible for the event was not included they voiced their disapproval and started to insist that Pat be included. Pat bowled out saying she had work to do. Alaska King crab was served at the reception. The Karloffs were [so] astounded by the size of the crabs that they begged the shells off the hostess. The next day Pat helped them clean them up, package them and mail them to somebody in England [probably Sir John] whom they thought would be interested in the large crustacean."[26]

Following the reception there was more socialising and the Karloffs attended a

i Lt. Gen. Frank A. Armstrong Jr. was the inspiration for Brigadier General Frank Savage, the main character in Beirne Lay Jr. and Sy Barrett's 1948 novel *Twelve O'Clock High*. Gregory Peck played the character in the subsequent movie version.

Rehearsals for *Arsenic and Old Lace*, Anchorage, March 1957 (Courtesy of Pat Christensen).

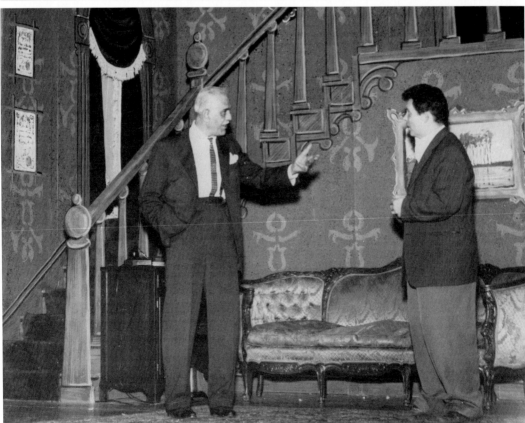

cocktail buffet at the home of Dr. George and Mary Hale. To herald their guest's arrival the Hale's children, Jimmy and Johnny, had built a snowman in the backyard and added a sign, "Welcome Mr. Karloff". At the buffet the Karloffs encountered yet more king crab. Following the soirée Dr. Hale drove the Karloffs to the 7:30 p.m. *Arsenic* rehearsal.

At 9:45 the following morning, local dog-racing champion Richard Beaulieu treated the Karloffs to a dog-sled ride through the Alaskan countryside. Although they enjoyed the excursion Evie later confessed they were a little disappointed not to have encountered any moose or polar bears. Still, they hoped they would be able to catch sight of them on a later date, she said.

Following the sled-ride the Karloffs joined the Beaulieus for the now seemingly obligatory king crab salad. However, despite the platter's frequency, Evie later confessed both she and her husband were "crazy about it"[27] and even ordered a crab cocktail that evening when they dined at the Travelers Inn.

Earlier that afternoon Evie had been thrilled when a 1957 Packard, with only 200 miles on the clock, was delivered to the Inn for their use during their stay. The couple could soon be seen driving it up and down Fourth and Fifth Avenues, checking the gift shops and purchasing postcards to send home.

That evening Karloff was back at the auditorium for rehearsals, followed by an informal gathering at the home of Frank Brink. To keep pace with the many Alaskan social engagements Karloff returned to

On an Alaskan excursion.

his habit of lying in, an approach he had adopted while treading the boards on Broadway. Evie, too, would follow her husband's lead, sleeping late and rising just in time for brunch.

On Tuesday evening, 19 March, following a sourdough hotcake brunch at the home of Dr. Lloyd W. and Margaret Hines in the Anchorage subdivision Turnagain By the Sea, and a radio interview on local channel KTMI, Karloff was back at the theatre to appear in a special dress-rehearsal performed for high-ranking military families who would be unable to attend the scheduled shows.

That evening, when the cast and crew had assembled, Karloff made an announcement. He had decided to donate his share of the gate receipts to the college group's building committee. He was very pleased, he said, to have an opportunity to help the college theatre group. He had been impressed with the "first-class modern theatre"[28] and the support proffered by the community, the cast and the director. "Brink has done a most incredible job and the enthusiasm of the group is marvellous," Karloff said.[29]

The star's generosity would allow Frank Brink to announce plans later for construction of an "intimate theatre" building. This new theatre, as planned, would be a concrete structure measuring 30 by 80 feet with a proscenium arch, and would seat one hundred. It would be built on school district property near the school on Hillcrest Drive.

At 11:30 the next morning the Karloffs were collected and driven to Fort Richardson army base, five miles north of Anchorage, to attend a luncheon hosted by commanding officer Col. Alexander N. Slocum and his wife. Later, it was lunch at the Officers Club

followed by a trip to Camp Denali, the Alaskan National Guard armoury located farther
north, where they were given a tour of the post. An excursion, with military escort, to the
ski resort at Arctic Valley rounded out their day and they were dropped back at their hotel
at 3:30 p.m. Later, Karloff was interviewed by KTVA TV before attending that evening's
dress rehearsal.

Anchorage Times staff writer Dick Whittaker was present throughout that rehearsal. The
cast was happy, the crew was happy, Frank Brink was happy, Whittaker later reported. "The
play's star, Boris Karloff, was on and off the stage conferring with Brink as the most minute
details of movement and gesture were discussed to produce the greatest comic effect,"
Whittaker wrote.[30] "The Karloffs and Mr. Brink seemed to have a great relationship," John
Elliott later said. "During blocking, for example, Mr. Karloff rarely made suggestions and,
when he did, it would be one-on-one with the Director. The entire cast, professionals
and beginners alike, instantly got caught up in his dedication to the role, and everyone
seemed to step up their individual performances five or six notches higher."[31]

Since Karloff's arrival in Anchorage rehearsals had been consistently running late
in a full-ditched attempt to be ready for the opening night. The main problem faced
that evening, Whittaker explained, was the question of momentum – how to keep the
play moving swiftly enough to stay ahead of the audience. Another was 'corpsing', for
even after two months of rehearsals the cast still found it difficult to keep from laughing.
Rehearsals were called to a halt after 10 p.m. in readiness for the play's opening the
following evening.

By now Karloff had fulfilled all of his social obligations. So, the following evening
– 21 March – after having spent a day of leisure, Karloff arrived with Evie at the
Anchorage High School Auditorium and settled into his dressing room in preparation
for opening night.

Shortly before the play was due to begin Karloff
asked Frank Brink if he could provide him with either
a small stool or a ladder. When Brink duly fetched
a stool from the janitor's closet Karloff announced
he was now going to hang himself. "Needless to
say, I was startled," Frank Brink said. "After he had
his joke, he said, 'You needn't be alarmed. It's my
arthritis. By hanging from that pipe, I can stop
the irritation for a while.' I placed the stool under
the pipe, he climbed upon it, then I removed it
while he hung there, and replaced it when he was
ready to come down and go to the stage."[32] Karloff
would repeat this ritual every night, although he
insisted Brink told no one. Any concerns the cast
and crew may have should be with the play, he
said, and not with him.

The curtain was due to rise at 8:30 p.m.
but was delayed by 15 minutes due, journalist
Fritz Pumphrey later explained, to "traffic
and parking problems".[33] He added, "This
observer felt that this was the only minor flaw

Alaskan *Arsenic and Old Lace* program cover (1957).

– to hold up a production of this type beyond the starting time. Anchorage, like other communities where good theatre is the order of the day, should take traffic and parking problems in its stride – and get to the performance on time. The production of *Arsenic and Old Lace*, as given by the Theatre Workshop, deserves that."[34] Still, despite the initial hiccup, the evening was a great success. "The largest first night audience for any play presented in Anchorage," Pumphrey wrote, "turned out for the top performance by the Anchorage Community College Theatre Workshop… The magic of a first night flowed through the Anchorage High School auditorium – created by the rapt attention given by the audience, the intermission discussion by the first-nighters, the professional touches backstage. Seasoned actors like Boris Karloff, for whom the role of Jonathan Brewster was created, must have sensed the audience response, knowing that, it too, gave an admirable performance. History was indeed made at the first night performance. The appearance of Karloff marked another milestone in the cultural history of Anchorage – the first time a thespian of his calibre has acted in an Alaskan production."[35] After the show Brink joined Evie in Karloff's dressing room to discuss the performance. When the analysis was complete the three of them joined the rest of the cast and 75 guests at an after-show party at the Forest Park Country Club.

The first night's reviews appeared the following day. Jeanne Bannister of the *Anchorage Daily Times* wrote, "Boris Karloff probably could have carried last night's performance of *Arsenic and Old Lace* by himself, but the local cast saw to it he didn't have to. The Joseph Kesselring comedy opened to a full house at the high school auditorium last night…

The cast and crew of *Arsenic and Old Lace*, Anchorage, March 1957
(Courtesy of Pat Christensen).

Karloff subordinated himself in the local cast and refused to take special honours. He took his curtain calls with the entire cast and would not even take a bow alone."[36]

From the moment it had been announced Karloff would play in Anchorage, the college was inundated with requests for the star's time. Although he had been promised his performance days would remain event free, Karloff agreed to make further social appearances. So at 11:30 a.m. on

Aunt Martha's
ELDERBERRY WINE
1 gal. elderberry wine
1 tsp. arsenic
½ tsp. strychnine
pinch of cyanide

Mix well and come to Romig Hill Auditorium, March 21, 22, or 23 and see **in person, BORIS KARLOFF,** in **ARSENIC** and **OLD LACE.**

(Tickets on Sale at Anchor Book Shop)

All Seats Reserved . . . . **$2.50 - $3.00**

The recipe for the Brewster sisters' elderberry wine (Courtesy of Pat Christensen).

Friday, 22 March the Karloffs were collected by Mrs. Frances Clark, the Alaska manager for the Havenstrite oil interests, and driven to visit two major local companies: the Federal Electric Company and the construction organisation, Morrison-Knudsen Corporation. After spending time talking with the employees the Karloffs spent the afternoon at the 5005th USAF Hospital at Elmendorf Air Force Base where they toured the facility, chatting to staff and patients along the way.

That evening's performance, like the night before, began late owing to a reoccurrence of the previous evening's traffic problems. As the audience made their way to the auditorium Karloff indulged in his pre-performance ritual of hanging from his dressing room pipe to ease his arthritis. The evening's show was another success and after the curtain fell on that second night Karloff attended another after-show party, this time held at the house of the Anchorage Community College Director Dr. Leroy Good.

The following evening's performance – Karloff's final night with the troupe – was another hit and the audience clapped and cheered enthusiastically as the curtain repeatedly fell. "I did not know what to do after I had run the scripted curtain calls twice," John Elliott said. "Mr. Brink was uncertain. But Mr. Karloff in an easy and gracious manner was able to talk to the audience, bring Mr. Brink on stage and slip away quietly into the wings."[37]

Karloff had been touched by the audience's response to his brief tenure in Anchorage. "[He was] incredibly gracious, and perhaps a little overwhelmed," Elliott recalled. "He could feel the genuine nature of the outpouring of appreciation and perhaps realised it was not only for the play he had just finished, but for his whole body of works."[38]

Karloff, as the press had noted, had refused to be singled out for attention from his fellow players on the first two nights of the play's run. His unexpected taking of centre stage on that final evening caused his wife some concern, as Frank Brink later explained. "After a seemingly endless series of curtain calls, Boris walked out on stage, held his hands up to quiet the audience, and began to speak with them," Brink said. "Evie turned to me and said, 'Oh, Frank, he doesn't do that sort of thing! I'm worried.' She then listened, while I presumed to reassure her that the love Anchorage was trying to express would accept anything he did, even if he stood on his head. At that moment, he poured out a rare and unusual response to an appreciative audience who saw in him something more than great skill and talent. He revealed a sense of humanity and generosity that evidently went beyond mere courtesy when he said, 'This has been the most rewarding moment of my career.' I had the feeling that even Evie must have been surprised at such an extravagant response."[39]

That final performance was followed by the customary after-show party, this time hosted by the Anchorage Community College Theatre Workshop President, Don Gretzer. After the gathering Karloff took Brink to one side. "I want to give you a gift and I don't want it to be something stupid or useless," he told the director, "so I want you to tell me what you would like."[40] Brink's protests fell on deaf ears. "Boris merely said, 'I shan't leave until you tell me'. Realising he was adamant," Brink said, "I thought for a moment and suddenly blurted out, 'Your shoes!' I said, 'To have the shoes of the first great theatre talent to walk on the Alaska stage would be the most wonderful gift I can think of. But, if you can't part with them, I will understand!'

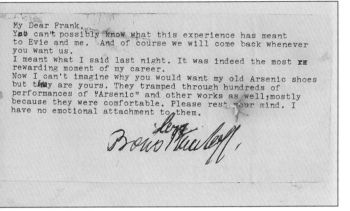

Karloff's note to Frank Brink concerning the actor's shoes.

With that, he said, 'I can't think why you would want these old shoes, but if you want them, they're yours!'"[41]

The next morning the Karloffs were up and out earlier than normal. The Alaskan trip had provided the star with the opportunity to pay a visit to the Havenstrite Drilling Company's operation and inspect the fruits of a long-term investment. "My husband has had a small interest in it for 20 years," Evie told the press. "It's one of the things which attracted him to come to Alaska."[42]

Karloff had been involved with the company since 1936 when the *Los Angeles Times* had announced, "The Iniskin Drilling Company, organised in Los Angeles by Carl Beal and Russell Havenstrite, with the latter as president, is about to shove off from Los Angeles Harbour on an oil exploration into Alaska, with upwards of $300,000 invested in its freighter Iniskin and the drilling equipment aboard. The company is taking its own derrick, drilling equipment, tractors, pumps, etc., and 55 men. It will operate on the Iniskin-Chinitna Peninsula, less than 20 miles from Anchorage. The company has permission to test more than 60,000 acres. After making a geological study of the territory, Beal and Havenstrite organised the company, in which some interest is held by Universal Consolidated Oil Company, Republic Petroleum Company, California Western Oil Company, Belmont Investment Company, George Pope – San Francisco capitalist, Charles Howard – San Francisco automobile man, Hal Roach, Walt Disney and Boris Karloff."[43] The operation completed the drilling of the first hole in 1937 but was then prevented from continuing explorations by the Interior Department. Operations were only resumed in 1955 when a second hole was drilled close to the old one.

Two Cessna 180 seaplanes were provided and at 10 a.m. on Saturday, 24 March a small party, including the Karloffs and Mrs. Frances Clark, boarded the seaplanes and set off on a trip to visit the operations on Chinitna Bay, on the west side of Cook inlet, some 130 miles south-west of Anchorage.

The party was met on site by John Havenstrite and camp supervisor Lee Brown who conducted them on a tour of the facilities. "There really *is* oil, then?" Evie asked. "I want a bottle to take home."[44] Following lunch at the camp Evie was presented with a small bottle of oil, as she had requested. The visitors then boarded the planes for the trip home, which included a sightseeing soirée through the mountains during which Evie finally got to see some moose. "I wanted to fly over an active volcano," she later explained, "so the pilot flew low over one to get a better view. Suddenly the cork popped out of the bottle of oil from the updraft from the volcano, and the oil spilt all over me. I took the remainder of the bottle back to New York, then to London with me, and said to Boris, 'Well – at least we have *some* oil.' Then we had to make a decision about whether to maintain the holdings – putting more money in, or what to do. Boris said, 'If it came in – it would be so much money that it would only be a burden – let's let it go.' So we let it go."[45]

The following afternoon, Monday 25 March, the Karloffs were driven to the airport to catch their flight back to New York. "When Mr. Karloff was leaving he thanked Pat for inviting him," Marcie Christensen recalled. "He said it did him a world of good to get a change of scenery, get away from the pressures of New York and the obligations and demands that he had saddled himself with. He had thoroughly enjoyed his vacation."[46]

Boris Karloff had earned around $1,500 from his Alaskan appearance in *Arsenic and Old Lace*, every penny of which he donated to the college. He also added to his generosity – against the protestations of the Theatre Workshop – by also insisting personally to cover his agent's percentage. Including Karloff's donation, the play's profits totalled some $7,500, a healthy start towards the $40,000 the new theatre was figured to cost.

On 29 March, four days after Karloff's departure, the Workshop's President, Don Gretzer, wrote a letter to Actors' Equity, informing them of the star's generosity. "We would like you people to know of the great good which Mr. Karloff has done for the theatre movement here in Anchorage," he added. "The wonderful personalities of Mr. and Mrs. Karloff, their understanding of people, and their wish to help us resulted not only in great admiration and respect for professional artists, but heightened community respect for local players which we may have had to strive for over a period of many years. It is difficult to say exactly how we feel about Mr. Karloff and his gracious wife. Superlatives can never tell the story of their effect upon the future of theatre here. Statistically, *Arsenic and Old Lace* drew the largest crowd ever to attend any performance of any kind of show in the history of the territory. But statistics can never say as much about the Karloffs as the lump in our throats at their departure."[47]

On 7 April Karloff wrote a letter of his own – to the play's director, Frank Brink. "Alaska is lucky to have you," he wrote. "You wondered how I could come to such a conclusion, so I will tell you. I learned that with every cast member you did far more than direct. You carefully and sympathetically taught the inexperienced. You cared more for their feelings than any director I have worked with."[48]

Karloff's tenure in Alaska had paved the way for other stars to appear on the stage of the Anchorage College Theatre. Frank Brink had already arranged for Theresa Wright to star in William Inge's play *The Dark at the Top of the Stairs*. "When I talk to Terry, I will tell her she need have no fear of being embarrassed," Karloff wrote to Brink. "She will be thrilled. As you indicated, you will be able to support her with professional quality talent right there in Anchorage."[49]

Later that month Karloff returned to television, appearing alongside Mary Astor and June Lockhart in *The Man Who Played God*, an hour-long adaptation of Gouverneur Morris's story. Broadcast on 25 April Karloff starred as a concert pianist who loses his hearing. After learning to lip-read he uses his skills to help people but, by these means, discovers that the woman he loves actually loves another. Three days later he joined Gertrude Berg, Edgar Bergen and Charlie McCarthy, Benny Goodman, Ed Wynn, the Billy Williams Quartet and Jack Miller's Orchestra on the *Kate Smith Hour* in a show which celebrated the singer's 25th anniversary as an entertainer. Karloff sang the popular Kurt Weill tune *September Song*.

The following month Karloff began rehearsals for his 17 May appearance on *The Dinah Shore Chevy Show* alongside Shore, Betty Hutton and Art Carney. One day, journalist Walter Ames discussed the forthcoming show over lunch with Karloff and Shore. "I was packing to sail to Europe for a holiday when the call came asking me to do this show," Karloff told Ames. "After the rehearsals I've been through I'm not sure but that I should have sailed. As it is, I leave right after the programme on Friday, fly to New York and sail Saturday evening for France. You can see I'm not taking any chances on you critics."[50]

After lunch Ames was invited to watch the show's rehearsal and noticed Karloff was having a lot of fun. When, however, Shore revealed Karloff would dance on the show, the actor seemed surprised. "I guess I didn't read far enough into the fine print of my contract," he joked.[51] In fact, Karloff was so content to appear on the show he had already agreed to make a return appearance.

On the broadcast Art Carney asked Karloff to be Dinah Shore's summer replacement and host the show. To celebrate his acceptance the show was renamed *Shiverolet* for the occasion and Karloff fronted a ghoulish band comprising of his co-stars, with the ladies suitably dressed in Morticia Addams-style attire. The group then proceeded to perform renditions of two current hits, with Karloff taking the lead vocals on Harry Belafonte's *Mama Look A Boo Boo*, and Carney leading on The Diamond's hit *Little Darlin'*. The next day Boris Karloff set off for England to make his first British horror picture in over 20 years – *The Haunted Strangler*.

HIS NEWEST AND MOST FRIGHTENING ROLE!
BORIS KARLOFF
in
CORRIDORS OF BLOOD
SEE!
BODY SNATCHERS!
CRUEL BEAUTIES!
BLOOD-CURDLING EXPERIMENTS OF DOCTOR BOLTON!
Directed by
ROBERT DAY
Boris Karloff
as Dr. Bolton
TOPS IN TERROR!

THE HOMESICK HORROR MAN

(1957-1960)

"There's an ugly rumour going around that I've retired from show business just because I've moved back to London. That will never happen. I will BE retired, but I'll never quit."[1]
Boris Karloff (1960)

With Karloff scheduled to return to England for the summer Bernard Coleman asked his friend for a favour. "One day I said to him – I hadn't got much money and I'd bought this old pub in Penge – it was a scruffy, run-down area... There were pubs everywhere – and I'd gone to an auction and bought this place for fifteen-hundred quid," he said. "And then I'd worked on it with a couple of friends to get it open, and it was a tiny little place, and I said to him, 'Would you open a pub for me?' He replied, 'My dear chap, I'd be delighted! I've always wanted to open a pub.' I said, 'What am I going to pay you?', because at that time people were opening supermarkets and everything and were getting a lot of money. He said, 'How about a pint of bitter?' [*laughs*]. Marvellous – he was wonderful. He always had a good line."[2] So, on the evening of 16 July 1957, Coleman collected the Karloffs and drove them to the Golden Lion pub in Penge for the opening. Despite the rain, the street outside the pub was bustling with onlookers keen to see the arrival of Karloff and Coleman's other guests, which included the cricketing brothers Alec and Eric Bedser.

Karloff had devised a novel way to open the pub, as Bernard Coleman would discover. "He'd got this old carrier bag, which he was clutching," Coleman recalled. "And I said, 'What have you got there?' 'Don't worry, boy, don't worry,' he said and he made a nice little speech, how delighted he was to open this pub, and he said, 'Now, stand there' and I stood there, and he reached into this bag and suddenly I heard and felt this big crash on the head as he hit me. He'd had these bottles made of plastic, like a champagne bottle and hit me! 'I declare this pub open!' he said, hitting me on the head with it. Then he gave me one. He said, 'Here's the other one. Now you hit me with it,' which I duly did. I mean, it was very kind. Fancy thinking of that! I mean – they were specially made for the occasion."[3]

Inside the pub Karloff was photographed pouring a glass of Merrydown cider from a cask. "We didn't have a spirit licence," Coleman explained. "In those days the licensing was very, very strict, and they wouldn't allow us to sell spirits. So all we sold was beer and cider, and sherry and wine."[4] In any case, the event was a big success due, mainly, to Boris Karloff. "Oh, he was marvellous, and he chatted to everybody," Coleman said. "And then, when I later expanded and took other pubs, he always would appear for the opening. Whenever he was available he'd always appear – always wanted to know what was going on."[5]

Advert for Cameo curtains, 1957.

Karloff had returned to England to make *The Haunted Strangler* for Amalgamated Pictures, a British production company created by Richard Gordon. Gordon and his brother Alex had emigrated from England to America in 1947. "I set up a business," he later explained, "to represent English and other foreign film production/distribution companies to license their films for them in the United States for theatrical and television release. So I got pretty experienced at how to make the deals, and then at a certain point in time, when it became very fashionable for English producers to get American actors to come to England and play in some of the films to make them more marketable, I also got involved in hiring the actors, dealing with the agents and setting up co-production deals. After a few years of that, I said to myself 'If I can do this for other people, I really should be able to do it for myself by now,' and that's how I started. I first made about half-a-dozen co-production deals in England and produced these films with English partners."[6]

Richard and Alex Gordon met Karloff for the first time in March 1948. Karloff was appearing in *The Linden Tree* at the Music Box Theatre on Broadway and the brothers went backstage to interview him for a British magazine. "We got along very well," Richard Gordon recalled. "He came back a year or so later in another English play [*The Shop at Sly Corner*] and I contacted him again. We sort of became friends on an on-and-off basis and he knew where my thinking was and that I was very keen to get into production. He was very keen to work back in England, and at one point in 1956 he gave me a story called *Stranglehold*, and told me that the story had been specially written for him by Jan Read.[i] He wanted to do the film and he wanted me to set it up for production in England, and if I could, he'd do the film with me. To use a cliché phrase, that was an offer I couldn't refuse. When I went back to England, being able to say that Karloff had agreed to do it, it wasn't too difficult for me to set up a deal.[ii] After that, I created my production company, Amalgamated Productions."[7]

Stranglehold was adapted by the author Jan Read and the picture's producer, John Croydon, writing under the pseudonym John C. Cooper. Retitled *Grip of the Strangler*[iii]

---

i Jan Read later wrote the screenplays for the fantasy pictures *Jason and the Argonauts* (1963) and *The First Men in the Moon* (1964).

ii On 3 October 1956 the *Los Angeles Times* announced Richard Gordon had engaged Karloff to star in *Stranglehold* to be shot in London the following March.

iii According to Croydon *Grip of the Strangler* was originally entitled *The Judas Hole* after the name of the music hall featured in the picture.

filming began in August at Walton Studios in Walton-on-Thames, with exteriors shot on the back lot and the immediate vicinity. To direct the picture Croydon had contacted 34-year-old Robert Day, who had co-directed the black comedy *The Green Man* (1956) starring Alastair Sim, and shot several episodes of the television series *The Buccaneers* (starring Robert Shaw as Captain Dan Tempest) for *Colonel March* producer Hannah Weinstein. "I guess they'd seen what I'd done already and liked it," Day said, "and figured that I could probably bring it in on budget."[8] The budget was small. "Certainly not more than one hundred thousand pounds," he said.[9]

Karloff played James Rankin, a writer, who investigates the 20-year-old murders of the 'Haymarket Strangler'. Although a one-armed man, Edward Styles, was hanged for the crimes in 1860,[iv] Rankin believes him to be innocent and begins to suspect the victims' autopsy surgeon, Dr. Tenant, to be the murderer. For, Rankin discovers, Tenant collapsed on the day of the hanging and was committed to hospital, but later disappeared along with a nurse. Rankin finds the murder weapon in Styles' unearthed coffin but is transformed into the murderer when he holds the blade in his hand. Following the slaying of a music-hall singer Rankin discovers that he is, in fact, the schizophrenic and murderous Dr. Tenant. Following the murder of his wife, the ex-nurse [Elizabeth Allan], Rankin confesses to the murder but is committed to an asylum. Transforming again into Dr. Tenant, he escapes and returns home where his attempt to kill his stepdaughter [Diane Aubrey] is foiled only when Rankin regains his sanity. He then attempts to return the knife to Styles' grave but is pursued by the police who shoot him dead.

A major production concern was how to achieve Karloff's Jekyll and Hyde-like transformation on the picture's modest budget. "We called Karloff, Robert Day (the director), and the make-up man to Walton Studios (now, alas, a housing estate) to discuss the metamorphosis," John Croydon recalled. "We talked about monsters, ghouls and ghosts and were not getting very far when I noticed a twinkle in Karloff's eye. 'Mind if I try my own?' he asked. 'Go ahead,' I replied. He turned his back and seemed to be remoulding his features. When he swung back again, we were stunned. He had removed his false left [*sic*. It was his right] upper and lower molars and drawn his mouth awkwardly sideways, sucked in his lower lip so that the upper teeth overlapped, his cheek drawn inwards. The left eyebrow and lid were lowered, his left arm drawn up and useless, as though he had suffered a major stroke. In a thickened tone, unlike his own softly modulated voice, he asked, 'Will this do?' What was there to say? Our psychopathic monster had materialised before our very eyes and that was how Karloff played the role. It was perfect."[10]

Croydon was a hands-on producer, shunning a life behind the desk and determined to retain his creative control. This attitude, he later admitted, brought him into direct conflict with the star. "The dash came," Croydon explained, "over a sequence between Rankin and his wife… I refused to alter the script unless Karloff could bring something better to it. He never did and the scene was played as written, although between Day's direction and Karloff's interpretation, it took on a dangerous degree of melodrama."[11] Still, most aspects of Karloff's acting *did* meet with the producer's approval. "As the madness took hold, so did the power of his performance," Croydon said. "It was frightening in its intensity, never allowing the personality to waver… Despite our differences, he had brought the character of Tenant/Rankin to life and we were well satisfied."[12]

---

iv Although the story is set some twenty years after the 1860 murders a box of evidence marked 'Jack the Ripper' is seen early in the picture. It is a curious inclusion, as the notorious killer struck in 1888.

Karloff's portrayal, though, had been the result of much careful consideration. "I think he treated every character, every script with respect; I know that he was very much involved in the portrayal of the character in *The Haunted Strangler*," Robert Day later said. "He didn't treat it just as another role; he was very, very deeply interested in what he was doing. We discussed the characterisation for hours and hours, the way he should look and everything."[13]

Day's work with Karloff signalled the beginning of a long friendship. "I met him for the first time on *The Haunted Strangler*, and he was a wonderful, wonderful man. We were very close friends, and we used to eat together almost every weekend – he would come to my house or I would go to his... I just can't say enough good things about him. He was kind, gentle, not a bit like any of the characters he's played in movies."[14]

"He was a wonderful man to work with," Richard Gordon later agreed, "of course the complete opposite of the characters he played on screen. He was a very gentle, typical English country gentleman. He was a very wonderful guy and very helpful to me, I will always be grateful to him for giving me that start."[15] Jean Kent, who was employed for a week to play Cora, the owner of the music hall The Judas Hole – "for which," she recalled, "I was extremely well paid",[16] – also thought highly of her co-star. "Mr. Karloff was a delightful man," she said, "with the most beautiful manners of any actor I have ever met in a very long career."[17]

It was intended that *Grip of the Strangler* would play as half of a double feature and both MGM and the British distributors, Eros Films, wanted another picture to play with it. "They quite rightly said, 'If you can't give us a second picture, we'll have to put it with our own picture and that won't be to your own benefit',"[18] Gordon said. He decided on a modern science-fiction story, *Fiend Without a Face*, which was shot back to back with the Karloff picture at Walton Studios, utilising much of the same crew. "Eros Films were so pleased with them," Gordon explained, "that each picture opened separately as a 'stand alone' in London's West End before the programme played the circuits on general release."[19]

Grip of the Strangler, now retitled *The Haunted Strangler* at MGM's request, opened at the Rialto in New York on 3 July 1958. The *New York Times* thought the picture, "for all its attempts to invoke Gothic atmosphere, has little more life than a chestful of old Victorian costumes. Blame it on the lack of real spirit in the screenplay by Jan Read and John C. Cooper, or on the flat direction by Robert Day. Whatever the reason, this film, which opened at the Rialto yesterday, seldom manages to free itself from synthetic posturing. The same goes for Boris Karloff, who plays a Jekyll-Hyde type who discovers beneath his crusading Victorian spirit an earlier murderous identity."[20]

A few years later Karloff was asked which of his horror films did he look back upon with a degree of satisfaction? He began by praising the work of James Whale, and his films for Val Lewton. "More recently a film of mine that I liked very much was *Grip of the Strangler*," he added, "made over here by a young British director, Robert Day, who has a real eye for period detail and realises, as I think a lot of other British horror-film makers don't, that ultimately it is the story values which carry a film, not an automatic shock every five minutes."[21] He had little time for the newer, more visceral, trend of horror pictures. "They are cheap, tawdry and disgusting," Karloff said. "They used to be classics – with respectable stories and serious overtones.[22]

He had the opportunity to discuss this type of X certificate film when he appeared on British television on Friday, 30 August on the final episode of *A-Z*, an alphabetical guide to showbusiness. "He is well qualified to speak from experience," one journalist wrote, "he was one of Hollywood's original monsters… Just in case you can't believe that the mild mannered man you will see on the screen has anything to do with horror movies, the B.B.C. has dug up pictures of some of the more gruesome make-ups that Karloff wore in spine-chillers like *Frankenstein* and *The Ghoul*."[23]

While in England Karloff also found time to pen an article for the British film magazine *Films and Filming*. The piece – *My Life as a Monster* – appeared in the November issue. In it he reiterated his long-held opinions of the genre that had made his name. "I dislike the word 'horror' yet it is a word that has been tagged to me all my life," he wrote. "It is a misnomer… for it means revulsion. The films I have made were made for entertainment, maybe with the object of making the audience's

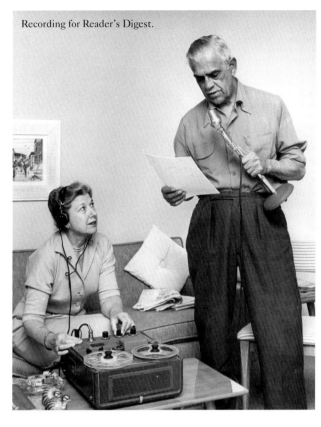

Recording for Reader's Digest.

hair stand on end, but never to revolt people. Perhaps terror would be a much better word to describe these films, but alas, it is too late now to change the adjective."[24]

The horror genre, he went on to explain, fulfils a desire by people to experience something beyond the normal range of emotions. He had seen an example of this on the set of *The Haunted Strangler*. "We were about to shoot a sequence in which a man is flogged," he wrote. "Suddenly the set was crowded by studio workmen and office girls all eager to have a look! There is a violent streak in all of us: and if it can be exploded in the cinema instead of in some anti-social manner in real life, so much the better."[25]

The fascination with tales of horror had long been inherent in the human psyche, Karloff observed. "Most people like to pretend that there is something just behind the door," he explained. "It transports the audience to another world. A world of fantasy and of imagination. A world inhabited by the characters of Hans Andersen and the Brothers Grimm. The 'horror' film is concocted more or less from the folk tales of every country. When I am asked if these films are harmful to children, my answer is always the same: Do Grimm's fairy tales do any harm to children? I have never heard of fairy tale books being used in evidence in a juvenile delinquency case! Naturally, good taste plays a very important part in the telling of a 'horror' story on film. Some have taste, others regrettably have not. As there are no rules laid down to give an indication of good taste it is up to the film's makers."[26]

It was, however, important, he said, that care should be exercised when creating such a picture. "You are walking a very narrow tight rope when you make such a film. It is building the illusion of the impossible and giving it the semblance of reality that is of prime importance. The moment the film becomes stupid the audience will laugh and the illusion is lost... never to be regained. The story must be intelligent and coherent as well as being unusual and bizarre... in fact just like a fairy tale or a good folk story. The 'horror' has to be for the sake of the story and not, as a few recent films had done, have a story outline just for the sake of injecting as many shocks as possible."[27]

Towards the end of September the Karloffs left England and made for France. "From Le Havre we caught a French Line freighter direct to Los Angeles and had the most wonderful voyage," Karloff later wrote, "three and a half weeks at sea through the West Indies and the Canal with stops at El Salvador and Guatemala en route."[28] Arriving back in Los Angeles he rented an apartment at the famous Chateau Marmont on Hollywood's Sunset Boulevard and it was here, on 19 October, Karloff sat down and wrote to his brother:

> Dear Dorothy and Jack,
>
> Your letter of September 16th was sent on to us here. Where the summer went I don't know. What with one thing and another it was rather disappointing and frustrating, not the least part of which was seeing so little of you two. But between fruitless efforts to find some place to settle permanently, which is our aim, efforts to get conclusive information on tax matters for the future, AND the film [*The Haunted Strangler*] which seemed to go on for ever, even to the day before we left, time just flew. We had no luck in reaching you by telephone in the closing stages and had to dash off to Le Havre without saying goodbye, which is dreadful... We expect to be here most of the winter and be back in London in February for another film [*The Doctor of Seven Dials*] for the same firm, and this time with any luck will be for good...
>
> Our love to you both and do let us hear from you.
>
> > as ever,
> > Billy[29]

At the end of October Boris Karloff made his long-booked return appearance on the Halloween edition of *The Dinah Shore Chevy Show* (27 October) along with Robert Cummings and Gale Storm. The Halloween festivities continued four nights later when he once again guest starred on Rosemary Clooney's show. A little over two weeks later, on 16 November, Karloff joined fellow guest Johnny Desmond on the *Gisele MacKenzie Show* and performed *Those Were the Good Old Days* – a number sung by Mr. Applegate (in reality, the Devil) in the musical *Damn Yankees*. He later joined Desmond and MacKenzie in a rendition of Harry Warren's tune *The Girl Friend of the Whirling Dervish*.

Days later, on Wednesday, 20 November 1957, Karloff, although not in the best of health, accompanied Evie to NBC's Burbank Studios to watch Ralph Edwards present another live broadcast of *This Is Your Life*. "Boris was not well at all," Evie later explained. "He had a throat infection... but not sick enough to stay in bed... And he thought we were going to watch the show, and then we were all going out to supper afterwards."[30] But Evie and Edwards had other plans.

The Karloffs settled down on one side of the studio and began to watch the live broadcast on a monitor as it unfolded in the studio. "Tonight," Ralph Edwards said, "let's turn the lights on over there by the double door and watch carefully to see what happens.

With Ralph Edwards on *This Is Your Life*, 20 November 1957 .

Our honoured guest whom we are about to surprise tonight is known to all of you as one of the truly great and beloved stars of the theatre, motion pictures, radio and television. Pan the camera quickly please. He's not coming through those doors because he's seated right there innocently, watching our producer's monitor."[31] The camera panned to Karloff as Edwards announced, "Tonight, this is your life, Boris Karloff."[32] Hearing his name Karloff looked up, smiled and waved graciously to the viewers. Then the penny dropped. He turned towards Evie and, for an instant, a combined look of horror, anger and betrayal crossed his face. "The look of horror on his face when he found that he was the subject – and I think the look of hatred that he gave me before he stepped on the platform – was something," Evie later said.[33]

One can only speculate as to the thoughts that ran through Karloff's mind as he joined Ralph Edwards for this most public biography. As a private man he was surely concerned the show might reveal facts he would wish remained undisclosed – his Anglo-Indian heritage, his mother's mental health problems, his brother George's shooting accident and the star's own multiple marriages. As it transpired, however, Karloff had nothing to fear. Edwards faithfully adhered to his guest's own version of events – despite knowing more about Karloff's private life than he revealed on air, as Bernard Coleman later explained: "I remember Jim [Laker] coming back and saying, 'You'll be amazed how many wives he's had!' and I only knew Evie because she was with him all the time I knew him."[34] Over the course of the next half hour Edwards introduced nine guests with varying degrees of success.[v] Karloff was clearly thrilled to be reunited with his old school friend, Geoffrey Taylor, and Edwards was even forced to step in while the old friends reminisced. However, Karloff clearly struggled to recall the next two guests. J. Warren Bacon, who had been the chief errand boy and general helper at Minot's opera house during Karloff's tenure with Harry St. Clair's company over 40 years earlier, had to prompt the star. "You knew my daddy," he said, "who was manager of the opera house – Fred Bacon."[35] Next came James Edwards who had shared a dressing room with Karloff at the Majestic Theatre in San Francisco during his stock company days. When it was revealed Edwards was now a sales manager and no longer an actor, Karloff commented, "I'm the only one who stuck with it!"[36]

He was, however, genuinely pleased to meet his next guest – Jack Pierce. "The best make-up man in the world," Karloff announced. "I owe him a lot."[37] Pierce then presented his friend with a gift – the monster's electrical outlets, or 'bolts' as they had become known. "I used to call it the Alemite nub," Karloff explained.[38] Next, Edwards introduced a film of *Arsenic and Old Lace* producers Howard Lindsay and Russel Crouse who happily recounted Karloff's involvement with the play. "Boris, we know that this is *your* life,' Lindsay said, "but, oh, it's a big part of our life too."[39]

A more recent theatrical acquaintance followed as Frank Brink was introduced. Despite Karloff's protestations Brink then told the audience of the star's generosity. "I'm going to tell it," Brink insisted, "because it needs to be told."[40] Then, as a clearly uncomfortable Karloff looked at the floor, Brink revealed, "When he discovered we were trying to raise the funds to build our own theatre he turned over every penny of his percentage of the profits to our building fund. Boris," he added, "I want you to know that the people of Anchorage have taken you into their hearts. They have designed a little golden trowel which we want to give to you to let you know how grateful we'll always be for what you've done for us."[41]

The star's love of cricket was addressed next, with the introduction of England and Surrey County Cricket Club star, Jim Laker, who presented Karloff with a cricket ball signed by his fellow team members. Then, Karloff's final guest – his daughter Sara – was introduced. Sadly, even on this occasion, Evie was unable to put aside her personal differences with her step-daughter, as this telling amendment to the show's format revealed. As Sara later pointed out, "The family is always brought on first. I was brought on at the last second."[42]

After the recording was completed Karloff attended an after-show party at the Hollywood Roosevelt Hotel where he chatted to his friends and colleagues. By the end of the evening, however, his cough had not abated. In fact, Karloff was now feeling worse and so Evie phoned the doctor who advised her husband be taken to hospital. There his cough, which was assumed to have been a chest infection, was diagnosed as emphysema,

v One of the background images shown during Karloff's *This Is Your Life* show was a photograph of a young boy sitting on a donkey while a girl stands close by. The image, which purports to show a young Karloff is, in fact, his nephew Harold Donkin – the son of Karloff's sister, Julia. The young girl in the photograph is Harold's sister, Dorothea, who later became a governess in California. Private Harold Donkin died in France, of pneumonia, on 22 December 1916. He was 19 years old.

the result of decades of heavy smoking. As a result Karloff was advised to quit smoking cigarettes. "He just gave up whatever he was told to and got on with it," Evie later said. "But I wish he'd given it up many, many years earlier."[43] Karloff, though, could not quit entirely and instead took to smoking a pipe.

Although he had remained amiable and charming during the television broadcast and after-show party Karloff had hidden his true feelings. "He was very upset about his *This Is Your Life*," Bernard Coleman later said. "He was *very* upset. What happened was I got a call from Evie, and then from others, to say could I get somebody to go out – a cricketer, you see – and I knew Alec wouldn't go. Jim Laker said he would go and Jim was a huge cricketing star. He'd taken 19 wickets in a test match. So Jim went out. But afterwards I understood he [Boris] absolutely hated it – hated it! And they were friends of his, the people who put this on – and he'd always said, 'Never, ever do this to me.' He was *very* upset about it. He didn't like it at all."[44]

In retrospect Evie felt she had made a mistake. Although she had promised her husband she would never let him go on the show, Ralph Edwards had told her he'd had a conversation with Karloff and now felt the star would be happy to appear. "So I agreed, I think wrongly," she later said. "Boris always said I'd sold him down the river for a gas cooker... It was a very difficult time trying to keep it secret... at the Chateau Marmont... So I would have to go down in the lobby to take telephone calls."[45]

It had been a very public exercise for a very private man and there was only so much Karloff would talk about, even to his closest friends. Bernard Coleman recalled that, of his family, Karloff only ever spoke of Sir John: "He was the man he talked a bit about. He said 'what a good man' and of how brilliant he was... He [Boris] was very proud of him. But he didn't say much and I would never discuss it. You know, I would never say anything to him about his family unless he brought it up."[46] Of his parents, Coleman said, "He never, ever mentioned them."[47]

Two weeks later Karloff had recovered sufficiently to return to television. On 9 December he appeared as Judge Winthrop Gelsey in *The Deadly Game*, an episode of the anthology series *Suspicion*. The drama told the story of a salesman who is invited to lodge in a small, nearby village when his car breaks down in the Swiss countryside. However, when he agrees to take part in a game with four, retired, elderly men he discovers they are a judge, a lawyer, a prosecutor and an executioner. His role as the accused soon seems too real. "During the course of one such trial," wrote the *Chicago Daily Tribune*, "you'll hear some intriguing discussions of 'guilt' and watch a snowbound traveller get scared out of his wits."[48] "Despite some contrivances in the plot," another journalist wrote, "this is a compelling thriller."[49]

In August Universal had turned over approximately six hundred pre-1948 features to Screen Gems, the television subsidiary of Columbia Pictures, for broadcast on television. "First of the Universal pictures to be shown will be a series of 52 of the studio's horror masterpieces," the *Los Angeles Times* announced. "They will be released under the general title of *Shock!*"[50] The first of these broadcasts was *Frankenstein*, which aired in Los Angeles on 1 October. In New York the season started two nights later with a screening of *Dracula*. The series proved to be a great success leading to another – *Son of Shock* – the following year. So, on 16 December, with a new generation discovering his horror pictures for the first time, Boris Karloff signed with *Voodoo Island* producers Aubrey Schenck and Howard W. Koch to make three pictures. The first, the *Los Angeles Times* revealed, would be called *Frankenstein 1975*.

Schenck had cast an eclectic mix of characters. In addition to Karloff, Don 'Red' Barry, Jana Lund and Charlotte Austin, the picture also featured TV host Tom Duggan, and even Duggan's television producer, Irwin Berke, as the police inspector.

Karloff would play Baron Victor von Frankenstein, the final descendant of the original monster maker. Scarred by the Nazis during the war, the Baron attempts to follow in his ancestor's footsteps and create a monster of his own. Unable to fund the purchase of a much-needed atomic reactor the scientist allows a television crew to use his German castle to make a Frankenstein programme. Then, with his reactor in place, the Baron successfully animates his monster, which begins to harvest members of the crew for body-parts. Even the Baron's butler Shuter [Norbert Schiller] and the Frankenstein family retainer Gottfried [Rudolph Anders] are sacrificed in the name of science. "We made that," the picture's producer, Aubrey Schenck, later explained, "because we had a three-picture deal with Karloff; we had to pay him $30,000[vi] whether we used him in a picture or not. So we went to the guys at Allied Artists – they wanted pictures – and we made it quickly for them. It was like a pick-up deal. I think we made it for $110,000, they paid us $250,000 for it – an outright buy."[51]

Production on the picture – which was soon renamed *Frankenstein 1970* – began at the Warner Brothers studio in Burbank on Wednesday, 9 January 1958. To maximise the picture's budget the director, Howard Koch, arranged to use a set from the Errol Flynn picture *Too Much, Too Soon* (1958) as a main backdrop in the picture. The set had originally cost Warner's $90,000 to construct, but Koch successfully negotiated to use the set, along with the backlot, for a mere $20,000. Schenck, meanwhile, was able to borrow a Cinemascope lens from 20th Century Fox, the studio co-founded by his uncle, Joseph.

The picture was made with breakneck speed. "Nine days' shooting – and I never had nine tougher days in my life, to do that picture in that time," Koch later explained. "I like directing – in fact, I enjoy directing more than producing – but as a director I don't feel I did such a great job on *Frankenstein 1970*, because I didn't have much time to really think."[52]

Koch had, of course, worked with Karloff before on *Voodoo Island*. While Schenck had not been present for that shoot, he would be for *Frankenstein 1970*, which afforded him some time with the star. "Karloff I had no trouble with," Schenck later said, "except he was the stingiest guy that ever lived! [*laughs*]… Well, when you'd go out to dinner, or to anything, he always liked to be treated. But he was a fine gentleman and he had a good mind, very erudite – exactly the opposite of what he was in pictures."[53] Charlotte Austin thought Karloff was "lovely, the 'last of the gentlemen' that there were, really… he was just a lovely human being… He was a very quiet, very private person. He really didn't talk much with anyone; I never saw him sitting down, having a conversation. He would do his work and then sit quietly, or go back to his dressing room. I think he was just doing a job and wanting to go home. A very quiet, gentle person that you didn't trespass upon; you didn't try to step within his boundaries. I felt sorry for him having to be in a movie like *Frankenstein 1970* – it was degrading. But that's a drive which I never had. Actors who love their craft and love acting will act no matter where it is, what time it is, how big the part, how small the part. *I* never felt that way."[54]

Frankenstein 1970 completed shooting in mid-January 1958. It opened in Los Angeles almost ten months later, on 11 November. at the Iris, UA Inglewood and 20 other theatres

---

vi According to Koch, Karloff was paid $25,000 for his work on the picture.

in a double feature with *Queen of Outer Space*, a sci-fi picture starring Zsa Zsa Gabor and *Rawhide*'s Eric Fleming. "It's the same old dank dungeons," the *Christian Science Monitor* wrote, "and the same old dank plot, and Boris Karloff is back again presiding over the cadavers and mouthing his gruesome lines as if they were particularly chewy caramels he could not get unstuck from... As he descends the staircase to his circular dungeon for the last time, a viewer cannot help thinking: There goes another square peg into a dismal round hole."[55]

Karloff, too, did not rate *Frankenstein 1970*. "I hope it's the last of that kind of film," he said. "I don't know how long these things can last. I guess they'll go on as long as people are stupid. We used to say something in the old pictures. Now they just hold up the monsters or whatever they have and say, 'Look how absolutely ridiculous they are'. It's sad, because it implies ridicule of people who are different and don't conform. There's no more sympathy."[56]

The Frankenstein film, though, was not the only problem. Karloff also took issue with the whole trend of 'freak-creature films' that were proving so popular. "Someone makes a new type of picture that accidentally catches on and makes money, and soon the whole town tries to copy it," he commented. "I honestly don't think these pictures would have gone over in our era because audiences were more mature. It's mostly the younger people who go to the movies today. No older person would stand for such rubbish."[57]

On Saturday, 18 January 1958 Karloff's 18-year-old daughter, Sara Jane, got married. The groom was a 26-year-old Air Force pilot, Richard Cotten. Neither Karloff nor his ex-wife – Sara's mother, Dorothy – had been happy with the prospect and Karloff, accompanied by Evie, had even flown to San Francisco to try to dissuade his daughter from the venture. It was, to Sara's recollection, the only time her parents ever met after their divorce.

The previous October, however, Karloff had mentioned the forthcoming nuptials in a letter to his brother, Sir John, and at the time appeared to be reconciled with the notion. "I am afraid I won't be with you on November 23rd," he wrote, "as that is my birthday and Sara Jane's, and to top it all off that is the day she is marrying a first lieutenant in the American Airforce and I will be in San Francisco to give her away! I have met the young man in question and I think it is going to be alright."[58]

The message, however, was not what it seemed. "That letter from my father to Sir John is very, very strange," Sara later said. "My wedding was never, ever scheduled for my birthday. It was always set for January 18, 1958 and he never agreed and then changed his mind! He and Evie objected to my getting married and especially to a big wedding and even offered us $2,000 to go away and get married quietly, instead of having a wedding of any sort in San Francisco!"[59] Rejecting the offer Sara asked her stepfather, Edgar Rowe, to give her away. "He insisted I ask my father, my father refused saying he would be in New York and thought Edgar should do it. I was angry and relieved. Edgar told me a joke going down the aisle."[60]

In early February 1958 the Karloffs took a holiday in France, during which he took some time out to act as Frank Sinatra's 'unofficial acting coach' on the war picture *Kings Go Forth*, then in production in the Maritime Alps in south-eastern France. Sinatra, as his valet George Jacobs later related, was a big fan of the horror star. "Mr. S got his one-take philosophy of acting from Boris Karloff...," Jacobs recalled. "He had met the horror icon on a studio lot in the late forties and had been bowled over by what an English gentleman he was... Whenever Karloff came over to visit Sinatra and to mentor him on roles he was considering by having Mr. S read lines for him to see how they sounded, he'd bring the most beautiful bouquets of freshly picked flowers. Mr. S never suggested this act of hospitality was a 'fag thing', as he would have if any other male had made the same gesture. Karloff's acting philosophy, in a nutshell, was simple: 'Say your lines. Hit your mark. Get out.' But Sinatra embraced this as the oracle of a legend and took it to heart. No multiple takes for him. In time, he became considered an efficient, naturalistic, often excellent actor. Whenever he was praised and asked how he learned to act, he didn't say Lee Strasberg or Stella Adler or Stanislavsky, but gave all the credit to Old Frankenstein."[61]

Returning from his holiday Karloff was soon back on television. On 12 February he joined Buster Keaton and his host in a trio of skits on *The Betty White Show*. Flitting between variety and drama, on 25 February Karloff joined Rita Lynn and Torin Thatcher in the episode *The Vestris* for the series *Telephone Time*. Directed by Arthur Hiller, the drama told the fictional, supernatural story of the ship *Vestris*. In 1828 the ship is en route from England to Boston when the captain's sickly wife has a vision on board. The ghostly visage [Karloff] leaves a message on a blackboard entreating the ship to change course but only when his wife's condition worsens does the captain comply. On the new course they find and rescue three shipwreck survivors, one of whom, Dr. Pierre, is the man from the vision. The *Los Angeles Times* wrote, "Some first rate drama here."[62] The episode was repeated five months later on 15 August, this time as part of the series *Tales of E.S.P.*, a short-lived paranormal series hosted by Vincent Price.

On 5 March Karloff appeared as the storyteller on *Shirley Temple's Storybook* narrating Washington Irving's tale *The Legend of Sleepy Hollow*. In the live broadcast from studio 2 of NBC's Burbank studios, Temple starred as Katrina Van Tassel, the object of affection of both the burly Abraham 'Brom Bones' Van Brunt [John Ericson] and the superstitious schoolmaster, Ichabod Crane. The pedagogue was played by Jules Munshin, perhaps best known as one of the trio of sailors on shore leave, along with Gene Kelly and Frank Sinatra, in the 1948 musical *On the Town*. "Shirley Temple, for the first time in a decade," wrote

the *Los Angeles Times*, "returned to acting last night and the results were, at best, adequate… The show itself continued the level of excellence that the *Storybook* series has brought to the screen this year, telling the old Washington Irving tale with a flair, and gaining good performances by Jules Munshin as Ichabod Crane and John Ericson as Brom Bones. Boris Karloff added much to the programme, substituting for Miss Temple as narrator."[63]

Karloff ended the month by joining Eva Le Gallienne in *The Shadow of Genius* on the television anthology series *Studio One* (31 March). Karloff played Professor Theodore Koenig, an unscrupulous nuclear physicist who is awarded the Nobel Prize after appropriating the findings of a deceased associate. The award, however, causes Koenig to wrestle with his conscience.

With Shirley Temple on *Shirley Temple's Storybook*, 5 March 1958.

The following day Karloff signed a contract with the Vanguard Recording Society in New York. He would be the narrator on a new recording of Prokofiev's *Peter and the Wolf*, accompanied by Mario Rossi conducting the Vienna State Orchestra. Karloff would receive $1,000 in advance of his royalties from the LP, which was released that October. "It would hardly seem that another addition to the vast collection of *Peter and the Wolf* recordings could attract much attention," one critic wrote. "One such addition has appeared (Vanguard VRS-1028), and it is well worth noting... Mr. Karloff's delivery is dramatic without being overdone, and he uses a magnificent speaking voice to great advantage. Mr. Rossi's interpretation of the score is skilful and meaningful. Together, they have produced a charming performance."[64]

Boris Karloff was now scheduled to return to England to make his second film for Amalgamated Pictures – *Corridors of Blood*. The story was not, however, the first choice for his second picture. "The deal I made with Boris Karloff when he consented to star in *Grip of the Strangler* was for two films," Richard Gordon explained. "At the suggestion of MGM, after they acquired the first film (and *Fiend Without a Face*) from me for distribution, we planned to make a film of Bram Stoker's *Dracula* as the second picture. It was to be filmed in colour and Cinemascope. The project was dropped when it was discovered that Universal still owned the copyright and was, in fact, in the process of arranging the Christopher Lee film with Hammer. Karloff certainly would have played the title role. We agreed with MGM to make *Corridors of Blood* instead."[65]

The picture went into production as *The Doctor from Seven Dials*.[vii] "The title change was agreed before the film was completed," Gordon said.[66] The screenplay, he added, "drew on a number of historical and factual accounts about experiments for the discovery of painless surgery. Horace Wells was one of the individuals researched by the writer. There were others."[67]

Horace Wells was an American dentist who, in 1844, began to use nitrous oxide (laughing gas) on his patients after experiencing its effects at a travelling circus. The following year, however, medical students harangued him when his demonstration of the gas's effects went badly wrong. The anaesthetic was administered incorrectly and the patient cried out in pain – an event that is depicted in picture. Wells left his practice in disgrace and became a travelling salesman. He soon, however, became addicted to chloroform and one day, in a deranged state, threw sulphuric acid at two prostitutes. He was arrested and incarcerated in New York's 'Tombs' prison where he later committed suicide. After inhaling chloroform to dull the pain Wells slit the femoral artery in his thigh with a razor and bled to death. He was 33 years old.

This picture, like *Grip of the Strangler*, would be directed by Robert Day. "I have a great admiration for him," Karloff later said. "Great respect."[68] Day, too, was pleased to be working once again with the star, and did so closely. "Well, he and I were deeply involved in characterisation," he said. "I enjoyed it again, because of Karloff mainly."[69] "By the time we got around to *Corridors of Blood*, we were shooting at the MGM British Studios in Borehamwood, and we had a bit more money in the budget," Day explained. "How much more I have no idea, but I would think it was probably twice the budget of *The Haunted Strangler*, about £200,000. And the shooting schedule was a bit longer, about four weeks."[70] Production began on Monday, 12 May 1958.

The story began in 1840. Karloff played Dr. Thomas Bolton, a philanthropic surgeon obsessed with the search for anaesthetic. Disagreeing with colleagues who believe that

vii The Seven Dials is an area of London close to Covent Garden. By the mid-18th century the area was a notorious slum.

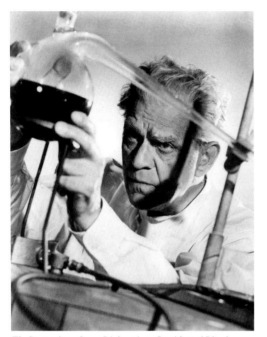

The Doctor from Seven Dials - a.k.a. *Corridors of Blood* (1957).

"pain and the knife are inseparable" Bolton experiments upon himself by inhaling his concoction of drugs. His growing addiction, however, distances him from his family – his son, Jonathan [Francis Matthews], his niece, Susan [Betta St. John] and his friends. Ridiculed by his colleagues when a demonstration of his anaesthetic goes wrong, he unwittingly falls in with the unscrupulous innkeeper 'Black Ben' [Francis De Wolff], Rachel [Adrienne Corri] and 'Resurrection Joe' who, like the notorious Burke and Hare before them, resort to murder to sell cadavers to the medical fraternity. In his desperation to obtain the necessary drugs for his experiments (and to feed his addiction), Bolton agrees to sign death certificates for these murdered souls, although his association with 'Black Ben' and his cronies inevitably leads to tragedy.

The casting of Resurrection Joe would later require an amendment to the picture's billing, as Richard Gordon later explained. "When Jimmy Carreras of Hammer Films agreed that I could have Christopher Lee for my film, and the role of Resurrection Joe was rewritten for him, the billing for the U.K. release was agreed," he said. "Later, when the film was released in America, we altered it because Lee was by then a more well-known personality."[71]

Born in London in 1922, Christopher Lee had served in the Royal Air Force and Special Forces during World War II. After demob a suggestion from a family member set him off in a new direction. "The Italian ambassador after the war was my cousin," Lee explained, "and he invited me for lunch in the embassy… He said, 'Have you ever thought of being an actor?' I hadn't really."[72]

In 1946 Lee was presented with a seven-year contract by the Rank Organisation and over the years that followed made appearances in such high profile productions as *Scott of the Antarctic* (1948), *Captain Horatio Hornblower R.N.* (1951), *The Crimson Pirate* (1952) and Powell and Pressburger's *The Battle of the River Plate* (1956). Then, in November 1956, he began his famous association with Hammer Films when he played the creature in *The Curse of Frankenstein*. His portrayal of Bram Stoker's *Dracula* the following year cemented his reputation as a new horror star – the new generation's successor to Boris Karloff and Bela Lugosi.

Although Karloff and Lee now worked together on *Corridors of Blood*, their paths had, in fact, crossed before. In 1953 Lee had appeared as Monsieur Jeanpierre, a murderous French dress designer in an episode of Karloff's *Colonel March* series entitled *At Night All Cats Are Grey*. "When I first met him, at Southall Studios," Lee later wrote, "he was in his middle sixties and had been famous for a quarter of a century... It did not bother him that he had become typecast. Types, he said, are continually in work. If they weren't types they wouldn't be popular. I wasn't myself desirous for being a type, though I could see the force of his argument… There was no reason for Boris to take note of me at Southall, but he was extremely kind. If I had a type at the time, I was cast right against it, in the character of a fruitily effeminate French designer. He very kindly did not discuss my performance in this. But he said to me that an actor must never be faceless, even when his face is obscured by bandages."[73] Now, on the set of *Corridors of Blood*, they would renew their acquaintance.

One day at the studio, while the two actors were talking, a journalist addressed Karloff. "He said, 'Well, of course it isn't your real name, is it – Karloff?' There was a silence," Lee explained. "Boris just looked at him. He [the journalist] said, 'Your name is a rather funny one really, isn't it?' or words to that effect. 'William Henry Pratt.' And I saw Boris's face set like stone. It was the only time I ever saw him lose his cool… he didn't shout, he didn't say anything – he just said, 'I don't think it's any funnier, or more amusing, than yours.' And a devastated journalist made a quick exit. It was the only time I ever saw him really, really annoyed."[74]

When *Dracula* [U.S. *Horror of Dracula*] opened in America in May 1958 Christopher Lee was afforded two weeks leave to attend the New York premiere. "It was my first trip to America and I flew over with a severe injury contracted when, after having acid thrown in my face and stabbing Boris to death on a bed, I crashed blindly into an iron stove," Lee said.[75] Returning to England and the *Corridors* set he refrained from discussing his recent successful ventures into the horror field – as the Creature in *Curse of Frankenstein* and the Count in *Dracula*. "Boris was above all things graceful," Lee said. "In the domain into which I'd recently stumbled and poached a couple of triumphs, he was king. When I returned from the heady whirl of the New York opening to finish off *Corridors of Blood* (as it came to be called), he never condescended to nor patronised me. He avoided any implication of my intrusion into the business and in fact we discussed everything save that."[76]

Francis Matthews, who played Dr. Bolton's son, Jonathan, had also recently worked for Hammer:

> I was cast for it very soon after completing **Revenge of Frankenstein** for Hammer Pictures. I recall being vaguely concerned at the time that I was in danger of being associated with the horror genre of films. In retrospect it didn't matter at all, and in fact many of the films of that kind and era are now regarded as undervalued works of cinematic art. However, in those days, as a young actor with his eyes on the future, you simply got on with them and kept quiet about it. None of these reservations, however, applied to the actual experience of making the film. It was at MGM-Elstree (long now disappeared) where only three years before I had been co-starring with Ava Gardner and Stewart Granger in **Bhowani Junction** under the direction of the great George Cukor. **Seven Dials** was obviously a less "elevated" piece of work but the pleasures involved were more than equal.[77]

One of the pleasures was to work closely with Boris Karloff.

> I recall being thrilled, if a little daunted, to know I would be working so closely on a film with one of its legends, which Boris certainly was, but nothing could have prepared me for the sheer fun and joy of the dear man's company. Curiously

what also struck me was that, having just worked for six weeks in close association with one of the profession's great gentlemen (and jokers!) Peter Cushing, I was now working with an exactly similar personality. It is interesting that two of the most celebrated stars, in the history of terrifying people, should both have been funny, friendly, likeable and lighthearted… Boris was very old by this time, and fairly frail… but his ebullience on the set and his interest in the processes of drug addiction, to ensure an authentic performance, were of the highest order.

I remember our director, Robert Day, was full of affection and admiration for him. I never recall a moment when Boris, despite his age, was ever late or unready with his lines or remotely difficult. In between takes he and I, as avid cricket fans, would be tuned in and riveted to the current test match scores. We developed a genuine father and son friendship. One of the running gags was that, at the end of each day's shoot, he would offer to sweep up the set before going home. He got his pay-off at the end-of-film party when we all, cast and crew, presented him with a huge studio broom with our signatures on it. God knows how he got it back to Hollywood, or if he ever did!![78]

The picture was completed in June 1958 but due to a change in MGM's policy remained unshown in the U.S. for almost five years. "A new management team had meanwhile been installed at MGM and decided not to continue releasing horror double bills," Gordon explained, "with the result that *Corridors of Blood* remained on their shelf for three years [*sic*] before finally being released in the USA through a newly-formed subsidiary company on a programme with a dubbed Italian exploitation picture that they called *Werewolf in a Girls' Dormitory* to which they added a specially-composed song *The Ghoul in School* that didn't help at the box office…"[79]

Corridors of Blood finally opened in Washington and Chicago in May 1963 and in New York a month later, on 5 June, at neighbourhood theatres. "*Corridors* starts with Mr. Karloff, as an altruistic surgeon determined to prove, through experiments, the existence of anesthesia," wrote Howard Thompson of the *New York Times*. "Opposing him are some selfish, bigoted colleagues. Some dregs of Old London are also blackmailing the poor guy, whose only aim is to benefit mankind. This portion is forthright, picaresque and carries ugly conviction, and Mr. Karloff is a persuasive, if lamblike, protagonist. Then the film turns into a plodding, shuddersome exercise in blood and pain. It's the old one-two, strictly for the sake of shock."[80] Regarding *Corridors* companion picture Thompson wrote, "Anyone who goes to see *Werewolf in a Girls' Dormitory* deserves exactly what he gets."[81]

"If it had not been for the falsity of the Seven Dials and Black Ben sequences, it would have been a better film," John Croydon later agreed. "Nevertheless, it is worthwhile and one of Karloff's best performances. He holds audience attention by his portrayal of a disintegrating man. Melodramatic it may be – but reading the life of Horace Wells' real life is even more so. His suicide was horrific and sensational. Despite our differences, a more articulate and erudite man than Karloff it would be hard to find. Had I been given the opportunity, I would have gladly worked with him again."[82]

"I find it odd that *Corridors* does not appear to arouse any interest in most anthologies of Boris's work," Francis Matthews later said. "I do think it was a script which contained many historical elements, with regard to the search for medical improvements and the battle against pain, which were vividly portrayed and were, in fact, based on the life of a real surgeon of those times. The reconstruction of a typical operating theatre of the time, and the people involved in helping the surgeons restrain struggling patients, was carefully researched and totally authentic. It should also be appreciated because of Boris's deeply moving portrayal of the downfall of a tragic figure obsessed with the search for a painless anaesthetic... Boris (Charles Pratt[viii]... another joke he was always indulging in) was a lovely man, and a joy to work with."[83]

After *Corridors of Blood* the Karloffs returned to New York and by Autumn were once more residing in the Chateau Marmont in Hollywood. In Los Angeles on Thursday, 6 November 1958 Karloff appeared in a live adaptation of Joseph Conrad's *Heart of Darkness* on *Playhouse 90*.

The loose adaptation of Conrad's novella was penned by Stewart Stern, who was thrilled when he learned Karloff wanted to play Kurtz. Stern first met Karloff at CBS after Evie had dropped her husband at the building. As the lift was broken Karloff and Stern climbed the stairs together. "He was somewhat frail," Stern recalled, "somewhat stooped, and had a very gentle handshake, and there was enormous sadness about that face when it turned to you. Great beauty. His eyes were deep and brown and looked at you directly. He had an enormous capacity for allowing you to feel received, and was keenly interested in who you were and what you had to say."[84] Roddy McDowall also admired his co-star. "I'll never forget him because he was arthritic," he said. "He was in great pain except he would never, ever complain. And it's just very indicative of what he was like."[85]

One day following rehearsals, after all the actors had left, Stern, the show's director Ron Winston, the art director and the cameraman sat around a conference table in the rehearsal room discussing the show. "Two hours after we thought the rehearsal had ended, I happened to turn, and noticed Boris in the corner, sitting very quietly reading the newspaper. I went over to him and said, 'Mr. Karloff, are you waiting for someone?' He said, 'No, no, no, no.' I said, 'Well, why are you still here?' He said, 'Because I haven't been officially dismissed.'"[86]

Lawrence Laurent of the *Washington Post and Times Herald* thought the broadcast, "the most unusual drama of the year... it was filled with mysticism and symbolism. At times, the drama was confused and confusing... With all of its minor failings, the sum total achieved powerful impact. It is quite possible that Roddy McDowall delivered the finest performance of the television season."[87] Karloff though, Laurent felt, "managed to trigger a couple of hard-to-suppress chuckles."[88]

Kurtz's dying words – "The horror! The horror!" – were tragically echoed six weeks later when Karloff's family was shaken by a real-life tragedy. On Thursday, 18 December Sir John Pratt's son-in-law, the 47-year-old Defence Ministry diplomat Tom Bromley drove home to his fog-shrouded house in Haslemere, Surrey. His two sons, Martin (aged 13) and Stephen (10), had returned home from boarding school days earlier to spend their Christmas at home. But upon entering the house Tom noticed a cricket bat and a pair of boots in the hallway. Both were spattered with blood. He called out for his boys but received no answer. Searching the house he found the bodies of his two sons, both clad in their pyjamas. Each had cuts and stab wounds. Stephen was discovered in the second floor

---

viii In a 1966 interview Karloff was asked whether his real name was William Henry or Charles Edward. "I don't know how that Charles Edward came about," he replied. "Somebody, when I was under contract at Universal, I think, made the mistake in the publicity department. If a thing ever goes out, you know, it never dies; it crops up again and again."

bathroom while Martin lay in the garage. While Bromley went to a neighbour for help his wife, Diana, was found wandering in the garden in tears. She was bleeding from a wound on her throat.

The police arrived and, while an officer stood on duty in the bloodstained hallway, others searched the Bromley's estate. They eventually found a knife in the grounds. Diana was, meanwhile, taken to hospital where policewomen waited at her bedside to hear her account of the slayings. "Our inquiries are not completed, but there is no evidence of any intruder," a police spokesman said. "Mr. Bromley has helped us greatly with our inquiries. Mrs. Bromley is still very poorly and has not yet been able to make a statement."[89]

Two days later Diana Bromley was arrested for the murders. She was released from hospital and taken before a magistrate in Guildford, where she was charged with the killings. Detective Inspector George Cornish told the court he was satisfied Mrs. Bromley had caused the deaths. Police pathologist Dr. A.K. Mant testified that Martin had initially been strangled while Stephen had been drowned. Both boys, he said, were apparently unconscious at the time of their deaths. Throughout the hearing the accused sat in silence, clenching her hands. She was held without bail and taken to the police station at Godalming.

On Wednesday, 25 February 1959 Diana was taken before the court at Kingston-Upon-Thames. There the court heard how she had first drugged her two boys before carrying them to the garage where she had made up a bed. She then backed the car into the garage and, after sealing the garage door with rugs, switched on the car's engine. When she later realised the boys were still alive she strangled Martin with a cloth belt and drowned Stephen in the bathtub before inflicting the knife wounds. She then cut her own throat and tried to drown herself in the lily pond before being found wandering in the woods. The court judged her insane and ordered her to be held in a mental hospital.

Diana's father, Sir John, was inconsolable over the tragedy. His great-niece, Elisabeth Crowley, recalled, "I vividly remember my mother telephoning Uncle Jack to say how sad she was to hear the news, and how he just couldn't talk to her. I learnt subsequently that Diana had become convinced that she should not be responsible for her sons and I imagine that she was committed to Broadmoor."[90]

In an interview over 40 years later 'J.T.', one of Diana's fellow patients at Broadmoor, shared her own recollections of Karloff's niece. "There were only women on our ward," she explained. "They've got two wards – you had Lancaster House and York House – but the men had all the other wards. There were several wards for the men… and… we used to go to the OT [Occupational Therapy] from there… they call it the Mini-Hanger… it's where you do things for factories and things like that, and they would put me in charge of all the people round the table… make sure they'd done the job. I'd do it, but some of them were very ill, they shouldn't have been in Broadmoor, because their minds had really gone... We had one girl there, Diana Bromley, and her uncle was Boris Karloff, the film star. And what she'd done, I think she put herself and the two children in a car – put the exhaust pipe on. It killed the children but didn't kill her, but gave her brain damage. And she would walk up and down all the time and say, 'Diana dies… Diana dies…' I think about every six months she would come round for about 20 minutes, and she would really talk posh… 'cause I used to take the mickey out her, and then she would get up, and walking up and down, and say, 'Diana dies…', and 'cause you'd got to feed her, [you'd] keep walking up and down, feeding her as you go along."[91]

The New Year brought with it Karloff's next excursion into television – a new 25 episode anthology series entitled *The Veil*. Karloff signed for the show on 18 December 1957. He would receive $2,000 per episode, plus an additional $1,000 in advance of syndicated re-runs. In total, Karloff expected to receive $75,000. For his part he would star, or feature, in the tales as well as introducing each episode. It was later announced he was expected to complete work on the series by 17 April 1959.

The Veil would be made at the Hal Roach Studios in Culver City, where the classic Laurel and Hardy shorts had been produced. In May 1958 the studios were purchased by the Scranton Corporation, a company involved in such diverse interests as the manufacture of electronics, photographic equipment and lace. The Corporation had, however, already sold a controlling interest to F.L. Jacobs Co. of Detroit, a manufacturer of motor parts run by Serbian-born (and, it later transpired, illegal immigrant) Alexander L. Guterma. It was a move that would later have serious consequences for Karloff's new series.

Three months later, on 18 August, the president and director of the film studio, Hal Roach Jr. – the son of Laurel and Hardy's famous producer – called a press conference to announce the expansion of the studios. He expected to make 20 feature films and six new television series, he said. One of these series, *The Gale Storm Show*, was already in the works. Another, soon to go into production, would be an anthology series entitled *The Veil*. Its host would be Boris Karloff. The series would be a chiller, the star later revealed, "but in an intellectual way".[92]

The Veil was the brainchild of Frank Bibas, a radio and television commercial producer who had an interest in the paranormal. "He *studied* it," his daughter Barbara later explained. "For instance, voodoo interested him – he just wanted to pick it apart and take its 'mystery' out of it. Then in a library, or wherever, he came across some files of actual case studies of the paranormal. And he decided that that would be a great series. That's how *The Veil* came about."[93] Bibas, therefore, hired writers who would provide him with tales of ghosts, reincarnation, premonition and precognition.

The first in the series was a Victorian story, *Vision of Crime*, in which Karloff was joined by Robert Hardy and Patrick Macnee. While aboard ship, 150 miles out at sea, George Bosworth [Hardy] sees the murder of his brother in a vision revealed in a bowl of water. He returns to England and tries to convince Chester Wilmore, a bluff, old, cocksure police sergeant [Karloff] and his assistant Constable Hawton [Macnee] that Albert Ketch, the man they had arrested for the killing, is innocent. Ignored by the police Bosworth later discovers his fiancée, Julie Westcott [Jennifer Raine], to be the killer.

Karloff's fellow Englishmen, Hardy and Macnee, would both go on to have distinguished careers on television and in film. At the time, though, Macnee was having problems. "Patrick was desperately trying to get work at the time," Robert Hardy later explained. "I think he was finding it very difficult to carry on – as we all do at some point in our careers. And he was out there in America and nobody was much employing him and I remember I used to lecture him and say to him, 'Stop giving up! Stop being so soft. Get on with it!' and things like that. And, of course, he did later when he came back here [to England]."[94]

Prior to *The Veil* Robert Hardy had already become a recognisable face on British television. "I'd done a mass in Britain," he said. "I was the BBC's first *David Copperfield*, and goodness knows what else. So it was more than a little bit, and I went out to America two or three times in the 50s with plays on Broadway and then I went out from one play when it folded to the West coast. I stayed there a long time."[95] Fortunately, Hardy was soon able to find work there. "Saved my bacon, because at that time television – which I did a tiny bit of in New York after the play had finished – was really moving out to the west coast. I went out with the movement and did a lot of work."[96]

Although *The Veil* gave Hardy the opportunity to work with Boris Karloff the two were, in fact, already acquainted. "I knew him much more on the side when I lived out in California," Hardy later explained. "He was a great, great friend of my mother-in-law, Gladys Cooper, and he was forever visiting. Boris and Evie used to come and he was the most enchanting man... He was a very courteous, kindly, sensitive man – I think in some degree appalled by his reputation – the Frankenstein sort of thing, with the knobs on his head and all. It just wasn't him at all. Any time his name comes up all I can say is he was a charming, kind, interested friend. I think he was a friend to young actors – which I was then, and whether he got me the part because he'd already been in it – I think it must have been that, yes... possibly. I don't know. And the agents who represented me at the time are long dead! So we shall never know!"[97]

Another *Veil* actor who, like Robert Hardy and Patrick Macnee, would go on to have a long career on television and in film was 19-year-old George Hamilton. Hamilton appeared alongside Karloff in the reincarnation tale *The Return of Madame Vernoy*. "Karloff was just a very nice man.... and he'd sit around and tell me stories about England," Hamilton later said. "He had a kind of strange way of walking which was pure Frankenstein."[98] Meeting Karloff, Hamilton later wrote in his autobiography, "was a thrill that mitigated the ignorance of my situation. That was something to write home about. Boris himself honoured me with a bit of useful advice: 'Never let your jacket gap[e] away from your neck. It's the mark of the bad politician and the bad actor'."[99]

According to the episode's director, Herbert L. Strock, the young actor initially proved rather troublesome. "George Hamilton was a rising young thing, and he was *not* the easiest character to deal with," Strock later explained. "It was only out of his respect for Boris that I got George to do *any*thing. George was rather difficult to move around, and would always want to be somewhere *else*. When Boris showed George that he [Boris] had faith in me, George then got faith in *me*. But up to that point, he wasn't the easiest guy to work with."[100]

Karloff, however, was a different matter. "This man was absolutely sensational," Strock later said. "He was as easy to work with as anyone I've ever known, he was like putty in your hands. He would always know his lines; he knew everybody *else's* lines."[101]

Although Strock would give the star a ten o'clock call Karloff and Evie would always be at the studio early. "Sometimes I would come on the set, figuring to be the first person there," Strock explained, "and there was Boris and his wife, Evelyn, sitting there, she doing her knitting and him reading. I would say to him, 'What are you *doing* here so early? I gave you a ten o'clock call.' (He was no spring chicken at the time, and I didn't want him to be worn out). But being the professional that he was, and having Evelyn at his side constantly, guiding him, and doing his own make-up, he wanted to be available if and when we ever needed him. That was greatly appreciated."[102]

Karloff was just as helpful during the filming. "I would tell him where to move and how to do things," Strock said, "and he would do whatever I asked him to do as pleasantly as possible, coming up with suggestions (as any actor will do). It was a pleasure working with this man... I think, of all the actors I've worked with over the years (including some of the better known actors), he was the most professional. *The* most willing. And a very capable actor – he could play from a bobby to a gentleman to... *any*thing! There was nothing this guy couldn't do, and I *loved* working with him. Even though the budgets were *extremely* limited I enjoyed these shows very much."[103]

Karloff was even willing to remain and help after his working day was done. "He would stay after I told him he was finished – I tried to finish with him earlier in the afternoon so he could get some sleep, but he would stay," Strock said. "I'd say, 'Don't *worry* about it; when I'm doing the other man's close-ups, I'll play your part off-camera and he can react to me.' But Karloff felt it was much more charming if *he* stayed and *he* did the part, and the actor could get the proper reaction from *his* eyes. I mean, they don't come like this anymore."[104]

Evie, too, was helpful, as Strock explained. "Mrs. Karloff was a charming elderly lady," he said, "and she did her knitting or read while he was working. She stayed there – came with him first thing in the morning and stayed with him. I *guess* she did the driving – I'm not sure. She saw to it he had his hot tea and that he had lunch, and she was actually very helpful in rehearsing lines with him, things like that. I liked her."[105] Robert Hardy recalled, "Evie was a *very* sparkly, amusing person – but again, gentle. There were no histrionics with either of them, there was no, kind of, actor-ish behaviour. They were just an enchanting couple. She had a glamour about her and, of course, he had a certain glamour about him because of his reputation – because everybody knew who he was... [I have a] very clear memory of the sweetness of the man, well, of them both. Which was kind of surprising because of his reputation as a performer – you know, the sort of parts he played. But he was the *gentlest*, most sensitive and understanding man. He was adorable."[106]

With Karloff at work in the studio the front office decided to capitalise on his presence and had him make a guest appearance on *The Gale Storm Show*, also in production on the lot. In the episode *It's Murder, My Dear* Karloff appeared in a dual role – both as himself and a look-alike intent on killing the star.

In the episode Susanna [Storm] and her friend Nugey [Zazu Pitts] visit the Hal Roach Studios. There they encounter Boris Karloff who talks to them of his new series, *The Veil*. Later, while the two women watch him filming an introduction for his show, Karloff's double takes a shot at him from a catwalk, grazing the star's shoulder. He is, therefore, taken to the studio hospital where he, Susanna, Nugey and a nurse are imprisoned by the look-alike – a disgruntled actor who cannot get work due to his uncanny likeness to the star. With the actor safely incarcerated the impostor returns to the *Veil* set and plays Karloff's scene. However, when his prisoners escape, the double surrenders.

This episode was broadcast on 31 January 1959. Karloff's series, however, was never aired. After only ten episodes were in the can[ix] the plug was pulled and, as a result, Karloff received only a small fraction of the $75,000 he had been contracted for. He would later struggle in vain to receive recompense. Things, however, would be worse for Hal Roach Jr. and his associates.

Hal Roach Studios and its controlling company, F.L. Jacobs Co., were in big trouble. "Boris Karloff put in several weeks on a projected TV series that may never see the light," explained the *Hartford Courant*. "Ten half-hour dramatic films under the general title of *The Veil*, an extra-sensory perception series, were completed at the Hal Roach Studio in

---

ix The final *Veil* episode, *Jack the Ripper*, (starring Niall MacGinnis) was *not* made for the series but was, instead, a British-made story appropriated for inclusion. As such Karloff only provides the bookends for the drama and does not feature in the story.

Hollywood. But then all work was stopped at the studio because of its involvement in the Guterma financial investigation."[107]

On 11 February 1959 the Securities Exchange Commission took action against the F.L. Jacobs Co. and its chairman and president Alex L. Guterma for alleged violations of Federal securities laws. "Last fall Mr. Guterma borrowed 'substantial sums of money' with his stock of Jacobs pledged as collateral," The *Wall Street Journal* explained. "Mr. Guterma borrowed the money from 'certain non-banking lending organisations and individuals' at rates of interest of about 2% a month, or 24% a year," the S.E.C. said. 'The lenders assertedly began selling the stock in December, but Mr. Guterma did not report the transactions, according to the commission. In [not] doing so, he unlawfully concealed from the investing public the fact that the principal 'insider' of Jacobs was liquidating his position, in conformity with his overall fraudulent scheme,' the S.E.C. has charged."[108] The Commission suspended the company from any over-the-counter trading and within days Guterma had resigned and was replaced by Roach Jr.

In September matters got worse when the Dominican government revealed it had signed a contract with three former officers of Mutual Broadcasting System, Alexander Guterma, Hal Roach Jr. and Garland L. Culpepper Jr. and had paid them $750,000. The spokesman for the Dominican government asserted the contract was to disseminate news in America, and not for the broadcasting of political propaganda. The following February Guterma was fined a maximum $160,000 and was sentenced to almost five years in prison on charges of deceiving the public in massive stock manipulations. Four months later Hal Roach Jr. was found guilty of failing to register as a foreign agent and fined $500. In March 1962 he filed for bankruptcy claiming he had debts of $1,050,802 and ten years later, on 29 March 1972, died of pneumonia at St. John's Hospital in Santa Monica. He was 53 years old.

After the collapse of *The Veil* Boris Karloff decided to go home. He would 'up sticks' with Evie and move permanently back to England. He had announced his intention to leave America prior to the production of *Frankenstein 1970*. Once his role in the picture was over, he had said, he would probably go abroad to live, possibly in England. "Such are the indications of changing times in the motion-picture industry," the *Los Angeles Times* had commented at the time.[109]

"It is important to understand that this is not a retirement," Karloff now explained. "I am rising 72, but I have never felt more like working, and I have commitments for more movies, television and possibly a stage play. It is just that my wife and I felt we would like to live in London, to make it our base from now on. It is possible for us to do this because of the great gains made in transportation. Once it was necessary for me to have my base in Hollywood. About 10 years ago speedier air travel made it possible for us to move our base to New York, where we maintained an apartment. I could get to Hollywood quickly for work, or I could hop over to London or the Continent for a job. New York was a good half-way point. Now, with the jets, I don't need a half-way point. It's almost as easy to get from London to Hollywood as it used to be to get from New York to Hollywood... And that will be it for us from now on, although I don't know how much we'll be able to enjoy it in the near future. I left behind in Hollywood a TV series that was interrupted when the Hal Roach Studio was immobilised by the present financial snarl in which it is involved. The series might be resumed there, and I'd have to go back. There are two Hollywood motion pictures [for Koch and Schenck] for which I'm on call. If a stage script being revised turns out properly, I hope to do it in London. If successful there, we'd bring the play to New York. I remember that after we settled down in New York, we scarcely used the apartment enough to hold the franchise, what with work in Hollywood and touring in plays."[110]

In mid-March, before he left America, Karloff appeared in *The Indian Giver* alongside Edgar Buchanan, Jackie Cooper and Carmen Mathews. Filmed on the Republic lot, and broadcast on 17 May, Karloff played a charming conman who, after arriving in a small western town, attempts to cheat the citizens out of money they believe will be used to erect a statue of a local hero.

Then, on 1 May 1959, Boris Karloff returned to England to live. "He always wanted to come back to England despite the ghastly taxation because he was English and it was here he wanted to be," Evie later said.[111] They purchased a top floor flat in a Victorian house at 43 Cadogan Square in London's Knightsbridge and on 21 May moved in. "They had a roof garden there," Bernard Coleman explained. "That was a nice apartment they had there. They were above the Dockers – Sir Bernard and Lady Docker. At that time Sir Bernard was chairman of B.S.A. [Birmingham Small Arms] and Daimler, and he was on the board of Midland Bank. He was one of the big tycoons of the time. Lady Docker was a very publicity-conscious lady who used to dress up – I mean, in tiger skin pants! And she used to get on the juice and she would get very boozed, and she was troublesome. And poor old Bernard Docker was a very quiet man, you see. And they had the apartment below Boris. And they would always invite them down and they [Boris and Evie] used to steer clear for years!"[112]

With the change of locale there would also be a change of direction. He was finished, Karloff told reporters, with the monster business. "I'm too busy with my other commitments for TV and anyway I want some time to catch up on cricket. After half a century in the United States one feels a little out of touch."[113] Still, he did not always find television to be a satisfying medium. "TV's quality may not always be as good as we would like it to be," he said, "there's more excuse for it than for bad movies. There is such an enormous amount of hours to fill, and of course it can't all be good because there is not that much good material. But the movies have nothing but time – and yet some of these degrading debaucheries they call 'horror films' are shot in eight days. The more they keep it up, the more they will ruin the movies. It's the old story of killing the goose that laid the golden egg."[114]

On 24 July Karloff renewed his Artists' Manager Contract with the Music Corporation of America (MCA) by signing for an additional three years. MCA was established in 1924 by Dr. Julius Stein as a music-booking agency. Later, under the leadership of Lew Wasserman, the agency began representing actors and actresses and grew into the largest talent agency in the world, boasting such clients as Clark Gable, Bette Davis, James Stewart, Marlon Brando, Marilyn Monroe, Charlton Heston and Gregory Peck. Although it was forbidden for a talent agency to produce television shows, in 1948 the agency did just that, after SAG president (and MCA client) Ronald Reagan granted the agency a waiver. In 1958 MCA purchased the 423-acre lot from Universal and renamed it Revue Studios.

Karloff's relationship with the agency was, he joked, all encompassing. Booth Colman, who had appeared with Karloff in a number of shows, including *The Veil*, recalled, "On one, the actors were taking a smoke break and Karloff joined us as we were talking about our agents, complaining about something. He said, 'Well, you know, I'm with MCA. MCA has offices all over the world. And when I'm out of work. I'm out of work *a-l-l over the world.'* [*laughs*]. I've always remembered that!"[115]

Karloff would call on both his agency and his union to mediate in his long-standing dispute with Howard W. Koch and Aubrey Schenck. On 15 October 1954 he wrote to SAG Executive Secretary John L. Dales concerning the pair's continued inability to produce the remaining contracted pictures. In April 1958, three months after the completion of *Frankenstein 1970*, it had been announced Karloff would star in *King of Monsters* for the producers. However, neither this project, nor any alternative, ever materialised, much to the star's chagrin. "As you may remember," Karloff wrote to Dales, "I have a contract with Koch and Schenck under the terms of which are two pictures remaining… and it is obvious to me and to MCA that they have no intention of making the remaining two films. The situation seems to have 'stabilised itself' as follows: Every time I do a job they request and receive an extension. Obviously the time will come when the sooty fingers will snatch me away during an extension period and my rejoicing widow will be left high and dry so far as the contract is concerned."[116]

Karloff even asked Charles Belden of MCA to try to force Koch and Schenck to film the two remaining films before July 1960 or pay him a cash settlement. "I am inclined to gather," Karloff later wrote to Dales, "that his [Belden's] view is that Koch would only offer a very token sum at best and that only to protect his reputation."[117] Questioned years later on their seeming reluctance to meet the terms of Karloff's contract, Howard Koch explained, "[Edwin F.] Zabel[x] and Aubrey didn't live up to the agreement with Karloff. By that time I had left them and gone to work for Frank Sinatra's company. They never made a third picture *or* paid Karloff, and I think it was an unhappy relationship at the end. Maybe Karloff felt badly toward me, too, but as I said I had already gone on with Sinatra and was not responsible. I do think, unfortunately, that before he died Karloff was unhappy with us, that we hadn't lived up to our agreement."[118]

As the matter dragged on Boris Karloff decided to accept another theatrical offer. So, on 12 January 1960, he returned to the stage, albeit briefly, opening the second annual San Juan Drama Festival in Puerto Rico with *Arsenic and Old Lace*. For six evenings he trod the boards of the Tapia Theatre as Jonathan Brewster. "We opened the season in their lovely 200 year old theatre and it was like a first night at the Met," he later explained. "The governor and his lady members of the cabinet and all the bigwigs were there."[119] Then two weeks later, on 3 February, NBC announced Hubbell Robinson Productions would present a new series to be aired the following season – a series named *Thriller*.

---

x Koch formed Bel-Air Productions with producers Aubrey Schenck and Edwin Zabel.

Chapter 22

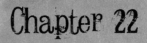 THRILLER

(1960-1962)

"I think the title leaves the stories wide open to be based on melodrama, not violence or shock. They'll be stories about people in ordinary surroundings and something happened to them. The whole thing boils down to taste. Anybody can show you a bucket of blood and say, 'This is a bucket of blood', but not everyone can produce a skilful story."[1]

Boris Karloff (1960)

Thriller was the creation of Hubbell Robinson, a 54-year-old producer who had been programme director, then executive vice president, at CBS. There he had produced the drama shows *Climax!*, *Studio One* and the Emmy award-winning *Playhouse 90*, all of which had, at one time or another, featured Boris Karloff. In 1959 he left CBS to create Hubbell Robinson Productions. Their first production was *Startime*, a series that, Robinson announced, would be different from the norm. "Our only formula," he said, "is to have no formula at all. No week will be like the week before. We want to cover the entire spectrum of entertainment. Our ambition – to try to realise on a weekly basis what television can be."[2] The series gave Ingrid Bergman her first television role in an adaptation of Henry James' *The Turn of the Screw*, while Alec Guinness, Dean Martin and James Stewart all featured in subsequent episodes. However, the viewing figures failed to reach the heights expected and on 31 May 1960, after 33 episodes, the series was cancelled. But by now, Robinson had moved on and was already in production of his new venture – *Thriller*.

"We're aiming at being the *Playhouse 90* in the field of mystery," Robinson announced. "That is in terms of excellence, story and production. Our plays will basically be stories of little actual physical violence. There will be no pistol whippings, no dark alleys. The bulk of the material will be about perfectly normal people caught in a terrifying situation beyond their control. They'll be stories in which no one gets killed."[3] By early February 26 scripts had been selected for production. "We're trying to do one-hour feature pictures, consciously and deliberately striving for excellence," Robinson said. "Each plot will be unique, unusual."[4]

The trend for anthology shows was to have a star introduce each week's episode. Series such as *Robert Montgomery Presents* and *Playhouse 90* both followed this pattern. As *Thriller*, too, would conform, a host was required. Hubbell Robinson chose Boris Karloff. For his services Karloff would receive $2,500 for each episode, above the title billing, plus an additional fee if he also featured in the drama.

Before starting work on his new series, however, Karloff returned to *Playhouse 90* for the First World War drama *To the Sound of Trumpets*. His contract for the episode, dated 6 January 1960, provided him with $10,000 for his services, plus 'round-trip transportation from New York to L.A'.[5] Broadcast on Tuesday, 9 February 1960 Karloff starred with Judith Anderson, Stephen Boyd, Dolores Hart, Dan O'Herlihy, Robert Coote and Sam Jaffe.

Boyd starred as Captain Leslie Cronyn, a British officer despondent by the constant stalemate of the conflict in Flanders. In his despair he quotes Voltaire: "All murderers are punished unless they kill in large numbers to the sound of trumpets." Cronyn plans to flee France and therefore steals the leave papers of a dead comrade. Before he escapes, however, he meets an America nurse [Hart] who plans to meet her husband on leave. The two embark on a weeklong illicit love affair before Cronyn sends her back to her husband. The Captain then returns to the front.

"Despite the fact that the trumpets had an all too familiar ring, John Gay's small drama came to the screen in a slick, gutsy production that occasionally flared with brilliant dialogue and contained several very moving scenes," wrote the *Los Angeles Times*. "Stephen Boyd as the Captain was a harsh, manly and eloquent hero: Dolores Hart was a properly winsome nurse. In a series of brief yet marvellous vignettes, Dame Judith Anderson, Boris Karloff and Sam Jaffe etched three unforgettable portraits – proving again that where acting is concerned they wrote the book."[6]

The episode was the first of eight high-budgeted 'special' plays that were scheduled in an attempt to revive the flagging series. "Frankly," producer Herbert Brodkin said, "the future of *Playhouse 90* is up to the public. If we get the ratings, it will probably be back next year. If we don't, it will probably die. And if it dies, I believe it will be a calamity for television."[7] Unfortunately the eight specials failed to revive the series as hoped and *Playhouse 90* was cancelled.

The following month, on 5 March, Boris Karloff appeared as Billy Bones, the pirate who bestows upon young Jim Hawkins the map to Captain Flint's hidden booty in *Treasure Island*. Shot in New York, this *Show of the Month* presentation was well received. John P. Shanley called it, "a brilliant television production... It was, in fact, one of the best telecasts of the season. Hugh Griffith, as Long John, a rogue with a twinkling eye, and Richard O'Sullivan, as Jim Hawkins, the innkeeper's son who embarked on a voyage for buried treasure, were outstanding. Billy Bones, the doomed possessor of the treasure map, was interpreted menacingly by Boris Karloff."[8]

Filming of *Twisted Image*, the first episode of *Thriller*, also began in early March. Each episode took, on average, five days to shoot and cost between $125,000 and $150,000. Karloff's contributions, when merely providing the introductory dialogue, were shot in batches, usually five at a time although the location of these shoots varied. Often they were filmed in Los Angeles at the Revue Studios but also, occasionally, in New York. The location of the shoot was determined by Karloff's current location and availability. As usual, in the periods he was not required, Karloff would readily accept other projects.

In April he played host on *Hollywood Sings*, a "nostalgic reprise of some of the popular song hits identified with the world of motion pictures" wrote television critic Jack Gould.[9] For an hour on Sunday, 3 April Eddie Albert and Tammy Grimes sang the tunes. "It was a warm and pleasant 60 minutes," Gould added.[10]

Within weeks of the broadcast Karloff had returned to England to begin rehearsals for *Upgreen and At 'em or A Maiden Nearly Over*, a musical melodrama for British television which aired on 6 June. Karloff played the role of the butler alongside Roger Livesey as the village squire, Stephanie Voss as his daughter, Tony Britton as the young hero (Captain Jack Falcon V.C. of the Life Guards) and Jimmy Edwards as the villainous Sir Caleb Chaselove. "Upon the result of the village cricket match depends the future of the squire's daughter;" explained *The Times*. "If her father's team loses, she will be forced to marry the

Karloff and Robert Florey during the production of the *Thriller* episode *The Incredible Doktor Markesan* (Courtesy of Gord Reid).

villain and her father will be ruined. The villain's eleven is unscrupulously stuffed with professional cricketers, but the traditional *deux ex machina* arrives – in the person of the squire's son unjustly disgraced by the villain – in time to save the day."[11] The newspaper called the melodrama, "a holiday diversion... near enough to complete success to make us regret the slight margin of error by which it missed the bull's-eye... It should be mentioned that the players gave their service for this production in order that a donation should be made to the National Playing Fields Association."[12]

"I think we did it once, live, and that was it," Tony Britton recalled. "The part about it I remember most of all was the day we spent filming the cricket. Thinking about it I'm not even sure we were filming the cricket for the television programme, or whether it was just that he [Karloff] came along to one of our cricket matches – one of the Lord's Taverners, probably – or the Stage Cricket Club... But what I can tell you is that the idea of actually meeting and possibly working with a man like that was thrilling indeed. But I didn't know what on earth he'd turn out to be like and, of course, he turned out to be one of the most gentle, one of the most extraordinary, enchanting, highly intelligent Englishmen. A most extraordinary kind – a total Englishman. I've been in the business for an awful long time, and I've done an awful lot of television and they come and go – and one tends to, sort of, not exactly wipe them out... but certainly not meeting a man like that. I just remember the Pavilion, standing and sitting in the Pavilion with him. It was a lovely sunny day, and we were sitting on the steps of the Pavilion and talking and chatting away and I was just so enchanted by the man himself, who was one of the dearest and, as I say, most 'English' men I've ever met in my life. This was the lovely thing about him – having seen all those horror movies of the day, with him playing, so brilliantly, these awful characters and then meeting this gentle Englishman, who was so happy to be back in England."[13]

Returning to America in early summer Karloff was soon back on television. On 23 June he appeared in *The Secret World of Eddie Hodges*, a musical written especially for the 13-year-old actor Hodges, and directed by Norman Jewison. "We had conceived the television special as a glimpse into the imaginary play world of a young boy," Jewison recalled. "All of his adventures were cast with Hollywood and N.Y. actors who not only brought star power to the cast but also were adept at specific stylised character roles including comedy. Boris was our pirate captain – re-creating Captain Hook. He was excellent. A charming and delightful man. Mr. Karloff was also an excellent fencer and easy to work with on the set. He was a very scary one-armed Hook."[14]

As a childhood fantasy *The Secret World of Eddie Hodges* was free of the increasing levels of violence that, Karloff felt, were becoming the bane of cinema. "I never go to see the so-called horror films anymore," he said. "But I'm told, and I believe judging from what I see on TV, that they go in for horror for the sake of horror. I think that's horrible."[15] Television, though, was not excluded from Karloff's criticisms. "We're in an era of insensate violence," he said during *Thriller*'s run. "Today it's shock, so-called horror and revulsion. I think the idea is to excite and terrify rather than entertain. The story is muck for the sake of muck. The overemphasis of violence on screen and TV has reached the point of being utterly absurd."[16] He complained further, "The whole thing has become ludicrous... and the fights that these magnificent doubles engage in is unbelievable. The sound men go to town and you hear such a tremendous wallop that the poor fellow's head should be on the other side of the room, yet he doesn't even have to take an aspirin. And isn't it wonderful that the leading men are so agile that they can dodge all the bullets? That's one thing you won't find on *Thriller* – violence for the sake of violence, shock for the sake of shock. The two skilful men who are in charge of this operation – Hubbell Robinson and Fletcher Markle – are going to prove that you can have all the suspense, mystery, adventure and excitement you could want without resorting to violence. However, like I say on the show, 'I promise you, this is a Thriller'."[17]

That name, Karloff felt, was entirely apposite. "*Thriller* is a good name for a series," he said. "It's an arresting title. And it does not tie you to one type of show. You can have suspense and excitement, without getting into violence. We are not going for any knife-at-the-throat style of acting. These will be stories of mystery in which everyday people get caught in unexpected situations."[18]

The series' first episode, *Twisted Image*, starring Leslie Nielsen, was broadcast on Tuesday, 13 September 1960. "There will be none of the horror clichés on this programme," Karloff had promised, "but there will be no lack of excitement either. We will deal with normal people involved in unusual situations."[19] He was pleased, he said, the series would not be suffused with famous players. "Isn't it wonderful," he exclaimed, "to use actors instead of stars... that abused word that has ceased to have any meaning. It is a sad thing," he went on, "the casualty... the awful waste of potential talent you find today. I'm often asked by young hopefuls, 'What do I do to get started?' How do you answer them now that the old days of stock and repertory – the training grounds for an actor to learn his ABCs – are gone?"[20]

Many young actors were now advocates of a new acting style, a technique Boris Karloff described as 'an abomination' – the Method.[21] "The chief lesson young actors and actresses from these so-called modern schools learn is complete and unerring egoism," Karloff said. "They are taught to relate everything to self. They care little for the words of the author, little for the dictates of the director, little for the efforts of the other actors in the play, and absolutely nothing for the audience. Take the case of Marlon Brando, who has been known to place rubber stoppers in his ears so he cannot hear the words spoken by the other players. He is afraid that the tone and delivery of his fellow actors might harm his own interpretation of his role. Now, I ask you, how can a player contribute to a play if he sets himself above it?"[22]

Despite Karloff's enthusiasm for *Thriller* the first episode was not well received. Both the reviews and ratings were poor. The following day journalist Larry Walters wrote, "No special blame and no special credit go to Boris Karloff, who lends his voice to the new whodunit called *Thriller*, launched on NBC-TV Tuesday night. All he did was a mediocre job of narration of a new horror series. This was an hour-long crime show replete with suspense, mayhem and murder. It also included the use of a child as a hostage in a murder chase. As we remember the television code, to which NBC stations are subscribers, this play was in violation of several of its clauses. One forbids horror for its own sake, and another prohibits the depiction of kidnapping in shows likely to be watched by children. From 8 to 9 p.m., many youngsters may have been watching. They must have been terrified. If the network proposes to present more of such gruesome fare, it might as well withdraw the series."[23]

The shows that followed fared little better. *Thriller*'s network, NBC, was very unhappy and after only six broadcasts threatened to cancel. Changes had to be made and as a result the show's producer, Fletcher Markle, was replaced. Instead, William Frye was asked to take over the series.

Frye was already familiar with the television anthology having produced episodes of *Four Star Playhouse* and *General Electric Theatre*. More recently he had produced the television western series *The Deputy* at the Revue Studios where *Thriller* was shot. "One of the reasons," the show's associate producer, Doug Benton, explained, "was that Bill knew Boris Karloff. Bill said yes, he would; all he requested was that I come over from the show I was working on and work *with* him, as the story editor. And off we went."[24] Now the series would contain both crime and horror stories. Maxwell Shane would produce the crime stories while William Frye would handle the tales of horror.

"The first thing Bill and I did was to sit down and look at the shows that had been done," Benton explained. "They weren't *bad*, but they were contemporary; they didn't have any of the old Gothic horror in 'em. When MCA had sold the thing, the network thought they were going to get something in the genre of Karloff, Lugosi, *Wolf Man* – Universal was famous for that sort of thing. And here they were, getting a lot of contemporary film noir stuff, which was not what they really wanted. What the network wanted, without being able to articulate it, was horror. Bill and I looked at this stuff and Bill said, 'It's not bad, but it's not *scary*. They want something that's frightening.' I said, 'We've got Boris Karloff. We can't do the Frankenstein Monster, but we certainly can do that kind of material' – which [the previous producers] hadn't done. Bill said, 'Well, we'll do horror. I always liked that when I was a kid anyway – Frankenstein pictures and Wolf Man pictures and stuff like that.' That was all fine – except that I didn't know anything *about* it! I mean, I thought it was... *childish*, to tell you the truth. But I thought to myself, 'I better find out [about it]'."[25]

However, the problem remained – what stories would they use? Benton contacted two of his friends, the writers Charles Beaumont and Richard Matheson, but neither was able to help due to prior work commitments. Beaumont did, however, have an idea. "What Charlie said was, 'Look, I just cleaned out my garage and I sold a complete file of *Weird Tales* to Forry Ackerman'," Benton explained. "'What you do is go over to

Forry's and buy them from him, let him make a profit. Those stories are *exactly* what you need for *Thriller*.'"[26]

Born in Los Angeles in 1916, Forrest J. Ackerman became a fan of horror, fantasy and science-fiction at an early age. His maternal grandparents would often take the young boy to the cinema. "They took me to see as many as seven films in a single day," Ackerman later said. "The first movie I ever remember seeing – in 1922 – was a fantastic one called *One Glorious Day*... Fortunately, Lon Chaney – 'The Man of a Thousand Faces' as they called him – began his great career about this time and my parents took me to see everything Lon Chaney ever appeared in."[27] Then, in October 1926, the nine-year-old Ackerman purchased a copy of the Hugo Gernsback magazine *Amazing Stories*. "There was a sort of 'lobster man' on the cover," he explained, "and he seemed to be saying to me, 'Take me home, little boy. You will love me!' That was the start of a lifelong love affair with science-fiction."[28]

After service in World War II Ackerman became a literary agent specialising in science fiction and successfully built up a clientele of two hundred writers including Isaac Asimov, L. Ron Hubbard, A.E. van Vogt and Ray Bradbury. After attending the 1957 World Science Fiction Convention in London, Ackerman visited Paris and while there picked up a magazine with a picture of *Werewolf of London* (1935) on the cover. Inside were stills and stories of the classic Hollywood movie monsters. On his return to America a publisher suggested they translate the magazine into English. "But, long story," Ackerman explained, "that didn't work out. So I spoke up and I said that I had 35,000 of these stills and memories of these movies ever since I was 5½ in 1922; and I think I can put together such a magazine. So the next thing I knew I was sitting in front of a smoking typewriter; it was going so fast and smoking so badly I was afraid it was going to die of cancer. For 20 hours a day I was writing the first issue of *Famous Monsters of Filmland*."[29] Initially intended as a one-off, the magazine was published in February 1958. Its great success, however, resulted in a further 190 issues being released over the next 25 years.

Doug Benton took Beaumont's advice and contacted Ackerman. However, the collector did not want to sell his new collection. Instead, Benton proposed to lease the comic books on the proviso that, when the series was over, Ackerman could buy them back for a cheaper price than he had sold them for. Ackerman agreed and the next day Benton took delivery of boxes of *Weird Tales*.

Every weekend for the next year Benton took home 20 magazines to read. From them he would select five suitable stories. Of these Bill Frye would pick two he felt the most promising and pass these back to Benton to make the final choice. "So then we started tracking down the writers and getting the rights to the stories," Benton said. "We were paying... I don't know, not a lot, maybe $1,250, $1,500 for the rights, but it was nice for the poor writers living out in Iowa or wherever, getting a call saying that somebody was willing to pay him five times what he'd got originally, for the rights to the thing! We were buying the rights to their *names* as much as anything else."[30]

Having a host of Karloff's stature it seems odd he was not featured in more episodes of *Thriller*. In the first year he appeared in only a single story. This was not, however, Karloff's doing. "The man was up there [in years] and we didn't want to tire him out. But *he* kept twisting Bill Frye's arm – oh, he loved to act, he would have acted every *week*!"[31]

In his first season's episode, *The Prediction* (broadcast 22 November 1960), Karloff played Clayton Mace, a phoney stage mentalist whose predictions begin to come true with tragic results. At the end of the episode Mace is knocked down by a car. So, when it came to shoot that scene, Karloff was required to lie in the curb in the rain. He refused a stand-in and, instead, dutifully took his place on the ground. "Here he was," said Benton, "this 70-odd-year-old man lying in the rain out there, at night, in the cold, and [the director] John Brahm, who was a great admirer of Boris, said, 'Look, we don't have to do it *this* way'. Boris said, 'Is this the best way for the *camera?*' John said, 'Well, yes it is, but, good Lord, you don't have to lie there and have that gutter water coursing up your britches like that!' Boris said, 'Oh yes I do! This is my *work*. I *insist.*' And he lay down there for a couple of *hours* while this shot was done. That episode was one of Boris's favourites."[32]

Audrey Dalton, who appeared in the episode as Mace's assistant, Norine Burton, recalled Karloff as, "just the perfect gentleman. A terribly British, wonderful, wonderful man. Just a very nice person. But very ill. When I worked with him in that – and I did *several* things with him – he was not in the best of health. His wife Evie was always with him on the set, to take care of him."[33] Dalton added, "Karloff was quiet. Very quiet. He went to his portable dressing room. Always."[34]

Make-up man Jack Barron had been engaged for the series and would prepare Karloff for his introductory segments. On set, Karloff's stature – his bowlegs and increasingly arthritic frame – was disguised by his wardrobe. "What he had was a kind of harness or belt around his waist," Benton explained. "It had a big elastic band that went down around his instep, and when he walked, that rubber band kept the pants legs straight and people couldn't see the awful curvature of his leg. Boris had one straight leg and one bowed leg, and his harness would straighten out the pants leg so his legs didn't look like parentheses."[35]

However, when featured in one of the stories, Karloff would call on the services of a long-standing and cherished acquaintance. "Karloff would have Jack Pierce come in and work on him some times!" Benton later revealed. "Pierce was too old to work regularly, but he did come around and was very friendly with Boris."[36]

Universal had dispensed with Pierce's services in February 1947 although the official news was the make-up man had left to go into business for himself. The studio announced he had, "resigned to launch a new idea in specialised creative production make-up which will be available to the entire industry."[37] In the years that followed Pierce went freelance and, to earn a living, often worked on projects clearly below his capabilities. In 1961 he was asked to be the staff make-up artist on the series *Mr. Ed* where he would remain for the next three years.

On 3 January 1961 the episode *The Hungry Glass* was broadcast. Starring William Shatner, this ghost story was based on *Psycho* author Robert Bloch's short story *The Hungry House*. With it the tide began to turn. *Thriller* was on the up.

Two weeks later, on 17 January, Karloff made a return appearance at the San Juan Drama Festival in Puerto Rico. The previous year he had starred there in *Arsenic and Old Lace*. Now he would take the stage of the Tapia Theatre in another favourite role, that of Gramps in *On Borrowed Time*. Then, two months later, on Friday, 17 March, he opened in the play at Monterey's Wharf Theatre and Opera House. With curtain up at 8:30 p.m. Karloff spent the following week trapping Mr. Brink in the 16-foot apple tree constructed especially for the production. The play came to a close on Saturday, 25 March with two performances; a matinee at 2:30 p.m. followed by the regular evening performance. Three days later he was back at the Revue Studios shooting more introductions for *Thriller*. Having completed these, Boris Karloff returned to England.

Thriller began its second season on 18 September 1961 with *What Beckoning Ghost*, the story of Mildred Beaumont [Judith Evelyn], a woman who believes she is being driven insane.[i] This final season contained the majority of Karloff's appearances as a featured player. In *The Premature Burial* (broadcast 2 October) he played Dr. Thorne, a man who uncovers the truth about a cataleptic patient's death. In *The Last of the Sommervilles* (6 November) Karloff played another medical man, Dr. Albert Farnham, in a tale of family intrigue, murder and deceit. The episode was directed by the actress Ida Lupino who, like Karloff, had been born in Camberwell. "She was a great favourite of Boris's," Doug Benton later said, "as both used to tell slightly off-colour English stories with a great deal of relish. He had a marvellous laugh. He really would laugh when he was amused, and she is one of the best storytellers I ever heard in my life."[38]

In the dual episode *Dialogues with Death* (4 December) Karloff appeared in two roles. In the first story, *Friend of the Dead*, he played Pop Jenkins, a morgue attendant who can converse with the deceased. In *Welcome Home* Karloff appeared as Colonel Jackson Beauregard Finchess, a Southern gentleman who shares the family's decrepit mansion with his sister, Emily [Estelle Winwood] – a woman who believes she can speak with the dead.

The siblings are visited, however, by their nephew Daniel [Ed Nelson] and his wife, Nell [Norma Crane], who are on the run after a hold-up in Chicago. They plan to hide out at the mansion and, while there, retrieve the family fortune before making for South America. However, the family had received a wire from the police claiming Daniel was killed in the hold-up. As a result Emily and the Colonel conclude the couple, despite their protests, are, in fact, dead.

When they later discover the money is stashed in a coffin in the family's underground crypt Daniel and Nell go to retrieve it during a rainstorm. The crypt, however, is no longer watertight and is slowly flooding. Still, the couple retrieve the money but before they can leave Emily locks them in, sealing their fates. "Daniel just isn't used to being dead yet," Emily tells her brother. "He won't accept the fact that he and the girl have to stay buried."

Not long after his birthday on 23 November, while London was nestled in snow, Karloff caught a plane to Los Angeles to make what would be his final appearance in a *Thriller* story – *The Incredible Doktor Markesan* (broadcast 26 February 1962). This story, of a man who can raise the dead, was the first to be produced by Doug Benton who had stepped in when William Frye had gone to Rome. The episode also marked the only time Boris Karloff would work with director Robert Florey, the man who had initiated *Frankenstein* at Universal 30 years earlier before being unceremoniously removed from the picture. The director, however, now seemed reconciled with the past. "Florey told me that when Universal decided to make *Frankenstein*, it was assigned to him," Benton later said. "He did all the spadework, got the script in shape, did everything."[39] The director was happy, though, to give credit where credit was due. "He said Whale did a hell of a job, he said it was *marvellous*!," Benton said. "He was honest enough to say, 'He probably did a hell of a lot better than *I* would have!'"[40]

In 1961 Karloff had flown, it was estimated, 75,000 miles travelling back and forth between work commitments. Although now 74 years of age and not in the best of health, he still enjoyed the travelling. "My wife and I get on the plane," he said, "they give us a

i Mildred's husband, Eric, was played in the drama by Evie Karloff's ex-husband, Tom Helmore.

good dinner – and then we're there. It's a pleasant way of life."[41] He fully expected this to continue. "We have always gone back and forth," he said, "and probably we always will."[42]

The New Year began with a return to familiar ground. In late January 1962 Karloff began rehearsals on another version of *Arsenic and Old Lace*, which was scheduled to be broadcast on 5 February. The production would feature Dorothy Stickney, the actress the play's author had sought decades earlier to take the role of one of the murderous aunts. She would now play Aunt Abby alongside Mildred Natwick's Aunt Martha. Joining this trio was Tony Randall as Mortimer, Tom Bosley (Teddy Brewster), George Voskovec (Dr. Einstein) and Dody Heath as Mortimer's fiancée, Elaine. The show was directed by Karloff's old acquaintance, George Schaefer. Tom Bosley recalled:

> The Director of the show, George Schaefer, cast me along with those wonderful other actors. At the time I was starring on Broadway in **Fiorello**. We rehearsed at a well-known studio below 14th St. Almost all the TV productions were live in those days and needed plenty of rehearsal spaces. I can't recall how long we rehearsed but the last day was on a Sunday.
>   At the time I owned a small Volkswagen, called "Bugs." In those days Tony Randall lived around the corner from me, and Boris was also staying in the area. I volunteered to drive them to the studio. Thanks to Tony, we were running late and I was speeding down the East Side Drive when we heard the police siren. Tony said, "I'll take care of it" and Boris said "I'll stick my head out the window and he will probably recognise me." When the officer saw me at the wheel he smiled and said, "Hey, I saw you in the show the other night." He paid no attention to Tony or Boris and just asked me to slow down a bit. The two stars were silent the rest of the way. Boris was a joy to know. We hit it off so well that we always had lunch together during the rehearsals.[43]

One day, columnist Alan Gill dropped in during rehearsals where, he said, he "found the actors behaving like a large and happy family at a Thanksgiving reunion."[44] Mildred Natwick, however, continually missed her cue, causing the cast to roar with laughter. "I think," said Karloff, "we had best have an organist standing by."[45] George Schaefer, meanwhile, directed the proceedings from a wheelchair. This was not a medical necessity, however, but merely a means to keep him off his feet during the rigours of the proceedings. "I'll tell you what I'll do for you, Millie," the director told Natwick. "I'll eliminate that lousy line."[46]

On another day things went poorly for Boris Karloff, as Tom Bosley later explained. "As you may know Boris was quite bowlegged," he said. "One rehearsal he was coming down the stairs and tripped and fell all the way down the stairs. I was the closest to him and I rushed to see how he was. I held him in my arms and he looked up at me and said, 'I will never play this part again'. We all laughed for a long time. He was not hurt. I enjoyed being his friend for such a short time. That is what happens with actors. We meet, work, and then say goodbye. Boris was a multi generous man who was totally unselfish as a person and as an actor. I'm sorry to say I never met his wife as she did not attend rehearsals."[47] Tony Randall also thought highly of Karloff. "He was humorous," Randall later told Scott Allen Nollen, "kind, very intelligent, friendly... He was a joy to work with and a good man."[48]

Unsurprisingly, only Karloff seemed at ease with his lines during rehearsals, although he did fear his familiarity with the full text might cause problems. "You know," he later told Gill, "this play has been cut from its 2½ hour running time to 75 minutes, and I'm just afraid that one of my old lines is going to come popping out of my subconscious in that final shooting. Then we'll be cooked, won't we?"[49] Still, Karloff was aware that his role was not the focus of the piece. "The ladies ARE the play," he acknowledged, "all the rest of us are peripheral. When I used to make my final stage exit, just as the ladies are about to poison that little old man, I could feel the hand of the audience heavily on my shoulder, pushing me off."[50]

Arsenic and Old Lace was broadcast live, and in colour, from NBC-TV's Brooklyn studios on Monday, 5 February 1962. "A good time was had by all but the most squeamish… It was very funny, quite mad and a real treat," one journalist wrote.[51]

A week later (12 February) Karloff appeared on *PM*, a talk show hosted by Mike Wallace. Joining Karloff of the show was a quartet of the star's former colleagues: Julie Harris, Tony Randall, Maurice Evans and George Schaefer. A month later (11 March) he returned to television, alongside Richard Basehart and Viveca Lindfors, in another dramatic role, this time as the defending counsel Sir Simon Flaquer in Robert Hitchen's courtroom drama *The Paradine Case*.

This hour-long drama was, like *Arsenic*, broadcast live and in colour from the NBC studio in Brooklyn. "Watching it caused one to yearn for more live television," one critic wrote, "such as that seen in the days when Coe [the show's producer, Fred Coe] produced the *Philco Playhouse* from 1948 to 1955. Richard Basehart was great in the role of the defence attorney for Mrs. Paradine [Lindfors], described as 'the soul of evil'. Members of the supporting cast – Robert Webber as the valet of the murdered blind Col. Paradine, Bramwell Fletcher as the judge, Boris Karloff, and Tom Helmore [Evie Karloff's ex-husband] – all were expert in their roles. This courtroom thriller was superbly played, unlike so much of TV's suspense stuff."[52] A week after the broadcast Karloff was back at the Revue Studios to shoot more introductions for *Thriller*.

When filming the series in Los Angeles Karloff would often take lunch with Doug Benton. "He liked to get away from the studio;" Benton explained, "he didn't like to go to the commissary because people were always coming over and interrupting him. He had a favourite restaurant. Sorrentino's in Toluca Lake, where the specialty was his favourite food, sand dabs, which is a miniature flounder that is found primarily between Los Angeles and Catalina. So that's where we'd go."[53]

During lunch Karloff would regale his companion with tales of his early days. "He told me that he felt the coming of sound had ruined him, because he had this pronounced lisp," Benton said. "He didn't realise it, but it was the distinctive thing about his voice, it's the thing that everybody mimics – when they do an impression of Karloff, it's that *lithp* that comes through!"[54]

Actor Ed Nelson[ii] was also privy to Karloff's recollections, as he recalled: "I was glad to get on *Thriller*, 'cause I wanted to work with Karloff so badly. He only came in and worked the show Tuesday, Wednesday, Thursday – Thursday night he would fly to London, stay in London two days, then fly back on Monday. He was very, very nice to the cast, but I just – pestered him, almost, sitting with him and talking about the old days and talking about

<hr/>

ii Ed Nelson appeared in four episodes of *Thriller*: *The Fatal Impulse*, *The Cheaters*, *A Good Imagination* (all season 1) and *Dialogues with Death* (season 2).

his friend Bela. He would tell me how sad it was, that Bela had been almost the No.1 actor in Europe, and when he came to the United States, because of his language problem, he became this creature here! How sad that was, Karloff said. So I just loved working with him – he was a very gentle man. He had window flowers in his flat in London, and he loved to talk about flowers!"[55]

The second series of *Thriller* ended on 30 April 1962 with the broadcast of a crime story entitled *The Specialists*. Although the series had never been a top 10 show it had consistently received high enough ratings to keep it on the air. However, things were about to change. "We were on the same network, and being made at the same studio as *Alfred Hitchcock Presents*," Benton explained, "and although I never heard this *directly*, I did hear it from people who worked on both shows: Hitchcock resented *Thriller* and thought that Hubbell Robinson had infringed on his franchise. He thought that if *he* was doing this type of material for MCA and NBC, then we *shouldn't* be. Actually, we weren't doing the same thing he was; he was doing some very sophisticated 'twist' material. Hitchcock was doing the sort of thing that they started out to do on *Thriller*, but were not successful with. We [Frye, Benton *et al.*] came along and improved the ratings considerably and got a tremendous amount of press, and Hitchcock didn't like competition. I don't think he ever came out and said, 'Get rid of 'em!' but he did allow them to enlarge *his* show from a half-hour to an hour, and that made it more difficult for us to stay on. Also, Hubbell Robinson was a CBS executive operating on NBC, so there were network rivalries there, too; the NBC executives resented Hubbell showing up on *their* network with an hour franchise. And the fact that *Thriller* wasn't an out-and-out blockbuster hit – all of these were factors in the fact that we all got nice letters saying, "Good *try*, but..." [*laughs*]."[56] Perhaps tellingly, following the show's cancellation many of *Thriller*'s directors found employment on Alfred Hitchcock's show.

Years later Karloff was asked if he had enjoyed working on the series. "Very much, indeed," he replied. "The man who produced it, Bill Frye, was a very good friend of my wife and I, and I have great respect for him. I think he's a wonderful producer and a great loss to television… he's gone to Columbia to make films."[57] Doug Benton, too, liked working on the show. "Everybody had fun," he said, "they enjoyed it, they looked forward to coming to work. For the actors, it was a throwback to the old days. Bill Frye always made his people feel like they were working in the biggest features on the lot – that was another talent he had, making everybody feel like what they were doing was quality work. And it *was* – for television, it really was. Boris Karloff – God, what a lovely man. I said to him one day. 'Boris, I've never seen you without a smile on your face.' And he looked at me and he said [*exuberantly*], 'Dear boy, I'm 75 years old and I *l·l·love* what I'm doing! Don't you realise?' Well, now that I'm 70, I do [*laughs*]! 'It's heaven!' he said. 'Heaven!'"[58]

Although *Thriller* was now cancelled Karloff's association with the series would continue, albeit in a new format. That October the first edition of a new comic book entitled *Boris Karloff Thriller* was published by Gold Key Comics. Released on a quarterly basis, the comic book featured new stories of suspense and the macabre, all introduced by a cartoon likeness of Karloff. Due to the demise of the *Thriller* television series the comic's title was changed after the second issue was published. The retitled *Boris Karloff Tales of Mystery* continued to be produced until its final edition hit the shelves in February 1980 – over a decade after Boris Karloff's death.

Returning to England, Karloff was offered a role in a remake of *The Old Dark House*, a William Castle/Hammer Film co-production that would now be played mainly for laughs. Karloff turned the offer down. "The new version they showed me in London was simply not to my liking," he later explained. "I sent back the script. Wanted no part in it. After all, I've been acting in the acting profession for more than half a century. High time to pick and choose my vehicles."[59]

On Monday, 11 June 1962 Karloff appeared as the guest star on British TV on *The Dickie Henderson Show* in an episode entitled *The Gangster*. "I looked for some improvement on ITV's *The Dickie Henderson Show* and found the plot tired and the jokes heavy-going," wrote the *Daily Mirror*'s television critic, Richard Sear. "Boris Karloff seemed never quite sure whether he was supposed to be an East End gang boss or just kidding. It turned out he had reason to be doubtful."[60]

On Saturday, 30 June *The Yellow Pill* – the first episode of Karloff's new series, *Out of this World* – aired in Britain. Created by ABC Television's only woman story editor, Irene Shubik, the series was similar to *Thriller* in concept, but science-fiction in nature. Over its 13-week run Karloff introduced hour-long dramas based on works by a variety of authors such as Isaac Asimov and Philip K. Dick. Originally the series was to have opened with an adaptation of John Wyndham's *The Dumb Martian* but instead the episode was moved to *Armchair Thriller*, although Karloff did make an appearance to announce the forthcoming series. A journalist for *The Times* found the new series to be intelligent and entertaining, if a little dour. "*Out of this World*... is not for the most part even superficially cheery," he wrote. "Science fiction writers on the whole tend to take a rather gloomy view of the future... the level of writing and direction has been encouragingly high, and if the ratings have corresponded, as it seems they have, *Out of this World* may well help to banish forever the view of summer as a time when just anything will do."[61] Unfortunately only a single episode – Isaac Asimov's *Little Lost Robot* – survives. The rest were wiped after transmission.

For almost three months Karloff refrained from additional television work, although, as he had made clear in March, he had no plans to retire. "As long as they ask me," he said, "I think it would be ungracious to refuse. As an actor, I believe it is an obligation to perform as long as they want you. Anyway," he added, "I obviously love it. Or I wouldn't have been at it so long – since 1910. But think how fortunate I am. It is given to so few men to find a walk of life in which they can earn their living by doing something they love to do."[62]

In September Karloff travelled to Chicago to begin work on an episode of the popular television series *Route 66*. The show featured the exploits of two men, Tod Stiles [Martin Milner] and Buz Murdock [George Maharis], who travel across America in a Corvette convertible, inherited after the death of Tod's father. The wandering nature of the characters meant that, each week, the duo could get caught up in new adventures. For a special Halloween episode Milner and Maharis would be joined by Peter Lorre, Lon Chaney Jr. and Boris Karloff.

In that episode – *Lizard's Leg and Owlet's Wing* (broadcast, 26 October) – Karloff, Lorre and Chaney arrange to meet at Chicago's O'Hare Inn to discuss the network's offer "to produce and star in the most terrifying stories ever seen on television". Lorre and Chaney want to bring back the monsters of old, while Karloff wants to strike out in new directions. To prove the classic monsters' worth Chaney dresses as the Wolf Man and scares the attendees of a secretary's convention. They later present their photographic evidence to Karloff explaining only a single woman, Molly Cross [Jeannine Riley], remained unaffected. Knowing the young woman to be in love with her boss, Karloff concludes that if they can frighten Molly, they can frighten anyone. He therefore appears as the Frankenstein Monster while Molly is kissing her boss. When she faints Karloff mistakenly attributes his make-up as the cause and agrees the old monsters were best.

Betsy Jones-Moreland, who appeared in the episode as convention attendee Lila, recalled, "We went to Chicago to shoot that, just after Labor Day [3 September] as I recall."[63] It was not, however, a pleasant experience for Maharis. "George Maharis got *very* sick," Jones-Moreland explained. "Very, very, *very* sick – he had hepatitis. I *think* that in the episode before that, they had him in the water at night in the cold. He got real sick, and they would *not* take care of him. They would not double him or do any of the things they needed to do to protect their star. And so in the middle of our shooting, he took off! Nobody could find him. We were there, as 1 recall, an extra two weeks, on salary, *all* of us. Finally he was found, or allowed himself to be found, or came back; he had tried to recover. They were not good to him."[64]

Aside from the appearances of Lorre, Chaney and Karloff the episode is also of note as it featured both Chaney and Karloff in horror make-up. Chaney appeared as the Mummy, the Wolf Man and even his father's role of the Hunchback of Notre Dame. Karloff, meanwhile, made his final appearance as his beloved Frankenstein Monster. Unfortunately, on this occasion, and much to Karloff's disappointment, Jack Pierce did not apply the make-up. "It was a quick job with no time to do the thing properly," Karloff later lamented. "In that show the Monster was just a distant cousin to the original – which was a pity."[65]

Lizard's Leg and Owlet's Wing would prove to be the last time Karloff and Chaney would work together. Chaney would continue in television making the occasional movie, most notably perhaps, Jack Hill's cult classic *Spider Baby* (1968). He died in 1973, aged 67, and left his body to medical science. Lorre, however, would soon appear again with Karloff – and Vincent Price – in a new picture for producer/director Roger Corman – a Poe-inspired comedy-horror entitled *The Raven*.

Chapter 23

KARLOFF, CORMAN & CO.
(1962-1964)

"The truth is, I am really a very gentle person. I do enjoy playing monsters, though, and I consider myself fortunate indeed to have frightened my way into the hearts of the public."[1]
Boris Karloff (1964)

Born in Detroit in 1926, Roger Corman began his career in the movie industry as a messenger at Fox studios. Following stints as a story analyst, and a grip at KLAC-TV, he got a job reading scripts for the Dick Highland Agency. While there, Corman managed to sell – for $3,500 – a script he had co-written called *The House in the Sea*. He quit his job and instead worked unpaid on the picture – now retitled *Highway Dragnet* – for which he received an associate producer credit. It was the start of Corman's long producing career. With his third picture, *The Fast and the Furious* (1955), Corman forged a multi-picture deal with James H. Nicholson and Samuel Z. Arkoff, the heads and founders of the American Releasing Company, an independent film production company soon to be renamed American International Pictures (AIP).

In 1960 Roger Corman produced and directed *House of Usher*, starring Vincent Price. It was the first picture he made that was based upon, or inspired by, the tales of Edgar Allan Poe. Following the success of the picture, which took almost $1.5 million in rentals against its original budget of $270,000, Corman continued in the same vein making more Poe pictures. *The Pit and the Pendulum* (1961) and *The Premature Burial* (1962) followed. Then came *Tales of Terror* (1962), a trilogy of tales that included *The Black Cat*, a comic segment starring Vincent Price and Peter Lorre. The success of this picture encouraged Corman to plan another comic-horror featuring the same two stars but this time adding Boris Karloff to the mix. The new picture would be based on Poe's famous 1845 poem *The Raven*.

To fashion a script from the poem Corman once more turned to 37-year-old writer Richard Matheson, the author of the science-fiction classics *I Am Legend* and *The Shrinking*

Man. Matheson had already penned the three Poe pictures that had starred Vincent Price – *House of Usher*, *The Pit and the Pendulum* and *Tales of Terror*.

Matheson later described the process of writing for AIP. "I hardly ever worked with Corman," he said. "On almost all the scripts, I would discuss them with [AIP head] Jim Nicholson mostly, sometimes Sam Arkoff. I would write the scripts, then Roger would come in and have some comments to make, and I would make changes, and then he would direct it. Sometimes I would go in and watch, but mostly I didn't, and that was the end of my relationship with Corman. I think he followed my scripts very carefully."[2] *The Raven*, Matheson said, "had to be a comedy because it's totally comic to take a poem and expect a horror film to come out of it."[3] Only Poe's title and the eponymous bird would be retained.

Instead, Matheson devised the tale of a sorcerer, Dr. Erasmus Craven, who mourns the death of his wife Lenore. When a raven appears at the window Craven discovers it is, in fact, his fellow magician Dr. Adolphus Bedlo, transformed into the bird by the malevolent Dr. Scarabus. Craven restores Bedlo and is shocked to learn that Lenore is alive and living with Scarabus. Bedlo and his son, Rexford, accompany Craven and his daughter, Estelle, to Scarabus's castle where they discover Lenore living as Scarabus's mistress. When Craven refuses to reveal his magical secrets, he and Scarabus indulge in a climactic duel that literally brings the house down.

Although Karloff had worked with both Lorre and Price in the past this was the first time all three would feature together in the same picture. The ensemble casting was welcomed by the stars, as Vincent Price recalled. "When Boris, Peter and I heard we were going to be in *The Raven* together we were really very excited," he said, "and we called each other up and Boris said to me, 'Have you read [the poem] lately?' and I said, 'Yes' and he said, 'What's the plot?' [*laughter*]. Of course there is no plot. So we just had fun with it, and sent it up. It ended up being a very funny black comedy."[4]

Production on *The Raven* began on Friday, 21 September 1962 and, in keeping with Corman's reputation for a quick turnaround, 14½ pages of dialogue were shot on that first day. Although the three stars were friends, with a keen sense of *bonhomie*, it soon became clear, when shooting scenes that contained all three together, there was something of a clash in their individual acting styles. Lorre was an ad-libber prone to adding unscripted lines as he saw fit. "Peter had a genius for not saying many of the lines in the script, but he knew them all," Price later explained. "He felt, and rightly so I suppose, Peter being as famous a character as he was, that what the audience wanted to see was Peter Lorre – and in a way he was right... he loved to invent. I think that it was part of his training in Germany; there was a lot of improvisation going on with pictures like *M*."[5]

Publicity shot for *The Raven* (1963).

One of Lorre's contributions occurs when Bedlo accompanies Craven down into the family vault. As they make their way into the dusty crypt Bedlo comments, "Hard place to keep clean, huh?" Vincent Price later explained the origins of this line: "We were talking about it and I had said to Peter, 'It always kills me that in these pictures I keep my family conveniently buried downstairs.' Well, this killed him, so that's where that ad lib came from. He was a very funny man, Peter... very funny man."[6]

In contrast Karloff preferred the lines to be delivered as written. Price was something of a balance between the two. "The thing is," Price explained, "that if you went along with Peter... you know, I'm a fellow who knows every line in the script because I don't know how else to do it. I am not geared to improvise. But if you're working with someone who is improvising, you improvise too. There's no other way to do it. You have to go along with their gags."[7] Karloff, however, felt otherwise. "With Boris and Peter, there was tension and an incredible clash of acting methods," Roger Corman revealed. "Boris frankly did not like Peter's way of doing things. It made him nuts and threw off his memorised reading of the lines. He told me a couple times he was not happy with his scenes with Peter."[8]

Still, when working together the trio could enhance Matheson's script, as Price later explained. "Boris, Peter and I wrote some additional jokes and brought them to Roger," he said. "He approved almost everything we'd done, added business to match, and integrated the result into the script. This was one instance where the actors and the director made a funny script into an even funnier picture."[9] Price devised the early piece of business where he continually hit his head on the telescope in his study. "Immediately the audience knew that something was a little wrong," Price explained. "Then, of course, it ended up with that marvellous line of Peter's: 'How the hell should I know?' – which is an absolutely gorgeous line"[10]

Despite any disagreements over acting methods it was a happy set, as Hazel Court later attested. "Here you have three very good minds. Peter, Boris and Vincent – they were all interested in art; they all had stories to tell," she said. "And oh! I used to sit and listen to them! Peter was absolutely fascinating, although he was very sick all the time. He was always pinching me on the behind!... Boris had a bad hip. He was a very gentle man, very soft, very kind. A real English gentleman. Vinnie was the healthy one, although he did frequently groan, 'Ohhh, my knees...' He always had a dirty story."[11]

Lorre had been ill for some time. Like Bela Lugosi, he had been prescribed morphine as a painkiller (in Lorre's case after a botched gall-bladder operation) and soon became addicted to the drug. Still, despite his ill health, Lorre soldiered on. "He looked frightfully funny," Karloff said, "like a chubby little black bird. Delighted the whole crew."[12]

Lorre's illness, however, did not quell his sense of humour. It had been his idea to make his character's son, Rexford, a fawning youth, a son who is constantly seeking his father's approval and affection – even though the father cannot abide the son. For the role of Rexford Corman cast 25-year-old Jack Nicholson. Nicholson had already appeared in a number of Corman's low-budget pictures such as *The Cry Baby Killer* (1958) and *The Little Shop of Horrors* (1960). "Roger gave me one direction on that picture: 'Try to be as funny as Lorre, Karloff, and Price'. I loved those guys," Nicholson later said. "I sat around with Peter all the time. I was mad about him. They were wonderful. It was a comedy, and Roger gave us a little more time to improvise on the set."[13] Years later, while making *The Shining* for director Stanley Kubrick, Nicholson revealed Karloff's lasting influence. "This is the way that I saw Boris Karloff marks his lines," he said, while underscoring each occurrence of his character's name in the script with a large tick mark.[i] "I've copied it ever since."[14]

Olive Sturgess, who played Craven's daughter, Estelle, had been a regular face on American television, but *The Raven* marked her first feature film. She soon fell victim to the stars' pranks. "They're darlings," she told a reporter on the set. "In one scene I am locked in a stock. I was in it when the break for lunch came. They all just walked off and waved and said they'd see me later. In another scene where I am roped to a post, Vincent Price kept tickling me."[15] All, however, were victims to the black bird of the title – a raven named Jim Jr. "One thing I remember about *The Raven*," Jack Nicholson later commented, "was that the raven we used shit endlessly over everybody and everything. It just shit endlessly. My whole right shoulder was constantly covered with raven shit."[16]

The picture's final duel – the face-off between Scarabus and Craven – also caused some concern among the actors, especially Vincent Price. "Well, making one scene frightened me," he confessed. "Boris was supposed to throw a scarf at me which turns into a snake and wraps itself around my neck. We were planning the scene and I asked Roger how we were going to handle it. He said he had this man who was a snake trainer and he was going to put this boa constrictor around my neck. He said not to worry, that it was a very tame snake and it wouldn't bite. The scene began with that snake around my neck, but Roger wanted it with its head facing the camera, but it wouldn't turn that way. We had to fuss for about an hour and a half to get the shot and then it took some prying to get him off me!"[17]

On the whole, Karloff had found the shoot an enjoyable experience. "One catch, however," he later explained. "I was told by Roger Corman, our director, that I must wear this long velvet cape, an immense garment which seemed to weigh a ton. After dragging the bloody thing around behind for a day or two on the set I approached Mr. Corman and suggested, in my most gracious fashion, that the character I played would look much more sinister and effective *without* the cape. But Roger caught on; he knew why I wanted to get rid of the thing. He just looked at me and said: 'Wear the cape, Boris'. So, that was that."[18] Production on *The Raven* ended towards the middle of October, having taken 17 days to shoot – but Karloff's work for AIP was not over yet.

After making a handful of Poe pictures Corman now felt familiar enough with the author's *oeuvre* to attempt a 'Poe-esque' picture of his own. One day, a week before the end of *The Raven* shoot, Corman had commented on how it was a pity to pull down the sets that had been built up and added to throughout the entire 'Poe cycle'. So, on a rainy Sunday, Corman decided it would be possible to shoot, in two days, enough footage on the still-standing *Raven* sets to use in a new picture. Corman called *The Cry Baby Killer* screenwriter Leo Gordon and asked if he had any scripts that contained a castle. When Gordon said "No" Corman invited him over to discuss his idea. "I want to shoot the week after next," he told Gordon. "I have to shoot 60 pages in two days. That means writing about 12 pages a day for the next work-week, which is not impossible."[19]

Although Corman had no idea what the story should be about he knew the ending should differ from his pictures' usual fiery climax – with their stock footage of the burning, falling timbers, originally shot for *House of Usher*. Looking out into the rain, inspiration struck. "The opposite of fire – water!" he exclaimed. "This castle will be destroyed by a flood."[20] So, as Corman completed *The Raven*, Leo Gordon worked on the new screenplay.

---

i Karloff's methods of marking his lines can be seen in his extant script from the play *The Lark*.

When his first choice, Vincent Price, proved unavailable due to a prior commitment Corman turned to Boris Karloff. "Boris agreed to the two days work – and no more," Corman said. "He was close to 80, in failing health, and he wanted to get home to England. I called his agent and we worked out a salary – AIP had paid Boris around $30,000 for *The Raven* – plus a percentage."[21] So, unknown to AIP, and with Karloff now engaged for the picture, production began on *The Terror*.

The finished picture would tell the story of Lt. Andre Duvalier, an officer with Napoleon's army who has become detached from his regiment. Riding along the Baltic coast he pulls a woman from the sea, but she then disappears. He is then attacked by a hawk and collapses, waking in the hut of an old woman. Duvalier's search for the mysterious woman subsequently leads him to the castle of Baron von Leppe [Karloff] where Duvalier sees a portrait of the mysterious woman. However, von Leppe claims it to be a picture of his long-dead wife, Ilsa. The lieutenant later discovers that, 20 years earlier, von Leppe had killed his wife when he found her to be unfaithful. The Baron's servant, Stefan, had despatched the young lover, Erik.

Duvalier and Stefan later encounter the old woman who reveals she is, in fact, a witch and the mother of the murdered Erik. In revenge, she called Ilsa from the sea and has been using her to drive the old Baron mad, hoping he will commit suicide and damn his soul. Stefan, however, tells the woman her son is not dead but is, in fact, alive and living in the Baron's place – for it was von Leppe, and not the witch's son, who had perished decades before. The years of deception have, however, taken their toll on Erik and he now believes himself to be the Baron.

In the crypt of the castle the Baron/Erik, encouraged by Ilsa, opens the sluice gates letting the seawater in. He plans to commit suicide by drowning. Duvalier and Stefan break in and the soldier once more pulls the woman to safety. Stefan and the Baron, however, perish and when Duvalier lays Ilsa upon the ground she decomposes before his eyes.

AIP co-founder Samuel Z. Arkoff was oblivious to the unauthorised filming until one day, after production on *The Raven* had ended, he wandered onto the picture's sets. There he was surprised to discover the cemetery flats still standing. The following Monday a suspicious Arkoff returned to the soundstage and found Corman and his crew at work on *The Terror*. Although he challenged Corman, Arkoff was relatively unconcerned by his discovery. "Because," he explained, "eventually I knew he'd put that film in his vault, finish, and come to us with a production deal. So it turned out to be our picture anyway."[22]

The filming of *The Terror* proved to be an erratic affair. The picture lacked a coherent script having, instead, only a rough story outline. As the actors were oblivious to their character's fates characterisation and motivation were difficult. Karloff's scenes were shot with only three additional actors. Corman had asked Jack Nicholson to play the young lead Lt. Andre Duvalier and Nicholson, in turn, suggested his wife Sandra Knight as his leading lady. For the role of the servant, Stefan, Corman chose 34-year-old Dick Miller. "One of the highlights of my career was the opportunity of working with Boris Karloff," Miller later said.[23]

Dick Miller had been a regular in Corman's films, having made his bit-part debut in the director's *Apache Woman* (1955). A few years later he was given the lead role of Walter Paisley in the cult classic *Bucket of Blood* (1959) before making further appearances in *The Little Shop of Horrors* and *The Premature Burial*. Corman's new movie, however, would be a little different. "The picture was put together hurriedly when Karloff finished shooting a picture with Roger Corman and had a weekend left over," Miller later explained. "It was half a script with some basic scenes for Mr. Karloff to shoot and no plot. I was given my script with a few days notice and we went to work. We had three days to finish it. We shot the scenes that Boris was in with such mysterious dialogue as 'Who was the young man last night?' and 'What was he doing?' etc. I spoke to Boris about his reading lines that made no sense and asked him how he did that. He said in pure Karloff fashion, 'When that happens I revert to Karloff.' Then he did an imitation of himself."[24]

Although Corman was a master at economising, by the second day time was running short. With a little over an hour remaining on Karloff's final day the director decided on a new, untried, method of directing. He told his director of photography, John Nicholaus, "Don't slate the shots. We'll worry later what to do with this film. We'll just start and stop the camera for now. When I'm ready to roll, I'll say, 'ROLL, ACTION' and you have one second to see if anything's wrong. If you say nothing, I'll say 'ACTION' a second later and you get it going. I'm going to print the whole thing. I'll remember what I shot."[25] This unorthodox method caused some hilarity later when the dailies were shown. Jack Nicholson later described watching them as "the funniest hour I have ever spent in a projection room... You first saw Boris coming down this long hallway in the Baron's blue coat. Then he'd move out of the shot. Then I'd come down the hallway and, after I'd cleared the frame, – Roger didn't even bother to cut the camera and slate the shots – Sandra would come down the hallway. Then it was Dick's turn looking weird in his black servant suit. And then Boris would come down AGAIN, this time in his red coat. All of this shot as if in one take with no cut."[26]

Watching Karloff at work, Dick Miller could see the actor seemed rather frail. "I didn't ask him about his health but he was obviously not well," Miller explained. "For example: the walk down a long flight of stairs was shortened to the last three steps. I drove him to the Chateau Marmont where he was staying with his wife. I met her and to this day I still regret having turned down an invitation to come in and have some tea."[27]

Despite his infirmities Karloff was still required to stand waist deep in water for the picture's climactic flood scene, as Roger Corman recalled. "He was supposed to die in a terrible flood at the end of *The Terror*," Corman said, "so we came up with a tank of water, which we placed him in for the briefest amount of time, photographing him with two cameras. After a little while, we then brought in a double to do all the really waterlogged scenes."[28] The scene was intercut with shots of pouring water filmed at the Hoover Dam.

At the end of the shoot the star said his farewells. "Karloff gave me a picture of himself which mysteriously disappeared," Dick Miller recalled. "Jack Nicholson swore he didn't take it but, to this day, I am still not sure. Boris was a perfect gentleman and professional at all times. It was a thrill working with him."[29]

Karloff was gone and Corman still had only half a picture. Scheduled to leave for Europe, Corman had to find a director to take over *The Terror*. "Since I was a DGA member, I needed a non-union director. So I went to my ace assistant, a young man I had hired months earlier just out of UCLA film school. His name was Francis Coppola."[30] Coppola put together a small crew from UCLA and went out to Big Sur with Nicholson and Knight to shoot exteriors. Unbeknown to Corman, however, Coppola decided to change the script on location. A week later the crew returned and edited the footage. Coppola then departed for Ireland to shoot his first feature, *Dementia 13*. Corman now needed yet another director.

He called upon Monte Hellman to shoot footage of Nicholson and Dick Miller on the cliffs in Palos Verdes. It had been a while now since Miller had worked on the movie. "About three or four months later, when we started to shoot the rest of the picture, I had forgotten that we had shot it," Miller explained. "Corman said, 'We're going to finish the picture' and I said, 'What picture?'"[31]

Hellman, it transpired, had also decided upon a rewrite. Then, when he too departed for another job, Corman called upon the services of Coppola's former UCLA classmate Jack Hill who had also worked for the producer. "Jack just about pulled the rest of the film together but was unavailable for the wrap," Corman explained. "We needed one more day of shooting."[32] When Jack Nicholson, therefore, asked to direct the final day's scenes Corman agreed and the actor finished the shoot. The picture had taken nine months from conception to completion. Roger Corman's impromptu idea had turned into the longest production of his career. Still, for some at least, it had been fun. "I had a great time," Jack Nicholson confessed. "Paid the rent. They don't make movies like *The Terror* anymore."[33]

By this time Karloff had signed with the Lester Salkow Agency on the recommendation of Vincent Price. Working at the agency was 36-year-old Arthur Kennard who had begun his show business career as a national tour director before joining the Wynn Rocamora Agency. Then, at the age of 26, he went to work for Salkow's agency where, two years later, he became the head of the television department. Soon, with clients including Vincent Price, Peter Lorre, Lon Chaney Jr., and now Boris Karloff, Kennard became the self-acknowledged 'spook agent'.

Whenever Karloff was due to arrive in Los Angeles, Kennard would arrange to meet him at the airport. At that time passengers would disembark from the plane and descend the steps directly onto the tarmac. Kennard, however, obtained permission to drive a limousine up to the plane for Karloff to enter as soon as he had descended the stairs. This set a precedent so, subsequently, every time Karloff flew to the U.S. he would find a limousine waiting for him at the bottom of the steps. Karloff never forgot Kennard's thoughtfulness.

The Raven opened in New York on Friday, 25 January 1963 at neighbourhood theatres. *New York Times* critic Bosley Crowther thought it, "Strictly a picture for the kiddies and the bird-brained, quoth the critic."[34]

To publicise the picture, Karloff had flown to New York to join Peter Lorre on a promotional tour, sponsored by RKO theatres. Arthur Kennard accompanied the stars, travelling on a greyhound tour bus, alongside 23 off-duty policemen.[ii] The police presence, it soon became clear, was necessary – for the sight of Boris Karloff and Peter Lorre set fans off in a frenzy and they often mobbed the entourage. A method was therefore devised to handle the crowds. A flying 'V' formation was formed by the policemen, with an American-Indian whom the police nicknamed 'Chief', at its point. "And Peter and Boris... just thought it was wonderful that we had an American Indian going through these crowds to protect us," Kennard said.[35]

At the RKO theatres the stars would enter and take the stage one at a time. Around the middle of the afternoon, however, Lorre would visibly fade, even almost falling from the stage at one point early in the tour. "Make no mistake," one journalist wrote. "Peter was weary, not beery."[36] A doctor was, therefore, engaged to help. He would arrive at some of the theatres, take Lorre aside and administer an injection. "It was all very hush-hush, very private," Kennard later explained. "When the doctor showed up, they would disappear in one of the backstage rooms or behind a drape. Nobody was to go near."[37]

With Peter Lorre and promoters for *The Raven* tour, 1963.

The weather in New York that February was atrociously bad. The city had been hit by heavy snow, but it was getting progressively worse and would eventually result in the cancellation of the tour. Even so, on one of the tour dates Kennard had made a date with Rica Moore, a lady he had met in California. The snow, however, now made the prospect of a meeting increasingly unlikely. "So I decided," Kennard later explained, "I've got to get out of this, so I can keep my date back at the hotel, and it's a good time to do it, because Boris and Peter will be out in theatres, signing autographs, and I'll be back at the hotel having a drink with this lady."[38]

Kennard began to feign illness, coughing and spluttering. A concerned Karloff suggested the agent return back to the hotel but Kennard stoically refused. "By one o'clock in the afternoon, there were snow drifts piling up," Kennard said, "and it was questionable whether or not the bus would even continue... At any rate, it did, and by 1:30, I said, 'Oh... I can hardly talk'."[39] Lorre, too, now suggested Kennard return to the hotel. Although the agent suspected Lorre had seen through his ruse he took the opportunity to leave and make his way back to their accommodation at the Hampshire House at 150 Central Park South.

There Kennard met the woman and the two went upstairs to the agent's room on the 25th floor, a two-bedroom suite he shared with Peter Lorre. As the woman's feet were wet due to the snow she left her boots in the hallway. Inside Kennard lit a fire, and began his planned afternoon's strategy. The actors were not due back until around ten o'clock that evening so he would order some champagne and let his romantic rendezvous play out. But at four o'clock, as Kennard and Moore sat in front of the fire sipping champagne, the door burst open to reveal Karloff, Lorre and the entire ensemble of policemen. As a shocked Kennard watched they all made their way into Lorre's half of the suite. "The girl turned white," Kennard explained. "She couldn't believe that here was Boris Karloff – Frankenstein – and Peter Lorre coming into this suite. It was pandemonium."[40] Kennard ushered the woman out, seeing her to the freight elevator before returning to the living room. There he found everyone staring at him. "We were fully clothed and all that," Kennard said, "but it looked bad because her galoshes were sitting in the vestibule when they came in. Fur top galoshes, very feminine. Something I wouldn't wear."[41] Then the 'trial' began.

Seated in the middle of the room Kennard was subjected to prosecutor Peter Lorre's questions as Karloff's judge kept order. "Peter, with that insane way he smoked cigarettes, would ask these vulgar questions," Kennard explained. "Did I have any intent of molesting this young lady? Well, of course I did. Why do you think I made this whole thing up to leave the tour in the first place? And Boris was saying, 'He does not have to answer that. That's an uncalled for question,' and so on."[42]

Throughout the trial the drink had flowed freely. Karloff and Lorre were light drinkers but Kennard and the police were getting more and more tipsy. Eventually Karloff called a recess and the stars called the kitchen and had tray after tray (at $80 a time) sent up to feed the policemen. The following morning Kennard awoke with a hangover and, upon entering the living room, found the 23 lawmen in a likewise state. "It was the funniest experience I've ever had in my life," he later said.[43]

The Raven opened in Los Angeles on 30 January 1963 where it played in 23 theatres and drive-ins in a double feature with *Warriors Five*, an Italian made war movie starring Jack Palance. "Lorre, Karloff and Price have a field day," the *Los Angeles Times* wrote, "squeezing each macabre scene dry, and still not overlooking comedy sensibilities."[44] After the picture opened in Chicago on 27 February one reviewer wrote, "It's fairly thin fare, made up mostly of camera tricks, and some very obviously false scenery, but Peter Lorre's performance is mildly entertaining. Youngsters may find it fun."[45] Despite mixed reviews the picture took, after distribution costs, $1,400,000 – a healthy return on the initial investment of $350,000.

Poster for *Black Sabbath* (1963).

Karloff's second picture for Corman, *The Terror*, opened in Los Angeles later that year on Wednesday, 25 September in a double bill with Coppola's horror picture *Dementia 13*. "*The Terror* is a spooky exercise in celluloid chills, starring Boris Karloff, that old terror himself," wrote Margaret Harford of the *Los Angeles Times*, "who spreads the creeps deftly over this American-International film... Nothing extraordinary about *The Terror* except that Karloff is more to be pitied than shunned, though he keeps up a fine pretext of villainy throughout most of the picture... It moves like a stately pavane but the authors exhibit some of that old Edgar Allan Poe touch for haunted happenings."[46]

In   March   1963,   not

long after appearing with Peter Lorre on Hy Gardner's talk show (3 March), Karloff flew to Rome to make *I tre volti della paura* (*The Three Faces of Fear*) for director Mario Bava.

Born in San Remo, Italy in 1914 Bava had been immersed in the world of movie-making from an early age, raised in the shadow of his father, the celebrated special effects designer and silent movie cinematographer Eugenio Bava. After serving his apprenticeship with his father Bava began to forge a career as a cinematographer's assistant, eventually becoming a director of photography.

He began directing second-unit scenes but in 1956 while shooting the horror picture *I vampiri* (a.k.a. *The Devil's Commandment*), the director walked out and Bava was recruited by Galatea Film to finish the picture. After he was required to step in and take over the direction on two further pictures Bava was rewarded with the opportunity to make a picture of his own. It was, he later admitted, a mixed blessing. "I didn't want to be a director," Bava said, "because, in my opinion, a director must be a true genius; besides, I was comfortable being a cameraman, and earned a lot of money."[47] Still, he had an idea about the type of picture he would like to make. "Because," he explained, "at that time, the [Hammer] *Dracula* film had been released, I thought I might do a horror film."[48]

From this desire came *La maschara del demonio* (*Black Sunday*, 1960), a tale of vampires starring English actress Barbara Steele. The picture was an international success and AIP, who had released an edited version of the picture under its banner in America, arranged to release further Galatea Film productions including *Black Sabbath*, the Bava directed anthology consisting of three individual stories with linking on-screen narration by Boris Karloff.

The trilogy of tales began with *Il telefono* (*The Telephone*), the story of a high-class call-girl who begins to receive threatening telephone calls. The second story, *Il wurdulak* (*The Wurdalak*), featured Karloff as Gorca, the patriarch of an 18th century Russian family who has been transformed into a vampiric creature, the

Top: With Mario Bava. Middle: Clowning with Bava. Botom: Karloff studies his script during the filming of *Black Sabbath* (1963).

wurdalak, a walking corpse that yearns to drink the blood of those it had loved in life. The final tale, *La goccia d'aqua* (*The Drop of Water*), told the tale of a nurse who steals a ring from the finger of a recently deceased medium – with chilling consequences.

Before AIP released the picture in America, however, a number of changes were made. The picture was dubbed in English and so Karloff's voice could now be heard on the soundtrack. Roberto Nicolosi's original score was replaced by one by AIP's resident composer Les Baxter. Different Karloff introductions were used and the order of the stories was changed. They would now run *The Drop of Water*, *The Telephone* and then *The Wurdalak*. Cuts were also made to *The Telephone* to excise the story's lesbian subtext and a supernatural element was added – the caller would now be a ghost. The picture's original parting shot of the wurdalak Gorca on a 'horse' was also excised, as Karloff later explained. "It was a most amusing ending, really," he said. "Sort of getting on this rocking horse and everything. The producers in Hollywood didn't like it, and they had a very valid point. If there had been any suggestion of comedy in any of the three stories, then this would have tied in. But there was no suggestion whatsoever, and this would have come as such a shock that it would have destroyed the film. I don't know if they were right. I think they must have been because they are very intelligent men and very successful [Nicholson and Arkoff of American-International]. They know their market, they know their field very well, and they've been extremely considerate to me. I'm most grateful to them."[49]

The deletion of the Italian ending probably came as a disappointment to Karloff despite AIP's reasoning. For, according to Mario Bava, Karloff had been more than enthusiastic when told of the planned ending. "Karloff embraced me," Bava explained, "and said that, in front of those huge fans, he would surely catch pneumonia... that he might even die... but that he didn't care, because it was the first time in his career he had enjoyed himself so much!"[50]

Black Sabbath was scheduled to open in the U.S. on 6 May 1964 in a double feature with another Bava picture – *The Evil Eye*, a thriller starring John Saxon. AIP's advertising-publicity director, Milton I. Moritz, announced full colour television spots had been produced to advertise the movie. It was a first, Moritz said, for both AIP and the horror picture in general.

Journalist Bob MacKenzie, writing for the *Oakland Tribune*, thought the picture, "a dandy little collection of three horror stories, a cut or three above most of the terror-in-triplicate films we've been seeing lately. Boris Karloff appears in only one of the trio but introduces the others á la Hitchcock. The old master's round-eyed, hollow-voiced spookery is more comic than scary these days, but he is a grand old charmer and always fun to watch."[51] The picture opened in Los Angeles two weeks later, on 20 May, at 30 theatres and drive-ins. It reached New York on 10 July, where it was relegated to second feature status, supporting *McHale's Navy*, the motion picture version of the popular television comedy.

Asked some years later if he had enjoyed the experience of filming in Italy Karloff replied, "Very much – except that it was brutally cold, and the hotel was a sort of marble palace. They don't warm up with one match being struck, and it was there that I got quite ill. I came back to England at the end of the film. I was able to complete it with a good deal of difficulty. I was desperately ill that summer. I had a very narrow squeak, and it left my lungs, as you can hear, very short winded. I had pneumonia."[52]

On 6 April 1963 Evie Karloff told the press her husband, after being bed-ridden for two weeks, was up and around the house. The cause of his illness, the newspapers claimed, was the inhalation of smoke on the set of the Bava picture. For five months Karloff refrained from film and television work. He did, however, indulge in less strenuous work and recorded more works for Caedmon Records. It was, in fact, his busiest period for the company.

Since his first Caedmon album, *Just So Stories*, was released in 1956 Karloff had lent his voice to many tales and poems. In 1958 he narrated Kenneth Graham's story *The Reluctant Dragon* and the poems *The Pied Piper* (by Robert Browning) and Lewis Carroll's *The Hunting of the Snark*. In August 1959 Caedmon released *The Ugly Duckling and Other Tales* by Hans Christian Andersen. "The 'gentle monster' reads beautifully with sincerity and tenderness the touching Andersen fairy tales," wrote *Billboard*.[53] In January 1960, when writing of the current spate of well-known performers – such as Julie Andrews, Joyce Grenfell, Stanley Holloway and even Eleanor Roosevelt – making records for children, journalist Herbert Mitgang expressed his clear preference. "Our favourite narrator of children's stories is Boris Karloff," he wrote. "That voice, coming from way down, has a resonance and storytelling authority that grips... He is heard on two Caedmon long-play records: *The Ugly Duckling*, which also includes five other tales by Hans Christian Andersen; and *More of Kipling's Just So Stories*, this set including *The Elephant's Child*, *How the Leopard Got His Spots*, *Armadillos* and *Old Man Kangaroo*. Mr. Karloff must like these stories; he sounds it."[54] The early 1960s, though, would see his largest Caedmon output. The first four years of the decade saw the release of numerous recordings ranging from works by Rudyard Kipling, Charles Dickens, classic fairy stories, Aesop's fables – and even a play by William Shakespeare.

In August 1960 Caedmon Records had announced it intended to make recordings of all 37of Shakespeare's plays and had signed such luminaries as Sir John Gielgud, Michael Redgrave, Trevor Howard, Ralph Richardson, Stanley Holloway, Anthony Quayle, Richard Burton and Margaret Leighton to realise the project. The plays would be released, in both mono and stereo editions, under the banner of the Shakespeare Recording Society. The recordings would all be made in London and the stars would be transported to the capital when required. The first recordings were advertised in the press in January 1961: *Macbeth* (starring Anthony Quayle), *Othello* (with Frank Silvera, Cyril Cusack, and Anna Massey), *The Taming of the Shrew*, starring Margaret Leighton, and Sir John Gielgud and Dame Peggy Ashcroft in *The Winter's Tale*.

Although Karloff had rejected Julie Harris's idea to play *King Lear*, claiming he was too old to tackle Shakespeare for the first time, he agreed to star in the titular role of the ancient British king in *Cymbeline*, alongside Claire Bloom, John Fraser and Alan Dobie. It is Karloff's only confirmed performance in a Shakespeare play.[iii]

Tackling 'The Bard' meant, of course, Karloff would be unable, as he was sometimes accustomed, to rewrite lines to accommodate his lisp. Still, Claire Bloom later said of her co-star, "I remember him as kind and polite, and having no troubles whatever with speaking Shakespeare."[55] One reviewer wrote, "Boris Karloff, in one way, has the easiest task of all as Cymbeline, for a monarch who has lost his way is something like an actor who has on the whole given up Shakespeare and who finds it difficult to articulate meaningfully the words that the true kings usc. Anyway, this characterisation is curiously right most of

---

iii In 1936 Karloff inaccurately claimed he was appearing in *Julius Caesar* when the 1912 Regina tornado hit. "Another time," he had said, "when I was playing *Julius Caesar* for $25 a week in Regina, Saskatchewan, with only a cambric tunic and a tin breast-plate between me and a 45 degree below zero temperature, a tornado blew down the theatre. The next day, I took the job of helping clear away the debris!"

the way through, whereas even the talented and sensitive Claire Bloom often errs by a kind of palpitating reticence. Nevertheless, the compete recording of a rarely performed and strangely interesting play has taken place; the reading is generally clear and tasteful, and in two or three cases (notably that of Pamela Brown as the Queen) eloquent and subtle: and both the ideas and the power of the poetry come through (sometimes, it is true, unassisted if unimpeded)."[56]

In September 1963 another two albums of Karloff's storytelling were released. Unlike his Caedmon efforts these were new stories of the macabre and the supernatural. Penned by Michael Avallone the tales appear to have been originally recorded by Karloff back in 1957 to be broadcast on a prospective radio show entitled *The Frightened* although, it would seem, no broadcasts of the material ever took place. In spring 1957 a *Tales of the Frightened* magazine was published by Republic Features Syndicate, which included stories by a selection of writers including Avallone and John Wyndham. The second – and final – edition appeared that August and included the tale *The Frightened*, allegedly written by Karloff himself.

A book, *Tales of the Frightened*, was also published to accompany the album's release. "Mystery writer Michael Avallone has authored a series of short horror tales to appear as pocketbooks soon from Belmont books," *Billboard* announced. "A number of these have been packaged into a moving series of records with narration in the hair-raising style of Boris Karloff. The scripting bears strongly Hitchcockian touches, as the master horror storyteller reads six tales on each disc, with suitable sound effects and musical accompaniment. A professional job all the way and horror fans will find plenty of excitement."[57] The *New York Times* considered the records which, it informed its readers, were "told with chilling relish by Boris Karloff", to be a "great thing to discourage too frequent visits by the less amiable members of the family."[58]

In addition to these retail recordings Karloff also continued to produce his short broadcasts for *Reader's Digest*, a practice he had indulged in since the late 1950's. "Evie and he used to do this tape," Bernard Coleman explained. "He would do this reading… and it was like a trailer to sell [the magazine] and it went out on the entire radio networks of America – this one reading of one story, which was his trailer. And that was his other big pension cheque that he used to get, and he did it for years and years and years. Wherever he was, he'd do this reading."[59] Recorded on reel-to-reel tape, these previews were pressed onto vinyl and distributed to radio stations for broadcast, one episode per day.

In September 1963 Karloff made his return to movies following his illness. Arriving back at the Producers Studio on Melrose Avenue, Los Angeles he began work on *The Comedy of Terrors*, his third picture for Roger Corman.

Following the success of *The Raven* AIP had approached the picture's screenwriter, Richard Matheson, and asked him to pen another comic-horror. Matheson then concocted a tale of two undertakers who, when business is slow, resort to murder to supply themselves with custom. Waldo Trumbull, the head of the company, would be played by Vincent Price while Peter Lorre would play his unwilling assistant, Felix Gillie. Again Karloff would feature, plus another of his old colleagues, Basil Rathbone, who was especially pleased to be included. "I wrote the script, and everybody loved it," Matheson recalled. "I remember a lunch we had just before they shot, where we all went out. They were so delighted with the script, especially Basil Rathbone who was just bubbling, burbling all over the place about it. He was supposed to play the part that Boris Karloff was gonna play… And then Boris Karloff by that time, his legs were in such a bad shape. The part that Basil Rathbone played required a lot of movement, a lot of action. He [Karloff] said, 'Let's reverse the parts', so he played their old father who didn't have to do much of anything."[60]

Rathbone was, indeed, pleased to be making the picture with his fellow actors. "We like each other," he said. "We respect each other. As an example, Vinnie (Price) said, 'I've asked them to favour you with the camera in this scene because it's your entrance.' This is not usual. You won't find this with many stars. Boris Karloff and I have been friends in pictures for a long time. Vinnie and I have done several pictures together. One was delightful with Bob Hope. I don't think it ever got released.[iv] We all know each other – three old pals."[61] Yet, despite his pleasure in making the movie, Rathbone was not enamoured by the picture's content. "It doesn't amuse me to chase someone down a corridor with an axe," he said.[62]

To direct the picture Matheson suggested 58-year-old Jacques Tourneur who had previously directed a Matheson-scripted episode of *The Twilight Zone* entitled *Night Calls* (1961), and had earlier helmed the British classic *Night of the Demon* (1957). Tourneur had also worked with Val Lewton, having directed *Cat People* (1942), *I Walked with a Zombie* and *The Leopard Man* (both 1943). "He was such a professional," Matheson later said. "He knew exactly what he was doing."[63]

Filming began on *The Comedy of Terrors* on Wednesday, 4 September 1963 on a 15-day schedule. "In movies there is very seldom any rehearsal at all," Vincent Price explained. "So Roger would get Boris and myself, and Peter and Basil and whoever was in the pictures, to come down and read. I think we were supposed to do one day of that and then we were to be paid. We would all get so carried away, though, knowing that the actual shooting schedule was so short. So we really welcomed the opportunity to be able to walk around the set and sort of familiarise ourselves with what the ambience of the story was. It was not so much a characterisation rehearsal, but a run-through. We'd walk around the set and Roger would say, 'Now this is what is going to happen here', and then we'd move on to the next scene. So he was very smart at that and, as I say, we all went along with it because it meant so much to us."[64]

Once again the stars were allowed to bring their own suggestions to the set. "Boris, Peter, Basil, all of us, we used to talk about what really scares people," Price said. "One time, we were trying to figure it out, and Boris said, 'Cobwebs'. And I said, 'Oh, come on, Boris, cobwebs don't scare anybody!' And he said, 'They scare men. Men hate cobwebs!' And it's absolutely true, you know; they're sticky. Women don't mind them; they just think you're a bad housekeeper. But men hate 'em! So we rigged up this huge cobweb, and I walked straight into it, and this thing went right across my face, and the whole male audience went 'Yeeech!'"[65]

Vincent Price also enjoyed the experience of working once again with his friends. "We had a wonderful time," he said. "One time, one of the big magazines, *LOOK* or *LIFE*, sent out a reporter to try and make fun of us. He came on the set and was really sort of grand, you know, and when he saw that we were really enjoying making the picture, he wrote the most wonderful article about the joy we had in making something that was really pure entertainment."[66]

Karloff's daughter, Sara Jane, occasionally visited her father during production, as she had on *The Raven*. "I had such a good time on those sets," she recalled, "mainly because all

---

iv *Casanova's Big Night* was released on 7 April 1954.

this remarkable men had such camaraderie, professional respect for one another, humour and enjoyment of what they where doing. It was marvellous to see."[67] Hearst Newspapers journalist Marianne Means also visited the set where she met Karloff and his co-stars. "They were all very kind to me," she later said.[68]

On Thursday, 5 December 1963 *The Comedy of Terrors* had a sneak preview at RKO's 86th Street Theatre in New York, followed by a cocktail reception held by AIP president James H. Nicholson. "It will be one of AIP's reliable moneymakers... *Comedy of Terrors* is a smart film... Without overstressing it, it is a good comedy too," wrote *Hollywood Reporter*. "There is not much about timing and attack to be learned by such as Price, Lorre, Boris Karloff and Basil Rathbone... Although these actors are all now in the character range, their names – particularly in combination – still have potency at the box office."[69]

The picture opened in Los Angeles (in 46 theatres and drive-ins with the thriller *Madmen of Mandoras*) and at the Palace in New York on 22 January 1964. Philip K. Scheuer of the *Los Angeles Times* was not a fan. "I found in it little of comedy and less of terrors; just a series of predictable gags repeated *ad infinitum, ad nauseum*; and besides, death isn't funny in the first place (unless occasionally, perhaps, when it is treated as high art). I felt ashamed to watch once reputable actors hamming it up all over the place, making a mockery of whatever is left of their poor images."[70] The critic for the *New York Times* agreed. "A musty, rusty bag of tricks rigged as a horror farce," he wrote, "spilled onto the screens of the Palace and the Brooklyn Albee yesterday titled *The Comedy of Terrors*. It isn't and it hasn't."[71] Yet despite such negative reviews the picture was another success for AIP. "It made money," Richard Matheson said. "Everything they did made money. I mean, they didn't spend enough to lose money."[72]

The author's comic-horrors for AIP were, in fact, so successful the company was soon

clamouring for more, as Matheson later explained. "They liked *Comedy of Terrors* so much," he said, "they thought, 'Well, we'll put them all in a picture again and add Tallulah Bankhead to it' – and so I wrote, I think, a very funny script called *Sweethearts and Horrors* about the Sweetheart family where Peter Lorre was a magician who had a fire sequence in his magic act and burned down every theatre he ever worked in – and Boris Karloff had a children's show, he was 'Uncle Dudley,' the kindly old television host who he hated children. Vincent Price was a ventriloquist and Basil Rathbone was an ageing music-hall comedy star, and Tallulah Bankhead was a movie actress, an ex-big star. And they were all completely vicious to each other, except for Peter Lorre, of course. You couldn't make Peter Lorre vicious. He had to be the victim, really. It was filled with sight gags. It would have made a wonderful picture. I don't

Karloff, Price, Lorre and Rathbone in a publicity shot for *The Comedy of Terrors* (1963).

know why they never made it… well, I *do* know… about three or four of them died before they could make it, so that kind of took the wind out of the sails."[73]

During the making of *The Comedy of Terrors* Karloff recorded the narration for a documentary on Hans Christian Andersen for CBS's *Chronicle*, to be broadcast on Christmas Day. "The programme, which will be on from 7:30 to 8 p.m.," the *New York Times* explained, "has no plot and no actors. Don Kellerman, the producer, is assembling 3,000 photographs taken by Marvin Lichter of Andersen's milieu – the Denmark countryside, waterfront and manor houses. A spokesman for Mr. Kellerman said: 'We are trying to get an impressionistic photographic survey of the place where Andersen lived and Denmark as it is today. It is an attempt to get away from the straight biography'."[74]

A week later, on 31 December, AIP announced their 1964 budget had been raised to $25 million – a 25% increase on the previous year. "Poe and beach parties continue to be the motif," wrote the *Los Angeles Times*, "largely due to the commercial draw of the former in an endless horror series with Vincent Price, Peter Lorre, Boris Karloff, Basil Rathbone, *et al*, and of the recent musical called, simply, *Beach Party*. Already completed is *Muscle Beach Party* and now on the drawing boards is *Bikini Beach*. *The Comedy of Terrors* will be followed by *The Graveside Story* – with the same nefarious gang of ghouls, plus Elsa Lanchester. And so it goes."[75]

From the beginning, however, there were problems with their new comic-horror. In November 1963 the New York hotel room of AIP president James H. Nicholson was burgled and among the items stolen was the script of *The Graveside Story*. Although it was not AIP's only copy Nicholson was concerned the thief would sell, or give, it to someone who would then steal the idea. Even though this did not happen *The Graveside Story*, like *Sweethearts and Horrors*, never materialised, despite numerous press announcements of the picture's imminent production.

In January 1967 the *Los Angeles Times* announced Vincent Price and Gloria Swanson were set to star in the picture, which was scheduled to begin filming in Toronto's 1911 gothic revival castle Casa Loma the following month. Then, in June 1969, Bette Davis and Mickey Rooney were touted as Vincent Price's co-stars in the picture, now set to start filming in Miami. Davis, though, soon denied any involvement. "Where did the story come from I'm going to star in *Graveside Story* in Florida?" she asked. "Can you imagine *me* doing this?"[76]

While the AIP pictures remained in the pipeline, a Karloff-penned article appeared in the January 1964 edition of *Reader's Digest*. "How NOT to be a Full-Time Bogeyman" was a single-page essay in which he explained how children's fairy tales, many of which he had recorded for Caedmon, were not so far removed from his own particular niche. "As one who has made a career of playing fiends, demons, mad scientists and other assorted monsters," he wrote, "I admit to what may seem an unusual interest – the study of nursery tales. But the truth is that many of these children's favourites rank among the most chilling of horror stories. Do you recall, for example, the witch who fattened up boys and girls for the oven in *Hansel and Gretel*? Or the wicked queen who commanded the huntsman to kill Snow White and bring back her heart? And what about Bluebeard, and that collection of murdered wives he kept in a closet? These characters, I submit, are fully as terrifying as any of the weird and twisted characters I have portrayed."[77]

The end of *The Comedy of Terrors* marked the beginning of a hiatus in Boris Karloff's horror film career. While the proposed AIP horror-comedies remained in production limbo the star would agree to appear in a curious collection of movies, the first of which, *Bikini Beach*, would be prompted by the untimely death of his long-time friend and acquaintance, Peter Lorre.

German poster for *Die, Monster, Die!* (1965).

Chapter 24

SOLDIERING ON

(1964-1966)

"Look at me at 78. I still have opportunities to do things. I really love the work. How many people can say they have spent their lives doing what they really love doing?"[1]
Boris Karloff (1966)

A t around noon on Monday, 23 March 1964 Peter Lorre's housekeeper, Beatrice Lane, entered the actor's bedroom in his West Hollywood apartment at 7655 Hollywood Boulevard. There she found Lorre lying beside his bed, still clad in his nightclothes. The cause of death, it was later determined, was a cerebral haemorrhage. Peter Lorre was 59 years old.

The actor's funeral was held on Thursday, 26 March at Pierce Brothers Hollywood Chapel. Rabbi William Sanderson conducted brief rites and Vincent Price delivered the eulogy before the collection of mourners that included Lorre's estranged wife, daughter and his brother Andrew, as well as friends and colleagues which included Red Skelton, Jerry Lewis, Phil Harris, Gilbert Roland, Sebastian Cabot, John Carradine and Edward G. Robinson.

"This man was the most identifiable man I ever knew," Price told the congregation. "No part of him was other than himself. His voice, his face, the way he moved and his laugh. He loved to entertain, to be a face-maker – and the audience which was his world loved him from the glimpses he gave them of his heart and mind."[2] Outside the chapel Skelton, who had stopped production on his television show, on which Vincent Price was appearing, to attend the funeral said, "We have lost a great actor, a man of great depth. I loved him and loved to watch him work."[3] After the services Lorre's body was cremated and inured in the Abbey of the Psalms at the Hollywood Memorial Park cemetery. "I miss Peter terribly," Karloff said three years later, "he was a delightful man and a truly original actor – there was none like him."[4]

With Lorre's passing, AIP was left with a problem. The actor had been scheduled to feature in the next of the company's popular *Beach* series, which starred Frankie Avalon and Annette Funicello as the surfer Frankie and his girlfriend Dee Dee. They found a replacement, however, in Boris Karloff who arrived on set to appear, albeit briefly, as an art-dealer in *Bikini Beach*.

With Jim Nicholson, Keenan Wynn and friend during production of *Bikini Beach* (1964).

The picture concerned Frankie's rivalry with a British singer known as 'The Potato Bug'[i] [Avalon, again] whose relationship with Dee Dee is causing the surfer some concern. To make matters worse the millionaire Harvey Huntington Honeywagon III [Keenan Wynn] plans to develop the beach into a housing complex for the elderly. Karloff made his appearance late in the picture when, during a fight scene between the surfers and the motorcycle gang, 'The Ratz', led by series regular Erich von Zipper [Harvey Lembeck], he examines, then agrees to purchase, a painting – unaware it is the work of Honeywagon's chimpanzee. "Have it sent to my place and there'll be a cheque for a thousand dollars waiting," he tells the artist/mechanic 'Big Drag' [Don Rickles]. "I must tell Vincent Price about this place," Karloff says to the camera before turning towards the ruckus exclaiming, "What monsters!"

Bikini Beach opened in Chicago on Friday, 24 July 1964 and at 30 Los Angeles theatres and drive-ins on 19 August. "A couple of truckloads of good-looking healthy kids, plenty of singing and dancing, and solid comedy from some old pros add up to two hours of mindless relaxation at theatres and drive-ins everywhere," wrote the *Los Angeles Times*.[5]

Aside from the film work, Karloff had also agreed to make a few television appearances while in the States. On 21 April 1964 he guested on *The Garry Moore Show* where he appeared in *Karloff's Kiddie Korner*, a parody of the children's television show *Captain Kangaroo*, and gave a rendition of the popular song *Tiptoe Through the Tulips*. Then, on 2 June, he appeared as a guest on Johnny Carson's *Tonight Show*.

This proved to be the last of Karloff's television work for 1964 and instead he spent the rest of the year in England, save for a brief mid-September sojourn to Ireland to attend the final few days of the Cork Film Festival. His short stay in the city naturally drew the attention of the press and on one occasion Karloff graciously tolerated an RTE reporter who had commented on how it must be rather monotonous for the star to play horrific monsters all the time.

Within months Karloff was back in the U.S. to appear as the special guest on *The Entertainers*, an hour-long variety show starring Carol Burnett. Broadcast on 16 January 1965, a bespectacled Karloff appeared with his host in a bookshop sketch. Burnett played a nervous sales assistant who is frightened when the horror star pays the shop a visit. "My dear girl, you have nothing to fear from me," he informs her. "You're making the mistake

i *Bikini Beach* director William Asher later revealed the script had originally been written for The Beatles. However, in the wake of their successful appearances on *The Ed Sullivan Show* in February 1964, the group dropped out and the character of The Potato Bug was written in as a replacement.

of mixing me up with the parts – the terrible parts, monster roles – that I play in films. In real life my great interest is in gardening. Why, only today I planted a new flowerbed!" "Who's under it?" Burnett asks. Later in the show Karloff gave a rendition of the *Mary Poppins* song, *Chim Chim Cher-ee* accompanied by the Lee Hale Singers.

Back in 1951 Karloff was asked if he had seen any of the then current batch of sci-fi pictures. "No, but I'd like to," he had replied at the time. "I understand they now have monsters who are vegetables. Fascinating!"[6] Now 14 years later, he would star in one for AIP – *The House at the End of the World*. Based on H.P. Lovecraft's 1927 tale *The Colour Out of Space*, the picture would be the first to be directed by Daniel Haller, the art director who had worked on all of Karloff's AIP pictures. Boris Karloff began work on the picture at Shepperton Studios in Surrey in late February 1965. "I end as a mass of fungus," he revealed to one reporter.[7]

The House at the End of the World told the story of an American scientist, Stephen Reinhart [Nick Adams], who arrives at the English village of Arkham intending to visit his fiancée, Susan Witley [Suzan Farmer]. When the locals refuse to give him directions to Susan's family home Reinhart makes his own way across some blasted countryside and arrives at the Witley house. There he meets Susan and her crippled father, Nahum [Karloff], who does not welcome the stranger. Stephen, however, reveals he had been invited by Susan's mother, Letitia [Freda Jackson], and is therefore taken to see the bedridden woman. Letitia, her form obscured by a veil around her bed, advises the scientist to take Susan and leave.

After the Whitley's servant suddenly dies, Stephen and Susan enter Nahum's greenhouse where they find strange animals and giant plants, mutations caused by a meteorite Stephen later discovers housed in the cellar. Susan's father, it transpires, has been using the rock in his experiments, intending to make the surrounding area lush with vegetation. However, its radiation has infected members of the household and later causes a crazed Letitia to attack Stephen and Susan.

After Letitia dies, a regretful Nahum tries to destroy the rock but is attacked by his (previously missing) maid Helga, another victim of the meteorite's radiation. Both she and the rock are destroyed but Nahum, too, is now contaminated. He begins to glow and change and, in his crazed state, chases after the young couple. Falling over the banister, however, he spontaneously ignites after hitting the floor. The young couple escape as the flames consume the Witley house.

Karloff's role in the picture was, he felt, reminiscent of the 'mad doctor' movies he had made for Columbia two decades earlier. "Here again," he explained, "the villain of the play isn't really a nasty sort of fellow. He was once a perfectly ordinary, kind man who makes a mistake of tampering with evil forces."[8]

By now, however, Karloff's health had deteriorated further. Off set he now used a cane to support his weak left knee, although he would later be fitted with a full leg brace as his joint continued to weaken. To accommodate his disability during the shoot Karloff was provided with a wheelchair, which had been unearthed in a London antique market. He would now play most of his scenes in this device. "It's rather a sinister contraption," Karloff said, "but somebody thoughtfully wrote it into my part so that I won't have to work my poor old legs too hard."[9]

Interviewed on set during production he admitted, once again, the important role providence had played in his life. "I've been darn lucky," he said. "Being type-cast is the best thing that could happen to an actor. I've had a good life and I intend to die with my boots – and all this make-up – on, I'm quite content with what I'm doing."[10]

The interview was briefly interrupted by a film official who wanted to run through the next day's work. "Any jokes?" Karloff asked, referring to his dialogue. "Not many," came the reply. "I think I can wing it," Karloff said, then turning to his interviewer he commented, "You know, dialogue can be reduced to a minimum in these films. It should be – the less spoken, the better."[11] When asked if Mrs. Karloff sees her husband's films, "Only under duress," came the reply.[12]

The picture, now retitled *Die, Monster, Die!*, opened in Connecticut on 27 October 1965 and in Baltimore a week later. The picture was released in Los Angeles at 20 city-wide theatres and drive-ins on 15 December in a double-bill with *Planet of the Vampires*, AIP's redubbed and retitled version of Mario Bava's *Terrore nello spazio*. "A standard but stylish piece of Gothic horror," the *Los Angeles Times* wrote of Karloff's picture, "this American-International picture has been directed with flair by Daniel Haller and acted with conviction by a cast headed by a pair of pros, Boris Karloff and Nick Adams. Pure haunted-house hokum all the way… At 77, silver-thatched Karloff retains the lovable menace that he has been projecting for the past 35 years."[13]

Karloff's involvement in his next picture was announced back in October 1965 when the press revealed – a little inaccurately – the star would lend his voice to the character of a mouse in *The Daydreamer*.

Five months earlier, on Friday, 28 May, the head of Embassy Pictures, Joseph E. Levine, hosted a luncheon at the Hemisphere Club in New York where he previewed recordings that had been made for *The Daydreamer*, a new animated picture the makers described as "the dream-adventures of young Hans Christian Andersen and his search for the Garden of Paradise".[14] Written and produced by Arthur Rankin Jr. and directed by Jules Bass the picture, which was by then half-completed, would feature a combination of live action and stop-motion animation. The live action sequences, starring Jack Gifford as Papa Andersen and Paul O'Keefe as his son Chris, were set to commence shooting on 15 June in six countries: the United States, Japan, Canada, England, France and Denmark. Hayley Mills, Patty Duke, Ed Wynn, Victor Borge, Terry-Thomas, Burl Ives, Sessue Hayakawa, Cyril Richard, Tallulah Bankhead and Boris Karloff would provide the voices for the animated characters. It was expected the picture would cost between $1,500,000 to $2,000,000 to produce.

"Hans' adventures lead him to Father Neptune's domain, where the Little Mermaid falls in love with him, then to the Emperor's palace for the famed 'New Clothes' episode," explained *Boxoffice*. "Later Hans meets Thumbelina, the Mole, the sneaky Rat and other famed fairy-tale characters before he awakens from a dream to find his worried father has been searching for him." Karloff, rather unsurprisingly, portrayed 'the sneaky rat'.

Although *The Daydreamer* was originally expected to have an Easter 1966 release it finally opened at the Warner Hollywood Theatre in Los Angeles on Friday, 29 July. It opened at RKO-Keith's in New York two months later, on Wednesday, 21 September. "This delightful film is answer to critics that the movies produce nothing that is acceptable for family entertainment," one journalist wrote. "*Daydreamer* rates five stars-plus… for family entertainment and enjoyment."[15]

After recording his dialogue for *The Daydreamer* Karloff began another period of rest, spending his time relaxing in his London flat. Still, he was available for the occasional interview – a less strenuous activity – such as the one he granted the BBC. The resultant programme, *Interval: Boris Karloff Looks Back*, was broadcast at 8:30 p.m. on Tuesday, 20 July 1965. Another interview of this period, however, did not go so well. Karloff had agreed to be interviewed for a new magazine, as Olwen Simmon later remembered. "I didn't do the interview. My husband did it while I stayed outside in the car," she explained. "You must remember he was very excited about meeting Boris and the interview, being the first one he had ever done in his life. He was very, very raw at this sort of thing and he took along his old tape machine. Firstly, Boris was quite old then and was not very well at the time, so [Karloff] told him he was not very professional. My husband didn't have a list of questions to ask, just what he could remember as he went along. When he played the tape back to me you could hardly understand it. During the interview he [Karloff] was more interested in talking about cricket than anything else. My husband, not being a sport person, was quite disappointed with it all."[16]

By now the health of the 77-year-old horror star played a deciding factor when it came to choosing work projects. A consideration would be the sheer physicality of the role. This, coupled with his desire to keep working, would sometimes lead to Karloff's acceptance of the strangest job offers. One such curiosity was his next television appearance – his final of 1965 – as the special guest host on the Halloween edition of the music variety show *Shindig!* Karloff signed his contract for the show on 5 October. The deal, which would earn the star $4,000, was handled at the Lester Salkow Agency by Merritt Blake, who recalled his charge as "a very elegant gentleman".[17]

The Halloween show was recorded a little over a week later, on 14 October, at the ABC-TV Centre in Hollywood. It was broadcast on Saturday, 30 October and featured Ted Cassidy ('Lurch' from TV's *The Addams Family*) and included music from The Spokesmen, Jackie and Gayle, and Bobby Sherman. Even Karloff had his own musical numbers.

Sitting in a large armchair, the moustachioed, bespectacled, horror star announced, "Ladies and Gentlemen, boys and girls. Now is the time for our nursery rhyme." He then recited, with musical accompaniment, the lyrics of Joey Dee and the Starliters hit 1962 song, *Peppermint Twist*. "You'll like it like this – the Peppermint Twist," he said. "Bubba Bubba Do Ba!" And, as he launched into the second verse, he was joined by a throng of female dancers who cavorted around his armchair. "Round and round and up and down," Karloff concluded, "and one, two, three, kick. One, two, three, jump, JUMP!"[ii]

This was one of two vocal renditions Karloff gave that night. The other was a cover of Bobby Pickett's 1962 hit *Monster Mash*, a song that had featured Pickett's own impression of Boris Karloff. Unfortunately, Karloff's *Shindig!* version is missing from available copies of the show. However, the audio for this clip, at least, still exists. For, on the night of the original broadcast, one far-sighted fan recorded the show's soundtrack on reel-to-reel tape. In 2007 he made the recording available on the internet.

1966 would prove to be another busy year for Boris Karloff for, despite his worsening health, he still had no intention of slowing down. The year began with a non-strenuous role in another picture for AIP – *The Ghost in the Invisible Bikini*.[iii] This would prove to be the

---

ii The day after Karloff's broadcast the press announced the show had been cancelled due to its consistently low ratings. The final show aired on 6 January 1966.
iii *The Ghost in the Invisible Bikini* went through several name changes before its title was settled upon. In March 1965 AIP announced the picture would be called *The Ghost in the Glass Bikini* and would star Frankie Avalon and Annette Funicello. This was later changed to *Bikini Party in a Haunted House*, which, in January 1966, was amended to its final release title.

With Francis X. Bushman and Basil Rathbone during the production of *The Ghost in the Invisible Bikini* (1966).

seventh and last of the *Beach* pictures and the first not to feature either Avalon or Funicello. Avalon had, by now, tired of the series while Funicello had decided to spend time with her new daughter, Gina. Instead, the couple were replaced by new characters played by Tommy Kirk and Deborah Walley.

Karloff appeared as the recently deceased Hiram Stokely who is visited in his crypt by his one time, and long dead, love Cecily [Susan Hart]. Cecily, who had died in a circus accident while performing as 'The Girl in the Invisible Bikini', informs Hiram he can regain his youth and enter heaven if he performs a good deed within the next 24 hours. Stokely's good deed is to keep the attorney, Reginald Ripper [Basil Rathbone], from eliminating Stokely's legitimate heirs and keeping the inheritance for himself.

According to Susan Hart both her own, and Karloff's, involvement had been a last minute addition. "The picture had been shot – without me – and it was such a mixed-up picture, it was not showable," she later explained. "You could make no sense of it!… After the picture was supposedly completed, it was unreleasable. I was not in the film at all initially; a month or a month and a half after they saw they couldn't do anything with it, the idea of shooting additional scenes with a ghost was thought up… For my scenes as the ghost, they put a blond wig and a black velvet bathing suit on me and they shot me against a black velvet backdrop. I was told where the people were in the scene into which I would be superimposed, what kind of instruments people had in their hands, so on and so forth – this went on for about two weeks. And then they had Boris Karloff come in and we shot our scenes in maybe a week."[18] She also said, "That was just a great experience. He was just so easy to work with! It was very natural working with him, and he was such a gentleman."[19] According to the picture's screenwriter Louis M. Heyward, however, both Karloff and Hart's involvement was assured even before the script was written.

There is some evidence to support both claims. Neither Hart nor Karloff have any interaction with the rest of the cast in the picture, which would indicate their scenes were shot separate from the others. However, a candid photograph exists showing Karloff, Rathbone and Francis X. Bushman (who played Karloff's butler) sitting all together in the studio.[iv] As both Rathbone and Bushman are wearing their screen costumes it shows Karloff must have been present at the studio for at least one of the days of filming although, of course, this may have been a purely social visit.

Whatever the truth of the matter, Heyward enjoyed his association with the horror star. "The Boris Karloff I knew was a studious, delightful, funny fellow," he later said, "and I don't think anybody has talked about him being funny! He had a wry sense of humour, and he would say sly, funny things. By 'sly' I don't mean 'naughty', they were just cute, they were words within words totally encapsulated. If you understood it, great, and if you didn't, also great. When he found that I understood almost half of his secret jokes, he would nod his head and his eyes would twinkle, which was a kind of precious thing to have with him."[20]

The picture went on general release on Wednesday, 6 April 1966. "Directed by Don Weis from a story by Louis M. Heyward and Elwood Ullman, the proceedings are completely nonsensical, of course, with much of the action laid in a supposedly deserted mansion," *Boxoffice* wrote. "There's just one shot on a beach but there are plenty of songs, including Miss Sinatra's belting out the lively *Geronimo*, Miss Hart and Karloff are outstanding and furnish a sock surprise finale and Rathbone and Miss Kelly perform like the old pros they are."[21]

On 14 February 1966, following his work on the picture, Karloff was admitted to the Good Samaritan Hospital in Los Angeles where, on 3 March, he underwent minor kidney surgery or, as he later called it, "surgical 'tidying up'."[22] He was still recuperating over a week later when attendants at the hospital explained their patient was "continuing to convalesce satisfactorily." Reporters were told, "His condition is good."[23]

Returning to England after spending five months in California, Karloff purchased two new homes and moved from the flat in Cadogan Square where for the past year he had lived next door to Christopher Lee.[v] "When we came out of our houses simultaneously, people expected to see body-bags dumped on the pavement," Lee later wrote.[24] Maintaining an accommodation in London, Karloff bought another flat, this time one situated in Sheffield Terrace in Kensington. "They had a very nice apartment there," Bernard Coleman said, "but no garden – and he'd had this lovely roof garden. He loved gardens. So they bought the cottage down at Bramshott and they had some garden there and that's where they finished their time."[25]

The ancient village of Bramshott is located some 18 miles south west of Guildford off the A3, the historic road that runs from London to Portsmouth. Perhaps appropriately for an actor primarily known for his horror roles, the village is reputedly haunted by a whole host of spirits, including a phantom coach, a boy piper, a highwayman, a cavalier, a drowned girl and even a pig.

"He lived at the house on the triangle at the bottom of Church Lane at the junction with Tunbridge Lane," village resident Wendy Moore later explained, "and there is a gargoyle reputed to be of him below the guttering at the back of the house."[26]

Like the majority of the buildings in the village, Karloff's cottage – 'Roundabout' – was an old building.

---

iv This may well have been the last time Karloff and Rathbone ever met. On 21 July 1967 Basil Rathbone died of a heart attack at his home in New York. He was 75.

v Karloff lived at number 43. Lee lived next door, at number 45.

The centuries old two-storey cottage was made of brick, built upon a stone plinth. The roof was tiled and the lower portions of the building were rendered, possibly during the 18th or 19th century to serve as a hop kiln or drying room. In the early 19th century the cottage had been the home of the Huntingfords, whose family had lived in the village from at least the late 17th century. Probably unknown to Karloff both William Huntingford and his wife Sarah had died in the cottage. William passed away in 1828. His wife followed 17 years later.

It did not take long for the locals to become aware that they were playing host to the 'King of Horror'. One Bramshott resident, Steve Reid, recalled:

> My friends and I used to walk past his house everyday. In the days when boys used to collect conkers we were always on the lookout for that special fifty-niner and it was no secret that the best conker tree for miles around was located in Mr. Karloff's garden on the opposite side of the road from his house. We used to see him fairly regular and then he would be absent for long periods of time, obviously now looking back he would be over in America and only be back at certain times. Anyway, we assumed he was away just as the conkers were getting to the best time. After much planning, or as much as eight-year-olds were capable of, we decided to make our assault that day on the way home from school. Armed with suitable sticks we proceeded to bombard his tree gleefully picking up our spoils. The pickings were so good even the lookouts were helping themselves when a strange pair of feet appeared amongst us gathering the conkers on the ground.
>
> On looking up we saw Mr. Karloff looking down at us asking what we thought we were doing. Even as kids we knew he was the Mummy and Frankenstein and fear of what he might do to us rendered us motionless. He just sat down with us and explained if we wanted the conkers to just knock on his door and he would lend us his ladder to remove the conkers rather than smash the living daylights out of his tree. This we duly did and after collecting our full bag of conkers he came back across the road with a glass of squash for us all. He was an absolute gentleman to us kids and he always spoke to us from then on whenever he saw us when he was home.[27]

One visitor to the Bramshott cottage was Karloff's eventual first biographer, the paranormalist Peter Underwood:

> I consider myself very fortunate in meeting and talking with 'the king of terror films' (he hated the word 'horror') on a number of occasions: at the Garrick Club, at film studios and on location, at his Cadogan Square [flat] (where I first met Evie, his last wife) and at his delightful country cottage, 'Roundabout', Bramshott, a few miles from my own home at that time, in Hampshire... He found peace at the cottage in Hampshire towards the end of his life but the garden was rather small and he rented some ground opposite where he grew apples. One morning, when he caught a neighbour's son helping himself, he gave the boy a severe look and told him to come and see him after school. When the crestfallen lad arrived after school he was given a basket of apples

and told, "If you want some apples come and ask for them, don't steal them."
It was a lesson the boy never forgot.

My first meeting with [Karloff] was more luck than judgement. My London
club was at that same time situated in Covent Garden, a stone's throw from my
office in Bedford Street, and the Savage Club had a reciprocal arrangement with
the nearby Garrick Club where I knew Boris was a member. One day a friend
at the Savage Club rang me and said, "I've just seen a 'friend' of yours go into the
Garrick Club." I asked who and he said, "Boris Karloff!" I lost no time in getting to
the Garrick. There I looked in at the members' bar and in all the rooms where
I thought he might be; not a sign – nor was he in the dining room. I walked up
the splendid staircase and entered the library. I might have known, there in a
corner, buried in a book, was Boris. I settled not far away. After a moment he
looked across at me, nodded and went back to his book. Gradually we began to
chat: about the weather, cricket, film-making in England and Hollywood, his own
films and the time passed. Some time before I had sent him the first draft of a
biography I had written – his biography – following some correspondence, but
he always said he was busy and anyway it was his films that interested people,
not him personally. We must have been talking on and off for the best part of
an hour when he looked more fixedly at me, his deep-set eyes piercing, yet not
unkindly: "I didn't catch your name... you're not a reporter?"... I told him who I
was and he thought for a moment, then it rang a bell. "Ah – my biographer!" he
laughed. We talked some more and then he said he had to go. "Well, you must
come and see me..." Later I visited him on a film set and several times at his
London flat, a comfortable place with antique furniture and lots of books. He
and Evie could not have been more pleasant and helpful. He read my first draft,
pointing out one or two errors of fact but making no attempt to alter or add
to the work. After his death Evie entertained me at the cottage in Bramshott
and we went over the manuscript together: later she complained about some
aspects of the book. She was not an easy person to get on with.[28]

A non-strenuous source of income for Boris Karloff was the one provided by advertising.
While many movie actors shunned the medium Karloff had embraced this additional
avenue of income since the early days of his post-*Frankenstein* fame. Over the years he
had endorsed products ranging from shaving cream and antacid tablets to automobiles,
curtains, light bulbs, razor blades, and had even licensed his name and image for use on a
board game – *Boris Karloff's Monster Game*. He would continue to promote products almost
to the end, shooting commercials for cigarette lighters and steak sauce.

Now he had agreed to participate in one of series of adverts made on behalf of the
Brewers' Society, an organisation founded in 1904 to promote the interests of the brewing
trade. In doing so he joined a host of other celebrities that included cricketer Freddie
Trueman, footballers Bobby Moore and Denis Law, author Hammond Innes and boxer
Billy Walker. Photographed with a jug of beer in hand, Karloff promoted the pleasures of
the British pub. "The American bar has a lot to be said for it," he said in the advert, "but
there's something about the British pub that no other country can quite capture... I still
go to California to work occasionally, and I appreciate my home and my local all the more
when I come back."[29]

By mid-May 1966 he was
back in California to make his
second picture of the year, a
political thriller entitled *The
Venetian Affair*, starring Robert
Vaughn. Vaughn played Bill
Fenner, an ex-CIA agent sent
to investigate an American
diplomat's suicide bombing
at a peace conference.
Karloff appeared as Dr. Pierre
Vaugiroud, a nuclear scientist
whose report may shed
some light on the incident.
Although the picture was, as
the title suggests, partly shot
in Venice, Karloff shot his
scenes at the MGM studios at
Culver City. The picture was
released in Californian cities
(including Oakland, Berkeley
and Alameda) on Wednesday,
4 January 1967. It opened
exactly one week later in Los

With Elke Sommer and Robert Vaughn during production of *The Venetian Affair* (1967).

Angeles co-billed with *The Sandpiper*, starring Elizabeth Taylor and Richard Burton.

"Producers Jerry Thorpe and E. Jack Neuman have come up with a competent espionage adventure yarn," *Boxoffice* wrote, "which casts Robert Vaughn as a less glamorous but more realistic spy than he usually portrays in the *Man From U.N.C.L.E.* TV series. This film falls into the *Spy Who Came In From the Cold* genre, which depicts the spy business as a grim, unpleasant, brutal game. However, unlike the latter, it does not tend to philosophise, but concentrates on action and intrigue… It's always nice to see old-time Boris Karloff, now 79, who has not worked for MGM since *The Mask of Fu Manchu* in 1932."[30]

By July 1966 Karloff had signed to lend his voice to another Rankin-Bass picture, this time a stop-motion horror comedy entitled *Mad Monster Party*. He voiced the character of Baron Boris von Frankenstein, the head of the 'The World Organisation of Monsters', who summons the organisation's members to a party in his castle on 'The Isle of Evil'. There he announces his retirement and names his nephew, Felix Flankin, as his successor. However, the choice does not prove a popular one and, instead, the monstrous members plan to eliminate their new leader.

It was the perfect way for the arthritic actor to earn an income. After all, his work could be completed from the relative comfort of a recording studio. According to the picture's composer, Maury Laws, Karloff recorded his dialogue in England, which was later mixed with the other recordings in a Hollywood sound studio. "Boris Karloff was the perfect gentleman," producer Arthur Rankin Jr. later said. "He was suffering from an illness at the time, but he gave us a great performance in *Mad Monster Party* and *The Daydreamer* as well."[31]

Mad Monster Party opened in New York on 8 March 1967. "Most of the so-called kiddie movies unloaded on weekends at neighbourhood theatres are absurdly awful," wrote Howard Thompson of the *New York Times*. "But *Mad Monster Party*, which Avco Embassy is showing today and tomorrow, at matinees only, is another matter entirely... As directed by Jules Bass and produced by Arthur Rankin Jr. with some gifted technicians, this party should make everybody chuckle, the tots and their escorts, and even monsters at heart."[32]

September 1966 saw the original broadcasts of two of Boris Karloff's television appearances. On 23 September he guest-starred on the popular television series *The Wild Wild West* starring Robert Conrad and Ross Martin. In the episode – *Night of the Golden Cobra* – Karloff appeared as Mr. Singh, a self-styled Maharajah who lives in an Indian Palace on the Pawnee reservation. Singh, in league with the Indian Commissioner, attempts to force James West [Conrad] to persuade the Pawnee to move on following the discovery of oil on their land. West, however, refuses and when the Commissioner threatens the life of the Maharajah's daughter, Vade, and Artemis Gordon [Martin], Singh dies trying to save them.

The episode reunited Karloff with one of his co-stars from *Frankenstein 1970*, Audrey Dalton, who now played his daughter. "That was great because I got to walk two cheetahs on a leash!" she later said. "That was fun, and so were the exotic costumes. That was a very 'different' kind of show, because it was so far out. Being a Western only remotely came into it [*laughs*]!"[33] Karloff, though, was frailer than he had seemed six years earlier. "My whole memories of him are always that his wife had to hover and take care of him, and there was always great solicitation of him on the set, by everybody."[34]

Four days later (27 September) he appeared in a very different role, that of a female assassin on *The Girl from U.N.C.L.E.*, starring Stefanie Powers. "I may say that *that* wasn't type-casting," Karloff said.[35] He starred as Agnes Twicksbury a.k.a. Mother Muffin, an assassin hired to eliminate April Dancer [Powers] and U.N.C.L.E. agent Napoleon Solo [Robert Vaughn], who also guested in this episode. Solo has joined Dancer on a mission to locate and safely escort a mobster's daughter to her father. In return for her safe delivery the mobster has agreed to furnish U.N.C.L.E. with important information about his organisation. However, Mother Muffin and her band of assassins have been hired to ensure the agents fail in their task. "A particularly funny, outlandish episode," one reviewer wrote. "Boris Karloff does a superb job as Mother Muffin... Don't miss it."[36]

Karloff's involvement had been the idea of the show's producer (and *Thriller's* associate producer) Doug Benton. "When we were doing *Girl from U.N.C.L.E.*, we got this script [*The Mother Muffin Affair*] and we were talking about Judith Anderson and people like that [to play Mother Muffin]," Benton said. "The writer of the script [Joseph Calvelli] was a great admirer of Karloff's, and he described Mother Muffin as being 'Boris Karloff in drag'. I looked at the damn thing and I said, 'Well, why don't we get Boris?' – I knew him and I knew that he would be amused by this. The people around Metro said, 'You're not gonna get him to play this... ridiculous thing!' and I said, 'I think we *will*. I'm gonna send it to him.' I think he got it on Thursday night, and I had a message from Boris in the office by the time I got there Friday morning – 'When and where??' He just *loved* making the thing, and he used to tell everybody that it was one of his favourite roles!"[37]

"In the make-up chair," Karloff's agent, Arthur Kennard, recalled, "looking in the mirror all dressed up with the rig on, he said, 'I look like a two dollar whore!' and everybody, of course, broke up."[38] Karloff's view was reinforced once day on location, as Benton later explained. "At one point while we were making the show," he said, "we were down under

Above: With Stefanie Powers and Robert Vaughn in *The Girl from U.N.C.L.E*
(1966). Right: Mother Muffin.

the pier at Santa Monica – it was one of the hottest days we ever worked. He had taken off
the top part of his costume and he was sitting in his trailer, wearing the wig and touching
up his make-up. It was so hot that he had opened up the trailer so that the sea air would
blow through; he heard this noise, he looked up and there looking in the window were
two 'urchins' – that was the word he used to describe them – about 4 and 6 years old. And
Boris swore to me that the bigger kid turned to his little brother and said, 'Jesus, Archie!
That's the *ugliest* old bag I ever saw in my *life!*' Boris would tell that story and *l-l-laugh*!"[39]

Within weeks of the episode's broadcast Karloff was filming his next television role. On
7 October 1966 he wrote in a private letter, "My wife and I are off to Madrid in a few days
to film a segment of the TV show *I Spy*, after that we expect to be back in California early in
December to finish up something for Roger Corman."[40] So, in the second week of October,
Karloff flew to Spain for another 'guest star' role, this time in *Mainly on the Plains*, an episode
of the popular secret agent series *I Spy*, starring Bill Cosby and Robert Culp. Broadcast on 22
February 1967 Karloff played Don Ernesto Silvando, a Quixotic rocket scientist who, despite
receiving death threats, refuses to believe the seriousness of his situation.

Karloff's next two offerings appeared during the closing months of the year. While
both featured narrations by the star one was destined for the cinema screen while the
other was made for television. Their intended audiences, too, were poles apart.

Mondo Balordo was a 'shock doc' – an exposé of peculiar customs, rituals and habits from around the world. Produced in Italy in 1964 Karloff had agreed to provide a narration for Western audiences. "In my career of nearly four decades in motion pictures I've played every monstrous role it was possible for writers to create," he announced in the picture. "But as you will see in the exciting film to follow, nothing invented by the human mind can be as macabre, grotesque and thrilling as the behaviour of people in so called real life." Then, over the course of the following 90 minutes, he introduced a series of clips ranging from a Vegas beauty contest to child drug addicts, and from smugglers to Jehovah's Witnesses.

Poster for *Mondo Balordo* (1967).

Although it is usually cited that the picture opened in the U.S. in 1967 *Mondo Balordo* did, in fact, play in at least one American city the previous year. In November 1966, the picture had opened at a drive-in in Gastonia, North Carolina with two showings a day. From there the picture made its way west, playing in Phoenix, Arizona in January 1967.

The picture opened in Los Angeles theatres and drive-ins on 8 March. "*Mondo Balordo* means 'foolish world'," wrote Kevin Thomas of the *Los Angeles Times*. "It also means still another of those conglomerations of mankind's primitive customs and frivolous practices that the Italians grind out like so much sausage... The whole specious affair benefits undeservedly from the tongue-in-cheek tone of Boris Karloff's narration."[41]

Christmas 1966, however, saw a more salubrious use of Boris Karloff's vocal talents with the first airing of a television animation that has since become a seasonal staple of American television - *Dr. Seuss' How The Grinch Stole Christmas!*

The idea for a half-hour seasonal cartoon short originated with Chuck Jones, the animator who had created the famous characters the Road Runner, Wile. E. Coyote and Pepe LePew. In 1963 Jones and his team were hired by MGM to create a new series of Tom and Jerry cartoons and it was here Jones had the notion of working with Theodor Giesel (a.k.a. Dr. Seuss).

The two men had known each other during the war when they had collaborated on *Private Snafu*, the Army's instructional cartoon shorts that followed the misadventures of the incompetent soldier of the title. Since then Giesel had become well known for his children's books such as *The Cat in the Hat* (1957) and *Green Eggs and Ham* (1960) – the ideal fodder, Jones thought, for an animated short.

"I really wanted to do something of his [Seuss]," Jones later explained. "So I went to MGM and told them I thought it was time we did something in that field and I thought that Dr. Seuss was the right person to go to. So I called up Ted and I asked would he be willing to think about doing it – he was anti-Hollywood because, after the war, they pirated a lot of his stuff and took his credits off some documentaries, one of which won an Academy Award and somebody else took it. He was pretty sour on that but I told him this was television… We talked about it and decided on *How The Grinch Stole Christmas!* Then I had to talk MGM into the idea of spending money for a storyboard. I did most of the drawings – about seventeen hundred – I had a few people who gave me very good help too… In those days though, it isn't like it is today – you had to sell it to a sponsor and then you'd go to the network and say, 'Well, here's the product. This guy's willing to pay for it'."[42] Jones, therefore, went out and gave 25 showings of the storyboard to the breakfast food and chocolate companies who all refused it. In the end the project was picked up by a rather unlikely sponsor – the Foundation for Commercial Banks.

Dr. Seuss's poem concerned the Grinch, a mean, spiteful creature who is afflicted by 'a heart two sizes too small'. Living atop Mount Crumpit, north of Whoville, the Grinch watches with irritation as the Who's merrily prepare to celebrate the festive season.

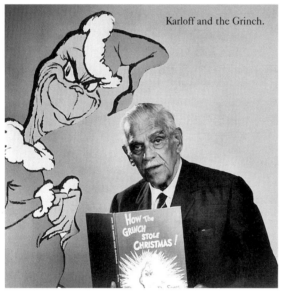

Karloff and the Grinch.

So on the night of Christmas Eve, in an attempt to halt the festivities, the Grinch steals all the presents and decorations from the inhabitants of Whoville. The next day, however, and despite their losses, the Who's Christmas spirit remains and as they sing, hand in hand, the Grinch's heart miraculously grows three sizes. "*How The Grinch Stole Christmas* is about a stinker who reforms," explained Dr. Seuss. "It pokes fun at the commercialisation of Christmas, but I don't set out with a cudgel to attack anyone."[43]

When it came to choosing a narrator for the cartoon Jones recalled a spoken word album he had heard and enjoyed. It was one of the Caedmon releases of Kipling's *Just So Stories* read by Karloff. It was an inspired choice. "To me," Jones later said, "one of the most important things was my getting Boris Karloff… He had this lovely, wonderful voice. Everybody thought of him as a villain. And he was so dear when he read it, you know. He really gave accent to each one and each note, and the narrator was important there."[44]

The cartoon reportedly took ten months to complete and cost CBS $315,000. Normally, Jones explained, animators would make three drawings per foot for a children's TV film. Jones and his team were making 15 drawings per foot for *The Grinch*. "You have to do this for believability," he said. "I have done 90 percent of the sketches myself. It's the only way to evolve things."[45]

In all, the piece required over 25,000 drawings and more than 200 backgrounds. "You have to work on the detail for a show like this to be believable," Jones explained. "Children are remarkable critics – if the drawings were not fully animated, they would be terribly disappointed. Dr. Seuss was so pleased with the result he has agreed, eagerly, to get started on the animation to another book, the popular *Horton Hears a Who*."[46]

According to one newspaper report CBS executives had claimed the total cost of the project was $600,000 making it, as Chuck Jones announced at the time, probably, "the most expensive half hour ever put on television".[47]

Broadcast on Sunday, 18 December 1966, the half-hour cartoon garnered mixed reviews. Clay Gowran of the *Chicago Tribune* wrote, "Telecast last evening, the special must have had the moppet brigade hanging on every minute. The cartooning, as might be expected with Jones at the helm, was excellent, a lively merger of Walt Disney and Rube Goldberg. Colour quality was superb. And old meany Karloff was just right as the off-camera voice for the tale about mean old Grinch, who first hated and then learned to love Yuletime."[48]

However, Hal Humphrey of the *Los Angeles Times* considered the cartoon, "a disappointment. It is my opinion that the book was better than this expensive half-hour colour TV adaptation proved to be… the result was much too mild, and I suspect the usually action-hungry small viewers may have shared my feeling."[49]

Despite the mixed reviews Chuck Jones retained his faith in the project and correctly predicted it would soon become established as a seasonal favourite. The reason for its success, he felt, was clear, as he later explained in a letter to Evelyn Karloff. "It now seems apparent that *How The Grinch Stole Christmas* will be a Christmas feature on television for as long as anyone can envisage," he wrote. "In my opinion the major reason for this is that Mr. Karloff gave such a thoughtful and understanding reading of the script. I think it is entirely appropriate that children for many generations will find joy and a deeper understanding of Christmas through the skill of your husband."[50] Dr. Seuss, too, was grateful for Karloff's contribution. "Working with him on *How The Grinch Stole Christmas* was a privilege, an honour and will be an inspiration to me always," he wrote.[51]

Within weeks of the broadcast Karloff was preparing the ground for his next venture. Back in England on 30 December, two weeks after *The Grinch* aired in the U.S., Boris Karloff completed his insurance papers for his next picture – *The Sorcerers*.

"REMARKABLE! TERRIFYING AND THRILLING!"

–JUDITH CRIST, New York Magazine

"I just killed my wife and my mother. I know they'll get me. But before that many more will die..."

PARAMOUNT PICTURES PRESENTS

TARGETS

STARRING

BORIS KARLOFF · TIM O'KELLY · NANCY HSUEH
JAMES BROWN · AND SANDY BARON AS KIP LARKIN

Screenplay by PETER BOGDANOVICH · Story by POLLY PLATT and PETER BOGDANOVICH
Directed and Produced by PETER BOGDANOVICH · COLOR · A PARAMOUNT RELEASE

SUGGESTED FOR MATURE AUDIENCES

Paramount
A Gulf+Western Company

Chapter 25

THE SORCERERS AND TARGETS

(1966-1968)

"To suggest as some people sincerely do that films about depraved creatures necessarily debase humanity – that fright is a sort of masochistic thrill instead of just another harmless, human reaction is, to me, complete and utter nonsense."[1]

Boris Karloff (1965)

In October 1966, while shooting *I Spy* in Madrid, Boris Karloff was approached with an interesting proposition – the offer of a starring role in a new picture to be shot in England. The enquirer was a young British filmmaker named Michael Reeves. His picture was a modern horror called *The Sorcerers*.

Reeves was born in Sutton, Surrey on 17 October 1943, the son of a wealthy solicitor, Derek Reeves, and his wife Elizabeth. After his father died the eight-year-old boy was sent away to attend Kings Mead, a boys' preparatory school in Seaford, Sussex. He continued his schooling at Radley College in Oxfordshire where his love of film prompted him to join the college's film club. He soon began making his own short films.

In 1960 Reeves accompanied his mother on a trip to Boston to see relatives and, seizing the opportunity, caught a plane to Los Angeles. He had already corresponded with his cinematic hero, *Invasion of the Body Snatchers* (1956) director Don Siegel, and now Reeves paid the director a visit. His impromptu trip paid off and the young man was rewarded with a brief period of employment as a dialogue director for some tests Siegel was shooting at Paramount.

His experience with Siegel, albeit limited, was enough to help procure further film work. While working as a runner on *The Long Ships* (1964), a Viking saga starring Richard Widmark and Sidney Poitier, he befriended production manager Paul Maslansky. When Maslansky later produced the horror picture *Il castello dei morti vivi* (*Castle of the Living Dead*, 1964), starring Christopher Lee and Donald Sutherland, Reeves was invited to Rome to work on the picture.

After another stint as a runner, this time on the picture *Genghis Khan* (1965), Reeves raised enough money to put towards a movie of his own, a self-penned horror picture, *The Revenge of the Blood Beast*, to be co-produced with Paul Maslansky. Reeves shot the picture in Italy with *Black Sunday* star Barbara Steele and Reeve's childhood friend, Ian Ogilvy.

Early in 1966 Reeves was back in London where he was hoping to develop a new picture for Christopher Lee. After this, and several other projects, failed to come to fruition he was introduced to John Burke, a one-time European Story Editor for 20th Century Fox who had quit for the more profitable career of writing 'novelisations' of film and television scripts. Burke had also written a treatment entitled *Terror for Kicks*, which Reeves promptly purchased for his production company, Leith Productions. In August 1966 he took an option on another Burke story, a haunted house tale called *The Devil's Discord*, hoping he could interest distributor/producer Tony Tenser in financing the picture. Tenser turned him down.

With no deal forthcoming for *The Devil's Discord* Reeves now decided to resurrect *Terror for Kicks* and contacted Burke, requesting a rewrite. The final

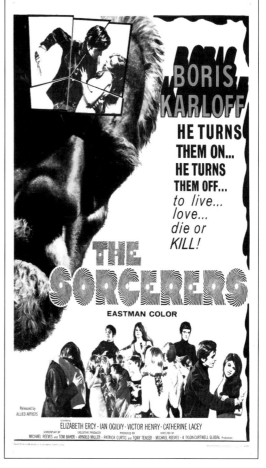

Poster for *The Sorcerers* (1967).

screenplay, which would reach the screens as *The Sorcerers*, was credited to Reeves and his school friend, Tom Baker.[i]

The script told the story of Professor Monserrat, a medical hypnotist who has spent 30 years living in poverty following the ridiculing of his work by the press. Disowned by the medical community, the scientist has been forced to earn a living by advertising his services in a tobacconist's window. Monserrat, however, never abandoned his work and has constructed a hypnosis machine, now installed in a clinical white room in his London flat. He tests it on Mike Roscoe, a bored young man who is tempted by the scientist's promise of "an unusual evening... [with] some extraordinary experiences."

Unknown to Mike, however, he has now become inexorably linked to the Monserrats who can now compel him to commit acts merely by the power of thought. It also becomes clear that the link is stronger than anticipated, for the elderly couple discover they can also share Mike's sensations.

His experiment a success, Monserrat now plans to write a report, hoping his work will be used for the benefit to mankind. A 'transmitter', he theorises, could be sent on holiday

---

i Reeves' friend, Tom Baker, is not to be confused with the famous *Doctor Who* actor of the same name.

and the elderly could experience the sensations by proxy. Before revealing the work to the medical fraternity, however, Estelle wants to use the youth for their own benefit. Her husband reluctantly agrees, with tragic results.

When Reeves was casting the picture he already had a clear preference for the role of Marcus Monserrat. According to actor Mel Welles, Reeves had talked "incessantly about wanting to make a movie with Boris Karloff,"[2] during the production of *The Revenge of the Blood Beast*. So, when *The Sorcerers* was in the planning stage, Reeves took the bull by the horns and flew to Madrid where the star was making *I Spy*.

He pitched Karloff the idea and agreed to pay him the requested £11,000 as well as to make certain changes to the script, as Tom Baker later explained. "In the original... the old folks use the transmission of sensation from the Ian Ogilvy character purely for their own gratification," he said. "No holds barred. But Karloff wouldn't buy that. He said his character had to have redeeming characteristics, or he would not do it. So we turned the ending round – he putting the brakes on his wife and ultimately sacrificing himself. To save the world."[3]

To set up a production deal Reeves turned to American producer Patrick Curtis. Curtis ran Curtwel Productions Inc. with his then-girlfriend (and later wife), the actress Raquel Welch. Curtis had hoped Welch would star alongside Christopher Lee in Reeves' project *The Devil's Discord*, which he also hoped to oversee. Later, after this picture failed to materialise, Curtis shifted his attention to *The Sorcerers* and contacted Tony Tenser with a deal.

"He came to see me with a young director named Michael Reeves; they had a script entitled *The Sorcerers*," Tenser later explained. "Pat told me they had already approached and gotten agreements from Boris Karloff and Catherine Lacey for the leading roles, and Michael's friend Ian Ogilvy had also agreed to be in it. Pat had a budget, and he asked me to put up half the money, help produce the film and distribute it in England and worldwide. The budget was low enough for me to afford. Boris Karloff was one of the idols of my youth. I had followed his career ever since I saw *Frankenstein*, and had always been in awe of him. I had heard of Michael, and I knew he had directed an earlier low-budget horror film, which was successful. From the way he spoke, he seemed to have great talent. After I met with Pat a couple more times, I knew I could trust him."[4]

Producer Arnold L. Miller and cinematographer Stanley A. Long were assigned by Tenser to assist Reeves on the project. The two had worked together many times, partnering each other in writing and shooting a collection of short 'nudie' films and documentaries such as *Nudist Memories* (1960) and *Nudes of the World* (1961) for their company, Stag Films.

Tenser had enlisted Stanley Long's help before. Tenser had financed Roman Polanski's psychological thriller *Repulsion* (1965), and when the picture went over schedule Long was brought in to shoot the final third of the picture. "He [Polanski] is a genius in many ways," Long later said, "but unfortunately he's the victim of his own brilliance – because he was very inexperienced as far as technical things were concerned. He's done some wonderful things but he was hard going to work with, I must say."[5]

Unfortunately, Michael Reeves did not provide an easier working experience. "Michael Reeves was, contrary to common opinion, very inexperienced," Long later explained, "and he had to be helped along a lot by the crew and, like all these young people, he had ambitions beyond the budget. That was the problem. I've worked with a lot of people like that. I was a very practical cameraman and I used to direct a lot of it through the camera, and I've worked with quite a few people like that, one way or another… But the problem with Michael Reeves was he really needed a five million budget and the budget was only ₤40,000. There was a bit of a shortage there! He was being ridiculous. He had too much ambition. He wanted to do too many things which were absolutely impractical on a low budget movie. My speciality is low budget movies… and you've got to cut your cloth according to the width. I had a reputation for being able to handle low budget movies and that's how I got to be involved with a lot of these things."[6]

In December 1966 Karloff had duly completed the obligatory insurance form on which he explained he had had bronchitis 'for years'.[7] He had also, he recorded, caught pneumonia in 1963 though his last x-rays had been 'favourable'.[8] Karloff also suffered from dyspnea – a sensation of breathlessness – and, for the past four to five years, had been plagued by a painful left knee, due to osteoarthritis. Yet the form filling was to no avail. His poor medical condition rendered him too high a risk and the insurance company refused to cover him. Nevertheless, the prestige of using Boris Karloff was worth the risk and the production went ahead regardless.

Filming began early in 1967. "It took three weeks," Stanley Long recalled. "15 working days – every weekday… It was very cold in the studios."[9] The interiors of the Monserrats' flat were shot at the West London Studios in Barnes. "It was a very small studio in Barnes," Long said, "and we rented it and put the sets in, a very small studio. I don't think it exists anymore. I think it's gone."[10]

Karloff was provided with a car and chauffeur who would pick him up from his flat in Sheffield Terrace and take him to the studio for the day's shoot. Evie, as always, accompanied her husband on the set. "She looked after him wonderfully," Stanley Long said. "She was much younger than him – but she looked after him like nobody's business… She was there all the time. I worked with him for seven days on that movie and she was with him the whole time. And we would go out to lunch. He was a very interesting man. He spoke about all the make-ups he used to have to wear – which he said was a cause of a lot of his problems. It was terrible. He was very disabled when I worked with him. He had a stick and was pushed about in a wheelchair but, nevertheless, a lovely man. It was a great privilege for me to have had the opportunity to work with him."[11]

Each day, before the shoot, Long would enlist the help of the lighting equipment to ease Karloff's pains. "I used to put the 10k – a very powerful spotlight – on his back in the morning and he liked that," Long explained. "He used to say, 'Where's my heater?' and he'd sit in his chair and I'd put the lamp on him… I think he had arthritis – very bad arthritis."[12]

To accommodate his medical problems Reeves would let Karloff remain as immobile as possible and, when not required on set, the star would often rest in a wheelchair. Yet, despite his poor medical condition, he was still willing to engage in physical activities for the benefit of the picture. During the scene where Estelle destroys the hypnosis equipment Karloff was required to crawl across the floor. Reeves, however, took so long to shoot this that Karloff, most probably in pain from his repeated efforts, looked up at the director asked angrily, "How much f--king longer?"[13] It was an uncharacteristic outburst from the usually placid star, but the director's insistence on multiple takes had pushed Karloff to the limit. "It's true," Stanley Long later said. "Michael was a pain to work with. He really was."[14]

On one occasion Long even found it necessary to restrain Reeves from some of his more excessive moments. This occurred during the first murder, when Mike stabs an old girlfriend, Audrey [Susan George], with a pair of scissors. "It was Kensington Gore, you know – the make-up stuff," Long explained. "But it was pretty nasty. That was the trouble – he had an obsession, you know, Mike Reeves. He had an obsession with blood. He was worse than Sam Peckinpah! I mean he was throwing it all over the place. I didn't like working like that. I don't like that kind of thing."[15] Long, like Karloff, preferred his horror to be understated. "It's much more effective," he said. "We [Long and Reeves] had many rows about that. The other thing I had rows with him about was the amount of set-ups that he expected to happen on the night shooting. I said, 'You have to be able to turn the camera round and make the best use of one location'. And I taught him how to do that. Whether it sank in or not, I don't know. Anyway, it was rather sad because he suffered with depression and I used to go out to dinner with him and talk, and he was a very depressive individual. It was sad really. I think he was really genuinely passionate about making movies and he was such a depressive person. It was terrible."[16]

Karloff mainly worked indoors at the studio, although he was required to shoot a few exteriors, which included his character's introduction in the picture, walking down a street on his way to a tobacconist's shop. "That was off the Kings Road, Chelsea," Stanley Long recalled. "There was a little back street where the tobacconist was. And the other shot of him walking down a lit street and going into a burger bar was done in Chiswick High Street. Otherwise they were locations all around London."[17]

However, Reeves was forced to cut corners when he had been unable to gain permission to shoot in certain locations. In order to shoot in the pool of the Dolphin Square Hotel in Pimlico, for example, the night-guard was paid £20 'to look the other way'. The most impressive example of his guerrilla filmmaking occurred at the end of the picture with Mike's fatal car crash. "We blew up a Jaguar car once on a building site somewhere in Notting Hill, I think it was, without permission," Ian Ogilvy recalled.[18] This style of movie making, though, was nothing new for Stanley Long. "That was a bit of a joke, that was," Long said. "We had no permission. But I used to go around like that in those days. I don't think I'd get away with it now. But I used to say, 'Come on, let's do it!'"[19]

However, the explosion was somewhat bigger than planned, as Patrick Curtis later explained. "I remember it like it was yesterday," he said, "If we could put, maybe, ten gallons of petrol at the bottom of the pit where the Jaguar goes over the cliff [sic] and it hits the bottom we can explode the ten gallons and it was, 'Well, if ten gallon's good, fifty will be even better!' And it blew the hell out of all of us. It shattered windows for blocks around. Our concern was that if we didn't get the shot and didn't get it finished within minutes, the police would arrive and we'd all be in jail for sure – and so we left this burning Jaguar at the bottom of this pit and we all took off in nine different directions figuring, 'Well, they'll catch one of us but we'll all keep our mouths shut.'"[20] Reeves escaped on his bicycle. Some of the crew, however, were not so fortunate and found themselves helping the police with their enquiries.

The Sorcerers opened in London at the Carlton, Haymarket on Saturday, 27 May 1967 in a double bill with AIP's historical pageant *Tower of London* starring Vincent Price. *The Times* film critic, John Russell Taylor, called it, "A striking debut in the British cinema."[21]

Monthly Film Bulletin also praised the young filmmaker's work. "Reeves manages to build a considerable charge," the reviewer wrote, "particularly in the second half of the film, with a superbly baleful performance by Catherine Lacey (Karloff is his usual reliable self, but a shade weary), and a script which comes as close to authentic *Sadisme* as anything since *Peeping Tom* in its detailing of the increasing urgency of Estelle's thirst for experience."[22]

Although making the picture had been a little difficult at times, Boris Karloff was pleased with the result. His satisfaction was shared by the judges at the sixth International Science Fiction Film Festival in Trieste the following July (1968), who awarded *The Sorcerers* their highest award, the Golden Asteroid, which Ian Ogilvy was despatched to accept. Both Catherine Lacey and Karloff were honoured, too. Lacey won the Silver Asteroid for best actress, while Karloff was awarded a Gold Medal.

"Boris Karloff was possibly the most famous actor I ever worked with," Ian Ogilvy later said, "probably the actor I'm most proud to have been associated with, and one of the nicest human beings on the planet."[23] Tony Tenser, too, felt highly about his star. "I can't say enough good things about Boris Karloff," he said. "He was a wonderful man, and a brilliant actor. He was nearly 80 then, but he remembered his lines and spoke them clearly. He interpreted his part absolutely correctly and uniquely, as only he could. He was the most unassuming man you could wish to meet. He couldn't even understand why people would want his autograph."[24]

"I think everybody got along with Boris because Boris was the kind of bloke you can't help but get along with," Stanley Long later said. "He was just a nice, gentle Englishman… I loved him. He was a lovely, lovely man. And he always had a lot of time to talk to you and he'd go back and talk about his days in Hollywood. There's a man who did some remarkable work and had a remarkable reputation in what he was doing."[25] He was, Long added, "a very kindly, old English gentleman who was very easy to talk to."[26]

In September 1967 Reeves began shooting his second picture for Tigon, *The Witchfinder General* (1968). It is generally considered to be his finest picture and was seen as the portent of greater things to come. Sadly, however, the promising career failed to materialise. Michael Reeves never beat his depression and on 11 February 1969 he died, the victim of a drug overdose. The low levels of drugs in his system indicted an accidental death and the coroner announced it as such. "I rather suspect he helped it on a bit, you know," Stanley Long later said. "He was taking pills and things but who knows with these things? These people have problems."[27] Michael Reeves was 25 years old.

In February 1967 work began on another Karloff picture – *El coleccionista de cadáveres* (*The Corpse Collector*) or *Blindman's Bluff*[ii] as it would be known for a time, a Spanish/American co-production shot in Torremolinos and at Estudios Roma in Madrid.

Karloff starred as Franz Badulescu, a sculptor famed for using animal bones as the armatures in his sculptures. Blinded in a car accident, the artist now works to complete a commission. Unknown to Badulescu, however, the accident had been planned by his wife, Tania [Viveca Lindfors], who had hoped to benefit from her husband's death. Along with her lover, the bistro owner 'Shanghai' [Milo Quesada], Tania has also been committing various murders and, after stripping the flesh from the corpses in a vat of acid, presenting the bones to her unsuspecting husband for use in his artwork.

Karloff had not, however, been producer Robert D. Weinbach's original choice for the role. Weinbach had wanted Claude Rains, but when Rains proved too ill to accept (he would pass away on 30 May 1967) Boris Karloff was offered the role.

---

ii The onscreen title of the picture is *Blindman's Bluff* and not *Blind Man's Bluff* as often cited.

Again, Karloff's poor health meant he would play the majority of the picture either seated or at rest. Although this was beneficial for the star the rest of the production was something of a farce, as he later explained. "Sometimes we make pictures under ridiculous circumstances," he said. "The weather was so bad... that plate glass windows blew in and we got no soundtrack because the wind went straight into the microphones. Not only that, there was no script girl either, to note down which lines had been said and in which shot. So we had to make up our own words all over again in the dubbing studio. The picture was up there on the screen with our mouths opening and shutting like fish in a tank, and we'd say to each other, 'What the hell were you saying then?' and 'I haven't the slightest idea'! So we made it up all over again ourselves."[28]

Blindman's Bluff remained unreleased for over four years, finally reaching the U.S. screens in August 1971, over two years after Karloff's death. Now titled *Cauldron of Blood*, the picture was paired with another horror movie, the British made *Crucible of Horror*, starring Michael Gough.

Cauldron of Blood opened at neighbourhood theatres in New York on 10 November 1971. Howard Thompson of the *New York Times* wrote, "It's painful to watch Viveca Lindfors and Boris Karloff, in reportedly his last film, balancing garbage like *Cauldron of Blood* on yesterday's double-bill. Made in Spain, the picture is a clanky derivation of *House of Wax*, whose anaemic colour even makes the Costa del Sol look dreary, which takes some doing."[29]

In March 1967 Karloff arrived in Los Angeles to finally start work on the "something for Roger Corman",[30] – a new picture entitled *Before I Die*.

Roger Corman, Karloff was told, had made a discovery. The horror star, he claimed, still owed him two days work. Not wishing to pass up such a golden opportunity Corman now planned to make an entirely new picture to star Boris Karloff. To direct the project he turned to 27-year-old Peter Bogdanovich.

Born in Kingston, New York in 1939, Bogdanovich had been a movie fan from an early age. After taking acting lessons at the age of 15 with Stella Adler, Bogdanovich embarked on an acting career before branching out into directing. "I had directed in the theatre in '59 and '60," he later explained, "and then in the early '60s, directed in the theatre in New York, and acted, and I'd been writing for *Esquire* for a few years. And in '64, I moved to California to get into pictures."[31]

Then one day at a movie screening Bogdanovich found himself seated in front of Roger Corman. Having read and admired the young man's *Esquire* articles Corman struck up a conversation during which he offered the writer a job as assistant on *The Wild Angels*, a biker movie starring Peter Fonda. Bogdanovich accepted and was put to work rewriting some scenes. He was even allowed to direct some ten minutes of footage. "They were pretty good sequences," Bogdanovich later said. "So I guess that's why Corman gave me the chance to do my own movie."[32]

This brief association would lead to bigger things, as Bogdanovich explained: "He called me one day and said, 'Would you like to make your own film?' I said, 'Yeah', and he said, 'Okay, here's the situation. Boris Karloff owes me two days' work. Now, what I'd like you to do is shoot about 20 minutes with Boris Karloff in those two days. You can shoot 20 minutes in two days – I've shot whole pictures in two days. And then... I want you to get some other actors together, and shoot for a week or two – say, another hour, or something – and then I want you to take 20 minutes of Karloff footage from a picture I made called *The Terror*. So, I'll have 20 minutes that you shoot with Karloff, 20 minutes of *The Terror* – that's 40 minutes – and then you add another 40 minutes with some other actors, and that'll be a new 80-minute Karloff picture. Will you do it?' And I said, 'Okay'. And financially, it was no great deal, but it was a thrill to get the offer, and my wife could work on it with me – Polly Platt."[33]

Roger Corman had stipulated that footage from *The Terror* should be used in the new Boris Karloff picture. Bogdanovich and Platt, therefore, spent a long time trying to decide how best to do this. Then one day, as a joke, Bogdanovich thought, "We'll start in a projection room, *The Terror* will end, and the lights will come up, and Boris Karloff will be sitting there. He'll turn to Roger Corman who'll be sitting there, and he'll say, 'Roger, that's the

Karloff as Byron Orlok in *Targets* (1968).

worst movie I've ever seen'. And I thought, 'Wait a minute, that's not a bad idea'."[34] A problem remained, however. What would the rest of the movie be about?

Bogdanovich recalled a conversation he had had months earlier with his *Esquire* editor, Harold Hays. Hays had suggested Bogdanovich make a movie about Charles Whitman, the 25-year-old student who, after killing both his mother and his wife, climbed the stairs of the University of Texas Tower where, for the next 90 minutes, he shot at people on and around the campus. When Whitman was finally shot dead by the police that day he had killed 16 and wounded 32 more.

Whitman proved to be the inspiration for the new movie. "And I thought if Karloff's in the movie, maybe he could be an actor," Bogdanovich explained. "Maybe he could be an actor who wants to quit because his kind of horror – this kind of Victorian horror stuff – was pretty old-fashioned compared to somebody who goes to a tower and just randomly picks people off. That was modern horror... that's how it started. We thought maybe we'd tell two stories, and since we only had Karloff for two days, we thought, well, that will make his story shorter and easier to shoot, 'cause we could cross-cut between the two stories."[35] With the general idea in place Bogdanovich and Platt began to work out the storyline and, once this was complete, Bogdanovich began work on the screenplay.

As Karloff's participation was assured for only the two days it was originally planned to have the star die half way through. It was an idea that dismayed Bogdanovich's friend, the director Samuel Fuller. As Bogdanovich recalled, "Sammy said, 'Why are you killing him off half way through the picture?' I said, 'I can't afford to have him'. He said, 'That's no reason. Don't ever think about budget. Never think about budget. Write it the way you want it.' And then, of course, he came up with the ending we used."[36] Bogdanovich took his friend's advice and began to rewrite. Now Karloff would be present for the entire length of the picture culminating in a face-to-face confrontation with the gunman.

He showed the finished product to Fuller. "And in about two and a half hours, pacing back and forth, he basically rewrote the script," Bogdanovich said, "giving me the most extraordinary ideas. I said, 'Jesus, Sam, this is fantastic. I've got to give you credit for this'. He said, 'If you give me credit, they'll think I did the whole thing'. I said, 'Well, you practically did'. He said, 'No, no, no – no credit, kid, no credit.' That's how generous he was. No credit, no money – just a favour."[37]

The final script told two stories: one of the disillusioned horror star Byron Orlok, the other of the mentally disturbed Vietnam veteran, Bobby Thompson. Orlok has decided to retire, believing his type of movies to be passé. "The world belongs to the young," he explains. "Make way for them. Let them have it." Thompson, meanwhile, shoots his wife, his mother and the grocery boy before buying more ammunition, telling the gun store owner he is going to "shoot some pigs" – a quote Charles Whitman, the real-life killer, had used in the same situation.

Thompson later begins gunning down drivers on the freeway until he flees in his car, pursued by the police. He finally escapes them by pulling into a drive-in. There he takes position in the scaffolding behind the cinema screen and, during a screening of Orlok's latest movie, *The Terror*, with Orlok himself in attendance, Thompson begins shooting at members of the audience. Panic ensues when the moviegoers realise a sniper is picking them off. When Thompson accidentally drops his ammunition, and then his bag of weapons, he climbs down from the tower to retrieve them. Orlok spots him and, as Thompson continues his killing spree, the horror star approaches him. With the star closing in on both screen and in person, Thompson takes pots shots with his pistol, grazing Orlok's head. Undeterred, the horror star approaches the killer and, in the only scene in the picture where the two characters meet, slaps him down. "Was that what I was afraid of?" Orlok asks Sammy as the police lead Thompson away.

The production was allocated a budget of $125,000. With the star's participation already assured Bogdanovich needed a suitable actor to play the killer, Bobby Thompson. He found Tim O'Kelly.[iii] "I liked him and I cast him," the director later said. "We got along very well. He was wonderful to work with."[38] The part of the filmmaker, Sammy Michaels,[iv] was written for Bogdanovich's friend George Morfogan, who ultimately proved unavailable. After considered using Henry Jaglom, Bogdanovich eventually decided to play the role himself.

Back in England Karloff had informed his friend Bernard Coleman of his new picture. "He told me – we were sitting watching the cricket match," Coleman recalled, "and he said, 'I've been offered this one', and he told me all about it and he said, 'I've met this young director. Very bright young man, very bright. Peter Bogdanovich. He's good.' And, of course, it was a great part, one of his wonderful parts. And people didn't realise what a good actor he was. They all used to link him, obviously, to the horror films and he was very grateful. He never, ever knocked them. He was always very proud of them. But he was very, very able in other areas."[39]

---

iii O'Kelly later played the role of Detective Danny 'Danno' Williams in the pilot episode of *Hawaii 5-0* (1968). When it came to making the series, however, O'Kelly was replaced by James MacArthur who would continue in the role until the end of the penultimate season (eleven) in 1979.

iv Sammy Michaels was named in tribute of director Samuel (Michael) Fuller.

In essence Karloff would be playing himself, a fact he was well aware of. Although star and director would not meet until the day before the shoot began they had spoken on the telephone a few times, and during one conversation Karloff expressed his concern with certain elements of his dialogue. "He said to me," Bogdanovich later explained, "'Since I'm obviously playing myself in this movie, can I not say so many terrible things about myself?' And I said, 'The audience will like you better if you put yourself down'."[40]

The Karloffs arrived in Los Angeles in mid-March 1967, a few days before shooting was due to begin and as usual were met at the airport by a limousine courtesy of Arthur Kennard. "We invited them for dinner to our first home, a modest rental out in the smoggy San Fernando Valley, the night after their plane landed," Bogdanovich recalled. "During the meal, Boris all of a sudden said to me, 'You know, you have written the truest line I've ever read in a script. I was reminded of it as we landed yesterday and drove about'. I was amazed and asked what line that could possibly be. Boris answered, 'The one when I'm looking out of the car window at the city streets and I say, 'God, what an ugly town this has become.' My Lord, it's never been truer.'"[41]

Work began on *Before I Die* on Monday, 20 March 1967. As Karloff's co-star Bogdanovich would share most of the star's scenes, many of which were shot, like the rest of the picture's interiors, in a small studio on Santa Monica Boulevard.

In the picture Byron Orlok, scheduled to make a new picture for young director Sammy Michaels, announces instead his intention to retire. The despondent young director later arrives at the horror star's hotel room and joins the star for drinks and conversation. As they talk Michaels watches a television broadcast of *The Criminal Code* (1931), the Howard Hawks picture that had featured Karloff in the role of the prison trustee, Galloway. "He really knows how to tell a story," the young director comments, watching the screen. Then Karloff, who was usually adverse to ad-libbing, added a line of his own – "Indeed he does." It was the star's tribute to the director who, he felt, had given him his first important role. Bogdanovich left the line in.

As a teetotaller, Bogdanovich had not been looking forward to shooting his drunk scene. Karloff, however, was encouraging as his co-star recalled. "It was wonderful to act with Karloff," Bogdanovich said. "We did this in one or two takes. He was just terrific... I think I am the only man who can claim to have been *on* a bed, at least, with Boris Karloff."[42]

Another troubling scene, though, was to follow and Bogdanovich found himself being directed in it by his star. "We had this scene where we're both on the bed together, and then we wake up in the morning," he later explained. "It was written in the script, he wakes up, turns, sees Byron Orlok... is shocked, and then starts to laugh. So, I said, 'Action', and we tried to do the thing, and... it's very hard to laugh on cue. Very tough. And I did it two or three times, and I kept screwing up. I said, 'That's no good'. And Boris finally turns to me, slightly exasperated, and he says, 'You know, just because you wrote it in the script that the character laughs doesn't mean you have to do it. I mean, you wrote it. You can also ignore it'. I said, 'Okay, thanks for the direction', and I did ignore it, and I just played like I was shocked, and we got it rather quickly."[43] The scene also featured another Karloff addition. Rising from the bed in his hungover state Orlok is startled by his reflection in a mirror. "And, that always got a huge laugh in the theatre when it was shown," Bogdanovich said.[44]

Karloff was out of the studio to shoot the drive-in scene with his climactic confrontation with the killer, Bobby Thompson. The original plan, however, was very different. As originally envisaged Karloff's character would die half way through the picture. Then Samuel Fuller had an idea and asked Bogdanovich if *The Terror* contained any footage of Karloff in a tuxedo. Bogdanovich replied there was. "Great! Here's what you do," Fuller said. "And that's where he gave me the idea," Bogdanovich explained "of having Karloff approaching the killer both on the screen and in life, which is a marvellous conceit that I think we pulled off. But it was Sammy Fuller's idea."[45] For the concept to work, though, and to allow Bobby Thompson to be arrested, the killer would need to have almost run out of bullets. Therefore, throughout his murderous rampage, the gunman is seen discarding or losing weapons from his arsenal.

That night's shoot turned into a long affair as Bogdanovich later explained: "It got to be about midnight and I said, 'This is going to take a little longer', and he [Karloff] said, 'Alright, it's alright, it's alright' and we went to about three in the morning with him. He was so sweet and he never complained. It was cold, as it always is in L.A. at night."[46]

Karloff started work on his final day at 8 a.m. He would remain in the small studio for the next 16½ hours while the last of his scenes were completed. One of these was the actor's recitation of an old fable. The idea had been a late addition by Bogdanovich who was prompted to add it after seeing the television broadcast of *How The Grinch Stole Christmas!*, with Karloff's narration.

In the scene Orlok is briefed about a personal appearance he is due to make at a drive-in presentation of his latest picture. Sammy Michaels suggests the horror star regale the drive-in audience with a story, so Orlok gives them a demonstration. He recites a story from a play by W. Somerset Maugham, a tale entitled *Appointment in Samara*.[v]

Bogdanovich had decided that the scene should be shot in a single take. While Karloff narrated the story the camera would slowly close in on the star, ending on a close-up. To facilitate this, a table on the set had to be moved during the shot to allow the camera to get closer.

As the story was a lengthy one the director suggested his star have his lines written on cards placed out of shot. "'You mean, Idiot Cards?' he asked, using the trade term," Bogdanovich later explained. "I nodded. 'No,' he said confidently, 'that's all right. I *have* the lyrics'. He always called his dialogue either 'the lyrics' or 'the jokes'. When we were ready, I called action and Boris started, but we had to stop after a few lines because the crew had messed up floating a table out of the path of the oncoming camera. We began again."[47]

Before shooting the scene Bogdanovich had quietly suggested that, upon concluding the story, Karloff should silently consider his own death. The star nodded and the director began to shoot the second take. "And when he finished that shot, 'cause that's the only completed take, the crew spontaneously burst into applause," Bogdanovich said. "It still moves me to think about it. And he was touched, I could see. He smiled and nodded. His wife, Evie Karloff, was on the set and I walked over to her and she had tears in her eyes, she was wiping her eyes and she said, 'Can you imagine how many years it's been since a crew applauded Boris?' It's a wonderful moment… and, perhaps, my favourite moment in the whole picture."[48]

Karloff completed his work on the picture on 24 March, having spent a mere five days on the production.[vi] Now, with the star's scenes in the can, Bogdanovich set to work

---

v Bogdanovich had seen the story quoted as an epigraph in John O'Hara's 1934 novel *Appointment in Samara*.
vi Karloff earned an additional £7,500 for working the three additional days on Bogdanovich's picture. This brought his total salary to $22,500.

finishing the rest of the picture. In all, the drive-in scene took a total of 12 days to shoot, over half of the picture's 23-day schedule.

Unable to afford many extras, Bogdanovich recruited family and friends to appear in the scene. The movie projectionist in the picture (who was, coincidentally, also named Byron) was the drive-in's actual projectionist. Mike Farrell, who would later become well known for playing Captain B.J. Hunnicutt in the popular television series *M*A*S*H*, was featured as a moviegoer shot down in a telephone booth. Future movie producer and director Frank Marshall played the drive-in's ticket boy. Even Polly Platt, who had recently discovered she was pregnant, was enlisted to walk past the camera.

Everything else in the picture – the bulk of Bobby Thompson's story – was shot in the remaining six days either on location or back in the studio. While the exterior of Thompson's house was a real home in the San Fernando Valley, the interiors were all filmed in the studio utilising the repainted and rearranged sets that were also used for Orlok's hotel room. When it had come to their construction, however, Polly Platt had discovered her plans had a serious design flaw. "When you work in the theatre, you have a proscenium and a stage," she later explained. "You always have to measure the stage – the height of the proscenium and the fly space you have. When I designed *Targets*, my first movie with sets, we had a whole soundstage. It never occurred to me to measure it, because it just seemed so big compared to what I had to work with in the theatre. As it turns out, it was one of the smallest soundstages in L.A. I designed a set for the house where the killer lived with his parents. We pre-built the set, and as we started to put up the walls, we realised that I had designed a set that was way too big for the soundstage. It just went right off the edge! We had a long hallway, which I had to shorten. I cut five-foot sections out of each wall in the hallway to make the set fit. I also shortened the size of the living room. I didn't get fired, because I handled the cheque-book. No one discovered my mistake! The set also converted into the hotel room for Boris Karloff. I saved money by making the set work for both scenes. I just plugged in doors and windows, added gold leaf and some trim for the hotel room of Boris Karloff."[49]

Platt had also designed a colour scheme for the picture, which was reflected in the two sets. The killer's home was bland with ugly decor. "It was cold and hard," she explained. "We used beiges and gold for the Boris Karloff character, and cold colours for the murderer. We wanted to avoid red. When the killer murders his mother, we wanted that to be the first time you ever saw red. We wanted it to be a big shock psychologically."[50]

To finish the picture Bogdanovich had to resort to an unorthodox style of filmmaking, as he later explained. "We shot on the freeway," he said, "and we'd looked into it, and you're not allowed to shoot on the freeway at all – on the freeway, at the freeway, near the freeway, anything. Well, you know, the thing I'd learned through Roger Corman was you don't pay attention to rules if you're going to shoot guerrilla warfare kind of filmmaking. And so we didn't pay any attention to the rules and we shot *on* the freeway, *at* the freeway and *staged scenes* on the freeway. I don't know how we got away with it."[51] To save money the entire scene was shot silent and all the sound effects were added in later by sound editor Verna Fields.[vii]

During post-production Bogdanovich and Platt decided to change the title. *Before I Die*, they felt, sounded too much like another picture they had seen – possibly Karloff's

---

vii *Targets* was one of Verna Fields last sound-editing jobs. She then concentrated on film editing and later won an Academy Award for her work on *Jaws* (1975).

own 'Mad Doctor' movie *Before I Hang* (1940). Then one day, while sitting around the pool at Bogdanovich's parent's house, Platt suggested the title *Human Targets*, which her husband promptly shortened to simply *Targets*. For six months Bogdanovich edited the picture entirely by hand on an old moviola. Prior to shooting he had shot test footage at the drive-in. Now, he cut every inch of that film into the finished picture.

Although Roger Corman had a deal with AIP to distribute his films, Bogdanovich wanted to try to sell the picture to one of the major studios. Corman gave his permission with one stipulation – he wanted his $125,000 investment back. Robert Evans, the head of Paramount, then saw the picture and eventually persuaded Charles Blühdorn – the head of the studios owning company, Gulf & Western – to buy the picture for $150,000. Roger Corman had made a $25,000 profit.

However, on 4 April 1968 – before the picture could be scheduled for release – the question of gun control was tragically brought to the fore when Martin Luther King was assassinated in Memphis, Tennessee. Then, two months later, Senator Robert F. Kennedy was gunned down. Paramount's front office was now divided. While some were in favour of shelving the picture, others wanted to release it right away. Eventually they agreed to give *Targets* a limited release that August. They made just eight prints, adding a written prologue to the movie advocating the need for gun control. Bogdanovich disagreed with the decision. "I don't think we have to explain or excuse," he said the following year.[52]

Targets opened at the New Embassy Theatre in New York on Tuesday, 13 August 1968. Howard Thompson of the *New York Times* wrote, "As director, producer and co-writer

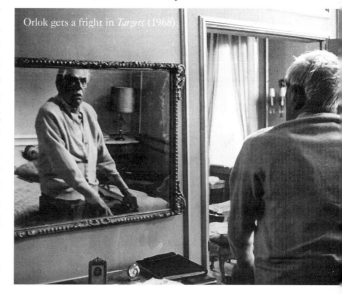

Orlok gets a fright in *Targets* (1968).

(with his wife Polly Platt) of the new Paramount release, Mr. Bogdanovich has nimbly sketched two case histories hinging on horror and joined them together, with an admirable minimum of blood-splattering, for the most grippingly clinical and freezing finale we have seen in ages."[53] The picture's only flaw, Thompson felt, was Bogdanovich's refusal to answer the question – Why? What had turned Bobby Thompson into a killer? "Aside from that one burning question," he wrote, "*Targets* scores an unnerving bullseye."[54]

Bogdanovich, though, had never intended to answer that question. "We did a lot of research," he explained, "and the most terrifying aspect of these crimes is that there is no answer. We find no reason commensurate with the size of the crime. I felt it was presumptuous to give an answer to something that psychiatrists, sociologists and humanists don't know. I would rather the audience come out saying 'Why?' because that's not so complacent an answer."[55]

Although *Targets* was not a financial success it brought Peter Bogdanovich to the attention of Columbia Pictures who expressed an interest in working with the young director. So, when Bogdanovich needed backing for his next picture, *The Last Picture Show*

(1971), he went to the studio who green lit his project. "It wouldn't have happened without *Targets*," he later said, "which wouldn't have happened without Roger, which wouldn't have happened without Karloff. And so that's how it goes in the movie business. One thing leads to another."[56]

Karloff finally got to see *Targets* for the first time in late May/early June 1968, a few weeks after the picture's New York premiere, and the day before he returned to England after completing work on what would be his final pictures. "It's a very timely movie," Karloff told the press. "The violence in this country is just appalling. I bet most of the homes in this very canyon have firearms. This country is close to frontier life, and we sometimes forget that."[57]

"Boris and Evie saw it and they really liked the picture," Peter Bogdanovich later said, "and they were very complimentary – and always referred to it as Boris's last picture, even though he actually did shoot some other stuff."[58] Although *Targets* would not be Boris Karloff's final film, it was, he considered, one of his finest.

On 6 April 1967, while *Targets* was still in production, members of the press and other invited guests arrived at the Magic Castle, the private magician's club situated up the hill behind Grauman's Chinese Theatre, for a special evening. The cocktail party had a two-fold agenda – to honour Boris Karloff while also promoting his recent album, *An Evening with Boris Karloff and His Friends*.

The album was the idea of musician, broadcaster and make-up man Verne Langdon, who had approached Karloff the previous year while the star was working in Los Angeles. Langdon's original script, however, had not met with the star's approval. "It was too flippant," Karloff later revealed, "too full of whimsy."[59] Langdon, therefore, telephoned Forrest J. Ackerman to tell him the bad news. Still, all was not lost, Langdon told him.

"Karloff says if I show him a new script by nine o'clock tomorrow, one he likes, he'll stay an extra day and do it."[60] The new script, Langdon proposed, should be penned by Ackerman. It was now 11 p.m.

Half an hour later Langdon arrived at Ackerman's house and while the new script was being penned Langdon played mood music (from Karloff's 1932 picture *The Mummy*) on a piano. "At two-thirty in the morning," Ackerman later explained, "I wrote 'The End' and thought 'lost cause'. Nobody – even in my autobiography – is going to know I ever tried this."[61] To Ackerman's surprise the script was approved. "Karloff loved it," Langdon told him. "His wife okayed it, the agent said fine, front office says 'all systems go'. Be here at 9 o'clock tomorrow and you can hear it happen."[62]

For an hour the next day Ackerman listened as Karloff spoke his words, as he later recounted. "The resulting recording session was a highlight of my life," Ackerman wrote, "one of my proudest, most satisfactory hours as every word that came out of Boris Karloff's mouth, I had put into it. I could hardly believe my ears."[63]

After the recording session was over, Karloff was

Karloff with (L to R) Arthur Kennard, Milt Larsen, Verne Langdon and Forrest Ackerman.

quickly surrounded by people, congratulating him on his performance. One of the gathered, Ackerman recalled, then asked the star, "Mr. Karloff, considering your advanced years, you've just done the job of a man half your age – can you give us any clue, any helpful hint as to how you accomplished it?" He replied with typical modesty, "Well, I don't know, gentlemen, I guess just good clean living." Then he rolled his eyes heavenward and added with a twinkle in them, "Up to the age of six!"[64]

In those pre-video days *An Evening with Boris Karloff and His Friends* provided, along with 8mm or 16mm movie prints, one of the few ways to savour clips from the old Universal horror pictures in the comfort of your own home. In January 1967 *Billboard* proclaimed it one of the magazine's 'four-star albums' – a recording "with sufficient commercial potential"[65] in its category.

"Karloff offers a soothing narration," one reviewer wrote, "that, in retrospect, is often amusing and reassuring… This record will probably have no appeal to the teenager because he has no way of judging its significance. But it is a collector's item for anyone who can remember those remarkable movies."[66] The LP was an instant success when it hit the shelves. At Hollywood's largest record shop the album, it was said, sold out even before it had been publicised.

At the press event that April, Boris Karloff, seated between Evie and Forrest J. Ackerman, fielded questions from the floor. "I hope my jury will be as kind as it looks!" he commented.[67]

One of the attendees that evening was Ackerman's assistant and colleague, Bill Warren. Now, at Ackerman's invitation, Warren was able to see the horror star 'in the flesh' for the first time. "It was the first time we had been to the Magic Castle, and were pretty well dazzled by it all," Warren recalled. "The press conference with Karloff took place in one of the smaller close-up magic rooms. I could hardly believe that I was actually in the same room with Boris Karloff, but there he was, genial and outgoing, answering all questions. I asked him about Lugosi; he related the anecdote concerning *Son of Frankenstein*, when he had to pick up Ygor's 'dead body'." He [Karloff] had been having back and leg problems, and was worried that he might strain himself – but he picked up 'nothing' (his words). He was impressed by, and grateful for, Lugosi's professional-actor behaviour: he undetectably stood up as Karloff made to lift him, almost eliminating the strain on Karloff's back. But mostly though, I just sat there with my mouth hanging open."[68]

"I'm a very lucky man," Karloff told his audience that evening. "Here I am in my 80th year… and I'm still able to earn my bread and butter at my profession. I am one of the very small family of the human race who happens to thoroughly enjoy his work. If I didn't enjoy it, I wouldn't go on."[69] He had no intention of stopping, he told them. "My leg in a steel brace… operating with only half a lung… Why, it's a public scandal that I'm still around!" he said. "But as long as people want me, I feel an obligation to go on performing. After all, every time I act I provide employment for a fleet of doubles!"[70] And what did Mrs. Karloff feel about her husband's film work, the star was asked. "My wife is a woman of great taste," Karloff replied. "She has seen very, very *few* of my pictures!"[71]

Returning to England, Karloff and Evie divided their time between their London flat and the quietude of their Bramshott cottage. Settling back into English life the star accepted a different role, as Vice President of Bramshott and Liphook Cricket Club. By now, however, the honour was purely titular, for his poor health precluded his attendance at many matches, although his love of the game remained.

By July, prompted perhaps by his failing health, Karloff's thoughts had turned to the question of his financial legacy. Although he had made his will back in June 1964, he now wished to arrange a few additional bequests. "Evie dropped you a line today with the boring news about this bout of our favourite bronchitis," he wrote. "However, as she told you, it is responding and clearing up well... In the meantime I have been meaning to write to you for some time about the copy of the letter you have which I left for Evie as to the disposition of certain funds later on."[72] After making some amendments to a new bequest Karloff concluded, "In the meantime I am behaving and doing what I am told and Evie, as always, is a tower of strength... how lucky I am."[73]

In Bramshott that December – Christmas 1967 – Boris Karloff's newspaper boy, Richard Randall, encountered the star for the first time:

> Every day I would cycle down that dark and eerie road, delivering to most of the properties, as it is a little way out of the village and since the old stores closed in Bramshott, there was nowhere else to get papers without a trudge to the village centre in Liphook.
>
> My meeting with "The Great Man" was two days or so before Christmas. I was just about to push the paper through the letterbox, when the door slowly opened. Now please bear in mind, I was 14 years old and it is the middle of winter and as it is only 7 a.m., it is still pitch black dark. Standing in the doorway under a very low light was Boris Karloff. We all knew that he was the monster in the Frankenstein films, and at that age, could only picture him as such. He slowly raised his left hand and took the paper, then he held out his other hand and gave me my [50p] Christmas tip. He spoke softly and slowly and thanked me for my services throughout the year. I can't remember if I said anything or not, I was that bloody petrified.[74]

Despite his continued poor health Karloff was still determined to keep working and, in February 1968, returned to the fold of Tony Tenser's Tigon British Film Production Ltd. to start work on another picture – *Curse of the Crimson Altar*.

Chapter 26

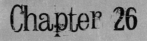

FINAL FILMS AND FADE OUT

(1968-1969)

"Well, I must admit the whole of my career has, shall I say, a familiar ring about it. They don't change the pattern very much. But I don't hanker for changes..."[1]
Boris Karloff (1968)

Boris Karloff's new picture, *Curse of the Crimson Altar*, would be a tale of witchcraft and revenge loosely based on H.P. Lovecraft's 1932 tale *The Dreams in the Witch House*. The picture's director, Vernon Sewell, had initiated the project after reading the original story. "I read it and decided I would like to make it," he said. "They already had Karloff for it but suddenly discovered they couldn't get insurance for him so he would have to be dropped. So we recast it with Christopher Lee."[2]

However, once again it was felt an uninsured Karloff was preferable to no Karloff at all, as the picture's producer Louis M. Heyward later explained: "He was confined to a wheelchair and I was told we could not get insurance. I said, 'Screw it. He goes on.' And no one came in as well prepared as Boris. He was the consummate, thorough professional, with respect for his craft and respect for his fellow workers. He was just a total delight to be with."[3]

Prior to the shoot, executive producer Tony Tenser had visited Karloff at his London flat but was disturbed to find a visible change in the star. "He hadn't been in the best of health during *The Sorcerers*," Tenser later said, "but in the year since, he had deteriorated quite a lot."[4]

Still, Karloff was back in the picture – but changes had to be made. "A week before the film started, the studio decided they had to have Karloff because they had to pay him, whether he died or not!" Vernon Sewell recalled. "So the whole script was rewritten a week before the start. Christopher Lee played the baddie and Karloff was written in as an extra character in a wheelchair, the goodie!"[5]

Left: As Professor
Marsh in *Curse of
the Crimson Altar*
(1968). Above:
Karloff enjoys
himself during the
production.

The final script would tell the story of antiques dealer, Robert Manning, who returns to his ancestral seat, the village of Greymarsh, to investigate the disappearance of his brother, Peter. Although Peter's last note was written on notepaper from Craxted Lodge the owner, J.D. Morley [Lee], denies all knowledge of him. Robert is, however, invited to stay at the lodge and later accompanies Morley's niece, Eve, to the annual 'Witch's Night', the commemoration of the burning of local witch, Lavinia Morley, some three hundred years earlier.

Despite being warned to leave by Morley's servant, Elder, Manning stays and that night experiences his first nightmare. He dreams he is a prisoner at a witches' Sabbath, where Lavinia attempts to make him sign a book, in blood. The experience soon seems more real, however, for waking from his second nightmare he discovers a knife wound on his arm.

The following day he discovers a secret panel in his bedroom that leads to a room at the top of the house – the room from his nightmare. After the local police sergeant dismisses his complaints, Manning goes to see black magic expert Professor Marsh [Karloff] who informs him he is a direct descendant of Lavinia's principal accuser.

Eve is shown the secret room but, after she leaves, Manning discovers Elder's body. Eve is later hypnotised by her uncle who prepares to sacrifice her for betraying the Morley name. Having also seized Manning, Morley now intends to bring Lavinia's curse to fruition by killing the last descendent of her accuser. Professor Marsh foils the plot, however, and Morley flees after setting the room on fire. Marsh, Manning and Eve escape and watch the spreading fire as Morley reaches the roof. As they look on, Morley transforms into Lavinia herself, who laughs at them as the building burns.

"It's about a warlock, a man whose ancestress was burned as a witch," Karloff explained. "He's a bit dotty, you see, and is running around seeking vengeance. Christopher Lee plays him. I'm bit of a red herring in the story, actually, and you don't know whether I'm doing the murders or [if] it's Christopher. At the end, it turns out I'm sort of trapping him and using the young leading man as bait, much to his annoyance I may say. I don't know which was worse, the script the producer got first or the one I saw first. He had to rewrite it at least three times, poor fellow. My main contribution to scripts is to see how much of myself I can cut out, to bring a four line speech down to two."[6]

Joining Karloff and Lee, as the 'young leading man' Robert Manning, was Mark Eden. Eden had made numerous appearances on British television in shows that included *The Avengers*, *The Saint*, *The Prisoner* and *Doctor Who*. His film appearances to that date included *The L-Shaped Room* (1962), *Séance on a Wet Afternoon* (1964) and *Doctor Zhivago* (1965). He is, perhaps, best known to British television audiences as the villainous Alan Bradley in the long running soap *Coronation Street*. "One of the reasons I took the part in *Curse of the Crimson Altar* was the opportunity to meet, and work with, a living legend: Boris Karloff," Eden later explained. "Boris was in a wheelchair for most of the film, and was not a well man, but he was always on time, and word perfect... He was such a charming man. A gentleman, in the true meaning of that word. I used to sit with him at lunchtimes and, at my instigation, [he] would regale me with stories of Hollywood in the 1930s and 40s."[7]

Virginia Wetherell was cast as Morley's niece, Eve. She had already appeared on British television in such well-known shows as *Doctor Who* and *Crossroads*. Then, following her work on the series *The Troubleshooters*, the actress was offered a five-picture deal by American International Pictures. "In the end, however," Wetherell said, "I only did one – for Tigon – and I had a super time. I thought Boris Karloff was wonderful: a gentle, lovely, sweet, sweet man. He was divine."[8]

While working on *Curse of the Crimson Altar*, however, the actress became subject to Tigon's whims, as the picture's director, Vernon Sewell, revealed. "They told me I had to have a naked woman in it somewhere," he said, "so I just showed a woman getting out of bed and that was it. I thought the whole genre was funny and I enjoyed doing those films."[9]

"Well, in fact," Wetherell later admitted, "in the scene where I look up from my book and say 'Who's there?' or whatever and then go to the door, that wasn't actually my body. I said 'I'm not doing that!' and they said 'All right – your stand-in can do it'. She was twice the size of me, and that taught me a lesson – you do your own nude scenes, or you check the body first!"[10]

Even so, Wetherell recalled the picture with affection. "I still think it's good, I really do," she said. "To be honest, at the time it was a case of 'Well, I'm not doing anything for the next six weeks – all right, I'll do it'. Those films were rather frowned upon. But now, one's remembered for those films and not the telly stuff that I did, which at the time I thought was much better. But there you go."[11]

Also featured, as the butler, Elder, was Michael Gough. It was the actor's second appearance alongside Boris Karloff. The two had appeared together, albeit briefly, in the television adaptation of *Treasure Island* (1960) on which Karloff, Gough recalled, "was just as lovely but we didn't talk so much."[12] *Curse of the Crimson Altar*, however, would afford the opportunity to get better acquainted. "I think Boris Karloff did the film because he came over to watch cricket as often as possible and used to travel on a Banana Boat," Gough said. "I don't think they run them anymore, a pity surely. So to be working in the purlieus of London watching cricket and doing a movie with very few lines to learn was a perfect holiday."[13]

Barbara Steele, who appeared in the picture as the witch Lavinia, had a lot in common with Boris Karloff. English-born, Steele had made a name for herself in horror pictures, working – as had Karloff – with directors Mario Bava, Roger Corman and Michael Reeves. Although the two had no scenes together Karloff and Steele did socialise on the set. "Karloff was the most gentle of personalities in private life," the actress later said. "You were immediately drawn into this beautiful soul that had such an aura of peace about him at the time we made this film. I believe he knew his time was short and he was fine with it. The entire crew adored him and so did Christopher Lee, who hovered about him like a guardian angel. I only worked on this film less than a week, yet I can still see that face of his with those soulful eyes that penetrated right into your innermost depths when he chose to really look at you. There was an unmistakable sadness in those eyes that had seen so much of this life in the spotlight, yet his grace and inner beauty made everyone in his orbit all the better for having known him. I do remember the publicity surrounding all of us on the film had labelled me 'the queen of mystery' or something equally daft... when Karloff heard this he took my hand and with a twinkle in his eye told me, 'Be careful, my dear, they will typecast you too'. I was then and still am honoured to have known him even if it was ever so briefly."[14]

One day, Tony Tenser called at Karloff's London flat to escort him to the shoot in the Middlesex village of Harrow Weald, only some 12 miles from the star's home. Evie answered the door. "I told her, 'I'm a few minutes early because I wanted to give Boris a chance to get his things together'," Tenser explained. "She said, 'Come in and have a cup of tea, because he's busy recording'. I asked, 'Does he have a crew with him?' She replied, 'Oh no, he's in his room alone, recording children's stories for the *Reader's Digest*.'"[15]

While some of the picture's exteriors were filmed in Ridge, a village some ten miles away, the majority of Karloff's scenes were shot inside, and in the grounds of, Grim's Dyke House, the former home of Victorian librettist William S. Gilbert, of Gilbert and Sullivan fame. Gilbert had, in fact, died in the lake. In 1911 he had attempted to rescue a woman in distress but, while doing so, suffered a heart attack and drowned.

One shoot in the house's grounds, however, would have repercussions. "We started out shooting night scenes in freezing rain," Karloff later recounted. "It's a bit different in the States. There they take you outside last of all and let you die in your own time. Much more sensible!"[16] Although Karloff joked about the situation at his age, and with his poor health, such antics could easily have proven dangerous, if not fatal. "He was actually taken ill during the shoot and had to go into hospital for a while," Mark Eden said. "When he returned he apologised to everyone for holding up the production."[17]

On 19 February Karloff entered London's University College Hospital for a 'routine medical checkup'.[18] Karloff's condition, a hospital spokesman said, was "satisfactory".[19] He left the hospital four days later when it was revealed he had undergone treatment for bronchitis. Despite his infirmities Karloff soldiered on. Christopher Lee later attested to his co-star's indomitable spirit:

> He was a remarkable man. During the last few years of his life he had to contend with agonising pain. He suffered from very bad physical disabilities: very, very bad arthritis, and of course, latterly, this very agonising trouble with his lungs. One part of me would literally shudder at the efforts that I saw him make and the pain that I knew it was causing to him and the other part of me

would stand there aghast in admiration and respect at the tremendous courage and vitality which he showed in the face of this very considerable adversity. He never complained; he always made light of his ills and his problems. He was a very sensitive man – a very kind man – always helpful, always polite, always courteous; I would say an outstanding human being in every way…

I saw him doing those takes from *The Crimson Altar* when he could barely breathe and yet, the precision, the sheer professionalism of it all, never faltered, never flagged, not for one second.[20]

With Karloff temporarily off the picture, measures had to be taken. "We had to shoot around him with a double for some exterior shots," Tony Tenser explained. "I went to see him at the private hospital where he was staying. I called at the front desk, and asked for Mr. Boris Karloff. The receptionist told me, 'I'm sorry, sir, but we don't have anyone here by that name'. I knew it was the right hospital. I thought for a moment, and then asked, 'Do you have a Mr. William Pratt registered?' The receptionist replied, 'Oh *yes*, we have Mr. Pratt'. I was shown up to his room, and in walked Boris. He had been out for a stroll along the corridor. He was so modest that nobody at the hospital realised that William Pratt was Boris Karloff."[21]

His work on the picture, Karloff recalled, "went through in jig time, about eight days",[22] and, although he had not worked on the picture long, he had certainly made an impression. "Everybody on the set respected him and really liked him," Michael Gough said. "He was a REAL GENTLEMAN!"[23]

"Before we parted," Mark Eden revealed, "he gave me a signed photograph of himself (which I had asked for) on which he praised my performance. It is on the on the wall of my study… I treasure it greatly."[24] Christopher Lee, too, would also receive a signed photograph from that shoot. *Dear Christopher, Many, many more together, I hope*, Karloff wrote on the picture. "And I can never look at that photograph without feeling rather sad," Lee stated. "I was very fond of him, very fond of him… everybody was."[25]

Although *Curse of the Crimson Altar* opened in the U.K. in December 1968 it did not reach the U.S. until over a year later. Renamed *The Crimson Cult*, the picture opened in Los Angeles on Wednesday, 15 April 1970 in a double bill with *Horror House* starring Frankie Avalon. "An admirable cast… plays it absolutely straight against knowing, frequently witty dialogue," wrote Kevin Thomas of the *Los Angeles Times*. "In short, a delight for horror fans, with Karloff in top form despite the infirmities of age."[26]

The picture opened at neighbourhood theatres in New York seven months later, on 11 November, in a double bill with *Count Yorga, Vampire*. "I should be hard-pressed to defend *The Crimson Cult* on any grounds other than affection for the subject and for some of the cast," wrote the *New York Times*. "But the special appeal… of *The Crimson Cult* [is] the last [*sic*] performance of the late Boris Karloff. He plays a Professor Marsh… and his role holds no surprises. But Karloff himself, cadaverous and almost wholly crippled, acts with a quiet lucidity of such great beauty that it is a refreshment merely to hear him speak old claptrap."[27]

In early February 1968 the press had announced that Karloff, now aged 80, would revisit the role of Jonathan Brewster for a new colour television adaptation of *Arsenic and Old Lace*. Joining him would be Helen Hayes and Lillian Gish as the murderous siblings, with *Hogan's Heroes* star Bob Crane as Mortimer.

However, when the show was produced at ABC's studios in New York the following month Karloff was not featured. Instead Fred Gwynne, of *The Munsters* fame, stepped into Karloff's shoes. When the show was broadcast in April of the following year the reviews were mixed and many reviewers found Gwynne a poor substitute. *Oakland Tribune* columnist Bob MacKenzie wrote, "*Arsenic and Old Lace* died of slow poisoning on ABC last night… There ought to be some way of bringing Fred Gwynne into court for his bad Boris Karloff imitation. Since Karloff originated the part of the mad nephew, Jonathan, Gwynne's interpretation was an out-and-out case of petty theft. But it wasn't even a good job of burglary, since poor Gwynne didn't seem to know from one line to the next whether he had a British accent or not."[28]

While Karloff's withdrawal from the show was not publicly explained it was most likely due to his continued ill health. Sadly, the night shoot on *Curse of the Crimson Altar* had taken its toll. The bronchitis had developed into a serious bout of pneumonia.

On Tuesday, 29 February Boris Karloff was announced as the winner of the Grammy Award under the category Best Recording for Children for his narration of *Dr. Seuss' How The Grinch Stole Christmas!* Earlier, Karloff's agent, Arthur Kennard, had called him to inform him of the nomination. "If I should win," Karloff replied, "why don't you accept the prize, put it on your desk and keep it for me."[29] So, the next time Karloff visited Kennard's L.A. office the award was pointed out to him. "It looks like a doorstop," the star commented.[30] "And with that," Kennard said, "he picked it up, opened my office door into the reception room, left it open and put it on the floor as a doorstop. And it stayed there for a long, long time – because I'm sentimental when it comes to people like Boris."[31]

Weeks later *Life* magazine celebrated the 150th anniversary of the publication of Mary Shelley's novel *Frankenstein*. While the article was solely concerned with the original novel, the magazine's cover featured a contemporary shot of Karloff, a seemingly disembodied head floating above a birthday cake.[i] The star later told the director Jack Hill it had been an honour to have been featured on the magazine's cover.

As Karloff recuperated after the bout of pneumonia he was visited by journalist Mark Shivas. "And the Karloff's London apartment isn't even slightly reminiscent of Charles Addams," Shivas wrote. "Instead, it's light, airy and in good Sunday afternoon taste. Mrs. Karloff is elegant, with a slight drawl and a pleasing tendency to chime in. He reached 80 last November, and still looks like a colonel from the Indian army, with skin the colour of old parchment."[32] Shivas found the star sitting, slightly hunched, in a winged chair. Although he looked frail, his condition, Karloff joked, did have its compensations. "I have a great advantage with my grey hair and this leg brace," he said. "The combination of that and bursting into tears at the right moment means that everything is done for me."[33]

Yet despite his ill-health Karloff had signed to make several more pictures. "Last year I did three films," he told Shivas, "this year I expect to make five. Four of them will be for a Mexican producer, a charming man, really charming."[34] This man was Luis Enrique Vergara.

Vergara had made a deal with Karloff to make the four pictures back to back, for which the star would receive $100,000 per film. Originally it was intended Karloff would make the movies in Mexico City but the star's health problems had resulted in the project being delayed. In July 1967 Karloff, then suffering from a bout of bronchitis, had written in a

---

i In the original photograph Karloff wore a dark roll-neck sweater. This was later modified to give the floating head effect.

private letter, "One only hopes that the Mexican deal can be postponed until I am fit again."[35]

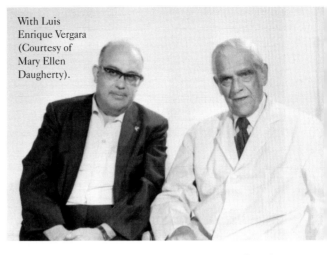

With Luis Enrique Vergara (Courtesy of Mary Ellen Daugherty).

As usual, Karloff mentioned his forthcoming commitments to his friend Bernard Coleman. "And then he'd say, 'I'm going off to South America [*sic*] to make a film'," Coleman said, "and he was pretty old then, and I said, 'What do you want to do that for?' He replied, 'Well, they offered it to me. We always work. You never stop working!'"[36]

The movies would be made by the Mexican production company 'Filmica Azteca' and co-funded by Columbia Pictures which, at the time, had a large South-American department. Karloff's poor health eventually ruled out a trip to Mexico City due to its high altitude, so the star's scenes would be shot in Los Angeles instead. The rest of the pictures would be completed later in Mexico.

To direct the pictures Vergara had hired 35-year-old American writer/director Jack Hill. Hill had studied film at the University of California where he had made several student films alongside his fellow classmate, Francis Ford Coppola. In 1963, after working as a freelance cameraman, editor, sound recorder and writer, Hill was offered a chance to work for producer Roger Corman. He wrote and directed additional scenes for Corman's *The Wasp Woman* (1959) to increase its running time for television release. Later that year Hill wrote and directed several scenes for Corman's film *The Terror* which had starred Jack Nicholson and Karloff, although, as he later explained, "Boris had long since done his work on *The Terror* by the time I became involved with it. I didn't meet him until just before the Azteca shoot."[37] Hill later gained a six-month writing/directing contract with Universal but one day realised his option had expired when he found someone else's name on his office door. He was now unemployed. Fortunately Hill's lawyer also represented all of the Mexican movie companies in the U.S. and recommended his client to Vergara. Yet, despite having planned for four pictures, the producer had only a single script. "And I read the script and it was impossible," Hill explained. "It had scene upon scene of somebody reading letters, slow, boring, it was never going to work. So I set about working out four different stories that would give Boris a chance to play four different characters."[38]

The first of Hill's outlines was called *House of Evil*, the story of Matthias Morteval [Karloff], a dying recluse who gathers his relatives to his secluded mansion to choose an heir. Next was the Caribbean-set zombie picture *Isle of the Snake People* in which Karloff would play Carl van Molder, the secret head of a snake cult. Then came *The Incredible Invasion*, the story of Professor John Mayer [Karloff] whose powerful nuclear ray is sought by both the military and aliens. This story, from a premise by Vergara, was not one of Hill's favourites. "I wasn't very happy with it, frankly," he said.[39] Finally came *The Fear Chamber*, which had a premise much more to the director's liking – a tale of a living rock that feeds on fear – "which," said Hill, "I thought was really a pretty terrific idea for a story – more of a science fiction thriller."[40] Karloff would play Dr. Carl Mandel, the scientist tasked with ensuring the rock remains suitably nourished.

The storylines were intended, as Hill later explained, to give his star plenty of "Karloffian stuff to do."[41] For the production to work Hill had to make special considerations when writing. "I had to write the scripts in such a way that all his scenes could be shot in Hollywood," he explained, "with the minimum of actors brought from Mexico, with sets that wouldn't have to be duplicated in Mexico."[42] Karloff's scenes would all need to be shot indoors as his health now precluded

With director Jack Hill during production of *House of Evil* (1968) (Courtesy of Jack Hill).

any exterior shooting. As a consequence, and whenever possible, Hill wrote scenes that the star could enact at rest, either seated or lying in bed.

After Vergara approved Hill's stories the director set about writing the four scripts. As time was short Hill's friend Karl Schanzer wrote the first draft of *The Incredible Invasion* from Hill's story outline while Hill did the final rewrite. The finished scripts were sent to Karloff for approval. "He liked them," explained Hill, "so we went ahead setting up production."[43] Vergara planned to have the films shot back to back in three weeks. Hill had known Roger Corman shoot two pictures in this manner but four pictures in three weeks, Hill later asserted, was "absolutely insane".[44]

Production was scheduled to take place at the General Services Studios at 1040 N. Las Palmas Avenue in Hollywood. The studios were built in 1919 and over the years many famous pictures, including Howard Hughes's *Hell's Angels* (1930), Korda's *The Thief of Bagdad* (1940) and The Marx Brothers' *A Night in Casablanca* (1946) had been shot on its soundstages. In the 1950s, with the increasing popularity of television, the studios became the venue for the filming of many popular shows, including *The Burns and Allen Show* and *I Love Lucy*.

In May 1968 the Karloffs flew to Los Angeles and were met at the International Airport by the star's agent, Arthur Kennard, who drove them to their house in Benedict Canyon where they would stay for the duration of the shoot. It was here that Jack Hill met Karloff for the first time when he "visited him briefly just to get acquainted".[45] Hill was pleased to have the chance to work with the star. "He was an idol of mine, of course," he said. "I had worked with Lon Chaney Jr. but never had a chance to work with Boris."[46] Chaney – whom Hill had directed in the cult favourite *Spider Baby* – had clearly expressed his opinion of his *House of Frankenstein* co-star. "Lon was very jealous of Boris because Boris was more successful," Hill explained. "He said, 'That guy isn't one bit better than I am'. But of course, Boris didn't drink."[47]

Although Hill and Karloff shared a common experience in working for producer Roger Corman it was not something the star wished to discuss. "The only thing he

Left: Karloff in *House of Evil* (1968). Centre: Karloff relaxes during the production of *House of Evil* (Courtesy of Bill Warren). Right: Resting between takes on *The Incredible Invasion* (Courtesy of Mary Ellen Daugherty).

said to me about Roger Corman was that he didn't want that name mentioned in his presence," Hill later revealed. "So I assume their relationship was not a happy one on Boris's part. I heard (hearsay) that Roger screwed Boris over very badly on a deferment of Boris's fee for *The Terror*."[48]

Each day Karloff was chauffeured to the studio. "We had him picked up in a limo," Hill recalled.[49] Upon arrival Karloff would leave the car and transfer into a wheelchair. "I'm sure he had an attendant or nurse," Hill said. "I don't recall if it was a man or woman. He had an oxygen bottle and mask with him at all times."[50] The star's poor health was very much in evidence. He had a brace on his left leg, and the ever-present oxygen tank attested to his breathing difficulties. He was, as Forrest Ackerman later said, "really… in a bad way, but what a trouper."[51] Although obvious to all, Karloff barely mentioned his illnesses. "All he said to me," Hill recalled, "was that, with emphysema, 'there were no spare parts, you know'."[52]

Forrest J. Ackerman, who had written the script for *An Evening with Boris Karloff and His Friends* the previous year, had been invited to the studio to watch Karloff in action. Ackerman, in turn, invited Bill Warren. On his first day at the studio Warren met Vergara. The producer was, Warren recalled, a "likeable, friendly man" who "took quite a shine to me when he realised both of us were Stanley Kubrick fans. We spent a good deal of time talking about *2001*, not much about the Karloff movies."[53] Vergara gave Warren an open invitation to visit the set as often as he liked although, not wishing to become a pest, Warren stayed away on several days. As it was his first time on a movie set Warren was understandably nervous and although he had tried to keep out of the way of the crew one *faux pas* drew him to the attention of them all. "I took one flash picture which got everyone excited," he confessed. "Apparently, you're supposed to call out 'flash!' when taking such a shot, so no one thinks a bulb blew out. I was deeply embarrassed."[54]

The weather outside was hot. On the soundstage, under the lights, it was stifling. After each take was completed the soundstage doors were flung wide and huge fans burst into action in an attempt to make the atmosphere inside more bearable. Unfortunately the heat was not the only problem. The entire shoot had not started well. In fact, as Jack Hill later confessed, "It was a disaster right from the beginning."[55]

When the actors arrived on set Hill discovered they were not the ones he had hired in

Mexico. Perhaps even worse, on a production where time was of the essence, they were often late. "They were never on time," Hill explained.[56] Even Vergara proved unreliable when his wife decided she wanted to visit Disneyland, "so," Hill recalled, "he was off at Disneyland when he should have been on the set where he had to make decisions."[57]

Unfortunately, some of the crew also proved problematic. "Actually," Hill admitted, "the main problem with the shoot is that I hired Roger Corman's production manager, Jack Bohrer, who was normally very good, but who took this 'Mexican' production very lightly – as a joke, in fact. Jack hired a friend of his as assistant director who had never done that job before and was completely incompetent."[58] This assistant director was a man named Beach Dickerson who, Hill recalled, "was mostly a sort of high-level gofer for Corman. He was a handyman of sorts and built some modifications to Corman's offices, which later caved in. Enough said."[59]

Fortunately, though, some crew members could be relied upon. The director's father, Roland Hill, designed the sets for all four pictures. Originally an architect, Hill had worked as a set designer at National Studios and Warner Brothers. In the early 1950s he joined Walt Disney Productions where he designed the interiors of Captain Nemo's submarine, *The Nautilus*, for the studio's adaptation of Jules Verne's *20,000 Leagues Under the Sea* (1954). His crowning achievement, though, was his design for the Sleeping Beauty Castle, the centrepiece of Disneyland, which had opened in Anaheim, California in 1955.

After time in costume and make-up Karloff was ready for the day's shoot. "He was thoroughly prepared every day," Hill recalled, "and suffered badly on several occasions because the schedule was badly drawn, so that sometimes he had to sit for hours before being called to the set. One day he sat all day on the stage and didn't work at all. I felt very badly about that, but he was very understanding about what I had to deal with, and didn't blame me. A lot of this was Vegara's fault, though, as he refused to engage a crew far enough in advance to get the best people, so that we had to take what we could get at the last moment. I must accept some blame, though, for trusting the production manager to take his job seriously, and I should have known that the A.D. was incompetent – although by the time I found out who it was, it was a *fait accompli*. It's just that prepping four pictures back to back in such a complicated structure kept me too busy to really stay on top of things. The shoot was planned to take only three weeks and it ran into four, right up against Boris's time limit. Many years later, when I was shooting another picture in Mexico, I heard that the people there thought that Vergara was crazy to try to do such a project. Apparently nobody there blamed me."[60]

When not required on set Karloff could often be found seated in his wheelchair, with his oxygen mask held to his face, studying his lines. However, his obvious tiredness and infirmities did not deter some from disturbing him. On one occasion Bill Warren saw a woman pull her son towards the star. "See?" she said to the boy. "He played Frankenstein."

"You mean Herman Munster?" the boy asked. Karloff ignored the dialogue until the woman addressed him directly. He then raised his head and smiled. Despite the intrusion, "he spoke, as before," Warren recalled, "kindly and sincerely."[61]

When it came to shooting, all eyes were on the star. When called to the set Karloff seemed rejuvenated, unshackled by his infirmities and keen to get on with the work in hand. He would rise from his chair unassisted and take his position ready for filming. "If there was any action in a scene," Hill said, "he would breathe the oxygen before starting, then do the action, then return to his wheelchair and sometimes take oxygen again."[62]

In one scene Karloff was required to bolt a door. Then, leaning on the wall, a wave of pain distorted his face. There was an audible gasp from the onlookers and several, unfamiliar with the script, stepped forward to help – not realising that Karloff was merely playing his role. Bill Warren later expressed his feelings about this moment. "Our concern for him," he wrote, "our apprehension over his courage, our awareness of his weakened physical condition, and a lifetime of loving the man on screen had made us all want to help."[63]

With Bill Warren and Forrest Ackerman (Courtesy of Mary Ellen Daugherty).

Watching Karloff at work, take after take, Warren noticed each time the camera rolled the star would alter his performance slightly. "I talked with him about this later on," Warren wrote. "He said that he had studied the script carefully, as always, so he'd know about his character not only from his own lines and actions, but from what the other characters said and felt about his character. He wanted to bring his part fully to life, knowing that in a fantastic movie, believability is of major importance. To produce believability for the audience, he had to achieve it for himself. That was one reason he varied his performance from take to take, while remaining within the boundaries of the character as he had interpreted them. 'I've done it all my film career', he told me. 'I've discovered that it keeps one from becoming too stale. This is a very great danger in working in films.'"[64]

As Karloff worked on the Azteca pictures he was visited on the set by Walt Daugherty. Daugherty was an ex-Hollywood stuntman, an enthusiastic Egyptologist, and devoted sci-fi fan who had been a committee member and organiser of the 1946 World Science Fiction Convention. In 1968 he was the principal photographer for Forrest Ackerman's *Famous Monsters of Filmland* magazine. Daugherty had met Karloff several times over the few preceding years. "Upon my first meeting with him," Daugherty later wrote, "I was immediately impressed by his gentlemanly manner, which had been written up by so many columnists. There was an overpowering impression which no one could fail to recognise from the very beginning of any association with him. There was a distinct and very sincere gentleness about the man."[65]

During the course of the shoot Daugherty and Karloff spoke several times. Invariably their discussions would turn to the topic of gardening. "We discussed at great length his garden in England," Daugherty recalled. "There was a sad smile on his face as we spoke.

You must realise that, because of his wheelchair condition, it was no longer a practical discussion based on a comparison of notes about the growing of various plants but instead a matter of 'what I used to be able to do'. Mr. Karloff was far from an amateur in the hobby of plants. Although no words crept into his conversation about this loss, it was evident in his eyes."[66]

"I used to garden, but because of my leg, I can't bend anymore," Karloff later told a journalist. "I used to play lots of games but *they've* given *me* up. So, you see, if I didn't work, I'd just sit here and grunt."[67]

Daugherty had long wanted to photograph Karloff and the Azteca shoots finally gave him the opportunity. During a break on the set, Karloff had been shown some of Daugherty's work. The photographer was then called over and the star enthusiastically agreed to a shoot. "He was ready to have the portraits done right then and there, and it was only after being assured that I would be on the picture for another few days, and could do it at a more convenient time, that he finally accepted the call of the director and went on the set for a scene. Later in the afternoon, off-scene where I had set up portrait equipment with the assistance of the crew, I finally realised a strong ambition and photographed Boris Karloff under my own controlled conditions."[68] While Karloff was filming, the photographer prepared for the session using Forrest Ackerman as the star's stand-in. Later that afternoon Daugherty shot the last formal portraits of Boris Karloff.

After the photo session ended an opportunity arose for one young fan to meet with the star. Writer Terri Pinckard had brought her nine-year-old son, Richard, to the set to see Karloff at work. Pinckard had adopted the boy – a Korean War orphan – after he had been abandoned by his G.I. father, and raised him on the classic monster movies. When Richard was introduced to the star he exclaimed, "Oh, Mr. Karloff, I've waited for this minute for years!"[69] Although Richard's statement raised laughter from onlookers, Karloff listened attentively to the boy. He reached out a hand and gently pulled the boy to him. Turning to Daugherty, Karloff said, "The next few will be of us together, the boy and I."[70]

During a break that day a few fans, including Ackerman, Pinckard and Warren, congregated in Karloff's small dressing room. There the star submitted to the usual round of questions. He seemed tired and as the session continued reacted less and less to the questions. Then Pickard spoke up. "Mr. Karloff, my 12-year-old is a handicapped little girl," she said. "She sometimes feels self-conscious of her braces. If I told her you wore braces on your legs exactly as she does, it would make her feel so much better for she, as [are] all my children, is an admirer of yours. But are you in pain?"[71] Karloff turned to her, stirred by her question. "His voice became animated at the personal interest and question," Pinckard later wrote. "He went into a discussion of the pain, the difficulty in movement that arthritis had brought to him."[72]

Pinckard and Karloff went on to discuss the merits of Britain's National Health Service before moving on to politics – where his strong political opinions were very much in evidence. Pinckard later recorded Karloff's views, including his belief that the United States, "beloved as it was to him, was sometimes betraying its people by not providing for them out of fear of socialism, the dirty word, the word that so many interpreted as communism."[73]

Karloff also bemoaned the general state of all political parties. "When any party gets into power and realises they represent the whole country," he opined, "they suddenly lose their extremism, their individuality and suffocate themselves with time-old ways of politics and politicians. It is as though they fear to be remembered in any way different from the previous administration. Not that that was good, but their position was at least known in history; a new edict might be received with less favour."[74] Still, despite the faults of the U.S. and the U.K., "they're still the best there is," he said.[75]

Such talk, away from the usual subjects of his movies, seemed to invigorate the star, for his face no longer seemed tired. Bill Warren recalled how he "listened to [Karloff's] lively discussion with Terri Pinckard about the founding of the Screen Actors Guild, and his intense dislike of the Motion Picture Academy. I think – but am definitely not sure – that he said he'd been approached to be the recipient of an honorary Oscar, and turned them down."[76] In fact, Karloff wanted nothing to do with the organisation. "An old friend of his," Warren explained, "perhaps Edith Evans (at this remove in time, I no longer remember to whom he was referring), was associated with the Oscar ceremonies that hot spring in 1968. He was irked that she was linked to the 'enemy' and darkly muttered that she'd regret it."[77]

The impromptu conference was bought to a close when Jack Hill appeared and told Karloff they were ready for him on set. As he left the dressing room Karloff turned to those present and said, with a laugh, "Well, I guess we've done all we could today to tear the United States' and England's present political policies to shreds and flush them down the drain."[78]

Back on set Karloff's dedication to his craft was as strong as ever, despite his frailties. "It was inspiring to watch him perform," Pinckard later said. "A glance at the script, his hand passed slowly over the brows and eyes that had haunted dreams of moviegoers, and the lines came. Sometimes he would say them, mouth them, shrug and turn to the director and say, 'They do not roll right on the tongue. I will say them this way'. And the director would nod, for [Karloff's] way was indeed smoother, better, more effective."[79]

This commitment – to produce the best work he possibly could – was also evident to Walt Daugherty. "I recall one scene," Daugherty recalled, "with Yerye Beirute (Mexico's Monster Actor) in which, after two rehearsals, Mr. Karloff called Mr. Beirute aside (within my earshot), at which time he told him, 'Yerye, this is your scene. I realise you are holding back because of me. Grab a hold of the part and play it for all it's worth. I repeat, this is your scene. Let me stay in the background and follow through.' In this day of fighting for recognition and scene-stealing by stars, it was so refreshing to see an actor give the scene to another."[80]

Walt Daugherty spent most of that night developing and printing the shots from the photo-session and the next day took several 16" x 20" pictures with him to the set where they were delivered to Karloff's dressing room. "I returned a short time later and you can imagine my great pleasure when he stated they were the finest portraits that he'd ever had taken – sentiments echoed by his wife. I gave him the copies that I had, from which they selected one to become his fan mail picture from then on."[81] Beneath this portrait Karloff wrote, *To Walt – I've waited 15 years for the finest pictures that have ever been made of me. Gratefully, Boris Karloff.*

Daugherty's recollections contain the only reference to Evelyn Karloff during the period of the Azteca shoot. Director Jack Hill never met Evie, either at the Karloff house in Benedict Canyon or at the studio. Only Daugherty mentioned seeing Mrs. Karloff in her husband's dressing room when she added her approval of the portraits of her husband. Possibly Karloff advised her to stay away due to both the heat and the chaotic nature of the shoot. Whatever the reason, Evie appears to have been uncharacteristically absent for the majority of the time.

She was in attendance, however, at a small dinner party held in honour of her husband by the author Robert Bloch and his wife. Also present was Forrest J. Ackerman and his wife Wendayne. Unable to decide upon a fourth couple to invite Bloch turned to Ackerman for ideas. Ackerman decided upon Fritz Lang, the director of *Metropolis* (1927). It was an inspired choice. "Yes," Ackerman later wrote, "these 'two old dinosaurs', as they put it, each touching 80, practically fell into each other's arms. They had been aware of each other's careers for 50 years but had never met... Usually Robert Bloch and I can be depended on to dominate the conversation at any dinner table, he being witty and I being half-witty, but this time the pair of us exhibited uncommon commonsense and shut our mouths and opened our ears – and drowned in anecdotes, reminiscences and observations that *should* have been captured on a longplay tape for posterity."[82]

Karloff's favourite late portrait (Courtesy of Mary Ellen Daugherty).

Boris Karloff's final film was *The Incredible Invasion*. After Karloff had completed his final scene Jack Hill stepped forward and announced to the cast and crew that the star's work was done. "Mr. Karloff rose from his wheelchair," Daugherty remembered, "and addressed the group, emphasising his pleasure in working with them and his pleasure at once again completing not one but four full-length pictures. It was evident for all to see that there were unabashed tears in his eyes, indicating his sincerity. Needless to say, the applause was resounding as his stand-in wheeled him off to his dressing room."[83]

With his final scene in the can Karloff then departed. "There was no party," Jack Hill said. "It was very tense at the end because we were very far behind schedule and, if Boris went over his time by one minute, the producer was in for a huge extra fee. We finished seconds before the deadline, and Boris left after the applause... He was always a very kind and gracious man. Everybody loved him."[84]

The shoot had given Jack Hill the opportunity to work with one of his idols although, unfortunately, the schedule had not allowed the two to become better acquainted. "I hardly got to know Boris personally at all," Hill said, "because the whole production was so chaotic and fast-moving that I had no time to socialise. And after the shoot he was very eager to get back to his rose garden in England. All I can say is that he was a fine actor and a real gentleman. And my limited experience with him was one that I'll never forget."[85]

Hill's work on the pictures also soon came to an end. He was supposed to go to Mexico to finish the pictures but Vergara disappeared. "He just took off," Hill exclaimed, "disappeared and I never heard any more about it. Eventually, he had a heart attack and died trying to scrape up the rest of the financing. I didn't find out until many years later that the pictures had in fact been finished. I finally saw one on tape and it just broke my heart to see what they'd done to it in Mexico."[86]

Karloff and the Hollywood Cricket Club,
Griffiths Park, L.A., 1968
(Courtesy of John Hayward).

During his stay in Los Angeles, Karloff paid a visit to the Hollywood Cricket Club and was photographed with the current team. "I was able to see Boris more than once at Griffith Park," team member John S. Hayward recalled, "the last time was when the team photograph was taken… When I last saw him he was using a sturdy walking stick. It is true that he was a very gentle man, with a most pleasing manner and not at all like his famous characterisations on film. At tea, several of our players (including myself) and other cricketers were able to enjoy brief conversations with Boris… You will appreciate that everyone extended the appropriate courtesy to this popular gentleman and former Hollywood Cricket Club player."[87]

Boris Karloff spent his summer in England at leisure, spending most of his time at the cottage in Bramshott where, for the next several months, he remained out of the spotlight. He was in England when, on 19 July 1968, Jack Pierce died. "The real father of Frankenstein is dead," wrote journalist Frank Taylor. "Jack Pierce, who invented the make-up for Frankenstein, the Mummy, Wolfman and dozens of other creepy characters, died in his Burbank home. His funeral at Forest Lawn drew less than 24 members of the movie industry, even though as a pioneer in make-up he had tutored most of today's make-up artists. Only Boris Karloff, who is in England, remembered to send a spray of flowers. Hollywood bids its own goodbye in the only way it knows – by staying away."[88]

Karloff broke his work hiatus when he was asked to appear on the season's premiere of *The Red Skelton Show*. Karloff had appeared on his friend Skelton's show before, but that was back in 1956 – over a decade earlier. On the new show he would be reunited with another old friend – Vincent Price.

As the show would be rehearsed and filmed at the CBS Television City in Fairfax the Karloffs flew out to Los Angeles. "I DON'T get calls for work in London, and that's fine with me," he told a journalist there. "It's not a big market for me. I'm much better known here. And besides, the fees for TV there are ridiculous. Imagine, $25 for a talk show. No, I'm happy to be able to pay my taxes here, contribute my fair share to a country that's done so much for me. I have no patience with these people who keep their money in Switzerland."[89]

Karloff's work on *The Red Skelton Show* was a bittersweet experience. Although the trio of Karloff, Skelton and Price laughed and joked together it was clear Karloff was not well. In the show's main sketch – *He Who Steals My Robot Steals Trash* – Karloff and Price played a father/son pair of scientists who discover Clem Kadiddlehopper [Skelton] asleep in their barn laboratory. Mistaking him for their experimental robot the scientists take their 'invention' to Washington for a disastrous demonstration at the Pentagon.

Originally, Karloff was to have played the skit from the comfort of his wheelchair, as Vincent Price recounted. "Boris with braced legs was wheeled into the scene by a midget in Frankenstein make-up – in the audience dress rehearsal he came off and called me over to ask if I had the same feeling he did, that the humour of the scene was deadened by the audience sympathy for a man in a wheel chair. I had to admit I did – whereupon Boris with infinite courage played the rest of the rehearsal on his feet and the show as well. Later Evie and I discussed this. She was naturally worried, but Boris's concern was for the show."[90]

With Red Skelton and Vincent Price on *The Red Skelton Show*, 24 September 1968.

In another portion of the show Skelton joined the two horror stars for a musical number, a song entitled *The Two of Us*, accompanied by the David Rose Orchestra. Spanky Wilson provided additional music when she sang two songs – *Alfie* and *Apartment 101*, while the Alan Copeland Singers performed *Nola*. "Red Skelton is back and hasn't changed a bit," columnist Bob MacKenzie wrote following the 24 September broadcast. "There are those who love him, and I wouldn't contradict them for the world. Boris Karloff and Vincent Price did some lumpish clowning in the monster vein, but the high point of the show came in a pair of songs by Spanky Wilson, a newcomer. She is cool, subtle, throaty and fine to look at. She will be very big."[91] Despite the difficulties Karloff later said the show with Skelton and Price "was a party for the three of us".[92]

Karloff's next television work – his last in a dramatic role – was in the television series *The Name of the Game* with Gene Barry. In the series' eleventh episode, *The White Birch*, Karloff appeared as Mikhail Orlov, a wheelchair-bound Czech author whose latest novel has been suppressed by the Communist government. Orlov enlists the help of publisher Glenn Howard [Barry] to smuggle the book out of the country in order to use the royalties to help fund the Czech freedom fighters. The episode also featured Roddy McDowall who had worked with Karloff on television over a decade earlier in *Heart of Darkness*. *The White Birch* was broadcast on the evening of Friday, 29 November 1968, six days after Karloff's 81st birthday. The episode's director, Lamont Johnson, later told Gordon B. Shriver:

> He was an obvious choice for **The White Birch** role, but we were kept in suspense until virtually the day of shooting his first scene because of his many health problems. When word came his car was coming through the Universal gates, I felt a signal of excitement and relief all around the set, only to be shocked into silence when he was wheeled through the stage door, looking pitifully emaciated and breathing with loud and disturbing symptoms of his emphysema.
>
> Then his nurse brought him to me directly, and he promptly dissipated the anxiety. As he shook my hand, he said in a loud, firm and witty voice, "What you see before you is not encouraging, I'm sure, but what is there is entirely at your service, sir."
>
> He was never so much as a single beat behind in anything relating to his role. A complete and heartening joy to all. His reminiscences of Peter Lorre were particularly delightful. The work and the community of his fellow actors, the crew and myself seemed to feed his energy and *élan vital*. He left more dynamically than he came to us, and always charming, humorous and strongly concentrated on his character and the telling of the story we had at hand.[93]

The Jonathan Winters Show – Karloff's last television work of all – was recorded on Monday, 14 October 1968 in CBS studio 43 at 7800 Beverly Boulevard in Los Angeles. It was broadcast a little over two weeks later, at 10 p.m. on Wednesday, 30 October.

Karloff was joined in this Halloween show by the actress Agnes Moorehead. A one-time member of Orson Welles' Mercury Theatre Group, Moorehead had appeared in Welles' famous 1938 *The War of the Worlds* radio broadcast and had featured in both *Citizen Kane* (1941) and *The Magnificent Ambersons* (1942). In 1968, however, she was probably best known for her role as the mischievous witch Endora, the mother of Samantha Stephens (Elizabeth Montgomery) in TV's popular comedy series *Bewitched*.

In one sketch Moorehead played the assistant to Karloff's mad scientist as he performed a transformation operation on the yokel Elwood P. Suggins (Winters). In a solo moment Karloff, accompanied by the Earl Browne Orchestra, sang the Frank Sinatra Top 30 tune *It Was a Very Good Year* with what one reviewer called a "Walter Huston approach".[94] Moorehead also told a horror story, accompanied by sound effects supplied by Winter, and music was supplied by the Craig Hundley Trio and singer Marjorie McCoy. "I found Mr. Karloff to be delightful," Winters later told Gordon B. Shriver. "I have long been a fan of his and that is why I wanted him on the show... He was very sweet to work with."[95]

Despite his ill health Karloff remained in demand. That October the press reported he was to join Frankie Avalon and Jill Haworth in the horror picture *The Dark* for Tigon. Karloff was slated to play the police inspector. However, his poor health later precluded his involvement in *The Haunted House of Horror*, as it was finally called, and he was replaced by Dennis Price.

Karloff's deteriorating health was very much in evidence when his long-time friend and biographer, Cynthia Lindsay, received a visit from him during one of his final trips to America:

> When she [Evie] brought him down to see me at the beach in Malibu the year before he died, she came in ahead of him and said, "I tried to get him to wait in the car, told him you would come out, but he wouldn't." I went out to greet him and the shock was terrible. He was holding the railing to the four short steps down to the house and literally dragging himself along. The look of pain on the beautiful face, the heavy tortuous breathing, the expression in the eyes… physically hurt me. He pulled the leg brace forward, shifted the cane to his other hand, embraced me, and said, "Here I am – a mess – but I'm here. The better for seeing you, old girl." I never saw him again.[96]

Returning to England after completing his work on *The Jonathan Winters Show* Karloff disembarked at New York's Kennedy Airport in order to catch a trans-Atlantic flight home. It was here the star caught a severe chill. After landing back in England, Karloff was immediately rushed to King Edward VII Hospital, in Midhurst, Sussex, less than ten miles from his Bramshott cottage.

In hospital Karloff received word that he had been honoured by the Count Dracula Society, a literary group established in 1962 for "the serious study of horror films and gothic literature".[97] Karloff had been voted the recipient of the Mrs. Ann Radcliffe Award, named in honour of the 18th century author of Gothic novels. So, on 17 January, Karloff penned a letter from his hospital room to the Society's president and founder Donald Reed. He was, Karloff wrote, "more than proud"[98] in being honoured but, in the circumstances, would ask his friend Robert Bloch to accept the award on his behalf.

A week later, on Thursday, 23 January 1969, while the star lay ill in hospital, the Karloffs home in Sheffield Terrace was broken into. Thieves took jewellery (including the charm bracelet Evie had received on her husband's *This Is Your Life*), silver, furs and even Karloff's gold medal from the Trieste film festival. Of some minor consolation was the fact that the thieves had neglected to take Karloff's gold SAG card No. 9 that he had so gratefully received in 1951.

At the hospital Evie fielded the calls to her husband allowing only a select few access. One of these was Karloff's agent, Arthur Kennard. During one of his long-distance calls Kennard informed his client that the celebrated Italian director Federico Fellini required his services. It was not true. "I dreamed up one of my typical agent-type lies," Kennard later explained. "I told him how I had this picture in the works for him and he was gonna put on the harness again and go to work. It made him feel good. I wanted him to go out on top."[99] Karloff's condition, by now, was deteriorating. As he had once opined to Jack Hill, there were no spare parts.

Now few were given access to the star. Evie had informed Bernard Coleman of her husband's condition but refused to let him visit. "She wouldn't let anybody go and see him," Coleman said. "She wouldn't let *anybody*. I said, 'Well, I'll go down to the hospital…' but 'No, No!' she said… I'd have loved to have gone. She was really very strict about that."[100]

Christopher Lee was a rare exception although, ultimately, he too was disappointed. "One of my great sorrows, of course, is the fact that I was not able to see him before he died," he later wrote. "I had spoken to Mrs. Karloff on the telephone two or three times whilst he was in Midhurst Hospital… She told me that he wasn't really at all well but was showing his usual tremendous guts. I said, 'Well look, I'd love to come down and see him. Do you think it would be all right?' and she said 'Oh yes. 20 minutes – 25 minutes – half an hour – he would love to see you'. I was planning to go down… when he passed away."[101]

On Saturday, 1 February Karloff, now in a weakened state, spent the day drifting in and out of sleep. Occasionally he would rouse and say a few words to his ever-present wife. Once, he suddenly whispered the name of fellow actor Walter Pidgeon and, after muttering the name once again, drifted back off to sleep. The next day Boris Karloff died. "I believe the end was peaceful and indeed it must have seemed a blessing," Christopher Lee wrote shortly afterwards.[102] The cause of death was recorded as a combination of cardiopulmonary failure, emphysema and chronic bronchitis.

At her home in Yucaipa, California, Sara Jane was oblivious to her father's passing. Then, on Monday, 3 February a neighbour suggested she turn on the television. There she was presented with news of her father's death. At 1:08 p.m. Sara sent Evie a Western Union telegram from the nearby city of Redlands. "So grieved to have just learned of Dad's passing," the telegram read. "Please call or wire arrangements for services. Love, Sara."[103] The message went unheeded.

The following day news of Boris Karloff's death hit the British newspapers. "The most faultless monster that the cinema ever saw, who for more than half a century turned audiences clammy with suspense, has died at the age of 81 in hospital in Midhurst, Sussex," announced *The Times*.[104] In America the obituaries continued, often illustrated with the almost compulsory picture of Karloff as the Frankenstein Monster – although the *New York Times* mistakenly accompanied their tribute with a photograph of Glenn Strange's monster.

Back in England Evie requested no flowers be sent and announced the funeral would be a private affair for family only. Boris Karloff's funeral service took place on Wednesday, 5 February in the chapel at Guildford crematorium. Considering the actor's worldwide fame it was a remarkably low-key affair. Although the chapel could seat up to one hundred mourners, only four people attended the ceremony on that dry, cloudy day – Evie Karloff, her sister Barbara and husband, and Evie's mother, Lina.

Although Karloff had two surviving siblings – John and Richard[ii] – as well as nieces and nephews, not a single one was present at the service. They were never invited. Also absent was his only child, Sara Jane, who was still waiting to hear from her stepmother. "She wouldn't allow anybody to go to the funeral," Bernard Coleman said. "She wouldn't allow it… It was a shame, really. But there you go. It's awfully difficult if people make those decisions."[105]

The star's cremated remains were buried in the open lawn in the 'Garden of Remembrance', poured down a two feet deep hole drilled in the lawn. Due to the large number of burials at the site there is little to see, no permanent memorial to mark the star's final resting place. The site, an area of grass, can be found only by its allocated code 2. H. 21 – Plot 2, row H, number 21. Evie had a rose planted in a nearby rose bed and an entry placed in the Book of Remembrance. The entry read:

---

ii David Pratt had died in Rochford Hospital in Rochford, Essex on 23 November 1952 (Karloff's 65th birthday). David was 81.

Karloff, Boris
1887 – 1969
A great man and a great actor.
Dearly and universally loved
By all who knew him.
"To live in hearts we leave behind,
Is not to die."

On 11 February a death notice appeared in *The Times*:

KARLOFF – On Feb. 2nd, 1969, peacefully, Boris Karloff, dearly loved and loving husband of Evelyn. Funeral held on Feb. 5th, privately, as he wished.

The 'King of Horror' was gone. "Doors will creak a little less ominously in movies now that our favourite fiend has gone," wrote journalist Donald Zec. "But the name Boris Karloff will continue to chill the spine of history."[106]

There had been notable exceptions to the horror roles, of course: Jonathan Brewster in *Arsenic and Old Lace*, Gramps in *On Borrowed Time* and Bishop Cauchon in *The Lark*, as well as countless others on radio, television and film. Still, to the masses Karloff will always be remembered, first and foremost, for his star-making role as the monster in Universal's *Frankenstein*. And if he had later been restricted as an actor by it he had never seemed too concerned. "After all," he once said, "I've always been a very happy monster."[107]

Chapter 27

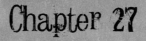

AFTERWORD

"I would hate to be un-typed. Every actor is typed, really. And it's rather wonderful when an actor can develop a trademark from his typing. After all, a manufacturer of boots or shoes spends millions developing a trademark – and here I had one handed to me."[1]

Boris Karloff (1962)

On 29 June 1969 the *Los Angeles Times* announced, "Actor Boris Karloff, who died in England earlier this year, left an estimated $250,000 estate to his widow. The terms of his will indicated he had left none of what was described as his American property to his daughter, Mrs. [Sara] Jane Cotton [*sic*] of Yucaipa."[2]

The will had also stipulated that, had Evie not survived her husband, $5,000 would be bequeathed to the Actors Fund of America. Karloff's friend Kristin Helmore (the daughter of Evie's ex-husband) would receive 'all right, title and interest'[3] to the Dakota building apartment[i] while his daughter, Sara Jane, would receive his residuary estate. In the event, everything went to Evie.

On 4 February 1969 – the day before Boris Karloff's funeral – Mexican producer Luis Enrique Vergara announced the star's salary for appearing in the four Azteca pictures – some $400,000 – now languished, uncollected, in a Mexican bank. According to Vergara, Karloff had requested his salary be placed in an account for him, planning to draw on it during his next Mexican vacation planned, the producer said, for 1972. Although no further mention of these monies is made in the press it can be assumed it, like the bulk of Karloff's possessions, eventually went to his widow.[ii]

After her husband's death Evie continued in her role as a movie star's widow, dividing her time between her homes in London and Bramshott. She attended functions and

---

i Had the apartment been sold before Karloff's death Helmore would have received $5,000. As it was, Evie later sold the apartment and presented Helmore with the monies – some $10,000.

ii Later estimates placed the value of Karloff's estate at the time of his death at the $2 million mark.

memorial services, meeting royalty and hobnobbing with politicians. Karloff's ex-paperboy, Richard Randall, had some dealings with her during these years. "I worked for a removal company," he later explained, "I moved many items of furniture for Evie, his wife, to her flat in London or from London to Bramshott. She always reminded us that she was Boris Karloff's wife."[4] "Evie Karloff was always polite," he added, "but also came over as a bit of a snob. She never failed to mention who she was and who she was married to. Having said that, she was always nice and polite to me. About 20 years ago, I moved some friends of hers to Lake Lugano in Switzerland. She actually lived next door to them in Bramshott Court (where she moved to after the death of her husband) and she went with them, for the ride, so to speak, and a short holiday. She recognised me straight away and we chatted for a while about that day when Boris answered the door to me, and her many removals. That was the last time I saw her."[5] "She could be a bit of a whatsit," Randall said. "When moving her effects from London to Bramshott or visa versa, she would rarely say please and thank you. It was more of an order than a request on where to place things. Having said that, she always gave us a tip when we had finished. Her tone was always, 'I'm paying for this, you do as I say'. Like I say – a bit of a snob."[6]

Even so, following her husband's death Evie did her best to honour his memory. She had a plaque erected in St. Paul's Church – the Actors' Church – in London's Covent Garden.[iii] The wooden memorial reads:

BORIS KARLOFF
(WILLIAM HENRY PRATT)
ACTOR
1887 – 1969
He nothing common did, or mean,
Upon that memorable scene.
(Andrew Marvell)

The two lines of poetry come from Marvell's *An Horatian Ode Upon Cromwell's Return from Ireland*, published in 1776. Far from honouring the Lord Protector the quote, in fact, refers to King Charles I upon the morning of his execution.

A second plaque was erected at Evie's instigation, this time in St. Mary's Church in Bramshott where she had paid £8,000 to have the bells rehung. "My husband always loved churches and this one in particular," she explained. "I thought it would be a nice thing to do in his memory."[7] Her biggest endeavour, however, was the establishment, on 18 June 1985, of the Boris Karloff Charitable Foundation (registered charity number 326898).

The foundation's remit still is to distribute funds 'to or for the benefit of such exclusively charitable objects and purposes as the trustees shall in their absolute discretion think fit'. "The latest Filed Accounts [to 5 April 2009] show an income of £75,745 which is paid out to a number of charitable causes," Peter Williamson of Peachy & Co. explained, "mainly connected with the acting profession but also including young cricketers, watching cricket being one of Boris's great interests. The Foundation has established scholarship Funds with RADA and LAMDA and supports a number of theatres including Shakespeare's Globe Theatre, the National Theatre and the Watermill Theatre in Newbury."[8]

---

iii George Bernard Shaw's play *Pygmalion* opens with pedestrians sheltering from the rain under the portico of St. Paul's church. It is here the phonetics professor Henry Higgins encounters Eliza Dolittle for the first time.

The years following Boris Karloff's death would also see changes in Sara's life. She had maintained a cursory relationship with her father since her parents' divorce and her marriage to Richard Cotten. Still, Sara's children were fortunate enough to become acquainted with their famous grandfather during his visits to America. "My father and Evie came to visit us in Dayton, Ohio after my first son, Michael, was born [1960] and in Scottsdale, AZ. after my second son, David, was born [1961] and visited us in Lompoc, CA. and in Yucaipa, CA. as the boys were growing up," Sara explained. "We visited them in L.A. when they would be there for work at the various places they would be staying... the Chateau Marmont or private homes. My father really enjoyed the boys and they, as they grew older, were very proud of him as they grew to understand what he did."[9] To avoid confusion, and allow the boys to differentiate between their grandparents, the Karloffs and the Rowes, Karloff suggested the boys adopt the Dutch terms when referring to Evie and himself. "They called him Opa, and Evie, Oma," Sara said.[10]

In 1972, after 14 years of marriage, Sara's marriage to Richard Cotten came to an end. She remained single until 1992 when she wed retired air force colonel William J. 'Sparky' Sparkman. It was a union that would last until Sparky's death in 2009.

Sara maintained an arms-length relationship with Evie. The two would lunch together whenever Evie was in California – but only once during each visit. Any personal correspondence was limited to just a few letters a year. Evie did, however, maintain friendships with some of her husband's friends, such as Bernard Coleman. "I got on very well with her," he said. "She was charming – but she cosseted Boris. They were so devoted, absolutely devoted and she didn't like anybody else [getting close]... it must have been a form of jealousy. I didn't realise how much it was until Sara Jane appeared and told me how difficult she had been. But as far as Boris was concerned she was marvellous to him, and marvellous with him – and she was good fun. When he died we used to meet her and take her out to dinner and she was very good. She was terribly upset when he died – but it was great fun. She was great fun. I liked her very much. I'm sure that she treated Sara Jane not well – I think it was very sad... and it was a great pity because she [Evie] was so nice but she obviously didn't get on with her stepdaughter."[11]

The old jealousies remained long after Karloff's death. On 18 January 1988 the Academy of Motion Pictures Arts and Sciences staged a tribute to the 'King of Horror'. *Boris Karloff: A Centenary Tribute* would include clips from Karloff's films as well as tributes from his friends and colleagues Peter Bogdanovich, Vincent Price, George Schaeffer and Robert Wise.

Although Evie was scheduled to attend Sara Karloff had not received an invitation. "I learned about it from Dinah Shore," Sara explained. "I called the Academy and they said, 'We've been looking everywhere for you'. Evie said she didn't know how to find you and didn't think you'd be interested. They sent a limo for me and my children three nights later."[12]

Sadly the next few years were years of loss for Sara and her family. First her stepfather Edgar Rowe died. Then, in 1991, her mother, Dorothy, died, aged 91. The following June, Evie became seriously ill but refused to see a doctor. Instead, honouring the dictates of her Christian Scientist beliefs, she decided to self-treat. Evie's condition worsened, however, and the following spring concerned neighbours broke into the cottage where they found her in a poor state.

In May 1993 Sara attended the 35th annual *Famous Monsters of Filmland* convention in Arlington, Virginia at the invitation of Forrest J. Ackerman. There she met two descendents of her father's old colleagues – Bela Lugosi Jr. and Ron Chaney (grandson of Lon Chaney Jr.). She discovered the two were actively involved in the licensing of their ancestors' memorabilia. They suggested Sara follow suit.

It was a timely introduction for, on 1 June, two days after the convention ended, Evie passed away. She was 89. Her funeral, like her husband's before her, was a low-key affair. "Her sisters… nobody was allowed to go," Bernard Coleman said. "It was very odd."[13] Evie's estate was later valued at £2.5 million and the majority of the monies (following a few bequests to friends) was placed in the Boris Karloff Charitable Foundation.

Even after Evie's death her influence remained. Four months afterwards Sara and Sparky travelled to England and were granted limited access to her father's old homes in London and Bramshott. Enquiring upon the plans for the disposal of her father and stepmother's estate, Sara was informed that no formal date had been set. It came as a surprise, therefore, when she later discovered the effects were sold off by auction at a priory in Newbury, Berkshire, only eleven days after she and her husband had returned to the States.

With Evie's passing Sara Karloff became the sole torchbearer of her father's legacy. Acting on information provided by Bela Lugosi Jr. and Ron Chaney she established a licensing company, Karloff Enterprises, to ensure the appropriate use of her father's image.

In 1977 Lugosi Jr. had unsuccessfully attempted to stop Universal Studios from profiting from his father's image. However this case, which concluded in 1979, proved a catalyst for the California Celebrity Rights Act, which was passed six years later. The act gave the heirs of deceased celebrities the right to profit from the commercial use of their names and likenesses. This right, initially established for a period of 50 years after the death of a celebrity, was later increased to 70 years.

In February 2000 Sara Karloff brought her own case against the studio, suing them for $10 million in damages. "Sara Karloff is owed millions by Universal because the studio ran roughshod over her rights," explained Sara's attorney, Allan Browne. "[Universal] used unsavoury business tactics and wrongfully used Boris Karloff's image and likeness."[14] On 6 December a Los Angeles Superior Court judge ruled in Sara's favour. Eight days later she reached a settlement with Universal Studios, the terms of which were ordered sealed. Sara is still not at liberty to discuss them.

Over the following years Sara was able to give her approval to projects she felt maintained a standard of good taste when using her father's image. On 30 September 1997 the U.S. Postal Service issued a set of five stamps commemorating the classic movie monsters: Lon Chaney Sr. as the Phantom of the Opera, Bela Lugosi as Dracula and Lon Chaney Jr. as the Wolf Man. Karloff featured twice – as the Frankenstein Monster and the Mummy. On 9 October 2002 he appeared on another U.S. stamp, this time featuring on the *Make-up* stamp in the series *American Filmmaking Behind the Scenes*. The stamp showed the star being prepared for his Frankenstein role by Jack Pierce and his assistant.

On 23 November 1998, the 111th anniversary of Boris Karloff's birth, a third British memorial – an English Heritage Blue Plaque – was unveiled, this time at the star's birthplace (then a Turkish restaurant) at 36 Forest Hill Road, Camberwell.[iv]

Members of the press and the public gathered to witness the unveiling by the star's good friend Bernard Coleman. "I got this call from English Heritage – a letter – would

iv Although Karloff was born at number 15 the house was later renumbered.

I open it?" Coleman later explained. "I said, 'Why me?' They said Sara Jane had insisted that I did it and not Christopher Lee – because while Lee knew her father quite well I'd been friendly with him over a longer period and had been a personal friend – and she insisted. I didn't think they [English Heritage] were particularly pleased about it, but anyway, I did it and he [Lee] duly arrived a bit late, but he did come. They were only interested in interviewing him – quite rightly – you understand that. As a news story it was not as good as if he'd done it. It was very flattering – I was extremely flattered, and I had to do the opening. I said a few words and it went very well. Everybody was quite pleased – I don't know about English Heritage [*laughs*], but there we are!"[15]

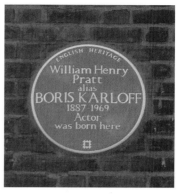

Karloff's Blue Plaque (Author's photograph).

Perhaps fittingly for an actor who made his name in the horror genre, reports of supernatural sightings began to emerge following his death, claiming the star had been seen walking in the grounds of his cottage 'Roundabout'. As such, his ghost has now been added to the list of the spectral inhabitants of the small Hampshire village.

One night in New York, sometime after Karloff had passed away, Dakota Building resident, writer and film critic Rex Reed, was awaiting the arrival of a taxicab. As the rain poured down outside he chatted idly with the Dakota's doorman. Speaking of the building's former tenants Reed announced the one he would most liked to have known was Boris Karloff. "He'll be back," the doorman informed him. "Wait and see."[16]

But, then again, he has never really gone away.

ENDNOTES

Foreword

1   Jarman, Peter J. "The House at the End of the World", *Boris Karloff: The Frankenscience Monster*, (Ace Publishing Corporation, 1969).

Chapter 1 – Origins (1796-1887)

1   Lindsay, Cynthia. *Dear Boris: The Life of William Henry Pratt a.k.a. Boris Karloff*, (Nick Hearn Books, 1995).
2   *Bombay Calendar and Register, 1813.*
3   Pratt, Frederick. *Letter to John Pratt*, 14 December 1948. Quoted in *Family History*, (Sir John Pratt Papers, PP.MS.5/32, School of Oriental and African Studies, London).
4   Pratt, Sir John. *Untitled Family History*, (Sir John Pratt Papers, PP.MS.5/32, School of Oriental and African Studies, London).
5   *Ibid.*

Chapter 2 – The Early Years (1887-1909)

1   Karloff, Boris as told to Arlene and Howard Eisenberg. "Memoirs of a Monster", *Saturday Evening Post*, 3 November 1962.
2   Langford, E. *Victoria R I.*, (Weidenfeld & Nicholson, 1964).
3   Ruddy, Jonah Maurice. "The 'Monstrous' Life of Boris Karloff", *Film Pictorial Annual 1938*, (Amalgamated Press Ltd., 1938). note: This article originally appeared, in two parts, in the British magazine *Film Pictorial* in May and June 1936.
4   *Ibid.*
5   Pratt, Richard. *Letter to Evelyn Karloff*, 23 December 1971.
6   *Daily News*, 17 September 1897.
7   *Meyers's Observer and Local and General Advertiser*, 10 September 1897.
8   Pratt, Eliza Sara v. Pratt, Edward – Court Minutes, J77/425/2969, (National Archives, Kew).
9   *Ibid.*
10 Pratt, Richard. *Letter to Evelyn Karloff*, 23 November 1971.
11 *Ibid.*
12 *Ibid.*
13 *Guy's Hospital Medical School Pupil Returns, 1886-1887.*
14 *Guy's Hospital Medical School Pupil Returns, 1887-1888.*
15 Pratt, Richard. *Letter to Evelyn Karloff*, 12 January 1972.
16 *Ibid.*
17 Ruddy, Jonah Maurice. *op. cit.*
18 Lindsay, Cynthia. *op. cit.*
19 Lindsay, Cynthia. *op. cit.*
20 *Ibid.*
21 *Ibid.*
22 *Ibid.*
23 *Ibid.*
24 Ramsey, Walter. "The Strange History of 'Frankenstein' Karloff", *Modern Screen*, February 1933.
25 *Ibid.*
26 *Ibid.*
27 *Ibid.*
28 Lindsay, Cynthia. *op. cit.*
29 *Ibid.*
30 *Ibid.*
31 *Ibid.*
32 *Ibid.*
33 *Ibid.*
34 Ruddy, Jonah Maurice. *op. cit.*
35 Karloff, Boris as told to Arlene and Howard Eisenberg. *op. cit.*
36 Ramsey, Walter. *op. cit.*
37 Karloff, Boris as told to Arlene and Howard Eisenberg. *op. cit.*
38 Ruddy, Jonah Maurice. *op. cit.*
39 *The Era*, 8 December 1894.
40 *The Era*, 1 January 1895.
41 Lindsay, Cynthia. *op. cit.*
42 Ruddy, Jonah Maurice. *op. cit.*
43 *Pall Mall Gazette*, 6 September 1897.
44 *Northern Echo*, 21 September 1897.
45 Ruddy, Jonah Maurice. *op. cit.*
46 "Between the Bolts: A "Found" Interview with Boris Karloff", *Monsterscene* No. 4, March 1995.
47 Ruddy, Jonah Maurice. *op. cit.*
48 "Between the Bolts", *op. cit.*
49 Karloff, Boris as told to Arlene and Howard Eisenberg. *op. cit.*
50 Ramsey, Walter. *op. cit.*
51 *Ibid.*
52 *Ibid.*
53 Pratt, Edward. *Last Will and Testament*, 28 October 1901.
54 *Ibid.*
55 *Ibid.*
56 "Between the Bolts", *op. cit.*
57 Karloff, Boris. *This Is Your Life: Boris Karloff*, (Ralph Edwards Productions, 20 November 1957).
58 Taylor, Geoffrey. *This Is Your Life: Boris Karloff*, *op. cit*
59 Ruddy, Jonah Maurice. *op. cit.*
60 *Ibid.*
61 Gifford, Denis. *Karloff: The Man, The Monster, The Movies*, (Curtis Books, 1973).
62 Taylor, Geoffrey. *This Is Your Life: Boris Karloff*, *op. cit*
63 Ruddy, Jonah Maurice. *op. cit.*
64 Ramsey, Walter. *op. cit.*
65 Gifford, Denis. *Karloff: The Man, The Monster, The Movies*, *op. cit.*
66 Karloff, Boris as told to Arlene and Howard Eisenberg. *op. cit.*
67 Pratt, Eliza Sara. *Death Certificate*, 1906.
68 Pratt, Richard. *Letter to Evelyn Karloff*, 5 November 1971.
69 Pratt, Dorothy. "Monster Attraction", *Everybody's Weekly*, 25 June 1955.
70 Dalling, Graham. *Email to author*, 10 April 2008.
71 Pratt, Dorothy. "Monster Attraction", *op. cit.*
72 Clutton, Sybil. *Interview with author*, 19 February 2003.
73 Underwood, Peter. *Karloff: The Life of Boris Karloff*, (Drake Publishers, Inc. 1972).
74 *Ibid.*
75 *Ibid.*
76 Underwood, Peter. *Letter to author*, 20 March 2003.
77 Ruddy, Jonah Maurice. *op. cit.*
78 *Picture Show*, 27 May 1933.

79   Karloff, Boris as told to Arlene and Howard Eisenberg. *op. cit.*
80   Ruddy, Jonah Maurice. *op. cit.*
81   Pratt, Dorothy. "The Most Celebrated Monster in the World", *Radio Times*, 27 November 1953.
82   Ruddy, Jonah Maurice. *op. cit.*
83   Clutton, Sybil. *op. cit.*
84   Ruddy, Jonah Maurice. *op. cit.*

Chapter 3 – First Steps (1909-1912)

1   Pratt, Dorothy. "The Most Celebrated Monster in the World", *op. cit.*
2   Underwood, Peter. *Letter to author*, 20 March 2003.
3   Ruddy, Jonah Maurice. *op. cit.*
4   *Ibid.*
5   Lindsay, Cynthia. *op. cit.*
6   *Hartford Courant*, 4 December 1932.
7   Johnston, John LeRoy. *Biography of Boris Karloff*, (Universal, 9 January 1932).
8   Ruddy, Jonah Maurice. *op. cit.*
9   *Ibid.*
10   *Ibid.*
11   Pratt, Dorothy. "The Most Celebrated Monster in the World", *op. cit.*
12   Karloff, Boris. *Letter to Sir John Pratt*, 17 February 1951, (Sir John Pratt Papers, PP.MS. 5/36, School of Oriental and African Studies, London).
13   Karloff, Boris. *Letter to Mrs. Claudet*, 18 March 1955.
14   Ruddy, Jonah Maurice. *op. cit.*
15   *Ibid.*
16   *Ibid.*
17   *Ibid.*
18   *Ibid.*
19   Karloff, Boris as told to Arlene and Howard Eisenberg. *op. cit.*
20   Ruddy, Jonah Maurice. *op. cit.*
21   Thomas, Kevin. "Karloff—Not Very Sinister", *Los Angeles Times*, 23 May 1966.
22   Pratt, Richard. *Letter to Evelyn Karloff*, 5 November 1971.
23   "Between the Bolts", *op. cit.*
24   Ruddy, Jonah Maurice. *op. cit.*
25   "Between the Bolts", *op. cit.*
26   Pratt, Dorothy. "The Most Celebrated Monster in the World", *op. cit.*
27   Ruddy, Jonah Maurice. *op. cit.*
28   Karloff, Boris. *Letter to Dr. Knowlton*, 22 April 1961.
29   Ramsey, Walter. *op. cit.*
30   Nesteroff, Greg. *Email to author*, 12 August 2007.
31   Karloff, Boris as told to Arlene and Howard Eisenberg. *op. cit.*
32   Pratt, Dorothy. "The Most Celebrated Monster in the World", *op. cit.*
33   Grafton, Samuel. "All He Needed Was One Good Scare", *Good Housekeeping*, August 1955.
34   *Lethbridge Daily Herald*, 20 February 1912.
35   *Ibid.*
36   Tarkington, Booth and Harry Leon Wilson. *The Man from Home*, (www.gutenberg.org/files/15855/15855-8.txt).
37   *Lethbridge Daily Herald*, 22 February 1912.
38   *Macleod Advertiser*, 29 February 1912.
39   *Calgary Daily Herald*, 12 March 1912.
40   *Calgary Daily Herald*, 15 March 1912.
41   *Calgary Daily Herald*, 20 March 1912.
42   *Morning Albertan*, 21 March 1912.

43   *Calgary Daily Herald*, 22 March 1912.
44   *Morning Albertan*, 22 March 1912.
45   *Regina Leader*, 3 April 1912.
46   *Ibid.*
47   *Ibid.*
48   *Daily Phoenix*, 13 April 1912.
49   *Saskatoon Daily Star*, 19 April 1912.
50   *Daily Phoenix*, 19 April 1912.
51   *Daily Phoenix*, 23 April 1912.
52   *Daily Phoenix*, 26 April 1912.
53   *Daily Phoenix*, 11 May 1912.
54   Pratt, Dorothy. "The Most Celebrated Monster in the World", *op. cit.*
55   Ramsey, Walter. *op. cit.*
56   Ruddy, Jonah Maurice. *op. cit.*
57   Pratt, Dorothy. "The Most Celebrated Monster in the World", *op. cit.*
58   *The Leader*, 4 July 1912.
59   Ruddy, Jonah Maurice. *op. cit.*
60   "Salt Lake Act Scores in New York, "A Star By Mistake" Is Coming West", *Salt Lake Tribune*, 11 April 1915.
61   Ruddy, Jonah Maurice. *op. cit.*

Chapter 4 – From Canada to California (1912-1919)

1   "Being a Monster is Really a Game", *TV Guide*, (Radnor, Pa., Triangle Publications, Inc., 15 October 1960).
2   Roman, Robert C. "Boris Karloff", *Films in Review*, August-September 1964.
3   "Decree Absolute of William Henry Pratt and Grace Harding", Microfilm No. B6311, File No. 202, British Columbia Archives.
4   Edel, Leon. "Boris Karloff, now of New York, Was Once Canadian Barnstormer", *Montreal Gazette*, 8 February 1941.
5   *Oakland Tribune*, 20 March 1932.
6   Ripley, Helene and Boris Karloff. *With a Grain of Salt*, 1913.
7   *Ibid.*
8   *Ibid.*
9   *Ibid.*
10   Ruddy, Jonah Maurice. *op. cit.*
11   *Ibid.*
12   *New York Clipper*, 11 November 1911.
13   *New York Clipper*, 13 March 1913.
14   "Karloff, Calm Menace", *New York Times*, 19 January 1941.
15   Lindsay, Cynthia. *op. cit.*
16   *Ibid.*
17   Bacon, J. Warren. *This Is Your Life: Boris Karloff, op. cit.*
18   *Opera House Reporter*, 13 October 1916.
19   Ruddy, Jonah Maurice. *op. cit.*
20   Lindsay, Cynthia. *op. cit.*
21   Ruddy, Jonah Maurice. *op. cit.*
22   *New York Clipper*, 7 February 1917.
23   "Lona Fendell Coming", *The Marshfield Times*, 12 January 1916.
24   *Ibid.*
25   *Daily Leader*, 30 April 1917.
26   *Oakland Tribune*, 20 March 1932.
27   Pratt, John. *Letter to Emma Pratt*, 6 December 1917, (Sir John Pratt Papers, PP.MS.5/30, School of Oriental and African Studies, London).

28 United States, Selective Service System. *World War I Selective Service System Draft Registration Cards, 1917-1918*, (Washington, D.C.: National Archives and Records Administration. M1509. Roll 1452381, Draftboard 1).
29 *Ibid*.
30 Lindsay, Cynthia. *op. cit.*
31 de Wilton, Olive. *Letter to Robert Anderson*, 2 February 1948, (Red Deer and District Archives, de Wilton fonds, MG 21 Series 1, sub-series c, File 1, Folder 24).
32 *Duluth News Tribune*, 21 August 1917.
33 *Idaho Statesman*, 13 November 1917.
34 Ruddy, Jonah Maurice. *op. cit.*
35 Lindsay, Cynthia. *op. cit.*
36 Ruddy, Jonah Maurice. *op. cit.*
37 *Ibid*.
38 Lindsay, Cynthia. *op. cit.*
39 Evening News, San Jose, Cal., 31 December 1918.
40 Urmy, Clarence. "New Year Vaudeville for Victory Patrons", *San Jose Mercury Herald*, 1 January 1919.
41 Ruddy, Jonah Maurice. *op. cit.*
42 de Wilton, Olive. *op. cit.*
43 *Ibid*.
44 *Ibid*.
45 *Ibid*.
46 Ruddy, Jonah Maurice. *op. cit.*

Chapter 5 – Early Films (1919-1931)
1 Gifford, Denis. *Karloff: The Man, The Monster, The Movies, op. cit.*
2 Ruddy, Jonah Maurice. *op. cit.*
3 Edwards, James. *This Is Your Life: Boris Karloff, op. cit.*
4 Ruddy, Jonah Maurice. *op. cit.*
5 Lindsay, Cynthia. *op. cit.*
6 Ruddy, Jonah Maurice. *op. cit.*
7 Lindsay, Cynthia. *op. cit.*
8 Ruddy, Jonah Maurice. *op. cit.*
9 *Ibid*.
10 *Ibid*.
11 Brownlow, Kevin. *The Parade's Gone By...*, (Abacus, 1973).
12 Gifford, Denis. *Karloff: The Man, The Monster, The Movies, op. cit.*
13 Ruddy, Jonah Maurice. *op. cit.*
14 *Ibid*.
15 Underwood, Peter. *Karloff: The Life of Boris Karloff, op. cit.*
16 *Manchester Guardian*, 20 November 1924.
17 Lindsay, Cynthia. *op. cit.*
18 Moffitt, John C. "Hollywood Makes This Man a Monster", *Hartford Courant*, 4 December 1932.
19 Ruddy, Jonah Maurice. *op. cit.*
20 Underwood, Peter. "Reminiscences of Boris Karloff", *Letter to author*, 12 August 2008.
21 Underwood, Peter. *Karloff: The Life of Boris Karloff, op. cit.*
22 Ruddy, Jonah Maurice. *op. cit.*
23 Lindsay, Cynthia. *op. cit.*
24 Ruddy, Jonah Maurice. *op. cit.*
25 *Kinematograph Weekly*, 26 November 1925.
26 *Los Angeles Times*, 19 July 1925.
27 Lindsay, Cynthia. *op. cit.*
28 *Los Angeles Times*, 20 July 1926.
29 *Variety*, 21 July 1926.
30 Underwood, Peter. *Karloff: The Life of Boris Karloff, op. cit.*

31 Gifford, Denis. *Karloff: The Man, The Monster, The Movies, op. cit.*
32 *Bioscope*, 24 March 1927.
33 Essoe, Gabe. *Tarzan of the Movies*, (Citadel, 1968).
34 Brownlow, Kevin. *op. cit.*
35 Gifford, Denis. *Karloff: The Man, The Monster, The Movies, op. cit.*
36 *Ibid*.
37 Ruddy, Jonah Maurice. *op. cit.*
38 *Los Angeles Times*, 26 January 1928.
39 *Los Angeles Times*, 28 January 1928.
40 *Los Angeles Times*, 24 April 1928.
41 *Los Angeles Times*, 6 May 1928.
42 *Los Angeles Times*, 25 May 1928.
43 *Los Angeles Times*, 30 May 1928.
44 *Los Angeles Times*, 4 July 1928.
45 *The News – Van Nuys (Calif.)*, 23 March 1969.
46 Pace, Terry. "John Carradine, Actor, Villain and Living Legend", *Fangoria* No. 52, March 1986.
47 Fine, Henry M. "Screen's Great Menace is 'a Lamb' at Home", *Screen and Radio Weekly*, 3 February 1935.
48 *New York Daily News*, 19 December 1932.
49 Lindsay, Cynthia. *op. cit.*
50 *Ibid*.
51 *Ibid*.
52 *Los Angeles Times*, 24 March 1929.
53 Roman, Robert C. *op. cit.*
54 *Los Angeles Times*, 27 February 1930.
55 *Los Angeles Times*, 26 February 1930.
56 Lindsay, Cynthia. *op. cit.*
57 Pratt, Dorothy. "The Most Celebrated Monster in the World", *op. cit.*
58 Lindsay, Cynthia. *op. cit.*
59 *Film Weekly*, 18 April 1936.
60 *Los Angeles Times*, 14 May 1930.
61 Lindsay, Cynthia. *op. cit.*
62 Bogdanovich, Peter. *Who the Devil Made It: Conversations with Legendary Film Directors*, (Ballantine Books, 1998).
63 "Between the Bolts", *op. cit.*
64 Lindsay, Cynthia. *op. cit.*
65 Underwood, Peter. *Karloff: The Life of Boris Karloff, op. cit.*
66 *Variety*, 7 January 1931.
67 *Bioscope*, 8 April 1931.
68 "Between the Bolts", *op. cit.*
69 *Kinematograph Weekly*, 8 October 1931.
70 Ruddy, Jonah Maurice. *op. cit.*
71 *Ibid*.
72 *Ibid*.
73 Nollen, Scott Allen. *Boris Karloff: A Gentleman's Life*, (Midnight Marquee Press, 1999).
74 Bogdanovich, Peter. *Who the Devil Made It, op. cit.*
75 *Ibid*.
76 *Ibid*.
77 Truffaut, Francois. *The Films in My Life*, (Simon & Schuster, 1978).
78 Bogdanovich, Peter. *Who the Devil Made It, op. cit.*
79 *Ibid*.

Chapter 6 – Frankenstein – (1931)
1 Karloff, Boris. "My Life as a Monster", *Films and Filming*, November 1957.
2 Shelley, Mary. *Frankenstein or The Modern Prometheus* (1818 Text), (Oxford University Press, 1998).
3 *London Morning Post*, 29 July 1823.
4 Shelley, Mary. *Letter to Leigh Hunt*, 9 September 1823.

5   Florey, Robert. *Hollywood: d'hier et d'aujord'hui*, (Éditions Prisma, 1948).

6   Curtis, James. *James Whale: A New World of Gods and Monsters*, (Faber and Faber, 1998).

7   *Universal Weekly*, 17 December 1932.

8   Curtis, James. *op. cit.*

9   Cremer, Robert. *Lugosi: The Man Behind the Cape*, (H. Regency Co., 1976).

10   *Hollywood Reporter*, 10 June 1931.

11   *Hollywood Reporter*, 18 June 1931.

12   Curtis, James. *op. cit.*

13   *Ibid.*

14   "Great Horror Figure Dies", *Famous Monsters of Filmland* No. 31, December 1964.

15   *Ibid.*

16   *Ibid.*

17   Taylor, Al. "The Forgotten Frankenstein", *Fangoria* No. 2, October 1979.

18   Curtis, James. *op. cit.*

19   Lennig, Arthur. *The Immortal Count: The Life and Films of Bela Lugosi*, (Putnam, 1974).

20   Curtis, James. *op. cit.*

21   *Ibid.*

22   *Ibid.*

23   Mank, Gregory William. *It's Alive! - The Classic Cinema Saga of Frankenstein*, (A.S. Barnes & Company, Inc., 1981).

24   *Evening Post*, 9 April 1930.

25   "Films Cast Up James Whale After 15 Years", *New York Herald Tribune*, 3 December 1944.

26   Curtis, James. *op. cit.*

27   "Film Producer Horrified", *Evening News*, 12 August 1932.

28   "James Whale and Frankenstein", *New York Times*, 20 December 1931.

29   Curtis, James. *op. cit.*

30   *Hollywood Reporter*, 1 July 1931.

31   *Hollywood Filmograph*, 11 July 1931.

32   "James Whale and Frankenstein", *op. cit.*

33   Curtis, James. *op. cit.*

34   *Ibid.*

35   "James Whale and Frankenstein", *op. cit.*

36   *Ibid.*

37   Curtis, James. *op. cit.*

38   Mank, Gregory William. *It's Alive!*, *op. cit.*

39   Curtis, James. *op. cit.*

40   Gifford, Denis. *Karloff: The Man, The Monster, The Movies*, *op. cit.*

41   Curtis, James. *op. cit.*

42   *Ibid.*

43   *Ibid.*

44   Beale, Ken. "Boris Karloff, Master of Horror", *Castle of Frankenstein Monster Annual*, 1967.

45   Thomas, Bob. "Bela Lugosi Disappoints Hollywood Gossip-Writer", *Big Spring (Texas) Herald*, 30 October 1953.

46   Lindsay, Cynthia. *op. cit.*

47   Gifford, Denis. *Karloff: The Man, The Monster, The Movies*, *op. cit.*

48   "Interview with Jack Pierce", *Monster Mania*, October 1966.

49   *Ibid.*

50   "Oh, You Beautiful Monster", *New York Times*, 29 January 1939.

51   Parry, Mike and Harry Nadler. "CoF interviews: Boris Karloff", *Castle of Frankenstein* No. 9, November 1966.

52   Whitacker, Alma. "Superior Intelligence Lurks in Grafted Brain", *Los Angeles Times*, 10 January 1932.

53   "James Whale and Frankenstein", *op. cit.*

54   "Between the Bolts", *op. cit.*

55   *Hollywood Reporter*, 17 July 1931.

56   Hutchinson, Tom. *Horror and Fantasy in the Movies*, (Crescent Books, 1974).

57   "James Whale and Frankenstein", *op. cit.*

58   Gifford, Denis. *Movie Monsters*, (Studio Vista, 1969).

59   Taylor, Frank. "Jack Pierce: The Man the Frankenstein Monster Made", *Los Angeles Times Calendar*, 11 August 1968.

60   Brown, Helen Weigel. "The Man Who Made the Monster", *Picturegoer*, 23 April 1932.

61   *Lethbridge Daily Herald*, 12 January 1959.

62   "James Whale and Frankenstein", *op. cit.*

63   Skal, David J. *Monster Show*, (Plexus, 1993).

64   "The Bride of Dr. Frankenstein", *Famous Monsters of Filmland*, August 1973.

65   Curtis, James. *op. cit.*

66   Karloff, Boris as told to Arlene and Howard Eisenberg. *op. cit.*

67   Nolan, William F. "Meal with a Monster", *Famous Monsters of Filmland* No. 22, April 1963.

68   Brown, Helen Weigel. *op. cit.*

69   Curtis, James. *op. cit.*

70   Gifford, Denis. *Karloff: The Man, The Monster, The Movies*, *op. cit.*

71   Karloff, Boris as told to Arlene and Howard Eisenberg. *op. cit.*

72   Underwood, Peter. *Karloff: The Life of Boris Karloff*, *op. cit.*

73   Gifford, Denis. *Karloff: The Man, The Monster, The Movies*, *op. cit.*

74   Mank, Gregory William. *It's Alive!*, *op. cit.*

75   Brown, Helen Weigel. *op. cit.*

76   "The Bride of Dr. Frankenstein", *op. cit.*

77   Curtis, James. *op. cit.*

78   *Ibid.*

79   Mank, Gregory William. *It's Alive!*, *op. cit.*

80   Parry, Mike and Harry Nadler. *op. cit.*

81   Hutchinson, Tom. *op. cit.*

82   Curtis, James. *op. cit.*

83   *Ibid.*

84   Mank, Gregory William. *Women In Horror Films, 1930s*, (McFarland, 1999).

85   Curtis, James. *op. cit.*

86   *Ibid.*

87   *Ibid.*

88   *Ibid.*

89   "Between the Bolts", *op. cit.*

90   Karloff, Sara Jane. "The *Frankenstein* Files", *Frankenstein* DVD, (Universal Home Video, 1999).

91   Mank, Gregory William. *It's Alive!*, *op. cit.*

92   Gifford, Denis. *Karloff: The Man, The Monster, The Movies*, *op. cit.*

93   Karloff, Boris as told to Arlene and Howard Eisenberg. *op. cit.*

94   Curtis, James. *op. cit.*

95   *Ibid.*

96   Gifford, Denis. *Karloff: The Man, The Monster, The Movies*, *op. cit.*

97   Curtis, James. *op. cit.*

98   "Clive of Frankenstein", *New York Times*, 15 November 1931.

99   "James Whale and Frankenstein", *New York Times*, 20 December 1931.
100 Curtis, James. *op. cit.*
101 *Ibid*.
102 Meehan, Leo. "Frankenstein review", *Motion Picture Herald*, 14 November 1931.
103 Hall, Mordaunt. "A Man-Made Monster in Grand Guignol Film Story", *New York Times*, 5 December 1931.
104 "As It Looks to Us", *Exhibitor's Forum*, 8 December 1931.
105 "Tradeviews", *Hollywood Reporter*, 8 December 1931.
106 Gifford, Denis. *Karloff: The Man, The Monster, The Movies, op. cit.*
107 Beacon, Guy. "The Letters They Write", *Film Pictorial Annual 1938*.
108 "Great Horror Figure Dies", *op. cit.*
109 Karloff, Boris. "Houses I Have Haunted", *Liberty*, 4 October 1941.
110 Lindsay, Cynthia. *op. cit.*
111 Gifford, Denis. *Movie Monsters, op. cit.*

Chapter 7 – After *Frankenstein* (1931-1933)

1   Bristol, O. "Boris Karloff: The Monster of the Movies in Real Life", *Picture Show*, 27 May 1933.
2   *Los Angeles Times*, 19 January 1932.
3   Karloff, Boris as told to Arlene and Howard Eisenberg. *op. cit.*
4   *New York Times*, 3 March 1932.
5   *Film Weekly*, 9 September 1932.
6   Priestley, J.B. *Margin Released: A Writer's Reminiscences and Reflections*, (Harper & Row, 1962).
7   *Ibid*.
8   Priestley, J.B. *Benighted*, (Heinemann, 1932).
9   *Ibid*.
10   *Ibid*.
11   Curtis, James. *op. cit.*
12   Stuart, Gloria. "Audio Commentary", *The Old Dark House* DVD, (Image Entertainment, 2003).
13   Mank, Gregory William. *It's Alive!, op. cit.*
14   Stuart, Gloria. "Audio Commentary", *op. cit.*
15   *Ibid*.
16   *Ibid*.
17   *Ibid*.
18   Curtis, James. *op. cit.*
19   *Ibid*.
20   *Ibid*.
21   Stuart, Gloria. "Audio Commentary", *op. cit.*
22   Bogdanovich, Peter. *Who the Devil Made It, op. cit.*
23   Curtis, James. *op. cit.*
24   Stuart, Gloria. "Audio Commentary", *op. cit.*
25   White, Rusty. *The Elegant Madness of Curtis Harrington*.
26   Mank, Gregory William. *It's Alive!, op. cit.*
27   Stuart, Gloria. "Audio Commentary", *op. cit.*
28   *Ibid*.
29   *Ibid*.
30   Curtis, James. *op. cit.*
31   *Hollywood Filmograph*, 9 July 1932.
32   *New York Times*, 28 October 1932.
33   *Picturegoer*, 28 January 1933.
34   "Rescuing a Classic: Curtis Harrington", *The Old Dark House* DVD, (Image Entertainment, 2003).
35   White, Rusty. *op. cit.*
36   *Washington Post*, 11 August 1933.
37   *Screen Player*, 15 May 1934.

38   "Between the Bolts", *op. cit.*
39   *Ibid*.
40   *Ibid*.
41   Nollen, Scott Allen. *op. cit.*

42   Kotsilibas-Davis, James and Myrna Loy. *Myrna Loy: Being and Becoming*, (Bloomsbury, 1987).
43   "Between the Bolts", *op. cit.*
44   Roman, Robert C. *op. cit.*
45   "Between the Bolts", *op. cit.*
46   *Ibid*.
47   Lindsay, Cynthia. *op. cit.*
48   *Variety*, 6 December 1932.
49   *New York Times*, 2 December 1932.
50   Kotsilibas-Davis, James and Myrna Loy. *op. cit*
51   McKay, Rick. "To the Manners Born: an Interview with David Manners", *Scarlet Street* No. 26, 1997.
52   Del Valle, David. *Zita Johann Interview*.
53   *Ibid*.
54   *Ibid*.
55   Mank, Gregory. "The Mummy Revisited", *Films in Review*, August/September 1984.
56   "Interview with Jack Pierce", *op. cit.*.
57   "Mummy Dearest: A Horror Tradition Unearthed", *The Mummy* DVD, (Universal Home Video, 1999).
58   Lee, Christopher. *Tall, Dark and Gruesome*, (Weidenfeld & Nicolson, 1997).
59   Terhune, Albert Payson. "How Hollywood Treats Its Dogs", *Modern Screen*, March 1933.
60   White, Rusty. *op. cit.*
61   Mank, Gregory William. *Women In Horror Films, 1930s, op. cit.*
62   Mank, Gregory. "*The Mummy* Revisited", *op. cit.*
63   *Chicago Daily Tribune*, 19 May 1935.
64   Del Valle, David. *Zita Johann Interview*.
65   *Ibid*.
66   *Ibid*.
67   Mank, Gregory. "The Mummy Revisited", *op. cit.*
68   Nollen, Scott Allen. *op. cit.*
69   *Los Angeles Times*, 23 January 1933.
70   Gifford, Denis. *Karloff: The Man, The Monster, The Movies, op. cit.*
71   *Variety*, 10 January 1933.
72   *Variety*, 3 January 1933.
73   *Kinematograph Weekly*, 19 January 1933.
74   Foster, Iris. "Just a Sentimental Monster", *Film Weekly*, 27 January 1933

Chapter 8 – The Transatlantic Star (1933-1934)

1   *New York Times*, 28 January 1934.
2   Lindsay, Cynthia. *op. cit.*
3   *Ibid*.
4   Nollen, Scott Allen. *op. cit.*
5   Lindsay, Cynthia. *op. cit.*
6   *Ibid*.
7   *Ibid*.
8   Ruddy, Jonah Maurice. *op. cit.*
9   *Ibid*.
10   Nollen, Scott Allen. *op. cit.*
11   *Ibid*.
12   *Ibid*.
13   Lindsay, Cynthia. *op. cit.*
14   Nollen, Scott Allen. *op. cit.*
15   *Kinematograph Weekly*, 27 July 1933.
16   Croydon, John. "Working with Karloff", *Fangoria* No. 36, July 1984.

17 Nollen, Scott Allen. *op. cit.*
18 *Ibid.*
19 Karloff, Boris as told to Arlene and Howard Eisenberg. *op. cit.*
20 Pratt, Sir John. *Letter to Cornelia Montell Arbutny*, 30 June 1946, (Sir John Pratt Papers, PP.MS.5/32, School of Oriental and African Studies, London).
21 Lindsay, Cynthia. *op. cit.*
22 Pratt, John. *Letter to Emma Pratt*, 22 February 1924, (Sir John Pratt Papers, PP.MS.5/32, School of Oriental and African Studies, London).
23 James, Rosamund. *Interview with author*, 27 August 2002.
24 Ruddy, Jonah Maurice. *op. cit.*
25 Lindsay, Cynthia. *op. cit.*
26 *Ibid.*
27 Ruddy, Jonah Maurice. *op. cit.*
28 Pratt, Sir John. *Letter to Cornelia Montell Arbutny*, 30 June 1946, *op. cit.*
29 Ruddy, Jonah Maurice. *op. cit.*
30 Nollen, Scott Allen. *op. cit.*
31 Ruddy, Jonah Maurice. *op. cit.*
32 Nollen, Scott Allen. *op. cit.*
33 *Ibid.*
34 Bristol, O. *op. cit.*
35 *Ibid.*
36 *Ibid.*
37 *Ibid.*
38 Lindsay, Cynthia. *op. cit.*
39 Nollen, Scott Allen. *op. cit.*
40 "Boris Karloff interview", (www.hotad.com/monstermania/2002/boriskarloff/).
41 "Between the Bolts", *op. cit.*
42 *Kinematograph Weekly*, 27 July 1933.
43 *New York Times*, 27 January 1934.
44 Karloff, Boris. "Oaks from Acorns", *Screen Actor*, October-November 1960.
45 *Ibid.*
46 *Ibid.*
47 Lindsay, Cynthia. *op. cit.*
48 Nollen, Scott Allen. *op. cit.*
49 *Variety*, 6 June 1933.
50 *Los Angeles Times*, 15 July 1933.
51 Nollen, Scott Allen. *op. cit.*
52 *Ibid.*
53 *Ibid.*
54 Brian, Mary. *Early Members: 1933*, (www.sag.org/early-members-1933).
55 Lindsay, Cynthia. *op. cit.*
56 *Ibid.*
57 "Between the Bolts", *op. cit.*
58 Anderson, Lindsay. *About John Ford*, (Plexus, 1999).
59 Bogdanovich, Peter. *John Ford*, (University of California Press, 1978).
60 *Ibid.*
61 Pratt, Dorothy. "Monster Attraction", *op. cit.*
62 *Los Angeles Times*, 20 September 1933.
63 *Ibid.*
64 *Washington Post*, 30 January 1934.
65 *Washington Post*, 9 February 1934.
66 *Washington Post*, 10 February 1934.
67 *Ibid.*
68 *Los Angeles Times*, 15 February 1934.
69 *Ibid.*
70 *Los Angeles Times*, 16 February 1934.
71 *Los Angeles Times*, 17 February 1934.

72 *Los Angeles Times*, 28 February 1934.
73 *Los Angeles Times*, 19 February 1934.
74 *New York Times*, 8 April 1934.
75 *Variety*, 3 April 1934.
76 Karloff, Boris. "Oaks from Acorns", *op. cit.*
77 Cagney, James. *Cagney by Cagney*, (Doubleday, 1976).
78 *Variety*, 2 October 1933.
79 Nollen, Scott Allen. *op. cit.*
80 Karloff, Boris. "Oaks from Acorns", *op. cit.*
81 Mosley, Leonard. *Zanuck: The Rise and Fall of Hollywood's Last Tycoon*, (Granada, 1984).
82 Arliss, George. *Letter to Darryl F. Zanuck.* (www.afi.com).
83 Howell, Maude T. *Letter to Darryl F. Zanuck.* (www.afi.com).
84 Mosley, Leonard. *Zanuck: The Rise and Fall of Hollywood's Last Tycoon*, (Granada, 1984).
85 *Ibid.*
86 *Ibid.*
87 *Ibid.*
88 Arliss, George. *My Ten Years in the Studios*, (Little Brown and Company, 1940).
89 *Variety*, 20 March 1934.
90 *New York Times*, 15 March 1934.
91 Bogdanovich, Peter. *Who the Devil Made It*, *op. cit.*
92 *Ibid.*
93 Hammett, Nina. *Laughing Torso*, (Virago, 1984).
94 *The Times*, 13 April 1934.
95 *Daily Herald*, 14 April 1934.
96 Bogdanovich, Peter. *Who the Devil Made It*, *op. cit.*
97 Cipes, Arianne Ulmer. Interview, *Universal Horror*, (Photoplay Productons, 1998).
98 Bogdanovich, Peter. *Who the Devil Made It*, *op. cit.*
99 McKay, Rick. *op. cit.*
100 Nollen, Scott Allen. *op. cit.*
101 Bogdanovich, Peter. *Who the Devil Made It*, *op. cit.*
102 *Ibid.*
103 Roman, Robert C. *op. cit.*
104 Bogdanovich, Peter. *Who the Devil Made It*, *op. cit.*
105 "Between the Bolts", *op. cit.*
106 Cipes, Arianne Ulmer. *op. cit.*
107 *Ibid.*
108 *Variety*, 22 May 1934.
109 *New York Times*, 19 May 1934.
110 *Film Weekly*, 15 March 1935.
111 Ruddy, Jonah Maurice. *op. cit.*
112 *Screen Player*, 15 May 1934.
113 *Ibid.*
114 Jensen, Paul M. *The Men Who Made the Monsters*, (Twayne Publishers, 1996).
115 Curtis, James. *op. cit.*
116 *Ibid.*
117 *Los Angeles Times*, 18 November 1934.
118 *Ibid.*

Chapter 9 – *Bride of Frankenstein* (1935)
1 Karloff, Boris as told to Arlene and Howard Eisenberg. *op. cit.*
2 Sherriff, R.C. *No Leading Lady – An Autobiography*, (Victor Gollancz Ltd., 1968).
3 *Washington Post*, 14 July 1933.
4 King, Clyde Lyndon, Frank A. Tichenor, and Gordon S. Watkins, *The Motion Picture in its Economic and Social Aspects*, (Arno Press, 1970).
5 Skal, David J. *op. cit.*
6 Sherriff, R.C. *op. cit.*

7   Gardner, Gerald C. *The Censorship Papers: Movie Censorship Letters From the Hays Office, 1934-1968*, (Dodd Mead, 1988).
8   Curtis, James. *op. cit.*
9   Gardner, Gerald C. *op. cit.*
10   Parry, Mike and Harry Nadler. *op. cit.*
11   Curtis, James. *op. cit.*

12   Cook, Page. "Franz Waxman", *Films in Review*, August/ September 1968.
13   Curtis, James. *op. cit.*
14   *Ibid.*
15   Mank, Gregory William. *It's Alive!*, *op. cit.*
16   *Los Angeles Times*, 21 August 1934.
17   Mank, Gregory William. *It's Alive!*, *op. cit.*
18   *Ibid.*
19   *Ibid.*
20   *Washington Post*, 21 April 1935.
21   *New York Times*, 3 February 1935.
22   Henderson, Jan A. and George E. Turner, ""Bride of Frankenstein:" A Gothic Masterpiece: Director James Whale and an Expert Team of Cinema Artists Defied the Odds in Creating a Memorable Sequel to One of the Most Famous Monster Movies of all Time", *American Cinematographer – The International Journal of Film & Digital Production Techniques 79:1*, January 1998.
23   Curtis, James. *op. cit.*
24   Ruddy, Jonah Maurice. *op. cit.*
25   Curtis, James. *op. cit.*
26   Karloff, Boris as told to Arlene and Howard Eisenberg. *op. cit.*
27   Mank, Gregory William. *It's Alive!*, *op. cit.*
28   Curtis, James. *op. cit.*
29   *Ibid.*
30   *Ibid.*
31   *Ibid.*
32   *Ibid.*
33   *Ibid.*
34   *Ibid.*
35   Mank, Gregory William. *It's Alive!*, *op. cit.*
36   *Ibid.*
37   Curtis, James. *op. cit.*
38   *Ibid.*
39   *Chicago Herald Tribune*, 19 May 1935.
40   Ruddy, Jonah Maurice. *op. cit.*
41   *Ibid.*
42   Mank, Gregory William. "An Interview with Valerie Hobson", *Bride of Frankenstein*, (MagicImage Filmbooks, 1989).
43   Curtis, James. *op. cit.*
44   Mank, Gregory William. *It's Alive!*, *op. cit.*
45   Curtis, James. *op. cit.*
46   Mank, Gregory William. *Women In Horror Films, 1930s*, *op. cit.*
47   Mank, Gregory William. *It's Alive!*, *op. cit.*
48   Mank, Gregory William. *Women In Horror Films, 1930s*, *op. cit.*
49   Lanchester, Elsa. *Elsa Lanchester Herself*, (St. Martin's Press, 1983).
50   Curtis, James. *op. cit.*
51   Mank, Gregory William. *Women In Horror Films, 1930s*, *op. cit.*
52   *Ibid.*
53   *Ibid.*
54   *Variety*, 15 May 1935.
55   Curtis, James. *op. cit.*

56   Gardner, Gerald C. *op. cit.*
57   *Ibid.*
58   *Ibid.*
59   Curtis, James. *op. cit.*
60   Mank, Gregory William. *It's Alive!*, *op. cit.*
61   *Ibid.*
62   Gardner, Gerald C. *op. cit.*
63   Henderson, Jan A. and George E. Turner, *op. cit.*
64   *Los Angeles Times*, 20 April 1935.
65   *Chicago Herald Tribune*, 23 April 1935.
66   *New York Times*, 11 May 1935.
67   "Bride of Frankenstein", *Kinematograph Weekly*, 6 June 1935.
68   *The Times*, 4 November 1935.
69   Mank, Gregory William. *It's Alive!*, *op. cit.*
70   *Chicago Herald Tribune*, 19 May 1935.
71   *Ibid.*
72   *Los Angeles Times*, 19 March 1935.

Chapter 10 – Home Again (1935-1936)

1   "Karloff Thinks Monster Roles Curtail Career", *Hartford Courant*, 9 June 1935.
2   *Los Angeles Times*, 8 June 1934.
3   *Washington Post*, 7 July 1935.
4   Nollen, Scott Allen. *op. cit.*
5   Shriver, Gordon B. *Boris Karloff: The Man Remembered*, (PublishAmerica, 2004).
6   Nollen, Scott Allen. *op. cit.*
7   *New York Times*, 5 July 1935.
8   *Christian Science Monitor*, 27 June 1935.
9   Jarman, Peter J. "The House at the End of the World", *Boris Karloff: The Frankenscience Monster*, (Ace Publishing Corporation, 1969).
10   *New York Times*, 13 April 1935.
11   *Washington Post*, 7 May 1935.
12   *Washington Post*, 9 April 1935.
13   Fine, Henry M. *op. cit.*
14   *Los Angeles Times*, 1 May 1935.
15   *Chicago Herald Tribune*, 19 May 1935.
16   Nollen, Scott Allen. *op. cit.*
17   *Ibid.*
18   *Los Angeles Times*, 16 August 1935.
19   *Washington Post*, 18 August 1935.
20   *Ibid.*
21   *Ibid.*
22   *Hartford Courant*, 9 June 1935.
23   *Dallas Morning News*, 16 September 1935.
24   *Los Angeles Times*, 26 April 1935.
25   *Los Angeles Times*, 26 May 1935.
26   *Christian Science Monitor*, 29 May 1935.
27   *Ibid.*
28   *Los Angeles Times*, 29 May 1935.
29   Ruddy, Jonah Maurice. *op. cit.*
30   *Los Angeles Times*, 30 January 1936.
31   *Ibid.*
32   Fine, Henry M. *op. cit.*
33   *Ibid.*
34   *Ibid.*
35   *Ibid.*
36   *Ibid.*
37   *Los Angeles Times*, 28 July 1935.
38   *Los Angeles Times*, 25 August 1935.
39   *Los Angeles Times*, 1 September 1935.
40   *Hammond Times*, 4 September 1935.
41   *Los Angeles Times*, 10 September 1935.
42   *Ibid.*

43   Shriver, Gordon B. *op. cit.*
44   *Washington Post*, 14 January 1940.
45   Nollen, Scott Allen. *op. cit.*
46   *Ibid.*
47   *New York Times*, 11 January 1936.
48   *Charleston Gazette*, 2 November 1935.
49   *Los Angeles Times*, 5 November 1935.
50   *Nevada State Journal*, 11 December 1935.
51   Nollen, Scott Allen. *op. cit.*
52   *Los Angeles Times*, 22 December 1935.
53   *New York Times*, 3 March 1936.
54   *Los Angeles Times*, 3 April 1936.
55   *Los Angeles Times*, 5 January 1936.
56   Karloff, Boris. *Letter to Charles Pratt*, 16 January 1936.
57   Nollen, Scott Allen. *op. cit.*
58   *Ibid.*
59   Karloff, Boris. "Diary of a Monster", *Atlanta Constitution*, 11 October 1936.
60   *Ibid.*
61   *Ibid.*
62   *Ibid.*
63   *Ibid.*
64   *Ibid.*
65   Nollen, Scott Allen. *op. cit.*
66   Karloff, Boris. "Diary of a Monster", *op. cit.*
67   *Ibid.*
68   *Ibid.*
69   *Ibid.*
70   *Ibid.*
71   *The Times*, 17 March 1936.
72   Karloff, Boris. "Diary of a Monster", *op. cit.*
73   Bledsoe, William. "British Filmview," *Screen Guild Magazine*, October 1936.
74   Karloff, Boris. "Diary of a Monster", *op. cit.*
75   *Ibid.*
76   *Ibid.*
77   Nollen, Scott Allen. *op. cit.*
78   *Ibid.*
79   *Ibid.*
80   *Ibid.*
81   Karloff, Boris. "Diary of a Monster", *op. cit.*
82   Karloff, Boris. *Letter to Sir John Pratt*, 6 November 1949, (Sir John Pratt Papers, P.P.MS. 5/36, School of Oriental and African Studies, London).
83   Bledsoe, William. *op. cit.*
84   *Ibid.*
85   *Ibid.*
86   *Ibid.*
87   *Ibid.*
88   Karloff, Boris. "Diary of a Monster", *op. cit.*
89   *Ibid.*
90   *Ibid.*
91   *Ibid.*
92   *Ibid.*
93   *Ibid.*
94   Karloff, Dorothy. "A Letter From the Karloffs," *Boris Karloff: The Frankenscience Monster*, (Ace Publishing Corporation, 1969).
95   *Ibid.*
96   Karloff, Boris. "Diary of a Monster", *op. cit.*
97   *Ibid.*
98   *Ibid.*
99   Karloff, Dorothy. "A Letter From the Karloffs", *op. cit.*
100 *Ibid.*
101 Karloff, Boris. "Diary of a Monster", *op. cit.*
102 *The Evening News*, 18 April 1936.

103 *Ibid.*
104 Karloff, Dorothy. "A Letter From the Karloffs", *op. cit.*
105 *Ibid.*
106 *Ibid.*
107 *Ibid.*
108 *Ibid.*
109 *Los Angeles Times*, 17 May 1936.
110 *Los Angeles Times*, 3 May 1936.
111 Nollen, Scott Allen. *op. cit.*
112 *Ibid.*
113 *Ibid.*
114 Karloff, Boris as told to Arlene and Howard Eisenberg. *op. cit.*
115 Bledsoe, William. *op. cit.*
116 *Ibid.*

Chapter 11 – A Lull in the Monstrosities (1936-1938)

1   *Chester Times*, 13 March 1937.
2   *Los Angeles Times*, 8 September 1936.
3   *Los Angeles Times*, 15 March 1936.
4   *Syracuse Herald*, 16 August 1936.
5   *Ibid.*
6   *Ibid.*
7   *Los Angeles Times*, 14 July 1936.
8   *Los Angeles Times*, 29 August 1936.
9   *Los Angeles Times*, 18 August 1936.
10   Levant, Oscar. *A Smattering of Ignorance*, (Doubleday, 1940).
11   *Ibid.*
12   Lindsay, Cynthia. *op. cit.*
13   Tuska, Jon. *Encounters with Filmmakers: Eight Career Studies* (Greenwood Press, 1991).
14   Lindsay, Cynthia. *op. cit.*
15   *New York Times*, 5 December 1936.
16   *Los Angeles Times*, 24 December 1936.
17   *Los Angeles Times*, 14 July 1933.
18   *Los Angeles Times*, 14 January 1934.
19   Lindsay, Cynthia. *op. cit.*
20   *Ibid.*
21   *Ibid.*
22   *Ibid.*
23   *Chicago Daily Tribune*, 1 January 1937.
24   *New York Times*, 11 November 1936.
25   *Nevada State Journal*, 31 December 1936.
26   *Salamanca, N. Y. Republican-Press*, 18 March 1937.
27   *Ibid.*
28   *Ibid.*
29   *Los Angeles Times*, 27 December 1936.
30   *Salamanca, N. Y. Republican-Press*, 18 March 1937.
31   *New York Times*, 19 April 1937.
32   *Fresno Bee*, 2 November 1936.
33   *New York Times*, 10 February 1937.
34   *Los Angeles Times*, 6 July 1937.
35   *Ibid.*
36   *New York Times*, 29 October 1937.
37   *Washington Post*, 4 April 1937.
38   *Ibid.*
39   *Los Angeles Times*, 10 May 1937.
40   *Hartford Courant*, 11 May 1937.
41   *New York Times*, 13 May 1937.
42   *Los Angeles Times*, 9 May 1937.
43   *Chicago Herald Tribune*, 21 August 1937.
44   *Ibid.*
45   *Chronicle Telegram*, 23 September 1937.
46   *Hartford Courant*, 27 January 1938.

47   *Circleville Herald*, 3 February 1936.
48   *Los Angeles Times*, 3 February 1936.
49   *San Antonio Light*, 8 March 1938.
50   Dunning, John. *On the Air: The Encyclopedia of Old-Time Radio*, (Oxford University Press, 1998).
51   *Chicago Daily Tribune*, 2 March 1938.
52   *Chicago Daily Tribune*, 23 March 1938.
53   *Chicago Daily Tribune*, 25 March 1938.
54   *Fresno Bee*, 30 March 1938.
55   *Christian Science Monitor*, 19 April 1938.
56   *Variety*, 27 April 1938.
57   *Albuquerque Journal*, 9 May 1938.
58   *Los Angeles Times*, 22 May 1938.
59   Lindsay, Cynthia. *op. cit.*
60   *Oakland Tribune*, 12 July 1938.
61   *Los Angeles Times*, 2 July 1938.
62   *Los Angeles Times*, 2 January 1939.
63   *New York Times*, 28 February 1939.
64   *New York Times*, 12 July 1940.
65   *Charleston Daily Mail*, 21 August 1938.
66   *Fresno Bee*, 4 September 1938.
67   *Ibid.*
68   *Ibid.*
69   *Los Angeles Times*, 13 October 1938.
70   *New York Times*, 21 November 1938.
71   *Christian Science Monitor*, 13 October 1938.
72   "Old Horror Pictures Pack Hollywood House," *Pampa Daily News*, 10 August 1938.

Chapter 12 – *Son of Frankenstein* (1939)
1   *Syracuse Herald*, 16 August 1936.
2   Curtis, James. *op. cit.*
3   Riley, Philip J. (editor), *Son of Frankenstein*, (Magicimage Filmbooks, 1989).
4   *Ibid.*
5   Youngkin, Stephen D. *The Lost One: A Life of Peter Lorre*, (University Press of Kentucky, 2005).
6   Druxman, Michael B. *Basil Rathbone: His Life and His Films*, (A.S. Barnes, 1975).
7   "Basil Rathbone, 75, Dies at Home Here", *New York Times*, 22 July 1967.
8   Sullivan, Ed. "Looking at Hollywood", *Chicago Daily Tribune*, 10 January 1939.
9   *Ibid.*
10   *Ibid.*
11   *Ibid.*
12   Weaver, Tom. "Donnie Dunagan", *Earth vs. the Sci-Fi Makers: 20 Interviews*, (McFarland, 2005).
13   *Ibid.*
14   Mank, Gregory William. *It's Alive!, op. cit.*
15   Lennig, Arthur. *op. cit.*
16   Cremer, Robert. *op. cit.*
17   *Ogden Standard-Examiner*, 2 February 1939.
18   *Ibid.*
19   *Ogden Standard-Examiner*, 25 November 1938.
20   *Kingsport Times*, 25 November 1938.
21   Parry, Mike and Harry Nadler, *op. cit.*
22   Weaver, Tom. "Donnie Dunagan", *op. cit.*
23   Jean, Gloria. *Email to author*, 30 June 2004.
24   *Ibid.*
25   Mank, Gregory William. *It's Alive!, op. cit.*
26   Bojarksi, Richard. *The Complete Films of Bela Lugosi*, (Citadel Press, 1980).
27   Riley, Philip J. (editor), *Son of Frankenstein, op. cit.*
28   *Los Angeles Times*, 14 January 1940.
29   *Washington Post*, 24 November 1938.

30   *Los Angeles Times*, 14 January 1940.
31   Mank, Gregory William. *Karloff and Lugosi: The Story of a Haunting Collaboration*, (McFarland, 1990).
32   *Lima News*, 4 Dec 1938.
33   Mank, Gregory William. *It's Alive!, op. cit.*
34   *Ibid.*
35   Jarman, Peter J. *op. cit.*

36   *Ironwood Daily Gloe, Ironwood, Mich.*, 17 December 1938.
37   Weaver, Tom. "Donnie Dunagan", *op. cit.*
38   *Ibid.*
39   *Ibid.*
40   *Ibid.*
41   *Ibid.*
42   *Ibid.*
43   *Ironwood Daily Gloe, Ironwood, Mich.*, 17 December 1938.
44   *Ibid.*
45   *Olean Times Herald*, 9 December 1938.
46   *Hartford Courant*, 11 December 1938.
47   *Ibid.*
48   *Hartford Courant*, 14 December 1938.
49   *Ibid.*
50   Beck, Calvin Thomas. *Heroes of Horror*, (Collins Macmillan, 1975).
51   Mank, Gregory William. *Karloff and Lugosi: The Story of a Haunting Collaboration, op. cit.*
52   Karloff, Boris. *Letter to Donnie Dunagan*, undated.
53   *Washington Post*, 3 January 1939.
54   Jones, Preston Neal. "The Ghost of Hans J. Salter", *Cinemafantastique* Vol. 7, No. 2.
55   Riley, Philip J. (editor), *Son of Frankenstein, op. cit.*
56   *Los Angeles Times*, 14 January 1939.
57   *New York Time*, 30 January 1939
58   *Oakland Tribune*, 23 February 1939.
59   *Ogden Standard-Examiner*, 11 December 1938.
60   *Los Angeles Times*, 23 March 1958.
61   Lennig, Arthur. *op. cit.*
62   "My Life of Terror, Robert Bean interviews Boris Karloff", *Shriek*, October 1965.
63   Glut, Donald F. *The Frankenstein Legend: A Tribute to Mary Shelley and Boris Karloff*, (Scarecrow Press, 1973).

13 – Medicine, Mysteries & Murder (1939-1940)
1   Karloff, Boris as told to Arlene and Howard Eisenberg. *op. cit.*
2   *Los Angeles Times*, 10 November 1938.
3   *Los Angeles Times*, 11 March 1939.
4   *Los Angeles Times*, 19 January 1940.
5   *Washington Post*, 31 January 1940.
6   *Ibid.*
7   *Washington Post*, 15 June 1939.
8   *Los Angeles Times*, 21 March 1939.
9   *Los Angeles Times*, 14 July 1939.
10   *New York Times*, 31 July 1939.
11   *Ibid.*
12   *Dunkirk (N.Y.) Evening Observer*, 16 October 1939.
13   Magers, Boyd and Michael G. Fitzgerald, *Westerns Women*, (McFarland, 1999).
14   *Ibid.*
15   Senn, Bryan. *Golden Horrors: An Illustrated Critical Filmography of Terror Cinema, 1931-1939*, (McFarland, 1996).
16   *Titusville (PA.) Herald*, 23 October 1939.
17   *Nevada State Journal*, 29 September 1939.

18 *Oakland Tribune*, 28 December 1939.
19 "Films Make History Expert of Roland Lee", *Washington Post*, 27 August 1939.
20 Underwood, Peter. *Karloff: The Life of Boris Karloff*, *op. cit.*
21 French, Lawrence. "An Interview with Vincent Price", *Vincent Price*, (Midnight Marquee Press, 1998).
22 *San Mateo Times*, 21 October 1939.
23 *Los Angeles Times*, 28 September 1939.
24 French, Lawrence. *op. cit.*
25 Nollen, Scott Allen. *op. cit.*
26 *Los Angeles Times*, 17 November 1939.
27 *Los Angeles Times*, 8 December 1939.
28 Fine, Henry M. *op. cit.*
29 *New York Times*, 13 January 1940.
30 *Dallas Morning News*, 17 March 1940.
31 Karloff, Boris. *Telegram to Sara Jane Karloff*, 19 August 1939.
32 Weaver, Tom and Michael Brunas, "Siodmak's Brain", *Fangoria* No. 44, May 1985.
33 Deutsch, Keith Alan. "Curt Siodmak: The Black Mask Interview", (www.blackmaskmagazine.com/siodmak.html).
34 Weaver, Tom and Michael Brunas, *op. cit.*
35 Mank, Gregory William. *Karloff and Lugosi*, *op. cit.*
36 Weaver, Tom. "Anne Gwynne", *It Came from Horrorwood: Interviews With Movie Makes in the SF and Horror Tradition*, (McFarland, 1996).
37 *New York Times*, 28 January 1940.
38 *Ibid.*
39 *Los Angeles Times*, 29 February 1940.
40 *Chicago Daily Tribune*, 1 March 1940.
41 *Ibid.*
42 *New York Times*, 22 March 1940.
43 Mank, Gregory William. *Karloff and Lugosi*, *op. cit.*
44 *Los Angeles Times*, 14 January 1940.
45 *Ibid.*
46 *Ibid.*
47 *Ibid.*
48 *Ibid.*
49 *Ibid.*
50 "The Screen", *New York Times*, 29 April 1940.
51 Karloff, Boris as told to Arlene and Howard Eisenberg. *op. cit.*
52 *Los Angeles Times*, 3 May 1940.
53 "Hedda Hopper's Hollywood", *Los Angeles Times*, 12 July 1940.
54 *New York Times*, 30 July 1940.
55 *Boxoffice*, 3 August 1940.
56 *Hartford Courant*, 21 July 1940.
57 *New York Times*, 3 October 1940.
58 *Boxoffice*, 8 November 1940.
59 *Ibid.*
60 Weaver, Tom and Michael Brunas, *op. cit.*
61 *Los Angeles Times*, 9 December 1940.
62 *New York Times*, 28 November 1940.
63 Karloff, Boris. "Houses I Have Haunted", *op. cit.*
64 *Ibid.*
65 Youngkin, Stephen D. *op. cit.*
66 Bojarksi, Richard. *op. cit.*
67 Mank, Gregory William. *Karloff and Lugosi*, *op. cit.*
68 *New York Times*, 15 November 1940.
69 Karloff, Boris as told to Arlene and Howard Eisenberg. *op. cit.*
70 Weaver, Tom. "Edward Dmytryk", *Science Fiction and Fantasy Film Flashbacks*, (McFarland, 2004).
71 Parla, Paul and Charles P. Mitchell, "Amanda Duff", *Screen Sirens Scream!: Interviews with 20 Actresses from Science Fiction, Horror, Film Noir and Mystery Movies, 1930s to 1960s*, (McFarland, 2000).
72 *Ibid.*
73 Weaver, Tom. "Edward Dmytryk", *op. cit.*
74 *New York Times*, 14 February 1941.
75 *Dunkirk (N.Y.) Evening Observer*, 16 October 1939.
76 *Ibid.*

Chapter 14 – Back to the Boards (1940-1944)

1   Othman, Frederick C. "Boris Karloff Calls Halt To Weird Film Make-ups", *Winnipeg Free Press*, 22 February 1944.
2   Parry, Mike and Harry Nadler, *op. cit.*
3   *Hartford Courant*, 6 July 1941.
4   *Los Angeles Times*, 13 September 1960.
5   Skinner, Cornelia Otis. *Life with Lindsay and Crouse*, (Houghton Mifflin Company Boston, 1976).
6   *Ibid.*
7   Karloff, Boris as told to Arlene and Howard Eisenberg. *op. cit.*
8   Crouse, Russel. *This Is Your Life: Boris Karloff*, *op. cit.*
9   Karloff, Boris as told to Arlene and Howard Eisenberg. *op. cit.*
10 *Ibid.*
11 Shriver, Gordon B. *op. cit.*
12 Karloff, Boris as told to Arlene and Howard Eisenberg. *op. cit.*
13 "Karloff, Calm Menace", *op. cit.*
14 Karloff, Boris as told to Arlene and Howard Eisenberg. *op. cit.*
15 *Ibid.*
16 Shriver, Gordon B. *op. cit.*
17 *New York Times*, 28 December 1948.
18 *Ibid.*
19 *Oakland Tribune*, 16 December 1940.
20 *Washington Post*, 16 January 1941.
21 Crouse, Russel. "Arsenic and Old Lace", *Life*, 3 April 1944.
22 Nollen, Scott Allen. *op. cit.*
23 Atkinson, Brooks. "Joseph Kesselring's 'Arsenic and Old Lace' Turns Murder Into Fantastic Comedy", *New York Times*, 11 January 1941.
24 *Wall Street Journal*, 13 January 1941.
25 Robb, Inez, "The Real Boris Karloff", *Mansfield News Journal*, 7 May 1950.
26 *Life*, 11 November 1946.
27 Shriver, Gordon B. *op. cit.*
28 *Evening Observer, Dunkirk, N.Y.*, 11 May 1946.
29 Lindsay, Cynthia. *op. cit.*
30 *Evening Observer, Dunkirk, N.Y.*, 11 May 1946.
31 Shriver, Gordon B. *op. cit.*
32 *Ibid.*
33 *Washington Post*, 27 June 41.
34 Atkinson, Brooks. "Murder For A Laugh", *New York Times*, 23 February 1941.
35 *Washington Post*, 9 February 1941.
36 *Washington Post*, 11 February 1941.
37 Skinner, Cornelia Otis. *op. cit.*
38 "South of the Border", *New York Times*, 1 February 1942.
39 Skinner, Cornelia Otis. *op. cit.*
40 *Washington Post*, 17 July 1942.
41 *Ibid.*
42 *Hartford Courant*, 26 April 1942.

43 *The Times*, 6 September 1962.
44 Shriver, Gordon B. *op. cit.*
45 *Ibid.*
46 *Hartford Courant*, 6 July 1941.
47 *Ibid.*
48 *Washington Post*, 5 July 1941.
49 Lindsay, Cynthia. *op. cit.*
50 *New York Times*, 26 November 1941.
51 Nollen, Scott Allen. *op. cit.*
52 *New York Times*, 24 December 1941.
53 *Ibid.*
54 Nollen, Scott Allen. *op. cit.*
55 *Ibid.*
56 *Washington Post*, 4 March 1942.
57 Pratt, Dorothy. "Monster Attraction", *op. cit.*
58 "Life Goes To a Party", *Life*, 30 March 1942.
59 Karloff, Boris. *Letter to Louise Stine*, 20 March 1942.
60 *Ibid.*
61 *Hartford Courant*, 15 March 1942.
62 *Ibid.*
63 *Ibid.*
64 Addams, Charles. *Drawn and Quartered*, (World Publishing Company, 1942).
65 *New York Times*, 9 June 1941.
66 *Hartford Courant*, 23 July 1942.
67 *Ibid.*
68 *Ibid.*
69 *Ibid.*
70 *Ibid.*
71 *Ibid.*
72 *The Gazette, Xenia, Ohio*, 23 July 1942.
73 *Ibid.*
74 *The Times and Daily News Leader, San Mateo, Calif.*, 10 October 1942.
75 *Ibid.*
76 *New York Times*, 12 October 1942.
77 *Boxoffice*, 20 March 1943.
78 Heffernan, Harold. "Hollywood Highlights", *Hartford Courant*, 21 July 1942.
79 *Los Angeles Times*, 18 August 1942.
80 *New York Times*, 4 October 1942.
81 Karloff, Boris. "Introduction", *Tales of Terror*, (World Publishing Company, 1943).
82 Nolan, William F. *op. cit.*
83 Karloff, Boris. "Introduction", *op. cit.*
84 Collins, Charles. "Bookman's Holiday", *Chicago Daily Tribune*, 7 November 1943.
85 *Los Angeles Times*, 2 September 1941.
86 Lindsay, Cynthia. *op. cit.*
87 Skinner, Cornelia Otis. *op. cit.*
88 *Ibid.*
89 Crouse, Russel. *This Is Your Life: Boris Karloff*, *op. cit.*
90 *Los Angeles Times*, 25 August 1942.

Chapter 15 – Lewton (1944-1945)
1 Berg, Louis. "Farewell to Monsters", *Los Angeles Times*, 12 May 1946.
2 Othman, Frederick C. *op. cit.*
3 *Christian Science Monitor*, 12 October 1944.
4 *New York Times*, 14 December 1944.
5 Weaver, Tom and Michael Brunas, *op. cit.*
6 Riley, Philip J. (editor), *House of Frankenstein*, *op. cit.*
7 *Ibid.*
8 *Ibid.*
9 *Ibid.*
10 Pace, Terry. *op. cit.*
11 *Ibid.*
12 Othman, Frederick C. *op. cit.*
13 Glut, Donald F. *The Frankenstein Archive*, (McFarland, 2002).
14 *Ibid.*
15 *Los Angeles Times*, 17 May 1941.
16 *Atlanta Constitution*, 9 May 1941.
17 *New York Times*, 25 September 1942.
18 *Hartford Courant*, 24 April 1943.
19 Eustace, Edward J. "A Witches Sabbath", *New York Times*, 10 December 1944.
20 *Ibid.*
21 *Ibid.*
22 *Ibid.*
23 Mank, Gregory Wm. "An Interview with Elena Verdugo", *House of Frankenstein* (MagicImage Filmbooks, 1995).
24 Coe, Peter. "Introduction", *House of Frankenstein*, (MagicImage Filmbooks, 1995).
25 Glut, Donald F. *The Frankenstein Archive*, *op. cit.*
26 *New York Times*, 16 December 1944.
27 Parry, Mike and Harry Nadler, *op. cit.*
28 Lindsay, Cynthia. *op. cit.*
29 *The Times*, 6 September 1962.
30 Wise, Robert. "Audio Commentary", *The Body Snatcher* DVD, (Turner Home Entertainment, 2005).
31 *New York Times*, 15 May 1944.
32 Siegel, Joel E. *Val Lewton: The Reality of Terror*, (Secker and Warburg, 1972).
33 "Karloff Undergoes Spinal Operation", *Winnipeg Evening Tribune*, 25 July 1944.
34 Stevenson, Robert Louis. *The Strange Case of Dr. Jekyll and Mr. Hyde and Other Tales of Terror*, (Penguin, 2003).
35 *Ibid.*
36 *Ibid.*
37 Mank, Gregory William. *Karloff and Lugosi: The Story of a Haunting Collaboration*, *op. cit.*
38 *Ibid.*
39 *Ibid.*
40 Bansak, Edmund G. *Fearing the Dark: The Val Lewton Career*, (McFarland, 1995).
41 Wise, Robert. "Audio Commentary", *op. cit.*
42 Lugosi, Bela. *Interview at the Metropolitan State Hospital*, August 1955.
43 *Ibid.*
44 Weaver, Tom. "Time Travelling Sun Demon", *Fangoria* No. 59, December 1986.
45 Wise, Robert. "Audio Commentary", *op. cit.*
46 Wise, Robert. *Letter to author*, 10 February 2003.
47 Wise, Robert. "Audio Commentary", *op. cit.*
48 Bansak, Edmund G. *op. cit.*
49 Wise, Robert. "Audio Commentary", *op. cit.*
50 Bansak, Edmund G. *op. cit.*
51 *Los Angeles Times*, 11 May 1945.
52 *New York Times*, 26 May 1945.
53 *Ibid.*
54 Green, J.L. (Chief Assistant (Policy), BBFC), *Email to author*, 9 November 2009.
55 *New York Times*, 8 September 1945.
56 Scott, John L. "Double Bill Mixes Horror and Laughs", *Los Angeles Times*, 23 November 1945.
57 Lindsay, Cynthia. *op. cit.*
58 *Ibid.*
59 Smith, Cecil. "Karloff—Arsenic, Very Old Lace", *op. cit.*
60 Lindsay, Cynthia. *op. cit.*

61   *Ibid*.
62   *Ibid*.
63   Smith, Cecil. "Karloff—Arsenic, Very Old Lace", *op. cit.*
64   Lindsay, Cynthia. *op. cit.*
65   Gunson, Victor. "Frankenstein's Monster Rebels! Film Boogey Man Tired of Scaring Folks", *Winnipeg Evening Tribune*, 10 December 1945.
66   Lindsay, Cynthia. *op. cit.*
67   Gunson, Victor. *op. cit.*
68   "Lighting Job Gives Karloff Loafing Time", *Hartford Courant*, 11 November 1945.
69   Weaver, Tom. "Anna Lee", *Science Fiction Stars and Horror Heroes*, (McFarland, 2006).
70   *Ibid*.
71   Gunson, Victor. *op. cit.*
72   *Ibid*.
73   Weaver, Tom. "Anna Lee", *op. cit.*
74   Mank, Gregory William. *Hollywood Cauldron*, (McFarland, 1994).
75   Weaver, Tom. "Time Travelling Sun Demon", *op. cit.*
76   *New York Times*, 20 April 1946.

Chapter 16 – Moving On (1945-1950)
1   Johnson, Erskine. "In Hollywood", *Daily Kennebec Journal*, 13 May 1946.
2   Berg, Louis. *op. cit.*
3   *Los Angeles Times*, 23 November 1958.
4   Lindsay, Cynthia. *op. cit.*
5   *Chicago Daily Tribune*, 2 December 1945.
6   *Los Angeles Times*, 27 February 1946.
7   Johnson, Erskine. *op. cit.*
8   *Ibid*.
9   *Ibid*.
10   *New York Times*, 9 November 1946.
11   *Chicago Daily Tribune*, 5 August 1947.
12   *New York Times*, 15 August 1947.
13   Lindsay, Cynthia. *op. cit.*
14   *Ibid*.
15   *Ibid*.
16   *Ibid*.
17   *Ibid*.
18   *Ibid*.
19   Karloff, Sara. *Email to author*, 22 April 2009.
20   Nollen, Scott Allen. *op .cit.*
21   Terry, C.V. "Gooseflesh Guaranteed", *New York Times*, 12 May 1946.
22   Fidler, Jimmie. "Chatter About The Stars", *Charleston Daily Mail*, 23 May 1946.
23   Brady, Thomas F. "Monster's Memories – Boris Karloff Views His Ghoulish Past And Finds He's Happier as an Indian", *New York Times*, 27 July 1948.
24   *San Antonio Light*, 28 November 1947.
25   *Portland Press Herald*, 28 November 1947.
26   Goldrup, Tom and Jim Goldrup, *Growing Up on the Set*, (McFarland, 2002).
27   *Ibid*.
28   *Billboard*, 23 November 1946.
29   Karloff, Boris as told to Arlene and Howard Eisenberg. *op. cit.*
30   *Chicago Daily Tribune*, 29 January 1947.
31   *New York Times*, 29 August 1947.
32   Crowley, Elisabeth. *Email to author*, 1 September 2008.
33   Pratt, John. *Letter to Emma Pratt*, 22 February 1924, *op. cit.*

34   Crowley, Elisabeth. *Email to author*, 1 September 2008.
35   *Ibid*.
36   *Cleveland Plain Dealer*, 21 March 1948.
37   *Ibid*.
38   *Ibid*.
39   *Ibid*.
40   *Ibid*.
41   *Ibid*.
42   *New York Times*, 27 September 1947.
43   Heyn, Howard C. "Karloff Bids Farewell to Frankenstein", *Hartford Courant*, 14 September 1947.
44   Crowther, Bosley. "Where We Came In", *New York Times*, 29 August 1948.
45   *Billboard*, 26 July 1947.
46   Monroe, Al. "Swinging the News", *Chicago Defender*, 16 August 1947.
47   Heyn, Howard C. *op. cit.*
48   Atkinson, Brooks. "At the Theatre," *New York Times*, 3 March 1948.
49   Karloff, Boris as told to Arlene and Howard Eisenberg. *op. cit.*
50   *Ibid*.
51   *Ibid*.
52   Kirkley, Donald. "Theatre Notes", *The Sun*, 22 February 1948.
53   Golly, Sydney. "Out-of-Town Opening", *Billboard*, 14 February 1948.
54   Atkinson, Brooks. "At the Theatre", *New York Times*, 3 March 1948.
55   Karloff, Boris as told to Arlene and Howard Eisenberg. *op. cit.*
56   Nollen, Scott Allen. *op. cit.*
57   *Ibid*.
58   Brady, Thomas F. *op. cit.*
59   *Los Angeles Times*, 1 December 1948.
60   Atkinson, Brooks. "At The Theatre", *New York Times*, 19 January 1949.
61   Lindsay, Cynthia. *op. cit.*
62   Parla, Paul and Charles P. Mitchell. *op. cit.*
63   *Ibid*.
64   *Los Angeles Times*, 5 September 1949.
65   Crowther, Bosley. "'Abbott and Costello Meet the Killer, Boris Karloff.' Opens at the Globe", *New York Times*, 19 September 1949.
66   Stein, Sonia. "Karloff Likes to Scare People", *Washington Post*, 11 December 1949.
67   *Ibid*.
68   *Ibid*.
69   *Ibid*.
70   *Ibid*.
71   *Ibid*.
72   *Ibid*.
73   *Ibid*.
74   *Ibid*.
75   Lindsay, Cynthia. *op. cit.*
76   *Ibid*.
77   *Ibid*.
78   Karloff, Boris. *Letter to Sir John Pratt*, 6 November 1949, *op. cit.*
79   *The Times*, 17 October 1949.
80   Karloff, Boris. *Letter to Sir John Pratt*, 6 November 1949, *op. cit.*
81   *Ibid*.
82   *New York Times*, 5 December 1949.
83   *Washington Post*, 21 February 1950.

84   Karloff, Boris. *Letter to Sir John Pratt*, 28 January 1950, (Sir John Pratt Papers, PP.MS. 5/36, School of Oriental and African Studies, London).

Chapter 17 – *Peter Pan* (1950-1951)
1   Atkinson, Brooks. "First Night at the Theatre: Jean Arthur and Boris Karloff in an Excellent Version of Barrie's *Peter Pan*", *New York Times*, 25 April 1950.
2   Foster, Inez Whiteley. "*Peter Pan*: Off on New Flights of Fancy", *Christian Science Monitor*, 1 February 1951.
3   *Los Angeles Times*, 17 September 1950.
4   Karloff, Boris. *Letter to Sir John Pratt*, 28 January 1950, *op. cit.*
5   *Peter Pan* theatre programme, (Programme Publishing Company, 1950).
6   *Chicago Daily Tribune*, 16 April 1950.
7   Robb, Inez. *op. cit.*
8   Foy, Peter. *Interview with author*, 12 August 2004.
9   Shriver, Gordon B. *op. cit.*
10   *Los Angeles Times*, 17 September 1950.
11   Foy, Peter. *op. cit.*
12   *Ibid.*
13   *Ibid.*
14   *Ibid.*
15   *Peter Pan* theatre programme, *op. cit.*
16   Bernstein, Leonard. *Letter to Shirley Bernstein*, 17 April 1950, (Bernstein collection at the Library of Congress: http://hdl.loc.gov/loc.music/lbcorr.00320).
17   Robb, Inez. *op. cit.*
18   *Ibid.*
19   Lardner, James. "The Wisdom & Wiles of Roger Stevens", *Washington Post*, 6 September 1981.
20   Atkinson, Brooks. "First Night at the Theatre", *op. cit.*
21   *Ibid.*
22   Chapman, John. "N.Y. Revival of *Peter Pan* is a Delight", *Chicago Daily Tribune*, 26 April 1950.
23   Karloff, Boris as told to Arlene and Howard Eisenberg. *op. cit.*
24   McCrary, Tex and Jinx Falkenbery. "New York Close Up", *New York Herald Tribune*, undated clipping.
25   Foy, Peter. *op. cit.*
26   Karloff, Boris as told to Arlene and Howard Eisenberg. *op. cit.*
27   *Ibid.*
28   Griffith, Robert. *The Politics of Fear: Joseph R. McCarthy and the Senate*, (University of Massachusetts Press, 1987).
29   Karloff, Boris. *Letter to Sir John Pratt*, 23 May 1950, (Sir John Pratt Papers, PP.MS. 5/36, School of Oriental and African Studies, London).
30   *Ibid.*
31   *Ibid.*
32   Persoff, Nehemiah. *Email to author*, 13 June 2006.
33   Shriver, Gordon B. *op. cit.*
34   Foy, Peter. *op. cit.*
35   *Ibid.*
36   *Ibid.*
37   *Ibid.*
38   Karloff, Boris. *Letter to Sir John Pratt*, 16 April 1953, (Sir John Pratt Papers, PP.MS. 5/36, School of Oriental and African Studies, London).
39   Nollen, Scott Allen. *op. cit.*
40   *Ibid.*
41   Walden, Dan. *Email to author*, 28 July 2004.
42   *Ibid.*
43   Persoff, Nehemiah. *Email to author*, 13 June 2006.

44   Foy, Peter. *op. cit.*
45   *New York Times*, 14 August 1950.
46   *New York Times*, 16 August 1950.
47   Persoff, Nehemiah. *Email to author*, 13 June 2006.
48   Walden, Dan. *op. cit.*
49   Karloff, Boris. *Letter to Sir John Pratt*, 18 December 1950, (Sir John Pratt Papers, PP.MS. 5/36, School of Oriental and African Studies, London).
50   *Ibid.*
51   Shriver, Gordon B. *op. cit.*
52   Lowry, Cynthia. "Karloff Likes Kids & Vice Versa", *Washington Post*, 22 October 1950.
53   Winchell, Walter. "Walter Winchell in New York", *New York Times*, 18 December 1950.
54   Foy, Peter. *op. cit.*
55   Graham, Sheilah. "Hollywood in Person", *Dallas Morning News*, 8 June 1951.
56   Foy, Peter. *op. cit.*
57   Karloff, Boris. *Letter to Sir John Pratt*, 17 February 1951, *op. cit.*
58   Foy, Peter. *op. cit.*
59   Cassidy, Claudia. "On the Aisle: Jean Arthur and Boris Karloff Bring 'Peter Pan' to Opera House", *Chicago Daily Tribune*, 28 March 1951.
60   *Ibid.*
61   Karloff, Sara Jane. *Email to author*, 1 May 2008.
62   Foy, Peter. *op. cit.*
63   Karloff, Sara Jane. *Email to author*, 1 May 2008.
64   Sagolla, Lisa Jo. *The Girl Who Fell Down: A Biography of Joan McCracken*, (Northeastern University Press, 2003).
65   Cassidy, Claudia. "On the Aisle: Joan McCracken Flies in the Window and Takes Over as Peter Pan", *Chicago Daily Tribune*, 16 April 1951.
66   *Ibid.*
67   Karloff, Boris. *Letter to Sir John Pratt*, 27 July 1951, (Sir John Pratt Papers, PP.MS. 5/36, School of Oriental and African Studies, London).
68   *Ibid.*
69   *Ibid.*

Chapter 18 – The Return of the Ghost (1951-1955)
1   Oliver, Wayne. "Ex-Villain Karloff Likes Respectable TV Roles", *Los Angeles Times*, 10 March 1955.
2   Crowther, Bosley. "The Screen in Review", *New York Times*, 14 May 1951.
3   Weaver, Tom. "Michael Pate", *It Came from Horrorwood: Interviews With Movie Makes in the SF and Horror Tradition*, (McFarland, 1996).
4   *Ibid.*
5   *New York Times*, 10 December 1951.
6   *Austin Daily Herald*, 28 May 1951.
7   Karloff, Boris. *Letter to Sir John Pratt*, 27 July 1951, *op. cit.*
8   *Hartford Courant*, 24 July 1951.
9   *The Times*, 24 July 1951.
10   *Ibid.*
11   Karloff, Boris. *Letter to Sir John Pratt*, 27 July 1951, *op. cit.*
12   Crowley, Elisabeth. *Email to author*, 10 August 2008.
13   "Screen Actors Guild Again Elects Reagan", *Los Angeles Times*, 12 November 1951.
14   Nollen, Scott Allen. *op. cit.*
15   *Chicago Daily Tribune*, 3 November 1951.
16   *New York Times*, 5 December 1951.

17 Gould, Jack. "Karloff Tilts With Windmills and Jimmy Savo Plays Sancho Panza in C.B.S. Workshop's Quixote", *New York Times, 16 January 1952.*

18 Weaver, Tom. "Michael Pate", *op. cit.*

19 *New York Times*, 26 December 1952.

20 Weaver, Tom. "Michael Pate", *op. cit.*

21 Simpson, Peg. "New Quiz Show Added to List Now Flooding Video", *Post-Standard*, 26 June 1952.

22 Hearn, Lafcadio. "The Soul of the Great Bell", *Some Chinese Ghosts*, (Roberts Brothers, 1887).

23 *Ibid.*

24 *Ibid.*

25 *Nevada State Journal*, 10 July 1952.

26 Mitgang, Herbert. "John Dickson Carr Is Dead at 70; A Master of the Mystery Novel", *New York Times*, 1 March 1977.

27 Bernstein, Walter. *Inside Out: A Memoir of the Blacklist*, (Da Capo Press, 2000).

28 *Ibid.*

29 *Ibid.*

30 *Ibid.*

31 *Ibid.*

32 *Ibid.*

33 *Ibid.*

34 Karloff, Boris. *Letter to Sir John Pratt*, 28 June 1952, (Sir John Pratt Papers, PP.MS. 5/36, School of Oriental and African Studies, London).

35 "The Return of the Ghost – That's Me Says Boris", *Daily Mirror*, 12 July 1952.

36 *Ibid.*

37 *Ibid.*

38 *Ibid.*

39 *Ibid.*

40 *Ibid.*

41 Sims, Joan. *High Spirits*, (Partridge, 2000).

42 Ibid.

43 Coleman, Bernard. *Interview with author*, 5 December 2002.

44 Cook, Ben. "Hollywood Film Shop", *Brownsville Herald*, 13 April 1953.

45 Nordell, Rod. "Boris Karloff Co-Starring In Comedy at RKO-Boston", *Christian Science Monitor*, 31 July 1953.

46 *Los Angeles Times*, 13 August 1953.

47 Hopper, Hedda. "Karloff to Make Film of a Jules Verne Story", *Chicago Daily Tribune*, 4 February 1953.

48 Karloff, Boris. *Letter to Sir John Pratt*, 16 April 1953, op. cit.

49 Nielsen, Leslie. *Letter to author*, 3 April 2006.

50 *Post Standard*, 30 March 1953.

51 Karloff, Boris. *Letter to Sir John Pratt*, 16 April 1953, *op. cit.*

52 *Ibid.*

53 *Long Beach Press-Telegram*, 23 April 1953.

54 Karloff, Boris. *Letter to Sir John Pratt*, 6 June 1953, (Sir John Pratt Papers, PP.MS. 5/36, School of Oriental and African Studies, London).

55 *Ibid.*

56 Coleman, Bernard. *op. cit.*

57 *Ibid.*

58 *New York Times*, 2 September 1953.

59 Parry, Mike and Harry Nadler, *op. cit.*

60 Brandon, Henry. *Letter to Scott Allen Nollen*, April 1989.

61 Remenih, Anton. "TV Claims Karloff in Whodunit", *Chicago Daily Tribune*, 16 February 1954.

62 Read, Jeremy. *Interview with author*, 13 March 2003.

63 Read, Jeremy. *Letter to author*, 23 November 2002.

64 "Partners in Crime: Authors' Campaign to Raise Prestige", *The Times*, 16 June 1954.

65 Coleman, Bernard. *Interview with author, op. cit.*

66 *Ibid.*

67 *Ibid.*

68 *Ibid.*

69 *Long Beach Independent*, 16 December 1954.

70 *Washington Post and Times Herald*, 12 December 1954.

71 Heimer, Mel. "My New York", *Didette-Messenger*, 7 January 1955.

72 Gould, Jack. "Television in Review", *New York Times*, 9 January 1955.

73 Gould, Jack. "Television: Boris Karloff. Beneath the Monstrous Make-Up Lies an Actor of Real and Diverse Talents", *New York Times*, 21 February 1955.

74 Shanley, J.P. "Nothing to Be Scared About", *New York Times*, 6 March 1955.

75 *Ibid.*

76 *Ibid.*

77 *Ibid.*

78 *Ibid.*

79 *Syracuse-Herald-American*, 1 May 1955.

80 *The Times*, "Night of 100 Stars", 25 June 1955.

81 Coleman, Bernard. *op. cit.*

82 *Ibid.*

83 Davis, Clifford. "On the Airwaves in America", *Daily Mirror*, 21 June 1955.

84 Lynch, James E. "The Case History of a Live TV Drama", *The Quarterly of Film, Radio and Television*, Vol. 11, No. 1, (Autumn, 1956).

85 *Ibid.*

86 *Ibid.*

87 Shanley, J.P. "TV: Karloff on Old Kick", *New York Times*, 1 September 1955.

Chapter 19 – *The Lark* (1955-1957)

1   Glover, William. "Finally No Frankenstein", *Cedar Rapids Gazette*, 29 January 1956.

2   *The Lark* theatre program, (Program Publishing Company, 1955).

3   Schumach, Murray. "Shaping a New Joan – Miss Hellman Discusses Adapting *The Lark*", *New York Times*, 13 November 1955.

4   *Ibid.*

5   *Ibid.*

6   *Ibid.*

7   *Ibid.*

8   *New York Times*, 25 July 55.

9   Brantley, Ben. "Stage View; When These Two Chat, an Era Is Speaking", *New York Times*, 14 September 1997.

10 *Ibid.*

11 *Ibid.*

12 Bikel, Theodore. *Theo: The Autobiography of Theodore Bikel*, (University of Wisconsin Press, 2002).

13 Karloff, Boris. *Letter to Sir John Pratt*, 9 December 1955, (Sir John Pratt Papers, PP.MS. 5/36, School of Oriental and African Studies, London).

14 Bikel, Theodore. *op. cit.*

15 Brantley, Ben. *op. cit.*

16 *Ibid.*

17 Bikel, Theodore. *op. cit.*

18 *Ibid.*

19 *Ibid.*

20 *Ibid.*

21 *Ibid.*

22 Shriver, Gordon B. *op. cit.*

23 Melvin, Edwin F. "Drama of Joan of Arc From Anouilh", *Christian Science Monitor*, 29 October 1955.

24 Karloff, Boris. *Letter to Sir John Pratt*, 9 December 1955, *op. cit.*

25 Calta, Louis. "All Critics Unite in Lauding 'Lark'", *New York Times*, 19 November 1955.

26 Brantley, Ben. *op. cit.*

27 *Ibid.*

28 Calta, Louis. "Prices at 'Lark' to be Increased", *New York Times*, 18 November 1955.

29 Karloff, Boris. *Letter to Sir John Pratt*, 9 December 1955, *op. cit.*

30 Coleman, Bernard. *op. cit.*

31 Glover, William. *op. cit.*

32 *Ibid.*

33 *Ibid.*

34 Nollen, Scott Allen. *op. cit.*

35 Coleman, Bernard. *op. cit.*

36 Bikel, Theodore. *op. cit.*

37 Plummer, Christopher. *In Spite of Myself: A Memoir*, (Alfred A. Knopf, 2009).

38 *Ibid.*

39 Harris, Julie. *Letter to Boris Karloff*, 2 June 1956.

40 *Billboard*, 7 January 1956.

41 Shriver, Gordon B. *op. cit.*

42 Crosby, John. "Western in Blank Verse Great, Unusual Play", *Hartford Courant*, 18 April 1956.

43 Gould, Jack. "TV: Western Tone Poem", *New York Times*, 16 April 1956.

44 *Los Angeles Times*, 14 May 1956.

45 "Bela Lugosi Seeks Cure", *New York Times*, 23 April 1955.

46 "Lugosi Drug Cure Progresses", *New York Times*, 3 August 1955.

47 "Actor Bela Lugosi, 72, Takes His Fifth Bride, 39", *Los Angeles Times*, 25 August 1955.

48 "Actor Bela Lugosi, Dracula of Screen, Succumbs After Heart Attack at 74", *Los Angeles Times*, 17 August 1956.

49 Jarman, Peter J. *op. cit.*

50 Thomas, Bob. "Summit Scare Conference Links Hollywood 'Monsters'", *The Galveston News*, 1 November 1962.

51 Brantley, Ben. *op. cit.*

52 *Ibid.*

53 *Ibid.*

54 *Ibid.*

55 Weaver, Tom. "Howard W. Koch", *Return of the B Science Fiction and Horror Heroes*, (McFarland, 2000).

56 Weaver, Tom. "Reginald LeBorg", *Return of the B Science Fiction and Horror Heroes*, (McFarland, 2000).

57 Weaver, Tom. "Howard W. Koch", *Return of the B Science Fiction and Horror Heroes*, *op. cit.*

58 Weaver, Tom. "Classic Creatures Revisited", *Fangoria* No. 147, October 1995.

59 *Hartford Courant*, 25 October 1956.

60 Wallach, Eli. *Letter to author*, 20 April 2003.

61 Gould, Jack. "Television: "The Lark", *New York Times*, 11 February 1957.

62 Glover, William. *op. cit.*

Chapter 20 – *Arsenic* in Alaska (1957)

1 *Los Angeles Times*, 13 September 1960.

2 Unidentified clipping, January 1957.

3 "Spotlight On: John Elliott, Volunteer Extraordinaire", (www.cottagetheatre.org/aboutus/newsletter/0103.htm#spotlight).

4 Christensen, Marcie. "Mom Remembers Boris Karloff", *Letter to author*, 11 September 2004.

5 *Ibid.*

6 *Ibid.*

7 *Ibid.*

8 *Ibid.*

9 Christensen, Marcie. *Letter to author*, 11 September 2004.

10 Unidentified clipping, March 1957.

11 *Ibid.*

12 Shriver, Gordon B. *op. cit.*

13 *Ibid.*

14 "Mrs. Karloff Likes Crab, Travel", *Anchorage Times*, March 1957.

15 Christensen, Marcie. "Mom Remembers Boris Karloff", *op. cit.*

16 "Spotlight On: John Elliott, Volunteer Extraordinaire", *op. cit.*

17 Elliott, John. *Email to author*, 18 July 2006.

18 *Ibid.*

19 Christensen, Marcie. "Mom Remembers Boris Karloff", *op. cit.*

20 Elliott, John. *op. cit.*

21 Christensen, Marcie. "Mom Remembers Boris Karloff", *op. cit.*

22 "Mrs. Karloff Likes Crab, Travel", *op. cit.*

23 *Ibid.*

24 *Ibid.*

25 *Ibid.*

26 Christensen, Marcie. "Mom Remembers Boris Karloff", *op. cit.*

27 "Mrs. Karloff Likes Crab, Travel", *op. cit.*

28 "Karloff Offers Proceeds to Help Build College Theatre", *Anchorage Times*, 20 March 1957.

29 *Ibid.*

30 Whittaker, Dick. "Theatre Cast Promises Top-Flight Production", *Anchorage Times*, 21 March 1957.

31 Elliott, John. *op. cit.*

32 Shriver, Gordon B. *op. cit.*

33 Pumphrey, Fritz. "Record First-Night Comedy Sees Kesselring Comedy", *Anchorage Daily Times*, 22 March 1957.

34 *Ibid.*

35 *Ibid.*

36 Bannister, Jeanne. "Karloff, Cast Take Curtain Calls Together", *Anchorage Daily Times*, 22 March 1957.

37 Elliott, John. *op. cit.*

38 *Ibid.*

39 Shriver, Gordon B. *op. cit.*

40 *Ibid.*

41 *Ibid.*

42 "Mrs. Karloff Likes Crab, Travel", *op. cit.*

43 Kegley, Howard. "Oil News", *Los Angeles Times*, 9 June 1936.

44 Lindsay, Cynthia. *op. cit.*

45 *Ibid.*

46 Christensen, Marcie. "Mom Remembers Boris Karloff", *op. cit.*

47 Shriver, Gordon B. *op. cit.*

48 *Ibid.*

49 *Ibid.*

50 Ames, Walter. "Karloff to Sing for Dinah; Sinatra Shuns Rehearsals", *Los Angeles Times*, 17 May 1957.

51 *Ibid.*

Chapter 21 – The Homesick Horror Man (1957-1960)

1   *Los Angeles Times*, 11 September 1960.
2   Coleman, Bernard. *op. cit.*
3   *Ibid.*
4   *Ibid.*
5   *Ibid.*
6   Lopez, Dan. "Face Behind the Fiends: An Interview with Richard Gordon", (www.digitallyobsessed.com).
7   *Ibid.*
8   Weaver, Tom. "John Croydon", *Attack of the Monster Movie Makers*, (McFarland, 1994).
9   *Ibid.*
10 Croydon, John. *op. cit.*
11 *Ibid.*
12 *Ibid.*
13 Weaver, Tom. "Robert Day", *Attack of the Monster Movie Makers*, (McFarland, 1994).
14 *Ibid.*
15 Lopez, Dan. *op. cit.*
16 Kent, Jean. *Letter to author*, 6 December 2002.
17 *Ibid.*
18 Lopez, Dan. *op. cit.*
19 "Fiend Without a Face: A reminiscence by Richard Gordon", (www.filmsinreview.com/2002/01/01/fiend-without-a-face-a-reminiscence/).
20 Nason, Richard W. "The Screen", *New York Times*, 4 July 1958.
21 *The Times*, 6 September 1962.
22 Brow, Rick Du. "Boris Karloff Shocked By New Horror Fans", *Hartford Courant*, 31 May 1959.
23 *Daily Mirror*, 30 August 1957.
24 *Karloff, Boris. "My Life as a Monster", op. cit.*
25 *Ibid.*
26 *Ibid.*
27 *Ibid.*
28 Karloff, Boris. *Letter to Sir John Pratt*, 19 October 1957, (Sir John Pratt Papers, PP.MS. 5/36, School of Oriental and African Studies, London).
29 *Ibid.*
30 Nollen, Scott Allen. *op. cit.*
31 Edwards, Ralph. *This Is Your Life: Boris Karloff*, *op. cit.*
32 *Ibid.*
33 Nollen, Scott Allen. *op. cit.*
34 Coleman, Bernard. *op. cit.*
35 Bacon, J. Warren. *This Is Your Life: Boris Karloff*, *op. cit.*
36 Karloff, Boris. *This Is Your Life: Boris Karloff*, *op. cit.*
37 *Ibid.*
38 *Ibid.*
39 Lindsay, Howard. *This Is Your Life: Boris Karloff*, *op. cit.*
40 Brink, Frank. *This Is Your Life: Boris Karloff*, *op. cit.*
41 *Ibid.*
42 Karloff, Sara. *Email to author*, 23 April 2009.
43 Nollen, Scott Allen. *op. cit.*
44 Coleman, Bernard. *op. cit.*
45 Nollen, Scott Allen. *op. cit.*
46 Coleman, Bernard. *op. cit.*
47 *Ibid.*
48 *Chicago Daily Tribune*, 9 December 1957.
49 *Hartford Courant*, 9 December 1957.
50 *Los Angeles Times*, 12 August 1957.

51 Weaver, Tom. "Aubrey Schenck", *It Came from Horrorwood: Interviews with Movie Makers in the SF and Horror Tradition*, (McFarland, 1996).
52 Weaver, Tom. "Howard W. Koch", *Interviews with B Science Fiction and Horror Movie Makers: Writers, Producers, Directors, Actors, Moguls and Make-up*, (McFarland, 2006).
53 Weaver, Tom. "Aubrey Schenck", *op. cit.*
54 Weaver, Tom. "Charlotte Austin", *It Came from Horrorwood: Interviews With Movie Makers in the SF and Horror Tradition*, (McFarland, 1996).
55 "Boris Karloff at the Twins", *Christian Science Monitor*, 9 August 1958.
56 Du Brow, Rick. "Boris Karloff Shocked By New Horror Fans", *Hartford Courant*, 31 May 1959.
57 *Ibid.*
58 Karloff, Boris. *Letter to Sir John Pratt*, 19 October 1957, *op. cit.*
59 Karloff, Sara. *Email to author*, 23 April 2009.
60 *Ibid.*
61 Jacobs, George and William Stadiem. *Mr. S – The Last Word on Frank Sinatra*, (Sidgwick & Jackson, 2003).
62 *Los Angeles Times*, 25 February 1958.
63 *Los Angeles Times*, 6 March 1958.
64 Gustafson, Robert. "Boris Karloff Reads 'Peter and the Wolf'", *Christian Science Monitor*, 28 October 1958.
65 Gordon, Richard. *Letter to author*, 4 February 2003.
66 *Ibid.*
67 *Ibid.*
68 "Between the Bolts," *op. cit.*
69 Weaver, Tom. "Robert Day", *op. cit.*
70 *Ibid.*
71 Gordon, Richard. *op. cit.*
72 Viner, Brian. "Prince of Darkness: A Rare Audience with Sir Christopher Lee", *The Independent*, 4 July 2009.
73 Lee, Christopher. *Tall, Dark and Gruesome, op. cit.*
74 Lee, Christopher. "Interview about Boris Karloff", *Curse of the Crimson Altar* DVD (DD Video, 2004).
75 Lee, Christopher. *Tall, Dark and Gruesome, op. cit.*
76 *Ibid.*
77 Matthews, Francis. *Letter to author*, 12 June 2002.
78 *Ibid.*
79 "Fiend Without a Face", *op. cit.*
80 *New York Times*, 6 June 1963.
81 *Ibid.*
82 Croydon, John. *op. cit.*
83 Matthews, Francis. *op. cit.*
84 Shriver, Gordon B. *op. cit.*
85 McDowell, Roddy. Interview, *Boris Karloff: The Gentle Monster*, (Van Ness Films, 1995).
86 Shriver, Gordon B. *op. cit.*
87 Laurent, Lawrence. "Playhouse 90 Managed To Top All the Comics", *Washington Post and Times Herald*, 8 November 1958.
88 *Ibid.*
89 "Boris Karloff Niece Slashed, 2 Sons Slain", *Chicago Daily Tribune*, 20 December 1958.
90 Crowley, Elisabeth. *Email to author*, 14 August 2008.
91 Trivedi, Premila. "Interview with 'J.T.' (1999)", *Mental Health Testimony Archive*, C905/14/01-04/VHS 01 of 01, (www.insidestories.org/node/16).
92 *Lethbridge Herald*, 12 January 1959.
93 Weaver, Tom. "Lifting The Veil." (Something Weird, Inc., 2001).
94 Hardy, Robert. *Interview with author*, 19 January 2009.

95   *Ibid.*
96   *Ibid.*
97   *Ibid.*
98   Beifuss, John. "Tripping the Life Tan-fastic; or, Tans for the Memories: A Talk with George Hamilton." (http://blogs.commercialappeal.com/the_bloodshot_eye/2008/11/tripping-the-life-tan-fastic-or-tans-for-the-memories-a-talk-with-george-hamilton.html).
99   Hamilton, George. *Don't Mind If I Do: My Adventures in Hollywood*, (JR Books Ltd., 2009).
100   Weaver, Tom. "Lifting The Veil." *op. cit.*
101   Weaver, Tom. "Herbert L. Strock", *Interviews with B Science Fiction and Horror Movie Makers: Writers, Producers, Directors, Actors, Moguls and Make-up*, (McFarland, 2006).
102   Weaver, Tom. "Lifting The Veil." *op. cit.*
103   *Ibid.*
104   Weaver, Tom. "Herbert L. Strock", *op. cit.*
105   Weaver, Tom. "Lifting The Veil", *op. cit.*
106   Hardy, Robert. *op. cit.*
107   "TV Notes", *Hartford Courant*, 17 May 1959.
108   "Guterma Resigns as F.L. Jacobs Chairman; Replaced by Hal Roach", *Wall Street Journal*, 16 February 1959.
109   *Los Angeles Times*, 31 December 1957.
110   Gaver, Jack. "Boris Karloff is Returning to England", *Oakland Tribune*, 31 May 1959.
111   "Karloff, A Legend in His Time, Dies", *Hartford Courant*, 4 February 1969.
112   Coleman, Bernard. *op. cit.*
113   "Karloff Returns Home to England to Stay for Good", *Los Angeles Times*, 2 May 1959.
114   Du Brow, Rick. *op. cit.*
115   Weaver, Tom. "Booth Colman", *I Was a Monster Movie Maker: Conversations with 22 SF and Horror Filmmakers*, (McFarland, 2001).
116   Karloff, Boris. *Letter to John. L. Dales*, 15 October 1959.
117   Karloff, Boris. *Letter to John. L. Dales*, 18 July 1960.
118   Weaver, Tom. "Howard W. Koch", *Interviews with B Science Fiction and Horror Movie Makers, op. cit.*
119   Hopper, Hedda. "Movies Overdo Horror, Karloff Laments", *Chicago Daily Tribune*, 13 September 1960.

Chapter 22 – Thriller (1960-1962)
1   Hopper, Hedda. "Film, TV Violence Absurd, Says Star", *Los Angeles Times*, 13 September 1962.
2   Smith, Cecil. "Startime to Shun Formula in $multimillion Specials", *Los Angeles Times*, 4 October 1959.
3   "John Crosby's Comment", *The Sun*, 21 August 1960.
4   *Ibid.*
5   *Standard AFTRA Engagement Contract for Single Television Broadcast and for Multiple Television Broadcasts Within One Calendar Week*, 6 January 1960.
6   Smith, Cecil. "Sound of Trumpets' on the Right Scale", *Los Angeles Times*. 10 February 1960.
7   Smith, Cecil. "Playhouse 90's Last-Ditch Stand", *Los Angeles Times*, 9 February 1960.
8   Shanley, John P. "TV: A Brilliant 'Treasure Island,'" *New York Times*, 7 March 1960.
9   Gould, Jack. "Eddie Albert and Tammy Grimes Star on 'Sunday Showcase' Narrated by Karloff", *New York Times*, 4 April 1960.
10   *Ibid.*
11   "Villain at the Wicket", *The Times*, 7 June 1960.
12   *Ibid.*
13   Britton, Tony. *Interview with author*, 1 October 2009.
14   Jewison, Norman. *Letter to author*, 9 June 2006.
15   Denton, Charles. "Ex-Monster Sighs for Gold Old Days", *Hartford Courant*, 8 January 1961.
16   Hopper, Hedda. "Film, TV Violence Absurd, Says Star", *op. cit.*
17   *Los Angeles Times*, 11 September 1960.
18   *Chicago Daily Tribune*, 7 September 1960.
19   *Chicago Daily Tribune*, 1 October 1960.
20   *Los Angeles Times*, 11 September 1960.
21   Langley, Frank. "Method Acting Schools Disgust Boris Karloff", *Hartford Courant*, 25 February 1962.
22   *Ibid.*
23   Wolters, Larry. "Karloff Horror Fare Horrifying for Kids", *Chicago Daily Tribune*, 14 September 1960.
24   Weaver, Tom. "His Life Was a Thriller: Part One", *Fangoria* No. 155, August 1996.
25   *Ibid.*
26   *Ibid.*
27   Hatcher, Lint and Rod Bennett, "Inside Darkest Ackerman", *WONDER* No. 7, 1993.
28   *Ibid.*
29   Fisher, Gary. "An Interview with Forrest J. Ackerman: 'Mr. Science Fiction'", *Armchair World*, 1997. (www.armchair.com/warp/ackerman.html).
30   Weaver, Tom. "His Life Was a Thriller: Part One", *op. cit.*
31   Weaver, Tom. "Licensed to Thrill: Part Two", *Fangoria* No. 156, September 1996.
32   *Ibid.*
33   Weaver, Tom. "Audrey Dalton", *Science Fiction Confidential: Interviews with 23 Monster Stars and Filmmakers*, (McFarland, 2002).
34   *Ibid.*
35   Weaver, Tom. "His Life Was a Thriller: Part One", *op. cit.*
36   *Ibid.*
37   *New York Times*, 31 January 1947.
38   Nollen, Scott Allen. *op. cit.*
39   Weaver, Tom. "Licensed to Thrill: Part Two", *op. cit.*
40   *Ibid.*
41   Smith, Cecil. "Karloff: A Jet-Age Monster", *Los Angeles Times*, 4 March 1962.
42   "The Lovable Monster", *Los Angeles Times*, 23 October 1960.
43   Bosley, Tom. *Email to author*, 8 December 2007.
44   Gill, Alan. "Television Today", *Cedar Rapids Gazette*, 26 January 1962.
45   *Ibid.*
46   *Ibid.*
47   Bosley, Tom. *op. cit.*
48   Nollen, Scott Allen. *op. cit.*
49   Gill, Alan. *op. cit.*
50   *Ibid.*
51   Lowry, Cynthia. "Arsenic and Old Lace Still Pleasing to TV's Audience", *Austin Daily Herald*, 6 February 1962.
52   Wolters, Larry. "'Paradine' Show is Case for Live TV", *Chicago Daily Tribune*, 12 March 1962.
53   Weaver, Tom. "His Life Was a Thriller: Part One", *op. cit.*
54   *Ibid.*
55   Weaver, Tom. "Full Nelson", *Fangoria* No. 104, July 1991.
56   Weaver, Tom. "Licensed to Thrill: Part Two", *op. cit.*
57   Parry, Mike and Harry Nadler, *op. cit.*

58   Weaver, Tom. "His Life Was a Thriller: Part One", *op. cit.*
59   Nolan, William F. *op. cit.*
60   *Daily Mirror*, 12 June 1962.
61   "Not Taking It Easy This Summer", *The Times*, 4 August 1962.
62   Smith, Cecil. "Karloff: A Jet-Age Monster", *op. cit.*
63   Weaver, Tom. "Betsy Jones-Moreland", *Attack of the Monster Movie Makers: Interviews With 20 Genre Giants*, (McFarland, 1994).
64   *Ibid.*
65   Nolan, William F. *op. cit.*

Chapter 23 – Karloff, Corman & Co. (1962-1964)

1   Karloff, Boris. "How NOT to be a Full-Time Bogeyman", *Reader's Digest*, January 1964.
2   Riordan, Paul. "He Is Legend: Richard Matheson", (www.scifistation.com/matheson/matheson_index.html).
3   Nollen, Scott Allen. *op. cit.*
4   French, Lawrence. "An Interview with Vincent Price", 1979 (and 1985).
5   French, Larry. "Vincent Price: The Corman Years", *Fangoria* No. 7, August 1980.
6   *Ibid.*
7   *Ibid.*
8   Corman, Roger with Jim Jerome, *How I Made a Hundred Movies in Hollywood and Never Lost a Dime*, (Muller, 1990).
9   *Ibid.*
10   French, Larry "Vincent Price: The Corman Years", *Fangoria* No. 7, August 1980.
11   Chase Williams, Lucy. *The Complete Films of Vincent Price*, (Kensington Publishing Corporation, 2000).
12   Nolan, William F. *op. cit.*
13   Corman, Roger with Jim Jerome, *op. cit.*
14   *Making the Shining: A Film by Vivian Kubrick*, (Eagle Film SS, 1980).
15   Ryon, Art. "Actress Enters Films With Creeps, Shrieks", *Los Angeles Times*, 10 February 1963.
16   Corman, Roger with Jim Jerome, *op. cit.*
17   French, Larry. "Vincent Price: The Corman Years", *Fangoria* No. 6, June 1980.
18   Nolan, William F. *op. cit.*
19   Corman, Roger with Jim Jerome, *op. cit.*
20   *Ibid.*
21   *Ibid.*
22   *Ibid.*
23   Miller, Dick. *Email to author*, 25 February 2009.
24   *Ibid.*
25   Corman, Roger with Jim Jerome, *op. cit.*
26   *Ibid.*
27   Miller, Dick. *op. cit.*
28   Naha, Ed. *The Films of Roger Corman: Brilliance on a Budget*, (Arco. 1982).
29   Miller, Dick. *op. cit.*
30   Corman, Roger with Jim Jerome, *op. cit.*
31   Miller, Dick. *op. cit.*
32   Corman, Roger with Jim Jerome, *op. cit.*
33   *Ibid.*
34   *New York Times*, 26 January 1963.
35   Nollen, Scott Allen. *op. cit.*
36   Wilson, Earl. "It Happened Last Night", *The Progress-Index*, 31 January 1963.
37   Youngkin, Stephen D. *op. cit.*
38   Nollen, Scott Allen. *op. cit.*

39   *Ibid.*
40   *Ibid.*
41   Shriver, Gordon B. *op. cit.*
42   Nollen, Scott Allen. *op. cit.*
43   *Ibid.*
44   Scott, John L. "*The Raven* Fanciful Horror-Comedy Film", *Los Angeles Times*, 1 February 1963.
45   *Chicago Tribune*, 6 March 1963.
46   *Los Angeles Times*, 28 September 1963.
47   Lucas, Tim. "Terror Pioneer", *Fangoria* No. 42, February 1985.
48   *Ibid.*
49   Parry, Mike and Harry Nadler, *op. cit.*
50   Lucas, Tim. *op. cit.*
51   MacKenzie, Bob. "Karloff in Treat for Horror Fans", *Oakland Tribune*, 7 May 1964.
52   Parry, Mike and Harry Nadler, *op. cit.*
53   "Reviews of THIS WEEK'S LP's", *Billboard*, 3 August 1959.
54   Mitgang, Herbert. "No Baby Talk at All", *New York Times*, 10 January 1960.
55   Bloom, Claire. *Email to author*, 9 March 2007.
56   Duncan, Chester. "New Records", *Winnipeg Free Press*, 2 March 1963.
57   *Billboard*, 21 September 1963.
58   *New York Times*, 12 January 1964.
59   Coleman, Bernard. *op. cit.*
60   "Richard Matheson Storyteller: Comedy of Terrors", (MGM Home Entertainment, 2003).
61   Alpert, Don. "What Ever Happened to Basil? He's Much Alive, Not Kicking", *Los Angeles Times*, 22 September 1963.
62   *Ibid.*
63   "Richard Matheson Storyteller", *op. cit.*
64   French, Larry. "Vincent Price: The Corman Years", *Fangoria* No. 6, June 1980.
65   Chase Williams, Lucy. *op. cit.*
66   French, Lawrence. "An Interview with Vincent Price", 1979 (and 1985).
67   Karloff, Sara. *Email to author*, 21 August 2002.
68   Means, Marianne. *Email to author*, 5 June 2003.
69   *Hollywood Reporter*, 26 December 1963.
70   Scheuer, Philip K. "*Comedy of Terrors* Film Monstrosity", *Los Angeles Times*, 23 January 1964.
71   *New York Times*, 23 January 1964.
72   "Richard Matheson Storyteller", *op. cit.*
73   *Ibid.*
74   Gardner, Paul. "'K' In Kris Kringle to Mean Karloff", *New York Times*, 2 December 1963.
75   Scheuer, Philip K. "AIP Millions for Poe, Beach Parties", *Los Angeles Times*, 2 January 1964.
76   *Anderson Daily Bulletin*, 4 August 1969.
77   Karloff, Boris. "How NOT to be a Full-Time Bogeyman", *op. cit.*

Chapter 24 – Soldiering On (1964-1966)

1   *Los Angeles Times*, 23 May 1966.
2   "Comedians Attend Lorre's Funeral in a Rare Tribute", *The Sun*, 27 March 1964.
3   "Peter Lorre Eulogized as Face Maker", *Los Angeles Times*, 27 March 1964.
4   Thomas, Bob. "Boris Karloff Likes Role Of Monster", *The News*, 12 April 1967.
5   Thomas, Kevin. "Younger Set Frolics Again in *Bikini Beach*," *Los Angeles Times*, 21 August 1964.

6   Thomas, Bob. "Monster He Created Still Haunts Him", *Austin Daily Herald*, 28 May 1951.
7   Feron, James. "Boris Karloff Separates Terror and Horror Films", *New York Times*, 17 March 1965.
8   Gilmore, Eddy. "Karloff Is Back at His Old Tricks", *Waterloo Sunday Courier*, 11 April 1965.
9   *Ibid.*
10   "Horror's an Ugly Word to Mr. Karloff", *Chicago Tribune*, 27 March 1965.
11   Feron, James. "Boris Karloff Separates Terror and Horror Films", *New York Times*, 17 March 1965.
12   *Ibid.*
13   Thomas, Kevin. "Karloff at Home in Haunted House", *Los Angeles Times*, 18 December 1965.
14   *New York Times*, 31 May 1965.
15   "*Daydreamer* Tells Tales by Andersen", *The Post-Standard*, 22 September 1966.
16   Simmon, Olwen. *Email to author*, 8 August 2008.
17   Blake, Merritt. *Email to author*, 19 September 2009.
18   Weaver, Tom. "Susan Hart", *Attack of the Monster Movie Makers: Interviews with 20 Genre Giants*, (McFarland, 1994).
19   *Ibid.*
20   Weaver, Tom. "Going AIP", *Fangoria* No. 96, September 1990.
21   *Boxoffice*, 18 April 1966.
22   Karloff, Boris. *Letter to Mr. Sokell*, 27 July 1966.
23   "Karloff Improving", *Dallas Morning News*, 12 March 1966.
24   Lee, Christopher. *Tall, Dark and Gruesome, op. cit.*
25   Coleman, Bernard. *op. cit.*
26   Moore, Wendy. *Email to author*, 7 September 2008.
27   Reid, Steve. *Email to author*, 6 September 2008.
28   Underwood, Peter. "Reminiscences of Boris Karloff", *op. cit.*
29   "Boris Karloff Looks in at the Local", *The Times*, 19 March 1966.
30   *Boxoffice*, 16 January 1967.
31   Goldschmidt, Rick. *Mad Monster Party: Unearthing a Rankin/Bass Classic*.
32   Thompson, Howard. "Screen: 'Monster Party,'" *New York Times*, 8 March 1969.
33   Weaver, Tom. "Snails and Smiles", *Fangoria* No. 189, January 2000.
34   *Ibid.*
35   Shivas, Mark. "Karloff, Still Eager to Scare Us Witless", *New York Times*, 14 April 1968.
36   "TV Previews", *The Milwaukee Journal*, 27 September 1966.
37   Weaver, Tom. "Licensed to Thrill: Part Two", *op. cit.*
38   Kennard, Arthur. Interview, *Boris Karloff: The Gentle Monster*, (Van Ness Films, 1995).
39   Weaver, Tom. "Licensed to Thrill: Part Two", *op. cit.*
40   Karloff, Boris. *Letter to Mr. Ronnie*, 7 October 1966.
41   Thomas, Kevin. "Italian 'Mondo Balordo' at Southland Theatres", *Los Angeles Times*, 10 March 1967.
42   Sito, Tom. "Chuck Jones: Archive Interview", *Archive of American Television*, 17 June 1998.
43   Gent, George. "Christmas Baubles, Old and New", *New York Times*, 18 December 1966.
44   Sito, Tom. *op. cit.*
45   Hendrick, Kimmis. "The Grinch: TV's Christmas Villain", *Christian Science Monitor*, 1 October 1966.
46   Kirkley, Donald. "The Grinch in Action at Christmas", *The Sun*, 18 December 1966.
47   Hendrick, Kimmis. *op. cit.*
48   Gowran, Clay. "Seuss Grinch Rates Christmas TV Kudos", *Chicago Tribune*, 19 December 1966.
49   Humphrey, Hal. "'Grinch' Disappointing Christmas Special", *Los Angeles Times*, 19 December 1966.
50   Jones, Chuck. *Letter to Evelyn Karloff*, 5 February 1969.
51   Dr. Seuss, *Letter to Evelyn Karloff*, 7 February 1969.

Chapter 25 – *Targets* and *The Sorcerers* (1966-1968)

1   Gilmore, Eddy. *op. cit.*
2   Halligan, Benjamin. *Michael Reeves*, (Manchester University Press, 2003).
3   *Ibid.*
4   Swires, Steve. "When The Movies Got Tenser", *Fangoria* No. 128, November 1993.
5   Long, Stanley. *Interview with author*, 8 January 2009.
6   *Ibid.*
7   Karloff, Boris. "Declaration to be completed by artist or principal in connection with Film Producers Indemnity Insurance", *Norwich Union Fire Insurance Society Limited*, (signed by Karloff on 30 December 1966).
8   *Ibid.*
9   Long, Stanley. *Interview with author*, 8 January 2009.
10   *Ibid.*
11   *Ibid.*
12   *Ibid.*
13   Long, Stanley. *Interview with author*, 20 February 2009.
14   *Ibid.*
15   Long, Stanley. *Interview with author*, 8 January 2009.
16   *Ibid.*
17   *Ibid.*
18   Ogilvy, Ian. Interview, *Blood Beast: The Films of Michael Reeves*, (Boum Productions, 1999).
19   Long, Stanley. *Interview with author*, 8 January 2009.
20   Curtis, Patrick. Interview, *Blood Beast: The Films of Michael Reeves*, (Boum Productions, 1999).
21   Taylor, John Russell. "Carlton: The Sorcerers", *The Times*, 15 June 1967.
22   *Monthly Film Bulletin*, July 1967.
23   Ogilvy, Ian. *Email to author*, 10 March 2009.
24   Swires, Steve. "When The Movies Got Tenser", *op. cit.*
25   Long, Stanley. *Interview with author*, 8 January 2009.
26   *Ibid.*
27   *Ibid.*
28   Shivas, Mark. *op. cit.*
29   Thompson, Howard. "Twin-Bill Highlighted by 'Crucible of Horror'", *New York Times*, 11 November 1971.
30   Karloff, Boris. *Letter to Mr. Ronnie*, 7 October 1966.
31   "*Targets* – an introduction by Peter Bogdanovich", *Targets* DVD, (Paramount, 2003).
32   "Peter Bogdanovich talks to Derek Malcolm", *The Guardian*, 21 February 1972.
33   "*Targets* – an introduction by Peter Bogdanovich", *op. cit.*
34   *Ibid.*
35   *Ibid.*
36   Bogdanovich, Peter. "Audio Commentary", *Targets* DVD, (Paramount, 2003).
37   "*Targets* – an introduction by Peter Bogdanovich", *op. cit.*
38   Bogdanovich, Peter. "Audio Commentary", *op. cit.*
39   Coleman, Bernard. *op. cit.*
40   Bogdanovich, Peter. "Audio Commentary", *op. cit.*

41 Bogdanovich, Peter. *Who the Hell's In It*, (Faber and Faber, 2005).
42 Bogdanovich, Peter. "Audio Commentary", *op. cit.*
43 "Targets – an introduction by Peter Bogdanovich", *op. cit.*
44 Bogdanovich, Peter. "Audio Commentary", *op. cit.*
45 *Ibid.*
46 *Ibid.*
47 Bogdanovich, Peter. *Who the Hell's In It*, *op. cit.*
48 Bogdanovich, Peter. "Audio Commentary", *op. cit.*
49 LoBrutto, Vincent. "Polly Platt", *By Design: Interviews with Film Production Designers*, (Praeger Publishers, 1992).
50 *Ibid.*
51 "Targets – an introduction by Peter Bogdanovich", *op. cit.*
52 Stone, Judy. "All Because of Boris Karloff", *New York Times*, 15 September 1968.
53 Thompson, Howard. "Screen: Two Case Histories of Horror Are Joined", *New York Times*, 14 August 1968.
54 *Ibid.*
55 Stone, Judy. *op. cit.*
56 "Targets – an introduction by Peter Bogdanovich", *op. cit.*
57 Prelutsky, Burt. "west/view", *Los Angeles Times*, 9 June 1968.
58 Bogdanovich, Peter. "Audio Commentary", *op. cit.*
59 Linden, Paul. "Karloff at the Magic Castle Pt. 2", *Famous Monsters of Filmland* No. 46, September 1967.
60 Fisher, Gary. *op. cit.*
61 *Ibid.*
62 *Ibid.*
63 Ackerman, Forrest J. "Long Live the King – My Evening with Boris Karloff", *It's Alive@85*, November 2001.
64 Ackerman, Forrest J. "Mr. Monster Remembered: Boris Karloff, February 1969 – February 1983", *Fangoria* No. 36, July 1984.
65 "Album Reviews", *Billboard*, 28 January 1967.
66 Laffler, William D. "Records – Popular", *Daily News*, 24 February 1967.
67 Linden, Paul. *op. cit.*
68 Warren, Bill. *Email to author*, 29 August 2008.
69 Thomas, Bob. "Boris Karloff Likes Role of Monster", *op. cit.*
70 Linden, Paul. *op. cit.*
71 *Ibid.*
72 Karloff, Boris. *Letter to Charlie* [Surname unknown – probably Karloff's executor, Charles H. Renthal], 15 July 1967.
73 *Ibid.*
74 Randall, Richard. *Email to author*, 2 September 2008

Chapter 26 –Final Films and Fade Out (1968-1969)
1 Shivas, Mark. *op. cit.*
2 *Ibid.*
3 Weaver, Tom. "Going AIP", *op. cit.*
4 Hamilton, John. "Beasts in the Cellar: The Exploitation Career of Tony Tenser", (FAB Press, 2005).
5 McFarlane, Brian. "Interview with Vernon Sewell", *An Autobiography of British Cinema*, (Methuen, 1997).
6 Shivas, Mark. *op. cit.*
7 Eden, Mark. *Email to author*, 21 January 2008.

8 Sothcott, Jonathan. "Interview with Virginia Wetherell", (www.hammerfilms.com).
9 McFarlane, Brian. *op. cit.*
10 Sothcott, Jonathan. *op. cit.*
11 *Ibid.*
12 Gough, Michael. *Letter to author*, 3 September 2002.
13 *Ibid.*
14 Del Valle, David. "Barbara Steele Remembers Boris Karloff", *Email to author*, 24 March 2009.
15 Swires, Steve. "Titan of Tigon Terror", *Fangoria* No. 129, December 1993.
16 Shivas, Mark. *op. cit.*
17 Eden, Mark. *op. cit.*
18 *Hartford Courant*, 21 February 1968.
19 *New York Times*, 20 February 1968.
20 Lee, Christopher. "A Tribute to Boris Karloff", Undated.
21 Swires, Steve. "Titan of Tigon Terror", *op. cit.*
22 Shivas, Mark. *op. cit.*
23 Gough, Michael. *op. cit.*
24 Eden, Mark. *op. cit.*
25 Lee, Christopher. "Interview about Boris Karloff", *op. cit.*
26 Thomas, Kevin. "A Double Bill of Shockers", *Los Angeles Times*, 17 April 1970.
27 Greenspun, Roger. "Screen: 'Count Yorga, vampire' and 'The Crimson Cult' Bow at Local Theaters", *New York Times*, 12 November 1970.
28 *Oakland Tribune*, 3 April 1969.
29 Kennard, Arthur. Interview, *op. cit.*
30 *Ibid.*
31 Kennard, Arthur. Interview, *op. cit.*
32 Shivas, Mark. *op. cit.*
33 *Ibid.*
34 *Ibid.*
35 Karloff, Boris. *Letter to Charlie*, *op. cit.*
36 Coleman, Bernard. *op. cit.*
37 Hill, Jack. *Email to author*, 14 July 2008.
38 Hill, Jack. "Audio Commentary", *The Fear Chamber* DVD, (Elite Entertainment, 2005).
39 *Ibid.*
40 *Ibid.*
41 *Ibid.*
42 Baumann, Marty. "Jack Hill", *The Astounding B Monster*, (Dinoship Inc., 2005).
43 Hill, Jack. "Audio Commentary", *op. cit.*
44 *Ibid.*
45 Hill, Jack. *Email to author*, 14 July 2008.
46 Hill, Jack. "Audio Commentary", *op. cit.*
47 Hill, Jack. *Email to author*, 14 July 2008.
48 *Ibid.*
49 *Ibid.*
50 *Ibid.*
51 Hatcher, Lint and Rod Bennett, *op. cit.*
52 Hill, Jack. *Email to author*, 14 July 2008.
53 Warren, Bill. *Email to author*, 29 August 2008.
54 *Ibid.*
55 Baumann, Marty. *op. cit.*
56 Hill, Jack. "Audio Commentary", *op. cit.*
57 Baumann, Marty. *op. cit.*
58 Hill, Jack. "Audio Commentary", *op. cit.*
59 Hill, Jack. *Email to author*, 14 July 2008.
60 *Ibid.*
61 Warren, Bill. "Karloff's Last Act", *Monster Kid Magazine* No. 2, October 2001.
62 Hill, Jack. *Email to author*, 14 July 2008.

63 Warren, Bill. "Karloff's Last Act", *op. cit.*
64 *Ibid.*
65 Daugherty, Walter James. "Final Act", *The Frankenscience Monster*, (Ace Books, 1969).
66 *Ibid.*
67 Prelutsky, Burt. *op. cit.*
68 Daugherty, Walter James. *op. cit.*
69 Pinckard, Terry. "I've Waited For Years!" *The Frankenscience Monster*, (Ace Books, 1969).
70 *Ibid.*
71 *Ibid.*
72 *Ibid.*
73 *Ibid.*
74 *Ibid.*
75 *Ibid.*
76 Warren, Bill. *Email to author*, *op. cit.*
77 Warren, Bill. "Karloff's Last Act", *op. cit.*
78 Pinckard, Terry. *op. cit.*
79 *Ibid.*
80 Daugherty, Walter James. *op. cit.*
81 *Ibid.*
82 Ackerman, Forrest J. "Mr. Monster Remembered", *op. cit.*
83 Daugherty, Walter James. *op. cit.*
84 Hill, Jack. *Email to author*, 14 July 2008.
85 *Ibid.*
86 Baumann, Marty. *op. cit.*
87 Hayward, John S. *Email to author*, 10 June 2002.
88 Taylor, Frank. "An Eye on Hollywood", *The News*, 25 July 1968.
89 Maays, Stan. "Meet Boris Karloff – Londoner Likes Work Here", *Waterloo Daily Courier*, 1 November 1968.
90 Lindsay, Cynthia. *op. cit.*
91 *Oakland Tribune*, 25 September 1968.
92 Maays, Stan. *op. cit.*
93 Shriver, Gordon B. *op. cit.*
94 *Valley Independent*, 30 October 1968.
95 Shriver, Gordon B. *op. cit.*
96 Lindsay, Cynthia. *op. cit.*

97 Doyle, James J. "Draculas Honour Gothic Greats", *St. Petersburg Times*, 27 April 1976.
98 Reed, Donald. "Homage to the Departed Hero", *The Frankenscience Monster*, (Ace Books, 1969).
99 Kennard, Arthur. Interview, *op. cit.*
100 Coleman, Bernard. *op. cit.*
101 Lee, Christopher. "A Tribute to Boris Karloff", *op. cit.*
102 Lee, Christopher. "Homage to the Departed Hero", *The Frankenscience Monster*, (Ace Books, 1969).
103 Karloff, Sara. *Telegram to Evelyn Karloff*, 3 February 1969.
104 Howard, Philip. "Boris Karloff Gave the Monster a Soul", *The Times*, 4 February 1969.
105 Coleman, Bernard. *op. cit.*
106 Zec, Donald. "The Gentle Monster", *Daily Mirror*, 4 February 1969.
107 Karloff, Boris as told to Arlene and Howard Eisenberg. *op. cit.*

Afterword

1 Smith, Cecil. "Karloff: A Jet-age Monster", *op. cit.*
2 "The Nation", *Los Angeles Times*, 29 June 1969.
3 Pratt, William Henry. *Last Will and Testament*, 3 June 1964.
4 Randall, Richard. *Email to author*, 2 September 2008.
5 Randall, Richard. *Email to author*, 3 September 2008.
6 Randall, Richard. *Email to author*, 4 September 2008.
7 "Karloff Name Lives On", Undated Clipping.
8 Williamson, Peter. *Email to author*, 20 April 2010.
9 Karloff, Sara. *Email to author*, 21 April 2010.
10 *Ibid.*
11 Coleman, Bernard. *op. cit.*
12 Karloff, Sara. *Email to author*, 22 April 2009.
13 Coleman, Bernard. *op. cit.*
14 *Daily News*, 8 February 2000.
15 Coleman, Bernard. *op. cit.*
16 Birmingham, Stephen. *Life at the Dakota: New York's Most Unusual Address*, (Syracuse University Press, 1996).

APPENDICES

Karloff: On Stage

This list contains details of Karloff's confirmed theatrical appearances, along with his character names, where known.

1911 – 1912
Jeanne Russell Players (a.k.a. Ray Brandon Stock Company)
The Devil (Hofmann), *The American Girl*, *The Man from Home* (Grand Duke Vasili Vasilivitch), *Emanuella* (a.k.a. *Two Married Men*), *The Half Breed* (Ross Kennion), *The Little Minister* (Rob Dow), *Cousin Kate*, *Moths*, *A Texas Ranger*, *The Squaw Man*, *Jesse James* and *The Moonshiner's Daughter*.

Other plays for the 1911/12 season included: *The Galley Slave*, *Friends*, *Paid in Full*, *The Flag of Truce*, *The Heart of Kentucky* and *The Young Mrs. Winthrop*.

1912 – 1917
Harry St. Clair Stock Company
Moths, *Facing the Music*, *The Young Mrs. Winthrop*, *Lena Rivers*, *Mabel Heath*, *A Terrible Tangle*, *Facing the Music*, *The Builder of Bridges*, *A Cheerful Liar* and *The Spendthrift*.

1917
Patti McKinley Players
Johnny Get Your Gun, *The Lure*, *The Girl I Left Behind Me*, *The Vampire*.

Lona Fendell Stock Company
Rebecca of Sunnybrook Farm, *The Whole Dam Family*, *Don't Lie to Your Wife*, *The Spendthrift*, *The Divorce*.

The New York Producing Company
The Virginian, (the Virginian).

1918
Robert Lawrence Stock Company
Unknown plays.

Alfred Aldridge & Co.
Bolsheviki (31 December 1918 – 1 January 1919), Victory Theatre, San Jose.

1919
Robert Lawrence Stock Company
Unknown plays, Majestic Theatre, San Francisco.

Fulton Players
Eyes of Youth (5 May 1919 – 17 May 1919), Fulton Theatre, Oakland.

1928
Reginald Pole Company
The Idiot (25 January 1928 – 28 January 1928), Parfyon Rogozhin, Belmont Theatre, Los Angeles.

Opera and Drama Guild
Monna Vanna (23 April 1928 – 2 May 1928), Guido Collona, Trinity Auditorium, Los Angeles.
For the Soul of Rafael (Opened 3 May 1928), Trinity Auditorium, Los Angeles.

Sprague Repertoire Company
Hotel Imperial (23 May 1928 – late June 1928), General Juskievica, Egan Theatre, Los Angeles.

Sarah Padden Company
Window Panes (5 August 1928 – 8 September 1928), Artem Tiapkin, Egan Theatre, Los Angeles.

1929
Kongo (Dates unknown), Kregg, Capitol Theatre, San Francisco.

1930
The Criminal Code (Opened 12 May 1930), Galloway, Belasco Theatre, Los Angeles.

1934
Mud, Blood and Kisses (17 November 1934), Little Theatre, Padua Hills, California. (Karloff appeared in this skit for one night only).

Annual Benefit (14 December 1934). Shrine Auditorium, Los Angeles.

1935
Show of Shows (1 December 1935), Shrine Auditorium, Los Angeles.

1936
The Drunkard (19 October 1936), Theatre Mart, Hollywood. (Karloff appeared as the guest of honour on the night of the 1200th performance).

1938
The Tell-Tale Heart (April 1938). (Karloff appeared in a touring production of Edgar Allan Poe's short story).

1940
Arsenic and Old Lace (26 December 1940 for two weeks), Jonathan Brewster, Maryland Theatre, Baltimore, Maryland.

1941
Arsenic and Old Lace (10 January 1941 – 27 June 1942), Jonathan Brewster, Fulton Theatre, New York.

Arsenic and Old Lace (13 April 1941), Jonathan Brewster, West Point Military Academy, New York
.

Night of the Stars (26 November 1941), Madison Square Garden, New York.

1942
Navy Relief Show (10 March 1942), Madison Square Garden, New York. (Karloff featured in 'The Floradora Sextet' alongside Eddie Cantor, Danny Kaye, Vincent Price, Clifton Webb and Ed Wynn).

The *Arsenic and Old Lace* Tour
(17 August 1942 – 23 January 1944)

(17 August 1942 – 29 August 1942), Jonathan Brewster, Biltmore Theatre, Los Angeles.
(31 August 1942 – 26 September 1942), Jonathan Brewster, Curran Theatre, San Francisco.
(28 September 1942 – 10 October 1942), Jonathan Brewster, Biltmore Theatre, Los Angeles.
(12 October 1942 – 24 October 1942), Jonathan Brewster, Geary Theatre, San Francisco.
(26 October 1942), Jonathan Brewster, Oakland Auditorium Theatre, Oakland.

The tour then left California and played in such cities as Chicago, Milwaukee, Boston and Washington. It ended, temporarily, after the 12 June 1943 performance at the Metropolitan Theatre in Seattle. It recommenced on 23 August 1943 in Washington D.C. After curtain down on 23 January 1944 at the Music Hall in Kansas City Boris Karloff left the *Arsenic and Old Lace* tour.

The *Arsenic and Old Lace* Pacific Tour
(February 1945 – June 1945)

1945
For almost four months Karloff toured the Pacific islands in a U.S.O. production of *Arsenic and Old Lace*. The tour played for the troops on such islands as Oahu, Midway, Canton Island, the Marshall Islands, Johnston Island and Kwajalein.

1946
On Borrowed Time (5 November 1946 – 24 November 1946), Gramps, El Patio Theatre, Hollywood. (This was followed by a stint in San Francisco).

1947
On Borrowed Time (March 1947), Gramps, Irish Theatre, Mexico City. (The weeklong residency was presented as part of the 'Teatro Americano' season.)

1948
The Linden Tree
(4 February 1948 – 7 February 1948), Professor Linden, Schubert Theatre, New Haven, Connecticut.
(Opened 9 February 1948), Professor Linden, Philadelphia.
(23 February – 28 February), Professor Linden, National Theatre, Washington, D.C.
(2 March 1948 – 6 March 1948), Professor Linden, Music Box Theatre, New York.

The Shop at Sly Corner
(25 December 1948 – 8 January 1949), Descius Heiss, Wilbur Theatre, Boston.
(18 January 1949 – 22 January 1949), Descius Heiss, Booth Theatre, New York.

1950
On Borrowed Time (16 January 1950 – 21 January 1950), Gramps, Penthouse Theatre, Ansley Hotel, Atlanta.
On Borrowed Time (30 January 1950 – 4 February 1950), Gramps, Penthouse Theatre, Ansley Hotel, Atlanta.

Peter Pan
(24 April 1950 – 30 September 1950), Mr. Darling/Captain Hook, Imperial Theatre, New York. (The play officially opened after a week of previews).
(2 October 1950 – 27 January 1951), Mr. Darling/Captain Hook, St. James Theatre, New York.

After closing in New York *Peter Pan* embarked on a national tour taking in such cities as Boston, Cincinnati, Cleveland, and Detroit. The final curtain descended on *Peter Pan* in Minneapolis on 29 April 1951.

1955
Night of 100 Stars (25 June 1955), Drunken butler, Palladium, London.

The Lark
(28 October 1955 – 12 November 1955), Bishop Cauchon, Plymouth Theatre, Boston.
(17 November 1955 – 2 June 1956), Bishop Cauchon, Longacre Theatre, New York.
(5 September 1956 – late September 1956), Bishop Cauchon, San Francisco.

1957
Arsenic and Old Lace (21 March 1957 – 23 March 1957), Jonathan Brewster, Anchorage High School Auditorium, Anchorage, Alaska.

1960
Arsenic and Old Lace (12 January 1960 – 17 January 1960), Jonathan Brewster, Tapia Theatre, San Juan, Puerto Rico.

1961
On Borrowed Time (Opened 17 January 1961), Gramps, Tapia Theatre, San Juan, Puerto Rico.

On Borrowed Time (17 March 1961 – 25 March 1961), Gramps, Wharf Theatre and Opera House, Monterey, California.

Filmography

Silent Films

1919
The Lightning Raider [15 chapter serial] (d. George B. Seitz), Extra.
The Masked Rider [15 chapter serial] (d. Aubrey M. Kennedy), Mexican.
His Majesty, the American (d. Joseph Henabery), Extra.
The Prince and Betty (d. Robert Thornby), Bit part.

1920
The Deadlier Sex (d. Robert Thornby), Jules Borney.
The Courage of Marge O'Doone (d. David Smith), Tavish.
The Last of the Mohicans (d. Maurice Tourneur), Indian.

1921
The Hope Diamond Mystery [15 chapter serial] (d. Stuart Payton), Priest of Kama-Sita/Dakar.
Without Benefit of Clergy (d. James Young), Ahmed Khan.
Cheated Hearts (d. Hobart Henley), Nei Hamid.
The Cave Girl (d. Joseph J. Franz), Baptiste.

1922
Nan of the North (d. Duke Worne), undetermined role.
The Infidel (d. James Young), The Nabob.
The Man from Downing Street (d. Edward José), Maharajah Jehan.
The Altar Stairs (d. Lambert Hillyer), Hugo.
The Woman Conquers (d. Tom Forman), Raoul Maris.
Omar the Tentmaker (d. James Young), Imam Mowaffak.

1923
The Gentleman from America (d. Edward Sedgwick), undetermined role.
The Prisoner (d. Jack Conway), Prince Kapolski.

1924
The White Panther (d. Alan James), Native.[i]
The Hellion (d. Bruce Mitchell), Outlaw.
Riders of the Plains [15 chapter serial] (d. Jacques Jaccard), Bit part.
Dynamite Dan (d. Bruce Mitchell), Tony Garcia.

1925
Forbidden Cargo (d. Tom Buckingham), Pietro Castillano.
The Prairie Wife (d. Hugo Ballin), Diego.
Parisian Nights (d. Al Santell), Pierre.
Lady Robinhood (d. Ralph Ince), Cabraza.
Perils of the Wild [15 chapter serial] (d. Francis Ford), Bit part.
Without Mercy (d. George Melford), Henchman.
Never the Twain Shall Meet (d. Maurice Tourneur), Villain.

1926
The Greater Glory (d. Curt Rehfeld), Scissors grinder.
The Man in the Saddle (d. Clifford S. Smith), Robber.

Her Honor the Governor (d. Chet Withey), Snipe Collins.
The Bells (d. James Young), Mesmerist.
The Golden Web (d. Walter Lang), Dave Sinclair.
Flames (d. Lewis H. Moomaw), Blackie Blanchette.
The Eagle of the Sea (d. Frank Lloyd), Pirate.
The Nickel Hopper (d. Hal Yates), The masher.
Flaming Fury (d. James P. Hogan), Gaspard.
Old Ironsides (d. James Cruze), Saracen Guard.
Valencia (d. Dimitri Buchowetzki), Bit part.

1927
Let It Rain (d. Edward F. Cline), Crook.
The Princess from Hoboken (d. Allan Dale), Pavel.
Tarzan and the Golden Lion (d. J.P. McGowan), Owaza.
The Meddlin' Stranger (d. Richard Thorpe), Al Meggs.
The Phantom Buster (d. William Bertram), Ramon.
Soft Cushions (d. Edward F. Cline), The Chief Conspirator.
Two Arabian Knights (d. Lewis Milestone), Purser.
The Love Mart (d. George Fitzmaurice), Fleming.

1928
Sharp Shooters (d. John G. Blystone), Cafe proprietor.
The Vanishing Rider [10 chapter serial] (d. Ray Taylor), The villain.
Vultures of the Sea (d. Richard Thorpe), Grouchy.
The Little Wild Girl (d. Frank S. Mattison), Maurice Kent.
Burning the Wind (d. Henry MacRae), Pug Doran.

1929
The Fatal Warning [10 chapter serial] (d. Richard Thorpe), Mullins.
The Devil's Chaplain (d. Duke Worne), Boris.
Two Sisters (d. Scott Pembroke), Cecil.
Anne Against the World (d. Duke Worne), Bit part.
The Phantom of the North (d. Harry Webb), Jules Gregg.

Sound Films

1929
Behind That Curtain (d. Irving Cummings), Sudanese servant.
The King of the Kongo [10 chapter serial] (d. Richard Thorpe), Scarface Macklin.
The Unholy Night (d. Lionel Barrymore), Abdoul.

1930
The Bad One (d. George Fitzmaurice), Monsieur Gaston.
The Sea Bat (d. Wesley Ruggles), Corsican.
The Utah Kid (d. Richard Thorpe), Baxter.
Mothers Cry (d. Hobart Henley), Murder victim.

1931
Sous les verrous [a.k.a. *Pardon Us*] (d. James Parrott), Convict.
The Criminal Code (d. Howard Hawks), Galloway.
King of the Wild [12 chapter serial] (d. Richard Thorpe and B. Reeves Eason), Mustapha.
Cracked Nuts (d. Edward Cline), Revolutionary.
The Vanishing Legion [12 chapter serial] (d. Ford Beebe and B. Reeves Eason), The Voice (voice only).

---

i With thanks to Dr. Robert J. Kiss.

Donovan's Kid (d. Fred Niblo), Cokey Joe.
Smart Money (d. Alfred E. Green), Sport Williams.
The Public Defender (d. J. Walter Ruben), 'Professor'.
I Like Your Nerve (d. William McGann), Luigi.
Graft (d. Christy Cabanne), Terry.
Five Star Final (d. Mervyn LeRoy), T. Vernon Isopod.
The Yellow Ticket (d. Raoul Walsh), Orderly.
The Mad Genius (d. Michael Curtiz), Fedor's father.
The Guilty Generation (d. Rowland V. Lee), Tony Ricca.
Frankenstein (d. James Whale), The Monster.
Tonight or Never (d. Mervyn LeRoy), Waiter.

1932
The Cohens and Kellys in Hollywood (d. John Francis Dillon), Self.
Behind the Mask (d. John Francis Dillon), Jim Henderson.
Business and Pleasure (d. David Butler), Sheik.
Scarface (d. Howard Hawks), Gaffney.
The Miracle Man (d. Norman McLeod), Nikko.
Night World (d. Hobart Henley), 'Happy' MacDonald.
The Old Dark House (d. James Whale), Morgan [billed as Karloff].
Alias the Doctor (d. Michael Curtiz), Autopsy surgeon.
The Mask of Fu Manchu (d. Charles Brabin), Dr. Fu Manchu.
The Mummy (d. Karl Freund), Imhotep.

1933
The Ghoul (d. T. Hayes Hunter), Professor Morlant.

1934
The Lost Patrol (d. John Ford), Sanders.
The House of Rothschild (d. Alfred Werker), Count Ledrantz.
The Black Cat (d. Edgar G. Ulmer), Hjalmar Poelzig [billed as Karloff].
Gift of Gab (d. Karl Freund), Cameo [billed as Karloff].

1935
Bride of Frankenstein (d. James Whale) The Monster [billed as Karloff].
The Raven (d. Louis Friedlander) Edmond Bateman [billed as Karloff].
The Black Room (d. R. William Neill), Gregor and Anton de Berghman.

1936
The Invisible Ray (d. Lambert Hillyer), Dr. Janos Rukh [billed as Karloff].
The Walking Dead (d. Michael Curtiz), John Elman.
Juggernaut (d. Henry Edwards), Dr. Victor Sartorius.
The Man Who Changed His Mind (d. Robert Stevenson), Dr. Laurience.
Charlie Chan at the Opera (d. H. Bruce Humberstone), Gravelle.

1937
Night Key (d. Lloyd Corrigan), Dave Mallory.
West of Shanghai (d. John Farrow), Wu Yen Fang.

1938
The Invisible Menace (d. John Farrow), Jevries.

Mr. Wong, Detective (d. William Nigh), James Lee Wong.

1939
Devil's Island (d. William Clemens), Dr. Charles Gaudet.
Son of Frankenstein (d. Rowland V. Lee), The Monster.
The Mystery of Mr. Wong (d. William Nigh), James Lee Wong.
Mr. Wong in Chinatown (d. William Nigh), James Lee Wong.
The Man They Could Not Hang (d. Nick Grinde), Dr. Henryk Savaard.
Tower of London (d. Rowland V. Lee), Mord.

1940
The Fatal Hour (d. William Nigh), James Lee Wong.
British Intelligence (d. Terry Morse), Valdar.
Black Friday (d. Arthur Lubin), Dr. Ernest Sovac.
The Man with Nine Lives (d. Nick Grinde), Dr. Leon Kravaal.
Doomed to Die (d. William Nigh), James Lee Wong.
Before I Hang (d. Nick Grinde), Dr. John Garth.
The Ape (d. William Nigh), Dr. Bernard Adrian.
You'll Find Out (d. David Butler), Judge Spencer Mainwaring.

1941
The Devil Commands (d. Edward Dmytryk), Dr. Julian Blair.

1942
The Boogie Man Will Get You (d. Lew Landers), Professor Nathaniel Billings.

1944
The Climax (d. George Waggner), Dr. Friedrich Hohner.
House of Frankenstein (d. Erle C. Kenton), Doctor Gustav Niemann.

1945
The Body Snatcher (d. Robert Wise), Cabman John Gray.
Isle of the Dead (d. Mark Robson), General Nikolas Pherides.

1946
Bedlam (d. Mark Robson), Master George Sims.

1947
The Secret Life of Walter Mitty (d. Norman Z. McLeod), Dr. Hugo Hollingshead.
Lured (d. Douglas Sirk), Charles van Druten.
Unconquered (d. Cecil B. DeMille), Guyasuta, *Chief of the Senecas.*
Dick Tracy Meets Gruesome (d. John Rawlins), Gruesome.

1948
Tap Roots (d. George Marshall), Tishomingo.

1949
Abbott and Costello Meet the Killer, Boris Karloff (d. Charles T. Barton), Swami Talpur.

1951
Cisaruv slavík [a.k.a. *The Emperor's Nightingale*] (d. Jirí Trnka), Narrator.
The Strange Door (d. Joseph Pevney), Voltan.

1952
The Black Castle (d. Nathan Juran), Dr. Meissen.
Colonel March Investigates (d. Cy Endfield), Colonel Perceval March.

1953
Abbott and Costello Meet Dr. Jekyll and Mr. Hyde (d. Charles Lamont), Dr. Jekyll and Mr. Hyde.
Sabaka [a.k.a. *The Hindu*] (d. Frank Ferrin), General Pollegar.

1954
Il mostro dell'isola [a.k.a. *Monster of the Island*] (d. Roberto Bianchi Montero), Don Gaetano.

1957
Voodoo Island (d. Reginald LeBorg), Phillip Knight.

1958
The Juggler of Our Lady (d. Al Kouzel), Narrator [short].
Grip of the Strangler [a.k.a. *The Haunted Strangler*] (d. Robert Day), James Rankin.
Frankenstein 1970 (d. Howard W. Koch), Baron Victor von Frankenstein.

1963
The Doctor from Seven Dials [a.k.a. *Corridors of Blood*] (d. Robert Day), Dr. Thomas Bolton [filmed in 1958].
The Raven (d. Roger Corman), Dr. Scarabus.
The Terror (d. Roger Corman), Baron Victor Von Leppe.
I tre volti della paura [a.k.a. *Black Sabbath*] (d. Mario Bava), Self/Gorca.
The Comedy of Terrors (d. Jacques Tourneur), Amos Hinchley.

1964
Bikini Beach (d. William Asher), Art dealer.

1965
Die, Monster, Die! (d. Daniel Haller), Nahum Witley.

1966
The Ghost in the Invisible Bikini (d. Don Weis), Hiram Stokely.
The Daydreamer (d. Jules Bass), The Rat (voice).

1967
The Venetian Affair (d. Jerry Thorpe), Dr. Pierre Vaugiroud.
Mad Monster Party? (d. Jules Bass), Baron Boris von Frankenstein (voice).
Mondo Balordo (d. Roberto Bianchi Montero), Narrator.
The Sorcerers (d. Michael Reeves), Professor Marcus Monserrat.
El coleccionista de cadáveres [a.k.a. *Cauldron of Blood/Blindman's Bluff*] (d. Santos Alcocer), Charles Badulescu.*

1968
Targets (d. Peter Bogdanovich), Byron Orlok.
Curse of the Crimson Altar (d. Vernon Sewell), Professor Marsh.
Serenata macabra [a.k.a. *House of Evil*] (d. Jack Hill, Juan Ibanez), Matthias Morteval.
La cámara del terror [a.k.a. *Fear Chamber*] (d. Jack Hill, Juan Ibanez), Dr. Carl Mandel.
Invasión siniestra [a.k.a. *The Incredible Invasion*] (d. Jack Hill, Juan Ibanez), Professor John Mayer.*
La muerte viviente [a.k.a. *Isle of the Snake People*] (d. Jack Hill, Juan Ibanez), Carl van Molder/Damballah.*

* Released after Karloff's death.

On the Radio

1932
California Melodies (3 January 1932) – Guests: Boris Karloff, Ken Murray, the Hallelujah Quartet, and soloist Vera Van.
Hollywood on the Air [a.k.a. *Hollywood on Parade*] (25 November 1932) – Host: Jimmy Fidler. Guests: Boris Karloff, Katherine Hepburn; Joel McCrea, and Others.

1933
Hollywood on the Air (7 October 1933) – Host: Jimmy Fidler. Guests: Boris Karloff, Victor McLaglen, and Others.
California Melodies (24 October 1933) – Guests: Boris Karloff, Ray Paige's Orchestra, and violinist Margit Hegedus.

1934
Hollywood on the Air (27 January 1934) – Guests: Boris Karloff, Maxine Doyle.
Forty-Five Minutes in Hollywood (15 February 1934): *The Lost Patrol* – broadcast of the motion picture's soundtrack.
Forty-Five Minutes in Hollywood (2 August 1934) – Guest: Boris Karloff.
The Show (27 August 1934) – Guests: Boris Karloff, Jean Sargent. [Karloff appeared in a scene from *Death Takes a Holiday*].
The Fleischmann's Yeast Hour (11 October 1934) – Guest: Boris Karloff [Karloff appeared in a scene from *Death Takes a Holiday*].

1935
Shell Chateau (31 August 1935) – Host: Al Jolson. Guests: Boris Karloff, Maxine Lewis, George Jessel, Joyce Wethered. [Karloff appeared in scene from *The Green Goddess*].
Hollywood Boulevardier (30 December 1935) – Host: Ben Alexander. Guest: Boris Karloff.

1936
The Fleischmann's Yeast Hour [a.k.a. *Vallee's Varieties*] (6 February 1936) – Host: Rudy Vallee. Guests: Boris Karloff, Kazanova Tziganes String Orchestra, Frank Fay, Anne Butler and Art Landry, and The Brown Sisters. [Karloff appeared in a scene from *The Bells*].

In Town To-night (22 February 1936) – Guest: Boris Karloff [BBC].

The Fleischmann's Yeast Hour (3 September 1936) – Host: Rudy Vallee. Guests: Boris Karloff, Arlene Jackson, Tom Howard and George Shelton, Eddie Green, and Doc Rockwell.

Camel Caravan (8 December 1936) – Benny Goodman and his Orchestra, Olga Albani, Boris Karloff. [Karloff appeared in a scene from *Death Takes a Holiday*].

1937

Concert Orchestra (2 September 1937) – Guests: Bob Burns, Mario Chamlee, Dolores Del Rio, Boris Karloff.

The Royal Gelatine Hour [a.k.a. *Vallee's Varieties*] (11 November 1937) – Host: Rudy Vallee. Guests: Boris Karloff, Tom Mix. [Karloff reads Horace Brown's Armistice Day soliloquy *Resurrection*].

1938

The Chase and Sanborn Hour (30 January 1938) – Guest: Boris Karloff [Karloff recites *The Evil Eye*].

The Baker's Broadcast [a.k.a. *Seein' Stars in Hollywood*] (13 March 1938) – Host: Feg Murray. Guests: Boris Karloff, Bela Lugosi, Harriett Hilliard. [Karloff read Kipling's *The Supplication of the Black Aberdeen* and joined Lugosi in the rendition of a short ditty entitled, *We're Horrible, Horrible Men*].

Lights Out (23 March 1938) – Play: *The Dream* – Cast: Boris Karloff, Templeton Fox, Mercedes McCambridge, Arthur Peterson, Ray Johnson, Bob Guilbert, Betty Winkler.

Lights Out (30 March 1938) – Play: *Valse Triste* – Cast: Boris Karloff, Templeton Fox, Mercedes McCambridge, Arthur Peterson, Ray Johnson, Bob Guilbert, Betty Winkler.

Lights Out (6 April 1938) – Play: *Cat Wife* – Cast: Boris Karloff, Templeton Fox, Mercedes McCambridge, Arthur Peterson, Ray Johnson, Bob Guilbert, Betty Winkler.

For Men Only (11 April 1938) – Guests: Boris Karloff, John Ringling North.

Lights Out (13 April 1938) – Play: *Three Matches* – Cast: Boris Karloff, Templeton Fox, Mercedes McCambridge, Arthur Peterson, Ray Johnson, Bob Guilbert, Betty Winkler.

Lights Out (20 April 1938) – Play: *Night on the Mountain* – Cast: Boris Karloff, Templeton Fox, Mercedes McCambridge, Arthur Peterson, Ray Johnson, Bob Guilbert, Betty Winkler.

The Royal Gelatine Hour (5 May 1938) – Host: Rudy Vallee. Guests: Boris Karloff, Eddie East and Ralph Dumke. [Karloff appeared in a play entitled *Danse Macabre*].

Hollywood (27 October 1938) – Host: George McCall. Guest: Boris Karloff.

1939

The Eddie Cantor Show (16 January 1939) – Host: Eddie Cantor. Guests: Boris Karloff, Burt 'The Mad Russian' Gordon.

Gateway to Hollywood (5 March 1939) – Play: *Empty Coffin*.

Vallee's Varieties (6 April 1939) – Host: Rudy Vallee. Guests: Boris Karloff, Irvin S. Cobb, Vic Oliver, John Doakes. [Karloff appeared in a drama entitled *Resurrection*].

1940

Kay Kyser's Kollege of Musical Knowledge (25 September 1940) – Guests: Boris Karloff, Bela Lugosi, Peter Lorre.

1941

Information Please (24 January 1941) – Host: Clifton Fadiman. Panellists: Boris Karloff, John Kieran, Franklin P. Adams, Lewis E. Lawes.

ASCAP on Parade (8 February 1941) – Guests: Ethel Waters, Deems Taylor, Boris Karloff.

Kate Smith Variety (7 March 1941) – Guests: Boris Karloff, Charlie Cantor, Minerva Pious, Smart Set Quartet.

Untitled (15 March 1941) – Guest: Boris Karloff.

Inner Sanctum (16 March 1941) – Play: *The Man of Steel*.

Hollywood News Girl (22 March 1941) – Host: Lydia Pinkham. Guest: Boris Karloff.

Inner Sanctum (23 March 1941) – Play: *The Man Who Hated Death*.

We, the People (1 April 1941) – Guest: Boris Karloff.

Inner Sanctum (6 April 1941) – Play: *Death in the Zoo*.

The Voice of Broadway (19 April 1941) – Guest: Boris Karloff.

Inner Sanctum (20 April 1941) – Play: *Fog*.

Inner Sanctum (11 May 1941) – Play: *Imperfect Crime*.

Inner Sanctum (1 June 1941) – Play: *The Fall of the House of Usher*.

WHN Bundles for Britain Program (14 June 1941) – Guests: Boris Karloff, Constance Collier.

Inner Sanctum (22 June 1941) – Play: *Green-Eyed Bat*.

Inner Sanctum (29 June 1941) – Play: *The Man Who Painted Death*.

United Press is on the Air (11 July 1941) – Guest: Boris Karloff.

Inner Sanctum (13 July 1941) – Play: *Death is a Murderer*.

Inner Sanctum (3 August 1941) – Play: *The Tell-Tale Heart*.

Gloria Whitney (13 August 1941) – Guest: Boris Karloff.

Inner Sanctum (26 October 1941) – Play: *Terror on Bailey Street*.

U.S.O. Program (23 November 1941) – Guests: Boris Karloff, Paul Lukas.

Time to Smile (7 December 1941) Host: Eddie Cantor. Guest: Boris Karloff.

1942

Keep 'em Rolling (8 February 1942) – Guests: Boris Karloff, Dorothy Maynor. [Karloff appeared in a drama entitled *In the Fog*].

Information Please (20 February 1942) – Host: Clifton Fadiman. Panellists: John Kieran, Franklin P. Adams, Boris Karloff, John Carradine.

Inner Sanctum (5 April 1942) – Play: *The Fall of the House of Usher*.

Inner Sanctum (19 April 1942) – Play: *Blackstone*.

Inner Sanctum (3 May 1942) – Play: *Study for Murder*.

Inner Sanctum (24 May 1942) – Play: *The Cone*.

Inner Sanctum (31 May 1942) – Play: *Death Wears My Face*.

Inner Sanctum (7 June 1942) – Play: *Strange Request*.

1943
Information Please (17 May 1943) – Host: Clifton Fadiman. Panellists: John Kieran, Franklin P. Adams, Boris Karloff, Jan Struther.
Blue Ribbon Town (24 July 1943) Host: Groucho Marx. Guests: Boris Karloff, Virginia O'Brien, Donald Dickson.

1944
Creeps By Night (15 February 1944) – Play: *The Voice of Death.*
Creeps By Night (22 February 1944) – Play: *The Man with the Devil's Hands.*
Creeps By Night (7 March 1944) – Play: *Unknown Title.*
Creeps By Night (14 March 1944) – Play: *Dark Destiny.*
Creeps By Night (21 March 1944) – Play: *Unknown Title.*
Creeps By Night (28 March 1944) – Play: *The String of Pearls.*
Creeps By Night (18 April 1944) – Play: *Unknown Title.*
Creeps By Night (25 April 1944) – Play: *Unknown Title.*
Creeps By Night (2 May 1944) – Play: *The Final Reckoning.*
Creeps By Night (9 May 1944) – Play: *The Hunt.*
Blue Ribbon Town (3 June 1944) – Host: Groucho Marx: Guest: Boris Karloff.

1945
Duffy's Tavern (12 January 1945) – Guest: Boris Karloff.
Suspense (25 January 1945) – Play: *Drury's Bones.*
Those Websters (19 October 1945) – Guest: Boris Karloff.
Inner Sanctum (23 October 1945) – Play: *The Corridor of Doom.*
Hildegarde's Radio Room (23 October 1945) – Guest: Boris Karloff
The Charlie McCarthy Program (28 October 1945) – Guest: Boris Karloff.
Inner Sanctum (30 October 1945) – Play: *The Man Who Couldn't Die.*
Report to the Nation (3 November 1945) – Play: *Back for Christmas.*
Information Please (5 November 1945) – Host: Clifton Fadiman. Panellists: John Kieran, Franklin P. Adams, Boris Karloff, Arthur Schlesinger Jr.
Inner Sanctum (6 November 1945) – Play: *The Wailing Wall.*
Theatre Guild on the Air (11 November 1945) – Plays: *The Emperor Jones* and *Where the Cross is Made.*
The Fred Allen Show (18 November 1945) – Guest: Boris Karloff.
Textron Theatre (8 December 1945) – Play: *Angel Street.*
Exploring the Unknown (23 December 1945) – Play: *The Baffled Genie.*
Information Please (24 December 1945) – Host: Clifton Fadiman. Panellists: John Kieran, Franklin P. Adams, Boris Karloff, John Mason Brown.

1946
The Kate Smith Show (4 January 1946) – Guest: Boris Karloff.
Request Performance (3 February 1946) – Guests: Boris Karloff, Frank Morgan, Roy Rogers, Allan Jones.
The Jack Haley Show [a.k.a. *Village Store*] (14 February 1946) – Guest: Boris Karloff.
The Bandwagon Show (24 March 1946) – Guest: Boris Karloff.

The Ginny Simms Show (5 April 1946) – Guest: Boris Karloff.
Show Stoppers (26 May 1946) – Guest: Boris Karloff.
That's Life (8 November 1946) – Host: Jay C. Flippen. Guest: Boris Karloff.
The Lady Esther Screen Guild Players (25 November 1946) – Play: *Arsenic and Old Lace.*

1947
The Jack Benny Show (19 January 1947) – Guest: Boris Karloff.
Kay Kyser's Kollege of Musical Knowledge. (12 March 1947) – Guest: Boris Karloff.
Duffy's Tavern (21 May 1947) – Guest: Boris Karloff.
Lights Out (16 July 1947) – Play: *Death Robbery.*
Lights Out (23 July 1947) – Play: *The Undead.*
Lights Out (30 July 1947) – Play: *The Ring.*
Lights Out (6 August 1947) – Play: *Unknown Title.*
Philco Radio Time (29 October 1947) – Guest: Boris Karloff.
The Burl Ives Show (31 October 1947) – Guest: Boris Karloff.
The Jimmy Durante Show (10 December 1947) – Guest: Boris Karloff.
Suspense (19 December 1947) – Play: *Wet Saturday.*
Kraft Music Hall (25 December 1947) – Guest: Boris Karloff.

1948
Information Please (16 January 1948) – Host: Clifton Fadiman. Panellists: John Kieran, Franklin P. Adams, Boris Karloff, George S. Kaufman.
We, the People (27 January 1948) – Guests: Boris Karloff, Connee Boswell.
We, the People (27 July 1948) – Guests: Boris Karloff, James Melton, Lillian Murphy, Al Capp, Mrs. Josephine Guerro.
Guest Star (12 September 1948) – Guest: Boris Karloff. [Karloff appeared in a skit entitled *The Babysitter*].
The NBC University Theatre of the Air (17 October 1948) – Play: *The History of Mr. Polly.*
The Sealtest Variety Theatre (28 October 1948) – Guest: Boris Karloff.
Great Scenes from Great Plays (29 October 1948) – Play: *On Borrowed Time.*
Truth or Consequences (30 October 1948) – Guest: Boris Karloff.

1949
Theatre USA (3 February 1949) – Guest: Boris Karloff.
Spike Jones Spotlight Review (9 April 1949) – Guest: Boris Karloff.
Twenty Questions (16 April 1949) – Host: Bill Slater. Guest: Boris Karloff.
Theatre Guild on the Air (29 May 1949) Play: *The Perfect Alibi.*
The Sealtest Variety Theatre (23 June 1949) – Guest: Boris Karloff.
Starring Boris Karloff (21 September 1949) – Play: *Five Golden Guineas.*
Starring Boris Karloff (28 September 1949) – Play: *The Mask.*
Starring Boris Karloff (5 October 1949) – Play: *Mungahara.*

Starring Boris Karloff (12 October 1949) –
Play: *Mad Illusion.*
Starring Boris Karloff (19 October 1949) –
Play: *Perchance to Dream.*
Starring Boris Karloff (26 October 1949) –
Play: *The Devil Takes a Bride.*
Starring Boris Karloff (2 November 1949) –
Play: *The Moving Finger.*
Starring Boris Karloff (9 November 1949) –
Play: *The Twisted Path.*
Starring Boris Karloff (16 November 1949) –
Play: *False Face.*
Starring Boris Karloff (23 November 1949) –
Play: *Cranky Bill.*
Starring Boris Karloff (30 November 1949) –
Play: *Three O'Clock.*
Starring Boris Karloff (7 December 1949) –
Play: *The Shop at Sly Corner.*
Starring Boris Karloff (14 December 1949) –
Play: *The Night Reveals.*

1950
The Bill Stern Colgate Sports Newsreel (13 January 1950) –
Guest: Boris Karloff.
Invitation to Music (18 June 1950) – Guest: Boris Karloff.
The Bill Stern Colgate Sports Newsreel (21 July 1950) – Guest:
Boris Karloff.
The Barbara Welles Show (18 August 1950) – Guest: Boris
Karloff.
Boris Karloff's Treasure Chest (17 September 1950) – Host.
Boris Karloff's Treasure Chest (24 September 1950) – Host.
Information Please (24 September 1950) – Host: Clifton
Fadiman. Panellists: John Kieran, Franklin P. Adams, Boris
Karloff, Richard Llewellyn.
Boris Karloff's Treasure Chest (1 October 1950) – Host.
Boris Karloff's Treasure Chest (8 October 1950) – Host.
Boris Karloff's Treasure Chest (15 October 1950) – Host.
Boris Karloff's Treasure Chest (22 October 1950) – Host.
Boris Karloff's Treasure Chest (29 October 1950) – Host.
Boris Karloff's Treasure Chest (5 November 1950) – Host.
Boris Karloff's Treasure Chest (12 November 1950) – Host.
Boris Karloff's Treasure Chest (19 November 1950) – Host.
Boris Karloff's Treasure Chest (26 November 1950) – Host.
Boris Karloff's Treasure Chest (3 December 1950) – Host.
Boris Karloff's Treasure Chest (10 December 1950) – Host.
Boris Karloff's Treasure Chest (17 December 1950) – Host.
Theatre Guild on the Air (24 December 1950) – Play: *David
Copperfield* starring Boris Karloff, Cyril Ritchard, Flora
Robson, Hugh Williams, Richard Burton, and David Cole.

1951
Duffy's Tavern (5 October 1951) – Guest: Boris Karloff.
It's News to Me (15 December 1951) – Guest: Boris Karloff.

1952
Philip Morris Playhouse on Broadway (10 February 1952) –
Play: *Journey to Nowhere.*
Musical Comedy Theatre (20 February 1952) – Play: *Yolanda
and the Thief* starring Boris Karloff and Lisa Kirk.

Theatre Guild on the Air (24 February 1952) – Play: *Oliver
Twist* starring Boris Karloff, Basil Rathbone, Leveen
McGrath, and Melville Cooper.
Dean Martin and Jerry Lewis Show (18 April 1952) – Guest:
Boris Karloff.
Theatre Guild on the Air (27 April 1952) – Play: *The Sea Wolf*
starring Boris Karloff and Burgess Meredith.
Philip Morris Playhouse on Broadway (1 June 1952) – Play:
Outward Bound.
Inner Sanctum (22 June 1952) – Play: *Birdsong for a Murderer.*
Best Plays (6 July 1952) – Play: *Arsenic and Old Lace* starring
Boris Karloff, Donald Cook, Jean Adair, Evelyn Varden, and
Edgar Stehli.
Inner Sanctum (13 July 1952) – Play: *Death for Sale.*
Musical Comedy Theatre (26 November 1952) – Play: *Yolanda
and the Thief* starring Boris Karloff, Lisa Kirk and John
Coote. [Probably a repeat of the 20 February broadcast].
Philip Morris Playhouse on Broadway (10 December 1952) –
Play: *Man Versus Town.*

1953
U.S. Steel Hour (5 April 1953) – Play: *Great Expectations*
starring Boris Karloff, Estelle Winwood, Melville Cooper,
Margaret Phillips, and Tom Helmore.
Philip Morris Playhouse on Broadway (15 April 1953) – Play:
Dead Past.
Heritage (23 April 1953) – Play: *Plague.*
Philip Morris Playhouse on Broadway (17 June 1953) – Play:
[The newspapers are at odds over the play presented
that evening. While some, such as the *New York Times*,
announced Karloff would appear in *On Borrowed Time*,
others stated the play would be *The Shop at Sly Corner*].
The Play of His Choice (2 December 1953) – Play: *The
Hanging Judge.* [British Radio].

1956
The Spoken Word (29 March 1956) – Guest: Boris Karloff.
Tales from the Reader's Digest – Narrator (until 1968).

1957
Untitled (19 March 1957) – Karloff interviewed on KTMI
in Alaska.

1958
Easy as ABC (27 April 1958): *O is for Old Wives Tales* –
Guests: Boris Karloff, Alfred Hitchcock, Peter Lorre,
Julienne Marie.

1960
Flair – Occasional guest (until 1961).

1963
The Barry Gray Show (26 January 1963) – Guests: Boris
Karloff and Peter Lorre.
For Young People (27 July 1963) – Play: *Peter Pan* starring
Jean Arthur and Boris Karloff. [Announced as a 'BBC
Science Feature' this was probably a broadcast of the 1950
recording of the play].

1965
Interval: Boris Karloff Looks Back (20 July 1965). [British radio].

Note: The following shows have been excluded as newspaper clippings reveal Karloff was not featured:
The Fred Allen Show (14 October 1945). The guest was Victor Moore, not Boris Karloff.
Inner Sanctum (14 February 1949) Play: *Birdsong for a Murderer.* This play starred Ted Osborn, not Boris Karloff.

On Television

1949
Chevrolet on Broadway [a.k.a. *The Chevrolet Tele-Theatre*] (7 February 1949) - Expert Opinion.
The Ford Theatre Hour (11 April 1949) – *Arsenic and Old Lace,* Jonathan Brewster.
Star Theatre (12 April 1949).
Suspense! (26 April 1949) – *A Night at an Inn,* Arnold Everett Scott-Fortesque (a.k.a. *'The Toff'*).
Chevrolet on Broadway [a.k.a. *The Chevrolet Tele-Theatre*] (9 May 1949) - *Passenger to Bali.*
Suspense! (17 May 1949) - *The Monkey's Paw,* Mr. White.
Suspense! (7 June 1949) - *The Yellow Scarf,* Bronston.
Celebrity Time (4 September 1949) – Guest.
Starring Boris Karloff (22 September 1949) - *Five Golden Guineas.*
Starring Boris Karloff (29 September 1949) – *The Mask.*
Starring Boris Karloff (6 October 1949) – *Mungahara.*
Starring Boris Karloff (13 October 1949) – *Mad Illusion.*
Starring Boris Karloff (20 October 1949) – *Perchance to Dream.*
Starring Boris Karloff (27 October 1949) – *The Devil Takes a Bride.*
Starring Boris Karloff (3 November 1949) – *The Moving Finger.*
*Starring Boris Karloff (*10 November 1949) – *The Twisted Path.*
Starring Boris Karloff (17 November 1949) – *False Face.*
Starring Boris Karloff (24 November 1949) – *Cranky Bill.*
Starring Boris Karloff (1 December 1949) – *Three O'Clock.*
Starring Boris Karloff (8 December 1949) – *The Shop at Sly Corner,* Descius Heiss.
Starring Boris Karloff (15 December 1949) – *Night Reveals.*

1950
Supper Club (19 February 1950) – Guest.
Masterpiece Playhouse (3 September 1950) - *Uncle Vanya.*
Lights Out (18 September 1950) - *The Leopard Lady.*
Paul Whiteman Revue (29 October 1950) – Guest.
Texaco Star Theatre [a.k.a. *The Milton Berle Show*] (12 December 1950) – Guest.

1951
Don McNeil TV Club (11 April 1951) – Guest.
Texaco Star Theatre (9 October 1951) – Guest.
The Fred Waring Show (21 October 1951) – Guest.
Robert Montgomery Presents (19 November 1951) - *The Kimballs,* Mr. Kimball.

Celebrity Time (25 November 1951) – Guest.
Studio One (3 December 1951) - *Mutiny on the Nicolette.*
Suspense! (25 December 1951) – *The Lonely Place.*
Lux Video Theatre (31 December 1951) - *The Jest of Hahalaba,* Sir Arthur Strangways.

1952
CBS Television Workshop (13 January 1952) - *Don Quixote,* Don Quixote.
Stork Club (30 January 1952) – Guest.
Tales of Tomorrow (22 February 1952) – *Memento.*
Texaco Star Theatre (29 April 1952) – Guest.
Studio One (19 May 1952) - *A Connecticut Yankee in King Arthur's Court,* King Arthur.
Celebrity Time (25 May 1952) – Guest.
Philip Morris Playhouse on Broadway (1 June 1952) - *Outward Bound.*
I've Got a Secret (19 June 1952) – Guest.
Curtain Call (27 June 1952) - *The Soul of the Great Bell,* Kouan-Yu.
Schlitz Playhouse of Stars (4 July 1952) - *House of Death,* Charles Brandon.
The Video Theatre (8 December 1952) - *Fear,* Larkin.
Texaco Star Theatre [a.k.a. *The Milton Berle Show*] (16 December 1952) – Guest.

1953
All Star Revue (17 January 1953) – Guest.
Hollywood Opening Night (2 March 1953) - *The Invited Seven.*
Suspense! (17 March 1953) – *The Black Prophet,* Rasputin.
Robert Montgomery Presents (30 March 1953) – *The Burden of Proof.*
Tales of Tomorrow (3 April 1953) - *Past Tense,* Dr. Henry Marco.
Quick as a Flash (7 May 1953) – Guest.
Plymouth Playhouse [a.k.a. *ABC Album*] (24 May 1953) – Sketchbook: *The Chaser* (with Karloff), *You Were Perfectly Fine, Nightmare Number Three, The Reticence of Lady Anne* (with Karloff).
Suspense! (23 June 1953) - *The Signal Man.*

1954
Colonel March of Scotland Yard (First broadcast 11 February 1954) – *The Invisible Knife,* Colonel Perceval March. Other episodes: *The Sorcerer, The Abominable Snowman, Present Tense, At Night All Cats Are Grey, The Case of the Kidnapped Poodle, The Strange Event at Roman Fall, The Headless Hat, The Second Mona Lisa, Death in Inner Space, The Talking Head, The Devil Sells His Soul, Murder Is Permanent, The Silent Vow, Death and the Other Monkey, The Stolen Crime, The Silver Curtain, Terror at Daybreak, Hot Money, The Missing Link, The Case of the Misguided Missal, The Deadly Gift, The Case of the Lively Ghost, Death in the Dressing Room, The New Invisible Man, Passage of Arms.*
I've Got a Secret (13 October 1954) – Guest.
The George Gobel Show (6 November 1954) – Guest.
Truth or Consequences (9 November 1954) – Guest.
Climax! (16 December 1954) - *The White Carnations,* Dr. Philip Nestri.
Down You Go (22 December 1954) – Guest.

1955
The Best of Broadway (5 January 1955) - *Arsenic and Old Lace*,
Jonathan Brewster.
Texaco Star Theatre (19 February 1955) – Guest.
The Elgin TV Hour (22 February 1955) – *The Sting of Death*,
Mr. Mycroft.
Max Leibman Presents (12 March 1955) *A Connecticut Yankee*,
King Arthur.
Who Said That? (20 April 1955) – Guest.
General Electric Theatre (1 May 1955) - *Mr. Blue Ocean*, Mr.
Blue Ocean.
Boris Karloff (15 July 1955) – Guest. [British TV]
I've Got a Secret (24 August 1955) – Guest.
The United States Steel Hour (31 August 1955) – *Counterfeit*,
George Redford.

1956
The Alcoa Hour (15 April 1956) - *Even the Weariest River*, Doc
Dixon.
The Amazing Dunninger (18 July 1956) – Guest.
Frankie Laine Time (1 August 1956) – Guest.
Frankie Laine Time (8 August 1956) – Guest.
The Ernie Kovacs Show (13 August 1956) – Guest.
Climax! (6 September 1956) - *Bury Me Later*, Vicar.
Playhouse 90 (25 October 1956) - *Rendezvous in Black*, Ward
Allen.
The Red Skelton Show (27 November 1956) – Guest.
The $64,000 Question (11 December 1956) – Contestant.
The $64,000 Question (18 December 1956) – Contestant.
The $64,000 Question (25 December 1956) – Contestant.

1957
The Rosemary Clooney Show (18 January 1957).
Hallmark Hall of Fame (10 February 1957) - *The Lark*,
Bishop Cauchon.
Untitled (20 March 1957) – Karloff interviewed in
Anchorage on KTVA.
The Rosemary Clooney Show (19 April 1957) – Guest.
Lux Video Theatre (25 April 1957) - *The Man Who Played God*,
Montgomery Royle.
The Kate Smith Hour (28 April 1957) – Guest.
The Dinah Shore Chevy Show (17 May 1957) – Guest.
A-Z (30 August 1957) – Guest. [British TV]
The Dinah Shore Show (27 October 1957) - Guest.
The Rosemary Clooney Show (31 October 1957) – Guest.
The Gisele MacKenzie Show (16 November 1957) – Guest.
This is Your Life (20 November 1957) – Subject.
Suspicion, (9 December 1957) - *The Deadly Game*, Judge
Winthrop Gelsey.

1958
The Betty White Show (12 February 1958) – Guest.
Telephone Time (25 February 1958) - *The Vestris*, Dr. Pierre.
Shirley Temple's Storybook (5 March 1958) - *The Legend of
Sleepy Hollow*, Narrator/Father Knickerbocker.
Studio One (31 March 1958) - *The Shadow of Genius*,
Professor Theodore Koenig.
The Jack Parr Show (22 April 1958) - Guest.
Playhouse 90 (6 November 1958) - *Heart of Darkness*, Kurtz.
The Veil (1958, Unaired)

- *Vision of Crime*, Host/Sergeant Chester Wilmore.
- *Girl on the Road*, Host/Morgan Debs.
- *Food on the Table*, Host/Captain John Elwood.
- *The Doctors*, Host/Dr. Carlo Marcabienti.
- *The Crystal Ball*, Host/Andre Giraud.
- *Genesis*, Host/Jonas Atterbury.
- *Destination Nightmare*, Host/Peter Wade Sr.
- *Summer Heat*, Host/Dr. Francis Mason.
- *The Return of Madame Vernoy*, Host/Charles Goncourt.
- *Jack the Ripper*, Host.

1959
The Gale Storm Show (31 January 1959) – *It's Murder, My
Dear*. Self/Lookalike.
General Electric Theatre (17 May 1959) - *The Indian Giver*,
Henry Church.

1960
Playhouse 90 (9 February 1960) - *To the Sound of Trumpets*,
Guibert.
The DuPont Show of the Month (5 March 1960) - *Treasure
Island*, Billy Bones.
Hollywood Sings (3 April 1960), Host.
Upgreen and at 'em, or A Maiden Nearly Over (6 June 1960),
Butler. [British TV]
The Secret World of Eddie Hodges (23 June 1960), Captain
Hook.
Thriller: Season 1 (13 September 1960 – 13 June 1961) –
Host.
*The Twisted Image, Child's Play, Worse Than Murder, The Mark
of the Hand, Rose's Last Summer, The Guilty Men, The Purple
Room, The Watcher, Girl with a Secret, The Prediction* [Karloff
as Clayton Mace], *The Fatal Impulse, The Big Blackout, Knock
Three-One-Two, Man in the Middle, The Cheaters, The Hungry
Glass, The Poisoner, Man in the Cage, Choose a Victim, Hay-Fork
and Bill-Hook, The Merriweather File, The Fingers of Fear, Well of
Doom, The Ordeal of Dr. Cordell, Trio for Terror, Papa Benjamin,
Late Date, Yours Truly, Jack the Ripper, The Devil's Ticket,
Parasite Mansion, A Good Imagination, Mr. George, Terror in
Teakwood, The Prisoner in the Mirror, Dark Legacy, Pigeons from
Hell, The Grim Reaper.*

1961
Thriller: Season 2 (18 September 1961 – 30 April 1962) –
Host.
What Beckoning Ghost?, Guillotine, The Premature Burial
[Karloff as Dr. Thorne], *The Weird Tailor, God Grant That She
Lye Stille, Masquerade, The Last of the Sommervilles* [Karloff
as Dr. Farnham], *Letter to a Lover, A Third for Pinochle, The
Closed Cabinet, Dialogues with Death* [Friend of the Dead -
Karloff as Pop Jenkins; *Welcome Home* – Karloff as Colonel
Jackson], *The Return of Andrew Bentley, The Remarkable
Mrs. Hawks, Portrait Without a Face, An Attractive Family,
Waxworks, La Strega, The Storm, A Wig for Miss DeVore, The
Hollow Watcher, Cousin Tundifer, The Incredible Doktor Markesan*
[Karloff as Dr. Konrad Markesan], *Flowers of Evil, Till Death
Do Us Part, The Bride Who Died Twice, Kill My Love, Man
of Mystery, The Innocent Bystanders, The Lethal Ladies, The
Specialists.*

1962

Hallmark Hall of Fame (5 February 1962) - *Arsenic and Old Lace*, Jonathan Brewster.
PM (12 February 1962) – Guest.
Theatre '62 (11 March 1962) - *The Paradine Case*, Judge Lord Thomas Horfield.
The Dickie Henderson Show (11 June 1962) - *The Gangster*. [British TV]
Out of This World (30 June 1962) - *The Yellow Pill*. [British TV]
Out of This World (7 July 1962) - *Little Lost Robot*. [British TV]
Out of This World (14 July 1962) - *Cold Equations*. [British TV]
Out of This World (21 July 1962) – *Impostor*. [British TV]
Out of This World (28 July 1962) - *Botany Bay*. [British TV]
Out of This World (4 August 1962) - *Medicine Show*. [British TV]
Out of This World (11 August 1962) - *Pictures Don't Lie*. [British TV]
Out of This World (18 August 1962) - *Vanishing Act*. [British TV]
Out of This World (25 August 1962) - *Divided We Fall*. [British TV]
Out of This World (1 September 1962) - *The Dark Star*. [British TV]
Out of This World (8 September 1962) – *Immigrant*. [British TV]
Out of This World (15 September 1962) - *Target Generation*. [British TV]
Out of This World (22 September 1962) - *The Tycoons*. [British TV]
Route 66 (26 October 1962) - *Lizard's Leg and Owlet's Wing*, Self.

1963

I've Got a Secret (28 January 1963) – Guest.
The Hy Gardner Show (3 March 1963) – Guest.
Chronicle (25 December 1963) – *A Danish Fairy Tale*, Narrator.

1964

The Garry Moore Show (21 April 1964) – Guest.
The Tonight Show (2 June 1964) – Guest.

1965

The Entertainers (16 January 1965) – Guest.
Shindig! (30 October 1965) - Special guest host.

1966

The Wild Wild West (23 September 1966) - *The Night of the Golden Cobra*, Mr. Singh.
The Girl from U.N.C.L.E. (27 September 1966) – *The Mother Muffin Affair*, Agnes Twicksbury (a.k.a. Mother Muffin).
Dr. Seuss' How the Grinch Stole Christmas! (18 December 1966), Narrator/the Grinch.

1967

I Spy (22 February 1967) - *Mainly on the Plains*, Don Ernesto Silvando.

1968

The Red Skelton Show (24 September 1968) – Guest.
The Jonathan Winters Show (30 October 1968) – Guest.
The Name of the Game (29 November 1968) - *The White Birch*, Mikhail Orlov.

Recordings

The following recordings were released during Karloff's lifetime:

1950

J.M. Barrie: *Peter Pan*. (Columbia ML 4312).

1955

Rudyard Kipling: *Just So Stories and Other Tales*. (Caedmon TC 1038)
.

1958

Kenneth Grahame: *The Reluctant Dragon*. (Caedmon TC 1074).
Lewis Carroll: *The Hunting of the Snark*, and Robert Browning: *The Pied Piper*. (Caedmon TC 1075).
Rudyard Kipling: *The Elephant's Child and Other Stories*. (Caedmon TC 1088).
Mother Goose. (Caedmon TC 1091).

1959

Hans Christian Andersen: *The Ugly Duckling and Other Tales*. (Caedmon TC 1109).

1960

Hans Christian Andersen: *The Little Match Girl and Other Tales*. (Caedmon TC 1117).
Tales of Mystery and Imagination – Washington Irving: *The Legend of Sleepy Hollow* and *Rip Van Winkle*. (Cricket CR 32).

1961

Charles Dickens: *The Pickwick Papers – Mr. Pickwick's Christmas* (read by Sir Lewis Casson) and *The Story of the Goblins Who Stole a Sexton* (read by Boris Karloff). (Caedmon TC 1121).

1962

Three Little Pigs, The Three Bears, Jenny Penny, and Other Fairy Tales. (Caedmon TC 1129).
Rudyard Kipling: *The Cat That Walked by Herself and Other Just So Stories*. (Caedmon TC 1139).
William Shakespeare: *Cymbeline*. (Shakespeare Recording Society SRS 236).

1963

Michael Avallone: *Tales of the Frightened, Volume 1*. (Mercury MG 20815 (M); SR 60815 (S)).
Michael Avallone: *Tales of the Frightened, Volume 2*. (Mercury MG 20816 (M); SR 60816 (S)).
Rudyard Kipling: *How Fear Came*. (Caedmon TC 1100).
Rudyard Kipling: *Toomai of the Elephants*. (Caedmon TC 1176).
Let's Listen Stories. (Caedmon TC 1182).

1965
Rudyard Kipling: *Gunga Din and Other Poems*. (Caedmon TC 1193).
Sergei Prokofiev: *Peter and the Wolf*. (Vanguard SRV-174 (S), SRV-174 (M)).

1966
The Daydreamer. (Columbia OL 6540) – Original Soundtrack.
Dr. Seuss: How the Grinch Stole Christmas. (MGM S-901/Leo the Lion LE-901).

1967
An Evening with Boris Karloff and His Friends. (Decca DL 4833 (M); DL 74833 (S)).
Aesop's Fables. (Caedmon TC 1221).
Come My Laurie With Me/He Is There. (Commander, ASCAP). M.O.L. 52 (45rpm Single).
The United States Air Force Presents Christmas. (non commercial release) – Karloff read a story entitled *Timmy Discovers Christmas* on side two of this album, which was distributed to U.S. radio stations.

1968
The Year Without a Santa Claus. (Capitol SL-6588).

Writings

(with Helene Ripley). "With a Grain of Salt", Registered for copyright on 21 October 1913.
"Cricket in California…", *The Screen Player*, 15 May 1934.
Film Weekly, 18 April 1936.
"Diary of a Monster… By Boris Karloff", *The Atlanta Constitution*, 11 October 1936.
"Houses I Have Haunted", *Liberty*, 4 October 1941.
"Forward." Charles Addams, *Drawn and Quartered*, (Random House, 1942).
Tales of Terror, (New World Publishing Company, 1943).
And the Darkness Falls, (New World Publishing Company, 1946).
"My Life as a Monster", *Films and Filming*, November 1957.
"Oaks from Acorns", *Screen Actor*, October-November 1960.
(with Arlene and Howard Eisenberg). "Memoirs of a Monster", *Saturday Evening Post*, 3 November 1962.
The Boris Karloff Horror Anthology, (Avon Books, 1965).

Bibliography

Books

Ackerman, Forrest J. *Boris Karloff: The Frankenscience Monster*, (Ace Publishing Corporation, 1969).
Addams, Charles. *Drawn and Quartered*, (World Publishing Company, 1942).
Anderson, Lindsay. *About John Ford*, (Plexus, 1999).
Arliss, George. *My Ten Years in the Studios*, (Little Brown and Company, 1940).
Asiatic Journal and Monthly Register for British Indian and its Dependencies, Vol. II. From June to December 1816, (Black, Parbury, & Allen, 1816).
Baumann, Marty. *The Astounding B Monster*, (Dinoship Inc., 2005).
Beck, Calvin Thomas. *Heroes of Horror*, (Collins Macmillan, 1975).
Bansak, Edmund G. *Fearing the Dark: The Val Lewton Career*, (McFarland, 1995).
Bernstein, Walter. *Inside Out: A Memoir of the Blacklist*, (Da Capo Press, 2000).
Bikel, Theodore. *Theo: The Autobiography of Theodore Bikel*, (University of Wisconsin Press), 2002.
Blackstone, Sarah J. *Buckskins, Bullets, and Business: A History of Buffalo Bill's Wild West*, (Greenwood Press, 1986).
Blake, Michael. *Lon Chaney: The Man Behind the Thousand Faces*, (Vestal Press, 1990).
Bogdanovich, Peter. *John Ford*, (University of California Press, 1978).
Bogdanovich, Peter. *Who the Devil Made It: Conversations with Legendary Film Directors*, (Ballantine Books, 1998).
Bogdanovich, Peter. *Who the Hell's In It*, (Faber and Faber, 2005).
Bojarksi, Richard. *The Complete Films of Bela Lugosi*, (Citadel Press, 1980).
Bombay Calendar and Almanac, (1827 – 1868 editions).
Bombay Calendar and Register, (1813 – 1831 editions).
Bombay Civil List, (Bombay Presidency, 1877).
Bordman, Gerald. *American Theatre: A Chronicle of Comedy and Drama, 1930-1969*, (Oxford US, 1996).
Brownlow, Kevin. *The Parade's Gone By…*, (Abacus, 1973).
Buehrer, Beverley Bare. *Boris Karloff: A Bio-Bibliography*, (Greenwood Press, 1993).
Cagney, James. *Cagney by Cagney*, (Doubleday, 1976).
Catalogue of Copyright Entries: Pamphlets, Leaflets, Contributions to Newspapers or Periodicals, etc.; Lectures, Sermons, Addresses for Oral Delivery; Dramatic Compositions; Maps, New Series, Volume 10, No. 7, (Government Printing Office, 1913).
Chase Williams, Lucy. *The Complete Films of Vincent Price*, (Kensington Publishing Corporation, 2000).
Coates, P.D. *The China Consuls: British Consular Officers, 1843-1943*, (Oxford University Press, 1991).
Corman, Roger with Jerome, Jim. *How I Made a Hundred Movies in Hollywood and Never Lost a Dime*, (Muller, 1990).
Cremer, Robert. *Lugosi: The Man Behind the Cape*, (H. Regency Co., 1976).
Crockford's Clerical Directory, 1938.
Curtis, James. *James Whale: A New World of Gods and Monsters*, (Faber and Faber, 1998).
Dick, Bernard F. *City of Dreams: The Making and Remaking of Universal Pictures*, (University Press of Kentucky, 1997).
Dunning, John. *On the Air: The Encyclopedia of Old-Time Radio*, (Oxford University Press, 1998).
Druxman, Michael B. *Basil Rathbone: His Life and His Films*, (A.S. Barnes, 1975).
East-India Register and Directory, (1812 – 1822 editions).
Ensor, R.C.K. *England, 1870-1914*, (The Clarendon Press, 1936).
Esshom, Frank Ellwood. *Pioneers and Prominent Men of Utah*, (Utah Pioneers Book Publishing Company, 1913).
Essoe, Gabe. *Tarzan of the Movies*, (Citadel, 1968).
Eyman, Scott. *Print The Legend: The Life and Times of John Ford*, (Simon & Schuster, 1999).

Film Pictorial Annual 1938, (Amalgamated Press Ltd., 1938).

Florey, Robert. *Hollywood: d'hier et d'aujord'hui*, (Éditions Prisma, 1948).

Forry, Steven Earl. *Hideous Progenies: Dramatizations of Frankenstein from Mary Shelley to the Present*, (University of Pennsylvania Press, 1990).

Forry, Steven Earl. *The Fantastic in World Literature and the Arts: Selected Essays from the Fifth International Conference on the Fantastic in the Arts*, (Greenwood Press, 1987).

Fowler, Gene. *Goodnight, Sweet Prince*, (Viking, 1944).

French, Lawrence. *Vincent Price*, (Midnight Marquee Press, 1998).

Gardner, Gerald C. *The Censorship Papers: Movie Censorship Letters from the Hays Office, 1934-1968*, (Dodd Mead, 1988).

Gifford, Denis. *Karloff: The Man, The Monster, The Movies*, (Curtis Books, 1973).

Gifford, Denis. *Movie Monsters*, (Studio Vista, 1969).

Glut, Donald F. *The Frankenstein Archive*, (McFarland, 2002).

Glut, Donald F. *The Frankenstein Legend: A Tribute to Mary Shelley and Boris Karloff*, (Scarecrow Press, 1973).

Goldrup, Tom and Goldrup, Jim. *Growing Up on the Set*, (McFarland, 2002).

Griffith, Robert. *The Politics of Fear: Joseph R. McCarthy and the Senate*, (University of Massachusetts Press, 1987).

Guy's Hospital Medical School Pupil Returns, 1886-1887.

Guy's Hospital Medical School Pupil Returns, 1887-1888.

Haining, Peter (editor). *The Frankenstein Omnibus*, (Orion, 1994).

Halligan, Benjamin. *Michael Reeves*, (Manchester University Press, 2003).

Hamilton, George with Stadiem, William. *Don't Mind If I Do: My Adventures in Hollywood*, (JR Books Ltd., 2009).

Hamilton, John. *Beasts in the Cellar: The Exploitation Career of Tony Tenser*, (FAB Press, 2005).

Hammett, Nina. *Laughing Torso*, (Virago, 1984).

Hart, E.P. (editor). *Merchant Taylors' School Register, 1851-1920*, (Richard Clay and Sons, 1923).

Hearn, Lafcadio. *Some Chinese Ghosts*, (Roberts Brothers, 1887).

Hibbert, Christopher. *Queen Victoria: A Personal History*, (Basic Books, 2000).

Hirschhorn, Clive. *The Warner Bros. Story*, (Random House, 1987).

Hutchings, Peter. *Hammer and Beyond: The British Horror Film*, (Manchester University Press, 1993).

Hutchinson, Tom. *Horror and Fantasy in the Movies*, (Crescent Books, 1974).

India List & India Office List, 1904.

Jacobs, George and Stadiem, William. *Mr. S – The Last Word on Frank Sinatra*, (Sidgwick & Jackson, 2003).

Jensen, Paul M. *Boris Karloff and His Films*, (A.S. Barnes, 1974).

Jensen, Paul M. *The Men Who Made the Monsters*, (Twayne Publishers, 1996).

Karloff, Boris. *Tales of Terror*, (World Publishing Company, 1943).

King, Clyde Lyndon, Tichenor, Frank A. and Watkins, Gordon S. *The Motion Picture in its Economic and Social Aspects*, (Arno Press, 1970).

Kotsilibas-Davis, James and Loy, Myrna. *Myrna Loy: Being and Becoming*, (Bloomsbury, 1987).

Laird, Paul R. *Leonard Bernstein: A Guide to Research*, (Routledge, 2001).

Lanchester, Elsa. *Elsa Lanchester Herself*, (St. Martin's Press, 1983).

Langford, E. *Victoria R.I.*, (Weidenfeld & Nicholson, 1964).

Langman, Larry and Finn, Daniel. *A Guide to American Crime Films of the Thirties*, (Greenwood Press, 1995).

Langman, Larry and Finn, Daniel. *A Guide to American Crime Films of the Forties and Fifties*, (Greenwood Press, 1995).

Langman, Larry and Finn, Daniel. *A Guide to American Silent Crime Films*, (Greenwood Press, 1994)

Langman, Larry. *A Guide to Silent Westerns*, (Greenwood Press, 1992).

Lee, Christopher. *Tall, Dark and Gruesome*, (Weidenfeld & Nicolson, 1997).

Leiter, Samuel L. *The Encyclopedia of the New York Stage, 1940-1950*, (Greenwood Press, 1992).

Lenburg, Jeff. *Peekaboo: The Story of Veronica Lake*, (iUniverse.com, 2001).

Lennig, Arthur. *The Immortal Count: The Life and Films of Bela Lugosi*, (Putnam, 1974).

Levant, Oscar. *A Smattering of Ignorance*, (Doubleday, 1940).

Lindsay, Cynthia. *Dear Boris: The Life of William Henry Pratt a.k.a. Boris Karloff*, (Nick Hearn Books, 1995).

LoBrutto, Vincent. *By Design: Interviews with Film Production Designers*, (Praeger Publishers, 1992).

Magers, Boyd and Fitzgerald, Michael G. *Westerns Women*, (McFarland, 1999).

Manguel, Alberto. *Bride of Frankenstein*, (British Film Institute, 1997).

Mank, Gregory William. *Hollywood Cauldron*, (McFarland, 1994).

Mank, Gregory William. *It's Alive! - The Classic Cinema Saga of Frankenstein*, (A.S. Barnes & Company, Inc., 1981).

Mank, Gregory William. *Karloff and Lugosi: The Story of a Haunting Collaboration*, (McFarland, 1990).

Mank, Gregory William. *Women In Horror Films, 1930s*, (McFarland, 1999).

Mason, Philip. *The Men Who Ruled India*, (Cape, 1985).

McFarlane, Brian. *An Autobiography of British Cinema*, (Methuen, 1997).

Miller, John. *Ralph Richardson: The Authorized Biography*, (Sidgwick & Jackson, 1995).

Mineka, Francis E. and Lindley, Dwight N. (editors). *The Collected Works of John Stuart Mill, Volume XVII - The Later Letters of John Stuart Mill 1849-1873 Part IV*, (Routledge and Kegan Paul, 1972).

Moses, L.G. *Wild West Shows and the Images of American Indians, 1883- 1933*, (University of New Mexico Press, 1996).

Mosley, Leonard. *Zanuck: The Rise and Fall of Hollywood's Last Tycoon*, (Granada, 1984).

Naha, Ed. *The Films of Roger Corman: Brilliance on a Budget*, (Arco. 1982).

Nollen, Scott Allen. *Boris Karloff: A Gentleman's Life*, (Midnight Marquee Press, 1999).

Ormiston, Thomas Lane. *Dulwich College Register, 1619 to 1926*, (J.J. Keliher & Co., 1926).

Parla, Paul and Mitchell, Charles P. *Screen Sirens Scream!: Interviews with 20 Actresses from Science Fiction, Horror, Film Noir and Mystery Movies, 1930s to 1960s*, (McFarland, 2000).

Plummer, Christopher. *In Spite of Myself: A Memoir*, (Alfred A. Knopf, 2009).

Pollard, Jack. *The Bradman Years: Australian Cricket 1918-1948*, (Angus & Robertson, 1988).

Price, Victoria. *Vincent Price: A Daughter's Biography*, (Sidgwick & Jackson, 2000).

Priestley, J.B. *Benighted*, (Heinemann, 1932).

Priestley, J.B. *Margin Released: A Writer's Reminiscences and Reflections*, (Harper & Row, 1962).

Quarterly of Film, Radio and Television, Vol. 11, No. 1, (Autumn, 1956).

Riley, Philip J. (editor). *Bride of Frankenstein*, (MagicImage Filmbooks, 1989).

Riley, Philip J. (editor). *Frankenstein*, (MagicImage Filmbooks, 1989).

Riley, Philip J. (editor). *House of Frankenstein*, (MagicImage Filmbooks, 1995).

Riley, Philip J. (editor). *Son of Frankenstein*, (Magicimage Filmbooks, 1989).

Riley, Philip J. (editor). *The Mummy*, (Magicimage Filmbooks, 1989).

Rohmer, Sax. *The Mystery of Dr. Fu-Manchu*, (Chivers, 1992).

Roosevelt, Franklin Delano. *Great Speeches*, (Dover Publications, Inc., 1999).

Sagolla, Lisa Jo. *The Girl Who Fell Down: A Biography of Joan McCracken*, (Northeastern University Press, 2003).

Schatz, Thomas. *The Genius of the System: Hollywood Filmmaking in Studio Era*, (Pantheon Books, 1989).

Senn, Bryan. *Golden Horrors: An Illustrated Critical Filmography of Terror Cinema, 1931-1939*, (McFarland, 1996).

Shelley, Mary. *Frankenstein or The Modern Prometheus (1818 Text)*, (Oxford University Press, 1998).

Sherriff, R.C. *No Leading Lady – An Autobiography*, (Victor Gollancz Ltd, 1968).

Shipley, Joseph T. *Guide to Great Plays*, (Public Affairs Press, 1956).

Shriver, Gordon B. *Boris Karloff: The Man Remembered*, (PublishAmerica, 2004).

Siegel, Joel E. *Val Lewton: The Reality of Terror*, (Secker and Warburg, 1972).

Sims, Joan. *High Spirits*, (Partridge, 2000).

Skal, David J. *Monster Show*, (Plexus, 1993).

Skinner, Cornelia Otis. *Life with Lindsay and Crouse*, (Houghton Mifflin Company, 1976).

Slide, Anthony. *Early Women Directors*, (A.S. Barnes, 1977).

Slide, Anthony. *Lois Weber: The Director Who Lost Her Way in History*, (Greenwood Press, 1996).

Stevenson, Robert Louis. *The Strange Case of Dr. Jekyll and Mr. Hyde and Other Tales of Terror*, (Penguin, 2003).

Sutton, Jean. *Lords of the East: The East India Company and its Ships*, (Conway Maritime, 1981).

Truffaut, Francois. *The Films in My Life*, (Simon & Schuster, 1978).

Turner, George E. and Price, Michael H. *Human Monsters: The Bizarre Psychology of Movie Villains*, (Kitchen Sink Press, 1996)

Tuska, Jon. *Encounters with Filmmakers: Eight Career Studies*, (Greenwood Press, 1991).

Tzioumakis, Yannis. *American Independent Cinema: An Introduction*, (Edinburgh University Press, 2006).

Underwood, Peter. *Guide to Ghosts & Haunted Places*, (Piatkus Books, 1996).

Underwood, Peter. *Karloff: The Life of Boris Karloff*, (Drake Publishers, Inc. 1972).

Uppingham School Roll, 1824-1931, (Deane & Sons, 1932).

Warren, Alan. *This is a Thriller: An Episode Guide*, (McFarland, 1996).

Weaver, Tom. *Attack of the Monster Movie Makers: Interviews With 20 Genre Giants*, (McFarland, 1994).

Weaver, Tom. *Earth vs. the Sci-Fi Makers: 20 Interviews*, (McFarland, 2005).

Weaver, Tom. *I Was a Monster Movie Maker: Conversations with 22 SF and Horror Filmmakers*, (McFarland, 2001).

Weaver, Tom. *Interviews with B Science Fiction and Horror Movie Makers: Writers, Producers, Directors, Actors, Moguls and Makeup*, (McFarland, 2006).

Weaver, Tom. *It Came from Horrorwood: Interviews With Movie Makers in the SF and Horror Tradition*, (McFarland, 1996).

Weaver, Tom. *Return of the B Science Fiction and Horror Heroes*, (McFarland, 2000).

Weaver, Tom. *Science Fiction and Fantasy Film Flashbacks*, (McFarland, 2004).

Weaver, Tom. *Science Fiction Confidential: Interviews with 23 Monster Stars and Filmmakers*, (McFarland, 2002).

Weaver, Tom. *Science Fiction Stars and Horror Heroes*, (McFarland, 2006).

Youngkin, Stephen D. *The Lost One: A Life of Peter Lorre*, (University Press of Kentucky, 2005).

Archives

Oriental and India Office Collections, British Library, London
Births, Baptisms, Marriages and Deaths: N/1/187/5, N/1/187/53, N/3/5/131, N/3/5/224, N/3/7/45, N/3/10/413, N/3/23/103, N/3/24/245, N/3/24/290, N/3/25/55, N/3/29/9, N/3/29/90, N/3/33/45, N/3/38/336, N/3/46/65, N/3/22/154.
India Office: Military Department Records 1708-1959: N/L/MIL/12/1.
Marine Ledger: L/AG/20/13/2.
Marine Records: L/MAR/7.
Financial Department Records: L/F/10/140.

Kings College, London
Calendar of King's College London, 1905-1906.
Calendar of King's College London, 1906-1907.
Guy's Hospital Medical School: Students Register, 1876-1895.
Pupils Returns – Guy's, 1886-87.
Pupils Returns – Guy's, 1887-88.

National Archives, Kew
Pratt, Eliza Sara v. Pratt, Edward – Court Minutes: J77/425/2969.

School of Oriental and African Studies, London
Sir John Pratt Papers: PP.MS.5/30, PP.MS.5/32, and PP.MS.
5/36.

Vital Records

Birth Certificates
de Wilton, Edith Doreen, 25 March 1898.
Harding, Jessie Grace, 16 December 1885.
Pratt, William Henry, 23 November 1887.

Marriage Certificates
de Wilton, Sussex Gerald to Holloway, Edith, 6 July 1895.
Pratt, William Henry to Harding, Grace, 23 February 1910.
British Columbia Archives, Reg. Number: 1910-09-062223,
B.C. Archives Microfilm Number: B11375, GSU. Microfilm
Number: 1983703.

Death Certificates
Pratt, George Marlow, 23 January 1904.
Pratt, William Henry, 2 February 1969.

Wills
de Wilton, Sussex Gerald, 13 August 1936.
Pratt, Edward, 28 October 1901.
Pratt, Eliza Sara, 24 November 1905.
Pratt, Emma, 28 July 1924.
Pratt, William Henry, 3 June 1964.

Probate
de Wilton, Sussex Gerald, 4 July 1939.
Pratt, David Cameron, 4 February 1953.
Pratt, Edward, 6 May 1902.
Pratt, Edward Millard, 2 May 1952.
Pratt, Emma, 13 September 1924.
Pratt, Eliza Sara, 2 February 1907.
Pratt, George Marlow, 11 March 1904.
Pratt, Richard Septimus, 19 February 1976.
Pratt, William Henry, 7 April 1971.

Other Records

Johnston, John LeRoy. *Biography of Boris Karloff*,
(Universal, 9 January 1932).

Divorce
Decree Absolute of William Henry Pratt and Grace
Harding: British Columbia Archives
Microfilm No. B6311, File No. 202.

WW1 Draft Registration Card
Pratt, William Henry, 1 June 1917. World War I Selective
Service System Draft Registration Cards, 1917-1918.
Washington, D.C.: National Archives and Records
Administration. M1509. Roll 1452381, Draftboard 1.

Red Deer and District Archives
de Wilton fonds: MG 21 Series 1, sub-series c, File 1,
Folder 24.

INDEX

References in BOLD indicate pictures